MOMENTS OF SOLITUDE

MOMENTS OF SOLITUDE

The National Library of Poetry

Chris Tyler, Editor

Moments of Solitude

Library of Congress
Cataloging in Publication Data

ISBN 1-57553-608-0

Manufactured in The United States of America by
Watermark Press
One Poetry Plaza
Owings Mills, MD 21117

Foreword

Throughout life, we store information collected from experiences and try in some way to make sense of it. When we are not able to fully understand the things which occur in our lives, we often externalize the information. By doing this, we are afforded a different perspective, thus allowing us to think more clearly about difficult or perplexing events and emotions. Art is one of the ways in which people choose to externalize their thoughts.

Within the arts, modes of expression differ, but poetry is a very powerful tool by which people can share sometimes confusing, sometimes perfectly clear concepts and feelings with others. Intentions can run the gamut as well: the artists may simply want to share something that has touched their lives in some way, or they may want to get help to allay anxiety or uncertainty. The poetry within *Moments of Solitude* is from every point on the spectrum: every topic, every intention, every event or emotion imaginable. Some poems will speak to certain readers more than others, but it is always important to keep in mind that each verse is the voice of a poet, of a mind which needs to make sense of this world, of a heart which feels the effects of every moment in this life, and perhaps of a memory which is striving to surface. Nonetheless, recalling our yesterdays gives birth to our many forms of expression.

Melisa S. Mitchell
Editor

Editor's Note

Common sense dictates that the shortest distance between two points is a straight line. From this assertion, one could extrapolate that the most effective communication is brief and to the point, requiring no flowery language or complex sentence structure. Why, then, do people use visual art or poetry to communicate? For example, in cubist art, objects and people are often distorted beyond recognition; the viewer must often struggle to decipher what is represented in a given painting, let alone what emotions the artist is attempting to convey. Poetic forms impose an artificial structure on language— few people speak naturally in rhyme or in perfect iambic pentameter. Frequently the meaning of a poem is not clear the first time one reads it; the reader must sort through a number of possible interpretations in order to decode the poet's true intent. It would seem, then, that art in any form is an extraordinarily inefficient method of sharing information, if one only imagines both the effort involved in imparting (or creating) and receiving (or interpreting) that information.

Yet visual art and poetry continue to thrive. The great writer William Butler Yeats offers one possible explanation for art's endurance as a form of communication: "Supreme art is a traditional statement of certain heroic and religious truth, passed on from age to age, modified by individual genius, but never abandoned." In other words, artists use their work as a way to express some universal truth, and each artist's creativity is his or her attempt to get as close to that as possible. In any event, it is likely that these universal truths are impossible to summarize in any concise terms.

One work in this anthology that attempts to explain some all-encompassing concept is Erich von Abele's "Only Human" (p. 1). In this piece, von Abele tries to describe the very essence of time. He begins, "Time is most itself when passing," a statement that implies the impossibility of the task he has undertaken; that people are too limited to be able to capture something so infinite yet so insubstantial. He elaborates:

> So bees wend high above the road
> Where a fine dust cloud rises
> And white birds appear in the gathered green.
> No painter here to take their wing to canvas,
> No inscrutable simplicity in a Buddha's cluttered mime,
> No poet giving voice to mute mud,
> No philosophic sap, swollen knot of superadded wisdom,
> Nor a Christ lodged in the slowing green snail . . .

Such statements imply that human efforts to impose order upon nature, to define it, whether through art or even through religion, cannot even begin to represent the true essence of time. These attempts are fleeting and ineffectual:

Such are limp hands white with sleep,
Hair as water burns on golden sand,
Or wooden dark in its stillness.

One cannot discover the nature of time by freezing a single moment; one can only begin to understand it by appreciating its immensity—"It be the blaze of afternoon brings the heat of world"—as well as its subtleties—"Listing here on slight breezes . . ."

Also present in this poem is a sense of the cyclic nature of time, an awareness of the rhythms of life, which are evident in a number of von Abele's references. For example, by alluding to Buddha in the second stanza, von Abele brings to mind Buddhism's doctrine of spiritual rebirth and growth. This cycle repeats until enlightenment is reached. Later, in the poem, von Abele mentions "a new old world," which also implies the cyclic nature of time. Finally, the structure of the poem itself reinforces its argument: It begins and ends with the same line, "Time is most itself when passing." This line both offers a hypothesis and confirms it; the evidence in the body of the poem leads to the inevitable conclusion.

Erich von Abele has presented his argument with remarkable skill and clarity, using imagery that is both vivid and cohesive. Therefore, the judges have awarded "Only Human" the Grand Prize in the contest associated with *Moments of Solitude*.

Another poem that offers a fresh perspective on a broad and timeless theme is Andre West's "A Poet Parts from His Muse" (p. 3). In this sonnet, the persona casts off his muse because she does not seem committed to playing the part. The Poet informs her:

"You fool, you haven't taken far enough
The notion that the artist must be dead
To everything except his vision, rough
As that philosophy must seem to him."

At this, the Muse recoils in "horror." Apparently she did not realize when she embarked upon this relationship the depth of the obligation she was expected to fulfill. The persona insists that the Muse must be as responsible for the art as is the Artist; because she is unwilling to be focused upon to the exclusion of all else, the Artist chooses to eject her from this role:

. . . Because she wouldn't cast her lot
With my endeavor I was forced to bar
The Muse from Helicon. Her fall was far.

Helicon is a mountain in Boeotia, north of Athens, Greece, that was believed to be the home of the Nine Muses of Greek mythology.

In this unusual poem about the artist/Muse relationship, the poem's persona asserts that creativity is as much the duty of the object of inspiration as it is of the inspired. In many other works that deal with this topic, the artist alone assumes the burden of creativity. If the artist and the Muse are forced to part, it is generally because the Muse either chooses to leave or dies, or because she loses her ability to inspire the artist. Rarely is it mentioned that the Muse is released from her function by the artist because of her unwillingness to concentrate exclusively on fulfilling the role. Hence, "A Poet Parts from His Muse" offers a new perspective on a familiar subject.

Steven Pratt's "Hale Bopp" (p. 9) also offers a fresh view of a familiar topic: love. The poet acknowledges his own insignificance in the grand scheme of things:

> *In celestial measure*
> *my boat's no larger than a*
> *salty drop of sea, . . .*

Conversely, the persona also says that the feelings he has for his beloved are timeless, covering the infinite vastness of space. He uses the comet Hale Bopp as a symbol of timelessness: This comet, which made headlines in 1997, made its most recent appearance in the inner solar system (thus being visible from Earth) in the year 2213 B.C. The persona asserts that what he feels now is no different from what people felt over 4000 years ago:

> *And my thoughts of you*
> ....
> *travel light years to the comet (and back)*
> *to recapture what Minoan lovers pondered one night*
> *in Phaistos, . . .*

The persona's love is thus capable of traveling immense distances and surviving for enormous amounts of time, even beyond the persona's own lifetime.

There are many poems in this anthology that are worthy of special attention. Examine the essence of faith in John Valentine's "Snake Handling at Mt. Zion Full Gospel Church, Georgia" (p. 7), or determine man's place in the universe with Sean Mack's "Some Breezes . . ." (p. 13). Place yourself in "Flushing Meadow Park" via Anna Kristen Ganey's unique and vivid imagery (p. 6). Get acquainted with the repulsive-yet-compelling title character of Katherine K. Dougherty's "The Lady in the Lake" (p. 8); or with the participants in the mechanical, but somehow vital, relationship in Christopher Koch's "Sarah Sitting" (p. 5). Decide whether or not you agree with Cynthia Eckles about the intoxicating nature of words in "WD-40" (p. 7). Empathize with the loved ones of an emotionally disturbed woman in Denise Brosat's "The Secret Garden" (p. 12). Or get insight into a gifted, but reclusive poet in Barry Winningham's "Emily Dickinson's 'Ars Poetica'" (p. 3). When reading through *Moments of Solitude*, bear in mind that each of these works is the poet's attempt to express some crucial idea; it is up to you, as the reader, to determine how close the poet has come to reaching that goal. Enjoy that process and all the poems contained within this anthology.

The publication of *Moments of Solitude* is a process to which a great number of people have contributed their talents and hard work. Many thanks to the editors, assistant editors, judges, and administrative, customer service, data entry, and mailroom personnel who have all collaborated on this project.

Diana Zeiger
Editor

Cover Art: Amber W. Johnson

Grand Prize Winner

Erich von Abele / Seattle WA

Second Prize Winners

Denise Brosat / Shelton WA

Katherine K. Doughterty / Ballwin MO

Cynthia Eckles / Emporia KS

Anna Ganey / Chandler AR

Christopher Koch / Alpharetta GA

Sean Mack / Fords NJ

Steven Pratt / Key West FL

John Valentine / Savannah GA

Andre West / Bronx NY

Barry Winningham / Bullhead City AZ

Third Prize Winners

Allison Adair / Spotsylvania VA

Martin Alejandro / Miami FL

Janet E. Arnold / Ronks PA

Jennifer Bricklin / Tacoma WA

FNA Cenidoza / Arteta CA

Daniel Corry / Madison WI

David Crowder / Palm Beach Gardens FL

Casey Cunningham / Spring Branch TX

Betty DeGuzman / Summit NJ

Anthony DeTommasi / White Plains NY

Kirsten Dooley / Toms River NJ

Peter Dorsey / White Salmon WA

Terra R. Dunn / Hendersonville NC

Michael L. Eby / Marion MA

Richard Eichman / Union Bridge MD

Gregory William Farrell / Monroe CT

Anita Lisko Gaab / Gladstone ND

Patricia Garcia / Monterey Park CA

Timothy Gavin / Pequannock NJ

Barrie Gellis / Flushing NY

Yobevita Gen / Lititz PA

Jessica Gifford / Bucksport ME

Pamela G. Greenside / North Miami Beach FL

Bill Hallinan / Helena MT

Leo Harrington / San Francisco CA

Stewart C. Harvey / Salt Lake City UT

Damion Michael Higbie / Mankato MN

Michael Hiratzka / Orlando FL

Alysan C. Hooper / Portland ME

John Igo / San Antonio TX

Maureen Kovach / Findlay OH

Donald Kuzma / Bend OR

Norma Laut / Elmhurst IL

Jorge Maldonado / San Diego CA

John Martin / Sedro Woolley WA

Sarah McFadden / Sudbury Ontario HI

Monica C. McTyre / Woodbridge VA

Lanny Morris / Washington DC

Eric Nesser / Tampa FL

Wes Nixon / Baton Rouge LA

Bob Okeefe / Bellevue NE

Kathryn Parks / Albuquerque NM

Joan Patrick / Duncan OK

Beth Pizio / Mt. Kisco NY

Cristina Rafols / Farmington Hills MI

Susan Rains / Temple TX

Jay Schwartz / Highland Park NJ

Nancy Shattuck / St. Louis MO

Richard E. Smith / Des Plaines IL

Dr. James Story / Brooklyn NY

Duane Tucker / Santa Monica CA

Lillian S. Varol / Charlotte NC

Nigal C. Wagner / Albany NY

Wm. A. Watling / Morris IL

Karen A. Weise / Quakertown PA

Josie L. Wilson / Spanaway WA

Tami Wilson / Snohomish WA

Ann Zalkind / Jackson Heights NY

Kay Zywicki / Concord CA

Congratulations also to all semi-finalists.

Grand Prize Winner

Only Human

Time is most itself when passing.

So bees wend high above the road
Where a fine dust cloud rises
And white birds appear in the gathered green.
No painter here to take their wing to canvas,
No inscrutable simplicity in a Buddha's cluttered mime,
No poet giving voice to mute mud,
No philosophic sap, swollen knot of superadded wisdom,
Nor a Christ lodged in the slowing green snail . . .

Such are limp hands white with sleep,
Hair as water burns on golden sand,
Or wooden dark in its stillness.

It be the blaze of afternoon brings the heat of world,
Listing here on slight breezes, where
Over your radiant slumbers sugar cypress arms
Canopy my nodding vigil.
Invisible breath: guardian of our present
Steals through infant lips, of a new old world,
Secretly to stir the leaves around.

Time is most itself when passing.

Erich von Abele

Once

Partitioned in tight compartments
Memories unbidden
reflect in obscure glass
Images rent askew in false camera eye
As in a shatter'd mirror
silver backing worn away
seen by veiled vision
Great passions illuminate my pathway
hidden yet by tall grasses
Some bold memories recalled with grace
others timid, lost in time and space
Memory stone dropped in sunlit dappled pond
rippled reflections wavering
like a besotted drunken man
wearing a worn and shabby cloak
tightly clutched to hold all in check
Was it all perhaps a grand illusion?
A rage of memory clouds perception
Oh, to behold with perfect clarity
as they were once

Josie L. Wilson

A Poet Parts from His Muse

After she co-opted me, I said,
"You fool, you haven't taken far enough
The notion that the artist must be dead
To everything except his vision, rough
As that philosophy must seem to him."
She looked at me with horror as my eyes,
Illuminated by the fire within
My reassembled being, made her rise
From bed and lean away from me a bit.
Our union was a danger. She was not
Prepared to fully sacrifice to it
Her life. Because she wouldn't cast her lot
With my endeavor I was forced to bar
The Muse from Helicon. Her fall was far.

Andre West

Sonnet

In Horeb's wilderness the holy things
Were trusted to the loyal Levites' care;
Their God-directed duty 'twas to bear
All on their shoulders, in the journeyings
Of Israel's folk, from sacred ark to rings
That held the tabernacle boards. By glare
Of fiery pillar pass'd they, burden'd, where
The bitter brooklets turn'd to sweeten'd springs.
So you, call'd likewise, bore our hallow'd tongue,
Wand'ring a wilderness of minds, with God
And your good light to guide you through the gloom.
We could not see the wondrous torrent sprung
From flinty boulder cleft by Aaron's rod:
But, ah, we saw you make a desert bloom.

Richard Eichman

Requiem

Now I lay me down to sleep
I hope the cellulite not to keep
If I should die before I wake
I hope not to share my lotto take
Now I lay me down my worldly heap
I hope at least 10% compound to reap
If I should fail to have my cake
The Renoir in the hall will have to be a fake
Now that I've buried wounds so deep
I find it near impossible to weep
Will that celestial walk I make
or have I found elsewhere to bake

Bob Okeefe

Emily Dickinson's "Ars Poetica"

"If I feel physically as if the top of my head were taken off,
I know that is poetry," she wrote.
These were the mighty words of Emily Dickinson the poet
as she mused upon the art of poetry—
one rare, unique, and solitary bird
one singularly original, individual bard
one lonely, different, brightly shining star
who wrote her poems to wage a war
on all respectability and its bores
who trumpeted propriety, decency, and mores;
the Salem witches flocked unto her door in droves
unseen, unheard, unknown, unheralded in her grassy yard unmowed
and her garden of roses blown, of bees in drone, of winter snow
in Amherst, Massachusetts, where these wayward spirits roamed
to awaken the dead from all their woes
reciting Emily Dickinson's poems—
oh, let these same words of Emily Dickinson be heard again,
for these words are the words of sin, the cross, and death;
these words are the words of life, the empty tomb, and breath
heard again and again, tolling like a bell on New England winds

Barry Winningham

Peculiar

How toilets flushing seem to chuckle almost
Reminding you of someone silly you once knew

Or water swirls down the sink like so many
Slap-happy dogs seeking shelter. Your front door

Surges open and suddenly it's the screen door
Of your grandmother's summer cottage, gush of her spirit

Gusting it open. Later, in steam billowing
From the flesh of a fissured sweet potato,

You swear you feel on your cheek a butterfly's wing
Or her spirit's quick kiss. How notes of grassy

Rapture seem to leap into traffic from an old station wagon
bulging with balloons. Yet, even with all these

Embraces, the stubborn lighthouse shouts to the sea
Its single-minded plea.

And sometimes 'round fringes of clover you can almost see
the loneliness of the rain.

Duane Tucker

Last Night's Zinfandel

Lovers fall under the moon's spell.
Drugged by the nights fragrance
Soon to be awakened by the breakfast bell.

Quietly he sneaks out of the hotel room.
It was all an accident.
Lovers fell under the moon's spell.

Lying on the pillow his villanelle.
How convenient
to be awakened by the breakfast bell.

The pen still lying in the inkwell
the ink sill wets the parchments
lovers who fall under the moon's spell.

Now it awakens Jezebel
to see him absent,
her lover awakened before the breakfast bell.

She sipped last night's Zinfandel
reading the letter's content
lover's fall under the moon's spell
one to be awakened by the breakfast bell.

Kirsten Dooley

Word Weaver

Old spinning woman weaves her web,
Spins her yarns of wordy wool,
Knits, crochets until each pearl
Reveals itself in written truths.
Fragmented thoughts must first be collected,
Nouns and adjectives gathered in pairs.
Stitched with verbs, stretched with adverbs,
Peppered with patterns that may even rhyme,
Laced with a common thread throughout,
Bound by a scheme of acceptable shape,
Built on a warp of writer's rich store.
Such weft of words she weaves all alone,
Through neural fibers hidden from view,
Until with her hand the strings are laid down,
In rhythmic rows one line at a time.
Slowly the creation begins to take shape,
This fabric so carefully crafted.
Sadly, with time, the yarns become tangled,
The words become lost,
And poems unravel.

Susan Rains

Paradise July

Fireflies dance
Rise mingle
In the heavy, clover-scented air of a simple summer evening.

Celestial twinkling, earthbound constellations
Blaze, then dim
A hundred flickering oil lamps
Ascend from the quilted landscape
Frolicking above sheafs of wheat,
Skillfully arranged.
Haphazard cascades of
Living torches
Nature's fantasia
Light the way amongst endless rows of corn.

Fireflies dance
Swirling Chasing Urgently
Playful in a fleeting season.
Final flights of fancy
As the grey-green cushion
Enfolds the last light
In the sable skies of dusk.

Janet E. Arnold

Winter Poem

Red-capped and mittened,
My daughter peers anxiously
Beyond me, into a world of falling snow.

To her eight-year-old mind, I am an obstacle
Insisting on a longer scarf,
A warmer hat, more socks.

She is as impatient, as I am reluctant
To face this new storm.

She fears she will miss it;
I know the drifts alone are unavoidable.

The kitchen,
Warm with brewing coffee and rising bread,
Becomes the farmhouse of my past.

"Did I ever tell you how Grandma always . . ."
She nods impatiently.
Resigned, I open the door
To allow cold blue sprinkled white.

I watch my daughter lean into the wind
Waddling awkwardly—
A diminutive blue snowsuit and a red woolen cap.

Terra R. Dunn

From My 34th Avenue Window

There are no deer grazing in driveways.
There are only tracks of tires
coming and going in forgotten directions.
Wires, like impotent leaves, drape from poles.
A cat strolls nonchalantly down the sidewalk.
His faded memories of the taste of warm flesh
dripping from his mouth after the kill
are as forgotten as the farmland now buried
under the feet of Buicks and Chevrolets
below me, poised like faceless steeds,
signifying nothing,
ready to drive endlessly in circles.

Barrie Gellis

Kent State, May 4, 1970

Four found dead among the halls of higher education
A bullet does not discriminate
love from hate
passion from discontent
It holds no age boundaries
It has no political point of view
it only strikes those
found
in a straight line
so geometrically perfect
only to be disrupted from that perfect line
by those who cross its path
like the cross hairs of a rifle
found in the hands
of those with a political point of view

John Martin

Those Younger Years . . .

The sky wrinkled up like the old veteran
sitting in his well worn rocking chair
thinking of the good old days

In the distance his faithful, old black lab could be seen trudging
through the once-smooth grounds towards the dirty, musty house

Before the dog could reach his master
he collapsed with an exhausted sigh
Onto the weak, rotted porch

(soon both fall asleep)

Dreaming of their nature hikes,
hunting and fishing trips together
during the hot, Indian summer years before

Then the rain began to fall in sheets of sorrow,
mourning for those younger years

Tami Wilson

The Meaning of Life

My skin peels back like the burnt crust
of a marshmallow revealing
glistening pink, red, and orange
muscles with veins shot through
glowing liquid sunset burning below
leaving white bones bright
as a newly discovered constellation
only to fade in a few hours
leaving small lumps, organs
like fallen fruit in an orchard
rotting into richness, dirt
looking for the center of me
I find nothing
only my layers make me whole

Jennifer Bricklin

Not Yet Fallen

Purity is short-lived near heat.
Porcelain snow, untouched by man,
melts in hot, soiled hands.
Cool, muddy water can be found in any river.

Slow, sultry music saunters through the air
on thick, deep waves.
Pulse triples rhythm in the mind.
Dizzy, disoriented, the smell of black.
Apprehensive, sideways glances wracked by desire.

Hard, cracked ground; parched, sick, aching for relief.
The water can't be seen at night, strung from a charcoal sky,
Hung like sheets dancing in the wind.
Quenching thirsty lips; feeding hungry thoughts.

Steam rises when two such opposing forces touch.
The earth sweats.
In a fantasy, tidal waves of pleasure spill over guilty dams
and caress valleys of snow white roses,
causing them to blush with amorous red bloom.

Judging eyes would gladly watch our bodies drown
in a murky pool of deception and regret.

Casey Cunningham

On My Father's Shoulders above the Grand Canyon

Nine months out of Vietnam,
and there is still enough blood in your thumb
to find the hollow side of my knees,
remembering the feel of skin and tendon
cables and the love of a yellow girl's mouth.

Far below, the river mines the last vein
of sun from the west. A hawk cries
its woman's cry, and you walk us out
into the sound. My hands are above
me now, and I want you to know I'm not afraid.

We will have that absurd moment of lift
before the fall takes us, and the centuries
collapse in a ring of color.
If we're lucky, the war will drain from you
before we land. And lifetimes from now,

it will be safe enough to return,
search the ledges for that place where we died,
and with a hammer crack open
the lacy fossil of our past in stone.

Damion Michael Higbie

Sarah Sitting

The highways spill westward off the coast;
let me lay you down tonight someplace east from here:
Aluminum skies—standard—,
steel rivet seams,
and clouds, like fat cattle, drift emptily to the block.
Thick, you move into me cliche
and in a drink we share some misty velvet.
We decompose the composite selves.
The rust swims down the pipe
and we move free and run through
the loud layers of the motel room:
six bucks an hour for just-visible conversation,
six bucks for words that dry up into
every second and only the room grows one hour deeper.
One loud layer of the dead skin of human history:
spin it; stitch it with steel rivets.
you tell me I need no more than that,
(it's warm to-day, even through the rust) and
I believe you.
When the cows open up.

Christopher Koch

On Loving the Old

The last of the brandy, more aura than liquor
Loving the fragility of the gift, the older
Colder fingers touching the knots behind the tapestry

Old age whispers away
Barely enough breath to flutter a candle
The voice from elsewhere making now of then
The ceaseless invocation of faces-become-names

These eyes looking at me see past me, backward
I become part of the legend in dissolved time
The childlike vision, the simplicities that say,
I am, I have been

Memories in a button-box
Offered one I take a button
"That was then . . . remember it for me."

Holding the button I feel its warmth fading
"Tell me . . ." . . . "I forget . . ."

I could cry out at the tender desolation
The terrible beauty of fading
The grasp that cannot hold

I have come to love pastels

John Igo

Tectonics

The land moves on so untroubled, when it moves unaware.
Floating on itself it hears its own advice;
Repeats with firmness that endless escape
from its constant motions.

Cradled within, a magma flow yearns to mingle with air.
Pressures faulting over time do not suffice;
They only trouble the accrued landscape
with their blank eruptions.

Troubled figures gesture, but just uncover heated air.
Agile fingers cover holes with melting ice;
Circulating one and all ride that gape
of dissolving motions.

But let that igneous pacific, itself, be my share.
Indigents may pay the complemental price;
My shape where you once shaped or once will shape
bestows benedictions.

The land moves on so untroubled, when it moves on aware.
Floating on its selves it hears its own advice;
Repeats its fullness as the endless shape
of its constant motions.

Leo Harrington

Ascension

Light lifts in rays from cottonwood bark,
And around the trunk mist rises breath-like;
Not far below roots, the force of continents
Drives a forest sunward.

Propolis scented breeze nudges flaxen grass,
And like a lover nudging her love's ear
Whispers moist promises.

Waxwings sense both force and promise
And call sharp, shrill cries,
Admonishing one another to silence.

Children come to this place, pause,
And bend groundward, planting small warm hands
Into dark cool mud.

Damp-kneed, breath rising in pale clouds,
They crouch, waiting, rooted. Breathless,
They are drawn earthward, buried
By the force of their ascension.

Bill Hallinan

The Undisturbed

I woke up thinking
I still fit in ballet shoes
dusty pink,
molded to the shape of
a little girl's foot,
half the size of my own.
Was I once a ballerina?
I dreamt I was.

Holden Caulfield and I take long walks
through virgin wood where I
dig holes, write poems, get dirty
while he watches, content to be my critic.
"They'll never make me a movie," he says
while I spout Irish truth from "Rattle and Hum":
"This is a song Charles Manson stole from the Beatles.
We're stealing it back."

I wear my mother's wedding ring,
The first marriage; my father.
It gives me the best of both worlds.

Allison Lee Adair

Fayetteville

At the silent reveille of spring
azaleas rouse to blossom bright as pain,
as red as blood—or white
as flesh when blood is drained.

Long-legged pines through foaming blooms
are wading, like MacArthur toward a shore,
while overhill young men
with cadenced chant imagine war.

Voluptuous gardens, bright amid the pine,
bee-busy and bird-trilling, angel-breathed
and opaline—a strange vicinity
to Quonset hut and olive drab and dun,
and tramp of boot and parchute
and shouts in unison.

C-130, butterfly,
grenade and rambler rose. Oh, why
is life most lovely
juxtaposed?

Norma Laut

Mother's Altar

Dark walnut dresser
Oiled with lemon
Sits in the shadows
Of mumbled worship.

Red glass candles
Glow for the holy saints,
Winged reptiles
Rest by their feet.

Prayer put in order
By small lavender beads
Linked by chains that carry a cross.

Lily flowers
Don watery pearls, porcelain gown . . .
Wither for mercy.

Man on the cross, bleeds for our sins.
Nails, thorns, halo of light.

Pictures of the dead
Smile at the living.
Wish you were here,
Wish I was there.

Patricia Garcia

Beyond Recognition

A wish wasted on pity
easily fulfilled
like handing out nickels
at intersection tenements

Anything to make you feel better
as if that's what you've always been after
an appropriate gift
if you think it exists
and I'll be a child again
when you leave me alone

The phone calls come so often
ever-thinning air
broken like a record scratched
beyond recognition

Embarrassed to set out alone
vicariously dying
through lifetimes of making
second mistakes for the first time

Jay Schwartz

Flushing Meadow Park

Flushing Meadow Park on a Thursday afternoon
i send subliminal messages to the boys
reflected by mica mirrors
and shamrocks on
double death on 1st and 2nd base
and ice cream (i scream) nonchalantly swaddled in Styrofoam cups
spoon me some upheavals, thick milk
i know not mine
while obsidian ash performing on the street corner under
    the street lamp asks me
Jimmy Crackcorn
i don't care

that south bend where there are these spareribs
luxuriating in stumpy bottles of beer
and strawberry lingerie
noisier but fatter
i think patting on my stomach top
snap-snap-snapping at the celery
in my Bloody Mary
unborn is my child

Anna Kristen Ganey

Russian Roulette with a Cap-Gun

I sat like a child in the back seat
of the old Palomino as we tracked the
country outback roads in the town of
Kannapolis: A hot southern gauntlet
where truckers break and the town lives
twenty years behind the rest of us.

My cousin played with his static-filled
radio, his arm hanging out the window; his
bully-bulged stomach dripping through his
open flannel and over his tight, muddy jeans.

Through a coughing laugh, he told me
to load the cap-gun with the small, red caps.

I paused. The rumbling beneath my feet
continued; the spitting muffler that
jiggled and clanked as we hugged the
dark turns in the Carolina mountain.

I raised the cap-gun to my forehead,
eyes closed and released the trigger.
The small spark spit through the open chamber in a
crashing hush, clapped into the air and suddenly ended.

Lanny Morris

Esc

The dull orange glow on a summer's eve,
Bathes the world and calmness strives.
Strong is the hold of the branch to the leaves,
Not to let go until frost arrives.

A tired young man roams the shores,
Of crashing, far, and distant seas.
And when the orange light strikes the moors,
He stands to gaze as waters heave.

Then twilight sings its quiet song,
And shadows 'cross the mead do play.
He turns his tired head to long,
For unknown regions far away.

Peter Dorsey

Hollow

You have left me
hollow
carved out
my insides
stretched and fingered them
like so many pumpkin seeds
you have
emptied out
my eyes and smile
left me longing
if not for wholeness
then at least for a candle

Jessica Gifford

Untitled

For Peola and Calvin
Noonday and midnight the solitary
figures still come
to pace the chainlink fence,
read a poem,
caress a teddy bear, pray.

An a cappella hymn rises, floats
light as a bubble
bursting on shards of grief
hidden by routine.
The mundane will set us free.

Yet the air still shivers,
cold as grave-breath,
reverberating for all time
with their silenced screams.

Joan Patrick

WD-40

I was beginning to think, but
I decided against it because too much
Of a good thing kills itself eventually.
I imagine myself digesting book after book
Of mindless, empty saccharine
Romance novels just as a start,
WD-40 lube on a squeaky mind.
And even then, so much later in the day,
I crack open a couple hundred books of poetry—Keuroac my heroin;
Whitman my Ecstasy;
cummings like LSD, and Dickinson
Like a dark, dry wine.
Then more and more turning pages
Of heavy-heated high school prose,
Reading menu list material,
Abandoning the banned and profane,
Replacing them, underlining them, dissecting them
Until they are nothing more than
Displaced symbols, words, and phrases
On the side of a soda can.

Cynthia Eckles

A Man for All Seasons

In the silent peaceful stillness of misty dawn,
In the joyful welcome of soft daybreak, I dream of you.
Your beloved face, radiantly suffused with desire,
Serenely kissed by the vibrant luster of morning dew,
Lushly fragrant in the blossoming song of spring.

In the dazzling shower of pale, golden sunlight,
In the silver rays of a brand new day, I dream of you.
The cool oasis of your dear, captivating smile,
The sparkle and gleam of blue magnificence in your eyes.
As they bask in splendor on the glorious summer breeze.

In the mellow, cozy heat and shimmering haze,
In the glittering cocoon of high noon, I dream of you.
The promise of sumptuous delights in your caress,
The wonder and beauty of spellbinding magic moments,
Turning my world into autumn's dearest colors.

In the glimmer of lovely carnelian sunsets,
In the enchanted hush of sheer evening, I dream of you.
The precious gift of your deep love, a rare treasure,
Profoundly poignant, all that my heart could ever wish for,
A safe haven, in the warm glow of winter's fire.

FNA Cenidoza

Snake Handling at Mt. Zion Full Gospel Church, Georgia

The Spirit moves ominously,
rattles like dry seeds
in a gourd, waits in a dark box.
I'd see how grace stuns a man,
drops him with a quick hand,
splays him like lightning.
Or how the eyes
of a healer are feral,
the yellow translucence
cold as a snake.
But now the long and writhing
diamondback
curls like sequined strands, rises
in rings, spreads a pendant neck to neck.
It flicks a tongue,
the quick fork divining,
fumbling for speech.
It arcs, finds a sudden word:
the pink mouth opens,
is sibilant, whispers in the blood, tests.

John Valentine

Pavlov Remembered

here
beneath this pitted wood
that dots the eye, stanchioned in the now
hollow socket this shaft
and transom inscribed
windward leans
above the bone tamed by me.

this now maggot'd flesh
i extracted from chaos, soothed it
with the unctuous milk of kindness,
purged from its unworthy bowels, autonomy.

shapeless
erstwhile blood and sinew
i established regimen and form—
wreathed with collar, covered its chain
with roses.

here
beneath clay and sand exhume
this skull of enormously sad visage
resting uncomfortably on its crossbones.

Gregory William Farrell

Stealing Watermelons

In the heady parlance of our youth,
Stealing from a patch was called a raid.
Taking melons from a roadside stand
Just didn't seem to make the grade.
The farmer's field was in the open,
But the kids would have to climb a fence.
Sometimes the farmer had a shotgun,
With salt for shot at the boy's offense.
Sometimes the boys would pull a fast one,
Slip the melon into the irrigation ditch,
From which it was recovered downstream,
A heist neatly made without a hitch.
Now the farmer oft was not so naive
To think he was free from such forays—
He just let the kids take off with booty
And fondly remembered his youthful days.

> *Stewart C. Harvey*

The Queen of Nothing

She wears her rags as riches.
From her hand-me-down looks to her second-hand thoughts.
Eyes somebody already broke taped together with tears.
A cracked smile held on by quivering lips.
A broken heart stitched with memories.
Despair and distress make up her wardrobe.
Walking on feet protected only by her teardrops.
Her soul as a diamond necklace, her mind as a broach.
This girl lives in a cardboard mansion and has a metal
Limo with a wobbly wheel.
Lives her life for what?
A quick poke into society with its hob-nob, pish-posh
Wishy-washy way.
She is content talking to her mop handle and drinking
From a bag.

> *Timothy Gavin*

Untitled

Hark! The masquerade is on!
Beneath a sky of azure splendor;
Floating clouds in vestal white
Gently bow to hills of flaming sumac
While all the trees in gypsy costumes
Dance madly with the wind.
Air with magic madness filled
Intoxicates the human mind with yearning
Far beyond the ordinary reach.
But who would trade for any other season.
Circle, circle high bonfire smoke
Wafting rare perfumes of maple, oak, and pine
Charged with Romany dreams of wanderlust
I stand on a windy day with sea gulls crying overhead
And green, wild sea booming on the sand.

> *Lillian S. Varol*

Waterville, Ireland

In summers past,
Oona and oodles of Chaplin children
And carefree maidens and friends
Romped here
Like giggling neighborhood kids
Playing shadowy oak trees and darkened patios.

In summer present,
I saw
Space,
Sun
Stillness,

And a lonely boat

Empty of fish and men.

> *Betty F. DeGuzman*

Only Human

Time is most itself when passing.

So bees wend high above the road
Where a fine dust cloud rises
And white birds appear in the gathered green.
No painter here to take their wing to canvas,
No inscrutable simplicity in a Buddha's cluttered mime,
No poet giving voice to mute mud,
No philosophic sap, swollen knot of superadded wisdom,
Nor a Christ lodged in the slowing green snail . . .

Such are limp hands white with sleep,
Hair as water burns on golden sand,
Or wooden dark in its stillness.

It be the blaze of afternoon brings the heat of world,
Listing here on slight breezes, where
Over your radiant slumbers sugar cypress arms
Canopy my nodding vigil.
Invisible breath: guardian of our present
Steals through infant lips, of a new old world,
Secretly to stir the leaves around.

Time is most itself when passing.

> *Erich von Abele*

The Lady in the Lake

The lady in the lake clawed her crooked
Fingers pulling earth to her breast
Feeding it—all her children.
Two fish-lovers dance
A pizzicato (moving like this)
Roaring heels of alabaster
Shells rubbing ridges
Like washboards, together.

The sight of pleasure and object of fear
She-spawn. Not to be looked at. Stripteases,
The slow peeling away of layers
A guise revealing the good woman.

She is autoeroticism, as her parted
Lips move toward spectators.
Eyes, castrating tentacles,
She watches the fish-lovers
(Dip-like-this) around the heartbells.
She uncovers the shosheen whisper of a
shoulder and removes
Only a glove.

> *Katherine K. Dougherty*

Untitled

Venomous snakes
Inject my soul,
I shed my skin
To give you more,
We dance around
Between this life
And the next,
You crawl over me
To bite my flesh,
With you in me
I cannot fade;
The gods are greedy,
They want you, too;
Changes are unreal,
What you want from me
I could never
Be that way
I could never
Be a snake.

> *Kay Zywicki*

My Oak Tree

I climb
and reach
with dirty little fingers
for higher boughs
to watch the picture clouds caressing
slate-filled skies in the violet breeze.

You speak a gentle rock-a-bye,
with timeless voice of rain-soaked bark,
and long lost trunks;
of whitewashed fence days
and secretly-perfect fishing holes,

Of captured insects
exploding from mayonnaise jars
onto sun-dribbled leaves.

My ageless oak;
eternal
like squirming churchfuls
of musty Sunday sermons;
and the endless days of school
just before summer.

Monica C. McTyre

Hale Bopp

In celestial measure
my boat's no larger than a
salty drop of sea,
but my eyes see the bullet hole
the moon punctures in the dark,
my skin senses the wind
that can cast me aside
like a tear falling into a fan.
And my thoughts of you,
though they burn but a milli-amp of current
compared to the energy of suns,
travel light years to the comet (and back)
to recapture what Minoan lovers pondered one night
in Phaistos, when a star suddenly skidded
between bear and bull,
trailing ravelings of galactic glitter,
untying the universe.

Steven M. Pratt

Friendly Fire

Flickering, tickling, tongue of flames
Who dance before my eager eyes,
Beneath these sparkling stars I deem you,
Immortal and all-wise.

Crackling, cringing bright orange muses
Why are you not considered live?
Busied with ceaseless churning motion
Like honey bees in hive.

Tunneling, twisting bowels of power
While burning sinful, shady schemes,
Evolve past natural barriers
Disturbing all dark dreams.

Aromic, agile balm of mankind
When married to young virgin wood,
Consume the vig'rous night with longing
As only lovers could.

Weakening, dying ashen embers
Which, still, glowing in radiant heat,
Continue to defy the night
And warm my weary feet.

David Crowder

The Bracelet

I look down between the scars and the fine black hairs to the bracelet on my right wrist. Every day since I was fifteen it has been clasped there to remind me of the grandmother I never knew. As I stare at its rings and plates interconnected, I notice the wear forty years of scratches, rubs, tiny little dents; some fashioned by the Mexican silversmith, like an eye with tarnished lashes, on a silver platter with hammered-out clumps of scrub grass all about. The clasp is hidden, as though it should not be undone. I undo it anyway.
It comes off with a flat clank, like a muffled wind chime.
(the inside is much different)
The metal is smooth, there is no artistry here, save the shapes darkened by sweat and age, a tinge of sooty grime. It reminds me of the portrait I saw once: the small oval, brown paper framing, crinkling, as though time had bent its very fibers; and then the picture, shades of sand, dark at first then brightening towards the center, her head brushed by soft light; the half-smile; dark eyes; the resemblance is faint. She was about that age when she bought the bracelet somewhere in Mexico from an old, sunburnt man whose tired hands
had sweated to make the prize; she couldn't have known as she gave it to her daughter that I would wear it someday.

Michael Hiratzka

Definition of the Earth

When I walk in the mid-day heat
pound the rock of suburban streets
the houses look like newborns, cute
loved by only those who own them

Little maples flicker and yawn
threaten to grow this place warm and unsterile
but razor-tip jets still beat the wind eastward
scour the slowly hardening sky

My skin must be picket fence white
weed-whacker orange and swimming pool blue
I feel synthesized without you, sweet Mamma,
camouflaged with suburbia

But you and me blend
with such sweet lack of effort that
although nature can't be shed through evolution
or human convolution we make new definitions

so when twilight falls grainy
and I say its pixels
smile your honey-drip smile and know
natural is a relative term

Daniel Corry

Ode to Sold Souls

Le Démon Vient à Côté:
(the demon is coming near)

spawning from the seed of my sleeping mind,
being the unseen beating, flying thing
sinking slowly down a poisoned iron vine
beneath the dark spells of phantom chanting

in glass and under raining sand, trailing
blood from my torn and twisted, tattered soul
which has been anxiously sold sparingly
to Satan for all there is yet to know.

where i may be my only vanquished foe:
welcome Guests, to a feast where Devils dine.
come in, pretend as if rage conceals fear:
the pleasure and fortune is all of mine.

for, i mistook it for a Demon there,
yet it was only a shining Mirror . . .

Eric Nesser

For You Mama

Woe to the Downyfresh:

From the hall linen closet I gathered them all,
One lump of pluff after another;
Sheets of summer cotton and blankets and terrycloth,
Breeze-fresh basketball swabs of white after white
After pale blush and white.

And stripping as I carried, with wide eyes and teeth,
Sun on face, I piled them high;
A milky mass propped against the dustworthy walls.
One greedy combat boot to weight down the toppling marvel.

Alone . . . my heaving . . . and a splash,
I snapped in place one crooked match.
A spark, a smile, and an ethanol bath.

   Karen A. Weise

Afternoons

You cut your hand
A breathing wound
and weeping willow
this surrender pressing flags
white against a sky
too low for you to stand or cradle
the weight of dreams sound and sleeping.
And the afternoons lean the elbow of my tongue
And the afternoons unfold the mute,
without fear.
I dare to speak, my lips to swallow with kiss
your cherry stain sour with slow breathing
and shedding rainfalls,
a crimson gathering of sunsets, false.

   Kathryn Parks

Straight to Linton

if a woman saw a woman fall
like courtney from her throne
i'd hope she'd fix a parching fix
fixed to dry a bone
and persons seen in the obscene
(useless Porlock stroll)
i'll find a place, with resting face
where they finally feel the toll
i can never stand a hand in hand
while rosebuds left to drift
like a soul afloat, adrifting sole
and others—angels lift

i found my way past Jonson's art
that faired so straight like His straight part
and in that time i've lain apart:
a Don Quixote, minus heart

   Yobevita Gen

Sonnet in E♭

I have not yet removed her from my eyes
from the thrall of her slickly-quilted skirt
she is the grace eternal of such despise
as woeful cannot rise above the dirt

Your tears are such that I am left weak
and weakly wondering at modesty
contend with myself prevailing speak
why do you rob my words reluctantly

Beethoven has your form on variations
recorded from my lips onto the page
and the Earth and all the Earth's creations
wonder at such luster on the frame

but wait until I rid her from prison
she will have failed and already risen

   Wes Nixon

Incongruent Twosome in View

Softly doffing his dashing hat, fogey debuts his pale, thinning pate,
revealing faint fuzz on his slick-domed capitulum;
Eyes, lackluster, weakly look through lenses dulled by decades of sun

Slight hunchback bends his stoop, deferentially; head's down-
cast . . . as if encumbered by superlative knowledge;
Finely fishnetting his mellow, hollow-eyed visage
are deep-seated creases, slicing his age-spotted rind
(Wrinkles remind of relentlessly progressive time,
of mortality's tenuous continuity)

Archaic threads float on his bony frame,
evidence of attrition diminishing his weight;
Suspenders keep his pleated pants afloat,
and purple sneakers pamper his tender toes

Timid, shuffling baby steps slow-mo' his decrepit form;
He wades, laboring through hushed waiting room, at a cold molasses pace
(Never again to hurry, in nervous haste,
he has no wherewithal to scurry, forevermore)

Geezer scratches his scraggly beard, and cracks a smile;
Deifies a baby girl, ascended in a sleep induced exile;
Red gnarly cane's his friend for life . . . but not for long.

   Richard E. Smith

Mass: Dandelion Regression

In memory of John G. Watling
Please do not
Regress to your bad times,
She says, but she cannot redress my grieve—
Ances that are not about ounces but these hundred
Pounds upon my head, of the smashed
Oriental flower.
It is not her fault; I am faulted in my heart
And mind,
For not murdering
Those of us who flattened
Hoa, the friendliest flower of Vietnam.
Both she now
And the mourning, most loyal cohort
(Hoa, though hurt) did say of that feeling, "Do not free it."
Though many of you may be,
With my life and thought I am
Not this satisfied: the dandelion
Goes white; . . .

   Wm. A. Watling

2:00 a.m. San Diego

There was a time
when tools were taken from the earth.
Stone was fist
and trapped earthen pigment,
actions spoke of future,
of boundaries that did not exist
so welcomings presided all hours.

Ageless children
script false identities;
alienated data on brick walls
of the dilapidated town.
They discover their names
like a pre-human discovering its land—
choice materials are more modern

Marking boundaries
is like the lion
who rips at the bark of the tree,
who tears at the heated ground—
a person's world
of signs we can't read.

   Jorge Maldonado

Balseros

the under-tow of gasping breaths
surfs each worried rafter
praying for the tides to release
the ropes and shackles
fear is not in death but in living

under the reigns of the chicken king
ominous skies crack open a hell the raven would run from
so the ocean screams and whirls canvas and match-stick rafts
as if the cries of whales
send rings of radar crossing the keys
oh, save us, save us, please

every minute the sun steals
a layer of skin that has already been beaten and bruised
every wave hurls the salt and bile that lines the stomachs

guantanamo bay beds the survivors
reported are handed scraps of paper
"por favor 375-6343 Estrada"

families await notice
searching list after list
like the wives of POWs
   Pamela G. Greenside

The Introduction

(for David)
Even through the screen I catch fleeting glimpses of you—
peering beneath a participle,
lurking behind a linking verb,
grinning beside a gerund.

I don't think you realize how much is revealed by your small i's,
the way you throw away punctuation
(meaningless symbols discarded,
lying forlorn in abandoned heaps),
the long pauses before your responses.

It's the spaces between words,
the yawning chasms at the ends of sentences,
the things you don't say
that invoke more than any damp pressing of flesh.

You may be able to hide behind h's and curl up around c's,
but, out of the corner of my eye,
I see the graininess of your silhouette—
the light shining between pixels.

In these moments it doesn't matter that I've never met you—
I still sense of ghost of your smile
through miles of buzzing telephone line.
   Beth Pizio

Horse Latitudes

Every life has horse latitudes.
After a cancer was cut from my breast
and a fiftieth birthday,
I was snagged in the waves
of green Sargasso Sea,
faced death unless I changed.

So, I too unloaded
my most precious cargo:
real estate bobbed in the wake,
diplomas, books, career,
keepsakes, rainy day chores,
relationships, even tears
spun out in the drift.

As light as spirit,
   I prayed for the wind and wave;
As large as sky and sea,
set sail for the dubious future.
   Nancy Shattuck

Personal Space/Time

I have been dreaming cosmologies.
Red shifts. Curved space/time.
Metagalaxies. Black holes in space.

Finding "big bang" theories more congenial
Since my life sucks backwards
To such an event

And I cannot see my expansion
As beginning from nowhere.

The "steady-state" people
Are steady-state people.

Captured suns and imploding stars
Not for them.

I am enthralled by Olber's Paradox:

If space and stellar matter were truly infinite
All where we looked would be light.

I examine my life.
How can I believe in that?

It is easier to believe black holes in space.
   Dr. James Story

Morning

I slept in the folds of one whose dark, comfortable curtains slowly came
      undone.
Letting me fall for so long . . .
That time just let me go the other way,
Drifting closer to the ice stars than to the dust
I became intoxicated with the memory of childhood.

I am not done with night wanderings.
The urgency of beauty casts its shadow on the snow
Seeking out the dangerous ones who smell invisible wounds after love,
Leaving you to perish,
The persistence of memory pulsating against a grey gate.

And what of that sunlit dome that breaks from the highway at dawn
Promising some vague hope,
Coming closer to making you feel more good and loved than any man
      ever could
Even though it's made of the stuff of the dead.
They just breathe different now . . .
with the wind instead of their hearts.
   Ann Zalkind

The Snowman

the snowman my uncle will never build
stands frozen in my nana's mind:
a pipe in his mouth, a hat on his head,
with jamie's face, but oddly different:
no lines crease his brow;
no frown touches his eyes made of coal.
made of snow, the snowman is strong
it's not jamie at all,
but still a welcome change
from the stone that bears his name.
he should be building a snowman, nana says,
but he is gone.
i will build the snowman for her,
stop her icy tears:
the tears that would not be
if only he were as strong as my snowman:
made of ice and tears and pain and love.
she misses you, jamie . . .
look at the snowman i've made
to stop nana's tears.
   Sarah A. McFadden

The Secret Garden

We'll place her in a secret garden
With faded walls and drooping dahlias
A weathered bench where she can sit
with sweet alyssum at her feet
She'll find her own companions
tiny faces without bodies
If she remains completely still
they may not come too close
The wind brings snarling voices
Something moves behind the hedge
flying dragons brush her cheek
She'll simply close her eyes
The sun upon her face
will heal the jagged scar
the memories were almost gone
the day she pulled the trigger

Denise Brosat

When I Was Three

Grandma, whose hair is like a silver sheet of paper hanging
to her shoulders. It looks like a mystery to me after
seeing her all day with the braided coils on top of her
head . . . but not now . . .
It is down as she combs it flat and white against her shoulders
for it is time for her private prayer.
She goes to her room and I peer at her
through a crack in the curtain that is her bedroom door.

She kneels down at the side of her bed and folds her hands
around her prayer beads. She raises her eyes to the cross
on the wall above her bed. The lamp at the farthest wall
turns her hair to a shimmering white halo around her head.
She looks like an angel as she kneels there, raises her eyes
to heaven, and prays "Otce nas (Our Father)" and "Zdravas
Maria (Hail Mary.)"

Anita Lisko Gaab

A Time to Remember

To Rush and the others alike beset
Who spew their venom and call it wit;
Whose maculated, wrinkled words beget
Armed militias "mit ruhig festem Schritt."
Still the gentle people do work and play,
They earn a living and obey the law;
Forgetting the tremors of yesterday
And the booted thugs with their swastika.
But lies glibly forged remain ever blind
So launder and launch your words with care,
Lest they come to lodge in some twisted mind
And smoke from ovens will scorch the fetid air.

Donald Kuzma

Artefact

Lentiled clay
of the upper reaches
wafting pottery
from Homo erectus
on beaches made blue with August

She leaves the Ice Age
adroitly imprisoning Earth
at the ridge
where the highest tide detains
cracked mounds like picanthripi nipples.

Before your Neolithic utensil
spirits itself away
bury your undead tongue,
among the shells there is room
for the silence of a novel era.

Martin Alejandro

Spendthrift at 80

In days when I was profligate
with time
The disregarded clock moved on.

Without knowledge of its
speeding hands,
Or care that life was
circumscribed
I let the hours slip away
un-named . . .
Not even to be caught in
hazy memory.

A minute, an hour, a day,
A week, a month, a year . . .
Once only words in a child's
book of time,
Are now compass stars to
steer by
In a swift and towering
sea of years.

Alysan C. Hooper

So White

the only picture i thought would suffice
to capture my beauty
was the one the coroner took.

A hardwood floor
a black satin dress (flowing, clinging to white petal skin)
  —so white
Hands tucked under head rest upon a blanket whose embroidery
whispers a child's name

pictures of you,
poems of you,
candles and violets
encircling
your CD was on repeat, the one you signed
and i drowned the pills with a bottle of Turning Leaf, your
favorite wine.

Nigal C. Wagner

Christopher

My precocious little brother
grins as opportunistically as Columbus,
so eager to perfect his exploratory abilities.
Sailing his little Niñas, Pintas, Santa Marias,
he cruises down a sudsy western route
of imagination.
He splashes into his voyage, head first,
prepares his minute men
for the random adventures
of newly discovered lands.
Christopher the great,
so pleased with his discoveries,
until his heart sinks
like a tiny plastic ship,
washed ashore with the realization
that he is still in his bathtub.
Land ho! Land ho! He departs
from an ocean of foam,
only to retreat onto a fluffy
flag of Spain.

Cristina Rafols

Some Breezes . . .

Downtown was again a forest waiting outside . . . like a tired salesman;
I could see it through the sealed window
from the quiet heights of the building.

And I have no damn patience for any of it.
Something stole that away very easily one day.

Still, I can find strength to laugh because I might have missed something,
something depressing while I was making the living,
like that revolution talk I kept hearing about on the bus route.

That talk never penetrates office buildings . . . never will.

And though I felt like a bison slowly moving with its grunting herds,
I noticed something, even with my head full of foggy distractions.

The others didn't notice it following us home playfully, but I saw the
patches of grass dancing and the green leaves
waving like schoolchildren in the trees.

It was as if the sky had thrown down millions of perfect feathers without counting
them, but I knew what it really meant:

God had not forgotten us, the weakened but free spirits here
in the glamorless part of the city where nothing usually moved with any kind of grace.

Sean Mack

Realms of Gold

He who embraces blank verses, disperses
The ode, the sonnet and lay.
We who align with cadence and rhyme, climb
The mountain of Keatsian survey.

I propose free verse is prose.
A rich and creative art.
But it misses the scent of a bourbon rose
And the throb of an aching heart.

A poem is a magical musical thought
With measured regimen
Silent with style the explorer brought
To a peak in Darien.

Michael L. Eby

Samson and I (Version 2)

Even as the slayer of Ashkelon did my soul enchant and betray;
Wiles of veiled evil amongst the perditious depths, my heart to steal away.

With mirth and glee did she the one, find delight in my self-perfidy;
To hold this flesh unto my own was to embrace death and ignominy.

Cast as refuse betwixt the sodden earth and fragments of bone from those before;
To ail alone in expectant repose, to rise again no more.

Though my head be as bare as the soul I once knew;
I yet hold the mandible and my hair grows anew.

For now, I must wait, inexorable time, my friend, I am finding;
For it shall unravel my tethered spirit from within this internecine binding.

Upon my return, the strength shall not delay;
For though snakebit I am, it will not take me away.

Anthony DeTommasi

Build a House of Dreams

Houses are made of rock and stone, of brick and wood, of sweat and plans, of dreams.
Little boy with sticks and nails constructs a tower
Up to the clouds and beyond the sky.
The proud architect eagerly welcomes anyone daring enough to sign on for the complete tour.

"Clean up that mess and come inside!"
Seven years old, misunderstood, he packs his bag and travels
to the end of the driveway.
Beneath the shade of the ancient oak he contemplates the secrets of time.
Eleven more years he wages war with those who will not allow him validation.

Driving, riding, wheeling; singing, searching, reeling,
Rooted inexplicably to the warm earth, steadfast and single-minded,
He earns slowly, oh, so slowly, the respect of all those lizard-folk with
Cataracts and scales. (Granted, those things are hard to get rid of)

A young man now, hammer in hand, plans spread out before him,
The house of dreams teeters on the brink of reality.
A second time he welcomes them in, but leaves the back door ajar.
Maybe now they will see that honor abides within the dreamer's soul,
Not on page 179 of the text book.

Maureen Kovach

Monuments of the Moment

I look to the ruins of Elysium,
Slain by a reality I never knew.
Do I recognize something of myself
In the rusted flesh of those monuments?

Now, all that sits in the west is the sun
And a bleak promises which manifests itself
In the deep lines which deface my features
With little regard for my mortal pride.

The west whispers this perpetual promise,
Sealed by the former occupants of Eden
And perpetuated by pestilences
Either natural or contrived.

Glory knows only a moment
While strife knows a lifetime.
I do recognize something of myself
In the rusted flesh of those monuments.

    Phillip Collins

Untitled

She shed her skin of ancient husbands,
her sovereign beauty broke forth.
The peach ocean bled over the naked covers,
her reign of sleeping ended
And she emerged a butterfly queen.
. . . the ice caps melted over the wooden sink,
she thought of the tears
and almost died.

    Maggie Glenn

For Kent to Alison

When the garden is bare and the ivory trellis
weeps against the wall, sunlight shadows
the garden and the ground is cool.

Kent's season is one of tenderness, a season
to be kind to the garden . . .

And when she plays she sleeps by the hearth
in New England; keeping within the memories of
a snowflakes dance: isolation, belonging, and place;
keeping within the memories of the New England
winter.

    Vincent Bratcher

Spring in the Market

She sits there a sister to herself
the shelf of her lap a throne for
peanuts dropped down in taps
while pigeons play the pavement

Some gray God had swept the sky
thrown rays of bright thinned
silence sprayed here to
touch on people in passing

She cracks a knuckled claw on
one seed to sow in her belly and
inhales the washed air to rinse
her heart, chuckles sideways

Shucking the shells

    Cary Tracy

Youth Hostel

My mother had many dresses.
Their hems hung by my ears,
As I knelt inside her closet,
Waiting to be let out.

Silk ones were chilly against my forehead.
And my hair would get caught on the metal fasteners
Of her belts. They dangled like a python
With one barbed fang.

Other belts were stiff, coiled
Ready to spring upon command.
To make certain none were broken,
They were rotated in use.

I pretended I was in a theater.
Times when you enter before sunset,
You exit into darkness.
I imagined buttered popcorn, boxed candy,

The seat beside me, empty.
My head dismal against the door.
I had forgotten the reason for my punishment,
Forgotten to wear a warmer shirt.

    Susan Lien

Accosted
in a dimly lit café.
Faces from a broken beer bottle
look down from across a tattered lampshade—

sitting in a cushioned chair
rolling my neck back in ennui—
comments stationed behind a gas respite
cash register—

next to warm, screaming
people in foggy crowd—
look to the lights with the disconnected wires
The melodies—

strain through the voices of second hand
smokers—
the beats of a heart—
a happy guitar.

    Yuriko Kimura

Hope In March

The wind blows up from Mexico—
Sombreroed zephyr on the wing;
It passes through the wavy plains,
Where dusky scissortails will sing.
It brings an energy to us;
So long we've been in sleep as dead,
And cabin-crazed kids and iris bulbs
Awake and lift their drowsy head.
The blond-and-blue, the next-door girl
Appears and asks my princess out;
Together, they ride and run just like
They did before the light went out.
Too long, too long the blasts have blown;
The earth has kept her needed rest.
Today, discover that spring is here.
Today, I think this time is best.

    Robert Wyer

The Pause Phase

The only time life pauses, so we can take a breath
Is with the arranging, after we lose one in death.

Chores always looming we think has to be done
Patiently wait till our senses, are no longer numb.

We have to soon set a day to lay them at rest
Till then obstacles relent, the river stays its crest.

There are chosen ones, when this time phase evades
That are handed peace with the passing, not multifarious charades.

Goals are a blur others stress to achieve
While the grievous are straining to hold what they believe

We can't comprehend the effort to care,
Or need participles to nourish, the pain that we bear.
We float in a bubble, held aloft, with only breathing air.

Maurine Fergueson

Home

At times I reflect backwards to days that once were bright
The home of mine was perfect each morning, noon and night.

It sat upon a hillside and faced the morning sun
I knew that I belonged there and had no need to run.

And soon the flowers I did plant grew tall, four special type
The joy of heaven I did feel—I knew not tears to wipe.

I wanted to remain there, 'twas written on my face
But He told me that go I must and leave this special place.

The storm roared like a lion—too much for mortal beams
And never more would I behold the place of my true dreams.

Shocked and lonely I did weep to flee and start to roam
Shocked and lonely I did weep to find another home.

Homes of so many types I saw till one I'd not forget
In ways it differed from the first and faced the sun that set.

And though I cannot forecast what will become of me
This new home brings me comfort, I'm happy now to be.

Some men have tried a lifetime and gambled with their dice
In hope to find the type of home that I have now found twice.

This is the final time I'll move, no cause for me to roam
The Lord has blessed it from above, this place that's now my home.

Philip Oddo

I

Pattern and Sway

Barren trees stand like dry pipes and wait
Frozen 'til sweet breeze tiptoes warm
Lone spirits drift from time to time by freeze breeze and lean
Branches like thorns sting upon the eye and scream in storms
and rain a thundering
Creek, creek, creek go their elbows and yearn for mercy
Teaching continues, like blowing through straws and inspire
respect for loneliness
They speak to me of trust
Touching seas with vibrations and dropping leaves as proof of change
Humming through windows and weeping history's pain
Surviving spoils of war and bittersweet kisses beneath its bow
Gentle and tired limbs have scooped many a curious boy and
cradled him with memories to last a lifetime
A tree of a lifetime and centuries swept beneath its roots
To still stand and stand another chill of change until a spring
daybreak gingerly urges on the sprouts
And trees recall the pattern and sway.

Alexis Wilson

Our Gray Shingled House

There's a gray shingled house we grew up in
The rooms filled with laughter, the walls paper thin.
Mom cooking in the kitchen, Dad working in the yard,
Sharing much love, and trying oh so hard.
Many years have passed, we're all on our own
Mom and Dad waiting for our call on the phone
The room's getting dimmer, the loudness of TV,
Waiting for our visits like it used to be.
Mom is getting tired, Dad is slowing down
Their once smiling faces now wear a frown,
They keep on giving all that they can,
This wonderful loving woman, this kind gentle man.
It's our turn, Mom and Dad, to look after you
Making you comfortable in all that you do.
That gray shingled house will live with us forever,
Will our love ever die? The answer is never!

Frances A. (Damico) Hall

Destiny

I want to remember how to laugh,
I want to remember how to live.
Dear God, please don't let the trials of my life,
    impede upon the hope I have for the future.

Let me see the sun peak through the clouds,
Let me climb the mountain to reach for the stars.
Help me to accept that your way is best,
Help me to accept that your way is mine.

Karen Hoino

Filling A Space

When a person who you love very much dies,
    it leaves a space nothing can fill.
When one hears or sees certain things,
    it makes you think back.
Back to the days,
    when they were alive.
Remembering the times you shared,
    whether faint or clear.
It isn't always the same.
    Not being able to be with them.
And when you feel pain in that spot,
    just remember all the time you shared together.
It will fill the void until,
    that day comes again.
The day that you start,
    missing that person once more.

Marie Hadden

My Treasure

The treasure I hold within me
Has only been seen by one.
The only one is my true love;
The treasure of what we've cherished and done.

The truth stays within me.
My love shines out through
The depths of my loving heart
Longing to be with you.

I am much filled with happiness
With your beauty, with your love.
My hopes keep soaring high,
As high as the angel above.

You are the treasure I hold.
The only love of my life.
My soul, my spirit, my dreams . . .
From dawn 'til moonlight.

Roselyn Alviar

Our World

Our world is such a wondrous sight
It fascinates me day and night
But how can its beauty stay
When the smog sends it away

It seems we fail to realize
We're using up all the supplies
Another world we will not get
And all our losses we'll soon regret

Our mistakes we cannot erase
But some of the beauty we can replace
We must leave something for the rest
And hope that they will do what's best

For this world is not ours alone
And new seeds of life will be sown
Give them the chance to make their way
And bring beauty back to our world someday.

Samantha Hamilton

The Big Five-O

When we are born, our days begin
And don't slow down through thick or thin.
As we go on they turn to years
And multiply 'mid smile and tears.
Nothing can stop the march of time
As it carries us up through our prime.
They're only numbers, don't you see,
They really don't apply to me.
But alas, they take their toll,
Our bodies are somewhat less than whole.
But God does the counting so face the fact
That there are some things we can't subtract.
If these numbers cause despair and gloom,
It's time for you to grab a broom
And sweep them behind you, out of sight,
And press ahead with all your might.
So count your blessings as you go
And be thankful for "The Big Five-O."

Olaf Dahle

A Poem For Paul

My loves favorite flower is the rose.
It matters not what color or where it grows.
He planted one in a flower bed close to a swan and a heart of red.
When in the winter, it was covered with snow,
He sat, and pondered will it grow?
Then in the spring when warm rains caressed the ground,
And dogwood, tulips, and jonquils did abound,
Amongst the blooms was a sprig of green
It quickly grew and was readily seen
Clinging to the fence with the Swan and heart of Red,
A beautiful rose in the flower bed.

Barbara E. Jones

Desertion's Penality

You can take my heart and crush it
You can fill my eyes with tears
You can walk away, leaving me and your son
But you'll pay in future years.

You can break your vows without a thought
Leave us without a dime
But "The Lord is always with us"
Each hour and all the time.

You'll recall when you get old and lonely
Without a solitary friend
The life, the love, the family, you gave up
Yes—You'll Remember then.

Sherry Kersey

I Am Mars

So, now your intellect is mature enough for you to visit me.
We've gone around Sol six billion times since my veins went dry.
You went around father Sol while dinosaurs ruled.
After sixty million revolutions they're relics like me.
Then caveman worshipped Sol, spear or meat.
He had body and mind but no prophet to greet.
I am your sibling with past life extinct, very bland.
The Creator allows his time democracy to stand.
Now the stage is for men to expand future concepts.
Blending many minds toward other star precepts.

Craggy is my verse of rocky feldspar.
Yours is of flowing streams and sentimental tar.
Discipline unfolding slowly reveals beauty hailed.
My red sky and wind leaves rhymes veiled.
Your sentimental philosophy is often thin and prolific.
Born again am I with future growth strong specific.
Toward others stars I am your major shuttle.
Give life birth to galaxy with no rebuttal.
Each human sees the future through many bars.
Patience I have with vast time because I am Mars.

William G. Lawrence

Abyss

In a cold, lonely, dark room
I sit and wait for your love
Candles surround me,
I can feel them when I reach out
Out into the darkness
I have no love to light these candles with
You have taken that away
Please give me something to light my way
Just one word from you
And my room of darkness would disappear
In a flood of light
A flood of warmth and love

Corinne Yonker

Autumn Splendor

Autumn's here with all its splendor;
Its enchanting beauty blankets our town.
What elegant raiment on trees and shrubs.
As green turns to red, orange, yellow and brown!

Flowers, too, keep on giving us heaps of pleasure,
As their blossoms of color stay bravely on
To challenge the touch of Jack Frost's fingers.
As he gleefully shouts to them "Begone!"

Great pleasure we take from this soul-feeding splendor,
As we reflect and gaze on the season of Fall.
We thank our Creator, the master artist,
Who provides this resplendent nature for all.

Evelyn Copple Widner

The Dream Crushers

Dry your eyes my pretty child
Just be yourself, my littlest love
Keep your hopes and your head held high
Remember to rise above

Those disgusting cads who walk around
Will attempt to crush your dreams
They walk about everywhere
They even resemble you and me
Somehow, somewhere, something went wrong for them
So they try to destroy the sparks
Always remember who you are inside
I'll hold your hopes and your dreams in my heart.

Margery Mulberg Tuckman

Who

Our world is full of miracles.
Looking at the sky at night
You see the moon and stars so bright
Made up of gases and dust.
Who put together this miracle?

From winter's ice and cold
The sun starts to warm the earth
Tiny green shoots appear so bold
To bring color to our world.
Who produces this miracle?

Birds starts to chatter and sing
They call to each other to build a nest.
Soft and warm are the breezes of spring.
Wild animals awake from their rest.
Who accomplishes these miracles?

When two together produce a third
This is a miracle most glorious.
"With God all things are possible" is the word.
He alone performs these miracles!

Virginia J. Brady

A Proud Day

As I watched him walking slowly by,
Proudly holding his head up high,
I wondered where the years had gone.
It doesn't seem it's been that long
That I held him tenderly in my arms,
While he melted my heart with his child-like charms.
When I wiped away those tiny tears,
Because of a fall or some unknown fears.
When I first taught him his ABC's,
And he recited them off with such sureness and ease.
The first day I took him off to school,
And he tried so hard to remember the rules.
How he looked so handsome in his Cub Scout suit,
As he gazed at the flag in his best salute.
Then off he went to enter Jr. High.
Oh where, oh where did the years go by?
Now today he's going to be confirmed,
Hoping he remembers the things he has learned.
Dear God, hold him tightly by the hand,
My little boy will soon be a man.

Rose C. Devine

The Unknowledgable

Why is it when a person tries to break bad strings
and become well that there's always someone in the wings
ready to accuse them of hell?
Why make demands that are virtually impossible
when the ill try to heal?
That particular person is always trying to tell you
what to do, how to feel.
Why do people think they have the right to blame
the ill for their own woes?
They should be willing and able to help,
not strip the ill of their psychic clothes.
Why do they feel they are perfect
and tall when spiritually they are so tiny and small?
The ill try so hard to gain control and save face.
Most of the time they just fall.
The ill are ill and should be treated as much,
so why, tell, me why the "so-called" healthy mind
thinks they are qualified
but only appear to be the biggest population of the blind?

Lisa Lindstrom Publisher

Thank You

So many times we've called upon you.
So many times you've helped us through.
Everything that happens, all of life's living,
You are always there, always so giving.

You listen, you hear, you understand,
Then you provide your helping hand.
Giving from you heart in your special way
Has helped so many through a difficult day.

So it come as no surprise,
That you heard our troubled cries.
Of course we'll help, you quickly said
We knew to follow wherever you led.

You walked us through our time of pain
You helped us release the mental strain.
We are once more back on track
Ready for life's next attack.

We thank you for how much you care,
We thank you for always being there.
We sincerely hope that you know,
You're special to us, we love you so.

Sondra Eisenpress

Sons and Daughters

To have a son and daughter, too,
This is a dream one wishes comes true.
Fortunate were we, this came about,
'Twas enough to make one shout!
"Shout what, you ask?"
And well you may.
We've completed our task,
And are proud every day.
Asked I, "A son and daughter, just one?"
This I did, indeed!
However, before it was over and done,
Son and daughter found one to fill their needs.
And now we have sons and daughters,
Two very outstanding pairs!
Doing all they can do,
Claiming: someone cares!

John W. Kauffman

Forever My Friend

I dreamed of golden skies
And seas soft as lullabies.
Where upon a crystalline beach
A maiden danced in a gown of shimmering peach.
Nimble as an imp, she leaped up high
Plucking butterflies from beneath the sky.
She laughed and sang as she played by the sea,
Happy and free as I can only dream to be.
I called her name, but she did not hear,
Until my eyes they filled with tears.
And when she turned to look at me,
I saw in her smile what is yet to be:
One day I'll see my friend beneath golden skies,
And together we'll play by seas soft as lullabies.

Linda M. Fields

An Idea

An idea is a fleeting figment from God
That comes to mind at any time.
It must be written down right away with laud
So as not forever to be lost,
For it may be the spark of something great
No matter what the unpredictable cost;
But when left unnourished, it comes to naught
Because an idea is something which cannot be taught.

Frank Paul Benwell

My Adorable Bahama Land

Oh, adorable islands in the sun,
You are loved by everyone.
Tourists come to your palm fringed shores,
Seeking exciting pleasurable tours.

We Bahamian children love the sea,
The water is clear as clear as could be.
Yes we love to walk hand in hand,
And play in the pink and white glistening sand.

Potato bread, crack conch and more,
Is grounded in our culture for sure.
Oh, tourists come to our islands, please do.
We are waiting to serve people like you!

Mary M. Russell

Unfathomable Nature

Bright is the sunrise in the fall of the year
That signals the approach of winter, so near
The silent beginning of early morn's frost
Reflecting the end of summer, soon lost
Wintertime brings with it, snow flakes galore
floating through space to cover earth floor
Like each of earth's season that comes once a year
Its presence brings to us much need clean air
And when this season finally comes to an end
Springtime is with us, them summer begins

Milton C. Plummer

Ode to the Maple Tree

The French, the English, the Aborigine,
All came together under a maple tree,
They looked, and saw its tiny buds,
Struggling for the light,
Little did they know, there would come plight.

Leaves sprouted true, lustrous and free,
Upon the Ten branches of this Maple Tree,
Too soon came icy winds,
Trying to shake them loose,
They began to struggle, clinging to the tree.

As they were whipped and tossed,
They writhed in fear, flamed with rage,
But the winds were strong, their stems weak,
Soon it was plain to see,
All of them would fall, in their adversity.

Then one by one, they did fall,
And buried,
The French, the English and the Aborigine.

Lee Hamilton

Forever In Love

Taunted with confusion, lost in this web of deception.
I find my way by your words,
"Be strong baby; it won't be long."
Abandoned by those who said that they would never leave.
Here you are standing strongly by my side.
Hurt by letting myself go on things that seem
so real and vowing never to be taken in again.
Here you are making all of that change.
You are my reason for tomorrow.
You are all my hopes and dreams.
And now, because of you, all my
sleepless nights are spent with a smile.
Instead of tossing and turning, I lie facing the sky,
finding the same sparkle of your eyes in each star.
And my deepest thoughts come to the understanding
that there really is someone who loves me.

Rahkim Vickers

Judy, Dear

I see heaven when I look into your eyes.
I look and look, with many a sigh.
The impossible, possible could be,
That beside me, you would always be.

Now, Judy dear, for once, fate was kind,
And did have us in the same mind.
Impossible or not, now I have you
With me always, since I said, "I love you."

Now, Judy dear, I fear words do me fail,
For with your charms, no words do prevail.
The best I can say, your charm I see,
And you mean all the world to me.

Howard A. Deaton

Take The Old Road

The highways of today are wide and fine,
You get where you're going in record time.
The car speeds along, you've no time to wait,
You have to keep that important date.

But just a short way over the hill,
There's another road, so empty and still.
The old road is alone, not traveled today,
As it curves along on its narrow way.

It twists and turns through valleys dim,
And winds along through shaded glens.
Each bend in the road just seems to say,
Aren't you glad you came this way.

Wind through the trees and songs of the birds,
Are the only sounds that can be heard.
God's beautiful work you can see everywhere,
Forget all your worries, forget all your cares.

So take the old road, as you travel along,
And with the birds you will burst into song.
Thank God for His wondrous beauty today,
As you travel along stay on the old highway.

Anna Maxine Holt Leak

Day

The sun has gone down for the day,
I knew the night will be soon
Although it's restful and peaceful too,
I can see the dawn,
Breaking into the morning,
Coming day to stay.

I guess it's evening somewhere,
The noon was the second thing
By pass, the evening of the day
I bring the breakfast of the
Morning for the second end of my stay.

My stay was the beginning,
Of the day in March to May
By the way, the breeze felt good on my skin,
Of my bodily parts,
My hair is brown, my eyes are brown
My skin was soften with pink,
Beneath my feet and my height stood
Still and that is alright with me.

Sarah Nell Newton

Ice Storm

Have you ever woken to the early dawn light with
A feeling that nature was new?
When the stars in the sky,
When the sun and the moon invite a heartfelt embrace
When an ice storm at night made a wondrous sight,
All glistening in glorious time.
When the branches of trees
As they bowed in the breeze
Played a symphony of wind chimes
All emerald bright with sapphire light,
A miracle to behold.
It shatters the mind, it dazzles the eye,
It stimulates all of one's senses.
And if you see true all that's silver and blue
With threads that are made by the cold,
You must be aware, it was all done with care
By the Master who cares for His fold.

Rovert J. Campbell

The Dreamer

A pain like this no one should ever feel.
My heart hurts so bad, I don't know if it will ever heel.
She enlightened my soul when I asked her to share in my life.
Then as quickly as she entered my world, she was gone;
leaving me filled with misery, sorrow, and strife.
My love for her was unconditional, as only I knew.
Yet, that didn't seem to be enough, and I was left with no clue.
When I asked her to be my wife I was sure she was gift from above.
For only the hard could make something more beautiful than a dove.
When I held her in my arms she filled my every being with pride.
I couldn't believe she had promised to be my bride.
But, as fate would have the last resounding word.
An ending to my story had met yet been heard.
As she proceeded to tell me that she loved another, I became visibly shaken.
For I had come to the realization that the dreamer had awakened.

John Garcia

She Wiped His Brow

Imagine the face of the Virgin Mary
As the angel told her of the child she would carry.
Confused and frightened she had to confess
Yet she bore it all with faithfulness.
The pain she felt as she gave birth
To the most glorious baby ever born on earth.
This baby she raised like any child
When he was sick she wiped his brow.
She nursed and cuddled and held his hand
Until he grew up to be man.
Her son so young, yet so wise
She watched as he was crucified.
She wiped the sweat from his brow
As he laid lifeless in the crowd.
This little baby, she held tight
When he could cry on the night.
He ran and played, so full of life.
Now she wipes the blood from his stripes.
God and Mary's sacrifice.

Deborah Ranburger

Lonely

All by self no one by my side.
I feel all alone especially inside.
My life is so simple, nothing different, or unique.
This seems to bother me even when I sleep.
I understand that no one cares,
to take the time to notice no one dares.
Life goes on, so they say.
My loneliness will change, maybe, someday.

Elyce Kluz

Roberta My Child

Bobbi (Roberta), I planned for another child.
That made you third in line.
You were received with open arms and was proud you were mine.
From a small child you had a mind of your own.
Right or wrong you juggled it alone.
Your struggles in life were not what you planned.
You refused all who offered a hand.
I wanted so badly to be of some help but you built a wall
That said "stay out"
Our difference in life was like night and day
Your strong will would get in the way.
Your past can never be changed that's true,
Yet God in His Love and grace has turned it around for you.
No matter what, nothing in life can ever change my love for you.

My Love, Mother
Bette Saraceno Quartarone

Sunflower

The sunflower in its splendor
Can compare with no other,
With its big brown center
And Radiating petals of yellow color.
It stands in the garden tall and straight
As if staring at the sun.
This lovely flower seems to wave at me,
Saying, "Come on have some fun."
But, when the sun hides for the day,
The sunflower nods its head
As if to say,
"Now it's time for me to sleep,
Until the morning sun
Once again begins to peep
Over the mountaintops
So very high
And reaches the center
Of the bright blue sky!"

Dorothy Warren

Nautical Knight

It's late afternoon with a painted red sky,
We board our ship and wave goodbye.

Our rig is a tightly built craft, of mahogany and brass,
With sails of white and a black pirates flag.

We batten down our hatches and prepare to sail,
We chart our coarse with the wind and the gales.

We hit fifteen knots, as our ship leaves the bay,
The sextant and stars will lead us the way.

The seagull and dolphin soon come to call,
On the starboard side as we approach the squalls.

Our nautical vessel slices through the waves,
Soon the night will turn to day.

The first mate checks our position, a top the crow's nest,
With his telescoping periscope, from east to west.

With endless blue waves capped in white,
And sounds of silence, with nothing in sight.

What mysteries the sea must hold deep below,
Of sailors and treasures of long ago.

Bruce Jones

The Admiral

She sat so stoic by the edge of the sea,
She guarded the shore for years.
She reached out and took many in,
She silenced all their fears.

She welcomed the servicemen home from the war,
She made them have hope I'm sure.
They sat on her porch and soaked in the sun,
Until their wounds were no more.

People came from near and far,
To see her exquisite dome.
They rocked on her magnificent porch,
When it became their summer home.

Now she waits to be torn down,
She doesn't understand.
Cape May was her home,
She is part of its history.
How this could happen is such a mystery.

People soon forget of how she helped so many years ago.
They can only see how it will benefit them,
They are so selfish, I know.

Ann Gilmore Taylor

Ghost

Come down from the starlight
That place you've been so long
Moon shining, clock strikes midnight
Chill in the air, wind blows her long black hair
Evil in the night, something's just not right
Here you are before me, three years dead
Her face is pale white, lips red like flame
From the heavens and stars in the night she came

To see you again, is driving me mad
Features transparent, her face is just a haze
Soft kisses I feel as the wind blows
What power has delivered you to me
I will never know
But fast as you came
You vanish and go
Leaving me in the cold
Night all alone

John Stanley

The Belated Awakening

The day finally came when he had to wake up,
For he wasn't getting much from life's brimming cup.
He sat down and tried to figure out
How his predicament came about.

In high school he was the all-star tight end.
Everyone wanted to be his best friend.
As his ego inflated, he deserted his studies,
And began to hang out with the wrong kinds of buddies.

He lived for football; academics he did deplore.
He knew college coaches would be knocking at his door.
His ego was regrettably his downfall,
For no college coaches came to call.

His younger brother, no great athlete was he;
So he studied hard and won his college degree.
The foundation for his future was laid,
But the tight end saw his dream of greatness fade.

Margarette Combs Saunders

The Problem Solver

All the pain I have ever felt
Is coming to gather now.
Seeing what is and what will
Never be, breaks my heart.
I carried the pains of many others
For most of my life and now they are
All too busy to even look at mine.
If anyone ever had a problem or were hurt in the heart,
They would call on my always open ear.
Now is the time for my problems and my hurt,
But the only one who has the time to listen is me.
When these people are finished talking
Out their problems with me, they always feel better.
How can I feel better, when I'm the problem solver.

Michele Younger

A Daughter's Concern

Hello, mother. Where've you been?
I've called once. Now I'm calling again.
I bet you were up before the dawn
And outside planning to mow the lawn.
What are the plans for you today?
Is there a meeting? Are you going away?
If so, be sure, fill your car with gas,
And caution! Don't you dare drive too fast.
Lock your doors and set the light
For fear the meeting's long, and you return at night.
I don't like your traveling alone,
So be sure you take your cellular phone.
Keep your signal flashlight by your side,
And don't you dare give a stranger a ride.
No matter where you plan to go,
You call me first to let me know.
Take care of yourself and call each day,
No matter if you've nothing to say.

Now friends, if like me, these things you're told,
Your children think you've grown too old.

Roberta E. Howell

In Memory of You

The tears continue to fall
every time I hear your name;
I know you're never coming back
but, my life will never be the same.

I remember your beautiful smile
and how your eyes were sparkling blue;
I know, in time, the pain will be less
but, I'll always be missing you.

Your gentle ways and tender hugs
always brought a smile to my face;
I will continue to reminisce about
all our times together
and I'll always remember the
warmth from your embrace.

I still dream about you wishing it wasn't true; that you're
never coming back to stay; there's so much I never got a chance
to tell you so much more than I needed to stay.

You're an angel, high up in the sky I'll never forget the joy
we shared together; even though you are no longer here your
memory, I'll cherish forever.

Susan Jehrio

To Hold Forever

In the shadows of life, there are many shades
Black and gray with specks of puce and deep maroon
Sad pockets of pain mirrored
Whenever those certain thoughts recur

Yet, with all, there are lovely moments
When the heart soars in joy and passion
Walk along the great ocean, blue and deep,
Awe of sunshine, sand, sky, reflecting

How to keep forever pictures of the mind
To bring out when needed, to savor and enjoy
To help forget when lonely hours make paths
Deep and sad for those other times that depress

Friends help dark shadows dim
Lights appear, radiant intensity
Laughter, music, colors held, embraced
Crisis gone, never forever, but now

Maryann Fenster

Frosty

A letter to a snow-bunny who fell atop the lift.
Her ski got caught in a snowdrift.
To the lift man she demanded to speak.
"My contacts are lost!" she did squeak.
The lift was stopped to look here and there,
Unaware of a man stuck on the lift chair.
Nowhere to hide, nowhere to run,
The man got caught over a working snow gun.
Finally, at the top I heard a sound:
"The contacts have been found!"
This doesn't seem fair
Because this man's butt was frozen to the lift chair.
To the snow-bunny I would suggest
A pair of prescription goggles would be best.

Christopher Fremont

"Arise Servant"

Arise Servant!
Arise from the clutches of the silent grave
Where lie the bones of defeat and tormented souls of retreat

Arise Servant!
Arise!
Arise!

Prepare to conquer the unconquerable mountain
Let the waters of thy soul flow from a fresh fountain

Be thou healed

Unveil the power from within
And let the solider be revealed

Arise Servant!
Arise!
Arise!

Unweave the tangled web of hidden victory
May your name be carved in history

Arise Servant!
Arise!
Arise!

Carla Payton

Nothing Left To Give

You want me to mourn,
    And I need to cry;
But my soul is empty,
    And my heart is numb.
    I have nothing left to give . . .

The feelings I had
    Are no longer there;
Love and care have been replaced
    By nothing but indifference.
    I have nothing left to give . . .

Hurt and pain have formed a barrier
    Around my compassionate soul;
Am I protected,
    Or have I isolated myself?
    I have nothing left to give . . .

Something is opened,
    A porthole or a tunnel;
And a light shines through,
    Happiness peeks in.
        Finally, I have something left to give!!

Carolyn A. Yunker

The Gift of Grace

The gift of grace can be so quickly. Disguised and lost in the haze.
When disillusion strikes; anger flairs; fear greeds in
As a serpent slithering with a snappy tongue taking serenity
from the soul in a lick.
Going from the heights of grandeur to the depths of despair
Until we heed the heart voice as a pan flute on a mountain top
Play its hauntingly beautiful ode to God.
Grace is given that way as a gift that fills our souls
Spilling over to all who see with the wisdom of the third eye
That grace never left us
It was only hidden by our own humaness.

Sidney Gale Ulmer

Poor Little Sparrow

Poor little sparrow you've lost your mate;
Only God knows her actual fate.
Could it have been some stealthy cat
Who pounced upon her as she sat
Eating a much-needed meal
Not knowing upon her death would silently steal?
Or, perhaps, a car passing swiftly by
That crushed her small body while on the fly?

Everyday I watched the two of you building your nest,
Carrying twigs and such without a moment's rest,
Until at last it was complete.
And I must say it was some feat!

Now a pall hangs over your little home.
It breaks my heart to see you sitting there alone
Waiting and calling for the mate who will never return,
For whom in sadness your heart ever will yearn.
But time eventually will lessen your sorrow.
Happier days will come after many a tomorrow.
'Til then I'll mourn along with you.
I don't know what else I can do.

Amy L. Sanford

The Omen II

He brought me a snack;
It was good to be fed
A sandwich and iced tea
"I only have to see
The other half of the ship
And then I'll be finished" he said.
I went back to the chapel
And after eating my lunch,
I snapped a picture
Of the vase of flowers bunch
For my file, to paint it later on,
Another petal fell to the floor
And then I napped with ease
After I closed the door.
I dreamed of a soft grassy place
Surrounded by shade trees; so I lay
And an image came to me, all white and lace
"You'll find what you really wish for"
And faded away.

June Bromund

The Sentinels

I gazed upon the plains at eventide
After the mists had disappeared.
And strange monolithic forms arose,
Stark and gaunt and mysterious
Against a yellow sky.
They were monuments to ages past,
Now weathered and worn to pierce the sky.
Their bronze-colored shafts marked
By the forces of wind and storm,
To remain as sentinels over
A battleground no longer kin
To daily wars of rain and fire.

Gordon C. Pierce

All Alone

As I sat upon my windowsill,
I began to pray with all my will,
that what was happening was all a big scheme,
or maybe even a long, long dream,
and then I realized I can't lie:
my best friend was really saying good-bye.
There and then I began to cry,
asking the Lord "Why, no, why?"
He answered with a shower of rain,
as if saying, "Let out your pain,"
and that's just what I tried to do,
but I couldn't do it in front of you,
so now I'm at home on my bed,
with all these feelings in my head.

Kara Williams

Ode to Theresa Saldana

You are the bravest of the brave
You stand with Joan of Arc
As a role model
For all young women of today

You came through that awful nightmare
And the difficult and painful recovery
And in your pain, you reached out
To help others

Integrity and compassion are yours forever
You are the world's finest actress
And one of its most beautiful women
May God bless you and keep you.
Theresa.

Charles D. Ross

Fireball

He started work at Drexel when he was just a teen
And Fireball is the name they quickly gave to him.
He was fast as a whiz and did the job so swell
That no other name described him quite as well.

Fireball goes to work early and comes home late.
He thinks Drexel furniture just cannot wait.
Everyone depends on him to get the job done
So he puts in his time and tries to make it fun.

Fireball never misses work if there is any way
That he can get there and put in his day.
This is always true unless he's close to death
And almost too sick to draw his next breath.

Drexel Heritage is the place and Morganton the town
Where almost any day fireball can be found.
For half of a century, he's given his best shot
To make Drexel furniture the best of the lot.

Soon he will retire and leave the job behind
And then someone else will take his place in time.
Fireball's work and loyalty will be hard to replace
For he is one of a kind among the human race.

Elizabeth B. Arney

My Love My Friend

Heart and soul you will always be . . .
The sweet important part of me.

You have opened my love like one other . . .
For you are my friend, companion and lover

The sweetness of your lips . . .
Your subtle loving touch . . . are worth so much.

My heart beats quick when you are near . . .
My body quivers with your loving touch . . .
All because you mean so much.

You could look for you will never find . . .
A love like yours and mine.

Communication, trust and love are held
In our life mirror . . . as we grow nearer and nearer

With your hand in mine . . .
Together catching the movement in time

Heart to heart
Soul to soul, the future is our to hold

God will be with thee and me . . .
Because forever you will see . . .
You and me.

Sandra Roman

Desperate Plea

On my bed I sit, crying an ocean of tears,
no one understands my hopes and my fears.
Can't contain myself anymore,
no one's here to comfort and reassure.
Can't overcome my condition,
with this low self-conviction.
Got a serious problem with hate,
towards myself and friends of late.
Can't buy a person to help me cope,
they say I'm far down the depression slope.
The pressure of life is taking its reigns,
it has a tight grasp and is inflicting pain.
Some say life deals you a bad hand,
but my bad luck is as vast as country land.
My eyes are swollen and blotched with red,
as I sit and cry on my unmade bed.

Allison Bryan

A Telegram From Somalia

Through the rising sand dunes
To the same old melancholy tunes
Roams a lass in the desert
Subduing her hunger and thirst

In the cold and chilly night
When all the world gets a fright
Clings a baby onto his mother
Suffering from the evils of the weather

Through the barriers of the bloody civil war
Even though death isn't so far
Copes a man to be fittest
Even though the hope is in the slightest

At least, that is what I saw
In the telegram from Somalia
That for our sins they suffer
While civilized men here have their supper

Abraham Sebastian

A Bud Is Afraid of an Early Rain

When it rains, I think of all our years together
Listening to the rain outside
And happy to be warm inside.

I still hear the sound on roof and window pane;
See the bed on which we've lain
To hear the sound of April rain.

The steady drone of rain that keeps the windows blurred
Revives a vision I can't dismiss
The tear I saw on our first kiss.

Love inside us dawning, you trembled when I held you.
The timid shining of your face
I held close when we embraced.

I likened you to a beautiful flower - still a bud-
With fluids stirred by warming grounds
It listens anxiously for raining sounds

Because a rain, too soon, would open up its petals
For belated frosts to maim,
A bud is afraid of an early rain.

Joseph S. Damico

God Chose Me

I had a little talk, just God and me,
About the way my life for him is suppose to be.
And he told me, "that I must decide.
Do I want to live my life for him? Or keep up the false pride?"

I wanted to explain to him and tell him the reason why,
But he said, "To me my child you cannot lie."
He said, I'll stand by you, I'll hold your hand."
I said "Okay my Lord, what is your plan?"

He said, "Do this my child, I know you can
You know that I'm a jealous man?
Love me first, so you will never thirst,
I chose you, you didn't choose me,
And this is so the world can see,

That you are my child,
You were just to wild,
All that running around,
I had to sit you down.

I had to get to you,
Before your life was through,
Now aren't you happy that I chose you?"

Alvaray A. Okolugbo

O Solitude

O! there is such sweet joy in solitude
　　That hours may be pined away in thought
　　Or 'ventures to imagination brought—
Lest over painful sorrow must I brood
Or pleasure by loneliness is o'er hued.
　　Of that abysmal darkness I want naught
　　Nor with bleak burdens my mind to be fraught
For in seclusion woe is e'er renew'd—
Nor yet! let me not to society
　　Where only fools striving toward the absurd
　　Are only with foolishness well endow'd:
The mundane, Love is overshadow'd by—
　　So once again I turn my thoughts inward
　　And walk in solitude amongst a crowd.

Steve Hendrix

O Gentle Breeze

O gentle breeze, surround me with a sweet whisper of fragrance.
Sing me a tune in this canyon of silence,
While I watch the birds glide, and clouds dance.
I will enjoy the gift of life, and this sight without pretense.

O gentle breeze, the peaceful waters begin to ripple with delight.
Swiftly you change, clouds form into a storm to be.
The earth does rise, make dark rings, cones of fright.
All of nature, man, and birds change their flight with thee.

O tempest one, quiet, be peaceful, you can fan a fire
into the arms of a cloud.
You can carve like an artist, relax solid to take form,
In your wrath, there is nothing you do to make us proud.
So be silent, be calm, be peaceful, do not storm.

Be gentle O breeze, surround me with a sweet whisper of fragrance.
Sing me a tune in this canyon of silence,
While I watch birds glide, and the clouds dance,
I will enjoy the gift of life and this sight without pretense.

Louise E. Marsh

The Children's Song

We dare not peek beyond the veil
for fear of something gray
our cowardice is our welcome jail
our hell with heaven's sway

As a child we fear not one
nor a thousand more
our size belittles our courageous mind
but the truth is hidden in lore

Our numbers are great but not for long
the horrible plague still grows
it catches us with our children's songs
and turns us into a chorus

Conformity is the enemy here
it grips all but a few
the ones who don't change are the ones who can hear
the children's songs, can you?

Lindsey Kish

To Love

Some say the greatest accomplishment is being a great leader,
Some say making a lot of money is the key.
Many will say having many lovers is the way to happiness.
Yet I feel the greatest feat of all is to learn how to love,
And in doing so, getting love back in return,
And maybe even greater still is teaching others how to love.

Geraldine Tiboldo

Shadows

Here I stand within the darkness of mind
Seeing shadows
Hands clutching every sane thought I can find
Holding shadows
My thoughts fly swiftly from me and come back
Knowing shadows
I realize then they show me what I lack
Wanting shadows
I reach to touch what I have never seen
Feeling shadows
My mind goes to places I have not been
Thinking shadows
I search the darkness and see nothing still
Finding shadows
So I in my dream-world do what I will
Being shadows
Michele Egan

Another World

There is a world
That may not be real
With dragons and elves and talking seals
The people use magic and sorcery
And everyone living there is free
They get along fine, without any wars
They sleep very easy, don't lock their doors
Violence is a thing of the past
People are kind, guile comes last
Nobody dies from another's hand
That all happens in another land
Deaths are mourned, lives are cherished
It is remembered, in wars many perished
The people have learned, from their mistakes
Rituals are held, at fields and lakes
Warriors now lie, where they did die
People remember, prayer are cast
It is as I said, violence is past

There is a world, it may not exist
I would rather live there, than here, in this
Kendra Anne Marsh

Rain Rain Rain

This would be quite a day,
Don't you think, for making hay,
As those good old childhood pies are ready mixed,
Lots of milo not combined,
With shucking corn, we're far behind,
And the prospects for sowing wheat are fixed.

What I think, I guess I'd better,
Not dare to write in this letter.
The Post Office Department would get after me, I'll bet,
They would have a trial in a hurry,
A verdict of guilty by the jury,
And if you think they'd be lenient, you're all wet.
Lucille Crawford

Hearts

Heart are made to feel.
After all, that's how you know they're real.
Thankful for a heart like mine,
I have a chance to leave my heart behind.
To stay with you my love.
I'll be above.
And when I'm gone;
My heart lives on.
Don't weep.
It's for you to keep.
Connie Hart

Calvary

O Lord, you press the scalpel into our vitals
But you also heal.
I know you are a God of love
Though the starving die
And injustice grinds its heel into the face of the oppressed.
And though the lonely and those whose hearts are crushed
Weep bitter tears at night
I know you hear our appeals and care.

And I know the spikes that tore through flesh and bone
You suffered, stifling the groans—
Raw back scraping splintery cross
Skull-piercing thorns, that final lance thrust through the side—
To share our deaths and sufferings
In manner so complete.

That all who look to you upon that cross—
Naked, shameful death!—
That look to you in faith
Shall, in their suffering, by your death
And by your rising be redeemed.
Kenneth Canatsey

Is Justice Served?

A dead man is walking, the last of his life,
For crimes he committed while yielding a knife.
As he walked down the hall, his eyes filled with tears,
And visions of torture from his younger years.
When he was a boy, just a baby of three,
His life filled with fear and brutality.
The bruises he suffered, never would heal,
Put a hole in his heart that he always could feel.
As the poison went rushing into his arm,
His body went limp and his eyes became calm.
Overcome by the peace his life never found,
Unlocking the past from the chains he was bound.
He welcomed the freedom in death he would find.
The only release from the prison of his mind.
Were the scales of justice served today?
For the sins of the father, the son would pay.
People will say that it's just an excuse,
Did he die here today, or at three, from abuse?
Carol Gomes

Happy Birthday Grandpop

Just a line to hope you have a very special day.
Ninety you will be on the twenty ninth of May.
I thank the Lord for giving me the time I had with you.
I remember special times, and special things you'd do.
And every time I'm feeling low, or maybe just feel blue,
I think about those many times, and how much I love you.

As kids we used to sit and play for hours at your house.
We'd go to bed, you'd tell us to be quite as a mouse.
We'd laugh, and we'd giggle, and we'd play into the night.
And then before you know it we would all begin to fight.

You'd holler up the stairway for us to try to settle down.
It was awfully hard to play without making any sound.
Eventually we'd go to sleep, and morning we would wake
To Danishes, and cocoa, and that special coffee cake.

If you've gotten curious to why I reminisce;
It's to let you know that those days are really missed.
And memories are one thing I hold closely to my heart.
They take away the miles, that hold us far apart.
And every time it comes around to the twenty ninth of May;
I'll think of you, and hope for another special day.
Joyce Bourgeois

Distant Skies

The sun came up while the sky was clear
The fallen moon looked so near
Leaving an emptiness about the sky
For no clouds were around to roll by
The beauty lay with in a night of stars
The distance once didn't look so far
Throughout the darkness the forest becomes alive.
But without the morning light the forest cannot thrive
Each dew drop that drips off the leaves, down to the forest floor
makes taking each step carefully, a necessity, looking
deep, before wanting more
Foliage grows up and hides what's real
While the insects crawl through to the heart,
for a grand meal.

Jennifer Emery

Sparkle Flight

Sparkling lights in sparkle flight.
You shine so bright without a doubt.

There's this radiant light that
glistens off your fingertips
can feel so right.
The softness of light which is
always glowing is so coming in the night.
You have my soul caught up
in your sparkle flight.
I have seen and know so very
well, the touch is beauty
inside and out.
The night sky is forever and
always a friend of the deepness
of hope in the sparkling lights
in sparkle flight.

Donald R. Roberts Jr.

No Escape

Her stomach was in tight knots,
not wanting to let go.
Her oblong face was flushed;
Her deep-set eyes cautious.

She wanted to ask around,
to find out what was going to happen.
She wanted to cry;
the worst was to be expected.

As the crowd around her grew,
she wondered if the others felt the same.
Was some one they knew in the rolled-over Cadillac,
trying to escape from its clutches?

Her body tensed more
as the police arrived on the scene.
Their faces told her it was hopeless;
the driver and passenger were dead.

An extrication unit came to the site;
they still had to remove the bodies.
The woman knew then why she was so worried—
her best friends were the ones in the car.

Chris Konecke

Asylum

Awoke this morning to the sound of an alarm in my head
Journey into insanitary make my body feel dead
Sit around all day watch a phone that doesn't ring
People stop by just to say goodbye
No fun, no future, no friends, only pain, drugs, sex, boys, girls
People without faces only names pass through these doors
There are no clocks leave and never return that's why I say
I don't want your life and I don't want mine
Listen son I'm trap in the asylum of my mind

Mike Burke

The Wonders of God

As the darkness of the night fades away.
We see the light turn into another day.

We look at the beautiful mountains so high.
We see the rivers flow that never run dry.

We see all of the flowers of the fields.
And all of the beauty that it yields.

We see the awesome tree that stands high.
Painted against the white clouds of the sky.

In the midwest we look over the fields of grain.
In the west the winds blow across the baron plains.

With all the life and beauty all around.
God gave us some of the most beautiful sound.

As we hear the newborn baby cry.
The little precious life we cannot deny.

Oh how precious a little life can be.
That God gave special just for you and me.

As we look and listen to lifes gentle tone.
Through His wonders God is made known.

Jerry Wise

A Mother So Kind

How fortunate we are that you were the one to give us life,
Before us, Dad knew he had a great wife.

You continued to give us life by the care you gave,
With a gentle smile your love poured out like a wave.

You enriched our lives by the things you said,
But it was through your actions, that you led.

You were always there with a word of praise,
And rarely did your voice ever raise.

You gave a helping hand to us and those in need,
A note, a word, a call, or meal to feed.

You are passing through this journey and are leaving us all,
With the words, "Goodbye, I love you sweetie," for us to recall.

Donna Westemeyer

Our Little Lad

*Dedicated to my grandson, "Jay Boy," now seven—
truly a miracle baby.*
See his curly little head
Peekin' out from neath the bed,
Playin' hide and seek with mom and dad,
He's the cute little cuss
Over whom we make a fuss,
And we both, call him Our Little Lad.

In his funny little way
He smiles and seems to say,
How I love you, my mom and dad,
He's a bundle of joy,
And a very happy boy,
So we both, call him Our Little Lad,

All day long, he's mothers little helper,
When dad comes home, he becomes the house hold Jester

Now it's time to go to bed
Time to rest his weary head,
What a busy, busy day he had,
So we lay him down to sleep,
And pray the Lord to keep,
Our heavenly gift, Our Little Lad.

Joseph J. Jacovino

Sleepy Eyes

Do you hear me knocking at your door?
Will you open up and talk with me?
For my love is for you.
I've watched you from afar and my heart cried out for you.
I've told the Lord, I love you.
Now my love, it's your turn sleepy eyes, to cry for me.
I ask, will you love me?

Lorrie M. Schasiepen

The Golden Peace Cord

Delicate strands of glistening yarn
banded together to make a golden cord
wrapped around a small pedestal
which holds upon it a world of possible intelligence
deemed useless by the realm in which we live

Climbing stairs to a possible heaven
the nether world disappears from beneath
the substructure that holds the pedestal
all is quiet in a serene darkness

The golden cord sways silently in the air
still wrapped around the pedestal
which holds upon it a world of nothingness
now useless to the realm in which we live

Francine Yenner

Was It By Chance

Was it by chance that the world is round,
Or that we can stand on solid ground?

Was it by chance that some birds can fly,
Or that others can only try?

Where would the fish swim if there were no seas;
Or to build our buildings if there were no trees?

If there were no snow on top of the mountains,
Where would we get fresh water for our fountains?

Was it by chance that this just came to be,
Or was it designed for you and me?

God had it all planned out from the start,
We just have to look around and take it to heart.

Then the answer becomes very clear, you'll see,
That all of this was meant to be.

Frank Pfitzenmeyer

The Breeze

It came at me, spreading itself across the front of me,
Caressing my face, my neck, my arms.

A clean, pure scent and feeling, as if it were only for me
Something that I did not need to share, could not share,
It was for me alone.

I indulged myself in this selfish pleasure for as long as
I could and the desire to ingest it, to keep it with me,
To keep it a part of me, to never let it go,
Could only be a desire.

For it was impossible to keep something so precious for too
Long, something that I could not own, but just to borrow
For a moment.

And as it passed, soothing my ears, curling down around the
Nape of my neck, smoothing back the long hair that rest
Against my shoulder, I did not ponder, because I knew
That there would be another,
Just for me.

Violet F. Gaudet

Take Courage

Tho' the road be rough and thorny
And the path seems dark and dreary
Take courage as you journey
For there is a hand that carry.

Life has its joys and sorrows
Remember that they're only shadows
Take courage as you face the morrow
For there's a guide you'll follow.

Trials of life is like a dark cloud
Heavy on your shoulder as a load
Take courage as you travel down the road
For at the end, there's someone who'll unload.

When your life is tossed with rage's tempest
Give it to the Lord for better rest
Take courage as you do your very best
And lean upon the Saviour's precious breast.

After the storm, the sun is shining
In every cloud's a silver lining
Take courage and wear a face smiling
For there's One who's caring and loving.

Mary S. Panaguiton

Lost Dedication

How elegant you are
Can I kiss you softly upon your cotton candy lips?
Brush coyly by your left cheek?
Travel boldly to the nape of your neck?
How beautiful you are
lying innocently upon the sunlight rearranging it from time to time
with one movement of:

your hand,
your head,
your smile

how elegant you are

honey brown,
sugar sweet,
milk chocolate man of mine chiseled fancy fine

authentically woven in Mother Africa's Likeness
how mystical you remain

Margot D. Ellick

Can't Come Home For Christmas

Gently falling snowflakes
Land and melt on my face
As I look around God's creation
All woven in white lace.

As the crisp air catches up with me
It tells me Christmas time is near
I think of being home with you
And sadly shed a tear

A tear of loneliness
And aching heart for home
Thoughts of being without you
Make me feel so alone

The aroma of Mom's tasty baking
The smell of the freshly-cut pine tree
That's the memories I miss most
In my heart, where I hold you close to me

I know we all have our own families now
But I'd like to make a special wish
Let's hold each other close in our hearts
And dream of being home for Christmas.

Valerie Drader

You Inspire Me

Yes! It' true,
No matter where I go
Or what I do,
You're a vision on my mind
That I thought I would never find.
You have set my spirit free
With wisdom from the ages and my love
Is slowly growing for you in stages.
You've given me the courage
To face adversity, full well knowing that
Each time I do, it's a lesson I've learned
Well from you.
So believe me when I say "You inspire me,"
Each and every day.

M. Harring

The Swallow

A bird approached me, singing loudly,
Warbling notes sweet to my ear;
Then he faced me, hovering proudly,
Ablaze with happiness, showing no fear.

Nose to beak, we smiled our greeting.
We'd never met, before that day.
A lovely moment, but all too fleeting . . .
He flashed his wings, and sped away.

Brian J. Dooley

Friend

I am a traveler walking down the path of life,
Where it will lead, I haven't a clue.
The road before me is full of twists, turns, bumps and holes,
Which way to go, which way to turn?
My journey is long and full of doubts, so much fear and distrust,
that I couldn't see the sunlight which waited for me at the end.
I stumble and fall, pick myself up and walk on.

Then something wonderful almost miraculous happened . . .
This road became straight, and flowers lined its path, sun beams
and rainbows filled the sky, the dark clouds disappear.
Joy started to fill a doubtful soul,
as apprehensiveness was replaced by trust.
There was a familiar smile at the end of this road.
A friendly soul to light my way,
A extended hand to help me up,
A shoulder to lean on . . .
All this time you were there . . .
My friend!

Jeri Bielec

The Dream

Last night, I had a strange dream.
I was dreaming that I was opening my window to let the sun in,
But outside it was still dark.
Where is the sun? I asked,
But nobody was in the room to answer me.
I got dressed, and I went outside, looking for the sun.
At my front door, I found the rain,
So I asked her where is the sun?
She did not answer me.
I walked down the road, and I met with the wind.
I asked him about the sun,
But he was very strong to stop and answer me.
From above, I saw the dark clouds which were chasing each other.
I asked them if they had seen the sun,
But they could not stop and talk to me.
Nobody knew where the sun was.
I awoke up with tears in my eyes.
To my surprises, my room was golden bright.
The sun is here, the sun is here,
I cried, and I jumped out of my bed to welcome him.

Barbara Efpraxiadou

Deja Vu

I think I've walked these woods before,
Perhaps a century ago,
I know it's true, I remember it all
Or, did I dream it so?

That big old fir that's rotting now
Was once a stately tree
Its trunk so large; its branches spread
Its top you could not see.

Beneath that tree two lovers met
Their hearts and arms entwined;
Initials carved into the trunk
I think, I know, I'll find

I search and search for tell-tale signs
Beneath the moss so green
I tear and scrape it all away
Until the trunk is clean.

My throat gets tight! My mind goes wild!
For clearly now I see
Two bold initials inside a heart
Carved deep into the tree!

Rose Carolyn Johnson

Soul Mate

I've been looking, for a beautiful man
I've been looking, for a beautiful man, to love
Oh! Where is he, Oh where is this beautiful man I'm looking for
Oh! I've been dreaming, of this beautiful man, to love
I've been searching this whole world through
Looking for this beautiful man to love
I ask the Lord above, to show me where I can find
This beautiful man, to love
To find this beautiful man that's made just, for me
Oh! I truly believe there is someone, for me
It was promised at birth that we would meet here on earth
To share our love eternally
Oh! Where is this special love I've been looking for

Naomi Glissen

A Snowflake Is Love

As I look out my window,
the snow falls down so cold.
I just keep thinking of how warm,
I'd be if I had you here to hold.

Every snowflake in the sky is
a symbol of our love.
And as I look very closely,
it forms a turtle dove.

When a snowflake is in the sky,
it is falling on its own.
But when it soon hits the ground,
into love it's grown.

But soon the snow will melt away,
and all the love will too.
And next winter when that little snowflake drops,
I will fall in love with you.

Heidi Lewis

Miriah

The day you arrived put a smile on my face
that could not be erased.
Nine months of wondering if you were a girl or boy;
I knew you would bring me so much joy.
Before I slip off to bed,
I sneak in to kiss your forehead
and thank God for a little girl so sweet.
Now you're two, oh how the time flew.
We have many more wonderful years together;
let's make it last forever.

Amy Bowen

The Road Ahead

Far and away this was the most awesome site.
The road ahead.
Winding dirt and cobblestone.
Was it sad or wonderful?
Burning embers of gypsy campfires roar to the
night sky, only to burn into blackness.
Were they banished or blessed?
Salivating lonely men spu from roadside bars.
they merge with business men,
On their way home to know one.

William T. Ferrentino

In Motion . . .

My walk, the echo to a glide
The sway takes me from side to side.

Your hand reaches out for mine
Large, suggestive, open wide.

The breeze whispers soft—its flow
reaching your ear.
Unveiling the many things, you've waited
until now to hear.

We are in Motion
Traveling a vast, boundless ocean.
In motion . . .

Back and forth, up then down
This dance we do, has a mind all its own.

We are in motion
Traveling a rhythmic ocean.
So free! In motion
Truly . . .

Cleo Leaphart

The Man in the Glass

If you get what you want in your struggle for self
And the world makes you king for a day
Just go to a mirror and look at yourself
And see what that man has to say

For it isn't your father or mother or wife
Whose judgement you have to pass
The fellow whose verdict counts most in your life
Is the one staring back from the glass.

Some people may think you a straight-shooting chum
And call you a wonderful guy
But the man in the glass says you're only a bum
If you can't look him straight in the eye

He's the fellow to please never mind all the rest
For he's with you clear up to the end
And you've passed your most dangerous, difficult test
If the man in the glass is your friend

You may fool the whole world down the pathway of life
And get pats on your back as you pass
But your final reward will be heartache and tears
If you've cheated the man in the glass

Karen Emily Holmes

Purple Heart

Here are words of wisdom to you I will tell
Love is like war because war is like hell
It sends you off on a mighty crusade
Unknown to you it's just a charade
You'd give your life in the heat of the fight
Not even knowing of you're wrong or right
All that you know is what you must do
In order to win what you think is true
But when it's over and the smoke finally clears
The dawn's early light shines on you fears
That you had been fooled heart and lied to again
Leaving with you a wounded heart in the end

Mitch Whatley

Please Take The Time

For Lillie

Please take the time to give a farewell kiss,
To give a heartfelt hug, and a look that's full of bliss.
For we can never know if this may be our last,
Your loved one may be gone and her time has come to pass.

You've got to be at work, or the kids will be late for school,
These are just excuses, we can all bend the rules.
Stop and look around you at the beauty everywhere,
For it can be taken from you and it won't seem very fair.

Please take the time, to look at the lady in your life,
A friend, a mother, your partner, she's also your loving wife.
We always take for granted, that she'll be there to the end,
To wash and sew and bathe the kids and help she'll always lend.

You're sore from long hard hours and your boss has made you mad,
You tell her all your problems and the bad day you've just had.
You haven't got the time to say how good she looks,
Until all that you have left is her picture in some books.

Please take the time, to kiss your wife today,
To give that heartfelt hug to help her on her way.
Believe me when I tell you and please don't hesitate,
To tell her that you love her, before it is too late!

Peter S. Hill

Warriors

The roar of cannons a distant sound
The moment of truth on the battle grounds
Where brave men tread give their souls to God
In return for strength to complete their jobs

Master of weapons and of the arts
They fight in the open they'll tear you apart
With cat like moves as they stalk in the night
With vengence sweet that makes them fight

With just a few or a hundred full
They're living legends they're raging bulls
A hunter of prey with an eagle's eye
Get in their way you too will die

Now if you think they're just plain men
I think you'd better guess again
Cause out there lurking in the still of the night
It won't be long hear the battle cry of warriors

Chuck Davis

Greener Grass

Some think the grass looks so much greener,
On the other side of the fence
But those who wander to that side,
Must reap the waiting consequence
And now I find my only lover
Seeks a greener, greener field,
I wish him happy hunting
And a harvest of good yield,
He travels down a mighty dusty road
To reach that greener side
He thinks he sees a shiny river
But that old river is all dry,
And like that shiny, shiny river,
The green grass is a mirage
So he turns his weary foot steps
And he slowly homeward plods
For he knows his lonely lover,
Welcomes back her long lost stray,
The greener grass he was searching for
Was always here when he went away.

Mildred Silke

Doomsday

They met twenty-four years ago;
When the little child was born.
Throughout the years, he watched him grow.
But, now, their special bond is torn.

He became the brother he never had.
Their closeness deepened as time pass.
He tried to teach him good from bad.
Their brotherhood was solid glass.

Suddenly, it shattered into pieces;
Sharp edges cutting through the soul.
Deep pain and anger increases;
Wasted feelings feel into a dark hole.

A hole too deep to see the light.
There's no escape, with dangerous walls.
The ground opened drastically one night;
Caused by vindictiveness and alcohol.

Immaturity and attitude;
Changed a lifetime of memories.
Into total strangers; solitude.
It's lost forever; no apologies.

Ann Yanulavich

Creators In An Era

We are creators in an era that has lost the creator's glow
Creators in an era that really doesn't know
If the ideas of the attic science are real enough to try
If the ideas of the companies can really get us by
We are creators in an era of computers and machines
We are creators in an era of movies and magazines
The ones who still find poetry a satisfying art
Who still type down our fantasies and unlock our heart
Creators of the one thing that everybody knows
The hopes and dreams of a million heartfelt glows
Looking deep within our friends and foes to find our one idea
That we can share with the multitudes or just one other lia

Jeanette L. Brown

It's Who I Am

Can I express the painful frustration of having to live a lie?
Everyday waking up to ask myself a question never answered, "Why?"

How can I be happy with a part of myself no one else can see?
If they all knew what I kept to myself would they still love me?

Sometimes I sit awake at night and question everything in my life,
Can one little secret cause this much strife?

Would everyone really think it's so bad?
I don't want to make anyone hurt or be sad.

I won't even be able to share anything about the person I love,
For fear that the reaction would sting like an iron spiked glove!

No one knows how much I want to say that one word!
By now I must be sounding quite absurd.

But why can't I just say it and not give a damn?
For God's sake, it's Who I Am!

J. Allen

TRUE LOVE

Love	is a phenomenon that created, a nothing into a something.
Overcomes	all created adversaries, that are apart of unexplainable planning.
Virtually	eroding any possibility of comprehension and or understanding.
Everything	for the purpose of a friendship, to have relationship, with choice given and seldom demanding

Hazel A. Hamm Jr.

Love Matters

To keep tears back is hard
I have to stay right on guard
I tell myself your love really doesn't matter
All the while I feel my heart, all in tatters
With head high I feel this pride
I haven't called you! God I would get on
My knees and beg—if you would let me inside
Please let me see the love for me in your eyes
Stop the good-byes.
What I would give!
How can I live?
One day at a time
Out of the pits I will climb
Oh Lord make haste help me find
Better fruit and not the bitter rind.

Katie Reeves

Insides Cry; Eyes Boil

A whole roomful of angels, dancing and singing,
Cavorting with pride and joy for their most loved one.
Peeking with giggles as their bells go ringing
They thrill the heart they adore, that would never shun.

Yet even so, if you looked at one little face
Looked into the eyes of that tiny, angel child
You would see the forced fun that was so out of place.
You would see the seed that would turn the child so wild.

Why is it? How could it be? So easy to ask.
Easier to answer. The most loved one is gone.
Not there to be seen, not there to perform the task
Of nurturing and so a grim picture is drawn.

Unloved as an angel he never stood a chance.
Insides cry, eyes boil; grown he doesn't rate a glance.

Linda Parsley

The Dead Gods

The time was right to fight for life;
Death at our heels, we had nothing more.
Evil and chaos in the land were rife;
To fight and die would not be a chore.

We had no more will for livin';
All we had was taken from us.
Before us, our foes we'd drivin';
Our betrayal would be a fuss.

In our midst, the foul one talked;
At its dark lies none could guess.
Our trust led the way we walked . . .
. . . Plans to make us none and less.

We stood flaccid and immobile, thoughts deranged,
As some wondered about, in reel and rout.
And then, as we became aware, from the world estranged,
Caught in the dark, as the stars died out.

Doug Clark

You Know You Are In Love

When you tell each other your deepest secrets.
When you aren't afraid to say what's on your mind.
When you make a promise and actually keep it.
When you do things for someone else's happiness,
And not your own personal gain.
You are happy to see each other,
Even if you don't look your best.
When he calls you, just 'cause he misses you.
When you look into each other eyes,
And know each others thoughts without saying a word.
When you will do, say, or give up anything for the other
ones happiness,
And that's when you know you are in love.

Colette J. Palmerio

The Sands of Time

I want to walk with you on a white sanded beach,
To feel your hands, entwined in mine, to celebrate life and living.

You came to me on the sands of time; with each ebb and flow
Of the tide I see your face in the crystal waters of the sea,
I smile, for you bring me joy in all the right places of my heart.

I caress your cheek—you shudder, I gaze searchingly into your eyes
They reflect pain and sorrow, but then you laugh,
And the fire of life dances playfully around
Those almond-shaped orbits, reverberating into your soul.

The cadences of your unencumbered laughter
Texturizes the atmosphere with droplets of healing,
The sweetness of your essence unveiled, poured forth
And filled me with complete and utter happiness.

Suddenly I am lost—can't find my way . . .
Twisting, tumbling, turning—seeking, searching,
Desperately needing, what? Effortlessly you cradled me
In your arms and gently placed me on the shores of your life.

Our spirits' meet—now I am no longer lost, or alone,
Your spirit whispers, "Arise my love"
Alas, I awake to realize it is but a dream.

Harriett H. Mayers

Wicked Lover

He was there;
He was everywhere—in a subtle way
Like a butterfly kiss

The power, hidden beneath a mask of benevolence
Oh, that mask he wears
It is a beacon, a light
Me, a moth, drawn to its glare—so bright
What's within it remains shrouded

His voice, a sacred bell, rang through the air
Its song, soft and gentle
Is a warm breeze

The lyrics hint at betrayal
The uncertainty hangs like a cloud
Until the drops fall
Rain, bourne of my heart
Thunder from my soul as the lightning strikes
And I die inside

And he's gone

Rachel

Fourteen Again

Make time work its magic and instruct the moon to rest—
For today I am fourteen again.

Reach into my heart and unleash emotions that
Send explosive joy and penetrating pain
Pulsing together through me with pleasure
Before bursting out to intermix with like spirits.

Innocent thoughts mutate as self-confidence
Breeds with self-consciousness.
Watch me change.

White passion fuels my desire to
Shine once again on stage
While I blush instantaneously at successful
Attempts by friends to embarrass me.

Come, playful child, wake up within me and break rules
To prove that when I close my eyes and wish, I truly am
Fourteen again.

Janice Malone

Love

Love is like a willow tree
It starts to grow from a very small seed
That is carried by the wind from a place far away.
It begins in a place where there is nothing.
It depends on others around it for support and companionship
Without this it will wither and die.
It starts to put down roots
And its branches reach for the sky.
It will grow tall and strong.
The wind may blow strong and fierce
But it will not break
It has the ability to withstand many storms and hardships
Others around it will benefit
From its tall wide branches and deep roots.
Then someone will come along,
Who thinks it is not needed, and cut it down.
But it will not die, it will come back
From its very deep roots.
Soon it will grow back ten fold of what it was before
And produce many seeds that will spread in all directions.

Chris Miller

Patriotic Chore

I'm just a little boy,
I don't know what to do.
My mother has forgotten me,
my father left me too.
I'm looking all around me,
the walls are closing in.
I don't know where I'm going,
I don't know where I've been.
I'm falling in a fatal trap,
I see it's coming soon.
I heard it heading toward me, then I only heard ka-boom
Now I'm looking all around, all I see's debris.
It took me fourteen hours, to find that it was me.
Where are the paramedics?
There are no surgeons here.
I think that I am dying,
Oh God! Now I know fear.
The funeral is all over,
I didn't want that war, but I served and did my best,
My Patriotic Chore.

Lance N. Barkley

Fear of Life

She hides her pain from the world;
no one can touch her inner soul.

She sits in her room looking
at the walls, thinking of all
the pain her life has caused.

She stays in the house because
she's afraid to sample the world,
to take back her life to end all the pain
so there won't be anymore suffering.

She feels like life is passing her by;
she could care less if she lives or dies.

She needs to stop letting fear
take over her life and rage
against the fear of life.

Chantelle Simmons

Peace

Who has known Peace
And known how to describe it.

An overwhelming calm sounding the depths
Of one's innermost being.

A Warrior strong, freeing the soul
From the grappling hooks
Of fear and pain.
A Paradox—a strong force yet a serene calm.
With Peace there is nothing to fear.
Who possess it need not fear that it be taken away.
Two robbers there are of this heavenly calm.
Remorse from the past and solicitous care
for the future ahead.

And so, mindfulness of the Present Moment at hand,
A return to the center and Peace is restored.
Peace—a resounding joy! A silent calm within!

Mary Ann Stickel

A Word To Life's Weary Travelers

Take solace in the earth,
For there are a thousand eyes and ears
That have been there since the dawn of man.

Run to the river
And cry in its banks.
Your tears will flow with fellow brethren,
The floating fears and years of the many and few
Who have run there before you.

Hug the sky.
Reach out as wide as you can and squeeze,
For the sky has hugged our world everyday since
Those with sight could see
And no one has ever hugged back.

So pack your bags,
Save courage, faith, and love,
For these will be given to you
As your journey unfolds.

Remember, you're following in the footsteps
Of a thousand hearts before you.
Their paths speak volumes to life's lost souls.

Warren J. Eallonardo

Gold and Silver Days

If you have a day that is sunny and cheery,
Or one that is rainy and dreary,
Think of the former as your "golden day,"
And the latter as your "silver day."
Clouds have "silver linings," you know,
And rain helps the flowers to grow.
So when your "silver days" come around,
Add your own "sunshine" and spread it around.

Evelyn L. Fersch

An Autumn Violet

How refreshing to find your purple head
Peeping from among the fallen leaves
That crunch as we reach to grasp
Your slender stem.
What unseen power stays our hand
As we hesitate and admire your courage
To bloom amid the autumn's somberness?
Why can't we tear you from the earth
Which soon the frost will harden?
Why can't we take your hand in ours
And roam the fields together?
Why do we leave your delicate beauty there
In the fast fading splendor of the fall?

John H. Jenny

Reflections

There she is again,
That girl who sometimes is my friend.
Her spirit is as fiery as her red hair
And her emerald eyes are so rare.
The word for her is definitely beauty,
Where as timid and shy seem to be my duty.
I long for comfort and to just fit in
And to have a heart stronger than tin.
She runs around without a care in her life
And leaves me inside to deal with the strife.
For you see, to that fiery girl
I am only a reflection with perfect curls.
I want to put away my mask,
But to do that would be such a task.
To be myself out there
And to know that people will still care.
I guess for right now it must be
That only the mirror knows me.

Mary Rose Pellicane

Love

Once I said, "I love you."
Once was enough,
For love does encompass all life.
All life encompasses love.
Then I said, "We'll marry."
Once was enough,
For marriage ties a bond never to be broken.
A bond that ties forever.
Then I said, "Children we'll have,
For children are the offspring of God's creation.
God's creation are children, offspring of His love."
"Now we have God, each other, and children.
Now we have love."

Robert V. Ciccarelli

My Rainbow

A rose is soft and its fragrance sweet,
　but is it soft as air and can it compete?

With the fresh sweet smell after a gentle rain,
　When God's light shines through his windowpane,

For as flowers go a rose's beauty is most rare,
　but it can never even compare.

For a rose is rooted in the ground,
　and rainbows dance and float on air,

And you can't have a rainbow without the rain,
　so there must have been a hell of a heaven's stir

To have produced one so bright and beautiful,
　as my rainbow, Jennifer!

Charles A. Simons

The Children of the Streets

To blow on the thistles,
And scatter the spores to the gusty winds,
Where the thistle loses its identity.
Growing bare,
When they are the pods of the Gods sent
Down from heaven,
To become the creatures of the true heart.
The only sin they have committed is being born alive.
With no one to care for them,
Where their only aim is to survive.
As they must hide, unloved,
And unwanted to become unseen,
For fear of being caught where they know
Not what will become of them . . .
These children of the streets.

Consuelo Suarez

An Innocent Child

There is an innocent child so hunger for love
Her big brown eyes has so much pain and all so lost
Running, running for help but, no one is there
Her heart pounding, searching for help and feeling so scared
Her life seems to be endless and all so unfair
That innocent face, so sad and feeling out place
Wondering, is there a rainbow at the end of the road
Will there ever be warmed while she's feeling so cold
She wishes, for love, happiness and joy in her life
At times she's feel's weak and is ready to say good-bye
The little strength she has; searches for an answer
Hoping the pain, loneliness will come to an end
For the child laughter will ease the sadness apart
She await's for someone to offer her a warm heart
To forget the horror and pain that has left her with scars
An innocent child awaiting for a brighter tomorrow
Hoping for happiness, laughter, and joy, no more sorrow

Elizabeth T. Davila

Emptiness Within

Your life is like a dark filled hole,
The Goddess of depression that takes out your soul.
She leaves you to lie on the cold, empty ground,
But, when you look up there's no one around.

You sit in your house alone as can be,
There are people around but you can not see.
The music you play is all you can hear,
And the sadness of words brings you to tear.

You try to stand up but you fall to the floor,
On your hands and your knees you crawl to the door.
You attempt to get up but it pulls you back in,
The sadness of darkness and the emptiness of sin.

You're locked between walls where happiness dies,
Where your Mom always sent you for your telling lies.
You'll never escape the everlasting fear,
Of the fear-filled emptiness brought upon the year.

Amy Landell

Time Gone By

As I sit in this square of time gone by
I can't help but have visions with every blink of an eye.
The horse drawn carriages. The people in the streets.
The children laughing and playing marbles
Where the town roads all meet.

How I envy those people of yesterdays past,
When life wasn't based on one's modern day mass.
Yes, it was a simple life, one of great pride,
When poverty was a part of life, not something to hide.

The people of today have lost touch with mankind.
It's me first this, or no that is not yours, that is mine.
When will this madness cease to exist?
If it were all gone tomorrow, I would surely not miss.

I guess I will lie down and rest my tired and weary eyes
and pray that when I wake up it will be that great era of
time gone by.

Daniel P. Burbank

Walking In Your Love

Lord, as I strive to walk close to you.
I pray you will be there with me each new day.
As I make this promise to meet you in the morning.
I will strive to hear and obey your every warning.
I know that the "world's" way is wrong.
So, I will choose to trust upon God's word and stand strong.
It does not matter what obstacles may come my way.
My only prayer is that I may continue to walk in your love everyday!

Christine Dahl

The Game of Life

Enter an unknown world, as night turns to dawn
Where you stand, are you a soldier or a pawn

Were you taught all the rules, what is wrong and what is right
Which piece are you, Bishop, King, Queen, or Knight

Do you know where you're going, do you know where to look
If you don't watch the other, you may be captured by a Rook

With each move you make, some people maybe taken
You may find yourself short a few pieces, until the others do awaken

Moves are decisions, some come easy and some you may dread
It can all go a lot smoother if you plan well ahead

At times it may seem hopeless, as your friends slowly disappear
That's when you must move forward and let go of your fear

Examine that each can do for one another and what each can bring
Work as a team, back each other, to protect the Castle and King

No person—no piece—is better than the other
It doesn't matter what you are, King, Queen, Sister or Brother

It's not about the winning or losing, it's how you play the game
If you don't enjoy the company, you have only yourself to blame

Seek out and cherish each moment, be careful what you chose
The pieces remain on the board, whether you win, draw, or lose

Joseph A. Maxwell

Carlton Pierre Mitchell !!
A Legend In His Own Time!!

Born on August 9th in '66
Take a moment and remember, if you can,
That he was full of charm, sensitivity, and wits
And was an extremely exceptional man.

He adored his little children,
In which he fathered five.
And in them his spirit will remain alive.
And in their children . . . it will return
And until we reach Heaven, we all will yearn . . .

To see him again, feel his comfort and grace . . .
And hear his hearty laughter from his smiling face.
So if you wish to write him a letter,
Go on . . . Don't hesitate.
The postman will deliver it to the mailbox
on Heaven's Gate.

Carlton's soul is very much here . . .
In his daughters and in his first to his
last born son.
He didn't just drive a Legend,
He was one!!!

Tabitha Taylor

Life's Clock

The clock of life is wound but once
And no man has the power
To tell just when the hands will
Stop at a late or early hour.

To love one's wealth is sad indeed
To love one's health is more
To love one's soul is such a loss
As no man can restore, the present
Only is our own, live, love, toil with a will.
  Place no faith in tomorrow
  For the clock may there be still.

Sheryl Perkins

My Image

When to heaven I take my flight
And leave my friends with delight.

I loved to help those that sat
Along life's hurried stone-filled path.

A "Hello" to some, to others smiles
As we walked life's many miles.

There were always flowers for those who choose
To stop and pause a few hours to loose.

My crafts was glad to share
For all those who really cared.

Listening carefully to those with trouble
So their cares will float away like a bubble.

Rita Akin Sandlin

A Mother's Love

A Mother's love is not so easily explained,
The choices she makes causing her so much pain.
 To put aside her selfishness motherly desire,
She agrees to let them live with their father.
 Oh, she dies inside a thousand times,
As she reminisces their final goodbyes.
 She tries so hard as not to drop a single tear,
For in those innocent eyes she'd never bestow fear.
 She kisses and hugs them each individually,
With words of wisdom chosen so carefully.
 Glassy eyed; pounding heart, she puts her best face on,
Praying to be perceived as nothing is wrong.
 She walks toward the car shaky legs, trembling inside
Soon these tears she won't be able to hide.
 She starts the engine and kisses are blown,
With the car in drive her tears start flowing.
 She cries so hard as she drives away,
Knowing she'll have many tomorrows, but only one today.

Sandra Marie Jester

Let's Do Our Best

Let's give our heart, and do our part,
To help our God above,
Let's help each other, as our brother,
Let's do our bit to love.

For life is sweet, and more complete,
If we do this each day,
And love will lift, each wondrous gift,
We give to God that way.

The more we give, the more we live,
The more we find God's way,
It's living right, and giving might,
To help the Lord today.

Let's aim our life, for toil and strife,
To offer for our good,
So God may see, and ever be,
A friend to those who would.

For life is fun, when we have done,
Our best for God and man,
Let's always share, our every care,
Let's give our Lord a hand.

Leo N. Brubaker

The Muse and Her Master

She stands there,
Looking fashionably forlorn while
He chips away at a priceless block of stone
(Like her mind, it is yet unknown).
At night she dreams of her masterworks
While he sleeps on next to her,
Not realizing which of them is the real genius.

Sara Angelique Oswald

Follow That Dream

Everybody has a dream
Or is it called, a goal?
Whatever you would call it.
It comes from deep in your soul.
Although, at times it seems so far.
It's closer than you think.
You must prepare the steps to take
And find that missing link.
Do you have the support you need?
Do you want it bad enough?
Are you a fighter or a quitter,
When at times, it may be tough?
Don't let your lifetime slip away.
Don't regret what you haven't done.
You'll only get one life to live.
Set that example for your son.
No matter how long it takes—
Or how hard it just might seem.
You must listen to your heart
And follow that dream!!!!!

Marie Olsen

A Moment of Joy

My heart is beating faster.
My memories of years going by
Now are flashing in front of me.
My hands are sweating.
My body is shaking.
I am happy. I am smiling.
Now it's time for me to leave this world.
God finally called my name.
My joy will be with me always.

Filippo Bonasia

Life or Death

Life or death. God's greatest gift to behold.
Spring or winter. Warm or ice cold.
Heaven or hell. Life, what a wonderful gift to behold.
Pleasure and strife, the essence of life.
What a story to behold of glories to be told.
Death a waits with each breath we take.
Time ticks without grace or haste.
Haste makes waste of life I am told so;
Make the most of the greatest gift to behold.

Laura J. Hobson

Standing at His Grave with Good News and a Broken Heart

Grandpa, the Yanks made it; your dream came true,
But you're not here to watch anymore . . .
Can't believe they made it!
You always knew.

You would be so proud of all of us too.
I'm in college and Matt works in the store—
Grandpa, the Yanks made it; your dream came true.

You were taken from us; you left too soon.
Randy died, my parents divorced . . .
Can't believe they made it! You always knew.

They played and won today, we thought of you.
This pain is so real, it's hard to ignore—
Grandpa, the Yanks made it, your dream came true.

I'm here at your grave, standing before you
Tears streaming down my face, my feelings torn . . .
Can't believe they made it! You always knew.

I'm fighting tears to give you this good news.
If he can't hear me, tell him this Lord—
Grandpa, the yanks made it! Your dream came true . . .
Can't believe they made it! You always knew.

Ray Smart

Mars Forever Lives

See a place on a known to no one now.
Light and darkness mix together sightless
Dust has settled here, it is coldness and alone.
There is rust on the mountain trails.
The mountains here are reality.
As sightless since of time to see you
To dust the years have won
This land of ages forever washed
High of welts, motionless and sublime
Hills to thoughts alive and waiting motion.
Today they seem as oldness
These fields of rusting mountain dust.
On and on till sight is lost and stillness
Breaks over yonder hill
Water bears it mark here above and
Below this crusting landscape at last
To nothing more but itself is dried
Is it a sleeping giant about to wake?
No, it is a space in place at last.

Edmund Walker Goddard

But For A Moment

Oh God, but for a moment,
a morning ray of sunshine beam;
enjoyed, but for a moment **life**,
is but a dream!

I now find, tears of sorrow,
where, but for a moment, **Thy sunbeam shined!**
I truly thought, but for a moment,
'twas for you, this pity pined;

Yet, I know, with God eternal,
ye have gone, where the soul **never dies**;
and alas! but for a moment
Wish you were here, to dry my eyes!

Dismal mornings, one now envisions,
No more sunbeam! to enshrine;
But for a moment, **Poor little me!**
as brilliant Truth, began to shine:

This is Jesus; The Living Word;
God is Spirit! Doth not thou see?
Oh death, thy sting, but for a moment;
one now doth shine, in Liberty!

Gary Bitson

The Porch

Our lives had held times of both joy and sorrow
Together we remained strong and faced each tomorrow
We promised long ago to always be one
Never to part until our work on earth was done
The years passed and the time had come to live our life
A dream to share together as man and wife
A porch to sit on each night and watch the setting sun
Another day would be ended and still we would be one
A simple dream, a new beginning, never to end
You were my life, my love, my friend
So many years ahead to share so much
A dream so close, now never to touch
Only a porch, but it meant much more
The dream shattered when you walked out the door
Alone now missing you so, my heart is broken
The dream is gone, words never to be spoken
There will never be a porch to watch the setting sun
Only empty nights, for now I am just one

Joan Gubitosi

Calypso Music

Such a sweet rhythm,
can't help but
wine your waist and move your feet instantly.
Listen to de beat.
Calypso music, feel de beat, so sweet.

Hear de brass bands
with those thundering sounds.
Let de music intoxicate your body,
with its compelling rhythm.
Calypso music, so sweet, hear de beat.

As for de inexperienced,
When de music hit you
there's an instant surge of electricity.
A tantalizing heat in your feet,
that makes you start dancing,
prancing and winning all over de street.
Calypso music, so sweet, so-ooo swee-eeet!

Avonelle Lewis-Rand

Marigold Santana

Love comes so easy these days
As fast as it comes, as fast as it goes
Marigold Santana nobody knows
How we feel inside
Sometimes it hurts so much
You don't want any one to know
Are we friends, are we lovers,
Or are we sorry to say what we feel inside

Tears come, tears go
Only I know, how your feelings show
You're a fair woman, with dark hair
And dark eyes, you have so much love inside
Only I know how you feel, even if you don't tell me so

Marigold Santana, learn more about yourself
Then you can let yourself go

Love comes easy

Juan C. Gomez

Our Neighborhood

Most people here are pleasant and kind,
Among the nicest one could find.
Then, like apples in a barrel gotten,
There's always a couple completely rotten.
One, a dealer, plying his trade;
The other, a woman, a vindictive liar;
Neither of whom care for the Powers higher.
Both of these people obey not the law . . .
Are the worst type of people we ever saw.
The rest of us only hope and pray
They will pick up their belongings
And just move away!

R. M. Cox

The Twelve Months

A New Year in January, made up of happiness.
Valentine's in February inspires love.
March is spring, when all wear green.
Bluebonnets so precious, like April so diamond.
Fields with onion, remind me of May.
Flag Day's in June, when all honor red, white, and blue.
Fireworks in July, is Independence Day.
August is worthy, plenty of work.
Labor Day in September, resting of work.
October is skeletons, frightening and bloody.
November is Thanksgiving, in memory of Veterans.
December is Christmas Day, when a lovely child was born.

Precious Perez

That Is Why I Won't Let Go

Jesus loves us, so.
That is why, I won't let go.
I'll never let go, of his powerful hands.
Jesus is savior, he's in command.
The Lord is my world, don't you know?
He's in my heart and in my soul.
He is the lily a perfect flower.
The Lord is my fortress
and strong hightower
I exalt the Lord and thank him, so.
More precious than pure silver and gold.
Jesus I love you, so.
That is why, I won't let go.

Frederick L. James

Life's Fountain

The spring of life renews.
As the seasons change, the winter becomes spring.
The flowers bloom, the bees buzz,
The earth releases,
Yesterday becomes a memory.
Stop, look and wonder at creation.
The dark becomes light,
God in full bloom.
The forest of men, draw from your tree of life.
Life's fountain is in search of you:
Touch, feel and understand.

Ed McDonald

In Your Arms

I feel safe no cause for alarm
at least not when I'm in your arms.
In the course of a day I often pray
just to get a glimpse of your face.
Some-how I'm just not complete
unless I at least get to rub your feet
or touch you in some other way.
Some-how in the course of each and
everyday.
Just a smile, a caress, just looking
at you relieves my stress.
It's the one time I let it all go.
Your my rock, my best friend, my
confidante and my lover and I love you.
Especially when I'm in your arms,
you lay your head on my chest
I feel this is love; so I can finally rest
And I want you to know I love you.
  I love being in your arms.poem in tracker

Daniel Jay Letchworth

Hovering

Flying Saucer,
Flying Saucer,

I once saw a flying saucer,
right before dusk,
and with a pop from atop the clouds,
there were suddenly two.

Steadied astride, they sat motionless beside,
just outside the parachute ride,
right before my eye.

Dull gray in color, a lackluster,
"no" noise to muster.
As they sat, they each looked like a hat,
not to doubt,
for they were as close as a good shout.

Now the summer of eighty four will always be a chore,
no matter the score, to explain what I saw,
on the eastern sea board.

Daniel C. Mure

Keep Smiling

Now, keep smiling my darling.
I'll always remember you that way.
Clear your tearful eyes in parting,
As hugs and kisses close our day.

Tho your heart may speak truer,
Keep on smiling all the while.
When your kisses seem fewer
I'll cheer up on your smile.

Here in my arms,
Your winsome charms
Say to me alone you belong—
Don't tell me pretty eyes can be wrong.

Keep smiling; brighten my skies!
And tonight, after we part,
Let me dream of the gleam in you eyes;
Then I'll awake with a smile in my heart.

Spearman B. Jones

My Loving Friend Lathan

To a wonderful man and loving friend—I love you.
My very dear friend Lathan is as loving as can be,
He is such a wonderful man and a wonderful friend to me.
He has such a good and wonderful heart,
From the moment that I met him I knew
I liked him right from the very start.
He is so good in every way,
He always seems to make my day.
He is so very talented his heart is made of gold,
I love Lathan for what he is always to have and to hold.
He is a sweetheart and a love,
That God has blessed from up above.
You are so loving and so kind,
You always write what's on your mind.

Elaine Shanker

For A Blind Man Sees As God Sees

For a blind man sees as God sees,
The darkness without the light within
The pain below the love of sin

Dwelling in peace dwelling in dark,
Cannot see her shadow
Can her heart, yes, he is smart

Walk a careful path,
Far above beauty, far below God.
For if you love the shadow,
You shall have nothing to hold

What he knows I cannot view.
He is just a blind man, a blind man who can see.
The distance between him and me.

For a blind man sees as God sees
The man within the beauty beneath
The hidden men, the sword in its sheath

Oh, what does life hold for me,
Love and its sinuous seams, death and its dark dreams,
Is it all just and outward image for me to see,
Oh, how could that be.

George Shultz

The House

I have had many families live with me thru the years.
Newlyweds have lived with me hoping to start a new life together.
I had babies play on the floor that I offer with care.
I may be old and need fixing up now and again.
But I keep who live with me warm from the cold nights of winter.
My walls are solid to keep back to hollowing of winds and the
falling of the spring rain saying you will not enter.
And yes I have seen broken marriage and even death touched me.
Life goes on as I do for I know out there is a couple or family
to move in and live with me.

Curtis Le Mier

Daughter of Mine

Daughter of mine so young and free,
running through life
with skinned up knees.
Your beauty astounds,
your love surrounds,
your hair flies softly in the breeze.

Daughter of mine so young and wild,
with your impish grin,
such a precocious child.
Intelligence so amazing,
through bright eyes blazing,
your young mind so inquisitive and waiting.

Daughter of mine so young and open,
shyly giving
of Love's sweet tokens.
Innocently teasing,
sweetness so pleasing,
a mother's heart could never be broken.

Judy Jones

Still Standing

This new generation of age like
if lost and out of a cage, going wild
And with finance out of control playing
with credit cards like a toy or a child.
Helplessly wandering with no respect, no
morals, lost of guidance and family
values, it just doesn't cut it, nobody
is watching for their p's and q's until
it's too late and you're too far out
And now you get ready for the bout, then you
file for chapter seven, when it all comes
down to an understanding then you might
say "Am I still standing?"

Ventura Colon

Disillusion

We live in the world
Where diversity-chaos reign.
We live in the world
Where guns talk to doves
Some live in "heaven"
Another in bitter reality
Destined, like parallel vertices
Run a railroad around earth,
Equidistant in all points,
Their faculty hierarchy committee of brain
Each in own way dream-visualize
Their future paradise on Mars.
Disillusion for mankind when welcomed
By whimsical wind strumming inhospitable melody;
Freeze-formed an immortal monument by mortals from earth.
There will be no Adam and Eve;
Illuminated by sungleams Utopians will salute earth,
As a remnant after the gun-dove
Disharmonious atomic wars on Earth.

Helena Dante

Dreams

A lazy, but gazingly thought . . .
Lingering and wondrously brought
by the constantly dreamy and bored mind
which relaxingly endeavors to find . . .
desires of venture, triumph, and romance.
Appear one second, but gone in a glance!
Yet, its real and intangible treasure
is its manifolds of verve and pleasure
that we so hesitantly need . . .
forever, so ever, indeed!

Lizabeth M. Velando

Crushes

What is that causes us pain,
And has us so confused we can't gain?
What keeps life interesting for us,
And makes it so we always cause a fuss?
What makes life intriguing and fun,
But makes it so we always want to run?
What makes the most talkative person shy,
And works against us until we want to die?
What keeps the world on the go,
Wondering why they did this as so?
What makes us feel the urge to scream,
but always gives us a reason to dream?

Why the wonderful thing of such,
I do believe has been called a crush!

Tessa Louch

God's Love

God sent His Son to show us His love,
That we might be saved to return to Heaven above.
His guardian angels keep us from harm
If we will just let them take us each by the arm.
To save us from sin and strife,
He did bear thirty-nine stripes,
On His back He did wear;
The nails in His hands
Pierced all the way through.
He took all the pain,
Just for me and for you.
All that we have is just a big loan:
Our children, our home,
Will some day be gone;
What have we then but Jesus the Son,
Who paid the price, that we might be won.

Virginia L. Mayhue

Ghost Town

Among the derelict of house and hut
And narrow streets where grass and brush have grown
Through rooms where dusty weeds and cacti jut,
Through narrow doors where many suns have shone
Singing in joy the winds play round and round
Swaying and twisting, droning soft or shrill
Tossing on high some leaves that they have found,
Humming and laughing where all had been still.
Here is a town where joy was brief and young
Life could be bought for little, wild and gay
And in a waltz its funeral hymn was sung
As in a cloud the living waft away.

This is the town in paler desert dress,
It cowers now in silent wilderness.

Luella W. Lee

It Could Happen

It could happen, just wait and see
I will grow up, but what will I be?
A doctor, a dancer, now let me see
I gotta think about what I can be
My mom always says, kid you can do
Whatever you want to, just do your best,
Keep on trying, I'm so proud of you.
If I close my eyes, I can see—me,
Dancing up on stage, people watching
And clapping just for me
A dancer I will be, a ballerina that's me!
It could happen, just wait and see!

Rachel Harper

Birds

Birds are such beautiful things.
They soar on high with fluttery wings.
They glide on currents of air,
Their perfection evident most everywhere.

Up, up, up, to the sky,
Oh my, I wish I could fly.
Happy and free are the birds of the wild,
Just watching them can melt the heart of a child.

Some are large and some are small,
Beautiful, they are, one and all.
All, are different colors of the rainbow.
Some sing, some squawk, and some even crow.

No matter where you are, no matter where you go,
Birds are there, flying high and low.
So, look for them everywhere you go, you see,
They are God's gift to you and me.

Richard Lundy

Flowers

When I was young
I used to read Dr. Suess with Daddy
Play Candyland till bedtime
Watch Cinderella
And plant flowers with Mommy

Now I belong to a grown up world
And I read Hillary Clinton's book about raising a child
Listen to the President talk about making America a better place
Watch the world fight many wars
And plant flowers with Mommy

Sheila Rhodes

Deep Within the Forest

Deep within the forest.
I can't explain
When you step there you throb
With pain.
The pain hurts, the pain stings
But still the pain is not the same.
I will still sign my name
in my very own blood.
Deep within the forest no one is loved.

The sky roars with thunders
but soon you and your grave
will be six feet under.
Memories hold you and me up.
Still you hear the cries
of your little pup.
The cries, the whimpers
the pain, the splinters.
The rain in the sky, it roars and thunders.
All you can think of saying is, "Oh, my."

Kimberly Newton   age 11

Golden Packages

A small beautifully golden wrapped package
topped with a golden bow.
Is it empty or is it full?
No one but me will really know.
It sits on the table as a daily reminder
that it does not cost us anything to be kinder.
This package symbolizes encouragement, time, challenges
and good works, all of which are gifts.
These are things that we all can give.
Things that may give someone that needed lift.
All our words should be as golden packages
with bows on top.
So let us strive to let this be our
goal and never stop.
Never until the end of out time.

Pat Scott

Just One Word

He is ten feet tall and knows
All about animals, planets,
TV shows, and CD ROM too.
He always has time to ride a bike with you.
He is a whiz at Math and answers
All your questions with a smile.
He takes time to pitch a ball or two with you,
So you can try out your new glove.

He is tough at times.
He brings tears to your eyes.
Just remember . . .
That he carries you in his heart.
Who is this person that can do,
And be all these things?
Just one word describes him.
The word that is perfect,
And fits so well is "Dad."

Evelyn Filipovits

Lonely Night

Could I be with you alone?
I'm not sure where this will go cause we don't have the time need,
Just enough to make us bleed.
You'll be leaving soon, it's hard to say when you'll return,
And I don't want to lead you on.
So if you feel the need, close your eyes and share this dream.
It will be there to hold you through the night, forever for tonight.
I will love you forever for tonight.
As I look into your eyes, feelings much
Too strong for us not to try and fight we still have tonight,
So when you're far away I will always be alone.
So if you feel the need, take my hand and share this night.
It will be eternity.
I've been broken down by empty promises, like a sky without a star.
I've been having doubts that I could feel again,
But I believe that I'm in love.

Shane A. Webster

My Only One

My mother is like a bright red rose
As pure and sweet with perfect pose
There are many mom's in this world today
But only to one would this I want to say
If ever there was a choice that I would of had to make
I would of picked her with no fear of mistake
It would be her with her special ways
That guided me through my learning days
Her heart is so true and full of love
She had plenty to give with the help from above
I wish her today Happy Birthday from my heart
And hope she knows I loved her right from the very start
So this is the birthday wish I wish for you
Health, Love and Happiness All Year Through.
Not only this one year but for many to come
To my mom—my only one.

Mary Fritz

The Crack of the Bat—Whack!

The crack of the bat- whack!
The soda bubbling- fizzle, fizzle!
The hot dogs cooking—sizzle, sizzle!
The ball being caught in a leather glove—smack!
The rush of the wind as a player slides into home plate—swoosh!
The fans drinking their Cokes—slurp, gulp! slurp, gulp! ahhh!
The players blowing bubbles with their gum—pop! pop!
The butter melting on the popcorn—crackle, crackle!
The fireworks exploding when the hometeam wins—boom! boom!

"Oh, how I love baseball games!"

Dustin Watterson

Live Your Life to the Fullest

As I sat there staring ahead
My mind tries to focus on what I might say,
I live in a world where nobody knows me
And I cry myself to sleep everyday.

Money has no meaning to me
For love is what I seek,
I feel my life slipping away
As my days turn into weeks.

I wish to God my life would change
Sometimes I think that I'm living for nothing,
There must be someone out there
To let me know my life is something.

So as I drive to find a meaning
I do not notice that great oak tree,
Now I find myself more lonely
As I look down from the sky looking down over me.

Brandon Py

Junior High

You said you felt like we were in Junior High.
I laughed.
I hated Junior High.
I was taller than the boys.
Not anymore.
I was sure I was going to be something.
Not anymore.
It was awkward.
I didn't know who my friends were.
Not anymore.
I didn't know what I liked,
I didn't know what I wanted.
I'm more certain now.
I still don't know where I'm going.
I still don't know what I will do.
But I know where I've been,
And I know what I've done.
And this is not Junior High.

Lisa Trefsger

Our Family, Our Friends, Our Buddies

We grow with our family, our friends, our buddies.
We think they will be around till the end of time.
We forget that they will say good-bye one day,
Not to return like before.
We play, we sing and enjoy the days and nights.
We are people who love our family, our friends, our buddies,
Put the thought out of our minds.
Someday they may not be around till the end of time.
We as children don't look that far ahead down the road,
It's time to play.
Someday as they walk out that door waving a friendly good-bye
And a sunny smile. We pray that they will be back.
Now that they are gone, we are left with the memories of our
Family, our friends, our buddies.
We ask God, "When will the pain end?"
Trying to recall our love for our lost ones, to help cover the pain.
We look back to remember our family, our friends, our buddies
Whom we've grown up with or come to know.
With the love and memories, along with the help of time the
Pain subsides only the loss is still felt every time.

Ellen F. Butts

You're My Best Friend

Dedicated to Dr. Wells
A friend is someone special,
someone who really cares.
A friend tells you the truth,
Specially when the truth ain't fair.

A friend is someone who helps in time of need,
and not just because they want to do a good deed.
A friend is a friend always, to the end.
Even when you don't deserve them to be your friend.

You've been a teacher, a parent and a shrink.
You never let me get by when I forgot to think.
You were as hard as you had to be and soft as you could.
You did all you were able not just what you should.

I'm not easy to love but you found a way.
Truth be told meeting you was my real birthday.
I remember that you told me that the way to repay
Was for me to help others, I'll try every day.

It won't be enough but it's what you have asked.
I'd do anything for you, just name the task.
I know that you won't cause you do it for free.
'Cause of you, it finally feels good to be me.

Matthew S. Whitt

The Black Woman

Of the poets, I'm Giovanni and Angelou.
Writing and feeling things that I know.

Of the singers, I'm Vaughn and Holiday.
Speaking with songs towards everything I say.

Of the actresses, I'm Dandridge and Horne.
A star guiding me since the day I was born.

Of the writers, I'm Morrison and Shange.
Going through changes each and every day.

Not just images, not just names.
Women.
Different, yet the same.
Each has a face, a talent, a gift.
Neither needed a boost or a lift.
Just a mind, a body and a soul.
All in order to play life's
Ultimate role.
The black woman

Naya Wright

The Park

We used to go to the park late at night
We had fun and played games all of the time
Then our happiness turned into fright
As the park was introduced to crime

As kids, we went to the park everyday
We met new people and had lots of fun
The only thing we did was laugh and play
Until someone came carrying a gun

Very soon afterwards, the park met death
Death had many names and many faces
Then at the park, we would all hold our breath
And soon we played in different places

Now the park is no longer filled with cheer
But instead it contains nothing but fear

Bill Krenn

The Fall

I love the falls the rivers because there are part of my soul
Battles of light and darkness, mass of tire
A long curtains of lacework and woven foam; please of splendor
Greens and blues, purples and whites melt into one another fade

Emotion tumultuously forward I had have day by day
Dull omnipresent foam washes my face. It's a terrifying journey
The power that give, we a different sense of owe
Here the inhuman life and strength are spontaneous, active.

I saw in that place is a complete circle its circle of life
A noise of unspecified ruin old civilization, new civilization
The sight cannot recognize liquid in the masses that hurt past
It's pressed by the straits into visibly convex form of future.

I could not get out of my mind the thought of great
Planes of water, slide past like a spring of a wild beast
The art and beauty which give us the stream of life
In all comparison that rise in my heart, in joy, in sorrow in hope

Capacity for delight and wonder to the sense of mystery
Surrounding our life, our sense of pity and beauty
Over the falls, in the white cloud of human crying for the rainbows
Over the fall ending as inevitably as this dark flood of my thought

Geno M. Popescu

In The Cavern

The sun plummets over the edge of the world
when the bloody stars fill his head.
The cold gun falls. It crashes against the ground
before his body, while the sun continues falling away forever
from him, taking his pleasure, his pain, all.

Pieces of brain slide from the back of his head
like snails leaving wet trails.
He tastes the red on his lips, knowing it
stains them darkly as his skin pales.
Skin stark white except for a tiny black hole
in his forehead that goes into another
universe where the suns are black, a
universe from which bloody stars pour into his mind.

He smells a flash of blue sky.
A drop of moisture touches his skin.
It is not rain.
He hears someone crying. It is not him.

His spine twists like a headless snake inside his still body.
Wine flows from his mouth instead of words.

In a black cavern there is lightning.

William Coleman

Look For Me

I know that you are sad now, and sometime tears do fall.
But smile when you think of me, I'm with you after all.
We shared a lot of laughter, and at times we shared a tear.
But memories are beautiful, and love does not cause fear.

Find the beauty in a flower, and in the birds sweet song.
Time can only separate, but not for very long.
There is no greater gift from God, than a tender gentle love.
Though you cannot touch my hand, look for me in stars above.

Please don't forget our laughter, and the happy times we had.
Don't let the time you think of me, make you feel lost or sad.
When you feel you can not find me, just pick up this poem and know.
An angel stands protecting you, look for me come rain or snow.

So while you wait to join me, and while on earth you stay.
Take time to share the love you have, don't put memory away.
I walk with you in darkness, when the starlight fills the sky.
And I hold you oh so tenderly, when you feel the need to cry.

So touch the tender memory, of the love you have for me.
And remember I walk with you, our love will always be.
If a gentle rain is falling, and a tear slips from your eye.
Look for me, I'm with you, love just knows, does not ask why.

Alice Harris

The Laid-Off Blues

Now the listen, my children, and you all shall hear
Of the fallout from layoffs and wages of fear;
Of our shattered self-images, doubt, and depression,
Of trumped-up excuses and childhood regression.

We live in a world where the dollar is all,
Where their profit is king, so that greed makes the call;
Where their bottom-line numbers, through some twist or quirk,
Come ahead of the people who make them all work!

We've thus come to the point in our social evolving
Our plans, and our lives, are now quickly dissolving
In favor of corp's rate and stockholder paybacks;
We're worked to the bone and we're screwed to the max!

Afer spending our lives working hard for the man,
We're dismissed with a wave of some MBA's hand;
We are told after twenty or more years on staff,
That a kid fresh from college is cheaper by half!

It is clear, e'en to Liberal Arts majors like me,
That employers must profit or they'll cease to be;
But, oh, where is it written that Greed be enshrined
As the firm's Golden Calf—to all else they are blind?

B. A. Woodhouse

Searching for the Real Meaning

The reality of the mind is difficult to find.
Thoughts don't match the way it really is.
Feelings filter through layers of webbing,
Gauze veils that interface with the world;
Ideas misshapen by being too long in formation,
Kneaded too carefully in an effort to reach acceptability . . .
Like a poem—never finished.

A poem in constant flux,
With words crossed out and written in again,
Obliterated, deleted, altered,
An ever continuing process of metamorphosis
Approaching the core.
Creeping closer
But never achieving the precise meaning.

Donald R Clapp

Beloved Child, Forever Resting

I see the sunshine and the clear blue skies
And I remember the sparkle in your eyes
Standing by your place of rest
It's your laughter I remember best
An emptiness is filled within my heart
A bittersweet, loving, special part
My child, though you are gone from mortal sight,
You're in my thoughts, both day and night
Although many days since you were here
My heart cherishes you, forever dear
I leave as the sky becomes less blue
Still, you know I'm never leaving you

Gerry Pearns

I Am Me

I am one, a child of the earth.
I am a flower, blooming in my own way.
I am one of a kind, like a snowflake.
I am small compared to everyone else.
I am me.

I am lost in the jungles of life.
I am a ladybug in the tree of people.
I am a drop of rain in the storms of civilization.
I am an eighth note in the song of the sea.
I am me.

Kristin Hubbell

A Father's Love

Nestled warm and cozy, safely in their beds,
Their Dad comes by to kiss them gently on their heads.
He pauses for a moment; he looks upon each one;
His heart swells at the night of his daughter and his son.

Sweet dreams swirling silently in this morning hour;
But they can feel his presence, his love and all its power.
They'll never have to question his love, his pride, his joy;
They know to him they'll always be his little girl and boy.

He stands alone in silence and watches them in sleep
And prays for his sweet treasures to feel this love so deep.
They waken in the morning and the sun shines up above;
But in their hearts, the warmth they feel, comes from a father's love.

Kathleen J. Mancuso

The Piece That Makes My Heart Complete

Somewhere in every person's soul,
There is a place in their heart where there is a hole.

They look far and wide for a piece that fits right,
But they find out that it's always too tight.

So on they go looking for a mate,
Or searching all day just for a date.

That emptiness in their heart will not go away,
Until they're joined in love on their wedding day.

I was lonely, heart broken, and very afraid,
That I would never find the perfect piece for me God had made.

Then one day you came into my life,
And I knew someday I'd be your wife.

You made me feel special like no one else could,
You took away the bad thoughts and replaced them with good.

When I'm away from you I feel like apart of me is gone,
Like when the sun isn't there when it is down.

I couldn't imagine us being apart,
For I know that would surely break my heart.

I need you because I love you for always and today,
To love and stand by me to never go away.

Cheryl Mathis

Shades of Gray

Though the sun shines bright and lightens the day,
The reality of life has many shades of gray.
The darkest hue, we know as black,
Is when you lose something you'll never get back.
A lighter hue, if that's what you choose,
Is one of admittance, but a refusal to lose.
An even lighter shade, a real subtle gray,
Is when you should leave, but opt to stay.
The lightest gray, with black, just a trace,
Is when you find comfort in your lover's embrace.
The greatest of shades, the glimmering white,
Is when life is joyful and going just right.
In an instant, the danger, as white fades away,
Roll in reality, with its many shades of gray.

Susan Evens

Be Strong

I believe everything happens for a reason,
So when something goes awry
Please, please don't cry.

Instead search for the positive.
I assure you it is there
And God does care!

Be patient, the search may be long,
But never give up, do not fret,
And never, never regret.

What's done is done.
Just adjust, take the time you need,
But remember to follow His lead.

When the time is right,
The reasons, He will reveal,
All you need to do is kneel.

Remember this and all will be well.
If you do not doubt,
Trust God, all will work out!

Rebekah Milburn

What's In Your Heart

Maybe it's not love I feel for you
But it feels so right so true
I don't think you know the way
You have put my heart in such disarray
Every smile and glance
Gives my heart a chance
I wish I knew how you feel
It's the only way my heart will heal
Is it that you don't care
Or is it that you can't share
Whether the truth is good or bad
It is better to know than to hope and be sad
I've tried to stick it out and be brave
For it's not lust I crave
But a solid relationship with you
It has to be what you want too
Which brings us back to the start
What's in your heart?

Celina Booth

Close Your Eyes

I thought,
And I have been thinking for a long time now
That if you see
Something
It must be in your own view,
Personal perspective
Narrow focus
Vision, less looks
Blind optics
Blocks options
But if,
And this is what I think you should do
Just close your eyes
Use your heart
Control your emotions
Close your eyes
Open your mind
Trace your thoughts
Close your eyes,
See what's on the other side.

Marc N. Johnson

Life's Garden

Friends are the flowers in life's garden.
They can forever bloom if you water them.

Each will come in their own special color.
And each will slowly start to blend.

It may take time, but they will grow.
Their color will shine; this they'll show.

And once you've seen how wonderful they can be.
You'll always want them around; just wait and see.

You're a precious flower in my life's garden.
We have grown together, shared sunshine and the rain.

I can remember when you bloomed into my heart.
We have become a bouquet of friendship, each doing their part.

So, whenever you're sad, or no matter how tough its been,
Remember, friends are the flowers in life's garden.

Teresa Jane Yoakum

Yearning For You

Day in day out I yearn for you.
I can't do much but think of you.
Your look and embracing smiles
Can be felt by me for endless miles.
Have I seen the glistening of your eyes before?
Why then do I keep yearning for so much more?
Year in year out I find myself feeling and seeing
Your soul sparkling through another being.
Oh heart of mine, what shall I do?
Can't think of anything but you.
Can't fine you ever anywhere,
Yet do I know, you are always there.
Thus, hope swells on inside my heart
That one day soon I'll find the cart
To flee this world of hurt emotions
And find the awaited grave solutions
To be with you heart to heart, face to face,
With no more daunting, evil menace.

Clara Frame

What Was I Thinking?

Students
Students
Everywhere
What was I thinking?
Me?
A teacher?
Can I help them?
Can I teach control?
Can I be an influence?
Can I encourage creativity?
Can I cause a love of learning?
Can I nourish them in succeeding?
Can I inspire higher levels of thinking?
Can I help to solve the personal problems?
Can I provide assistance to their learning needs?
Can I show them they are masters of their destiny?
What was I thinking?
I was thinking I could!
Just need to do it one student at a time!
Just need to do it!

Ledru Ellen Gowin

Untitled

I don't care anymore, I can't.
All my cares have been relieved from me.
It may have been more of a robbery or rape
But the difference this time is that I wanted you to leave.
I hate myself for writing this but it's tradition, or habit.
It makes me stronger, yeah, it'd be nice not
To have to go through obstacle courses
With ropes to hang yourself, to be made the strongest.
But that's how the fates are twisted.
If only we could see the face of the master of tightropes,
Then we could understand the crazy routine
He's planned for this circus of a life.
That's all you were, a one-act circus show.
Well, sweetheart, looks like the crowd isn't interested anymore.
So you pick up your peanuts and move, on, or back.
You never really learned how to move on.
And you'll pull your circus into another town
While you perform your tricks.
The time will come again, most likely sooner than later,
And your own elephants will rain on your parade.

Rebecca Battaglia

Feelings

It's time for me to say what I feel
I can no longer hold these feelings that I have for you inside
You are the one I want to commit to for the rest of my life
I picture us in the future happy as can be
You are what I live for and will die for
Your words put me in confusion
You say that we are perfect for one another
And yet you try to keep a distance between us
Say what you mean and mean what you say
Your words are only hurting me and leave me in disbelief
Your words are beautiful at times and destructive on impact
Your words make me silent and trigger my tears
How can you say you love me and then expect
Me to forget about that special day
When we embraced our lips as the sun went to sleep
The feelings that stirred from the first kiss was like no other
A fire was lit in my heart and lead me to discover
A path that I've been searching for all of my life
And then you sting me with your words
That puncture the very heart I used to love you

Christina Ann Potoky

ll Mourner

A loss of life. A leaving of soul.
The direction of strife is to leave us not whole
And stagger us with its toll.
Brought to sorrow for all tomorrow
Is a widow left to grow old.
A pledge of heart. An aath to a known.
Feelings for one's counterpart will leave one alone,
To forever carve his stone.
Her madness plays throughout all the days
In a lingering undertone.
A touch of frost. A feeling of fear.
When all thought is not of loss a panic appears,
And that is all that she hears.
All she had spun cannot be undone
As she looks into her mirror.
A place of peace. A presence of flower
What was felt was the least upon the morning hour,
But it was the follower.
And what remains is all of the pain
Soon bestowed on an ill mourner.

Michael A. L. Morris

Soul Spark

As one soul ignites the other,
And brilliant blaze defeats the night,
Rest in one corner, just beyond the light.
Darkness hides me from your eyes.
Cross the boundary now, spill dewy desire,
And bathe me in the radiant fire.
Mold me in your arms, let me become your clay.
Shape my soul into goddess form.
In your hands I am reborn.
If a curse overcame,
And the light did spoil and break upon my eyes,
Let that wicked shard that pierced my heart—
Bleed until I die.

Elizabeth Coughlin

A Potable Paradox

Did you ever stop to think about how contradictory
The thinking in our culture often seems to be?
To concoct a simple cocktail seems to bear this statement out
To prove the point I'm making without the slightest doubt.
You start it out with alcohol to give it lots of "clout,"
Then weaken it with soda to take the power out.
You add a little lemon to give it lots of "zip,"
Then sweeten it with sugar before you take a sip.
You cool it down with ice, chopped from the freezer shelf,
Then raise your glass, say "Here's to you!"
And drink it down yourself.

Mary C. Mahon

Pyre

The cold embraces,
Picks up the soul to surf the cascading breeze.
Frosty hands caress the skin,
Shiver the spine, blind the mind.
The never ending ballet of sin,
Sick from misery, played through
A gauntlet of desire.
Once again only cold is friend.
Not a funeral fire dares
Quench the solitude of cold
Washing over time.
Sacred ballet, the tapping of toes beckons me,
Lost soul drawn unto fire.
Still so cold, like the dead growing old,
The unknown knows.
Bliss of the desolate unknown to the pyre
Mounting a symphony scribed by a squire.
Ruins of time the cold whisks up,
Channelling fear through the heart of love.

Michael A. Goodman

My Lachrymose Eyes

I live this labyrinth life,
Alone with nothing but my mind
Latent, lucid I am to people,
For they do not know me, the real me,
Here I sit and write at the age of,
Of 90 such a longevity life I know,
But my words, as old as I they are,
A largess to me like candy to a child
For once I had someone dear to me,
Beautiful by light she was,
By night invisible to all but I,
A sickness among her for time would tell,
How long with me her presence would stay
My lachrymose eyes she could not see
Laudable was I for an answer,
Answer to my prayers that the day, the day would never come
The day she, her life and love would distinguish
Distinguish like a candle's flame to a draft
And my heart lacerated without her
Alone with these lachrymose eyes.

Christopher Flythe

A Friend

A friend is a person who just cares,
Who has always been there,
To love, to care, to inspire, and to share,
Throughout those memorable years.

A friend is a person who helps guide you through;
To be there just for you,
During the worst and best of times of your life,
And sees the best in you.

A friend is there to stay awhile,
And a friend is there to offer a smile,

Only a friendship that a friend can give will last
Forevermore.

Friends are forever!

Paula Pearson

Red

Poetically inclined, technically lost in another
Dimension, head spins into a tremendous aching
Pain, mind lost and confused in all the thoughts,
Tears flow from the eyes like a river flows into the
Ocean, damaged, hurt, crying, all the while the
Earth still spins, just like your heart, you grab the
Razor, cut slices into your wrists, just to see if you
Could possibly end this, your mind is a time bomb
Waiting, racing, ticking its life away
Thought after thought, as you make the final choice,
Life or death, which one, evil or good, all the time
Messing everything up, always in the wrong, or so
It seems, slice, slice, as you watch your blood, slowly
Drip away, your breath begins to stagger, all you see
Is red, you hear faint voices, all you can make out
From these voices are the words help, still all you see
Is red, red, red, red,

Jessica Corwin

White Rhinos of South Africa

Twilight had turned from a sunning-dusk, to a nasty, filthy
pitch black storming lake, that roared over Thunder-Bay;
Our Light had faded to a slow moving peek, winds danced in violence
across the once quiet-seas of grass, we had no choice but to stay:

Night had fell in a swift cadence, Natures, raining deluge
passed as the pouncing, lusting King of Beast; Bright Moon
-Beams broke open the silence of darkness, but, only the
hunted remained still, when they move they fall as spent prey,
and, yes, the hunters will Feast:

Cast on adventuring plains as nomads the weak soon stumble
to locking jaws, this contest of food in "Africa" is called
life Giving; Bask the victors do on tearing, bleeding, raw
flesh they are carnivorous, and, love death amongst the Living:

Along the great grass plains roams a hulking "African" armored
beauty, of pure violent locomotion, who quavers on Low;
Belong, this awesome land roving water quencher is Nature's
armored tank, they are few, yet, they stand not alone these,
White Rhinos Of South Africa.

P. Vincent Nee

Spring

Winds that make the howling sound of winter's wrath have all come
to pass and spring awaits the newborn day, when calm and warmth
are now to stay. Spring eases the heart of burdens and weights of
winter's day, burdens and weights that have now gone away. Birds
greet the leafy faces of the tender trees, as gentle breezes ease their
young in their nests when done. Bird's song enhances the glory of
the dawning of morning in God's heavenly glory. Flowers blooming
and crops booming, with sunshine everywhere, there is no reason
to really fear. For spring is a second chance, a welcoming commit-
tee, an angel's dance. The rhythms rapture and soothe the soul with
the calm following the storm, the calm of God's warmth and heavenly dawn.

After winter there is always spring, after darkness, light does beam.

Ruth Goldfarb

Surprise!

What a delightful shock to glance out at the pasture
Where the two horses usually graze in peaceful stature;
To discover a surprising addition to the serene look
An adorable long legged foul had arrived beating the time book.

Now this little surprise was not supposedly due for awhile
But you can bet this palomino filly brought quite a big smile.
With two white socks to give her some special adorning marks in place
She also has diamond-like marking on her darling face.

The veterinarians calender date was in the middle of July
Yet one such estimated timing you can not always rely.
So into this world came this charming filly of June 6th in early morn
Defying all date projections, she decided it was a good day to be born.

Her long legs seemed to be surprisingly strong
She took everything in stride, apparently feeling here she did belong.
In two days those little stilts were racing across the pasture
A sight to see, the mare chasing and calling the filly trying her energy
    to capture.

Nadine M. Bushong

It's Harvest Time

There are many souls to be harvested,
But only a few workers to harvest them.
Let's pray to God who owns the harvest.
He will provide the workers to go out, and gather for Him.

Many of our youths and adults are slaves to illegal activities,
Drugs, crimes of passions, shootings, and other sins.
Christians have been commanded to go out into the world.
Unite in Christ's compassionate forgiving attitude, and bring them in.

We must engage ourselves in a ceaseless war
Against the evils of this dying world.
Let the peace of Christ rule our hearts.
Go out into the highways and hedges and bring in our boys and girls.

God specializes in finding and changing lives.
Those we may consider unreachable or unworthy.
When we harvest for God, he can take their lives
And use them effectively in His services.

Alice M. Jones

Life Cycle—One Perspective of Abuse

Newborn. Infant. Toddler. Raped. Silenced. Beaten. Stitches.
Bruises. Broken bones. Repetition creates its own normalcy.
Parochial school. Behave yourself. Keep up grades. Be obedient.
A good little girl. Submissive. Quiet. Shine those shoes. Fold
your hands. Confess sins. Pray. Memorize. First Holy Communion.
Stations of the cross. Meditate. Jesus hanging on an immense
cross. Suffering. Ten years old. Molested. Fondled. Raped.
Priests were no different. Feeling sorry for men. Time passes.
Now too old for pedophiles. Reprieve. Thank God. Build a new
life. Embrace celibacy. Celebrate life. Several years pass. Raped
again. That rapist got a five to life sentence. So did I. Some
wounds need to be remembered throughout eternity. Like the
one's in the Savior's hands and feet and side. Not a pretty
autobiography. One in three women have a similar history before
age eighteen. I am not alone.
Thank God? Is the goal one in one women by the 21st century?
Does anyone hear our cries? Not much response. Few results.
Blame the victim, not the man. Sacrificing women and children is easy.
Supporting the law is difficult. Condolences are easier to give.
What is the message? Actions speak louder than words. The past,
present, future doesn't just go away. These are the pieces of eternity.
Awareness, not forgetfulness, brings wholeness. So scars remain.
What is identity? Here am I. Where does it end? With me.

Lauren Jones

Suzanne

Your beauty arrested me and held me without bail.
A witch could not have cast a stronger spell.
But you were sent by heaven, not from below.
You woke me up and turned me from my pointless path,
and drew me out from my safe academic haven, the world
I created for me—to protect me from a world that terrified me.
Then I saw you in that world and dared to leave mine to enter yours.
When I kissed you that night on Ocean beach,
I began to dare to live. With you, everything came together—
attraction, desire, yearning, passion, satisfaction, and, yes, love.
Like an angel, you could not stay for me to have you.
Four times you left me. Only three times you came back.
Once I went to you but that was only to tell you goodbye,
and send you back from where you came. One time more
I hope to come to see you. Then we will never be parted again.
Welcome me with a kiss to complete the journey we began
with a kiss so many years ago.

Jack Gordon

The Word

The "word" has lost its meaning
    Feelings are no longer felt.
        We live in a world where power is overrated—along with the "self"
            No tears are shed, and there is no pain.
                People die—again and again.

The "word" has lost all meaning.
    Feelings can no longer be felt.
        Life passes and leaves us behind . . .
            We don't even know to cry for help.

Teresa Novacek Flood

Remember When

Remember when: life was a skip and a jump, a day full of fun?
Remember when: fun was not a gun?
Remember when: crime did not pay?
Remember when: getting high was not a twelve-year-old's goal in life?
Remember when: Charles Manson was not a teen's Idol?
Remember when: kids could play outside without being kidnapped?
Remember when: a parent's priority was their children and not the night life?
Remember when: the word "crack-baby" did not exist?
Remember when: life was a skip and a jump, a day full of fun?
Remember When?

Loretta Richard

Mania

What is this madness inside of me, and why does it challenge me so
Causing so much pain to those I love the most,
oh why oh why will it just not go

Its dominion over me is dividing my heart and it wants to seize my soul
I battle so hard to repress it; will only bitterness linger when I am old

I gaze into the mirror to see this evil and dare it to look at me
It doesn't even attempt to, because the real me is the person I see

My heart is full of love and anger; I can't discriminate between the two
This evil that won't leave me alone, and takes all my strength to renew

One day it may go away, but oh the scars it leaves behind
Hurting those I love the most; this illness of my mind

Trust me if you can to fight it with a brutal force, brutal and unkind
To make it disappear forever, never capturing my soul or my mind

I know this thing that has hurt me so; I've known it for all my life
I know it will be my fight or flight

So please bear with me and encourage me along
Stand with me and together we can be strong

What is this madness inside of me and why does it challenge me so
I will fight until my last breath is drawn, and forever away it will go

Debbie H. Nichols

The Opening

Her love for him mirrors his for her. And yet self-imposed shackles
deny him the key—the key to unlock his true self—
opening his full capacity for love—to give and to receive.

Entangled in another's web of shackles;
While society's propriety fetters the freedom of his soul mate.
His freedom flounders. His loneliness lingers.

His love for her transcends the flesh,
And yet, temptation he tempts when 'ere they meet.
Lips touch, yet do not part. Bodies caress, yet do not entwine.

Their love so real, denied to feel.
Remembrance of past kisses and embraces he holds tight.
Closing his eyes, he relives the ecstasy of those nights.

The door to full fulfillment remains open, yet he will not free himself.
Perhaps the door lies within himself—the door he cannot see.
Perhaps the door lies within his forbidden lover's constrained desire—
the desire to consume his self-control

She ruefully respects his rationale,
While gently opening her harbor.

When once he enters this powerful portal,
His lonely trap unsnared—his soul to soar.

Carol J. Boyer

The Ghost of Corporate Racism

Born from the depths of social hatred and bigotry,
Raised up from the tar pit of hell, there rises a ghost; a ghost
That haunts the halls of corporate America, energized by bigotry,
Social hatred and ignorance; a ghost whose only mission is
To destroy and divide Americans by race. This ghost roams the
halls Of corporate America, bringing fear and pain to all employees;
A ghost that lives beneath a glass ceiling, preventing minority
Employees from advancing within that corporation; "a ghost that
Has lived for years," roaming the halls of corporate America;
And a ghost that will always live in corporate America, because
As long as man hates his brother for the color of his skin,
The ghost of corporate racism will always live,
Roaming the halls of corporate America.

Lester Nesbitt

Heaven's Gate, 1997

Stay in your place, Hale-Bopp!
Totally unexpected visitor —
Small world unto yourself.
But you, perchance, may think we visit you
If you can think at all.

While going about your life
—Your long trajectory—
For a brief moment, here,
Every few thousand years, you share our sun.

Its rays awaken motes of dust and gasses
Sleeping within your frozen core.
Excited now, they spring to life and
—Flinging themselves into the emptiness—
They shimmer behind you, enhancing your glamor.

Your glamor calls to souls.

And just this week, not far from San Diego, thirty-nine men and women
Clamoring, tried to pass through Heaven's Gate,
Leaving behind their bodies —
Trying to reach behind you to the hovering, hidden spacecraft

And Eternal Life.

Marion Perkus

Love Never Dies

My sweet love blows a breath into my chest
And starts a fire within me
You are my desire.
Yet, you're a danger zone I should not enter.
Your anger feels like a knife in my chest.
I'm having trouble breathing like I'm losing my breath!
Once again you take me deep down to the depths of despair,
Sucking the life blood out of me, devouring me, leaving me
drained and weak, still wanting more, still needing you
To feed my soul—I have tried to escape this.
I want us to go back to a place called ecstasy.
We should stop denying it, for it was written in blood long ago!
We were two maddening spirits who became one.
Breathing as one,
Hearts beating as one, connected
For always, throughout eternity.
It is destiny,
For love never dies!

Bon Stewart

The Hand

Water, food or chips are the stomach's investment
    But did you know that the hand, represents The New Testament
There are 27 Books in The New Testament, 27 Bones in the hand
    More than a mere coincidence, just listen and you will understand

The thumb represents God and the fingers man
    You cannot hold with your fingers, what you can with your hand
The thumb is Jesus Christ, the fingers (Matthew, Mark, Luke and John)
    If we began to follow these men, we can serve The Lord as one

Some things you pick up with your fingers, you can't hold onto
    But when your thumb joins in, that means God will see that you do
Think of God's hand and the gift that we all cherish
    His Holy Son, who will never perish
Just look at your hands, from your wrist to your nails
    And forever trust in God, because for us He never fails.

Radford P. Savage

Capacities of Life

Who am I now? I am All I cam.

I am sorrow and sunshine. I am tears and triumphs. I am loud
and yet I can sound as a mouse. I am unknown and I am also
predictability. I am touched and I am outraged. I am quiet and I
am Thunderous! I am still

Tomorrow I will be raucous.
And the next I could be coy and sleepy.
    If I wish!

I could yell in church and wear a stained had and smoke even
though I'm prone not to. I could spit on the sidewalk and go
barefoot in a museum and frolic in a boutique...if I wish.

I could be late . . . I could shout obscenities . . . I could be all of
    these if I wish!

I can and should and might and won't and will and could . . . if I wish

You see My "I Am's" used to be my could's and might's and wont's
    and should's. And now I am.

My Am's are growing and changing and seeking. Because I wish
them to. I can be whomever I wish now.

No guides or destructive patterns. I have created a clean slate
and I can put on it any Am's I wish. I a can add and erase and
scratch out because I now have the eraser.

You can't cram any of my Am's! My Am's are my Am's
Am I Am's what I Am's! If I Wish.

Christine Lewis

Never

Never again will your eyes open
To see me laugh or smile
Never will they look at me with such love
Will the tears ever stop?

Never will your lips taste my kiss
Never will they speak the words I love you

Never will your arms draw me near
Never again will they hold me tightly
Will mine ever stop reaching for you

Never again will your hands hold mine
Never will they gently touch my face
Will mine ever stop shaking?

Never will your legs run to me
Never will they lead us in dance
Will mine ever be able to turn and walk away?

Mary Ann Johson

Sound Asleep

Rock-A-Bye Baby, Little Bo Peep,
hush little baby, fall fast asleep.

Peter Cottontail, and Jack and the Bean Stalk,
3 little mice ran up the clock, tic-toc . . . tic-toc . . .

Mary's little lamb and Willie's factory—
I sing softly to the sleepy baby

Winken, blinken, nod sailed along the darkened sky
Jack Be Nimble makes the baby weep and cry.

King Cole was a jolly old man
Robin Hood, Tinker Bell, and Peter Pan . . .

The Baker's man, and baby too.
The Little Old Woman Who Lived in a Shoe.

Aladdin's lamp, and The Three Little Bears,
Goldilocks and her flowing gold hair.

Alice in Wonderland, the Rabbit and Spade.
Her weird adventure and precious masquerade!

Robison Crusoe and Huckleberry Finn
The Little Mermaid that loved to swim.

The Gingerbread man, Hansel and Gretel
The evil witches and pot's and tea kettles

The baby loves each and every one;
t falls asleep and then the story's done!

Meghan E. Williams

Dear Dad

Winter winds, so fierce they blow,
But when I gaze at them I know
They carry angels from above
That guide you to
God's arms with love.
As I wonder why
We had to part
And I try to mend
My broken heart
I hope the winds
soon turn to breeze
and replace my tears
With memories.
Til then your strength
Will get me through.
With my undying
Love for you.

Dedicated in loving memory to my father,
Charles L. Bloom, Sr.
September 14, 1942 - January 9, 1997

Love, Susan

Susan J. Campbell

At The River's Edge

As I sit upon the River bank and watch as you go by,
I find your grace and beauty are something you can't hide.

Where is it that you come from . . . where have you already been?
I wonder where you're going as you travel without end.

I've seen your mood change quickly as you rage beneath the storm,
Yet when you cease the raging you're so gentle an so warm.

The sunlight wakes you up at dawn . . . And fills your way with light.
You burst into a prism . . . And sparkle with delight!

And when the moonlight adds its friendship . . . to aid you on your way,
You become a mirror . . . full of wondrous golden rays!

And if the rains should come your way . . . what would they bestow?
The beauty and the elegance of a brightly colored bow!

I close my eyes so I can listen . . . to the things I cannot see.
Hoping that you're willing . . . to share your thoughts with me.

And as I listen carefully to the words that you would speak,
You take me places in my mind that I could never reach.

I could spend a lifetime just watching as you play . . .
Your gentle ways and tender smile . . . They take my breath away!

Your peace and your tranquility can bring me to my knees,
And then I thank the Lord above . . . for sharing you with me!

Suzette Ovenshire

Why Shoud This Be A Racial World

Why should this be a racial world
When there are so many other things that need to be taken care of?
What is a life without love? Every heart is so cold and bitter of.
No one truly witnessed the first execution,
Other than the Father above, who gave us all His dearest love

Why should this be a racial world? Why should this be a racial world?

Seems like no one cares. White against black, black against white,
People, you know that's not right. Why should this be a racial world?
Somebody tell me why should we live in racial violence.
The Bible says the love of money is the root of all evil.
If you plant a seed it will grow.
He also said if you have the faith the size of a mustard seed,
He will take care of your every need. Remember the first commandment,
Thou shall not kill; thou shall not steal.
All you have to do is get on your knees,
Ask the Lord to give you the will, because prayer changes things.
Why don't you give the man a chance. The Lord made me, the Lord made you.
Our Father which art in heaven, hallowed be thy name.
Why can't we all be the same? Why should this be a racial world.
I don't understand why

Mary E. Ricks

There's Something I Must Say

There is someone I appreciate that has made my world new,
She is someone very special, and mother it is you.
I am proud that you are my mother, you make me feel alive.
These are my true feelings that I express from deep inside.
You have given me many things, things only you can give.
They are very special feelings that help my will to live.
I feel that I am becoming a man, I say with pride and joy.
But I know I let you down in many ways we both know this is true.
But now I plan a worthy future, and this I will show you soon.
Yes I know I hurt you many times and know I cause you pain,
But even though that is the pasted, I will remember that with shame.
I have these special feelings they come from deep inside,
It is knowing that you are my mother, and it is filling me with pride.
These things I have said please believe they are true,
I would like you to remember and believe that,
I love you.

Deion Matthew Walker

He Is

His eyes are like a cloudless sky . . .
His smile is as radiant as the sun's rays on a warm, summer day . . .
His skin is creamy white . . .
His body is like that of a horse, hard and rugged . . .
He is like a beam of sunshine, wearing proof upon his head and heart
That he was sent from above . . .
His shiny, golden halo glimmers in the splendor of his brilliancy,
Creating a great illumination around his intense strength . . .
He looked "Godly" upon the saddle of his snowy colored horse . . .
Not a hair out of place . . .
A stern, yet bewitching look upon his face . . .
When he turns, his profile is fixed and firm,
Causing even more admiration from all who see him . . .
He truly is, a heavenly body. . . .

Michelle Diley

Charlene

Tonight my heart is heavy with the memory of someone whom I love deeply.
Though I cannot see her, I feel as if she's in the room.
I feel like screaming out loud—into the darkness.
I will miss her eternally.
Without her I feel like dying, I feel like hitting something,
But it would do no good.
I may be able to understand why someday, somewhere, somehow . . .
Today my heart still aches—I doubt the pain will ever go away.
As the years pass I let go, but the pain is still with me.
The pain and the missing will never die completely.
The memory will be . . .
But I must let go . . . I must.
I've been clinging to her, not loosening my grip.
I try to be just like her, but it doesn't work.
I need, not only for her, but for myself, to let go.
She should be free completely, but her memory I will keep,
And her soul will be set free.
I finally let go, and we are both at peace.
But I have a memory, and the pain is still there.
It only tells me how much I love Charlene.

Joanna Griffin

War-Torn Love

A dried red rose among faded pink ribbons,
Wrapped around musty love letters.
Mute testimony of a love lost to war.

He and she were only just wed
When the cold voice of war bade him "come."
He left unwilling, a babe on the way
And she promised to wait forever.

Letters arrived ever week-then suddenly they ceased.
Months passed-no word forthcoming,
Yet faithfully she waited: first hopeful,
Then prayerful, and finally fearful.

A knock at the door, a grim telegram:
"We regret to inform you your husband is dead."
Gowned in black, she remained ever faithful, living only for her babe.
Quietly awaiting the glorious day death would take her to him.

I found my mama in her old rocking chair
Lap full of letters dated 50 years past,
Red rose in one hand daddy's picture in the other,
A sweet happy smile on her lips.
Her lonely wait over-at last reunited with love.

Meredith Sue Allison

Love and Respect

What's wrong with our society? Are we going to hell?,
Let's sink our teeth into the story I'm about to tell,
Maybe we should dial 911 up in the sky and ask for help,
A light sprinkling of love dust on this earth to grow and develop,
If parents and teachers aren't allowed to discipline,
Child Abuse is mentioned and the story begins,
TV and movies show all that trash, sex and drugs remain,
When teenagers idolize such heros as Kurt Cobain,
Sex used to be a Act of Love and Marriage,
Today it's on the first date, followed by a baby carriage,
Gang fights, girls and boys, drive-by shootings seem to be the fad,
Not looking back to see the damage is what's really sad,
Hating and hurting parents without any shame,
Raping and killing five and six years old seems to be their game,
That ol' saying "Spare the Rod and Spoil the Child,"
Is what we've done to our society that's so wild,
Treat others like you want to be treated should be our strife,
With parents, teachers, neighbors, bosses to partners in life
Who should set the rules and give them their goals?
Parents save our future, and put love and respect back in children's souls.

Anna May Cranny

The Answer

There's another of those men who reek of filth and new drunk gin
Their clothes are rotten their way forgotten
As they slump along coughing some dissonant song
That used to kindle hope within—both of them are growing dim

You know what that woman did when she was still a little kid?
Shot her daddy in the head. He was still in the bed
Where he'd done the thing that will always cling.
She found the gun where it was hid, pointed, pulled, took off his lid

Then there was the corporate exec, biz was great but life's a wreck.
Kids in boarding school, wife sits on a stool
In some dingy place longing for a friendly face.
He vows to get his life correct when he ends his corporate trek.

How about the little boy who immigrated from St. Croix
He was not the same, his peers played the game
Of tease and ridicule every day at school.
His only friend a store bought toy, sadly t'was his only joy

How should we begin to feel—pretend misfortune isn't real?
Are we to be saints—welcome all complaints
Or chose to ignore deadening our core?
The answer is to kneel and pray to the Master who can heal.

R. H. Powers

Stone Footprints

I gazed across the desert waste and looked at the burning sand,
Where cavemen at one time hunted and wild creatures ran.
To time of man with club and spear and a cave in which to lie,
To wrestle life from a primitive land to slay the beast or die.

Back, back in time to forest and fern, of animals strange and grand.
Of dinosaurs and mastodon, of swamp and palm.
To time of misty seas and fish and frond.
Of minty beasts stalking in the land.

A land of fire and water without life at all
Only molten earth and sky
To wonder at billion suns or stars that gleam on high
Back, back in time when we were but a dream to God.

Now I gaze at footprints that took centuries to mold
What future life this earth will hold
When we are but bits of dust scattered by the winds
And our souls by death set free, have vanished into eternity

Frances Ruth Rhodes

Love Bug

I have a bug in my heart so big I can see through.
only intestinal insecticide can save me now.
I have too much love, but to little all the same.
But what would love be if there wasn't a word for it.
I have bugs all around me they surround me.
Bugs tattooed in my heart, ingested in my throat they become a part.
but climbing my legs like so many hopes and dreams.
For tomorrow I see, maybe I will see without a bug in my eye.
or a style in my cry. Who knows?
Not I said the fly.
I walk about in a dreamy haze like an unknown soldier
with liquid eye gel, yet maybe it's just a phase.
Life would be perfect if only I could see what I'm meant to see.
Waterfalls in specific patterns, for it's the little things that matters.
Death all around, yet not a still sound.

Beth Lapping

Tired

I'm tired, my world strung out on some distant reality.
Quarter to ten.
Broken traffic signal blinks, click, click, click.
The stench of neon and drunken men lingers the air.
"Two twenties, two twenties."
Black guy tells me what he's tired, of clogging the air in my throat.
Virginia stands and loses what is left of her mind.

Alarm clock buzz, grab a cigarette.
"I know, I know, you're tired."
It's seven A.M., here's the traffic, "No, I said Camel lights."
"Did you ever have those nights when you didn't dream?"

11:01, I'm concentrating on your answering machine.
"What do you need?"
Something stable that won't make you choke.
Maybe just to breathe.

Jason Todd

Valentine's Day

Ten tons of inert helium are coldly supporting two thousand
square feet of filmy foil, a dozen florid red roses with prickly
chartreuse stems, nine paychecks, and a year of toil, industrial
treasures from here and abroad, brand names scream out from
the expensive packaging, an enchanting trail of petals as exactly
described in this week's publication.

He has saved up all year for this one single moment, a thousand
and one tricks from a book, a romantic sound track from a
trickling clarion mountain stream in the Andes, rambling poetry,
his young heart beats with that sly sensation that he can make
up for all his faults with money, coldly shivering because he
can't and he won't and he doesn't and he cries.

Alone in the emerald valleys that roll like water beads on the back of
one's hand, among the sparkling sunflowers that turn their silent faces
skywards, accompanied by a jittering procession of vivid wildlife
just out of the eye's reach, simplicity, kindness, and concern,
trust and respect that he has worked hard to earn.

He knows that he is lucky, and he thanks God for what he is able
to attain, because when his world turns into a dark dungeon she is
there to keep him sane, a daisy he clutches, his young heart
beats with the honest sensation of satisfaction, warmly em-
braced because he is and he was he does and he cries.

Mike Ahlering

Out of the Shell

My shell is breaking wide open. There are still a few pieces stuck
to me, but I'm peeling them off now. What a sight the world is!
And what a sight I am. I have so much to share, so much beauty
inside me that I have never shown people. I haven't even seen
it all myself. But I feel it oozing out. I'm seeing it on people's
faces, mirrored in their eyes. I am beautiful; I am unique, a marvel.
I am aching to open myself up to the whole world, open for
people to "see" and to "see" other people. I want to visually,
psychologically, physically experience life. The feeling is beautiful.
It is Love. I am in love with life.

Brenda Bernwanger

Ruthie's Heart

"How be 'ya? How's your Ma?"
A visit home always included a short walk to Cousin Ruthie's,
Her greeting the same as years went by and
The seams deepened and multiplied around the wise old blue eyes.
Her warm little house stretched out to take in another generation,
But its pulsing heart was always the bustling kitchen,
Redolent with essences of Ruthie's activities:
Baking, canning, gardening, trout-fishing.
Then each year as the late fall warnings of bitter winds and lowered sun
Would send shivers through the creaking rafters,
Ruthie would leave to visit warmer climes out west.
While she was gone, the snow would cuddle and caress the tiny porch,
Wrapping the doorstep in cold embrace,
Holding the empty house in snowy sleep
'Til she returned to warm her bones.
Back she'd come as smells of Spring spread 'round the house,
Dandelions poking through the moist front lawn,
Dainty lilac buds showing on the bushes near the front door.
And once again, from the core of the house, came the steady rhythm
Of her busy days and nights, the healthy beat of life resumed.

Judith Lee Whitney

A Wanted Dream

The sun is setting now over an iridescent extent.
The world continues to voice its routine.
Families finishing dinner, kids going for one last swim.
Somewhere soon a mother will be gently lulling her baby to sleep.
I lay back in the motionless grass,
Looking above at the vast nothingness that separate us.
My mind wanders closer to you as it is penetrated by the dark blue,
silent sky.
I look for comfort in your outstretched arms.
As I enter the realm of your passion and tenderness,
You heal all my pain and take away my sorrow.
Not a word is spoken, but yet, I am no longer afraid.
I am in your arms now, where I belong, so I shut my thoughts to everything.
The realities of your death are swimming through every ripple of my mind.
Yearning for my dream to become truth, I fall asleep.
The soft, angelic movements of your breath my only condolence.
When I awake I find you nowhere but in the boundless abyss of my heart.
I need you here with me.
And I beg night and day to live life as a dream
Because I know that if I could, you'd always be in my life.

Danielle Duffy

Reflections On The Man In The Moon

Saturday night on the back of a truck
Racing toward home from a day in town
Lying on a quilt and a pillow of feathers,
I watched the darkened sky rush by.
The low hanging clouds partially hid the full moon.
I gazed in wonder at it surrounded by billions of stars.
Was there a Man in the Moon? Was it made of green cheese?
Little did I envision my own precious son, yet undreamed of, yet unborn,
Would help others who also gazed in awe.
Marveling and seeking the answer.
He helped them walk on that planet of wonder.

The telegram came one bright spring day,
Announcing your NASA scholarship to explore
Space where so long ago, I first viewed
The man in the moon and wondered.
My childish musings answered through you, my own dear son.
Your acceptance of the scholarship,
Your grasp of communication led you to design the historic link.
Now I hear and see the man in the moon.
The voice and face of God, translated because of you.

Ruth B. Morgan

My Poor Mother-In-Law

My poor mother-in-law, her kids they number three,
But their tormented childhood has left its legacy.

The eldest left the country after doing time in jail,
Convicted twice for dealing drugs, his life seemed doomed to fail.

The youngest is a junkie, addicted to gambling and drugs,
She lives off Mommy's money to atone for lost childhood hugs.

My husband was the great hope, a successful lawyer was he,
But he had a dirty secret, he beat up his family.

See, my deceased father-in-law was wealthy in his day,
And that was all they cared about, their kids were just in the way.

Her only grandchildren are loving and smart, she'd tell me "They're great!"
But when I left her abusive son, her "love" for them turned to hate.

My husband never visited her, he hated it when she was near,
But when needed to hide money from me, she became his "Mommy dear!"

Mother and son will not see the boys, father, grandmother no more,
'Cause if he must pay child support, together they'll walk out the door.

And my poor mother-in-law, now her losers number three,
Her family has no future 'cause she left the winners with me!

Randee Karch

The Moments

For that one brief moment I could just be and I could truly see
The beauty of the mountains above and the valleys below
Touching my soul, making me whole

Windless, crisp air, a bird's whisper in the distance
The stillness and quiet is hardly met with resistance
And I am humbled by this brief moment onto which I have stumbled
Nature's splendor is such a majestic sight, enveloping me with all its might

As I stand high above on my perch
I think this is for what I've searched
For life's journey is but a series of moments
To captive and motivate and quench our thirst
And, above all, this should be first

For the moments come and go and quickly pass us by
But the memories stay and linger if we only try
For when we can just be then we are truly free
Letting us see life's purposed and key

This moment will stay with me forever
Beyond belief and beyond measure, and become something I
truly treasure
As I strive to be in all that I do and see

Cynthia Kay Berryman

A Birthday Wish

A child celebrated his Birthday don't you know
With a party and a cake with candles all aglow,
there were eight for he was turning eight year old.
He extinguished the candles with one big blow
His eyes lit up when told that his wish would come true
He kept the secret to himself as if his lips were glued
Later that night the brother asked if his wish had come true
The little boy looked at a Birthday card from his party that day
and shook his head, No, as he looked away.
What was your wish his brother inquired
That I could read and spell, he said as his voice expired
As the boys were climbing into bed, the older one patted his head
Your wish can still come true for on my birthday it will be my wish too!

Connie Blue

Any Single

Any single person can blend into a crowd.
They are individuals with particular habits and arrangements.
A crowd is a large mass of them with no certain person identifying another.
Their movements are alike and each has his or her own search for a mate.

When one is connected with one, the single then becomes two.
Now the pair determines whether or not they are to stay matched.
A series of examinations and rituals begin so one another
can figure out, if this is the life companion.

Time will elapse and the two will endure a scroll of tasks—
Love
Hate
Pain
Happiness

If the two accomplish the list with substantial success,
then they will no longer journey within the group.
They are free to travel separated from the mass.
No more can another identify the two as a single.
Identity is now a couple, and a couple can always be seen inside a crowd.

Traves W. Eisenhauer

Strange Weeds

Digging with a pitchfork
Has revealed kernels of possibilities
Hoarded by the ancients many years ago

Sown carelessly or with care
They grow in the fertile humus of my mind
And seed themselves in yours

I didn't know the root systems would be so tenacious
I would have tried to stop in the face of improbability I am glad that
Nobody told me

Bursting wildly like black-eyed Susans of furious patch of lilies
Possibilities break through the concrete sending long cracks into the
Corners of held convictions and fears

Flaring up and out demanding to be looked at the possibilities look less
Ridiculous in daylight after one has lived with them for a while

Pernicious weeds common as dandelions
Flood heretofore rational minds (I know I am supposed to dig them out;
Sometimes I water them)

What will the harvest be? Senseless acts of beauty? Acts of insane
Kindness? voices of protest? Seeds of change? I refuse to let
Possibilities die they are invited to grow in my garden

Julie Meltzer

To Those Killed By Belief

We were horrified and saddened to see you lying there,
your purple-shrouded corpses arranged neatly everywhere.
Before becoming members of that terrible temple of doom,
did you feel, in ordinary society, for you there was no room?
When you forsook conventional religion, did you incur others' hate?
What really happened to your hearts and minds, we can only speculate.
Were the materialistic pressures of modern life so very great,
you chose to abandon your earthly forms and enter Heaven's Gate?
What made you feel so empty, so vulnerable and alone,
that on your own planet Earth, you felt you had no home?
Was it harsh remarks and gossip that made you turn away?
Were you desperately seeking solace in that cult's new way?
Could anyone have saved you, if anyone had known?
Did we drive you to destruction when you felt forlorn?
We ask these questions of you—we know your souls are listening—
because we stand here hurting, tears on our cheeks glistening.

Carole Judge

Clouds

As clouds go by in the sky
Giving pleasure to my eye,
How relaxing.

Often when I see them, I think,
"Just what do they remind me of?"
for they can have such interesting form
of animal, of people, and of various things, too.

Also they can seem ominous as in storm clouds:
dark; thunder roaring; lightening flashing; wind blowing
and rain coming down.

As they perform their primary duty in the ecology of our
land, who knows, the One who made them might have had
an additional plan. That plan might have been for clouds
to serve as a source of inspiration to the poet, the song writer
and to the artist; or to be casually observed by anyone who
would dare view them as they cascade overhead.

So whatever the reason, whatever the season, take time to look
skyward. What you see there might be of interest in some sort of way,
If no more than as a spark to brighten up your day.

Clouds can work magic. Are you a magician?!
Ida Mae Miller

Untitled

I have longed to return from my many journeys to a woman
worthy of the tribulation from my quest.

Can there be such a woman?
Of loyal body and patient mind.
The one who will cast my mask aside and see me for my true self;
find me in the dark forest of mind.

Who will peer into the corners of my soul and allow
the light of tranquility to nourish it?

As I wade into the river of destinies, I search endlessly
for the spirit of my own evolution.

Strange, this body through which I wade is not as wide as is deep.
The current flows swiftly, and dangerous does this make the
waters for there are destinies for all eternity, but only one per being.

Christopher Michael Collins

The Letter of Symbiotic Polarity

My Dear Nubian King,

You are the king of my domain. You need me, but I need you
every day after I dwell in the face of this nation's ugly ways. I
need you for comfort, I need you to hold me close to you for
reassurance. You are the shield I look for in the world. I want to
lose my thoughts in your embrace. I can talk to you, and I need
you to be able to talk to me. We must communicate with each
other correctly. I need you to support me in my endeavors as I
do for you. I don't need to be disrespected, but I do need
respect respectively. I don't need for you to put me down, the
world does that enough. I need you to lift me to the pedestaled
throne I resumed on the Nile, and I will place you at the top of
the pyramid that you built. I don't need your hands on my
throat or across my face, but on my hips, around my waist.
Never let me go as I take on my submissive role and you your
comforting dominant one. Because I love you and I need you.

Love,
Your Nubian Queen
Stephanie M.

The Great Questions

How much longer will it be possible for you to endure this heavy burden?
How much longer will you continue
to present us with small warnings of things to come?
How much time is left, before all patience with us, is lost forever?

Will we even take notice?
When will be the time, that we, the ones given the gift of choice,
will become awakened by the great signs you give?
When will we stop just scurrying on from day to day,
believing that it is someone else's fault; not theirs?
When will we finally become frightened enough
to heed the eminent warnings filling the air?

Are we going to heed the omens?
Are we out of time to learn what all other living things
have known since time began?
Are we out of time, to stop the destruction
and repair the damage that has been done?
Are we out of time to have earned the right to even try?

Is there even any time left to learn?
Donna Meredith

The Peanutbutter Fantasy

As the smoke filters through the thickening air, the candle burns
and we all must stare. I hear a noise, but am not sure, a night of
distinction is what's in store. In tune, without making a sound,
the laughter is felt
through the soul's ground. Don't stop the rhythm, don't stop
the rhyme. Feel, feel it become alive. Alive as the sun with wild
fire eyes, as cold as the breath of the thundering skies. Embrac-
ing the moment, yet letting it laugh, the beauty of words and the
overwhelming craft. If it were not for love, if not for hate, what is
in between these, that's your fate. Your fate is emotion, your
sight is deceit, a handful of puzzles fall beneath my feet. Could
you be with, it's not my choice, you can't decide in the truth of
your voice. Falsity and the future go hand in hand, I don't know,
do you understand? Understand the apple as it is with the tea.
Within the key of knowledge lies the peanutbutter fantasy.

Why now? Why then? You, me, Zen. Buddha, Christ, mystery,
unknown, beyond dreams. Beyond the horizon and engulfed in
the rain, the echoes of the canyon are saturated in my brain.
Release of emptiness, being with infinite time, I can't see the
future for the past is far behind. As we cross the placid sea,
there's a flame ahead of me. A bright light of gold, but the
statelines of old Preserving a light, not knowing what is right,
indecision in the vision, but always seeing our sight. Life is now.
What can tomorrow bring?

Kevin J. Barry

Elegy to a Grieving Friend

All pass this way but once, leaving their trace in memory;
By slow steps, one by one, our forebears pass.
We thought of them as immortal, assuming they'd always be near—
Depending on them all the while,
Knowing they could always be leaned upon,
Resting in the assurance of being understood.
We turn to our life's companion to fill the void and to steady us.
And when our parent passes, we feel the loss more acutely.
We'd not withstand the loss without love
From family, from friends, from dear contemporaries.

So I send to you all of my love. Because, at such a time,
We all need to know that someone cares.
I care, your family cares; likewise, friends and contemporaries care.
But the greatest need is Biblical—that our Heavenly Father cares,
That Jesus Christ is still our Best Friend,
That the Lord cares for us and wants to lighten our burdens.
He wants to strengthen our spiritual walk;
He wants to make our hope abide.
See the day the Lord has made!
There's so much beauty in it that the heart is inexorably quickened!

Richard K. Colley

Heated Night

Sometimes you wake me up at night, to tell that you're mad.
You may as well phone the neighbors too, they can already hear
That you think that I'm cad.

Sometimes you make me feel I can do nothing to please.
I'm sorry that you feel this way, but I'll not be the one to leave.

As someone wrote long ago, to conquer is divine. You already
Have got all my soul, and I beg of you, please, don't take my mind.

I think to myself, I've got to be strong, will this night of hell ever end?
I've done everything that I know to do, now I'm asking, dear
God, Please step in.

And, as fast as the fury had started, it all has begun to descend.
The fire that your eyes have been burning, now show a content to
The end.

And now the night is silent, from which there was such turmoil
I wish you sweet dreams, with kiss of my love, my beautiful new,
Baby girl.

Murry Eggleston

Oh Mommy Dear

I'm sitting here wondering, why, when, and how the end will come.
The times are growing so near and I can feel my fears.
I'm trying to be so strong, Mommy dear,
only knowing that you feel my tears.
I see and feel your sadness,
and share your tears that I see from your eyes.
And then, it makes my insides feel so afraid.
You being so scared of following the light to a much happier place
that you will love and cherish and wait for all of us to follow someday.
Please Mommy dear, keep your eyes closed and follow the light
as far as it goes to help you see ahead of all your fears.
Oh Mommy dear, I will miss you so much,
I will always cherish the love and bond that we have shared, and I
know you will always be there to help me through the rough times.
Remember Mommy dear, I love you more than words can never say,
I love you so very much and
I will miss your hugs and smiles today and always.

P. Monnell

Teach Us, Lord

Lord, I just want to thank you and praise you too for being so
loving and kind all of the time. When I'm in trouble you are right
there to show me how much you care and answer my prayer.
Your love and mercy have brought me through the roughness,
the sadness and gladness too.
If it wasn't for you I don't know what I would do.
I'm so glad that your darling son Jesus Christ have came into my life.
Lord, there is sadness and trouble everywhere we go.
It makes me wonder are we sowing the right seeds
for our children to grow.
They are going astray; there are drugs and alcohol everywhere.
They don't really seem to care or have any hope;
they just want to smoke dope.
Teach us Lord, how to cope and take these guns from our children
and please, Lord, teach them they don't need to use coke or
smack, to turn their lives over to your love and guidance.
There will be no need to smoke, shoot, or use dope.
Let's get high on our Lord and Savior Jesus Christ;
He will straighten out our life.
Lord, are we trying to put peace in our life without Jesus Christ,
Who is the prince of peace the essence of life?

Maggie Pearl Evans

Time, Eagle and Wind

Time keeps on slipping into the future the song says.
I want to fly like an Eagle far above the sea.
I want to fly above the clouds into the heavens far above where I can see.
Time keeps on slipping into the future.

I want to fly like an Eagle with my wings stretched far across the sea.
For you Dear God are the winds beneath my wings and
being in the heavens with you is what the future holds for me.

So, Dear God, let time keep on slipping and let me
soar in the skies like the Eagle with my wings
spread far and wide, and you Dear God, the wind beneath my wings.

Judy Mahurin

You Felt Like a Father to Me

My love was tall, I thought I had it all
Why days were so slow, I didn't know
Until you walked away, oh what could I say
You felt like a father to me.

I grew to be strong, thinking about you all day and night long
A real lady I grew, but my life's still not through
Fantasies still to see, you left us alone Mom and me
Life is still there, but you don't seem to care
You said that you loved me
So you felt like a father to me.

Hopes and dreams for me to share, lots more tears for someone to care
With you or without, my life goes on no doubt
But I don't know how it could be, you felt like a father to me.

And what I can't understand, is when you told me about those bad men,
You showed me your love and then
Like a bird you flew off and left me again
But remembering what you said before, about love I wanted more
Even after all you did to me,
Even if it was something you didn't realize or see
You felt like a father to me.

LaToya D. Tuck

FREEDOM

I am a free spirit. You cannot possess me . . .
You can hold me, caress me, soothe and delight me.
But do not take me for granted.

For when you do that, you trap me in your thoughts . . .
You hold me static . . . when in truth,
I am always in transition . . . states of alteration.

I am a free spirit. I must be free as a bird on the wing.

Free to soar high as an eagle.

To survey the scene from a . . . different perspective.
Free to crawl on my hands and knees as a small child.
To burrow in the dirt and hide like a worm.

And after I have soared, and crawled, and hidden myself away . . .
Then I will calm myself and seek reason, and common sense will be my Guide.
And I will become a homing pigeon,
And return to the place where in Truth I have never left.

That place in my heart where love remains a constant flame.
Where the duties of the day are my favored companions.

I will find my freedom in the joy of service to those around me.
And I shall be as faithful as a dog at your feet
who has been allowed to run free in field . . . and gratefully comes home to his Mast

Kate Barker

I'm Looking through the Window

I'm looking through the window and what do I see?
I see the hole entire world, and everything in it except for me!
But where am I and where are you, are you looking through a
window to?

And if you're looking through a window somewhere in the world
What do you see? Do you see a bee in a path of flowers, or someone
standing on the Eiffel tower? Tell me what do you see? And
when you're looking through the window where are you,?
Where am I? I'm looking out the window still with my looking
eye, And playing with the key that goes in the keyhole in the
door that leads outside.

And now what am I doing? now I am putting the key in the keyhole
in the door that leads outside, so I don't have to look out the
window anymore, Crank goodbye!

Chelsea A. Jones

Legacies

What will I leave my children when I die?
Money, I hope. But it must be divided many times.
We're not disciples of zero growth. And one disastrous choice
Could wipe them out, even so.

A healthy start. But from there the choice is theirs, to make or break.
Safe place to live, I can't assure it
Nor do I wish them safer than their neighbors.
I wish them peace on earth, but know it cannot be
Peaceful, when all these angry hearts are struggling here.
Goodwill; freedom from hate.
I wish them those to give them their own peace.

I wish them to seek truth, not satisfied but tranquil still,
Trusting eternal universal laws I hope they'll learn and to live by.
And last, I wish them joy.
To laugh is the best gift we mortals have.

Lucile Corbin

All I Ask Of You Is You

You walk by my side, nights we are joined together as one,
Of your love I can be sure, why then do I have to run.
I need you

I cannot be strong enough to believe, I cannot be strong enough to trust,
A fear tearing away inside me, I know a life of loneliness is a must.
I Love You

When I'm with you, I care, but when you care, the hurt is there too,
A hurt that tears away at life, so help me please, what am I to do.
I ask nothing of you but you

Heaven and hell is forever, life is just a moment in time,
Why can't I accept you, instead of this tormented mind.
I need you

Be patient and give me your strength, of you one day I'll be sure.
Help me to trust and believe, and together our love will endure.
I love you

Continue to give me your heart, as I have given you mine,
And soon I will learn to believe, and our moment will be forever in time.
All I ask of you is you

Carol Bushar

Depression

Depression nibbles at the edge of my consciousness,
Trying to consume me. I fight it and try to conquer.
Sometimes I succeed and it leaves me,
But soon it returns, and the nibbles become bites and more is consumed.
I fight harder, the faster it bites,
Then an urgency takes over and I know I am fighting for my life.
bring in reinforcements, happy thoughts, memories,
And tears keep the enemy, depression at bay.
I fight to overcome and I hope to destroy, so I can live.
Before the core is reached and I am completely consumed
And I cease to be.

Carolyn Ingles

Untitled

We as people must surely know the time will come
When we will have to go.
We have used our planet we have mined her gold.
We have smelted her ore we have burned her coal.
We have felled her trees we have destroyed her swamps
We have ruined her oceans with our many wants.
We must have known for we have been shown
The damage we did all on our own.
We didn't have help she didn't partake
of the garbage we put in her lakes.
But yes there is time as there always is
To leave her still for our little kids.
But do not be tardy do not be late.
For she is not happy she is starting to hate
She may not come back she may not be able
Then who will fill our table? We must act now to stop this cancer.
We should look to ourselves for the answer
Shes a beautiful place this planet called earth
We must treat her with respect and know her worth.
And maybe that day when our kids are in charge
She will still be able to show them her charm.

David Neaves Jr

The Rain

As I sit here staring out my window
I notice it's raining and sadness overwhelms me.
I begin to reminisce, thinking of what we once had.
The thought that you may be gone,
Gone forever is too much for me to bear.
Oh how I cried, my thoughts are enveloped
In darkness and devoid of light.
As dark as the skies above, my heart is aching.
I don't want to be alone and without you.
The thunder is like a crescendo of sound
And the lightning brightens the skies but still I'm heavy-hearted.
I can sit here no longer I must go outside,
Outside into the rain.
No one seems to notice the tears that stream down my face
As I walk these lonely streets without any place to go.
There must be I've got to know is there a place for me in your heart.
Until I know I feel empty and incomplete.
So I keep walking lost and alone in the darkness of the night,
In the rain.

Timothy Alexander

Angel Wing

Angel wing on puff white cloud, poor Angel lost her wing.
Searched high and low, she found a soul, trembling in his boots.

Angel embraced this shattered soul, in her one wing that remained—
administered tender loving care to the bruises on his heart.
Then Angel firmly nudged soul back on the road to destiny—
an envisionment of life fulfilled, blessed, and unburdened
by a troubled past.

Finishing her work, Angel soared up high through the
clouds that reached to Heaven. She came upon that puff
white cloud where her gossamer wing shone bright.

Angel sewed her lost wing with a thread of light. Happy
with a job done well, Angel flew right on to her home in paradise.

Monica Iroegbu

The Best of Friends

The best of friends stick by each other, through thick and thin.
The best of friends never say good-bye forever, they're always back to share.
The best of friends have to fight sometimes, to show they really care.
But most of all,
The best of friends are the ones you look straight at, not up or down.

Valerie Goodwin

Colorful Memories

From the sky, the sun so big, so bright, a ball of iridescent yellow.
A bouquet of wild flowers laced the fields, colors of a Picasso painting.
In a nearby pond, fish swam lazily by, while the bullfrogs play hide and seek.
The aroma of fresh-cut hay spiced the air, with warmth of a summer breeze.
The stars blinked and lit the sky, fire-flies became flashing neons.
The leaves of Autumn emerge from the trees, tinges of color flutter to the ground.
Like a ghost from out of the past, Jack Frost lays his blanket down.
Quiet snowflakes float from the sky, a disguise of white innocence.
While angular shapes of feathery crystals lie unruffled and tranquil in a mound.
Sculptures of ice figures clung to the trees, proving a sense of loyalty.
From the sky droplets of water did fall, with a flash of light and a crack of angry thunder.
Look quickly overhead—a palette! A palette of rainbow colors: blues,
greens and reds, with a vision of faded yellow.
As I sit on a blanket of grass, green like an emerald gem,
My nostrils fill with a fragrance . . . a rose, a rose of ruby red.
The sun so big, so bright, softly a snowflake fell, fire-flies fly and lit up the sky, a fall
breeze caressed my cheeks, images of colorful memories.

Wanda Reagan Shelley

The Trucker's Poem

As I walk out the door to sit on a bench
I hear beautiful birds singing away.
As I look up in the sky I could only see the clouds rolling by.
Now it makes me stop to think . . . if clouds keep rolling by and by
I wonder how you must feel driving day by day, hour by hour
Without a few days to rest.
I wonder if I'm still on your mind or if I'm just an old flame
And no more to be seen.
I know I said I won't be around for awhile but Babe . . .
One things always on my mind, and that's you Babe!
I know you roll in and out of here like the clouds above,
But one things for sure—my feelings for you will never roll out of me.
You probably don't know how much I miss you
Or how badly I want to see you again,
That every time I see an eighteen wheeler roll on through
It always brings back those sweet memories of you.

Tara L. Paules

Memories of Home

As I sit and look over the back to the river where we once played,
I can hear the laughter of a memory I know will never fade.

As I sit, I can see across the yard to where my swingset used to be
and there you were Mom, always smiling back at me.

As I sit, I can look upon the mountain trail, which we climbed many times before.
I know those happy childhood days will be no more.

As I sit outside this house, the place I've loved so all my life,
I am filled with loving memories of you Mom and Dad
That often make me smile, and sometimes make me cry.

Sheila D. Maynard

Untitled

What do two friends mean to each other that would cause you to go
and leave in the way you did.
What did she do or was it something she said.
Why did you choose to leave all she wanted was to know why and
how could you do this.
You promised that you would stay with her forever and never leave
unless you had to leave.
She loved you so much but yet you still felt that you had to leave.
Now she wants to know why and what were you thoughts and feelings.
Where you empty and felt like no one could help or was it just what
you felt would end the pain.
How is it if you loved her and cared then why couldn't you call with a final goodbye.
Your friendship she thought was strong enough to go through
everything and now she's left with one less friend who she loved.
Now there's a hole in her heart that will never mend.
So why is the question that I can't answer and no one can answer for Liza.

Heather Lewis

The Dark Journey

As I walk down the path,
Theres fear up ahead.
I'm trying to, find my way back
But yet I'm mislead.
Wandering what should I do
About, this long dark path.
There's darkness every where
And I'm how wandering, how long will I last.
down this crucial and dark aisle,
That I'm walking.
I feel that I'm all alone,
But I hear voices talking.
Telling me to go on and don't be afraid.
Take the dark journey, that lies ahead.
Indeed I did, And I didn't surrender,
What happen at the end, I don't remember.
Rather it was a reality,
Or was it a dream.
But the Journey was dark
And that was seen.

Stevie Hickmon

Road Kill

Squeak, squish, splat
Another pathetic victim
Only this time it's reversed

You are the victim
and I am the . . . the . . .
The despicable Monster?

Devastated, Destroyed, Distraught
Where could I turn
You appeared, disappeared, and reappeared

I saw your glowing eyes
like a call from afar,
but what could I do?

You destroyed my life,
You or another of your kind

I'll never know,
It doesn't matter
They're all weasels.

Akilah Ponds

Fayetteville

At the silent reveille of spring
azaleas rouse to blossom bright as pain,
as red as blood—or white
as flesh when blood is drained.

Long-legged pines through foaming blooms
are wading, like MacArthur toward a shore,
while overhill young men
with cadenced chant imagine war.

Voluptuous gardens, bright amid the pine,
bee-busy and bird-trilling, angel-breathed
and opaline—a strange vicinity
to Quonset hut and olive drab and dun,
and tramp of boot and parchute
and shouts in unison.

C-130, butterfly,
grenade and rambler rose. Oh why
is life most lovely
juxtaposed?

Norma Laut

Moms

Moms are always there
correcting you when you're wrong

Moms are always there
helping you be strong

Through the good times and the bad
she'll never lead you wrong

You may have disagreements
that's what makes the bond so strong

She's seen you in the bathtub
she's seen you sound asleep

She brought you into the world
she comforted you when you weep

It must have been a hard job
But you were commended in the end:

With my everlasting bond with you
and love until the end

Through your long hard journey
you won forever a best friend

Shilo Dillon

For Labor Day

It is the roads that we walk on,
the parks that look so great,
It is the buildings we live in
which labor did create.
It is all the assembly lines
which give us our production
it is our press working hard
to keep informed our Nation.
It is our Congress at work
our President so dear
and all our services in our land
which put all things in gear.
We the workers of our land
in every occupation
we have built what we have today
In fact we build our Nation!

Sophia Demas

Celebration

Christmas Eve down on the farm
Grandpa's house was cozy and warm.
His brood came for a celebration
That became an annual tradition.
Grandma gave love, hugs and kisses
To tiny tots, gawky lads, prim misses.
All brought food of holiday appeal.
After thanks, we ate a hearty meal.
Men gather, guffaw at tall tales.
Women exchange recipes, tell of sales.
Students on vacation are of good cheer,
Talking of schools and their peers.
Happy children roam to and fro,
How they change; how they grow.
Sometimes, outside is fallen snow.
Good-byes are said; time to go.
We drove slowly over icy streets,
Little ones already fast asleep.

Christmas Day is time to remember
Baby Jesus in Bethlehem's manger.

Rachelle Stephens

This Moment We Live

This moment we live!
Every sixty seconds of it
is ours to accept and to
render a benefit.
This moment is filled with
many breaths, even strife.
Do what we can; make each breath count,
as breath is the elixir of life.
This moment is a gift in time
all part of life's cycle—with breath
and spiritual existence
transcending physical death.
Momently, we move forward
noting our movement and acuity.
It seems we are bound to this life
with stability, love and continuity.
Within the measure of a moment,
we build stepping stones to the future.
Let's give as our spirit prevails . . .
in the presence of this moment we live!

Cesarina Maria Rossetti

What Will Tomorrow Bring

Yesterday is gone;
Remember it well.
Today is here;
Use it well.
I dream of tomorrow,
And to there dwell.
Tomorrow is yet to come,
And there I will dwell.
Yesterday, I dreamed of today.
Today, I dream of tomorrow.
Tomorrow will bring new dreams
Upon which to dwell.
Yesterday is gone.
Today is here.
I dream of tomorrow,
And there to dwell.

Mattie M. Stewart

Forgiving and Unforgivable

Forgive their foibles
Their fretful frailties
And their "woe is mees."

Forgive their bewilderment
At the finding of horses tails
Then exclaiming "golly gee!"

Forgive outrageous rodents
Angry at salivating thieves
Who cunningly conspire
To steal their moldy cheese.

Forgive grammarian's
Dem, dose and deese
Learn dem "by your leave"
And a courtly "if you please."

Unforgivable ramblers
Ensconced in a balmy breeze
Judiciously disappear
Amidst a vapourizing sneeze
Endowing for posterity
Their ever haunting wheeze.

Joseph Binder

Snowflakes

Snowflakes, oh snowflakes
Falling from the skies
Just to hold you is
Like catching butterflies

After the long journey
I caught you in my mouth
But you stung my lips
I never let you out

Rainer W. Raumer

Will of the Lord

One or the other must leave,
One or the other must stay,
One or the other must grieve,
That is forever the way,
That is the vow that was sworn,
Faithful "til death do us part.
Braving what had to be borne,
Hiding the ache in the heart.
One whosoever adored,
First must be summoned away,
That is the will of the Lord.

Clara Lansing

The Grievance of Sound

The snow is falling to the ground;
You can hear it thudding all around.
Yet no one seems to hear the screams,
Of the snow;
Or so it seems,
That no one seems to hear the cry,
Of all the people who do die.

Heather A. Smith

These Raging Tides

Oh bitter sky, oh angry sea,
doth thou described the depth of me?

I ponder not on tranquil times,
but dwell instead on fury's rhymes.

I Have no wish to tarry long;
my torrid soul, my final song.

I Choose instead to burrow here,
inhale the chill, embracing fear.

And ever care not how I fare
in wakeless sleep, departed there.

And only thee doth, understand,
my inspiration, last command.

Oh with your wrath your glorify
a kindless fate, my heart to cry.

The tempest wane cannot repair
the grave of sorrow, buried there.

Marie St. Hilaire

A Mother's Love

A Mother's love is endless
Like a river flowing to no where
A Mother's love is forever
Like a storm that never stops
A mother's love is secret
Like a prayer you say to God
A mother's love is being together
Like on a peaceful day in a field
A mother's love is endless
So, know that there is no end to
A mother's Love.

Carolyn Hall

Sacrificial Triumph

A meadow of flowers,
allowed only one;
a palette of colors
press up toward the sun.

To choose but one flower
among such a cast,
preserving an image?
Creating a past?

I choose it on merit
of beauty possess,
hold captive its offering
while causing its death?

Refrain from the challenge
smile up at the sky;
disturb not the artist
of nature's outcry.

Marie St. Hilaire

He Is Gone

Here today, gone tomorrow.
Gone for ever into the new life.
He said he would not leave me
But he did.

Swiftly, silently, completely.
Without a care, a word, a good by
Or a by-your-leave. He left
No mess, no trail.

He said "When my time is up,
I'm ready to go. I'm not afraid
Of death! It's a challenge.
I like challenges!"

He troubled no doctor,
No nurse, no pharmacist,
No hospital, no clinic.
He accepted his fate.

He worshiped his little mother.
He cherished his loyal wife.
Perhaps he and his mom
Will ready a place for me.

Constance A. Warren

Fenton III, Our Son, Upon His Dying

What were his thoughts,
As he lay dying there,
Alone, in darkness, in pain?
Fenton our son, was he afraid?
Did he cry out, for sibling,
For friend, for Mom, for Dad?
There was no voice to comfort him,
No hand to hold.
Did he feel deserted, betrayed?
Was he aware that God was
calling him? Did he hear?
Did he understand?
Was he at peace, at last?
God, keep him.

Fenton F. DeSilva

My Black Rose

My rose, my black rose.
Sweet love, secret love.
My secret shade, my other beauty.
Lovely, lovely, but lonely.
My hidden talent, my secret treasure.
My rose, my black rose.

Opal Mabry

Remember Me

When heart no longer taps its beat
And limbs are stilled in silent sleep,
Beneath a quilt of earth and stone
In quiet repose, I rest alone,
Remember me!

Remember not my faulty ways,
My jealous nature, silent days.
Think only of the time we shared
The smallest deed, to show we cared,
Then bury me!

Bury me deep within your heart,
So far that I become a part
Of all you were and still remain,
All you plan to be again;
And there, my love, is where I'll be
As long as you—remember me!

Jean Ann Kaitner

Chance It

If you look for fault
in life it surely
will be there.
If you look for goodness
it may seem
kind of rare.
Skepticism haunts you
It tells you to beware.
Throw your fate to chance
decide to take a dare.

Kathy Tenorio

Do . . .

Do the people know what is
Under their feet
More than earth, more than rock
It is something beyond
The movement of feet and a
Chorus of voices
Who are leaving their marks
On concrete and steel
But all is pushed under and
Passed off as trash
And the true meaning shunned
Because they are afraid
A future not yet come
So they scoff at the marks
Below archways of stone
Which circle the city
Revolving in turn,
Being changed and evolved
As the grains of sand grow
Right under their feet

Amy Lynne Holland

Some Hue

1000 colors of the seas
A million shades of sun
And the glass of temperance
Flows upon our guns
And her rainbow water
Pure, sweet and clean
Cures sorrows of broken men
Helpless children, blood and gin
Battered women, slaughtered, shaven
All religion, accused, exiled
But the Earthen daughter
Knows no queen
The search for peace and order
Was paid for in utter chaos.

Kelly Queener

Runaways

Clouds scantily clad in gray
Whiteness protruding from their tops;
Moving quickly like runaways
Searching for a place to stop.

The clouds are loose and thin
Appearing thready and frayed;
Roaming with only a whim
Uncertain and disarrayed.

Thinning with distance they flow
Pursuers seem to fade away;
Unsure which way to go
They meld with other strays.

Lost in the company of clouds
Identities merge with others;
Joining a cobweb of fuzzy crowds
Left to be free or smothered.

With only a veil of life allowed
Existence becomes a tenuous vision;
Deserting the family of clouds
Portrays a future to oblivion.

Orell La Montagne

The Eagles

An eagle soaring to heights unknown,
Searching for prey to carry home.
His beak and talons ready to claim,
Any small animal on the plain.
When he flies back to his nest,
The eagles will feed from his quest.
The female, also, brings feasts galore,
From far away, off the shore.
The eagles will soon learn to fly,
Gliding and soaring through the sky.
As generations fall asleep,
They the cycle will repeat.

Bill Sleasman

Autumn Rose

The last rose of summer
So beautiful so fair,
Like the last love of life
Growing on faith and a dare.

Blossoming late like love
Sometimes does, dear and strong,
The pink and yellow rose
Will last through many a dawn

Sometimes I wonder why
Love does come about late,
Like the last rose, so special,
Making life worthwhile
To contemplate

Marion Kangiser

Superman

A Superman you may be
Climbing mountains for all to see.
But the Superman who beckons me
Is the "inner" man who sets me free.

Kind, gentle heart has he,
Surrounded in humility,
A soul reaching, compassionately
To all of his friends and family.

A Superman you will be
Now, and through eternity.
A Superman who holds the key.
A Superman you are to me.

Mary Lou Paquette

What Is Your Name?

A name is a gift,
Bestowed at birth
Pure and undefiled.

In the course of your life
When your name is spoken,
Things are recalled
Which you've stood for,
Which you've done.

Your name becomes a token,
Of the value of your word.
It's a reminder of the integrity
That you have, or have not.

When you have passed
From out of this mortal existence
What would you have
To be left behind,
To be remembered,
Each time your name is spoken?

Sofia Palacios

The Prickly Refugee

I have a cactus plant, at home,
Now a relic of the past.
It came from a patch of desert,
Of which, we've seen the last.
I came upon that cactus,
When I walked by where it stood,
And got the urge to dig it up.
I wondered if I should,
Cause I had heard some people say,
You're not to move those plants away.
But, with gloves on, I got it free,
Though several prickles got to me.
Now, that it's safely in my den,
And I walk by that patch again,
I see that I must have been right,
Cause bulldozers had cleared the site.
Had I not dug it from the ground
My cactus plant would be mowed down.
And I would not have had the pleasure,
That one gets, from such a treasure.

Frank Greenberg

Faith

Like a flower
Unfolding gently
Petal by petal
Responding
to the warmth
of His light within
Slowly, vulnerably
Radiating joy
To dance silently
on the wings
of Spring. . . .

Lesley Parsons-Tomes

Love And Hate

Love is like a row of flowers
    as beautiful as ever
But hate is like a forest fire
    more lifeless than ever before
This is why I chose love
    for it is better
Better than a beautiful river
    or a blooming rose
Love lasts longer than you
    can possibly imagine
So love from head to toes.

Matthew Rose

Pain

The pain in my life
Is causing my heart
To break in two.
I just don't care
About anything anymore.
Why does it have
To happen to me?
So much pain-
On myself and other-
And I've caused it all.
I don't know
What to do with my life.
Will this pain ever end?
Will I ever be happy?

Bridget K. McGuan

Meditation

God gave us thoughts
With which the world to roam!
And far countries see
He gave us dreams
That we might not lonesome be
When all alone!
He gave me inner eyes
With which to see
In distant skies
A hope that is to be!
So
All in all
He who notes
The sparrow's fall
And clothes the lilies white
Gave not to us
A vacant wall
But wondrous inner light
In which the soul takes flight!

Anne Marie King

"Please"

Moms and Dads are crying
Girlfriends and wives saying
Sons, husbands, and boyfriends dying,
    "Please no more"

Men and Women stealing,
young girls having babies,
trying to find love,
Boys and girls in gangs,
trying to survive,
    "Please no more"

Life is short
Here today, gone, tomorrow,
Brother against brother,
A life for a life,
    "Please no more",

Let's all try to love each other,
Let's all try to help each other,
Maybe if we try to live together,
then we won't be saying,
    "Please no more."

Alice Boswell

Sunny Day

Day so bright
Heat of light
Soft wind blows
Flowers grow
Birds are singing
I love being.

Rebecca S. W. Dranchak

Things of Mother

Things of Mother take me back,
The memories dusty and faded.
Special reminders of long ago,
Stacks or recollections to be raided.

A handkerchief of lavender
To wipe away our tears.
A warm embrace with gentle words,
To wipe away our fears.

Costume jewelry galore,
So beautiful and sparkling.
Appearing as royalty, all dressed up,
And off—to go out dancing.

Roses in a vase of glass,
Portraying Dad's devotion.
Star dust sounding through the air,
Stirring up deep emotion.

Yes, things of Mother
Remind me so
Of special times
So long ago.

Lu Lineberry

Thinking About You

When the moonlight glows
and the energy flows,
you know what's on my mind.
I've been thinking about you.
You're like a dream in real time.
I've never felt this way
so it's hard for me to say,
what is yours and what is mine.
When the moonlight glows
and the energy flows,
you know what's on my mind.
I've been thinking about you.
You're like a dream in real time.
I've never felt this way
so it's hard for me to say,
what is yours and what is mine.

Brad David Buckley

Snow

Oh, my God
What pure delight
When you blanket
Your earth is snowy white
And silently cover
Every flaw that's around
Spreading quiet beauty
All over the ground
You whisper in whiteness
And seem to say
I created this wonder
I give you this day
Life's joys are in simple things
Your riches never buy
Like the beauty of these snowflakes
Falling from the sky

Bonnie D. Kirkland

The Moon and Stars

Today when everything was through,
I thought only about you:
The stars and the moon
which are so bright,
I pictured your smile
in the moonlight.

Ami Mangold

Life

How smart I thought myself to be,
When I was twenty-one;
Life stretched out
Ahead of me,
Now's the time for fun.
At thirty-one things were much
The same;
Nothing now to worry me,
Life is but a game.
At forty-one and fifty-one,
I did not step so high;
What a shock it was to me
How quickly time went by.
At sixty-one
I really am concerned,
How little time is left to me,
How much I've yet to learn.

Nita Cross

Dedicated to a Lost Friend

Before do you remember
The fun we had,
How we always made it through
The good and the bad.

Remember together
How much time we spent,
The days and nights
We came and we went.

Where did those days go?
Those days that meant so much to me.
How come things changed?
Didn't you like how it used to be?

If you did, I think
Those days would be here.
That's what I keep telling myself
As I wipe my tears.

If they don't come back
I don't know what I'll do.
I can't think anymore
Because all I think of is you.

Erika Kalkan

Renaissance

I've fallen into the shadows of time,
  life standing still,

Living in a world,
  within one,

My only freedom,
  I've mastered in my dreams,

My thoughts in be free,
shaken by memories of my past,

Searching within "myself"
  struggling,

Like a new born,
Meeting my father
His son, and the holy ghost,
For the first time.

Mark Baeta

Alcatraz

Here I am
Caught up in
Your world
A world of darkness
A world of deceit
A world of control
Your world
you keep me locked
in this house like
I'm a caged animal
I can't breathe
I feel smothered
You abuse me
I don't deserve this
I tried to love you
Here I am
A prisoner in Alcatraz!

Pedro Abad

Thoughts of You

I live alone with company–
Myself and thoughts of you.
The mem'ries of the times we had
Most always leave me blue.
But despite the gnawing emptiness
Your departure leaves in me,
The exciting kind of life we had
Leaves a glowing memory.
There are times that I loathe fate
For taking you away, my sweet.
Yet often times I think me blessed
That our lives were so complete.
I may never love like that again
Because of ling'ring memories.
But as you died yours was a wish
That new love would give heart's-ease.
Yet I sit here with my company
Myself and thoughts of you,
And thinking that new company
Could not a love like ours renew.

Stewart C. Harvey

Best Friend

Let me tell you about
my best friend,
There always around,
when I'm happy as sad
Rich as poor, sick or well
Not as fair-weather friend
I can call on them twenty four seven,
And never brake your heart,
And always forgiveness,
No need for money,
My best friend lives everywhere,
Alone and below.

Bernadette Marian Thompson

I Wish I knew

Used to wish . . .
What it feels like to be you
What gives you pain or happiness
To be with you
The sentiment sac, called skin
To know what think likes you . . .
Convolution of your puzzled brain . . .
And mystic thinking that you do
To walk the hallways of your thoughts.
Wonder what it feels like to be you

Leo Uliczny

Heaven Up Above

I wonder what's beyond the sky
Or up above the air? I wonder
What it's like to fly and see
what lies up there,
To see what heaven looks like?
Would be an exciting thing?
Oh, what a wonderful sight
That Jesus Christ could bring,
Praising God with all our hearts.
He found us when we were lost.
Thanking Him for what he did
When he died upon the cross.
Glory, glory, glory.
Is how heaven might be,
To let God know I love Him,
And how much He loves me.
Heaven, heaven, heaven.
Is such a wonderful place
With Jesus and His angels
Bringing a smile to my face.

Latoya Lovick

Pressure Builds

Pressure builds
Voids unfilled
Give love with smiles all the while.
Pressure builds
Tears are spilled
Give love with smiles all the while
Pressure builds
Rage instilled
On the verge, feel so impaired.
Inadequate?
Give love with smiles all the while.
Pressure, voids, tears, rage
Still the pain remains
Why?
No love with smiles
All the while

Ann Marie Geisser

Season of Hope

Spring is a season of hope,
there is beauty all around us.
New hope is born in
bold green scenery
of leaves budding on a tree.
the budding flowers are
ready to burst and lift
their eyes to God,
and when the rain begins
to fall, it refreshes
every leaf, flower, and
blade of grass.
Then the warmth of glowing
sun shines down upon them.
All trees and flowers then
give thanks to God by
showing forth their radiant
beauty for such great gifts.

Jillian Therese Alderete

Untitled

I will take the early morning walk
Yet I must not ask the time,
For those shadows creeping toward me
Will turn me back soon enough.

Irving Seidenberg

Mother's Heart

A gentle sigh, a timid shower
A trembling hand, a delicate flower;
A broken dream, a sudden storm
A life not lived, a child still born.

A distant look, a well kept grave
A mother's child we could not save;
A heart cries out with muffled sobs
The angel of death too quickly robs.

A memory lives by God's rich grace
A dimpled smile, a baby's face;
And violet eyes who spoke the words
That only mother's heart has heard.

Rachael Rebekah E. Purpel

I Am A People Lover

People lovers never—
Crack bad jokes, borrow money,
Collect taxes or talk finances or say
"I told you so"
All they do is stay close by and
Radiate affection.
Be a "people lover" cause
"People lovers" "love people"

Velma Groves

Humanity

If you only knew my name
would it be easy to ignore,
the only place I have to live
is a box without a door.

Would you come and visit,
sit down without a chair,
if all I have to offer is
conversation and fresh air?

You refuse to look into my eyes,
what is it that you see?
A small reflection of yourself.
Afraid you could be me?

If you only knew my name,
could you reach out to shake my hand?
For if you did, you would see,
that I, too, am just a man.

Daronda Cross

Why Can't The World Come Together

Why must the world be split apart,
Why can we not agree?
Why can't the world come together as one
So it's a better place to be?

Everyone takes their own path,
But soon they lose their way.
We need the help of others
To guide us every day.

If everyone asked one another
To help them make the right choice,
Then the world would come together,
And the world would have one voice.

This is the dream of many people,
Not just one or two.
But this does not begin with others,
This begins with you!

William James Kenny

God's Blessing

God's Blessing
is wisdom,
knowing our
right and wrong.

God's Blessing
is caring,
having the
heart to
share whether
times are
good or bad.

God's Blessing
is praying,
knowing that
you can go
to Him and,
by faith,
knowing that
there will be an answer!!

God's Blessing

Linda K. Evans

Made It Out

Made it in through vows
Vows to treasure,
Love and protect
Then the beast released
Vows broken-blood shed
spirit broken-broken heart

Will stepped in
Saved my Life
Introduced me to God
In a private way
He forgave my promise
He shut me down
To lift me up
He renewed my Life,
Healed my wounds,
Revived my spirit
So I could
Make it out.

"I Made It Out"

Veronica Scott

The Garden

As I sit in my garden
I am, so alone
And I speak to the flowers
I tell them
I have no love of my own
Then a warm breeze disturbs us
And whispers in my ear
Turn around and look
Your love is right here
As I walk toward the Trellis
I see
A beautiful face, longing for me
We rush toward each other
Our bodies entwine
Then you gave me your heart
And I gave you mine
So we wed in the garden
Our garden of love—
Our love is forever
As the heavens above

Carolyn Luce

Evening Shadows

Evening shadows grow dim
with the fading light
what once was day
will soon become night.
The noise of day, will soon drift away
only to be replaced by the silence
of night.
Along with the darkness, comes
a tinge of fright
which will pass away swiftly
with only a glimpse of
morning's first light.

Bill Collins

The Actor

Upon his stage
He did act
Supposed fooling all the others
For no emotion did he lack

Through con artistry
Did he paint
His own life's facade
Simply too raw and only faint

All to gather some approval
And fake his foe
He had all the power
To dismiss and so

But to me he was a novice
At his art of word
Being too superficial
Made him only absurd

Fooled only but himself
For all the others now do see
All his life an actor
Himself he'll never be

Angela Tezak

Trapped

My words can't express what
I feel inside; it's so hard to say.
It's so hard to write; I myself don't
understand. I feel trapped, but I know
someday and somehow it'll all workout.
Let's take it one step at a time
and soon you'll find out.

Janet Moreno

Ode to a Mother

She is the one held in esteem,
She is a lady so serene;
She is the one you can turn to,
When all the world, to you seems blue.

She is the one to hear your cries,
She dries the tears from little eyes;
Her time is always your time too,
Her caring matched by few.

Her wisdom seems never ending,
And tiffs she is always mending;
A main stay in the family tie,
Her love for us will never die.

Carole Kuczajda

Desert

Nothing all around me,
In the middle of nowhere.
Nothing all around me,
Nothing but despair.
Never touched by humans,
Never seen by man.
Tales gone by here,
Lost upon the sand.
Dusty little stones,
Tiny bits of glass.
Nothing all around me,
Let alone a blade of grass.
Tiny broken branches,
Skyline smooth and straight.
Endless miles around me,
If I make it out, the desert shall I hate.

Karen Alderfer

Me

God made the world
with me in mind.
I am like no other,
I am just my kind.

Russell Davis

Sacred Water Spirits

Sacred water spirits
Rain down hard
To clear all darkness away.

Cleansing winds
From the north
Bring wisdom and truth
For those who have traveled astray.

The bird tribes take flight
To spread forth
Their sacred messages
From every height . . .

While water gathers
Into pools of light;
Of Spirits reflected
On into the moonlight night. . . .

Susan Wright

The Frail Ends of Sanity

Drowning in the world
I cry to man for answers
No Comfort in Sorrow's hands
Yet Love's dagger is cold too
Wondering aimlessly
amid this darkness
I look for Sweet Misery
in the bosom of Society's crutches
Embracing the chains of Life
I'm weighted down
with Burden's thoughts, I cry
Hollowness raped my sanity
and Pride my liberty, they enjoy
Dictated by Choice, I stay
Conscience ran when he had the chance
left me with Morality
who hides in a dark corner
So I drown in my tears
and reach out to the world
Left to myself, no one else

Mike Best

The Ocean

As the deep blue
waves roll
the sea gulls glide
overhead with
peacefulness and grace.

The soft sand
sifts gently
through my
smooth hands
with its own passion.

The roar of the water
sings out as the waves
crash along the beach
making a rhythmic beat.

The sweet scent
of salty water
invades my soul
as I sit on the shoreline.

Christie Gardner

From God's Love

God chose me.
His essence
brought my soul forth,
and willed me here
with His greatest intentions;
therefore, I am—
my spirit must be.

I endure,
I survive,
I strive and flourish,
holding His love
as the highest reward,
until He calls me
to His heavenly sanctuary.

Bridgett M. Bethune

Fear

Fear, run, run, hide, darkness
That's not I; I'm strong
I see light
Evenly from the inside
There a always light.
Burning through and through
Bright bright, dim dim.
But there is light
Fear no man.
Not running
Not running
No more darkness.

Ruth Rainey

Untitled

No matter what's been said
    hurtfully or in anger
I'll love you.
No matter what trials on tribulations
I'll stand by you.
With your hand in mine
I'll defend you.
And as God is my witness
    I'll always love you.

Charlotte A. Rogers

Freedom

As we live, live so sweet
People die standing from their feet

When slavery was born
Blacks were ripped and torn

Why was this unfairness there
Everyone should be fair

Slavery is not here now
But things didn't change somehow

Why the difference between the skin
Everyone's heart is within

Amber Buis

My Erin

My Erin rose to greet me
Like a green velvet carpet
Shining through the morning mist

I glimpsed her rolling hills
and they warmed my heart completely
For I knew that love and friendship
Were gently touching me

She has warmed the hearts of strangers
And welcomed all who came
She is waiting there with open arms
Innocent as her name

Oh Erin, my Erin!

Pauline J. Doyle

A Shot in the Dark

I am a penlight,
trying to pierce the darkness
that shrouds the muted night;
I am the crystal rains
trying to douse
the burning souls of men
so they can further roam
in the naked forests
they raped and plundered;
I am the grain of rice
that wanted to feed stomachs
aching with hunger
to calm the spirit in anger.

But with futility and hopelessness
darkness looms
despite the penlight,
souls turned into embers
despite the rain,
stomachs ached despite the repast.

Jose P. Mariano

Beautiful Brown Eyes

The guy I see in my beautiful
brown eyes has made my world
around me die. He has the
most sensational eyes, but all
in all I don't recall if I can ever
try to call the things he has done.
He makes me shiver deep inside.
But the guy will always be seen
in my beautiful brown eyes.

Karlotta Bivins

My Miracle Is You

So many people don't believe
That miracles are real and true,
But as for me, I believe.

Just as I was feeling
There was nothing left to believe in,
God heard my heart cry,
He felt my soul become heavy,
And he saw the darkness deep inside.

For my unspoken prayers of despair,
He worked a wonderous miracle,
Of which I was unaware.

To believe in things we cannot see,
To have our hopes and our dreams,
Is sometimes harder than is meant to be.

And when we feel we can't go on,
And our hopes for love and joy are gone,

The Blessed hand of God is there,
And pulls us near, for he cares,
He sends us little miracles,
My miracle is you.

Deborah L. Nischan

Because She's My Friend

She maybe six kinds of a liar,
She maybe ten kinds of a fool:
She may have faults that are dire
And seem without reason or rule.
There maybe a shadow above her
Of ruin and woes that impend:
I do not dislike, indeed, I love her—
I love her because she's my friend.
I blame her, I know, but I do it
The same to her face as away;
And if other folks blame, well, they rue it
And wish they'd had nothing to say.
I never make diagrams of her,
No maps of her soul have I penned;
I don't analyze—I just love her,
Because—well, because she's my friend.

Seretha Wilson

Tonight You Will Be My Bride

I have watched you both night and day
And I found high morals and pride..
For your love I wanted and craved
so tonight you will be my bride.

Before we met my heart was sad,
I've been hurt and had wept and cried.
But you comforted me and I'm glad,
That tonight you will be my bride.

We must have honeymoon of course,
Will be the order of the affair,
And may we have joy forever more,
Tonight I'll make a wish and a prayer.

We shall have a nice cozy home,
I hope we'll have a lovely child.
Greatest moment I've ever known,
Is tonight you will be my bride.

Eddie Hanee Hamdani

Mother

Yours was the face
that was held so near
Yours was the voice
that kept me from fear

Yours was a fragrance
That made life so dear
You made me complete
You're the reason I'm here

You stayed with me at night
To chase the monsters away
And when the sun rose in the morning
You stayed with me all day

And as I grow
To become an adult in this world
My mother you will always be
And I your little girl

Jessica Marie Parker

Moments

Listening and learning
Brings on a strong yearning
To keep on going,
Even though I am unknowing.
Life isn't a game
And I'm not to blame.
Time is my friend,
In which there is no end.
I do my best,
No matter how much unrest.
Dreams are thought,
Which mean a lot.
Having no career
Only brings on more fear.
Today I am able
And somewhat stable.
There are demands
And no one understands.
Caring is sharing, as living is giving,
And most of all "Hang in there."

John Kelly

Life

What is wrong with the world today,
with everyone killing each other.
Whites killing blacks,
sisters killing brothers.

We should be happy
that each one of us is liven.
And be grateful with the many chances
our beloved God has given.

Because once this world is gone
what then will we do?
Good water will be all gone,
and the sky no longer blue.

And all because of us,
and the bad things we did.
Because when we were given warnings,
to them we did not bid.

So before it becomes to late
And our time come close to the end.
Be sure you have done all you can,
for yourself and a friend.

Kimberly Benham

She Is My Mom

She is as pretty as flowers of spring,
That April showers bring.

She is as gentle as a kitten,
And was always there to listen.

She curled my hair, as I slept,
She held me when I wept.

She worked hard everyday,
And always, had a lot to say.

She taught me right from wrong,
And her love, made me strong.

She would sometimes, read to me,
Or maybe sing a song.

I will always love her,
"She" is my Mom.

Gerri Frasure

Friend from the Heart

She has been there
Through the good and bad.
She listens, laughs, and cries
Sharing our lives.
More than another person,
More than a friend.

Sitting behind the counter,
Her eyes brighten when we enter.
Caring to ask how we are.
Caring to talk when needed.
More than just a friend.
More than what words can describe.

A friend from the heart.

Charles E. Harles

Racism

When white doesn't like black
And black doesn't like white
We tend to argue
Scream, fuss, or fight
The object of the game
Was to love one another
Treat everyone equal
Not just your "brother"
If we learn to love
Which brings forth peace
The world would be better
From the west coast to the east
So the point of this poem
Is to release the imprisoned
From hate, pain, anger
And of course Racism!

Lowanda Johnson

Rasinbrain

I lie on my bed,
Trying to believe,
Someone so smart,
Could be so naive,

I thought I was perfect,
I couldn't understand,
How truly wrong,
I could be about raisinbrain.

It is unbelievable,
How sweet it can be,
Even though I had to fight,
It's worth it now that it's all for me!

Emily Lawson

Great Art Thee, O' Lord

Great art thee O' Lord.
That thou hast saved thy people,
From death, hell and destruction.
May thy coming be soon.

I will sing a new song of joy.
We are married to Jesus.
Will be the hymn is which, I'll sing.
I will bow down
And worship thee.

I want to be pleasing in thy sight.
Help me in thy way.
Keep me and protect me.
Receive for thyself the victory.

Over the enemy, satan,
Jesus, I love thee.
There is no greater love than thine.
Bless thy name thou,
Holy One.

Frederick L. James

My Friend

I have a friend who knows my name;
We have fun playing great games.
We never push or pout;
We always help each other out.
I have a friend and you do too—
That's true because my friend is You!

Myra Walker

Bonded

A week of love and laughter we shared.
Reunion of hearts and souls that care.
Sky above, grass below
wide open spaces together to roam.

Time stands still yet flies too fast
parting again comes at last.
Sad farewell, tears too near;
sorrow and loss too deep to bear.

Separate lives, yet forever entwined
Searching always to be together.
Bonded as only wild wolves do;
One mate forever me and you . . .

Robin R. Miller

A Midnight Call

Listen, listen very carefully
can you hear
A Midnight Call?

If you can; then you'll know
the fear of a mother when
her child is lost; you'll know
the beat of a racing heart

The frantic pace of a
mother's mind—her fears

Listen, listen very carefully
can you hear
A Midnight Call?

The call of a mother's cry
as she's racing to her
child's side asking
Why? Why?

Listen, listen, very carefully
can you hear—can you hear
A Midnight Call?

Mary Lithgow Sarganis

The Best Revenge Can Be

You'll find me in your mind.
As you eat or walk or sleep.
My voice rings in your ears.
That will make your arms go weak.
With every tear you cry,
Your eyes will be clear to see.
And whenever I come by,
You'll know what you did to me.
And every time you close your eyes,
With your pillow behind your head.
I'll be in every dream you have.
Until the day your dead.
Perhaps my anger and bitterness,
Should not be a victims trait.
But for the life you took from me,
I have no choice but to hate.
I will never walk again,
But you'll never be free.
The way my life will plague your soul.
Is the best revenge can.

Stacy McKenzie

Forever, Ever and Always

You were always there
There to listen when I talked
There to hold me when I walked
There to teach me when I learned
There to reach me when I yearned

You were there, always there
Now you're in Heaven, in God's care,
I can feel you, but I cannot see
But in my heart you will always be.

God took you young
God took you early
Through Heaven's gate
So white and pearly

I'd love to touch you one more time
One more time and I'd be fine.
But that can't happen and I know
Each day stronger I must grow.

I love you forever, Father Don
Through this poem, you shall carry on.

Suzanne Kranak Griesbeck

Rare Affair

Your Body is so beautiful
No other can compare
Your Shape stands out in a crowd;
And people stop and stare.

Your "Top" part, draws attention;
With your "Arms spread out so wide.
Your "Bottom" part, how lovely!
You fill my heart with pride.

Your "Shoulders" are so silky
As my fingers and toes run through.
Your "Attitude" is magnificent
That's one reason, "I love you."

You are the best, in every way.
I couldn't love you more.
Michigan, my Michigan;
From shore, to shore, to shore.

Brenda S. Landers

The Shell

The body is the shell
In which the soul resides
For only a finite existence
For the soul is expelled
From the body, as is the
Infant from the womb
Eternally evolving
Weaving destinies
Newly threaded
Like wool, forever turning,
In the loom.

Nelwyn Lisa Flowers

The Wondering

The paradox of love,
The inelegance of its expressions
The exaltation of love,
The ebb, the wane of its depression.
I love the fairness of his face,
The beauty of his form,
His movements full of grace
And Jupiter's eyes of storm.
Were it not for poet's heart
And sweet sentiment enduring,
All lovers soon would part,
Love's sickness quickly curing.
For, filled with beauty though they be
Cupid's darts they'd gladly flee
If they but knew
Why they woo!

Dorothea Holober

Mr. Bill Retires

Mr. Bill . . . it's perfectly clear,
You're no longer for hire.
You leave us with many a tear,
Now, it's your time to retire.

Thirty years "here" . . .
A blink of the eye.
Twenty more "there" . . .
A lifetime of "try."

We are better off now,
Those touched by you.
You have taught us how,
From a different view.

Work was hard, it's plain to see,
You always gave it your best.
You earned this right to be free—
Now there is more time for rest.

Schedules and time clocks
Are no longer a fuss.
So . . . in between walks,
Come and visit with us.

If you will . . . Mr. Bill.

Alan J. Hemmen

The Ocean

Ever so mighty yet ever
so serene
The roar so beautiful
as it soothes us
Us, who wonder who
respectfully watch
The mountains so tall endless moving
Giving to us a feeling
a longing as we
beckon to its call

Kathleen Melvin Kaler

Rainbow

Soil tossed
Blackening the skies
As angels begin
To soften the ground
For their garden.
Spading the sky
So their seeds will have a home.
Patting the soil firm
And then taking out
Their large watering cans,
Showering earth.
Watering cans emptied,
The flowers begin to bloom.
Spreading glorious reds, oranges,
And yellows,
Mystical greens, indigos, and blues
Up into the sky,
For angels and humans alike
To admire.

Shayna Freedman

Once in a Lifetime

Only once in a lifetime,
But just at the right time,
You meet your perfect match.

It's always unexpected,
Seemingly misdirected,
But just what you had hoped for.

It's exciting and it's fun,
It's things you have never done,
But everything that you dreamed.

Your world suddenly alive,
Heart ready to take the dive.
Still, you wonder if it's real.

"Is this too good to be true?
Or could it really be you?"
Only one way to find out.

So you'll put it to the test,
Vow to give your very best,
The rest only time will tell.

Robin Renea Frederick

Israel

Live in the Promised Land
Enjoy the Golden Sun and Sand
See the Eternal Light,
Seek the Lord with all your might.
Dream of a new Justice for man.
Live in the Promised Land.

Feel the truest joy of life.
Seek the strength Free From strife.
Know your fellow man.
Understand how your history ran,
Live in the Promised Land.

Find your long lost Love
Pursue the pure white dove.
Judge for yourself anew.
See how your people grew.

Find your place in the sun
Know your race was won.
Thrill to every moments feast.
Live and Love the Eternal Peace.

Robert T. Goldberg

I'll Never Do It Again

An innocent child in school
I disrespected the rules.
"When are you going to learn,
Go sit in the corner!"
And I cry teacher, teacher,
I'll never do it again.

An innocent teen at home
Acting out for attention.
"When are you going to learn,
Go to your room!"
And I cry mother, mother,
I'll never do it again.

A lonely adult in the world
Wanting love and affection
Still acting out for attention.
"When are you going to learn,
You have the right to remain silent!"
And I cry Lord, Lord,
I'll never do it again.

A promise I now keep.

Robert Cummings

As She Sleeps (My Beautiful Wife)

To Shannon Johnson.
Her body is still,
Her eyes tightly closed.
And her minds in a world,
That only she knows.

Her dreams will now take her,
To a paradise within.
A swim with a dolphin,
Or a talk with a friend.

For now she won't worry,
About problems in life.
As she sleeps in my arms,
My beautiful wife.

Kermit L. Johnson

Heavenly Delight

As I sit reading my Bible and it
Explains heavens to me,
O' how I wish I were there, with
Jesus, and the hosts of the heavenly.

Heaven is a beautiful city made
Of pearls and jewels, and its streets
Are paved with pure gold as if it were
Transparent glass.
It is made of holy material that will
Eternally last.

The Old and New Testament saints will
Be there with the Master, face to face,
And I'll he there with them,
By His grace,
In that magnificent, delightful,
Heavenly place.

Claudette Estes

Untitled

I wrote a poem,
It wasn't long.
But it had the melody of a song.
Love is the breath of life,
Saves use from destruction's knife.

Peggy Start

A Warrior's Love

Off to battle with a kiss
Knowing all the things he'll miss
Her hair blowing in the wind
Her face he might not see again.

He left her to fight
For glory and might
And he'll be back
When the day is bright.

While she is waiting at home
Hoping to sing the victory song
She'll hear the bids above
Sing a song of a warriors love

Debbie Jernigan

To Be With Someone

To be with someone
A special someone,
This is what I once had.

I loved him dearly,
I still do.
But sometimes love isn't enough.

You think it is
But then you begin to see
You're not the one he loves.

But still you love him so
And it hurts when he has to go.

So now you're all alone
Again.
You wonder if you'll ever have
That special someone that you love,

The one you loved—and lost.

LaDonna McIntosh

Question

Life!
Is it
A disease of planets?
A disfiguring pox
That festers in clusters
To defile and putrify?
That penetrates the innards
To ravage and devour?

Will it consume
With fatal fever?
Or will it run its course?

Some planets seem
Immune to
Life!

Beth Browning James

Grumpy

Wind knocking endlessly on my door.
Hitting restlessly on my window,
throwing cool breezes through the
cracks of my window banging my skin,
telling me to let him in so he can soar
through my house. Outside the wind is
grumpy, hitting against the wall while
changing colors and scaring my sister.
Daylight comes and the wind turns to
a breeze and goes away to
chimney sweep a peaceful family.

Jamie Biss

Am I?

I live within a faceless shell
Where nothingness and pity dwell
My empty head filled to the top
With clouded thoughts that matter not.

Barbara A. Buehler

Untitled

Close your eyes
Shut them tight
Can you feel me
All that I have to offer
Everything I keep inside
Open your eyes
Imagine my dreams
Know who I am
So selfish is the heart
No thought of letting go
A tight grip on the past
Where there are no words
I have memories
Stories in my hand
Quivering naked inside
Too scared to speak
Where do you come from

Ronda Styles

Night-time Skies

Vivid night skies
Void of all stars.
The coldness of the moon
In circled by a ghostly glow.
While moonbeams slide across
a wide open sky.

Skies of black,
Storm clouds brewing.
Great swells of the sea
White tipped and angry, waiting.

Night-time of black
Great thundering waves.
White swirling foam,
Hitting craggy rocks
And smothering the sands.

Black clouds move slowly by,
The great storm passes
While skies turn to iridescent blue.
Quiet shadows of the moon
Upon a midnight sky.

Dolores J. Rosebrough

Alibis Work, Sometimes

I told them why I could not do it—
No time, no talent, energy;
Obligations, family.
They nodded, "yes," they understand,
Someone else would be more able
To handle such a great demand
Although they would prefer just me.

Years have passed, my life goes on
Excuses, alibis, prevail
To save me from that extra mile
Or the fear that I might fail;
Expose my inability.
And not I know that when they asked,
I convinced not them, but me.

Marilynn J. Storms

Friendship With Jesus

Jesus is my friend
Divine, almighty one.
Jesus is my friend
Who sits in heaven above
Ever interceding for me.
Jesus is my friend,
Never ending friend.
He watches and cares for me
Whenever I call upon his name.
He is the son of God
Who died upon a cross
To rescue all the people
Who were lost in sin.
By this sacrificial death
Everyone became free
To accept Jesus.
His death paid the ransom
And paid the penalty.
Oh, what a friend I have.
He cares so much for me.

Margaret Rahn

Mommy's Wish

Tiny little baby holding you
In my arms
Protecting you from all the
Things that might harm.

Loving you gently with every
Breath you take
Guiding you with every step
You make.

Helping you to grow and learn
New things each day
Laughing as we go with all
The things we play.

Learning as you grow to let
You go your own way
Knowing not how to help sometimes
Or even what to say.

Hoping for a future filled
With happy times
Praying that I've done my best
Raising this child of mine.

Ladonna J. Murdaugh

To An Eagle

To you mankind is the enemy,
The blue sky is your home,
The nation's symbol strong and proud,
Forever you will roam.

When I see you soar above,
Great pride is in my soul,
With freedom in our hearts,
Peace—our common goal.

You sit upon a mountaintop,
High up in a tree,
And watch the world far below,
Forever to be free.

James Paulette

Lest We Forget

Bells that chime, carols sung,
Excited kids, stockings hung,
Sales off the grids, Christmas cheer,
In every clime, this time of year.

But what is it really all about,
Besides the salesman's talk and shout,
Besides the tree, the lights, the fuss?
Did we forget who was born for us?

Who gave His life upon a tree?
Who took our sins and set us free?
T'was Jesus Christ. It's not a fable,
For He was born in a lowly stable.

Shepherds came to shout His birth,
Love one another, Peace On Earth!
Wiseman came, presents to bring.
Isn't all this in the carols we sing?

Have we forgotten that this is true?
That He was born for me and you?
Do you remember, remember yet?
What will happen, if We Forget?

Lillian L. Leeds

Cat Bit

Reluctantly I do admit it:
I am not smarter than my cat.
Losing patience, clearly showed it,
When I snapped at her, "Just scat!"

In general a furry love,
She's sweet and gentle as a dove,
But here with aching hand I sit;
The hand that slapped is hand she bit.

Twice before she tried to teach me.
Today I think she really reached me.
A message shows in feline eyes.
One hardly needs be super wise
To know what pitch in her meow
Means, "Do my bidding. Do it now.
The pantyhose you're struggling with,
Just leave. Come on. I won't allow
more time at all. Don't stall."
Stir up anger in this pet;
She'll give you something to regret.

Mary E. Van Pelt

Only Me

The first day I saw you
I knew it was meant to be
I thought you felt it too
But it was only me
Before I knew it
I fell in love
A love so deep
A love so true
There was nothing that anyone
Could say or do
I kissed you
And I thought you felt it
But I was wrong
And that made me feel like ****
I fell in love
And I thought it was meant to be
But it wasn't for you
Only me

Jennifer Kramer

Self

Oh, lover of self,
How many you slay.
Their covers of paper,
On cold streets they lay.

You see not their plight,
No need to, you say.
Their lives, what they've made it,
Be out of my way,

Your in a great hurry,
You drive to your gate.
In the castle behind it,
Your dinners in wait.

If greed has consumed you,
Are you blind to your fate?
Do you know now for sure,
If nows, not to late?

Carmelita C. Steger

Isabella Grace

Celebrate
She is great

Gift of love
From above

Life burst forth
Taking course

Now we know
The special glow

Of her face
Isabella Grace

Susan Collins

A Mother's Wish

To have you again in my care,
To brush and comb your hair,
To watch you fly your kite,
Play marbles right into the night,
To see you hug your brother.
While I wander where is your father.
If I could turn back time
I will hug and kiss you more
These words come from my heart
I send my love on the wings of
A dove, I'll say goodbye
Without a tear.
And hope it won't be long
The birds will sing the song
That tells you I belong.

Betty Aikman

I'm Late

I'm late!
I'm late, I'm late!
I thought I set my clock for 6:08
But that was a big
Mistake!
What? No way!
I gotta go,
I'm going to ruin.
The show!
There,
I made it!
My costume?
Uh-oh!

Jason Bernheimer

Untitled

The delicate
love
bitter of
life
Ask sad, deliberate breast
Woman
felt beneath the
stare
Worship
but do not cry for me

Mary Catherine Perotto

I'll See You Tomorrow

You think you're smart
'Cause you took my job
And left me here in sorrow;
I finished ahead,
You flunked instead,
But I'll see you tomorrow.

There must be a reason
For choosing you
As a leader for someone to follow;
You put on the white collar,
And earn the bright dollar,
But I'll see you tomorrow.

I'm tired of being pushed
'Cause my skin ain't like yours,
And my head is said to be hollow;
Believe what I say,
I may not catch up today,
But I'll see you tomorrow!

Larry W. Colwell

Black Coffee

Half-empty cup
With black coffee
Made too strong to sip.
The dirty cup
Cries out to the walls,
But the walls remain still.

Half-cup of sweet coffee
Sipped long ago,
Now sits waiting,
While the winter wind
Rattles the table
Beneath it.

Elana Goldstein

Harlem Girl in the Caribbean

Standing, looking at you.
I see myself, mirrored
in your faces.

I stand in awe
Of the beauty of
Our diversities
And our commonalties.

I feel the intensity of
Our ancestral ties
That bind us in a
Totality of love.

Come,
Let us look
Homeward

Together,
For we
Are one.

Gayle V. Dancy-Benjamin

Daddy

Daddy, my sweet Daddy,
How I've loved you so.
You are always in my heart,
For my thoughts could tell you so.

Daddy, you have left me,
And my tears can surely show.
The loss that I have suffered
And the friend I lost for sure.

Daddy, God has called you
To a grand and special place,
To the heaven of our dear sweet Lord,
And angels every place.

Daddy, on those golden streets
Our friends and families stroll.
They're happy that you've come home
To share the love of the Lord.

Daddy, I must let you go,
For I know that's what you'd say
But Daddy, I do love you,
More than these few words can say.

Mary Walker

Anger

Anger is red
It looks like fire
It tastes like hot peppers
It feels like broken glass.
It sounds like a broken violin
It smells like a dead skunk.

Edan Wickersham

Little Bird

Little bird at my window,
Gazing at me,
I sit and I wonder,
What do you see?
Can you see that I'm lonely?
Have you just come to cheer?
Little bird at my window,
I'm so glad you're here!

Kay Haney

True Love

In today's
Artificial world
Made up of
Concrete cities
And
Plastic people
The only thing
Real to me
Is my
Love for you.

Gregory Johnson

Beautiful Slave, Beautiful Mother

*In loving memory of African women
enslaved in America.*
Through the womb of a beautiful slave
So I am
Life given to me by God
Through the womb of a beautiful slave
So I am
Intelligence, strength and beauty
Through the womb of a beautiful slave
So I am

Naomi Stewart Reaves

My Best Friend

Dad, you were my shelter from the winds,
You were also one of my best friends.
You'd lift me up when I was down,
You'd pick me up right off the ground.
What do I do now that things have changed,
Now that all your future plans have all been arranged.
I know life without you is going to be tough.
The short life I had with you, just wasn't time enough.
There were a lot of good times that we shared together,
And the memories of those, I will cherish forever.
Throughout your misery, I'm glad I was there,
Although seeing your pain was hard to bare.
I wouldn't have had it any other way,
Because I love you more than words can say.
I know my pain will ease in time.
And strength to continue on, I'm sure I will find.
But for now I will have to swallow my pain.
And I know when I need you, I'll still call your name.
And although our life here together has come to an end,
I will always still call you, my best friend!

     Joetta (Tessie) Purvis

You're The Only One I Love

You're the only one I love
Sent to me from heaven up above
You're always by my side
On your shoulder I have cried
In my life you hold a place
That nothing can erase
So, together in life we live
And to you I'll only give
My heart, soul, and mind
And you shall only find
That my love for you has grown
From the day we were a known
Please always keep in mind
When you look inside your heart you'll find
That life goes by so fast
So, lets make each moment last
Because one day we will be old
But our love will still be gold
For, God made us to see
That forever we will be.

     Jaimi Melissa McIlraith

Forests

Deep in the forest there does lie peace.
It is only created by those who own it—
The creatures of the forest.
Like the sweet singing bird
Who fills the forests with its melodious sound.
And the chittery squirrel
Who collects its nuts on a cool autumn day.
The trees sway gently in time with the wind,
And the deer leaps freely across the forest ground.
As I walk through all this,
I feel like it has always been my home.

     Carley Nicole Cunningham

Shattered

Breathe in a breath that shortens my life,
And blow out the candle of hope.
Look into the layered sky for clouds of insecurity.
Run through a field until I grow weak;
Faint in the grass;
Close my bloodshot eyes.
A sharp wind wakes me up
Shattering my dreams,
Like voices in a dark room.
Breathe in a breath of fresh air,
Breathe out a sigh of relief.

     Tim Hapgood

Unnamed

I never really knew why they were ever put here.
They criticize us, disrespect us, fill our lives with fear.
And yet without one I never would have been born.
My head filled with questions, my life tattered and torn.
And still I wonder what would the world be like without them?
No one to caress you the only way that they can,
To tell you it would be all right, to ease your pain.
To make your life into sunshine when there's been nothing but rain.

To make you proud because you're a woman, a beautiful black queen.
They tell you that you're just the finest thing they've ever seen.
Even if it is a lie, they give you that feeling
To where you just want to die.
They give you visions of glorious passionate love, then,
It's gone. Floating away, flying free like a dove.
They take you to ecstasy and back again.
Showing you places you've never seen or been.
And to think all that can be caused by just one three letter
Word . . . Ha ha! Men!

     NaLonni Evins

Son Et Lumiere

A shawl of dust upon my hand
As monsoon stalls above the land,
Sitting on a summer's morn
I am crossing paths with June . . .

Sticky heat surrounds us all
And clouds don't rain they just grow tall,
The lightning flash makes us so small
While crossing paths with June . . .

We wait and wait for cool sweet rains
To come up from the south again,
Tho desert rules with heat insane
We're crossing paths with June . . .

Cruel morning wakes a wicked sun
That puts cool shadows on the run,
Now tempers flair we're all undone
Here crossing paths with June . . .

There nothing left to do I guess
But sit and wait like you I guess,
And ponder cooling thunderstorms

That hotly kiss the moon . . .

     David "Bugs" Kowalski

Fate, The Oppressor

Down on my knees, this thing called fate
Has conquered once again another foe.
Grim laughter seems to echo through its hate;
What causeth me to be maltreated so?

Life at its best is but a bitter thing,
A little laughter sprinkled with the tears;
Alas, the circumstance of fate can only bring
Naught but pain and sadness through the years.

What power controls this black design
Which clutches our hearts and leaves them cold?
Men to this monster-foe their fate resign
Within its bosom doth the destiny of man enfold.

Yet out of the blackness and the pain,
One light alone keeps our hearts young,
As shedding sunlight to the rain,
The chord of God's sweet mercy softly sung.

     Franklin Trask

The Dog Across The Street And Me

As my weary eyes expand
To take in the magnificent spring
The matted creature appears,
Heavy hearted, soul in tow
To obstruct my picture-perfect view.

A throughbred true, yet now blue,
The pick of this Collie litter, for sure . . .
His eyes, once alert and alive,
Now stare into space . . . just like mine.

Neglect will not kill us,
Nor ticks in our feet.
That we are kindred spirits
That's a fait accompli.
Have patience, gain strength
And we'll leap once we are fit.

Since our mutual creator, The Lord,
Just might have designs for us both
Which will be exciting, and exuberantly rewarding
For all of those desolate paths we have walked
That we dotted with kisses, caresses and love.

Gina S. Hernandez

Digging For Treasure

Tell me about a child that comes to school
And I will show you someone who deserves to learn
Tell me about a child who goof off in class
And I will show you a child who wants to be heard
Tell me about a child who has "no hope at all"
And I will show you a child who has not been reached
Tell me about a child who is an "air head"
And I will show you a child who is misunderstood
Tell me about a child who is a "dumb jock"
And I will show you a child who has unlimited gifts
Show me don't tell me about students
They have more good than bad
It is up to us to find out what they have
Don't give up on a student because he or she is not perfect
Being a teacher can be very hard and time consuming
Sometimes, almost like looking for a hidden treasure
That treasure is in all of our students
It is up to us to look and dig for it
The richness that we find will be far greater than gold or jewels
Those riches are enjoyed by only a few

Anthony J. Wilkinson

Victory

I'm often in wonder, and amazed at my own inward
Description of the outside world,
I seek to understand, but still I'm amazed and not satisfied,
Little by little I find pieces of a whole, but I can't
Seem to grasp that elusive whole,
The faster I run, the slower I become,
The more I endeavor, there stands someone more clever,
But never will I doubt the outcome, what the end result will be,
For I will rise above my insecurities, stand face to
Face with my accusers,
And defeat my enemies, the rulers of darkness
In this world gone mad, this world gone mad,
So beware snakes that slither, worms that burrow,
Into the ground,
For I will rise from the ashes of my infirmities,
From the afore mentioned insecurities, and stand
Looking into the eyes of my maker, as he affirms,
Well done my good and faithful servant, well done!

Tillmon Meadows Jr.

Untitled

As the curtain of darkness falls
The imprisonment begins, but it is
Not a jail full of guilty persons,
It is a meager world lacking any light,
Burdened by the physical obstacles
That had seemed neutral in the daylight,
But now loomed ominous and destructive,
Searching me out like a fugitive,
Only to strike me down as I escape the prison.

In my attempts at liberation,
I find myself struggling-not to move forward,
But only to maintain the position I held
Just moments before.
The struggle lasts until dawn,
Until the peacekeeping sun makes his presence felt
To every creature that tried to escape the prison.

Chris Steinmeier

Would You

Would you say I do, would you say it to me?

If I had the key, the key to your heart
Would you say it to me, would you do your part?

Would you hold my hand when I'm feeling blue
And would you believe that I'll always love you?

Would you dry the tears that life seems to bring
And tenderly kiss me, make my heart sing?

Would you work with me in building our dreams
And show me you are what you seem?

Would you wait the day my love to come through
When at last I can say "I love you?"

Philip A. Brooks

POISONOUS POWER

My power is my poison
I strive to get strong,
No step taken wrong,
And even so with each move
A poisonous dosage I consume.
Slowly increasing its strength,
The more infected I become.
My power is fueling my poison,
Total complete empowerment.
Leaving me isolated, by myself
Scared of the final result.

Confined isolation
Am I to die alone with my power?
Should I block off this poison
And live powerless?
Incomplete?
Deny myself of a poison that must take its course
In order to control the strength . . .
Of
My poisonous power. . . .?

Marilyn Sharpe

Untitled

You've changed my life, and made me see.
There are others more important than me.
See a child's love, given without strings.
It bears the fruit a lifetime brings.
See friends in need, never asking please.
Who receive great wealth, which you cannot see.
See a wife who has managed to change a stone.
Without cracking its core to stand exposed.
See yourself, who indeed, is shaped anew.
From the haunting past you wondered through.
You've changed my life, and made me see.
There are others more important than me.

Robert Hamman

A Lasting Autumn Stay

The night glows and speaks heavenly
Amid the ferns of grace, a trail of beauty goes

When it is hard to see your life
When others do not know your name
Walk in the light, caress your heart the same

And I do not know why beauty has to cry
The cold wind flies again
The morning brings a willow tree, soul swaying

Yes, it is bound to be a life
I do not know the song
Stand in the chord, see where I belong

Growing traces of one day
A lasting autumn stay
Come sit and weave with me
The love I have seen just come my way.

Susan Minnick

Reason For Doubt

I am a child, in need of attention and love.
I ask God for help, there is no answer.
I turn and walk away, alone.

I am a young man
in need of guidance and understanding.
I ask God for help
there is no answer.
I turn and walk away, alone.

I am an adult
in need of knowledge and wisdom.
I ask God for help
there is no answer.
I turn and walk away, alone.

I am an old man
stricken with the disease of time.
I ask God for help
there is no answer.
I turn and walk away
for the last time
still, alone.

Mike Bachman

My Father's Care

Father you are always near,
You are the one who always cares,
Although I'm not worthy of your love,
You still bless me from heaven above.

As each day unfolds, I know I'm in your plan,
I know for each battle, for me you stand,
When everyone is my enemy and offender.
You are my friend and my defender.

When I'm down and low, father you help me grow,
When I am confused and sad,
You make me contented and glad.

You turn life's failures to success,
You transform each curse to a bless,
You make everything impossible to reality,
You recreate opportunity available to me.

That's why my voice I'll lift up high,
I'll always sing my praises to the sky,
I would always uplift your name,
'Cause I know for me your Son was slain,
And when I call, you never restrain.

Tamiko Prescod

Seasons

Snowflakes drifting on a still winter day,
Descending from above like crushed white pearls,
Eyelet trimmed blankets covering cold beds of earth,
Soft icy cotton, enter my world.

Rain pouring down on a moist spring morning,
Drizzling from above, so piercingly cool,
Crystalline drops from goblets on high,
Ending the reign of the morning dew.

Rays beaming down on a hot summer day,
Halos of luster on a quiet earthly scene,
Sunshine glistening from heaven on high,
Radiating sparks and warm golden beams.

Leaves blowing around on a windy fall day,
Twisting dried hues of brown and bright red.
Unassuming seasons of majestic change,
Bring forth your splendor for years ahead.

Ethel H. Guinyard

Our Love Survives

I go to bed head in hand,
it feels like a clanging pan.
To go to sleep I must try,
to help this night go quickly by.
One day soon my heartache will end,
in through our door will walk my Ken.
My loneliness will go away,
my love will be home to stay.
Then our future we will start,
never more to be apart.
Our love will bloom, our love will last,
we will forget these sad months past.
Each day will start with love and cheer,
each one knowing the other is near.
Our love is now, our future clear,
for this we waited all this year.
The love in our hearts will forever glow,
our love is true this we know.
Our hearts beat now as one,
see what true love has done.

Willie M. King

Auburn Hair and Eyes of Emerald Green

There is a story that I want to tell to thee,
About a trip I took back in 1943.

As I approached the British Isles, I saw this fair land.
Then I thought to myself, this was made by God's own hand.
When I landed on the shore, everything was quite serene,
And all the men and women were wearing of the green.

I asked the name when I landed on this fair land,
And the answer they gave me, "Why, it's Ireland!"

It was there that I met this sweet girl called Colleen.
She had hair of auburn color, and eyes of emerald green.

That was many years ago, but still in my dreams,
I see the girl with auburn hair and eyes of emerald green.
Now when I leave this world behind and enter Heaven's gate,
I know I won't have long to wait.

For waiting there to greet me, when I enter Heaven's scene,
Will be an angel with auburn hair, and eyes of emerald green.

I may not see her again on earth but that's alright with me,
But soon I will be with her throughout eternity.

So when we (you and I) get to Heaven, you will get to meet this
sweet Colleen. The one with auburn hair and eyes of emerald green.

Howard Ditmer

To Be Like Thee

Why oh why can't I be,
Like the beloved one that raised me
So understanding, loving and wise.

Why can't I be the sun so bright
Always cheerful, helpful and full of life.
Knowing how to love and be loved.

Why can't I be the mother of the year
Getting praise, love and roars of cheers,
By only kissing and giving a big hug.

Why can't my children love me
The way I shall always love thee.
For you are the world of peace.

Why can't I be like you mother dear,
Because you are far away and I am here.
Away from your inspiration and loving ways.

As I write you this day,
I shall kneel and pray
That God above will bless me
For mother, it's like you I want to be.

Beverly J. Harvey

Our Lives As A Christian

Our Heavenly Father saves us from sin,
When we open our hearts, and let him in;
He gave us our lives,
That we might spread His word and baptize;
But on the other hand,
Christians must obey His command!
They must set aside a time each day,
To read His word, and pray,
They must be a teacher to others,
Including their sisters and brothers;
They will tell y-o-u
That you can become a Christian too,
For His word, you do not have to search,
Just read your Bible, and go to church;
Above all your daily needs,
You must truly believe.

Carolyn Harmon

Boulevard of Broken Dreams

Little Lisa, she was a looker,
Her face should be up on a screen.
Her dreams it seemed, in the would lead,
To the boulevard of broken dreams.

At eighteen, she hit the road running,
Memphis just couldn't hold on.
She's a poor country girl, with her sights on the world
And a room on the boulevard.

But like so many before her,
She believed all the lies that were told.
No more lonely nights, her name's up in lights,
And now, she can't let go . . .

They found her down by the seaside,
Her beauty, a memory.
God rest her soul, now they're sending her home,
From the boulevard of broken dreams.

Dreams weren't made to be broken,
But fortunes were made at a cost.
All the promises crossed, all her hopes were lost,
On the boulevard of broken dreams. . . .

Timothi Le Romack

Untitled

Why fuss with my hair?
And make it just so.
A dress that is short, or one to the floor.
Shoes that are high, or ones that are flat.
Whether I'm tall an thin, or short and fat.
Does anyone see the real me that is there?
When the real me's inside and no one cares.
One must care in order to see where loves
reply lives in side of me.
If no one cares and no one sees.
Will it wither an die? Or can it live on,
as long as I share the love that is there in me.
But there is God who knows how I feel.
If he weren't so far away I could touch him.
But then he can be o-so near, an he can touch me, so.
Alone I am not.
And lonely I'll never be.
As long as I let him into share with me
A love of all loves that can never compare
with any other kind of love any where.

Jacquelyn Weaver

Jessi, My Friend

While I was only a pebble dull
You were a luminous marble of perfection.
Somehow we became one
A friendship in stone
Grown together as one star
The sun.
Above all as long as we had each other
No boundaries,
There were no walls.
At times we shared one heart,
One soul, one mind,
How close you can come to owning someone else's voice
Or calling it your own.
The inspiration to put pen to paper now
Came from your ability, expression.
Nothing that can be put in words was withheld;
The laughter, the comfort, the acceptance
We found in one another
We found ourselves, each other.

Erica Grauerholz

A Love Poem

The warmth and compassion that her eyes convey can be
compared only to the stars in the heavens. The sweet melody
of her laughter fondles the senses and soothes the anxiety.
Oh, she is so much more than woman. What is this
healing light that I feel in her soul? It caresses me
and fills me to the very core of my being. I am humbled
by her charm and elegance. I am also alive with passion
and desire. A desire so great, I fear it may consume me.
And yet, my actions are restrained. Though it is not
by willpower, but by her disarming smile. For as I
live and breathe, it is that smile, affecting and enchanting,
that nurtures me and preserves my sanity.
Though I may never know the gentleness of her touch,
or experience the ecstasy of her kiss, she has awakened
in me a stirring ensemble of emotions I never knew existed.
I feel strengthened, and I feel saddened. For I
know this gallant quest can never be realized.
She will forever remain as distant and elusive
as the stars themselves.

Gino Anthony Peccia

Apples

The wind blows delicately,
The sun shines brightly,
The people come and look.
They take what they want,
Friends come and go.

The people still come,
I'm still here, waiting.
Someone sees and touches me,
He takes a bite,
Leaving me on the tree.

He sees a shinier apple,
Abandons me and goes to it.
He takes a bite,
But there is a worm.
He drops it and tries to come back.

I have fallen,
Not knowing whether I will be picked up.
He stares at me and walks away.
I stare at him and wonder if he will return.
I am dying.

Jennifer E. Seyler

Ginko Tree

On my faith journey I sought thee

Your stalwartness, your uniqueness, your other centeredness
Enraptured me from of old

Whence have you come? Where did your spirit generate?
In admiration I fail to grasp what has come to thee so naturally

Do not our journeys converge yours and mine?
Do we not face the seasons? The elements?

Yet is not the sun, there within our grasp?
The moon and stars are put on our doorstep.

Is not the secret of life...the mystery of life?
Borne within us by the sun?

You and I need to grasp from within and without
The center of our being

For our Creator defined us,
Unique as we are . . . unique as we have been

Diann Theresa Cousino

Desert Loneliness

If you were ever alone on a moonlit night,
Away out on a desert plain
Then you know what I mean I speak of the thing;
That feeling that comes over a man.

It seems that a mist comes out of the sand,
Filled with memories and thoughts of home;
The things like a wall as it gathers around,
And it chills a man to the bone.

You know how you feel when you look at the moon,
And it drifts along in the sky;
And you long for the things that belong to you;
Things that money cannot buy.

Then a cloud comes along and covers the moon,
It seems to hide the things that were there.
And the mist settles down and goes back in the sand
And the desert once more is bare.

But you go right on from one day to the next;
And in your heart you never forget and you know, that the day
When you go back home will be the happiest you've known yet.

James O. Self

My Angel Child

In loving memory of Charline.
Charline, Charline, my angel child.
Sweet and kind but a wee bit wild.
Left this world so long ago;
Took our hearts but left her memories glow.

Now she stands in God's light,
A shiny star, bold and bright.
Still sweet and kind but a wee bit wild.
Charline, Charline my angel child.

Karen Davis

One Face

One face among the many massed against
That cold December hill creates a ghost
Who lies in mind forever dormant there;
Until the specter sprouts a memory
That's warmed and watered by a tear from some
Such well of time ago revived. Look back
And see the quilted figures crouched around
A fire, so much like the one we stood
Beside, across that barren frozen patch
With weapons dangling by our sides. One face
Looked up and stared until my gaze met his.
I read his look as if it said, "My God,
What are we doing here within this bleak
And frigid land when we should be at home."
"Agreed," I nodded, Mona Lisa smile
Upon me then. One face was all it took.
We parted eyes that haunted ever since.

J. L. Quick

I Will Love You

I will love you till, the sun no longer shines.
Until words no longer rhyme.
I will love you till, the sea no longer
Flows, Until my love ends, only you will ever know.
I will love you till the mountains
Never peak, Until my lips shall never speak.
I will love you till the winters have
No snow, until forever, and ever, only you will know.
I will love you till the end of time,
Until no love you'll ever find.

Georgia L. Weesner

Mom Too

I am a Mom too
This could only come true
Because of you
I know you took time before you
Had to choose

The choice was between me and you
You knew what you had to do
Now is my turn to say thank you
Because it was life that you did choose

The Mom I got because of you
Did the best she could, and it's true
Because of you
I am a Mom too
Two times two

I thank God for guiding you
I thank you for you
I thank God for the Mom that stepped in for you
Mother's Days come and I think of you
For now I see clearly what a Mom can do
Because I'm a Mom too!

Mary G. Mary

Ennui

Chemically induced or life induced?
Floating lethargically through the day
Hours, minutes, seconds, milliseconds
Clock ticking,
metronome of my life
Heart beating
Moving inexorably towards its ceasing
Rhythm of Live
Inhale! Exhale!
Watching the sun's snail-like progress
Across the wasteland of the universe
Waiting impatiently for the sun to melt into nothingness,
Pooling golden eddies on the sea's surface
yearning for Morpheus' respite
Briefly, and then watching the clock, yearning for the sunrise,
And end to my self-imposed exile from light
I am a prisoner of time
Locked to its marching gait
Incarcerated?
For what crime?

Mary E. Best Lamalie

Butterfly

Butterfly with satin wings
Flying through the pasture greens.
Blossoms and leaves hide you completely.
Beyond the wind that smells so sweetly.

Fly, fly, up so high through
The clouds that reach the sky.
Beyond your way little butterfly,
Your beauty is with in the sky.

Don't wait for me with your satin wings,
Fly, fly, up so high
Past the planets and the stars,
Good bye my little butterfly.

Elaine A. Tencza

Esc

The dull orange glow on a summer's eve,
Bathes the world and calmness strives.
Strong is the hold of the branch to the leaves,
Not to let go until frost arrives.

A tired young man roams the shores,
Of crashing, far, and distant seas.
And when the orange light strikes the moors,
He stands to gaze as waters heave.

Then twilight sings its quiet song,
And shadows 'cross the mead do play.
He turns his tired head to long,
For unknown regions far away.

Peter Dorsey

Doll House Wishes

Doll house wishes and little pink dishes: make believe wishes.
Ice cream sticks, mud cakes and make-up kits.
Make believe tea, dresses, straw hats, and old shoes
Beads and flowery things, even a ring or two.
Mothers old pearls, caught haphazardly in her curls;
Gazing at her looking glass, thinks she's grown up girl;
With powder and make-up all about her face,
Can't tell where she started, not even a trace.
Dolls, dresses, make-up cakes, and little girl wishes:
In her own right, she's such a lovely sight.
Just having fun playing all grown up:
Serving tea in pink dishes
And all her doll house wishes.

Mary Francis Day

Thomas, The Tank Engine

Choo-choo-choo says the train.
Thomas is what they call him by name.
He's so full of play,
And I'm here to say,.
That with Thomas, there's never a dull day.
Toot-toot-toot goes his horn.
The other trains with him usually do scorn.
But when all's said and done,
And after Thomas has had his fun,
He's still one of the best on the run.

Janet E. Keitel

Family

We hear but ignore the voices and we rarely understand
Without years of confrontation or someone's final stand
But given time we find an answer and overlook the cost
Thrive on our achievements taking time to mourn our lost
As our family stretches out

Home is of great importance but there are always those who stray
Solutions are easy in black and white but we live in shades of gray
No matter how we abuse it, the hurt is directed in
But the house would remain standing with the loss of all our kin
And our family reaches out

This family bickers among itself and the battle always rages
The problem is as old as time as people learn in different stages
Family grows and home grows small, as we reach into the black
Honor those who push us on and hope they all come back
Our family's arms are long

G. B. Reith

The Last Tear

Can you take and hold the trust I give to you,
I'm tired of being strong and I would like to cry
It's not a tear of fear, but the damned ocean of my time
With the last few years,
So you see I really would love to cry,

But will you let me—can you induce me with your trust,
Hold to protect me in my moment of nakedness
Let me forget all and take me back into your love
I want to cry only the depths of men would know,
Tears torn by values and fears calmed by thoughts
Of masculinity lost

Do you care enough to shelter me in this time of need,
To hold, and understand with your eyes speaking softly to me
While you blanket me in your body's warmth, be my earth and water,
Let me be your wind and sky.

I just want to cry, people make it so hard to do,
Can you help this weak man's plea for strength,
And if after I look to you and give a foolish smile,
The last tear coming down means "thank you."

Michal John Duveneck, Ph.D.

Brown Forest Lake

Brown forest lake in the middle of my mind.
It is a special place that only I can find.
Eyes of fire flash though the dark of night.
My soul stands naked at the edge of the light.
Waiting for answers that I know I can't reach.
Talking of truth that I know I cannot teach.
Clouds of wisdom whisper as they float softly by.
Telling me it's a short time before those that die.
That I must leave behind for those that wait.
A way for them to able to open the gate.
To find me here always for their soul's sake.
Knowledge to share at brown forest lake.

Dennis Brigge

The Chill

Listening, casually, to familiar sounds
I drift into a trance.
Then unbidden my ear
Hangs upon a gentle phrase.

Deep within . . . a connection is made . . .
And faerie fingers trace my spine.

Rapt, my eyes blur and close,
Embrace the delicious frost
That dimples the skin
And captures the soul.

How elusive!
How sweet!

Child of passion, would that I could
Lose myself in your chill kiss.

Stephen Rolston

What's a Poet?

What's a poet? Is there a precise description?
See below.

Sensitive? Full of fun?
Deadly serious? That's not a pun!
Affectionate? To nature tuned in?
A discerning eye—or a lonely cry?
A message hard-driven for a cause striven?

A warning to heed?
A passion to bleed?

Agitator? Mediator? Meditator?
Condenser of wordy pages into world-shaking ideas?
Shaper of broad scene-scapes into heady descriptions?

Refrainer of pithy elements?
Disposer of chaff by way of a laugh?
Thrusting knowledge and beauty
Onto barren nothingness?
Feeling a sense of time
To record moments sublime?

All of these? Maybe none of these?
Will you geniuses out there tell me, please?

Carol H. Ross

A July Respite

Yuccas' white blossoms
On slender white stalks
Rising taller than the orange of the tiger lilies.
Birds splashing
In the bird bath
Sheltered from the blistering sun
By the dogwood tree now in leaves of green
Having blooms long gone.
Early evening, a rabbit, maybe two.
Nighttime dusk.
Relief from the oppressive heat and humidity.
Today approaches yesterday
Tomorrow comes.

S. Davison

Mask of Pain

We've opened our hearts to pain again
Both to scared to let the other one in
Our wounds have scars our cuts to deep
Our hearts alive but wants to sleep

If we feel nothing but a touch to the skin
Never will our hearts feel love again
Must we laugh as our hearts carry shame
We wear a mask to cover our pain

Karen Pollard

Yellowstone

In Yellowstone's fields
The daisies grow
Between the buffalo
Row on row
And mark their place,
While in the sky
The vultures greedily shrieking fly.
These are the dead.
Scarce days ago
They lived, grazed, and wandered.
Now they lie
In Yellowstone's fields.

(During the winter of 1997, over 2,000 of
Yellowstone's buffalo were shot as they
crossed into Montana seeking lower,
less icy pastures. This represented 2/3
of Yellowstone's buffalo.)

W. Ulysses L. Fowler

A Gloomy Day

Today is a gloomy day,
Gray clouds
And fog in the distance.
Today is a sad day.

The sun is hiding in the clouds,
Drops of water are dripping off the tree petals,
There are no birds in the sky
To fly
Or turtles on the grass.

The wild turkey are not out
To play.
It's a gloomy day.
The roses and tulips are sad;
They have no sun to make their way.

Today is a gloomy day.
Today is a writer's day.

Morgaine Witriol

Joys of Life

When you are born, everything is new,
the grass is always green, the sky is always blue,
and the sun is always shining.
As a youth, discovery and learning are the constant joys of life,
every day more intriguing than the next.
In adulthood, you realize the concept of
similarity and contentment,
discovery and learning become the precious joys of life.
And as you near the end of your path with discovery
and learning in the past,
you still hope the grass is always green,
the sky is always blue, and the sun is always shining.

Drew H. Zimmerman

Essence

I see you softly as the stars shine upon you
Your essence abide with me in the evening light
I hear your soft whisper in the forest too
The stars sparkle, glisten and beckon your sight.

I have walked among the stars in your pursuit
Calling, yearning for your hand in mine
Travelling near and far to seek out your spirit
Yet, you walk with me each night, our spirits intertwine.

My very soul reaches, extends with time
I am but a traveler whose soul touches many
It was predestined that your soul found mine
For your soul's essence, I find better than any.

Frank Orr, Jr.

The Sullen Walk

Her face came to me again last night.
All warming expressions erased by my
Appearance

Turning hands that feel the desire pulling,
Griping on a memory cast by springtime flowers

The bed I lie in knows my tears.
The air I breathe yearns to know my
Thoughts

Where must I go?
My footsteps can not be silenced.
The bleeding sounds of worry
Echoes

Through my body as if it were a tomb
A death not
Finished
James Ryder

Valentine's Day

*To my fiancée when she was in the hospital
on Valentine's Day in 1987.*
In this year, and on this day;
One needs to show love in every way.

Send the flowers, candy, or cards;
Dine in the night, with a loved one, underneath the stars.

Share in the moonlight with the one you love;
Touch them with the gentleness of a snow white dove.

One might even simply do this:
Say "I love you", give of yourself;
Sealed with both a hug, and a kiss.
Steven M. Dietrich

Untitled

My life is that of a nomad
Moving steadily over the expanse of reality
No roots have I to nurture
Nor a settled point of return
Quite vainly in my hours of solitude
Do I ponder on past journeys
The desired lessons learned
As well as those undesired
My only stable possession is myself
Everything else is tangible
But somehow my being gets lost
Into the road I have traveled
For the two become one
And I have become my own journey
Amy M. Phelps

Moment

As my eyes open with the new day sun
I have a moment of calm
Though it lasts but a minute, it feels like hours
During this moment,
I have no worries
No responsibilities
No cares
I hear nothing but the morning bird's song
See nothing but the golden rays over the tree tops
Through the window
I taste nothing but the sweet, crisp morning air
As the sun slowly rises, the calm disappears,
Until the next morning when it appears once more
Jessica Logatto

What Is Love

Love is the feeling in your heart and mind
when you meet the one you're going to marry.
Love is what comes out once in your lifetime,
the one thing in your life that's real and pure and true.
When you feel it you know what it is,
it's a never ending feeling of happiness,
like nothing else in the world.
It's a beautiful pink and purple sunset,
but only more, you have to look beyond the warm feeling
that you get when you see it.
Love is the only thing that you need,
and when you have it your life is complete.
Love is like caring for something like nothing else,
knowing that you would do anything for the person.
That is love.
Jonathan M. Thiel

Pleasure or Punishment

Silence is what I call it
I clench onto my feelings
For fear of a minuscule drop
To drip from my lower lip.
To endure the pain of my own
Feelings is like a self inflicting disease.
This is my silent motivation
Lack of speech is a painful act
Of eating my words.
I try and try again
But I cannot digest unused words.
Silence is broken.
J. Bacho

A Woman's Lament

At times like these I fail to see
The humor in the human being

I cook and clean
And work and strive
At times it seems
My home's a hive

Taking care of a sick man
Taking care of a sick child
Loving them both as best I can
But at times they both drive me wild

When he is down, he walks out the door
When she is down, she lets me know
I try so hard, but I can take no more
My cork is slipping, I'm gonna blow

A little less love is the solution to this
To make once more a home with bliss

For I have no escape nor do they care
There can be no mistake nor a sudden dare

For I will have no love left to shout
Nor two careless loves to worry about
Cathleen A. Kennedy

Mistakes

I have made mistakes and so have you
I have lied and you have too
Nobody is perfect this is true
We all make mistakes and there is nothing we can do
But if we allow ourselves to dwell upon the past
In our hearts, our mistakes will forever last
For the mistakes I have made, I have forgiven myself
My mistakes and my pride I have put upon a shelf
We must forgive ourselves and let the past go
We must look inside and let our true selves show
We must live our lives day by day
And soon in the past our mistakes will stay
Ron Guffey Jr.

He Touched My Hand

He reached over to count all of my fingers and toes . . .
He touched my hand.

He guided my tottering steps . . .
He touched my hand.

He held on tightly as we walked up to the school . . .
He touched my hand.

He balanced my bicycle as I curved down the road . . .
He touched my hand.

He grabbed hold of the steering wheel as I tried to drive . . .
He touched my hand.

He helped me with my cap and gown . . .
He touched my hand.

He walked me down the aisle . . .
He touched my hand.

He held his first-born grandchild . . .
He touched my hand.

He lay dying.
He touched my hand.

     Phyllis F. McMullen

Tic Tock

Expressing explicit fear
Shamelessly shedding a single tear
Powerful urges come from inside
A darkened corner run and hide
Sorrows I give my relinquishment
But, no, they do not get the hint,
The severity of my life increases
Today my world crumbles to pieces
Their dissuasive ways keep me from enjoying life
I am left in this awful strife
Do you know how I feel
Have you been through the same tragic ordeal
I tried to leave but their pandemonium scared me still
I long for something peaceful, hopeful, tranquil
But my utopia is out of reach
Happiness is not something you can teach,
Run a mile and walk a block
My life is beating away like a clock
The alarm has been set
I am just not ready to leave yet

     Alyssa Stafford

Inspired

When the lights are dim and you are near,
I love the feel of your hands so clear.
Oh what we can do when the lights are out,
But What more we can do when the lights are not.
Your hands are here and there and everywhere,
What shrills and shivers it sends up my spine,
to have the feel of your hands so fine.
How long it will last no one can say
but lets enjoy and have fun while we are in the hay.

If only time would stand still for us,
so we can love each as we wish,
and not have to blow each other a kiss.
Things get harder and harder each day.
If only we could back up time as we would say.
Then things could be different all the way,
and we could have each other in our hay,
to love and cherish to this day.
Our love is strong as strong can be,
that way it will last you will see.

     Doris M. Zimmerman

The Death of a Dream

Unable to live the American Dream
With the world and lives coming apart at the seams.
Vandals, Thieves, and sickness roaming the night,
These are examples of America's plights.

No solution in sight, No one really cares,
No answers, No respect, it's all blank stares.
Where does it end, and where do we go?
Why can't the insanity leave us alone?

No respect of what belongs to others,
And yet we're to believe, these are our brothers.
Whatever happened to simpler times?
Of laughter, of morals, and bright sunshine.

A cloud has covered the life we've worked for,
And opportunity is no longer at the door.
All you see are people and their vanity,
It's hard to maintain and keep your sanity.

It's a downhill ride we've been on for years,
Not seeing the hurt, or thousands of tears.
Yes this is the end of the American Dream,
Of peace, tranquillity, peaches, and cream.

     David Wisser

The Showing of the Tress

Before our eyes a magic scene.
These wooded hills so lately green
Have been transformed to bright array
Autumn presents her Rare Bouquet.
With purest paints that glow and gleam
a wondrous Artist passed unseen
and with a masterstroke he makes a masterpiece
with no mistake!
From tinty tints to tones so bold
Sun-beige, amber, flaming Gold!
No fairy kingdom could compare, with this
our hillside glory fair.
Some land rich gems and sculptors prize
In some impressive buildings rise.
We're blessed above such things as these.
Our regal Showing of the Tress!
Created as our master wills
Designed with grace upon our hills.
The Painter Royal, hands Divine
Displayed for Common eyes like mine!

     Juanita White

No One Was There

No one was there, to say goodbye. Its just not fair.
You should of called me, I would of known and I would,
have been there, to hold your hand and tell you that;
"Mom I'm so sorry, I didn't
Try harder, to be a good daughter,
I always love you and dad."
I know ever since dad, all you've been inside is sad.
I should of done more to try to ease your pain,
And to help you feel you weren't alone.
I wish I could go back and tell you so many things.
When I got there, you were already gone,
And lying there, all alone.
No one was there to say good-bye it's just not fair,
You know I would have gotten there.
We took you back to Cameron,
And placed you next to dad.
The ending should never, have been like that.

     Tammy Alley

Solitude

There are times when I feel alone,
times when there is no one else to hold.
A distant planet with only me,
dreams and hopes that no one can see.
The sun sets beneath the sky
and fades its purples to the night.
The night is warm and dark.
It comforts me as I confide
and share unknown secrets.
I ask it questions and the stars shine bright
There are no answers but that of life.
A planet exists among us all!

Briana Caldwell

Angel

Could you be an angel sent from above,
sent to earth on a special mission,
to teach me the true meaning of love.

You introduced yourself to me,
for me it was a pleasure.
After talking for hours,
I knew you were truly one of God's treasures.

You were different from all the other's,
you were kind, caring, you were very sweet,
for once I truly felt happy
I finally felt complete.

You held me on a pedestal
as if I were your queen
I of course felt undeserving for
this love like I've never seen.

You were truly sent from God,
for I've never felt like this before
you answered all my prayers
you helped unlock my heart's door.

Could you be an angel, sent from above?

Cindy Tetkoskie

Eagle

An eagle struggles from her nest, her wings reach out in pain
to lift her faded feathered frame to fly on once again.
Her eyes no longer see the ground and every moving thing,
her ears are worn, for time has robbed, and never hear the day.

She stretches out with weary cry and strains to find the wind
where gentle might some stream arise to lift her body free.
But there is nothing left in her, she tumbles from the nest
where once she raised her eager young, felt their warmth beneath.

Down, down the mountain side she slips, too weak now to resist,
and looking up, she sees the sky, her queenly domain, fade.
All her days pass by her eyes, dimming as she falls,
but suddenly she's free again and rising up . . . up . . . up . . .

The pain now gone, the body strong, she sails the morning breeze,
and leaving earth far . . . far below, she rises to the heavens.
A broken mass on mountain lies, blood and feathers strewn.
High above the eagle soars, reaching for the sun.

Helen Maynard

The House Across The Street

In the house across the street
There is the stomp of feet
They pretend it is about money they are fighting
But despite they're acting there is no hiding
The reason that they shout and scream is me
Because I'm the girl who lives in the house across the street

Courtney Barbee

A Silver Palace

Silver puddles glisten from the sun
As tree branches touch it to become one

With a leaf as a finger a limb as an arm,
To shelter the weak from any harm

The wind is a partner, dancing with life
The birds are its chorus and the storm is its wife

The sun is a fire's light in the blue ocean sky
And clouds are its waves splashing silently up high

Falling matter is to decay,
As life begins and ends each day

As upon the soil, as infinite grounds and a rock, a throne
And a forest, a kingdom that still isn't fully grown,

Comes its rulers that have many names,
That creates all, from seas to wide open plains

The mother of the nature and the father of the time
As poets come into this court to capture its very rhyme

Laura Manthey

Depression and Back

I am suffocating, drowning in the blackness.
No way out, I'm trapped in despair.
My hands are bleeding from the struggle;
I've fallen too far, I'm gasping for air.

There is no light at the end of my tunnel.
All light has ceased to exist.
I fear my world is ending.
I can't go on like this.

I don't know why my spirit has died
And cannot be revived,
But it has left, not return.
Just sadness has survived.

I have fallen, but not too far.
Each day I regain ground.
A new beginning has started
Where happiness can be found.

I was a prisoner, caged but fighting,
I would not be defeated.
Life is not worthless, nor am I.
I've won, I have succeeded.

Stephanie Harris

The Upside-Down Monkeys

I saw two monkeys at the zoo,
their tails were like a curly cue.

They'd climb a bar and hang upside down,
and then they'd turn and look around.

They'd eat bananas and throw out the peel,
and then they'd start to laugh and squeal.

They drew a large crowd with their comical acts,
sometimes they looked like acrobats.

Monkeys mimic human beings,
It helps to boost their self-esteem.

They like lots of attention,
and work hard 'til they get it.
Just like people,
they appreciate credit.

If you clap your hands and stay awhile,
Their faces light up,
and then they smile.

A trip to the zoo is a nice day out,
And you get to see what life's all about.

Dolores Butter

Life

The seas of life sometimes over-flow to drown, ropes
attempt to bound, twisting the mind preventing the
race set before us to be run; won.

There are chains attempting to bind and the courts
with the power to confine, riding life's roller coaster
causes one to become stuck in mid-air between
the real and the imaginary, causing one not with
the mind but the hand to reach for a resting place.
This place becomes uncomfortable, crowded, and to be
Left with despair, feeling life isn't very fair.

Dreams are portions taken from daily living with chance
to organize while we're sleeping, then the surge to become
free and real. The portions of one's daily life
materialized in our dreams now to manifest into the real
world, in spite of over-flowing seas, binding/bounding
ropes or chains, even confining courts, just the need to be free.

Success isn't given—taken.

Lee E. Byrd

Love Abides

A virgin peach, which the sunshine ripens.
While the rain fills the empty places.
Growth is slow, but surely will come, with the passing of time.
So to savour every moment of youth, freshness and innocence.
Enjoyment, laughter and sorrow that passes, when love abides inside

In the passing, of fruits untimely damage,
The struggle is yet to begin.
For in a companion, you hope to discover, a closeness love brings

Soon disappointed time after time. For winter continuously comes.
The empty cold soon battles and convinces,
Given way for bitterness to come in.

The foundations of youth has now been shaken.
For without sunshine and rain a peach will surely die.
With every struggle it is over, when love no longer abides.
In the fog, faith is anew for the foundations was not destroyed.

Reaching, clutching, hoping, praying, and yes trusting..
Thru the mist a beam breaks through.
For the one above has paid the price,
The peach has now ripened and love still abides.

Naomi S. Smith

Soul

I stand before you, looking deep in your eyes,
searching for a glimpse of your soul.

It has to be there, waiting for someone like me,
to steal away and hold.

A game of cat and mouse it plays, flitting about,
denying me possession.

And what of my soul, you so unfairly borrowed
without even a hint of discretion?

How easily you took, that which I never gave,
and used in such careless fashion.

Now, I'm jaded and crushed with no hope at all,
of ever fulfilling my passion.

My restless heart aches for what might have been,
had you given yourself to me.

Instead, I clumsily grasp the cold, cruel hand of
what I know to be reality.

Roberta L. Henry

Ode To Love

To My Ed
The day that will always mean so much,
Is when your fingers had that magic touch.
While walking through the yellow pages
And found the number which changed our lives for ages.

That's the day we began our undying love,
Which swept us away on wings of a dove.

And on that day our everlasting friendship was found,
Which will always carry us through life's ups and downs.

I will be by your side all of my life,
Because I am very proud to be your wife.

Sheila P. Deeb

Behind These Doors!

Since early in her youth, she'd often been called a fool
And, some even said she must've never gone to school.
Some made an effort to be polite and kind
But on special occasions, she was often left behind.
She'd been to the funny farm, it's true,
But, so were many others, too.
She knew she wasn't very smart
And, just knowing that, tore her apart.
Why was she so different from the ones, she loved so dear?
And, sometimes she felt as if she didn't belong here.
But, going back behind these doors wouldn't do her any good
Cause all her friends and loved ones would help her if they could.
But, one day her eyes were opened, and she finally saw the light.
She realized to be somebody she might have to put up a fight.
And what relief she felt when all her fears were gone
And she decided that day by day she'd make it on her own.

Kathleen Duos

Magic

Magic of the flooding light
Magic of the sky, magic of the radiant face.
To go on with a thousand masks
And turn back with the face.
Magic of the face aglow
Like a halo of clouds.
To know to float against the light like a bird,
And to know when and how to turn back.
How top survive the brilliant moment?
How not to miss a face in the light?
To tug at the brightness like a sad blanket
To pass alongside the bright-hued graves
And go on forever with a face of light.

Baruch Link

Demonic Angel

Another sense of evil is brewing up inside,
I see the doors to darkness are swinging open wide.
Again the demon greets me, to show me his way,
He shows me to the minds, of those who must pay.
This demon is an angel, but only in the light.
When darkness falls across my soul, he comes to help me fight.
Vengeance, is his duty, to those who kill my hopes.
Vengeance is his law, for the world with which he copes.
When darkness falls and gives way to the light,
This demon becomes an angel, with anticipated delight.
As an angel, his love is true,
Kindness and blessings for all of you.
Basking in the light of the Almighty divine,
Drinking in the love, like the finest of wine.
In this light, that he much admires,
He sees the hopes of my desires.
The demon and the angel are one and the same,
The darkness and the light are what gives him his name.
My life is a whirlwind of his unseen grace,
But when I look in the mirror, I can see his face.

Chris Michael McDaniel

The Girl of My Dreams

The girl of my dreams,
Is the girl of my life.
No matter what life has in store,
Your name will always come to mind.

The girl of my dreams
Is the girl of my heart.
Now the fantasy isn't too far.

No matter how distant,
No matter how far,
You'll always have a special place in my heart.

And now I end by saying good-night.
And you'll always be a special person in my life.

Michael Eitniear

Memories of My Dad

I sit on the bank with deep thoughts of my dear dad,
and a tear rolls down my cheek,
My tears flow more,
and they solemnly land in the creek,
I look at the reflection of the moon
on the creek with care,
It reminds me of my dads
shimmering silver hair,
As I hear the crickets making their sweet harmony,
they seem so near, yet their very far,
The beautiful music that I hear, reminds me so much
of my dad singing and playing his guitar,
The times I spent with my dad were so precious to me,
I loved doing everything with my dad, from camping,
to just talking, as I sat upon his knee,
As the moon glows brighter in the sky far above,
My dad will always be in my heart,
for he is my dad, the dad I'll always love.

Terry L. DeVore

We're Not Dead

If I could count all the shed tears
It would seem like an ocean to me
If my heart were a clear glass window
All the pain and scars you could see

I have questioned the loss of your love
Our parting was so fast final cold
Maybe we'll see each other again some day
Before we get wrinkled and too old

Tears are not welcome in your heights of glory
Cause you care not the heart breaks evermore
The presence of your lust is for many
To approach, tease, taunt, love and adore

May God lead, guide, direct and forgive you
For the pain you put on many others and me
May your heart be filled with much happiness
And you may your life feel untangled and free

Tears are drowned in this Watonga home
But there is no death wreath on my door
Teardrops aren't welcome in your presence
You're used to broken hearts before o'er and o'er

Phala Dooley

Spring Snow

I watch the snow falling, falling,
heaping piles of whiteness everywhere.
Trees bending, branches breaking . . . outages.
The silent visitor picks up speed
Then breaks into little howls of wind
and scatters more snow.

In the morning snow is piled everywhere,
covers everything; then at noontime the sun
turns on its magic splendor
upon a spotless landscape.

Eleanor Murley

Grandma's House

Dedicated to my favorite grandma, Jean Osborne.
Oh, how I love going to Grandma's house,
for she is special to me.
I love how she pushes me up and down
on the swing by the olive tree.

As I walk into her bright yellow house
I feel so loaded with cheer!
It feels so cozy and warm inside,
Just knowing my grandma is near.

She feeds me, bathes me and treats me nice.
She gives me kisses with sugar and spice!

We sing and walk in the garden all day,
and she sets up games so we can play.
Peasants? No, that won't do.
Though all I ask from her is a simple,
"I love you!"

She waves goodbye as she stands by the door,
But I'll be back at Grandma's house,
to see her face once more.

Deena Williams

The Gift

I've already written your pardon in red
So go live again I died for you instead
And all of those things
That brought you such pain
I'll remember no more
Now that you wear my name
I've already written your name in my hand
So go live again I'll help you to stand
I've already written your pardon in red
So go live again I died for you instead
And all of those fears that
Brought all of those tears
I'll wipe them away with joy everyday
I've already written your pardon in red
So go live again I died for you instead
And all of those things
That brought you such pain
I'll remember no more now that you wear my name
I've already written your name in my hand
So go live again I'll help you to stand

Carl Maness

Fading Away

She's lead a full life
She's had some ups and some downs.
Now she's fading away

She grew up on a farm
with oil lamps and wells
She worked from sun up to sun down,
Her brother and sisters as well.

She's been there for me
When I was hurting or laughing
She patted me on the back for a job well done
Or put me in my place when I do wrong
What can you say to bring back something
That's fading away.

I guess you can't.
Just I miss you, love you and
Will see you someday in Heaven.

Helen Kay Brown

Swept Away by Night . . . .

Swept away by night.
Wayward, westward this is our ships destined flight.
Tomorrow by day our journey begins;
Somewhere in time where houses are roofed with tin.
The small town's here seem in some disarray;
Although everything fits in all the right way's.
Cool and alluring these island's seem thin;
Like sheets of white linen swaying in the wind.
They capture your soul time and time again;
Like pirates abound on every rim.
Water's seem sacred abundant with light;
Cleanse my heart penetrate my life.
Rainforest's here are always a delight;
Things are mysterious and never in sight.
Smell the air this is where it begins;
The trail to heaven no one knows where it ends.
Journey's well looked at will last forever;
These island's were given to us as one of God's greatest treasures.
Behold their splendor and their beauty;
To protect them forever, be our duty.

Diane Armstrong

And God Created Adam

From the beginning of conception in his Father's womb.
A flood of information, raining down on him.
Absorbed by his soft, black clay body.
A body forged in heat of not fire, but electricity.
And all consuming light.
Within him and without him.
Omnipotent light laced with probing heat.
Brilliantly white, sinisterly dark, consuming heat.
Extreme, unbearable, peaceful, soothing heat.
Soft, cold touches on the soft, black body. Molding. Shaping.
Steady, exact, unseen hands of an anxious, quivering, unseen artist.
Shaping. Molding. Sculpting into perfection.
One critical element needed. The artist reaches inside Himself.
Pulls out a seed, named Fallibility.
Plants His seed. The seed of the fruit called corruption.
He bakes the clay with His breath of life.
The clay hardens. Slowly the seed grows.
In His image. Perfect

Jerry Don Smith Jr.

If You Were A Bird

Many times you've said, you wish you were a bird.
But where would you go? Or is this question absurd?
Would you fly like an Eagle? Just to soar in the sky?
Or behold God's beauty, from a cliff way up high?
Would you be a hummingbird, flapping so fast,
Pecking each rose 'til you got to the last?

Maybe an owl would suit you just fine
Because you are wise, so observant all the time.
Or a seagull so white, sailing beautifully so bright.
Or maybe a dove, staring down from a steeple,
Seeking a friend as you observe all the people.
Or maybe a hawk, swooping down, fierce as can be
To protect those you love with strength, cry, and plea.

My heart is sincere with this statement so true.
With your own loving wings, to see us, you flew
Thousands of miles. It didn't matter how far.
You were determined to make it just as you are.
And now that you're here we enjoy all of your stay.
We love you Mom. This is what we all want to say.
May God grant you great peace on this Mother's Day.

Emily Galvez

The Message Is I Love You

In your eyes I seem to see, a future that is clear
One that lets in happiness, and throws out all the fears.

Looking at those wondrous eyes, stores joy within my soul.
For in them I see you and I, and the love that is truly whole.

Only this can make me feel, like I'm truly blessed
Just one look at those brown eyes, and I see only the best.
Visions seem to come to me, of what could surely be
A future that is filled with love, that contains both you and me.

Every frame seems perfect, or better than the last
For we enjoy what we have now, and forget about our past.

You see my love that is my wish, to share my life with you
And hope that we can find some joy, in everything we do.

Once we have accomplished this
And our Life here is no more
We will continue loving
When we stand on Heaven's floor.

Until then remember this
For you need no be so clever
Our love is not till death and part
Our love is love forever.

Carlos Ramos

A Little Girl's Guardian Angel

Looking down from Heaven one day
God saw a girl and turned to say
"There's no doubt that this girl is strong
But she'll need help to get along.
The world can be a cruel harsh place
And she'll need help through life's tough race"

"He's there to help her with her math
To help with struggles down life's rough path."
"He's there to buy her food and clothes
He meets her needs, he always knows."

"He'll teach her how to love all things
And if she's patient, the joy it brings."

"He'll show her love so strong and true,
No other love will ever do."

She'll need help there's no doubt
But her Grandad's there to help her out."

"And when it's time for him to go
This will hurt her much I know."

"Oh he's still help with lots of things
Only now, he'll have wings."

Angie Loria

Stephanie

With eyes of green and painted nails
A flowered dress and pig tails
barefoot running over the farm
Stephanie has never done any harm

Although she is only four years old
Stephanie has a little heart of gold
With he arms stretched wide for a hug
At your heart strings she will tug

Like the sun that brighten your day
Stephanie make you laugh in her own funny way
Watching the baby calves being fed
You wonder what is going though her head

One day Stephanie will leave us all
But I know she will always give us a call
When she grows older and there is little time
I know she will let us know she is fine

Debi Moore

My Son

My son, my son
You are who you are:

I know you were brought here, and put on this land
To grow and grow, into a wonderful man!
This takes time and many years,
My tears will flow, in lots of fear:

I know you will make it, and know that you can;
But I won't always be there to hold your hand
You've been taught right from wrong,
Now it's up to you, to hold on strong.

I know life's not easy and has many ups and downs
But don't let your friends mess you around;
So, think about what you do, there are so many who care about you

I know our relationship is from a far,
But, my son; you are who you are!
I can only help if you let me, and tell me what's wrong,

So, my son; when you feel you're falling
You can reach out for me, Gramps or Granny!
This is your Mom, speaking to you straight from my heart . . .

I love you, my son: you are who you are!

Paula Ezell

Modern World?

This is the 90's, some will say
The world is changing every day.

Out with the old—and in with the new—
The time far change is overdue.
But . . . think back to yesterday—
The things that made you smile.
The right to choose, whether wrong or right.
The freedom to enjoy with all your might.
Take that away, and soon . . . you'll see
You'll miss the way it used to be.

Thelma J. Steinback

Love

Love is patient, love is kind,
Envy and fault, it does not find.
True love is priceless, a genuine treasure,
Its depth and value, you cannot measure.
Love is unselfish and understanding,
Always trusts and is undemanding,
Love is not forced or planned in advance,
It comes without warning with only a glance.
Love protects and has no fear,
It gives the heart strength to persevere.
Real love is elusive and happens to few,
I know all this because love brought me you.

Lisa D. Patrick

Think

Close your eye and you will see,
Dreams and visions come to thee.
Follow your thoughts and ride on the groove,
Maintain your focus with every move.

Don't panic when you are losing track
Use your memory to think back,
Mistakes are what we all have seen,
Remember you are a human being.

Patience is what it is all about,
Only stupidity, the reason to scream and shout.
Quite funny how it all makes sense,
Once you have established self-confidence.

Now open your eyes and look around
Make your goals a reality and your life will be sound.

Larry Wein

Rubber Ducky

A child's first toy for his first bath in the sink,
A happy rubber ducky just for fun.
The color so brilliant, of course not pink,
Just as bright and clear as the sun.

Bath time now was much desired,
So much laughter came about.
Little rubber ducky was admired,
You would never see him pout.

But the time came soon,
When the yellow duck grew old.
Instead there was a loon,
Little rubber ducky was sold.

Great memories there were,
Right now he was all by himself.
Their favorite he was sure,
But here he remained on a shelf.

The past is still just the past,
The little toy has to move on once more.
Rubber ducky thought of last,
With the memory of love from before.

Michelle Wright

Untitled

I have watched a beaver be Christ
slapping lakes with his tall.
Salvation and a day.
I have haunted The Halls of Heaven.

I have become the sun-circle,
a phoenix rising from the ashes of night.
slowly, purples, pinks, oranges, reds,
I have haunted The Halls of Heaven.

I have heard the bullfrog chorus
echo love through my throat.
Creaking, raspy-bass, swelling with breathe,
I have haunted The Halls of Heaven.

I have joined the Angel chorus,
singing midnight praises to God.
Peepers, bullfrogs, crickets and I,
I have haunted The Halls of Heaven.

I have put a stop to the world
with tobacco smoke and a piercing hawk-call.
Smoky spirit on the wind and voice,
I have haunted The Halls of Heaven.

T. J. Miller

Music

Music is my life
I wonder sometimes will I go far
I play the flute sometime called a fife
Or will I just get stuck in tar

Music, music, is all I care to have
I wonder sometimes will I go far
Or will I just stay home all day and wonder
What will happen next

Is music the way to go
Or maybe I should just wait a while
Or maybe I should go on
To see what will happen

And maybe I will and maybe I won't
I guess I'll just have to wait and see.
The answer is there
What do you think?

Katie McClellan

My Father

He entered my heart willingly,
when it was in need.
My father heard the weeping of my heart
and sheltered it with his majestic kind of love.

My father began touching my heart
but now he holds it.
My father has been the flowers in my garden,
the sand on my beaches,
and remains the love in my heart.

My father is my believer,
and I am his admirer.

Jamie Patterson

Pathways

There is a little pathway between your heart and mine;
Filled with love's sweet memories, that will not fade with time.
The memories grow sweeter as the years go slowly by;
And though I know it's over I never will know why.
If I could take this pathway and find my way to you,
Would you meet me on the pathway and make my dreams come true?
Would you let the memories take us back to the early years,
Or would this little pathway only bring more tears?
There is a little pathway between your heart and mine
And it will always be there until the end of time.

Millie Wilson

What Is Love?

My meaning of love is quiet and at ease,
For I believe love is something that people should cherish and see.
Love is taking the time to listen to each other,
To show gentleness and passion within one another.
I believe love is holding each other tight,
To be understanding within a fight.
Love should be guided through our hearts,
As if an angel struck us with the love of her dart.
I believe love is something that shouldn't be taken for granted,
Something that shouldn't be forgotten and abandoned.
Love conquers all, each and everyone, those big and small.
I know that it's hard to express feelings of emotions.
But when we're together love becomes a potion.
I believe love is being yourself
and not hiding within a shell,
Telling the truth and not being put through hell.
I believe love is always knowing what to do.
To always express the words "I love you."

Suzanna M. Pearson

Freedom

You were the vine, I was the tree.
I was steadfast, you circled me.
You used my trunk, lunged for the sky
you sapped my strength, and passed me by.

Another tree, another view
long down the lane, attracted you.
I felt bereft, asked you to stay.
You clambered down, and slunk away.

Your shadow gone, my branches grew.
Light shed on me; you'd blocked my view!
I saw the world, I breathed the air,
grew tall and strong without a care.

You saw the change, my leaves of green,
tried to return where you had been.
The workers came; they nurtured me.
I sheltered them. They cut me free.

Now you are gone, and I am me.

Julia Foca Ceravolo

A Memory Passed Away

A beautiful memory that you once have with a friend
just disappeared in the thick air as if forgetting a dear
person who just passed away, a very dear person to you
because you love that person very much and
when he/she dies unexpectedly without you knowing it,
all of a sudden the person that you love turn into a hatred,
asking God why He suddenly get the person that you love.
But that's what happen to us, our life's come from God
and in the end God will get what He had given to mankind.

Alicia A. Aguinaldo

Marriage

Marriage is another word for matrimony,
A couple making vows to one another,
Vows that they will carry out
During their lifetime together.
It is the union, of a man and a woman.
The union, although physical, is spiritual as well.
There are times filled with ups and downs, joys and sorrows.
It is working toward mutual gains and accomplishments.
Marriage changes like the times,
But the changes should be for the better.

Mari Anne McKinnie

The Mist and the Moon

The mist rises out of nowhere,
a Ghost from the Grave?
Creeping upon the land, covering it without warning.
Revenge! His heart aches for the one he truly loves,
but the one he is forbidden to touch,
He tries to reach her, but he fails.
Every night he waits for her, his Goddess in the sky.

She rises only at night, she is the moon!
She sits on her throne of endless Black.
Her Jewels are but the stars scattered in Heaven's domain.
She does not linger after revenge,
yet she only cries the rain, she sees him.
Her heat breaking a little more.
She longs for him to be by her side.
She speaks softly with her beams of light!

They say "goodbye" in the early morning light.
And they disappear like a Dream disappears as you wake!

Melissa L. Pennington

Reflection

Today the sun was shinning
But I did not appreciate.
It's just another day I thought
On the calendar, another date.

As the day went on,
I was too blind to see
The sky, the ocean, nature's beauty
And all of God's blessing flowing over me.

I missed the sound of the children laughing
Not even a nice music I wanted to hear
I was so involved with my own depression
I started wondering if God was near.

As I continued along with my life journey,
I saw situations that I couldn't stand.
It was then that I realized how blessed I was
To have my life in God's hand.

If I can give someone advice
If I can share with someone a word or two
I would say, "Enjoy life and don't be so blind,
Don't take for granted God's love for you."

Jane Elisabeth Clark

Alone Except One Other

There are those who always look for love
But seldom do they find
Another who will love them back
And that is why they cry

They know they have so much to give
But no one to receive
The feelings they hold deep inside
And that is why they grieve

They want so much to have someone
That they can call their own
Someone to hold when times are tough
But they are all alone

And so they go on searching
For the true love of their life
They go through all the heartaches
The struggles and the strife

But every now and then we find
That somehow one succeeds
They find the love they're looking for
The love that we all need.

Corey Hendricks

Am I Special

Dedicated to Nicole Marie Jennings
Am I special, you bet I am
I arrived on this earth one of God's little lambs.
He gave me life, he gave me pride
So don't even think you can kick me aside.

I'll fight for my rights, but never abuse
Showing love and forgiveness you can't refuse.
You may have been taught bi-racial is wrong
If you search your heart we can build a bond.

No matter what color you were born
Black or white, yellow or bronze.
It's what's inside your heart and mind
To give your best to all mankind.

Give me a chance and you will see
That I am special and it came from Thee.
He gave me a place here on earth
To show the world just what I'm worth.

Am I special, you bet I am.

Mary Urton

God Said It's Now Or Never.

I was livin' my life, as if I was in control, the drugs was
what made me feel right
Only cryin' to God, when times got so bad, when I dug myself
in a hole, and couldn't get out!
God please, can you help me! I promise I will do better
if you help me, outta this mess
Known', when he did, I was back to what I was doing
My life was going up in smoke, the devil was about to
serve me his deadly blow, with the wave of his hand
God came to me ! my son, you are again comin' to me,
Please, please! help me!
I don't know if I want to help you, you said you will come to me
God said, it's now or never.
Come unto me, give me your heart, soul, let me
have control of your life
All the things that brought me to this point, I cried,
Oh, how I cried; God said, it's now or never; It's now!

Dwain F. A. Morrison

Relative Sadness

I might have seen you yesterday
in the midst of a foggy crowd.
I might have seen you, because you look like every stranger
that passes before my eyes.

We might have the same color hair, "mom",
"Dad", we may have the same color eyes.
I guess I'll never know.
I wouldn't know your face
if it were in front of my eyes.
I wouldn't know your touch
if you bumped into my empty body.

I might have seen you yesterday
swimming above the clouds,
I might have seen you.
coming down the tree.
I might have seen you yesterday
flying in my dreams.
I might have seen you.

Kathleen Pydynkowski

My True Love

Her eyes are bright. Her smile is so sweet.
My heart fills with joy every time that we meet
When I look at her lovely face, I know
That I will never give her up or let her go.
Reminiscing about the first time that we met
A memorable experience, I will never forget.
We looked at each other with such a surprise
Like a secret package coming out of disguise
As we started to get close, she was whisked away
Only to return to me in a better way.
From that day on my heart has been filled with love
And I give my "thanks " to the Lord above
A gift so precious, he has given to me.
A beautiful baby girl for the world to see.
As I look into her eyes that I will cherish forever
Nothing can be so sweeter, than the two of us together.

Jodie Thomas

For Want of a Name

For want of a name let's call him John Doe,
He is one of those boys that cannot say no.
When entering a barroom a smile would appear
As he would tell the bartender, "Give me a beer."

This day no exception with a bunch of refills
He was feeling his oats, actually soused to the gills.
He staggered a bit as he aimed toward the door,
Then turned to the boys, "Tomorrow 'bout four?"

He was making up time down a back road he knew
When he saw the taillights of a car come in view.
While in the process of passing he came to a rise
Saw the headlights too late through liquor blurred eyes.

The crash that ensued was never quite clear
His brain was too numb from the tankards of beer.
Thrown from the car with nothing but bruises
He walked toward his victim with mumbled excuses.

From where the drunk stood he saw the brown hair
And the ashen white face, the blank vacant stare.
Recognition then name, bloodshot eyes with tears filled
As he cried, "Oh my God, that's my daughter I've killed."

Anton F. Weidemann

Sunshine

If I could pour the sunshine
I know exactly where it would be.
I'd pour it over two close friends
Such as you and me.

If I could pour the sunshine
I'd pour it from on high
And watch it closely as its beams
Embrace two friends, you and I.

If I could pour the sunshine
Your heart I'd hope it would capture
And turn to me with open arms
To fill its empty rapture.

If I could pour the sunshine
On you light would always be
And where the light shines brightly
I would dream it would capture me.

If I could pour the sunshine
Happiness would never have to end.
For under a radiant beam of light
You and I would forever be walking hand in hand.

Ronda J. Watkins

April Things

Since last April, much has grown, as
April things so aptly blossom,
Grown from spring which brought forth days of
Mellow breeze and lilac fragrance:

Laughter which rings new and fresh, and
Oh, for once it comes sincerely,
Lips that whisper just for me the
Words my heart has longed for hearing—
Arms of love (they come in spring,
I've heard), which hold me warm and close—
You, who raised me high on wings of
Angels over troubled seasons—
Angel wings, they carried me through
Winter's chill and stormy trials
Safely to another April,
Once again amidst your garden . . .

April things! Your laugh, your lips, your
Arms and wings which bring the sun's mirth!
Spring is born within my soul, in
April's rest a spirit's rebirth.

Cynthia Wallace Paxton

Lost In Love

In all the wanderings of my life,
I've found no one like you.
And until you came along,
I was always sad and blue.
You fill my heart with joy,
And make my life worth living.
You overwhelm my mind and soul,
With your love and giving.
And when I am depressed,
You lighten up my life.
You fill me up with gladness,
And I forget my strife.
Now you've gone and done it,
You went and stole my heart.
And if you ever leave me, I'll surely fall apart.
'Cause now I really love you, you're everything to me.
I need you here by my side, forever faithfully.
I'll love you 'till the day I die, as long as time goes on.
I'll always want to hold you, and say that you're my own.

Les Clippard

The Sanctuary

You are too strong sometimes
And hide away your heart behind a wall
Where it cannot be reached by love and broken
The hiding place is safe, and does not fall

And keep every thought, emotion, and feeling inside
Words are left unspoken; which ears are waiting to hear
But it keeps you safe; from your own pride

And hold on to the loneliness ever so tight
Holding desires back there where it is safe
You know of no time to give them that is right

And you walk away from me, yet you stumble to your knees
I know how to reach your hiding place, and your heart
You know my love will not hurt you, it will set you free

And, I am alone again and wanting you near
But, your wall has been replaced by another
Keeping you apart from me, and all that you fear

And I will leave you to your own place and time
But, know it in your heart that I am waiting
For the time when your heart changes your mind

You are too strong sometimes

Sherry Calvert

Listen

We are all free spirits soaring and low; some with aggression,
others more subtly so—Seeking pureness within our souls:
looking for the great divine to soothe away our woes of time—

Casual friends may come and go, good ones are all around;
however, authentic friends are seldom found—
"We must learn to listen to the sounds,
we must learn to listen to the sounds all around

We are all beings of mankind, some of us are proud;
others act like cowards, we all need pride in our lives
and within ourselves—We must choose a lifestyle
to reflect our true inner-selves, and to come full circle
of our own self-worth.
"We must learn to listen to the sounds,
we must learn to listen to the sounds all around—

Yesterday can be put away to reminisce,
tomorrow is another day for potential
and sweet blissfulness; today can be
what we make it to be, it is our GOD-given gift

Sandra L. Bruce

Passages of Time

Sometimes there is nothing to say
But I still manage to have my way
I don't seek attention, or find much given
Still I think life is worth the livin'
I find others pressing for the mark
By taking shots in the dark
A lot passes by me, including the occasional near miss
Yet we are all striving to find self bliss
While Gurus and Prophets are leading the masses
I'd just as soon polish my glasses
Shining them up to see reality
Seeing some comedy, seeing some calamity
This world is changing, I think it's affecting our youth
Like creating a new telephone and everyone jammed into a booth
I'd like to say I've seen a lot, as if I were life's tutor
But it's nice to know I've yet to see what's to learn in the future.

Daniel R. Page

Not Anymore

Whenever I would say to you
"Darling, I have something
I want to tell you"
"Not now" you would say
"Tell it to me some other time."
And so, disheartened, I would silently walk away.

"Darling—do you know
what happened to me today?
It's really very funny!"
"Oh what is it?"—"Not now," you would say.
And so, disheartened I silently turned away.

"Darling—I want to show you what I bought today."
"I have no time—not now,"
you would say.
Again, disheartened I walked silently away.

"Darling, why is it you never have time for me?
What about our vacation to Florida, or our trip to Italy?"
"But we have lots of time," you would say.
"Not now! We'll talk about it another day."
But the pages of the "Volume of Tomorrows" became so very few . . .

Nicolina Pileggi

Tears Why Do I Cry?

I cry because I am happy
I cry because I am sad
I cry because I'm in pain
I cry because I am lonely
I cry because I am hurt
I cry because I am alone
I cry because I love
I cry for the world I cry for you, I cry for me
I cry when I remember how things used to be
I cry for what I had
I cry for what I've lost
I cry for what I thought I had
I cry for what I want to have
I cry because I've been misled
I cry because I'm disappointed I cry because I am in love
I cry because that's all I can do I cry because I need to
I cry for those who no longer have tears to shed
I cry for those who do not know that it's okay to cry
I cry in order to heal but most of all
I Cry Because Tears Make Me Feel Better!

Cecile Accilien

My Children: I Can't Carry You Now

You are now grown-ups and well
Responsible for every step you do
Kind nature lets you feel
That help is in every place you go.

I can't carry you anymore
Your weights have exceeded mine
I could not walk you about like before
Your strides put me behind the line.

When you're small and cried so loud
I lifted you cautiously and quickly,
Your life reached up to the cloud
That comforted you endlessly.

When you were on my shoulder
Footprints were deeper and a bit rough
Imprints now are virtually clear,
More in number and fairly tough.

As I scan the clean pages of time
I can see your dreams with brighter chance
Though I can't carry you now, aim is divine
Keep your faith, love it and enhance.

Policarpio F. Ferrera

Colorblind

The world would be so sublime
If everyone was colorblind

If we were oblivious to race, creed or color
Maybe then we could learn to love one another

Separation and hatred are destined to begin
When a person is judged by the color of their skin

But who are we to judge anyway
For there will be only one judge on judgement day

When that day comes and judgement begins
We will not be judged by the color of our skin

The hereafter must be so sublime
Because God Is Colorblind

Barbara J. Turner

Forgiveness

Forgiveness is a broken dream, which hides itself
within the corner of the mind, "often called forgetting,"
so that it will not bring pain to the dreamer.

Forgiveness is the mother who remains at your side,
when ones burden puts shame upon her.

Forgiveness is the aunt who never forgets you,
even in your days of despair.

Forgiveness is the flower or tree which still stands
up straight with its leaves when mother nature is mighty.

Forgiveness is the cousin who never throws it back at you,
even though she told you so beforehand.

Forgiveness is our Father in Heaven who will not leave
our heart and soul, after all we've done wrong

Laverne L. Wissinger

Paradise July

Fireflies dance
Rise mingle
In the heavy, clover-scented air of a simple summer evening.

Celestial twinkling, earthbound constellations
Blaze, then dim
A hundred flickering oil lamps
Ascend from the quilted landscape
Frolicking above sheafs of wheat,
Skillfully arranged.
Haphazard cascades of
Living torches
Nature's fantasia
Light the way amongst endless rows of corn.

Fireflies dance
Swirling Chasing Urgently
Playful in a fleeting season.
Final flights of fancy
As the grey-green cushion
Enfolds the last light
In the sable skies of dusk.

Janet E. Arnold

New Day, Pure and Wonderful

Delightful, the daylight dapples
New dawn fresh with wonder.
Another day wakes from its rest,
Still young in dream's hope not yet shattered.

Hours still open and waiting with challenge
Time's log yet ready to fill.
Oh, to return the day in its same glorious way,
Well-used, not abused, as it came gifted to us.

Linda Cunningham

Dagger

Every time you lie to me
Every time I catch you in deceit
You look at me and smile at me
And let a tear run down your cheek

You tell me that you're sorry
That it'll never happen again
Each time I take these lines you feed me
Though I know that they are poisoned

Each time I take you in my arms
And tell you not to cry
I know that you are waiting
To tell you your next lie

Even though I know all this
And I know that you won't change
I'll take you back with your poisoned lines
Despite that dagger in your eyes

Donald G. Lipps

What God Allows

God allows things to happen,
Sometimes I think they are rough.
If I can't find the good of it,
I'm not looking to God enough!

Each trial, each sorrow or set-back,
That happens to one of God's own,
Brings much comfort, many blessings.
For with God, I am never alone.

So when some days I feel depressed,
Wondering, why, oh, why can this be!
Has God truly turned His back,
Allowing this too happen to me!

Then I must remember God's love,
And that what ever happens, God knows;
I must always praise God, and be thankful.
For the mercy and love that God shows!

When things happen that makes me doubt,
And makes God seem far away, unreal;
Then I remember I belong to God.
Because of His love, not how I Feel!

Ruth Wise

The Weddding

So near in thought . . . but far in time
It seems like only yesterday
I prayed God one child . . . and was blessed
With a son . . . my Mingo Ray.

Now I sense this is not just another friend
This girl you've brought into our life,
But possibly your soul-mate,
The woman you'll ask to be your wife.

I wish you health and happiness
And I'm touched you found true love
I wish your union trust and longevity,
With the blessings from your father above.

I pray you perseverance, and strength to endure.
For although I know now it all seems like fun,
Your trails and lessons in life have just begun.

Christine, I give to you my man-child,
With a prayer that you'll never part.
Please love him, Grow with him, Stand beside him,
For you now have my heart!

Deb Schneider

Barbed Wire Box

Trapped inside,
Tearing and ripping to abide.
Laced with barbed wire so sharp, almost fake
Cuts through flesh like butter to ones in escape.

People stare, counterfeit humans stare,
Prototype people don't care to beware
They don't understand your tampered mind,
Beasts are outside, different creatures of a kind.

Nowhere to run, nowhere to hide
Split personalities soon to collide,
You run your mistakes through again and again,
But no one can escape these treacherous pens

Ashley Simko

Angels

Big and tall working for me
Sitting, waiting just to see

Where I will send them one by one
On a mission to be done

Hearkening swiftly unto my voice
God-given power by His choice

One—two—maybe three
Read King James and you will see

A legion is what you behold
[that's 12,000 I am told]

Angels, angels await your call
They keep us safe even when we fall

I send them out before I go
to ward off things I do not know

Angels are spirits that soar and fight
In the day and through the night

Mounted with wings they are prepared
Formally trained to give us care

So there is no place that I can be . . . When an Angel
of God is not watching over me.

Carla Mebane

Untitled

In a miniature treehouse
I sit by the window
trying to catch wisps of smoke in my hand
from cigarettes long forgotten
nostalgia throbbing at my temples
caught in a labyrinth of synapses
where all I can do is search—endlessly
for a destination never reached
always close but never
never reached
and all I can do is search
blindly until frustration conquers
and I stare blankly at bad graffiti
and the smell of mildew and urine
penetrates my nostrils
and no one answers my desperate call
my hopeless plea for companionship
long forgotten
mingles with smoke from a cigarette
that I try to catch in my hand

Patrick Drury

The Leaf

A small branch snaps on an old oak tree,
setting brown and red leaves free.
They twist and swirl and spin in flight,
as if small colored ships on a stormy night.

On a sea of wind,
these small ships flew,
red and brown and orange in hue.
One small red leaf landed on the street,
another; orange, at an old man's feet.

Soon only one small leaf was left,
and in my hand it came to rest.
One small brown leaf,
all alone,
So very far from home.

Jon Michael L. Lang

I'll Be Seeing You

Leisurely, I am strolling down the boulevard;
Today, the traffic does not bother me.

The seagulls appear a bit more graceful,
And I can taste salt in the air.

The throngs of tourists flocking to side-shops,
Picking out their memories, holds my interest.

Brightly colored bikinis, piles of wind-blown hair;
Tanned, toned, bodies releasing coconut oil into air.

Knowing my time in paradise is limited . . .
Obtaining as many pleasure as I can is my goal.

This is what I have waited for, all year long,
To feel the sun upon my face, and hear the ocean's song . . .

I will not waste this opportunity; nor my obligation
To do nothing, yet everything, which is to be my vacation.

Todd Rousseau

The Red Man's Doom

When our country was one vast plain
And the Indians hunted its forest for game.
They planted their corn by the river side
And made their homes from the buffalo hides.
It must have been beautiful and serene
With the forest so fresh and the fields so green.
The fish in the brooks and the birds in the air
If there was a paradise, it must have been there.
Then came the white man from over the sea
They were looking for India and thought this was she.
So they anchored their ships and began to land
And got their first glimpse of the native red man.
They were made welcome and invited to stay
And the red man's doom was sealed that day.
They accepted their food, their shelter and drink
But the way they repaid them. It grieves me to think.

Alma Wetona Brown

Merry Christmas!

A brilliant star, all through the night,
To Bethlehem shone the way,
Where in a manger, smiling bright,
The beautiful Christ child lay.
Since he was born, we celebrate
The holy Christmas feast.
We honor Him and contemplate
The many blessings we've received.
To one and all, this time of year
Is wished much joy, and all the best.
A blessed Christmas with loved ones near,
And holidays filled with happiness!

Helga B. Hiott

A Birthday Wish

This wish is sent along its way
in hopes of brightening up your special day.
Another year has come to past;
and here's hoping it is a really big blast.

Celebrate your day, go out and have some real fun.
Try to make this the very best one.
Indulge yourself, have a little spree . . .
Be the best party animal you can be.

And when you are finished
When the partying is all done;
Remember, my friend . . .
Next year you can have another one!

Irene Kent

Dad

You gave the love I share today. It's hard to see
you fade away. You caught the stars I needed most.
But now I see you as a ghost. I know you watch
beneath the clouds. I try to catch the one you're on.
But the ones I've caught you're still not there.
I miss you Dad and love you so.
You taught me things like I taught you. I know
a lot because of you. Things I do I would not
know without the love you'd always show.
I miss you Dad and love you so.
You brought the moon. You brought the stars.
Never I could show the same. I will once
when I am old, I'll teach a child what I
was told. But 'til that day that I do so,
I miss you Dad and love you so.
With the morning you will rise and all the stars
will fade away. You shall lie and we shall pray.
I miss you Dad and love you in every way.

Kristy Lee Koobation

The Season's Change

Nothing's like it used to be,
the grass is no longer green.
The trees are bare without their leaves,
and summer is just a dream.
I wish that there was sunlight,
for all of us to see.
I wish there was an answer,
to why nothing's like it used to be.
Why is there no splashing of water in the pools?
Why are there no noises of summer's happy fools?
Nothing's like it used to be,
everything has changed.
I wish I could go back to yesterday,
and feel the sun's warm rays.

Nicole D'Agostino

My Child

Take your first breath as you lie upon my arm.
Believe that nothing can do you harm.
Whimper and fuss upon my chest.
Never speak, I'll do the rest.
I will rock you to slumber in my lap.
I will feel your heart going tap.
Give you love and room to grow.
Watch with wonder at the seeds we sow.
Through the years I'll learn to let go.
I'll hope I taught you all to know.
My boy once so small,
Now you are so big and tall.
I hope I did all I can,
To help my boy become a man.
You are my love, my life, my child.

Peggy Breeding

Darkness

Deep velvety inky blackness
A sheer joy to behold; the joy of
Inane laughter and tears and fear.

Grasp it to thyself if you can.
Stumble here and there; 'tis difficult perception,
A small quarter your lot.

Traumas are few within this comfort zone.
Muffled by despair, pain, intricacies,
Yes . . . but

Strictures gone abated to nothingness.
See with humble tears wisdom that fulfills
Your being, always great gladness.

Heaving blackness; grasp pervasive knowing,
Belonging, worthy, competent joy.
Permit darkness fall away.

John W. Ghumm Jr

Games

As a child, I enjoyed games.
Games were meant to be fun,
The challenge of winning, of besting your opponent;
Oh, the sheer joy of winning.

You didn't win all the time,
But it was the thrill of competition,
The excitement of outsmarting your foe;
These were your reasons for playing,
And most importantly, even when you lost,
You never got hurt!

But now some games are deadly.
Your heart and emotions are badly damaged.
How do you tell someone love is too important
To be toyed or played with?

Winning isn't so important anymore, either,
Especially, when you would like nothing better
Than not to participate.
So, please, listen carefully,
"Stop playing games!"

Darla Latrice

Home

Home is where I long to be
Home beside the deep blue sea
The rippling waves, the sweet smelling air
Home is something I cannot bear

Sina Tu'u

Flight of the Angels

Soft and weightless breezing right by,
not all of us see the angels fly.

A knowing exists that's deep in the heart
for every soul to make a fresh start.

To search for the love that's always around
to lift up our spirits off of the ground.

The knowledge is there, it's ours for the taking,
to help guide us through each decision we're making.

Through life's ups and downs we'll remain standing tall
if we listen intently to the angels' call.

Guiding us like a driving force within,
they know what we need and where we've been.

So when in need, just look to the sky
and with your soul see the angels fly.

Linda Carfagno

Home Street Home

Does anyone remember, does anyone care
About the hopeless, pitiable wretches
Who call the streets their home

We pass over their forms
Lying on the streets
We step around their figures
Begging for some change

We justify our actions
We allocate the blame
It is all their fault
They have caused this pain

For some this may be true
Addictions have brought many down
But for many more this is not so
The hidden demon within is to blame

Distracted by the madness
All reason, all sense is gone
Delusions fill their heads
Destroying the souls, shattering the minds
Of the pitiable wretches who call the streets home

Patricia Anne Di Noia

Untitled

In our longing to understand
life we may come upon many a conclusion.
Not a one is the same for every person.
We need only enjoy life
and in our efforts be prosperous.
In enduring its hardship and trials
let not what you have be taken for granted,
for just as it was granted,
it shall someday be taken away.
The simple things are the finer things,
a chance to run, a sweet kiss, a good friend,
or a cool summers breeze.
Things we don't realize
are the things we could be unfortunate to miss.
With these words I shall leave you
to perhaps ponder this blessing called life.

Jared Welfl

Red

I am the hope that is needed here,
in this world of ruin that is full of flame,
although I am the flame that burns,
For I am Red.

People call out, needing help and dying,
I rush in, but I cannot interfere,
although I am the blood they run,
For I am Red.

I warn others of arriving danger, and they run,
they keep their lives, while others die,
although they keep their lives, they feel for the deaths,
For I am Red.

Why I am hated, I'll never know,
I start the fire that keeps them warm,
although it's their fault they die of flame,
For I am Red.

I have saved this world many times,
and I'll do it again, so help me God,
although I am abused without respect,
For I am, and never shall be, Red.

Danny Stark

Hobo Was His Name

I was out walking one foggy night.
When I came across a hoboes' site.
They said, "Please sit down and talk to us.
But, watch that Gus; he's a mean old cuss."
One started to talk and said, "See that puppy over there?
He gets into some pretty bad fights and, loses his hair."
He asked me if I would please take him home,
For it's for sure we can't even afford a bone.
I took him home that very night.
He stayed out until the morning light.
He crawled in and what a sight,
For he had been into another fight.
"Hobo what I'm I going to do with you?
If you don't behave you and I are through.
You didn't have a place to go, you know?
That's how you happened to get your name Hobo."
He looked at me with those big sad eyes.
As if to say, "I'll try; just don't cry."
He was so happy when I picked him up and gave him a big hug.
Now Hobo knows what it's like to have someone with a special love.

Sandra E. McNeely

Harriet

One dark summer night, while the north star was shining bright,
The moon shined down, and let Harriet Tubman see the whole town.
Everyone told her to wait, even the guy at the gate
Harriet had to get away.
No matter who or what was in her way.
Harriet went to the slaves
Even the ones who worked at the graves.
Some of them had their doubts,
But Harriet would not let them pout.
Harriet took them to the border.
Even the ones who would not take her orders,
Harriet told them, "Even you have the right
to be treated as a white."
She lead them to freedom
So that no one else could beat them.
She would return back
To her slave owner, Jack.
Her name means honor and pride,
So that no one else would have to hide.
Do You Have Pride?

Carin Marie Lockhart

Crucifixion

The words below tell a miraculous story
of a victory not lost but won
Where a once hopeless city received a miracle
And when God sacrificed his only Son.

The crowd shouted their cheers like puppets
A sentences of death they gave him
They carried him off like the common criminal
And was flogged from limb to limb.

The women wept tears of death
A sponge dipped in vinegar he was fed
His whole body writhed with pain
A crimson-stained robe the lot ripped to shreds.

He risked separating from God
A life-giving sacrifice he made
All of their sins were forgiven
And now all of their debts were paid.

His life gave hope to all humankind
An atonement for our sins he did pursue
Took one last look at heaven and said
"Forgive them, Father, for they know not what they do."

Michelle Beaulieu

Fireworks

It all started on the Fourth of July
You were wild and I was shy
Then a friend fixed us up together
And since then I felt like I could love you forever
A friend of yours asked to dance with me
And I noticed that you didn't like what you had to see
So when you asked me to dance
I knew it was my one and only chance
So I said yes and added a smile on your face
And then you placed your hands on my skirt made of satin and lace
I felt a tingle run through my heart
And I hated the thought of having to part
After the dance we sat on the swings
And listened to the glorious fireworks as they would ring
When you said good night to me
I kept you in my mind all through the night and in my sleep
What I felt for you was nothing but true
And now my heart is waiting for you to say "I love you."

Brittany Kinneer

Dreams

Dreams can make or break most great ideals
They can make us realize what is fiction or real
Dreams can bring two people close in heart
When in real life they may be worlds apart
When things start looking really bad
A simple dream can make us glad
Dreams of a moon lit walk on a beach
Seem to be brought into our reach
Just one thing to keep in mind
When bad news strikes you from behind
When you are awaken from a bad nightmare
Just close your eyes and I'll be there
To share in the pain and your fright
I'll help you make it through the darkest night
No matter how bad or alone life seems
I am always as close as a simple little dream

David Taylor

If

If the world could share together, how great our lives would be
No longer filled with evil, every soul would be set free

If everyone could share their happiness from deep within
Such goodness would become outstanding, no longer with deep sin

If everyone shared their life and radiated goodness all together
The world would be like sunshine, no matter what the weather

If everyone united and helped with one another
Perhaps just shaking hands and calling you my brother

If, together we united with goodness deep inside
This life would be so wonderful, violence would subside

If everyone prayed for this, just for once a day
The world would soon enlighten, everything'd be ok

If only we had faith, our inner goodness we could spread
No longer filled with sadness, no tears we'd have to shed

If each day on this earth, our true purpose we fulfilled
The Lord would be so happy looking down from his grand seat
Elated with contentment, his glory quite complete

Lorraine Haskell

You

My bags are packed and I'm about to go
You said you needed time to be alone
But just incase you have a change of mind
Here's my number where I'll be tonight
You know it's hard for me to understand
But I'm going to try and be an understanding girl
I'm hoping you will have a change of heart
Cause without you I'm going to fall apart.
I don't want to be lonely
I don't want to see a day without you
I'll give you anything you want
I don't want to lose you
Cause I love you so much.
With every inch, every part
With every little bit of my heart

Sylvia Mari Escobedo

Dreams

As night falls and I lie in bed,
Wonderful visions run through my head.

Of fighting a dragon and being a knight,
Saving a damsel out of its bite.

I could fly like a bird up in the sky,
Or be lying on the ground, looking up high.

I could even swim in the deep blue sea,
Or live in the jungle peaceful as can be.

And after I wake up from the visions I see,
I think to myself, "What will tomorrow night bring?"

Dreams are so special like most things are,
And can even be better than wishing on a star.

Jerisa Ropelato

Fade Away

Paint peels like skin, waves crash like bones;
Your body is a jungle and I'm the fire;
Drive across your head on a highway;
Sun burns your eyes, fog clouds your head;
Walking across the bridge to nowhere;
Wind blows your nose, snow blankets your soul;
Hail pounds your ears, rain washes your face;
Thunder drives your heart, sleet blinds your veins;
Hair pulls roots, wrinkles divide your tissue;
Blood heals, tears hurt, sweat goes nowhere;
Running up the stairs to somewhere;
Life fades away, pain lives on.

Jacob Patrick Gonyea

Flame and Fire

Now, in the small, secretive hours of a dark new morn
I consult with my dilemma of purity torn;
While my weakness of body leaves me forlorn.

For just last night with temptation I slept
And through throws of passion I secretly wept;
To be giving something sacred I had always kept.

In a coffin of flesh I yield up my soul
To be damned unto hell which has now stole;
My will and my self and my Heavenly goal.

Having accepted the dangerous dare of my desire
I fell into flame and I fell into fire;
Now I must live a faithless life wholly dire.

Chamron Hunsley

Moving On

She was full of nothingness, void of color,
Her energy she expounded was solar.
as my eyes traveled outside to inside,
I was perplexed by her inner beauty.
Her bleak first impression fashioned a lie,
That may show her as moderately moody.
Her feminism shows through her forepart,
It glows as a vibrant magenta,
Growing a searing fire within her heart.
Her foundation ran with an agenda.
Her lucid endowment of indigo,
Sparkled with an immense intensity.
I see her age, and she will fall as snow.
I abandon her and look towards the city.

Machelle L. Marin

Racism

What is racism? It happens everyday
In many different ways.
People discriminating one another,
Just because of color.
Why are we this way
Each and every day?
Treating people of one color
Different from another.
Why can't we look inside?
They could be very kind.
I wish I could go back in a time machine.
And wipe the slate of racism clean.
It might have come back?
It might have stayed away?
If it would have stayed away,
Just think how much better the world would be today.
I know it may be just a dream,
But you never know.
Martin Luther King Jr. had a dream too.
Maybe mine will come true.

David Shaffer, Jr.

Two Angels for this Year

Say, have you heard the latest flash?
The Fishburne's are 'spectin' again!
You know the darlin' bunch I mean
Mom, dad and little Ben!

They stormed the gates of heaven
And here is what they planned:
A "babe" in '97
To hold young Benjamin's hand!

"Well, since you've prayed so very hard"
The Lord said "Never fear"
I'll send another cherubim
"Two angels for this year!"

Mary C. Sperrazzo

Rape—No Justice

The most beautiful act in the world is the creation of a child.
The way it is done should be both tender and mild.
But when a senseless person gets it into his head,
To have sex with someone until she's hurt or left for dead;
Knowing that he is not wanted—not now—not ever.
Refusing her no because he says she means yes; but knowing better.
That is when justice can never be swift or painful enough.
While he got what he wanted when he wanted it . . . rough.
If it were for me, the man would not live.
And no sympathy in my heart would I give.
I don't believe in any kind of murder;
But I also don't believe in the rape of a girl.

Jamie Richardson

Little Beacons of Light

Fireflies in the night skies,
The twinkle and sparkle in a child's eyes.
Fireflies in the grass,
Raindrops shimmering on the glass.
Fireflies in the fields at night.
Shine like stars in heavens light.
Fireflies on the 4th of July
Fireworks dancing high in the sky.
Fireflies little golden glow,
Glimmering sunshine through God's rainbow.

Pearl L. Saville

Morning Sound

My peaceful dreams danced all around
But were soon interrupted by the morning sound
I just lay there still and quiet
And listened to Mom's kitchen riot

The bacon shouted sizzle pop
The eggs just hissed and wouldn't stop
The plates rattled, the toaster clang
The dog barked, and our phone rang

The tea kettle's whistle started to blow
Mom was running to and fro
The floor was squealing and squeaking like crazy
I should have offered a hand, but I was too lazy

After the noise died down a mite
I went to the kitchen to get me a bite
The food was all great, as I soon found
Oh how I love the morning sound

Shannon M. Smith

The Grocery Store Blues

It's pay day, the day I dread,
No wonder I have a pain in my head.
With a grocery store only a block away,
Please help me before my cart looks like Santa's Sleigh!
For as I walk in the door before my eyes,
Are donuts, cakes, and mouth-watering pies!
The next aisle is even worse, with cookies and puddings
to drive me berserk,
If I put them in my cart, I'll feel like a jerk.
For I've finally decided thin is the way for me,
Yes, that's the way I want to be!
Please help me stay on a path that's light,
Until I go to bed at night!

Debra G. Mills

Angel In Disguise

Dedicated to Kelly Ann Gleeson,
who passed away July 12, 1996
A year has passed, my daughter,
since that fateful day you turned and went away.

God looked down through Heavenly eyes,
and saw you, An Angel In Disguise.
He spread his arms to you and smiled,
Come to me, my lovely child.

My love for you grows stronger
With every passing day,
and I miss you more than words can ever say.

I know in my heart your love will never end,
And in Eternity we will be together again.

Donna Gleeson

My Window

Each day I sit here and ponder.
My mind always seems to wander.
I look at all of God's Glory
For someday I will know the true story.

How many times I have thought
What I could have done or bought,
Then again I think of what is true value,
Is it to pick up a phone and call you?

I dream of many things in the past,
Thank God they were not made to last.
We do so many things in life we regret,
God grants a form to use to forget.

Most assuredly that is called prayer,
Having faith we know He is always there.
It's truly amazing as to what He gives
He cares about hunger, strife and how each of us lives.

I quite often think of a very dear friend,
To him my eyes I would like to lend.
But then to God I would surely offend;
You see, His rules were not made to bend.

I think of my mother, sister and wife,
For so many ways HE has blessed my life.
There are so many times when I was hateful,
Now is a different time for which I'm grateful.

Ernest Haws

The Old Country Road

The old country road was once brand new
With a surface quite flawless,
And ruts that were few.
Pleasure rides ringing with family cheer
Emulating gaiety;

Minor cracks did appear.
The new trail was parched by the sun in the sky,
Etching small lesions,
Barely visible to the eye.
Gradually erosion, corrosion; call it what you might.
Wore down that old road
Visibly pocked to the sight.

Everyday stress, and an occasional breakdown
Made lasting impressions,
Like a face with a frown.
Now that old road, hardened by abuse
Had character of its own, no less for the use.

The lines in that road no one could erase
They had stories to tell; you see,
That "old road" was my grandmother's face.

Linda Clarke

Off to College

It's a sad time to part with a boy, grown
And leave him at a college hall;
It's a lonely time to say goodbye
To a son, so young, yet tall.

A mother wants to linger in his college room,
And makes up his bed smooth and neat;
While father carries luggage,
Gives him money and advice, mother worries,
Will he get enough to eat?

So parents drive off and wave farewell
To a lonely boy standing tall;
With a wish in their hearts for all that is good,
They leave him at the college hall.

Hilda Hatlen

My Fernando Fantasy

I have dreamed all my life of finding love that is true.
A love sharing and forgiving and unending too.

But my past has been filled with disappointing romance.
Now my heart's at a point where I question a chance.

Regardless of the pain, hurt and confusion,
I still imagine only the perfect delusion.

I'm tough and maybe cold, with a wall most do not climb.
It will now only break down through a test of time.

Then you enter my life—however briefly and out of reach,
And I begin to dream again "Is it possible you're here to teach?"

Teach me to trust and want and fall in love again.
To wish for life to share and be with one, and only one man.

I'm ok on my own you know. Quite happy I think in fact.
But I far prefer to share my life. I see nothing wrong with that.

I hope it's ok for me to say "If you and I are meant to become one,
It now depends on the road we take, and steps we've already begun."

　　Maurine Baker

Raistlin

Darkness of heart and blackness of soul
Watching the world through eyes tinted gold
His quick mind flashing, cunning and wise
He creates his next plot. Another innocent dies
Always formulating to further his own ends
To the torments of the Abyss his souls slowly descends
Quick-tempered, impatient, and scornful of advice
He hates all of those who try only to sympathize
Quite the contrary when the plot is his
He is ruthless yet patient, sipping herbal fizz
Magic ecstacy running through him, adrenalin in his veins
His next spell is cast, his body's energy drains
The air explodes, fire burning his lies
And of his enemies, everybody dies.

　　Steven Corenflos

Undersestimating Infinity

The warm are emits reassurance.
It's friend that gives life,
But just as quickly can expel it.
Without second thought or remorse.
It has no friends, no enemies.
It's infinite.
Ever constant and changing.
Her daily routine is never the same.
Man cannot modify her authority,
Nor measure her intensity.
She alters instantaneously.
So destructive, yet so enjoyable.
Her strength is underestimated by some,
Others remember her past lives, the legendary tales.
It's a never ending story.
It continues for generations to come.

　　Carolynn Costantini

Spring and Fall—A Poignat Duet

Two school girls pirouetting across the spring-green meadow
Faces radiant with joy and anticipation,
Looking for blackberries and plums,
Listening to bees' hummings and birds' songs,
Surprised by a cluster of iridescent butterflies.

Two elderly ladies proudly wearing their new fall tennis shoes,
Careening merrily through the halls of the nursing home,
Relieving for a while the monotony of Alzheimer's disease,
Faces aglow with movement and found friendship.
Love, a common necessity, is for all seasons.

　　Kay Baines

God's Signature

The power and majesty of God on high,
Is captured in the splendor of the evening sky,
Amidst the shadows and the setting sun,
The colors of the evening have just begun.
Look to the heavens and enjoy the sight,
It will remind you that God holds you tight,
Within the clouds and the vivid hues,
My awesome God's love shines through.
The spirit of God may bring tears to your eyes,
With the powerful splendor of heavens skies,
The beauty may even take your breath away,
When God writes his signature on the day.

　　Margaret George

Seconds

Tick it's gone, tick it's gone
Relentlessly from dusk to dawn
Don't waste a one, they're so precious few
But far, far, to many people do

Time drags on, it seems so slow
Tick, tick, tick they go and go
I'll do it tomorrow. There's always then
But the ticks will stop, you don't know when

Take your time, no need to worry
There's plenty of ticks left, what's the hurry
I'd like to get back one or two
To tell them again that "I Love You"

It all comes down to taking or giving
Which one for you makes life worth living
I don't know how many I must confess
But just one more is just one less

444, 441, 380 tick, tick, tick no more to play
My little boy he died that day
833, 637, 600 tick, tick, tick no more to play
My little man he died that day

　　Donald M. Dougherty

My Life

To my father (28 January 1973)
I've spent my life raising hell,
But still there isn't much to tell.

Because of you, I'm only twenty three,
And I haven't much of a life ahead of me.

I've spent most of my life living a lie,
And the only place it got me was to sit and watch life pass me by.

Then one day someone I loved was taken away from me,
It was then I realized how much love really meant to me.

That someone was my father, a man I loved and was very dear to me,
I realized then all the joy I'd been missing.

By not saying those three simple words, "I love you"
I only hope I can start a new life, and hope it's not to late.

Maybe I can now that I know what it like to love and not too hate.
There is one thing I would like to find,

Before I leave this world,
I'd like to find happiness and love with peace of mind.

So if you are living a lie,
Take my advice and learn what love is and to love.

Or you will find life will pass you by.

Your Daughter, Fran
　　Fran Mason

A Smile Unchanged

I kneel to feel your trembling hands
Beneath the blanket's warmth.
Your straw hat and flowered sweater
Remind me that it's you.
The hills of green your backdrop.
Budding crocus at your feet.
Silent clouds walk slowly by and blend from white to blue.

I lean slowly in and whisper your name touch your cheek—
But your gaze remains unchanged.
What is it you see beyond the hills beyond the flowers and trees?

I look out to yesterday
When you were tall and strong, lifting me
Into the apple trees.
Never too tired for a story or a smile.

I push your chair through the budding gardens—
I hear my childhood giggles
And see your bright young face and I reach to wipe a tear
For all the seasons gone by and all those yet to be.

Looking out across these hills
I squeeze your hand and you smile.

Susan Farrell

Night School

Now when it came to schooling,
There was never any fooling.
My folks gave me the best they could provide.
Later on I had yearning,
To go to night school learning
How doors to hopes and dreams to open wide.

But when 'twas time to go,
I did not have the "dough."
All my hopes and dreams seemed smashed.
I don't know where my wife got it—
She just scrimped and saved and brought it—
And handed me the cash!

Then to get a plan in motion,
Drafting class with Mr. Grothen;
I was on Dunwoody's path!
And to keep my course on center,
Loren Blanchar was my mentor—
Machine Shop, Tool-Making and Math.

Herbert W. Lee

Feelings

Doubt, Confusion
Together in madness
Fear, Passion
Clinging to each other never willing to let go
Ideas, Dreams
Working together to achieve what they want
Tears, Anger
Both who nurse a wounded heart
Smiles, Hugs
Hoping nothing will shatter this dream
Caresses, kisses
A show of affection
Staring, Gazing
Trying to memorize every inch
Chills, Sighs
Trying to hold onto their sanity
Blushing, Giggles
Both so scared to make a mistake
Beating hearts, Racing blood
It's all so very right

Dawn Ryan

Nous Ne Savons Pas Le Morte

Dear Tibet,
How you learned life so well
Venture into death
Without fear
But Oh
How you scare the masses.
Perhaps that is why
You are persecuted in China
Because you scare the Taoist
Who studies his arts
And does not worry about multi-colored demons
Who will haunt him at death.
He finds his nothingness through the Way
And does not worry about the Bardo Thodol.
I must agree, Tibet,
With China
I find my happiness in the Way
Not in waiting for the moment of death to arrive.

Alfred Cormier

Wasted Time

Dedicated to Dustin Kurz
I tried to tell you, I knew you meant well,
It wouldn't work out, for that I could tell.

I know the promises, you thought you could keep,
I began to believe you, I got in too deep.

For now I know no one can be trusted.
My heart is too sick, my mind is too cluttered.

I don't wanna see you, for I can't find the words,
It's too much to take, for that I have learned.

My mind has been set, my heart has been blocked,
No one shall enter, it shall remain locked.

You've hurt me too much, and dragged me so far,
It never did last, to find who you are.

You make me feel sad, but I hope you still care,
Love's hard to find, but I hope you're still there.

I'll never be with you, for that I decide,
You're not worth the heartache, or feelings inside.

So now it's all over, this is the end,
I'll miss your charmed lies, and remember your intends.

Jamie Van Atta

The Alamo

There was a man named Davy Crockett.
He came from Tennessee.
He wanted to help the Texans
Along with Jim Bowie.

Texas's army was small but strong.
The Mexicans had more men.
When the two sides met in battle
Mexico thought they would win.

The battle did not last very long.
Jim Bowie and Crockett died.
When all of the fighting was over
Women and children cried

Texas lost the Alamo.
They fought at San Jacinto.
They got their revenge and yelled the phrase
Remember the Alamo!

Royce Ballard

When It's Over

It's really hard for me to believe that it's over.
Part of me is numb and doesn't really comprehend
That it's over.

On good days, I can see that I got the healing
I needed to get from this relationship.
And so it's time for me to move on, to realize
That it's over.

And now we spar over who gets what,
When really it's our hurt feelings we are expressing.
And we sometimes laugh and talk
As though nothing is happening, ignoring
That it's over.

And sometimes I hear a song, or I'm awake late at night
And I cry, for all that it could have been, but isn't,
For all that it isn't but could have been,
For all that we are and are not,
When it's over.

Linda L. Johnson

One Of Three Idylls—By The Brook

Today I heard the waters of the brook,
Oh, what a sparkling and enchanting sound,
Like silvery laughter, and this forest nook
Was filled with water music most profound
This little rill went singing on its way
With innocent and unpretentious glee,
As if it were forever more at play,
And blessedly from worldly care set free
And, as I pondered, how I deeply yearned
For that self-same serenity of soul
That from this water muse I might have learned
To have and hold, while weary years may roll
Perhaps, some day when I am very wise,
And cease to fret about dull, earthly care
I'll learn the art, and true contentment prize
That in the rippling brook was always there.

Julia Burns Holland

One Perfect Rose

I awake every morning with you on my mind,
And within my heart, a peace I find.

This incredible feeling is so unexplainable.
It's an honesty and truth, that's never changeable.

It's a gift of love, that only the heavens could bring.
It's the rhythm and harmony that make my soul sing.

How thankful I am for all that you give,
Especially for this precious life that I live.

And I am thankful for all of my family and friends,
Because their care and support never ends.

Until I found you, I was lost without a way,
But now you light the path that I follow each day.

By one simple prayer, you ease my thoughts and sorrows,
And the truth of your word makes joyful my tomorrows.

Yes I once was blind, but now I can see,
Because faith and love have strengthened me.

So as I grow faithfully in your garden of love,
I long for eternity in heaven above.

When you planted that seed Lord, it was me that you chose.
And now I blossom in your garden as one perfect rose.

Jennifer Artell Bendy

WindMill

Her eyes reflecting in a half moonlit night
She stands as a Sentinel on a silent hill
   Longing . . .
      Anticipating...the return of her beloved

She listens to the surge of the lovers below
   Rising . . . falling . . .

Suddenly, gently
   She feels the warm touch of her lover
      As he gently caresses her flaxen arms
         Intensity grows
            Energies joined in the depths of passion

As suddenly, as he appeared
   He is gone

She waits..listening to the ceaseless sounds of lovers below
   As a silent sentinel she waits
      Longing . . .
         Anticipating . . .

Dennis E. Royer

I Sometimes See You, But Never Hear You

Your eyes touch me with a certain sort of
gracefulness, softly, as you pass by

Longing and wondering, memories pass by
They are only pieces and fragments of
broken up happiness floating in the midst of
imagination, creating a small, chaotic
person inside

Touched by your presence with breathlessness
I let free, free from reality into your world—
No longer searching for myself, for I've found
within you piece of mind

Forever and ever, until all life perishes,
I'm captured by your love and helpless to your heart
in complete infinite charm.

Heather Hollis

Night

As night covers the earth,
as darkness takes away the light,
I see the tiny fire flies take to flight
Just a tiny glow of light out in the night,
Soon the moon appears so big and bright,
A million twinkling stars cover the sky,
Sparkling like diamonds they glisten and shine
The crickets sing a sweet melody as the gentle
breezes blow through the trees,
Night has fallen, day is at end, the world lies
in slumber till morning comes again.

Nancy Noe

Mother

A mother's love is the greatest gift of all.
The joy that comes when she smiles.
The tender touch of love when receiving a hug.
She knows your greatest fears,
And knows how to chase bad dreams away,
A simple kiss on my cheek at night.
"Goodnight my angel so sweet, I love you"
Is the whisper in my ear.
For all the thousands of seconds I ask her to wait.
And all the seconds she will wait.
Now that I am grown and want to be loved,
She guides my way through the seas of tomorrow.
My mother, my friend, my hopes and joys
My listener, my teacher, my everything
You have made me to be.

April M. Adams

A Thousand Words

A thousand words, none the same
Each one describes why I'm insane
Each one is about you, everything you do
Each time I close my eyes visions of you appear
Every time I think of you I have no fear
Now that I'm in love I cant think of anything better
Than being with you from now until forever
You are my heart without you I would die
All I can do is sit here and cry
Thinking of you makes me wish you were here
So I could hold you close and whisper in your ear
Everything I need, you have, everything I look for is in you
Now that you're in my life
Theres nothing anyone can do to change my love for you
Ever since I met you I wanted you to stay forever
Now that that's coming true I hope we stay together
Our love is the strongest thing ever
Nothing else matters as long as we're together
I love you always and forever

Rick Plant

Dream Catcher

Dream Catcher, dream catcher,
Catch me a dream

Every Kid should have a home
No kid should be lost and have to roam
Kids should have warm clothes and food to eat
Not beg and scratch out a living on the street

Dream Catcher, dream catcher,
Catch me a dream

Help parents along the way
Kids get confused and sometimes stray
Teach kids and parents that to love-is to understand
Parents, do not lose control reach out-ask for a helping hand

Dream Catcher, dream catcher,
Catch me a dream

The Earth is not heaven—that is something we all know
Think about it—there is not much choice on where to go
We can make the world a beautiful place
Let us all work together protect the kids and keep them safe

Dream Catcher, dream catcher,
Catch me a dream

Stephanie Ray

My Little Voice Is Silence

Big people, grown-ups and tall adults,
My little voice is silence and quiet.
I'm shy to speak loud in front of people.
My little voice won't come out!
I can hear you!
I can read your lips!
People, adults, and grown-ups won't listen.
They don't care about me being deaf!
Blind hearts, deaf hearts, and handicapped hearts.
Big people, grown-ups and tall adults,
My little voice loves to talk with my little friends!
Little kids, young kids, teenagers, and my little dog.
Kids help! And give a big smile to the deaf,
Blind, and handicapped.
And you don't feel shy,
Embarrassed about being deaf,
Blind, and handicapped.
But life is hard!
Do hearing people love deaf people?
My little silence has a feeling about the world!

Olivia Andrews

The Rainbow Road

The rainbow road stretches out past my sight
filling my eyes with its colorful light
as I step on the road, I hear a faint laugh
mocking me, as I walk past

The rainbow road starts making me cry
As I year to reach its end
happiness awaits me there
and life will make me its friend

The rainbow road starts giving me chills
I cannot wait for its wonderful thrills
but I don't see any children at play
and as I look behind me, the road has turned grey

Mike McDonald

It Isn't Love

I really want him to be mine,
I know he will be in time.
When I look him deep in the eyes,
I feel that I just want to cry.
My love for him is very deep,
I even have dreams of him in my sleep.
But now, I withdraw the fact
That he'll be mine,
And that my love for him will end in time.
My love for him will never end,
And I know he'll always be my friend.
I hope our friendship really lasts,
So we can laugh at our thoughts of the past.
I felt so special when he kissed me,
But now I wish it was a fantasy.
I feel that I am being pushed and shoved,
And now I know that what I feel,
It isn't love.

Kimberly Latoya Laws

The Man of Steel

A sheet of steel is what I am,
even though I look much like a man.
In the past, many shapes I have took,
but I have never been given this sort of look.
I can't imagine how wonderful it must be,
to be able to walk, talk, hear and see.
I'll stand here alone, as quiet as a mime,
a soldier from the past, now frozen in time.
I am not the tin man from the Wizard of Oz.
I represent all people who have fought for a cause.
The gift of freedom and the ability to choose,
a gift so many lives you had to lose.
How proud you should feel to walk around free.
God bless the people that made this be.
To you I honor, with appeal,
for I am, "The Man of Steel."

For awhile, I was him.

David M. Higgason

Bitterness

Bitterness creeps in, it can control your life.
When you recall years of trouble, pain strife.
Anger seeps in, adds more pain to the mess.
People who know you would never guess,
The feelings you hide from those who should care,
Who have forgotten their Mother, now that Dad isn't there.
Dad would be so hurt, if he knew the rewards she gets,
For their years of sacrifice, but, she isn't done yet!
God will let her live to see her kids reap their harvest,
Then wonder, worry, and, cry, because they are forgotten!

Alberta Price

I Am Me

I am a bird who has not yet leaned to fly and a fish who cannot yet   swim,
I wonder about those who have no wonders and those who can   answer their dreams,
I hear the silent screams of those at war and want to ease their pain,
I see the end of the rainbow and stare at the pot of gold in vain,
I want to be different and like everybody else,
I am a bird who has not yet learned to fly and a fish who cannot yet   swim.
I pretend I am an emperor but,
I feel no new clothes,
I touch the sky, but with each handful stars,
I worry about those who cannot reach,
I cry for those with broken hearts who may never trust again,
I am a bird who has not yet learned to fly and a fish who cannot yet   swim.
I understand value of listening though I say I'll never need it,
I try to make myself be heard,
I hope someone has heard every word,
I am a bird who has not yet learned to fly and a fish who cannot yet   swim.

   Dominique Rogers

Empty Chair

I manage to get through thanksgiving without the one I loved
There were plenty of turkey and dressing, and lots of goodies were there
The day was spent with my children whom I loved and who cared
But there were sadness because we had an empty chair

There were times I wonder if I could make it through the holidays
Thoughts of Christmas which would be coming in a few days
Tho' I knew my children would be around to show love everyday
Also, I knew that across our table would be an empty chair

I trimmed our Christmas tree which I hoped would bring cheer
But somehow this tree would bring back memories of past years
I knew my love would not be around to share Christmas this year
This Christmas would not be the same, we faced that empty chair

I guess I thought my love would always be here
Now I faced an empty house and my love's empty chair
Time has change my life that I loved so dear
I guess I never thought of life without the one I loved to be near

   Marjorie Marie Privett

Daddy, Do You Know?

Daddy, do you know that our love for you will last throughout creation?

Daddy, do you know that without you here our lives have lost foundation?

Do you know that the time we had will never leave our minds—
and an eternity of memories we'll hold for all of time?

Daddy, do you know that our family will reunite some day?

Daddy, do you know that each one of us is never far away?

Do you know that our trust in you will never, never die?
For you have taught us- we have listened-and you will always be our guide.

Daddy, do you know that tomorrow brings the joy of all redemption?

Daddy, do you know that the promise holds . . . and there are no exceptions?

Do you know that in all our eyes you were our perfect light,
and that we're gathered here together to celebrate your life?

Daddy, we all know you'll not be here again to feel our loving touch.
But our hearts are full of love for you—we miss you, oh, so much.

With the strength that comes from loving you we thank God for all we've had.
And we'll go on our way together because of you—Our Precious Dad.

   Nancy N. Price

I Can't Help It

I can't help it I'm only, thirteen
They call me names and say I'm mean
They say I'm just plain out rude
They say I have a attitude

I cry all the time when I'm alone
I wish I had another family and home
I wish that I could run away
But I'm afraid I won't have a place to stay

I will admit, help I need
I need help with life, that's indeed
Every time I start to cry
I wish I could lay over and die

It's sad for me to think that way
I only feel good when I go out and play
I hate my life in every way
I can't wait till the day I move away

I desire love in every way
I need somebody with love every day
I'm all alone here and there
I'm all alone everywhere

   Andria Nicole Parker

Fishy

Fishy, fishy how I wishy,
That you'd swim round in your dishy,
But you don't, you just float,
Like some endlessly drifting boat

My fishy, fishy sleeps and sleeps,
He never swims, he never eats.
When I try and wake him up,
He just rolls over and

It just sits there, it isn't fit,
There might be something wrong with it.
I think I'll take it to the vet,
There's something not right 'bout my pet.

His body's fat, his face is green,
It can't be cause his bowl's not clean.
I just don't care what people have said,
I won't admit my fishy's dead.

   Michael Chino

Night's Vision

In the black void of night,
With all its bitter splendor,
Reveals an inner being.
One of tremulous reality.
This other side, a darker half of my soul.
Like a black rain of acid
That forever thunders on my heart.
A grip of death that clutches my throat.
Stealing the breath of sweet life.
Mournful beauty that I long to have, to be.
Yet, it is a mere void in the night.
I search never finding that restless peace.
A piano player in a tomb,
That knows no sanctity in his solitude.
I ask you,
Where is my sanctity in my dark world?

   Julee Robinson

I Couldn't Pass You By

Oh my love, oh my dear, there is poetry,
It's words carried on the wind, I can hear.
It's saying: I couldn't pass you by.
And the only understanding is in my heart,
For it alone knows why;
Sounding like words of love,
Saying: I couldn't pass you by. No, I couldn't pass you by.

You ask me to pass you by, but no matter how I try, I just couldn't pass you by.
I can clearly hear these words on the wind;
I have two loves, and it's no sin. With each different in their own way,
This love is not the same, so loving you is not a shame.
The first is gone, but you are here, both are in my heart, it knows why.
Please listen for those words, my dear,
Think again and again and express your love for me,
Those winsome words on the wind, I will hear.
And so my words of love will also be on the wind,
Please listen my dear, and you will hear those words:
I couldn't pass you by.

Norbert Watson

Finish What You Start

Your insecurities and fears that gathered on your shelf,
That one by one throughout the years just grew within yourself.

No longer do they grow in you, courageously you've severed,
The crutches that you held onto and through it all you weathered.

You've jumped the hurdles in your way and climbed each mountain crest,
You've conquered fears from yesterday by striving for the best.

You've labored for your children's sake, your will for them unbroken,
Each painful step you had to make are now a cherished token.

Through the window in your soul you aim and strove for each endeavor,
Unblemished by the daily strain defeat you've shown not ever.

For nothing in life can make you as whole than to feel pride within your heart,
For only till then is piece in your soul When You Finish What You Start . . .

Jennifer Lisa

The Revelation of His Essence

And so her hair danced
It danced the dance of a thousand Mozart's
and still bore the aroma & softness;
That of a crisp mountain spring with a translucent rose petal dust.

The golden locks hypnotized as time stopped to laugh

Ocean window eyes touched me gently . . . or so I thought
They were merely borrowed by her soul for the unveiling
Exposed was a trembling, naked inner man
A spirit with nowhere to hide and yet ironically at peace.

She replaced his camouflage, the clock chimed and he waltzed with her hair

Amy Davison

A Soldier In Hiding

The mist covered my eyes as I walked through the night.
   The darkness was thick, and pitch black it became.
I am breathless as the air thickens through the night.
   I am a soldier hiding in the leaves out of sight.
I breathe at a small pulse rate, as if I am silent in the leaves.
   The others listen but hear nothing, but the wind whistling through the trees.
They walk closer, almost at my bunker.
   I reach for my gun, the question racing through my mind, "Shoot or Not?"
My gun rises through the misty air as though the three shots were almost silent.
   I stay at my bunker, but the odor of the bodies makes me pass out.
I lie almost dead, I am never found.

Robbie Reams

Mother

Mother is a word that everyone has heard.
But not often do we stop to give thanks to our mothers of
whom we all have heard.
Mother tells you when you're right or wrong; she keeps
your spirit going strong.
Mother picks you up when you are down; she gets your
feet back on the ground.

Mother gives you hope when you can't find any
and her words of wisdom, well there are so many.

Mother holds you in her arms when you have to cry
and there's never any quitting, she'll say you have to try.
Then when you go on a trip afar, it's mother who wonders
where you are
As she lies awake at night.
But she knows you have become an adult
and everything will be all right.

It's to my mother I owe the most as I'm stopping now
to make this toast.
For everything you've said and done, I send these words
to number one.
My mother.

Adam Edwards

Loving Your Friends

Loving your friends is not always easy.
Sometimes it seems they make you go crazy.
Not knowing how or what they feel.
Not knowing what they're thinking of you, everyone else,
or even themselves.
You think they need to open up tell you their problems,
worries, fears, and dreams.
Maybe they think the same of you.
Maybe they can not trust you.
Maybe you can not trust them.
Maybe you shouldn't be friends at all.
You never talk about important issues.
So what's the point.
Try for the friendship you enjoyed once before.
The memories, the fun, and even the tears.
Why even try?
Try because it's worth it to get close to them.
'Cause no one knows how long either of you will be here.
Or if you will ever meet again.

Mary Lenneman

Reflections of Hope

As I sat one winter morn on the balmy coast of Maine,
I thought of how unfair life can be, and the sorrows we retain.
I thought of the pain endured by some when battling just to live,
and the frustration felt by family when they have nothing but love to give.
Then the sun started to rise out of the ocean on that cold brisk morn,
and I watched life begin again as a brand new day was born.
The dull red glow grew brighter as time seemed held in place,
it took away the darkness, and left a smile upon my face.
A voice cried write this down it's too beautiful to forget,
if you don't capture this on paper, the loss you may regret.
Another voice came to my mind saying don't worry about this part,
I've taken this wonderful moment and written it upon you heart.
It will be there forever, so use it again and again,
to tell of that glorious morning and God's promise to sustain.
Our faith in God will help us through the darkest moments of life,
giving us strength to endure the pain and easing us in our strife.
When realities of life assail me and I bow my head to pray,
I'll always think back to that winter morn and the start of that
beautiful day.

Nils Granquist

Circle of Life

We all know you have to work to get to the spot you want,
to believe in yourself, and not give up, you can be seated in front.
But there will be times when you want it to end,
keep trying, things will suddenly blend.
You will be seated on top of the list, and those bad times will become a mist.
You have fought the race, the challenge of life, the giver of
hopes and dreams,
And in the end, you have won, by all your beliefs and means.

Sarah Wiggins

The Person Inside

You say you're never going to get it.
You live a life of protection and serenity.
Then one day it suffocates you pulling you in.

You thought you were never going to get it.
When you look in the mirror you realized you weren't the same.
You're a different person on the inside and on the outside.
You try to fight it, but it won't go away.
You struggle through the painful tauntings, barely surviving each day.

People always staring through uncaring eyes.
They look at you in disgust and think you're not wise.
You wish it didn't happen.
You wish it would all would just leave and go away,
but it just won't, it just won't.

It haunts you everyday of your life.
It makes you sick and you want to die.
You can hardly walk around.
You can hardly make a sound.

Family holds you; friends comfort you.
All you say is at least they understand.
Is there a person inside or is it just me?

Alexis Brown

My Blessing

All I saw were the gloomy clouds of this world and my misery.
My heavy load could not be eased.
With each passing day my river of sorrows flowed.

What am I living for? What is destined to happen?
I saw no future for me.
All I saw were the long, lonely days of my life,
No one to love, no one to care for.
I saw no reason, I saw no hope.

And as I chose my fate, a Light shined upon me.
For I was near the Golden Gates of Heaven.
The glimpse filled my soul with joy I could not explain.
And like a child I was marveled by the wondrous, illuminating Light.
Then I saw no more,
Then did I know it was not my time.

For the Light had assured me my life was precious and did have purpose.
He showed me a way,
A way of happiness

And now I see with each passing day a silver lining in the clouds.
The blessing of God's smile on me.

Lisette Garcia

Togetherness

Inspired by my boyfriend, Chad Siegler
Why does this world have so many winding roads?
Why does this darkened world cast a shadow among our love?
For our only goal is togetherness, and we are separated.
We fight to stay together, and we lose.
Not by fault of the heart, but by fault of distance.
And as we lose ambition for life, the world still turns and we are lost.
Lost in the fantasy of being together.
And shortly our wish comes true.
And we are frolicking in meadows and holding hands, and the
sun seems brighter and life seems easier.
And in a blink of an eye we are awaken by a lonesome alarm
clock, and find that our fantasy world was only a dream.
So we hold on to this dream and carry it gently for it is fragile.
And we realize that we can't be together now, and we haven't
lost the fight yet because everyday is a step closer to that
wonderful day of togetherness.

Jennifer Truran

Summer's Night

Like two candles burning bright on a breezy summer's night:
One is strong and does not flicker with each breeze that comes
through my bedroom window;
The other is weak and fragile and I fear it will go out.
But if it does, it will not be lost, for the winds will
Carry its smoke into the deep, dark, summer's night.
Will I ever hear its flickering flame?
Will I ever hear its sweet childish song, full of innocence and warmth?
I venture out into the night looking for my candlelight.
But I cannot find it; it's gone to my past, and there it will stay.
The other candle still stands, unharmed, and untouched.
And when I look in the mirror will I still see the same face?
For only one candle now brightens my room through the deep,
dark, summer's night.

Shannon Delaney

A World of Three

In the mind of the real, resplendent my sense.
Indulgence and anguish of the soul—so intense.
This potency balanced with heedless routine
That I strive to restrain, but slips in between . . .

My hands by a momentary encounter of forever.
The Surreal disconnects me from the exterior, where I
Contemplate why and how I've arrived. And I perch inside
An indiscernible hindrance, numbing my senses and stopping . . .

To sail and soar. Denuding unrevealed, the dream world's moan
Drowns my nacreous floor—my inhibitions blown, my fears thrown
Like hail at my core, while I feast on desires I thought I'd outgrown.
Until lucidity pours my spirit on the throne of truth—I am alone.

"How real I truly am" is just an echo forsaken once uttered.
Even mortality is a lost reminiscence as the blur of another inflames
My wonder, if they too can be spellbound, if they too share the daze,
Awaken only slightly from reverie—to behold something sturdy . . .

Like today, tomorrow, the clock's punctual power.
Responsibility is my soul-purging shower.
I declare the rest nonsensical. The real's come to stay.
But I fathom it's hopeless, and perceive myself drift away . . . .

Danielle L. DeMailo

Now That You're In My Life

When it all started I never imagined what it would be like,
Or the way my heart would beat when your words would strike.
Whenever I am hurt, confused, or sad,
You make me smile and I no longer feel bad.
I have turned to you in many times of need,
On one of those days our relationship began as a freshly planted seed.
You can always find a way to make me laugh and smile,
And afterwards I just sit and think awhile of what the future may hold,
What would or could become of us?
I know my heart will always hold for you a special promise,
You have occupied a special place in my heart that I know will never part.
I don't know what I'd do without you around,
Because in you a true friend I've found.
I can tell you my deepest thoughts, secrets, and fears,
I've shared with you many smiles, laughs, jokes, and even some tears.
It sometimes scares me to think of what may come to be,
I can only hope that it is a never-ending bond between you and me.
I have grown on the inside as well as the outside because of you,
Yes, I feel all of this and even love too!

  Johnna L. Devine

Creation's Lullaby

There came a little child to earth a long, long time ago.
Angels of God sang out His birth, they sang both high and low.
Throughout the stillness of the night their song rang loud and clear
For they knew that a Child had come to grace those with hearts sincere.

The Virgin Mother meek and mild sang "Hush, my Child, don't cry.
"Listen with love while creation sings its sweet lullaby."
"Thank You, my God, for showing Your love to the creatures You have made.
"Your Son now is God with us! Rejoice! Rejoice! Our debt is repaid."

Joseph stood throughout the night to wait on Mother and Child,
Pondering words that the angel said, "You're so chaste and mild."
"How is it that God has chosen me for such a worthy task?
Prophets long awaited Him and now His reign is here at last!

The shepherds gathered around to see the Babe in swaddling clothes.
They wondered how we could be saved by a Child who merely dosed
He opened His eyes and looked at them, the look, it was a sign.
From eyes so human there came a gaze that saw from hearts divine.

Then from the distance came a sound of bells from a tired camel train
Men from the East lead by a bright star, they sang this glad refrain:
"We bring gifts of gold and myrrh and incense to honor this Child
Born in Belen' on this Holy Day, to Mother Mary, meek and mild."

  Marlene Miller

A Transcendental Trip

The wind whips my mind, stirring my soul, sending a shiver
Down my spine. Goosebumps engulf my body as thought
And emotion collide. The ebb of perpetual feelings harkens me
To ride and ponder on life's wondrous reelings.

God beckons as Winter's icy fingers caress the nape of my neck.
Listen my son, the answers are all around. They travel on the winds'
Whisper. Gargantuan gusts are no louder than the supple serenade
That gently guides an autumn leaf to the welcoming arms of the earth.

August's angst-filled searing heat is no more penetrating than the Cooling comfort of
Autumn by a brooding brook. Cloudless star-filled Nights are no more revealing than
the cumulous clouds that cascade A full October moon. Swept away by the feelings
of this world, the Sunrise speaks to me when I am ready to sleep as the sunset rises
me From slumber. Reality and thought merge as I conceptualize these revelations.

Mindful meanderings in the woods reveal no more color than those Spent on a
bustling city street. Ralph's words whisper in the breeze,
"The world, this shadow of the soul, or other me, lies wide around, its
Attractions are the keys which unlock my thoughts and make me
Acquainted with my self." My friend speaks to me as I look for my part,
"Keep searching Kimosabee, it's closer to the heart." FOR TER-RIP

  Adam Robinson

Imagination

I would like you to find a special quiet place and relax your mind.
Use your imagination, and cherish what you find.

Look up at the stars shining all through the skies,
find the brightest one and imagine my eyes.
Are they full of tears from pain, glowing with gleam, or do they
tell you I've lied? It's your imagination, so you decide.

Now remember my eyes, as you close yours. Take a deep breath'
the scent you now smell will remind you of me. It's your imagination,
So what scent will it be? Is it Sunflowers, or have I just gotten
out of the shower? Is it the smell of us making love, or maybe
it's CK-One? Now remember that scent as you look back above.

You see my eyes in the sky, and smell me all around; Now listen
up— how do I sound? Am I singing a melody of my favorite
song, or am I laughing at your jokes? Or maybe I'm yelling from
pain because you've been gone for so long.

When you feel you have failed, and have nothing to say—
Just relax and let your imagination take you away!
Before you question my suggestion—
Try it out, see if you can feel me deep in your heart.
It's amazing how much you can feel, yet still be apart.

Michelle Lemmer

A Blind Love

Goodbye, my love, I should have seen it coming,
But my eyes were covered by my heart, you see
And my heart, well my heart wasn't thinking very rationally.
My love, I've loved you far too much,
Too much to see a love as such,
A love that someday will no longer be,
Because you need someone other than me.
I thought love was enough, and if I gave all I had,
We would be perfect forever, I'd be there, you would never be sad.
But I'm not enough, me to have and hold,
Your dreams are much larger, stronger and bold.
I wish I could follow you, I know my love won't die,
But as for individuality, self worth, it is no lie,
That most of that lies in you, your love, your eyes,
When you said we were both so very different
You know I didn't want to hear,
I didn't want to listen just wanted to have you near.
I'm starting now to uncover my eyes, stop telling my heart these lies,
And look into that soul of yours, and confess what I despise.
That maybe I'm not your soul mate you see,
But I'd give anything if I could be.

Jaclyn Loew

Behind the Shadows of Darkness

Behind the shadows of darkness, why I see no light.
I see the shadows of people moving about,
If wondering about darkness was a crime I'd be in jail.

To fulfill a place of emptiness that needs to be healed,
As if there was a great big whole being covered by something.
It makes you look around and keep wondering.

It's like a circle being shaded in with no hope of space never again,
But as you think and wonder even more, the time will come.
If we keep thinking of what we could find behind,
The shadows of darkness wouldn't be so kind.

If we could see behind the shadows of darkness, things in need
Could be fulfilled with a problem that could never be healed.
The shadows of darkness would never be seen or heard,
It's only the hole to be filled if you mind is mislead.

Tammy S. Bush

Unity Divided By My Own

Such isolation never any participation. Creations—situations—
savaged nations words cannot convey the grayness of each day.
Environmental destruction—feel so numb, so very glum—children
dying —parents crying. Priorities gone insane. Toxic substances
remain. Man and beast—maybe the same. Look around that should
explain. Can't make no bread—body's bought on streets instead.
Political corruption bomb interruption. Power structures abused
10,000 more annhilations—missiles flying straying shell—life is
violent, as a world sits silent. Mother Earth and forms of life are
dying—we are, our own worst enemies— signs of change are
grim—oh how saddened I become from the heavens to the oceans
to forests and mountains creatures are crying, Is our love for life
dying? Why aren't we trying?

Many aspects of life, forever perished;
shame, shame, we are all to blame.

Joshua D. Dickson

Words

Where has my heart gone?
Have meaningless words overtaken my meaning?
The meaning in all words that seems to become more meaningless
every time we utter or make the sounds that are our words.
I can say that love is good as to hate is my sin.
That doesn't tell you exactly where or how I've been or even where I'm going.
Has my heart travelled abroad
Came close to home again and again like a lonely homeless friend?
I can say that I love you
But that won't mean a thing, just a saying, not a beginning, not an ending,
not a damn thing.
I can say that I'm sorry, that I didn't mean the things that I said
The words that were going through my head
Haunting me in my sleep every night as I lie alone in bed.
Words, meaningless in sound, all around, Silence is the only thing found.
And with this hollowness inside my broken heart, I only ask of you
Before you say anything that you don't mean or even anything that you do
Think about the meaning, or the feelings, and the consequences of being
With the sounds of the words that you or even may not mean to say.

Kommany Sinlapasai

Untitled

Gazing at the world spread before me, I feel anger throb in my body,
I feel sorrow in my eyes for the men who neither know
nor care what they have done.
I feel pity in my heart for the innocent that suffer,
both man and beast, at these men's hands.
In his greediness man destroys the beauty and peace of
the earth without blinking an eye.
In his selfishness he takes what is not his to take
and bleeds it to satisfy himself . . .
with his pride and ignorance he cannot feel remorse.
Yet, amid this circle of grey, I still can see patches of brightness.
The beauty that once covered the whole earth,
peace and harmony still survive in these places.
There are forest and lakes, flowers and blue sky instead of con-
crete, glass and steel.
Simple pleasures still abound there,
with love between both man and creature.
The sides of these patches are being forced inwards
and soon will be the size of a tear.

Linda C. Cherp

Love Signs

Two constellations, stellar configurations
Binary attractions, condescent illumination
Perfection personified in the heavenly astrological combination
Under the eclipse of Venus, Taurus was warned
Unconditional love comes with a price and you may be scorned
He took no heed to the advice and gave his all to Capricorn
Attentions were appreciated and one time commencerated,
but her heart belonged to another
An unknown symbol which he would soon discover
The former suitor of his universe now turned once again into a present lover
Self doubt raised questions . . . where along love's line did he squander
Some unseen mistake, now alone he lay but his heart grew fonder
of his missing nebula
No sun set without him thinking of her on a regular
A comet left a blazing trail of hope for the Taurus,
and it did not take the fates to foresee this
To know he would see his Capricorn one day,
someday again under the eclipse of Venus.

Tony Moser

Tonight

I really saw you tonight like I never saw before
Naked and exposed, skinless with only blood and bone to bare
You looked like Andromeda burning against the black
I really heard you tonight speaking in a familiar tongue
And deciphering my code you sang songs I'd almost forgotten
You made the trumpets seem loud
Tonight I realized what we could be
    yet I have to wonder what you did see
You made me think of amnesia and wanting the wanting again
You made me think of you; in a shameless way and wish
    to capture your soul
Suddenly I wanted your secrets to be mine, our laughter shared
Suddenly I wanted nothing more than to know you
Yet you walked away again (for another six months?)
I really loved you tonight, beauty was no more an illusion
Your blade slipped into my heart, may it never emerge
May tonight be every night and you be always in it
Tonight I love you (shall we do it again?)
If only evening could murder the dawn, tonight belongs to us
If only you knew I really saw you tonight
Raw underneath with all your demons exposed
Now can you see me tonight? Let's blow out the sun

Mark Rasmussen

Life and Time

As I lie here and I cry, my father yells, my mother sighs.
Over time I lay and wait till I am old enough to open the gate.

The clouds shift, the sun falls yet no peace in my black halls.
I full asleep yet still awake while my brother stays out late.

I wonder, I dream yet all does seem like life is taking its eternal time.
For me to climb my highest mountain my biggest fall.
Then I hear my mother call.

My brother is home once again
Then it starts all over again.

Why must life take its time,
I am punished but committed no crime.
Still I wait to escape.
Here I lay and I cry, once again I ask myself
why does life take its time.

Nicole Claire Kraut

Thoughts of a Broken Heart

Oh tragedy of tragedies, what pains beset my life.
For I have lost the most precious of things, the love of my dear wife.

I tell myself all through the day. Hey, you've been here before.
But, alas, it doesn't help, the pain grows more and more.
I should be thankful, I say to me, there are others worse off then I.
But even this, cannot hold back, the many tears I cry.

It isn't as this is enough, the grief continues on.
My darling daughters, I miss them too, for they are also gone.

So they're not of my own blood, I miss the all the same.
Oh what bliss, it would bring. To hear them call my name.

What could I offer, give, or say, to get back my dear girls.
For they are of a greater value, than a house of costly pearls.

The answer here, is all too clear, oh what a woeful day.
There is no cure for a broken heart, the pain is there to stay.

Charles Petrosky

Untitled

Throughout the years of my life, I have seen many sights
Those of love and those of hate, those of smiles and those of tears
Those of good times and of bad, those of life and those of death
Through it all I still stand, at times holding myself up with both hands
I have my chances to take a fall, yet I always choose to stand up tall
Some wonder why I don't break, some are curious why I still awake
But with each day comes a new challenge, with one more doubt I
    have to battle
Some say "I can", some say "I can't", some say "I will",
    some say I won't"
Some say "I'll stand", some say "I'll fall", to prove I can and
    will stand tall is
The biggest challenge I'll ever face, so to this day each day I wake
I look at each challenge I have to face,
When each day is done and sleep comes near
One more challenge has been conquered and I have not fallen
Tomorrow is another day with a new challenge and a new battle
When morning light awakes me, I will stand tall and
Greet the challenge waiting to push me down
But I will battle and I will win and
I will stand tall until the end

Tracy Diane Willoughby

Why Did Daddy Die?

Why did daddy have to go? she was too young to understand.
I told her daddy's better now, for he's in the good Lord's hands.
But why did he leave us? Was all that she could say.
We told her it was just his time and yours too will come one day.
But he was suppose to take care of us, he wasn't suppose to leave,
She didn't know any different that's what she was always told to believe.
Didn't daddy love us, I always thought he cared?
She couldn't understand, she always thought he'd be there.
"What did we do so bad to make daddy go away?"
"Why did daddy have to leave, why didn't daddy stay?"
It was daddy's time to go so we tried to explain,
Of course she couldn't understand, all that was there was the pain.
"Will daddy ever come back?" She murmured as she cried,
All we could say was no Sarah, daddy had died.
She looked at us with a puzzled face as tears rolled out of her eyes,
She then said with her soft little voice, "then why didn't daddy say good-bye?"

Tabatha Farless

The Wall

Memories fly about their heads
    as they remember their loved ones who now are dead.
They're wives, sisters, and daughters all,
    back to visit their family's fall.
Make a rubbing, remember their name;
    missing from this world, it will never be the same.
They leave, they're gone, away from this place,
    never to forget their beloved's face.

Samantha Aishman

For Comfort In Bereavement

Consider the great eagle, and the grandeur of his flight
As he surveys the whole terrain below from majestic height.
See the power and the beauty as he spreads his wings to fly
With joyous freedom, the winds of heaven he can now apply.

Long ago this eagle lay cramped safely in his shell;
And then the egg became the eaglet—confined to nest as well.
With time and determination the eaglet learned to use his wings;
And found wonder and exhilaration, soaring above earthly things.

We stand and watch the eagle as he dips his wings in farewell.
He stretches magnificent feathers, and soars in wondrous flight
To a destination only he and God can tell.

Which one of us, in earthbound status, who have yet to "win our wings"
Would call the eagle back to eaglet and restrictions that it brings?
With open arms and open heart we wish him "Godspeed" on his way
Knowing full well we will see him again—some other wondrous day.

Joy Morris Buffington

Storm Of Hate

The hate of a nation is like a silent storm blowing in on a north wind.

When the initial winds begin to blow in, carrying hate in like a
bird, people ignore the taste of saltiness which their own hate creates.

Then the clouds make their grand entrance. They become dark
ebony in regards to hate. These clouds, hold in hate,
storing it like a safe; unbreakable.

Only when the clouds become too full, unable to hold their
internal rage, does the hate fully emerge. Raining down on
people like a waterfall, intense and never-ending.

Before people even have a chance to prepare, the silent storm
has reached its full fury. Wild and mad like a caged animal.

People are afraid of what the storm of hate can do, but still even
more afraid to go against the storm. Like small children clinging to
their parents, people stay inside, shutting all doors and windows,
waiting for the storm to pass.

Only a storm of hate won't die like an old man tired and weak.
It becomes stronger with time.

In the end, only when people step outside with umbrellas of accep-
tance and understanding, will the storm die and the rainbow appear.

Ashley Younger

The Secret

Whispers are all around me
I have no clue what is the talk
Is it about me?
I hope so dearly that it is not about me!
It could rumors, it could be the truth.
So many people whisper through the night.
It is not fair, but then again nothing is.
I need to be part of the secret.
Only those who are 'normal' can be part of the ever so tightly closed circle.
So, as I lie here and dream, while I hear the whispers
And don't gossip with the others.
My secret is better than theirs though,
Because I know that I will always be stronger and they may not
always be,
Because I was once a listener instead of a whisper.
And they have been protected by their whispers,
But their whispers fade away and mine grow stronger.
I will know who is better.
And along with my letter,
I will whisper my secret. I will always be free.

Renee Gause

The Real Me

Open up my mind,
Shocked at what you see.
In your mind, what you've found can't possibly be me.
My outer shell you crack,
In this my hidden inner core is suddenly revealed.
The wax you pour has hardened,
As you burn it melts away,
And there I stand before you, not at all what I had seemed the other day.
You're tall and mighty queen, that had once seemed so proud,
Now a huddled puppy, thrown amongst the hungry crowd.
Frightened and worried, scared and unsure,
Out of control, a boat wrecked upon the rocky shore.
What lies underneath, my flesh now bloody and torn,
Open and unprotected from the relentless scorn.

I scream to get out,
I scream to break free,
I scream to let out what has become the real me.

Yvonne Bratcher

The Beginning Of Life

Time has begun; Power and energy, my constant companions.
I find stress upon me, exhilarating yet exhausting, I rest.
Warmth, contentment, gentle motion.

A tingling surge of energy bursts forth; I Am Moving!
I have fingers, toes, and a mouth, a heart within beats steadily.
A heart beyond beats life, my comfort, I rest.
Warmth, contentment, gentle motion.

Suddenly, a pressure, movement is a struggle!
Discomfort, confinement, pain!
My heart beats frantically within me, the other frantically around me!
Exasperating pressure!
Release! Freedom!
I am moving: I hear, I see, I cry.
My heart beats rapidly within me; the other heart?
I lean against it, hearing its comfort, I rest.
Warmth, contentment, gentle motion. Time has begun.

Sharon Simon

Don't You See What You Have Done?

Don't you see what you have done? To abolish of me,
delete me out of your life.
To tantalize my love for you was wrong.
Left me to yearn for a piece of your dream.
Don't you see what you have done? You have such a mysterious way.
Closed up inside a murky dream.
Release this torture, reveal your secret to me.
Trapped in a shadowy night, a foggy place, without a loved one in sight.
Don't you see what you have done? Destroyed an honest heart.
To talk so persuasive, so convincing to warm my soul and heart.
Don't you see what you have done" leaved and abanded me.
Neglect to tell the very truth, perplex my state of mind, you see.
Tremendous pain and immence sorrow, walking alone with
fears of tomorrow.
Never could I be the one your eyes could desire,
never could I be the one to set your soul on fire.
Don't you see what you have done to me?
You stold, then sold my heart and made me bleed.
I'll never be the same person again, you destroyed my faith and
took away my only dream. To the one who broke my heart,
"Rob," don't you see what you have done?

Stephanie Nicole Aragon-Vandeventer

Lot

I am a good man and I live alone now.
I reflect with sorrow as I walk amidst the ashes; for, three good
Men would make the difference here.
I searched! I begged!
My friends and neighbors closed doors, hearts and ears to me lest
The government retaliate.

"My children!" they said, "My food!" they said, "My job!"
They warned me against meddling, day upon day.
I should have had the plague for how I was shunned.
I then begged for one good man, yes, for one good man!
With renewed faith I bargained with all but my soul.
As I leave Chernobyl with nothing in my keep,
I carry a burden I can hardly bear.
My pledge to find one good man here, has failed.

I have traveled to America and I am a just and fair man.
Yet, I live on the street with cold and hunger as my friends.
I am homeless and alone. I have pledged in this vast nation to find ten good men.

I am homeless and alone, but God willing, I will find ten good Men!

Jill Fahey Johnson

In The Stillness Forever

In the stillness
the pillows cradle his head,
and blankets try to warm a body
that will never feel warmth again.
A TV commercial (from the TV in corner) tries to entice a mind
that will never again undergo thoughts.
The irritating sound of harsh rain upon the window,
won't bother him anymore.
A petal on a wilted flower wants to fall
but seems to be held up by the stillness.
I sit there almost as still as him, but my chest heaves as I breathe,
His will never do the same.
He is in stillness forever.

In the stillness I cry.
Perhaps no one else cares.
No one else knows of the stillness, and how horrible it is.
Maybe they care.
I see them walk by, I notice they are afraid,
afraid of the stillness and the thought of forever.

Katherine Michael

Letter To A Girlfriend

I spent my whole life yearning for that closeness
Seeking intuition and that feeling
Of closeness somewhere underneath the skin
And my search took me to many places
To Peru in my sixteen year
To Greece in my eighteenth year
To the false promises of little boys
And elsewhere
And beyond
But only to realize that I could spend
A lifetime trying to make a man understand
But they would never be able to feel my being the way you can
You map me out and give sense to me like an equation
You have made me realize that beyond rapture
Beyond inhibitions and disappointments
And the shame that my mother and society inflict upon me
Past the limitations of the utmost love that man can conceive for a woman
There is a love much closer
A love on the inside

Leigh Wisner

Effects of Love

You're weak in the knees,
you can hardly breathe.

You feel an embrace
and see a kind face.

You have nothing to fear,
you're comforted here.

When you leave it's not quite with haste.
You wish that you both could just stay in one place.

You count the days, hours, minutes, and seconds till you meet again.
You loose all direction and fall in the end.

Because you weren't careful when you first started
you fell too far; now you're broken-hearted.

Love plays games that have traveled through time.
Those games, that were yours, now are mine.

They've twisted my thoughts and destroyed my trust.
Now I can't tell if it's me or just lust

that draws you ever so nearer to me.
I can't fall much farther! Please let me be!

Let me return to my once well-shaped form,
to repeat the process as stated before.

Juli Boeglin

Don't Cry For Me Now

In memory of Lawrence Horton
Don't cry for me now for I am finally home,
soaring through the clouds is where I'm to roam.
I walk with God on streets of gold,
and there are so many miracles to behold.
Now for me there is no pain,
and everyday it seems ten times my strength I gain.
So don't cry for me now because I'm soaring through the
air under God's wing, as free as a bird and in no pain.
With the key in my hand, I'm suddenly at the gate,
just for a moment in time I stop and hesitate.
Because you see now, my long hard journey is through,
and all of my thoughts become suddenly on you.
I want you all to remember in your moment of despair
not to worry 'cause I'm still there.
So don't cry for me now, all you have to do is wait,
and remember when it's your turn I'll
be there with the key to God's pearly gate.

Holly Horton

I Am Special And Unique

I am special and unique
I wonder what it's like to die
I hear a whispering voice calling me
I see the world as a prison
I want to leave it soon
I am special and unique

I pretend to love the world, it pretends to love me
I feel like a leaf that is falling and never hits the ground
I touch the smooth, deep, ocean leading to nowhere
I worry about life and always will
I cry for no reason, but to feel the pain deep inside
I am special and unique

I understand the word peace, and think, why don't we have it
I say life is like a trail, you have to run no matter how tired you get
I dream of nothing, but wishes, wishes that never come true
I try to help the world but can't,
I hope for something that can.
I am special and unique.

Katherine Biggs

Descending Leaf

A falling leaf, not knowing its destination or course
Detached
Blowing in the wind
From here to there
It travels, no destination
Withering with every blistering beat of the sun
Pelted by the hard, yelling rain
Comforted only by the sweet, soothing, rare touches of an
optimistic breeze
Searching for a quiet place to gently rest its torn and tattered edges
Looking for a niche, you might call it
Floating on the river to the vast, mysterious ocean
Lost in its course, lost in its life
I am the leaf

Shana Singh

Life

The years have come and gone, like the rain drops in a stream
Sometimes it's at a standstill, other times it's gone in a dream

People take it for granted, the way things are
But time has a way of it's on, not going so far

If everything were to stop, what would happen then
I guess people would wonder, where in the world have we been

Time is every where, yet not so far have we gone
I wonder if time will be here for a long time,
Or maybe not till the next dawn

With time all around, we slip into our own dreams
I wonder if we can hold it all, or will it bust at the seams

I would like to catch it, hold it for as long as I can
Just maybe to learn from it, but who am I to try to hold it in my hand

But time cannot be held in ones hand,
Nor will it stand still for any soul
For it passes like the breeze, and it consumes you whole

In our busy world, who stops to watch a butterfly any more
Nobody has time for play, it's all become one big chore

Ray Griffin

Holocaust

The past is not of me.
The love of the future is behind.
I can't say that of what I wish I were
But yet, I wish I were not alive.

The love of death is what I share, the light of life is that of comfort.
Is that the pain of which I bring?

For death is that of comfort and life is that of death.
And at the tomb of which I lay.

But if at that I could stare at deaths door
and walk in the light in which comfort is.
And without death I stare at my tomb.
Then so I do, and so will I be.

The fear of what is to become
knocks at my door and sings to my soul.
As if it feels—makes me blind unto the truth of life.
Sing no more of death to my soul but of life, and the comfort therein.

So soon I will forget of pain and death, and the suffering of my soul.
Then can life comfort my heart.
Until that day I can never be free.
But my thoughts make me endure the pain.
I can't ever come back, and I can't ever leave.

Carly Newton

September 28, 1996

It was a Tennessee's night.
The sky was low, and I walked among the stars in a field.
The chill air reminded me to feel.
Without it, I should have been lost in wonder.
I lay on the midnight grass
and drowned in its dew.

The mud walls did not imprison our thoughts or bodies.
A path of crystal led us into a narrow and complete darkness,
as we searched for Knowledge.
Evil was weak that night, but we were not out to slay it.
I stumbled across it lying on a ledge, shined my light on it,
began to tease it.
When it tried to bite me it fell into the water and retreated under a rock.
Cursing us silently for disturbing its wounded rest, it vowed revenge.

We never made it to the end, but along the way we found peace,
and covered our faces in it,
Taking some home for the family.
Cold water and midnight would rinse it away.

Gregory Kessler

Sadness

Sadness, a cold grave which upon I weep. I come bearing flowers for
whom I've lost. For no apparent reason at no apparent time, a bad time.
A time where they were unwanted and unneeded in this world.

Now a fog sets in and takes over the night. I bend down to place
the flowers on the grave for whom I've lost. Yet in the sadness I am
confused, so I look down the grave and wipe away the damp
leaves and stare, for I am looking at a person I know better than
anybody, myself.

Becky Ton

The Restaurant

The sound of white noise fills my ears.
People talking and laughing
A woman screaming at her child for spilling his water.
Chairs scooting in and out
The sound of silverware scraping at each dish
The cash register rings, the hostess is saying,
"Thank you, come again"
A baby begins to cry, the mom says "Oh no, not again"
A sizzling plate rushes by me off to satisfy someone's hunger.
The sound of a lighter keeps on clicking, a rough voice asks for matches
Smoke fills the air
Elevator music fills the background, does anyone enjoy?
No rhythm, no harmony
No beat, just sound
The chaotic white noise
I take a bite of my salad.

Rachel Piccioni

Nostalgia

All through the purple haze of noon, high and light, and bird-song joyous
clear across the sun-baked meadow the children's voices reach my ear.
Short-lived anguish and fleeting joys, rising and falling with the
tide, and never-flagging energy: it is all there for me to hear.
Oh Paradise, when life is new and filled with the rising of the sun,
turning ever toward the new, naturally, and without fear.
So whole, unscarred as yet by strife, and all times filled with newer
finds, growing, gathering, day by day, child-memories, forever dear.
These wild, young years—so short the time of sweet unencumbered livin
The world is clean, the stream is pure; the end of childhood is so nea
Oh! I would trade experience for just on day of innocence!

Eveline van Lidth de Jeude

The Hospice Nurse

You are a Hospice Nurse because you believe in a Special Kind of care . . .
It is love and understanding that only a Hospice Nurse can share . . .

We observe the devotion and tenderness You so freely give.
It is these actions through which the Hospice Sprit can live.

We have witnessed the Many lives you have touched . . .
The end of Dreams, Broken hearts and such . . .

For Each new day you choose to stay . . .
You continue to guide the Hospice way.

Life is a Journey Destined to end . . .
It is reassuring knowing you are not only a nurse, but also a friend . . .

From Heaven to Earth Angels have been sent, We know this is true.
We witness the miracles daily in the work our Hospice Nurses do . . .

Next time you are down and feeling blue, remember the lives that you have touched . . .

And remember Everyone at Hospice loves our Nurses very, very much!

Serita Brame

Where I Am Now

Distant waves splash upon glistening rocks which overpower the shoreline.
Translucent water seems to meet sunset each night in a different design.
This vision I see as I'm laying on a silk over coat that is upon sand.
Pearls sit on polluted area that I'm ashamed to call my land.
Blue diamond dew is on my flowers, roses, and daises all the same.
Ferns which hang in jungles in far away places, while I stay in one place.
Only time is to blame.
Tears of joy soon approach the happy face.
Sand flies fast so set your pace.
Dunes ride on misty hills of the heated desert terrain.
Illusions of water spouting from the oasis may drive you insane.
Welcome to the desert the place no one wants to be.
Beyond what is real is a hard thing to see.
Lots of places to venture both near and far.
Though changing location don't forget who you are.
If the world were a rose, I'd be the stem.
But I'm proud were I stand and I'm proud were I am.

Erica Yvonnet

The Added Years

When I chanced to glance in my mirror
I wanted to turn away
To close my eyes on a new line or wrinkle which wasn't there yesterday,
But something compelled me to stare and realize time put them there.
My mind said, "Do not have fears, for these are the added years."
Do not yearn for the used to be;
Remember graceful age has the beauty of a willow tree.
Remember, too, for each thing time takes it gives something in return,
For it is in living that we learn.
We learn kindness, understanding, humility and patience we lacked   in our youth.
We must also learn to look in the mirror and face the truth.
We learn to hold unkind words on our tongue,
Which isn't a virtue of the very young.
With each added year thank God;
He lets us see not only the sun but the rain,
And only then will our added years not be in vain.

Dorothy Nickel

Someday Orchard Grove

The blindman of the ocean saw and said come sit and sing with me.
We'll run away to clouds above the orchard grove where nothing hurts but nothing grows,
Where I can whisper sweetness into your ear and you will cry altruistic tears.
She'll water the trees and plant the ferns for the love of mine for her that burns,
And maybe someday it will be okay to say but not today because it is my child's birthday,
The child for which I constantly weep and mourn her loss though she isn't gone
To the place where we all are alike,
Not heaven, not hell, but here in my cell,
To the soft, to the free, where everyone is like me,
And someday, I shall laugh.

Summer Keenan

The Saint's Call

I caught a glimpse of heaven
As I lay upon my bed.
I heard the voice of Jesus,
And this is what He said:

"You've finished your work,
Ran gallantly the race.
Well done, My child.
Welcome to My holy place.

A great cloud of witnesses
Has awaited your arrival.
All your seeds have been planted
For the endtime revival.

Don't worry about family,
Acquaintances or friends.
For upon My triumphant return
You'll see them again.

Come now and be with me,
Without pain, pill or suture.
Because in Me and only Me,
"You still have a future."

Gloria Nichols

Mother

Mother
Loving, caring
Spiritual bond
Always signing my referrals
Buddy

Jasmine Walker

In My Dreams

I see you in my dreams
walking along the water's edge
as the sun slowly sets

Your white dress blowing in the breeze
is slightly wet where the
water has danced around your ankles

The sun's last rays fall
on your beautifully soft skin
giving it a golden glow

I see you in my dreams
turn to me with hands out stretched
and together we walk

As the moon lights our way
I turn to look at you
and realize my dream has come true

Johnny F. Young Jr.

The Purpose Road

Your life will have a real purpose,
As you carry a heavy load,
Getting educated and rearing a family,
Will keep you on the purpose road,
But up ahead you meet the challenges,
And this lightens the load.

Give meaning to your life,
As you travel the purpose road,
Show some accountability,
No matter how heavy the load.

Since every life has a purpose,
And we mold it as we see fit,
Remember, the purpose road we travel,
Can be bright or dimly lit.

Bertha Harwe da Bingham Osborne

Life Is What?

Is life such of that as a rose that grows, blooms, and dies?

Is love a twisted sense of fate or a chance of whether your romance
will last or die depending on how hard you try?

Isn't strange how people can live on someone's mere word,
but die for money?

Is it a true thing dictionaries definitions are correct or is it all a
matter of aspect and allowance into a society who judges right or
wrong everyday often by looks and color.

I often wonder if my thoughts or feelings really do make a difference
or is life just a meaningless existence?

Why do we try so hard to be perfect when it is not our own
impurities that cause the problems, but mere miscommunication.
Talk, speak, read, love, cherish, hope, for what, who, why?
Is there a God?
Isn't that what you wanted? Are you happy or was it me?
My fault, my bad, my wrong. Oh, not it's just a mere song.

Listen closely or you'll miss it.
What will I miss? A chance at bliss?
Utter existence is but a change, just like the rose and even romance.

Melissa Bradbury

Hornet's Nest

The slums, those savage streets, I recall, with sleigh sliding by
the slushed sidewalks, most of all when going to kiss my small head,
my father gently wraps my cold arms and legs, instead, with his coat,
And slowly pulls my sled, by stone gray rows of streets filled with
winters's worst mud, slime and silt.

Along this city swamp, quietly, stealthily, my father pulls my sleigh,
almost escaping, but not quite the swarming horde. Our hornet's nest,
no honey-comb, those trashed stacked tenements, still stale and
stagnant, they abominate me, my memories, my loathing of mother.

They tell of times tinkering almost joyless in misshaped seconds,
and still remind me when I make my visits distant and dreaded,
while I watch my mother rocking in her chair near the wall.
There leans my old sleigh rusted (once, almost brand new).

Now rotted wood, all rust smelling mildew like her,
Worn out, an old unvarnished frame, which bold light and brazen air
eat away at peeling paint, and make putrid wasting that darken deep.

My thoughts taint more, down where the mind moulders
Senseless I sit somniferous, sifting through sick memories. I see stale
slums and rotted tenement stair, reeking of foul garlic and raw garbage.

Where ruffling mother's hornet like wings meant her sting to strike a blow

Maxine J. Norden

Policy Of Love, When Love Is True

Love has rules and love has punishments
Those who are addicted to disobeying its truth,
Must pay the price of living in cold madness.
With out joy, or memories to live life through,
Causing one's heart to crumble and fade away to a cold
World of woe, and live within the darkness of shadows.
Becoming a dweller in the halls of utter regret,
And purely living for awaiting death to reposes.
Only to live in a world of pure darkness and in total loneliness

Love has rewards of passionate fruit for true lovers,
Grown in a garden with celestial soil from heaven's
Earth, and heaven's chaste water.
Its juices of pure zeal from me to you, give strength to,
Life's new set of lovers. Who share both love and laughter.
Giving two lover's a chance to bloom together,
To build a future which will last forever and ever . . .
Our roots will pierce the earth profoundly to forbear, lies of love
from intruding, giving our love a true meaning and our passion more
burning satisfaction, polsifying strength to combat exotic beings with
impure actions, and proffering a venomous-serene of predestined Love.

Alfredo Lopez

Untitled

Love,
How infinite in bearing,
How baseless in foundation.
How possessive in nature
And assaulting, threatening;
Evoking a willing destruction of self.

How frustration to know longing,
And yet, how glorious to feel it.
How evasive and fickle
Unable to grip it.
Love, you are a demon,
An imp from halo to hoof.

This is treachery!
And you, soul, are the traitor.
I demand you give me back myself
I demand . . .
I demand . . .
I demand you take me.

Luke Diliberto

Maui Morning

Soft noe noe
Quietly filling Hana Bay
Where is Kauiki?

Harry L. Garnham

Ideals

Ideals are ours to cherish,
They start in youth and last,
Until with time they perish
And then become the past.

There are those who have commended
Work well done, thus joy complete.
But as each task is finally ended,
What is the joy, tasks to repeat?

Others sing of bright parades,
Of happiness and joy divine,
But, with time, that also fades.
I too once thought, love was mine.

Ideals belong to all mankind.
And many struggle to do right
But at the end what do they find,
Oblivion, eternal night?

Dan Mchenry Hicky

Being So Much More

Floating weightlessly in
My silent chaotic sea
Oars electric extend beyond
The hull of me—
Out, into the other,

Never so much more than this
Have I felt the intricacies of being.
Evolution a survivable being
Brings slowly and so,

I am arriving continually
In wavelike motion
To the shore that is
That survival of
The arrival of
The silently anchoring
Chaotic me.

Amy M. Collins

Daysend (Western Minstriel)

Around the prairie campfire the tired cowhands rested,
listening as they never did before.
And they watched the agile fingers hold the guitar as he tested,
every string to hear them ringing true once more.

Say now boys I have a story and since we have time,
I'll tell you of the places I have been.
Of the people that I met there, of the beauty and the clime,
and the things I've done he added with a grin.

As he began the mighty tale each cowboys eyes grew bright,
their nerves on edge they strained for every note.
packed with violence, he made it, crammed it full of outlaws might,
even told about the weapons that they tote.

When the wondrous tale was over, you could hear each in drawn sight,
the applause rang loud from every fellow there.
How it might of been the truth or it might have been a lie,
either way they really didn't care.

They just begged him for another just as rough and just as fast,
to while away again an hour or so.
And they listened to the music and they tried to make it last,
they'd be mighty sad to see this fellow go.

Dolores Regan

A Mother's Love

Raising children in this age is not an easy task.
Parents are bewildered; "What should I do?" they ask.
My daughter's smoking pot; I know, my son, he's snorting coke.
Our lives are turning upside down, my friend this is no joke!
We have talked and we have prayed; We've screamed and we've cried.
We've whipped them and restricted them; Dear God you know we've tried!
We live in fear from day to day, why can't they understand?
That all we want is to watch her grow and his become a man.
My father say's to "tighten up!" my mother says "Be nice!"
My friends are always right on hand with all of their advice.
Well I don't know if I am wrong or if perhaps I'm right.
But their futures lie within my hands so I'll put up a fight
There's going to be some changes here, there's going to be some rules!
Don't try to fancy talk me kid, I'm stubborn as a mule!
I love you and I need you, I don't want to be alone.
But if you can't obey them, find yourselves another home!
This may seem strict, this may seem mean, but this my child is true,
There is no love any greater than the love I have for you!

Katheryn Shepard

When To Stop?

I lay awake, thinking, staring, wondering—
thinking of yesterday, today, tomorrow;
staring into the darkness of future;
wondering whether a river exists for me to sail on.
Unaware, drifting into yet another sleep of uncontrollable thoughts;
a dream captures my mind, providing life to the conscience,
suggesting direction with a compass of the heart despite mind;
so that true feelings race about in fury before my sights.
A dream, a hope, mapping my course, suggesting a need;
that a synergy of two on one vessel may forever tame turbulent waters,
and provide balance with strength amidst darkness;
a need fulfilled by the blessing of a friend's eternal presence during the voyage.
Awakened unknowingly, senses focusing, thinking, staring, wondering again,
thinking of my dream, staring into the new day's sun, wondering who, when, how?
Who will fulfill the need set forth during my heart's flight in the night;
when does one truly know the best from the many good;
how might this search reach fulfillment without subconscious inhibitions?
Unknowns to which I now find a heart fluttering answer,
my search ends without regret and forever sparks with excitement,
for today I found you—tomorrow, us.

Stephen E. Belisle

Suffering

Here I sit so broken hearted,
No one care's how it got started!
If I happen to die tomorrow,
Who would have any sorrow?

Pain, pain and more pain,
What the heck has other's gain!
Grief, sorrow, never really joy,
I've just been a man's toy.

I've loved hard and always lost,
Just look and you'll see the cost.
I have gotten nowhere in life,
Nothing existing but all the strife!

Take away my kid's, my man, my life,
I've placed to my wrist a kitchen knife.
Failure, evil, Satan's sin,
Only through God can we ever win.

Mary E. Hudson

The Path of Life

The path of life brings us all
to where we sit proud and tall
on the path of life there are many turns
with each of these a lesson is learned
on the path of life we shall all fall
but we get up and stand just as tall
on the path of life we shall all cry
right before we learn to fly

Carolyn Grable

Jerry's Love

When we were young and filled with fire,
Our bodies burning with desire,
I was thrilled just to know,
that Jerry loved me.

As time went by and the fire's roar
was banked against the daily grind,
I was happy just to know you
that Jerry loved me.

When voices raised with bitter words
became the thing to fight against
I always knew days down inside
that Jerry loved me.

I am alone now, he is gone,
my eyes fill with tears that glisten,
and I shout to anyone who'll listen
that Jerry loved me

Irene M. Evans

My Talk With God

Dear Lord I pray to you above
Watch over this man with tender love
Although we are many miles apart,
I love him Lord with all my heart.
Please let him know in some small way.
My prayers are for him everyday
I pray Dear Lord please help me see
His love for me just could not be.
I pray so hard to you today
Please make this hurting go away.
And when our lives on earth are through
Please carry us safely home to you.

Grace Bojarski

Painted Dreams

Gravity holds me but
time confines me.
An acre of field and one lone marigold to brighten its day.
To be free is what?
Is it the seagull that flies overhead,
or is it the marigold alone in thought, with only the careless wind
to disturb its solitude?
I sit on the edge of my eternity
and throw grains of sand into the sea,
who carries them on
and laughs at my childish ways.
The dream that suspends me over the moon
only prolongs the inevitable drop in to the ocean of time.
Meditation ceases
reality bites
the wind delights the lonely marigold.
Artificial light dwindles in moonbeams
asking timidly if his existence matters in the realm of the sun,
and the moon replies, as the sun implies,
that he only counts for as much as he gives.

Elizabeth Forsyth

Love Taken

Rainbows glow, and color smiles on the man who gives his heart.
To those who share the happiness cup all days are filled with love.
But when the mind is filled with doubt, the colors red and dark.
The love that shared to each as one can be no more and must part.
To understand, and it be clear, this I cannot do.
The love we had, the passion we felt, the heat just burned within.
And now it has been replaced with winter's arctic freeze.
Thanks to you it is no more, the happiness we felt.
Two Jacks for sure come into play on everything that's said.
To be as one; you'll never feel with anyone but me.
Away from you, eliminated from me to find happiness can never be.

Elfrun M. Allan

Untitled

Desolate eyes hunt an empty rink,
Searching for the sights and sounds that still echo in their hollow hearts.
But the moment is gone.
Seized by red winged vultures, flying so high in their glory,
That they cannot feel the pain that is lain on these war-torn bodies.
Blood and sweat are diluted in tears of defeat,
Combining to make a sickeningly sweet concoction of meaningless
shrugs and excuses. Blame is passed sinlessly—
From error to error,
Person to person,
But defeat has no face.
Only a feeling of utter hopelessness and despair—
Challenged by many,
Overcome by few,
Understood by even fewer.
For it is not the strength of your body but of your character that matters.
Broken hearts and shattered egos
Must be mended with pride and filled with determination
As a single thought pulses through each body
As they beat as one on their quest for revenge.

Monica Samec

Sun On My Face

Oh, cease you wicked rain,
Let the sun shine on my face.

Oh, gloomy clouds be gone,
Let the sun shine on my face,

Oh, puddles dry up soon,
Let the sun shine on my face.

Nature be, oh, so beautiful,
Let the sun shine on my face.

Let me feel the sun's warm embrace,
Let the sun shine on my face.

Valarie Quinones

Druggie

You are such a hypocrite!
You tell me "Stay away from them,"
Then you go smoke a joint.
I put you on a pedestal,
And you pass out and fall off.
Then, when you wake up,
You blame me for your fall.
You put me up there,
Is the excuse you use.
Well, I've got news for you:
You put Yourself on that pedestal
That summer seventeen years ago
When you decided to get laid.
But nothing really matters now,
You've burned your pedestal.
You're nothing but a druggie.

Rea Strother

My Mom Taught Me

How can I describe
What my Mother is to me
When the memories of her being
Start in eighteen ninety three.

A century of loving kindness
Shared with those she held so dear
Leaves me full of prideful awe
For the special times I had with her.

For over such a lifetime
Many pressures came to bear
And I, just one of many,
Yet she always was right there.

Of course were times that I recall
When I firmly took a stand
And in her loving understanding way
My backside felt her hand.

At times I feel it's frightening
When my thoughts turn inwardly
For much of what I am and do
'Tis 'cause my Mom taught me.

Edward J.

Untitled

Can you tell me my friend
can you tell me the way back home
can you show me with your everlasting
strength
I doubt it
for there is only one somebody who can
seldom lie in the bed that I have made
for myself
that body is me

Jack Josel

The Winds of Change

Our souls float on the winds of
life, like leaves in the breeze
Every so often two souls meet
and for a time journey together
When and if the winds should
change and separate the two
they should be thankful for
the time they shared
But if the union was meant to be,
the winds shall come full circle
and once again unite the two
so they may continue the
journey they started.

Joel C. Long

A Lazy Winter Day

Cozy, cuddled up by the fire
With a book in my hand
That I read to myself.
I soon will find I'm in another land
Filled with adventure, mystery, and fun.
My book will take me anywhere, I can.
I find myself devoured in time,
While my book swallows me up,
As the snowflakes gently fall outside.
Then my mother calls, "dinner time,"
And I have to leave my adventures
behind.

Laura Beth McClinton

Friends

Play with them,
Help them,
Hug them,
Invite them over
to your house.
Sit with them,
Talk to them,
Eat with them,
Friends!

John Kopp

True Love

True love don't die
Don't go away
Memories grow stronger
Each passing day

I'll never forget you
Tho' sometime I try
I'll always love you
True love don't die

Sometime I feel angry
Since you're no longer here
Often feel lonely
Sometimes it's just fear

Tho' you're no longer with me
I still feel your embrace
And when I close my eyes love
I can still see your face

I know you're happy
In your new home above
Someday I'll join you
You're my true love.

Pearl L. Ham

Let Me Sing

I have flowers on my table.
I have sunshine at my door.
Let me sing while I am able,
For soon I'll be no more.

Leaves of gold, mornings frosty,
Autumn's chill against my door.
Let me sing while I am able,
For soon I'll be no more.

Rafters white, a fire now crackling,
Winter's silence at my door.
Let me sing while I am able,
For soon I'll be no more.

Now comes Spring, a new beginning,
Things will bloom just like before.
'Tis now birds that do my singing,
Praising God forevermore.

Katrina Staggs

Would You Survive My Life?

Could you handle my troubles?
Can you survive my horrible dreams?
Can you conquer my fears?
Can you deal with my problems?
Can you withstand my pain?
Can you live with the pressure?
Could you survive the heartache I do?

Lindsey Brown

The Lamb

Blessed is He,
The lamb upon the throne;
For all people should praise
The day He was born;
For it is He whose flesh
Was beaten and torn;
All for our sins
And denied of His throne.
But now He's our savior;
We can call Him our own;
For only through him
Can man be reborn.
We must receive all of Him
For our lives to transform,
And have faith in His promise
To take us all home;
So give Him glory,
And let the truth now be known.
Blessed is He
The lamb upon the throne.

Kelly V. Doyle

A Timeless Dove

A dream so soft
A timeless dove
That sows the seeds of everlasting love
Descending now, but soaring on
It gives my soul the wine of dawn
Whose gentle sadness, like a dart
Delves deep into my sleeping heart
A timeless dove that took to fight
Gracefully pierces each peaceful night
Those autumn leaves that spin me 'round
Fail to leap love's endless bound

Gigi Shames

Lisa, My Gem

Through the crystal waters of life
A gem among the waves
Unique as each individual snowflake
which touches the earth
So you touch the inner souls
of your friends
You certainly do shine with kindness
toward every human being
treating all
as you would a friend
This is you
My daughter
Lisa

M. Levite

If We Never Met A Stranger

If we never met a stranger
What a wonderful world this would be

Everyone would show so much love
Just wanting the best for you and me

There would be no more hunger
For our love would feed the world

There would be no place for disaster
For everyone would truly care.

Race would not be an issue
Through all eyes we'd see a friend

Someday, someway, somehow
Will all meet a stranger
And treat him as a friend.

Carl Cunningham

Oh Angel, My Guardian

Your eyes open wide
Those of a child
A view through the window
Of your soul, there inside

I walk to your bed
The years slip away
Memories flash by me
All the words not said

Speaking so calmly
You accept without fear
The future awaits
Of one I hold dear

A life that was troubled
Full of pain, yet the Lord
Awaits 'round the corner
It is time, strike the cord

For God, He is gentle
Our wishes He hears
Our life may be short
But our souls will have years

Sylvia Fitzpatrick

Soil Deep Within Us

The bounds of earth
Center core, core of
Mankind, is breath,
Then gives no more
Doth twine with earth's
Crust.

Lucille Dobrzynski

Figure of an Angel in the Sky

Do you see what I see
Though the sky is cloudy
Do you see the beautiful figure
How beautiful art thy
So shimmery, So bright

There is shimmer of silver
In the sky tracing the figure
Look there my child
It is a beautiful angel
So beautiful and divine

Oh how I wish
I could be like
The figure in the sky
That beautiful angel
That floats in the sky
With silver around it's figure
So beautiful and bright
My beautiful, beautiful angel in the sky.

Kimee Spidell

Mind Games

I may never cross your mind
But if you ask you will find
You're in my mind everyday
Sometimes I wish you'd go away
How can I love you so much
When I will never touch
That cold, cold heart inside of you
Which will never let you do
Anything to let me know
If you return the love I show
To you in every little glance
But I still can't take the chance
That you will learn just how I feel
And break my heart and it won't heal
Then cold like yours my heart will stay
And gradually I'll fade away
For if your love I'll never know
It is best that I don't show
The burning love I feel for you
Because this dream cannot come true

Brenda M. Hudson

To My Son

Infancy, childhood, and teen-age
All are falling behind,
As from the great roll of living
Your 21st year doth unwind.
The training and briefing are finished
The do's and do-not's are your own
Your dependence on others diminished
As older and wiser you've grown.

Was I patient when patience was needed
Was I firm when firmness was due
Was I gentle and understanding
When life was perplexing you?
Does the love of God and of virtue
In your inner soul abide?
Have you honor, faith and courage
And an honest and loving pride?

One can know not all of the answers,
But when the query is done
There is joy and pride abundant
In the man that you have become.

Marie E. Bernell

Julie's Doll

Living and loving,
Tugging at mama's leg.
Big sister always abreast,
Peeling her shiny Easter egg.
Baby sister's fast asleep.
So, peaceful.

A child born to search.
A child born to pain.
A child born to long,
Long for love so strong.

Always wishing.
Hope for the ballerina.
The doll for Julie.
Her nursery school friend.

Climb upon the box,
Rising to the apex.
Just within reach.
Almost triumph.
As I tumble into mama's arms.
Mama whispers, that's Julie's doll.

Janice M. Hollander

My Feathered Friends

They migrate in the winter
And fly free in the spring,

I always look forward to it
Just to hear them sing

In the day they entertain,
And at night they softly calm,
With just a gentle coo.

Blue, red, brown, and yellow
They're all so beautiful

They fly so elegantly,
My favorite sight to see,

Just by luck far and near,
My favorite sight can be seen.

If I could be any creature,
A bird is what I'd be.

Heather N. Guice

Protected

Though blazes of fire
may light up the sky
Smoke covered cities
that sting your eye.
Shaken by earth's
most angered fears.
Drowned by the sorrows
of lonely men's tears.

No harm shall come near thee

Fever may spread
in the wealth of kings
Scars shall appear
on the faces of thieves.
Mountains may tremble
buildings will fall.
Blood will spill
in the heart of it all.

But no harm will come near thee.

For blessed and divine are the souls
of innocent children as life unfolds.

Elizabeth Talbot

Untitled

His unwashed hair has never seen a
comb,
Looking unkept, looking ungroomed.
She stands here with a brush in hand,
Every hair in place, pretty face.
It's expected of her,
Yet, would be exceptional of him.

Laura Newton

For V.M.D.

On my knees at your feet
I give me to you
To betray, to beat, to marry
To be loved, my heart you can bruise
Or love as you choose
Please let me be with you
Even five minutes a year
To love you always
Do you love me?
I don't hear
Your voice I adore
Like chocolate and money
I always want more
Than I will ever need
But I need you more
Than you will ever guess
Or know unless I can tell you
But the words fly away
Like a thousand clouds in a windstorm
And I still want to give me to you.

Stacy Yingling

My Dog

My flowers bloom in the summer;
In the autumn it will rain.
The face of my Maggie
I would love to see again.

You left us, oh, so suddenly;
The shock was so severe.
We never thought for a second
That such grief was very near.

I miss the sound of your panting
And your bark since you have gone,
And though I no longer see you,
In my mind you still live on.

It broke our hearts to lose you
But you did not go alone,
For part of us went with you
The day you left our home.

Though you are gone forever
And your paws we cannot touch,
We're still so very lucky to have
Memories of the "Dog" we loved so much.

Anita Ellen Carroll

Your Best Friend

When day are long,
and night never end.
When there are many trials to bear

And no one seems to really care
When your mountains seem to erupt
And you feel like giving up
And your plans gone away.
You just can't face another day.
Don't give up
You have a friend in
Jesus Christ.

Queenie E. Jones

Untitled

I look upon the heavens
As the clouds prepare the day
The sun dawns the morning
While the darkness fades away
Our world provides life
happiness
We share throughout the land
The Lord carries my sadness
Forgiving the sins
Of man
Faith rules my spirit
I'm a soldier, The helping hand
Protecting Gods children
On his mountain
I will stand

William M. Hoppe

You

You made my heart sing to the stars
And soar like a dove.
I find myself searching for
The moonlight in the heavens above.
I feel like I'm on a cloud
Looking down below,
Seeking and searching,
Not knowing where I should go.
What should I say
Or what should I feel?
I find myself reaching out
To see if you are real,
Wanting to hear your voice,
To touch your face,
Hoping I'm not dreaming
Or my feelings out of place.

Edna M. Crunelle

A Taste Of Me

I hear voices of all who know me,
they cheer when I come around.
But by myself, they do not know,
my tears begin to sound.

Not always sad, I mostly shine,
when those I love are near.
But by myself, they do not know,
what forms in me is fear.

Fear of being left alone,
For I am scared and unsure.
But by myself, I hope they know,
My love is truly pure.

I may seem like a strong one,
Who does not feel sorrow at all.
But by myself, they do not know,
My tears begins to fall.

Please don't think that I'm unhappy,
For happiness makes me complete.
I just don't know where I'm going,
And I need you to guide my feet.

Dana Lee Childress

You And I

You and I, we are no more,
I pray for your knock upon my door.
Daylight has the darkest hours,
Night time dreams with mystical powers.
Take my thoughts to another place,
Moonlight kiss my tear-stained face.
So hurt and so alone,
Now that you and I are gone.

Tammy Turner

Free

If I could bring a touch of life
from every thought I feel
As I lay my head upon your breast
So gently where I kneel

My heart cries out
My soul sings out

Let me ride the tide of your life

Let me taste the breath in you
As it mellows - smooth as wine

So sweet, the taste of your nectar
As it welcomes the morning light
Mother natures juices flow
That greets the birth of life

If I wrap my mind
Around your body
Will you comfort me
Nestling on a bed of clouds
absorbing all to be
As I humbly lay before you
Your angel sets us free.

John C. Bailey

Phobophobia

I'm afraid to say
That I'm afraid
Of everything around.
I'm afraid to walk,
Afraid to talk,
Afraid to just sit down.

I'm afraid of water,
I'm afraid of land,
I'm afraid of grass,
I'm afraid of sand,
I'm afraid I'll shrink,
I'm afraid to expand.

I'm afraid to laugh,
I'm afraid to cry,
I'm afraid to live,
I'm afraid to die,
And worst of all, oh dear, oh dear,
I'm most afraid of all my fears!

Christopher Long

On Differentiation

Struggle!
Work!
Over and over
Again and again I struggle.
He's there
Critical,
Contemptuous,
Unloving.
Stand up!
Speak up!
Say what is you!
Say what is yours!
Say what is his!
Know what you want!
Stick to it!
Don't back down!
Don't give up!
Struggle!
Joy!

Peter S. Hashim

The Arrival

The space had grown,
I should have known.

The touch was warm,
I sensed no harm.

The light was bright,
I was full of fright.

They sounds that were heard,
They must have been words.

The meaning unclear, yet
I was so near.

The rhythmic sounding
I once felt as synchronized pounding,

Ceased.

I had arrived.

Anita Nisbet

Love Is

Love is a cloud
Love is a dream
Love is a feeling
Nothing comes between
Love is wishing well
A fountain of youth
Love is no secret
And only the truth
Love is kind
Love is true
And any hard feelings
Love will see you through
'Cause I found love
When I found you

Linda M. Farias

Please Remember Me

No matter what you do,
Please remember me.
For in my heart,
Though we're apart,
You will always be.

My heart cries out for you,
Although you're far away.
But what a thrill
If someday you will
Come back to me to stay.

Meantime, I will wait;
And hope soon I will see;
Your smiling face
Some how, someplace
So, please remember me.

Carrie Knowles

Our Friendship's Over

My friend I hate to do it,
But our friendship just can't last.
The time we shared together,
Has faded to the past.
I told you it would happen,
Our friendship was bound to end.
Even though I know you care,
I don't consider you a friend.
For I look at you in a different way,
I've fallen in love with you my
Friend!

Vianney Wilkerson

Dreams, Wishes and Tears

If dreams were given to me
And my dreams came true,
I'd force myself to sleep at night
Just so I could dream of you.

If wishes were given to me and
I was granted just two,
I'd wish for you to always love me
And the other I'd save for you.

If tears could write a love song
And the love song was made for two,
You would know just how I feel inside
And how much I truly love you.

But dreams are just for dreamers and
Wishes seldom come true,
My tears won't write a love song but
When they fall they will fall for you.

Kurtis Baumgart

A Glimpse of Heaven

As the sun creeps above the mountains
and the deer waiting to feed,
Our Father is so caring
and fulfills their every need.
I see the frost upon the ground.
I hear the geese fly south.
I feel the breeze upon my face;
no words come from my mouth.
A sunrise so spectacular.
a peaceful, quiet scene;
Purples, pinks and oranges
bleed through the evergreen.
The hands of God at work,
as the tapestry unfolds,
The beauty and the wonder are
revealed each time it's told.
So when you see that sunrise
it's a gift for your today,
And recall that glimpse of heaven
and take the time to pray.

D. Priar

A Child

An experience unlike any other
Something one could never imagine
The coming of a new life
The dawning of a new era
Watching the days pass by
Wondering. Asking. Hoping.
Wondering if everything is OK
Asking for guidance
And hoping they will grow with happiness
A new experience
Days turned around
Chaos everywhere you turn
Love. Embrace. Enjoy.
Love a new life
Embrace the tiny body
Enjoy the best years of your life
A child, a being, a person.

Erica Brown

Genius?

He thinks of himself
As a clear thinking man
A man who stands
—for logic
—for reason
A man to believe in.

The strings of his mind
He plays like a harp
For reason is an art
available to
a chosen few.

His children do not think right.
They worship false gods.
Despite his erudite advice,
They do not see
That he can never be wrong.

"Go and see," says he.
"God thinks just like me."

Patricia Marion

Unity

Take my hand
and walk beside me
into the future
with love as our guide.

Take my heart
and preserve it with yours
in the union
of all that we share.

Take my soul
and know that I am
your life long companion, your friend,
your eternal love.

Accompany me in the beauty of
two hands interlocked forever,
two hearts pulsating,
two souls submerged . . .

One life.

Donna Maria Gulla

A Life With You

I'd live with you
Down by the riverside
In that old brick house
Where the fields stretch wide

I'd walk with you
In fields of gold
Across the bridge
Past the swimming hole

I'd lie with you
Under the stars so bright
And touch your face
Deep into the night

I'd kiss you softly in the setting sun
And forever hold you in my arms.

Tate Nuckols

Untitled

Close to the ground
spreading like wild fire—
covering vales and mountains
with yellow flowers and greenery.
Have I forgotten, what you are called?
Of course, not.

Ingrid D. Larson

Farewell To Sierra

Blossoms float in the gutter of rain,
ripped from our sturdy branches.
We could not stop her hell, her pain,
her reckless race of chances.

Soaked of will, of joy, of life,
and wasted, fickle lovers,
she cut her losses with a knife.
She needed more from others.

A life snapped off in early spring,
cherry blossom time.
She cannot shout, she cannot sing,
we can't undo the crime.

Her spirit's gone, like rising fog
whispered into bleakness.
Our hope decays, like rotted log
broken down with weakness.

In morning chill we cling together,
shuddered into oneness.
Silent in the somber weather
we hug the soul between us.

DessyeDee Clark

Awakening

Silence, and
All of creation lies,
Eager, awaiting the entrance of
Morning

Graciously,
Dawn lifts her head as a
Tress of black splendor from morning sky
Passes

Brilliantly
Shimmering, dancing 'cross
Rivers of waters, her music, her
Laughter

One open
Eye to behold the new
Day and the greatest of trials and
Triumphs!

Felicia Renee Evans

Untitled

Today we step in the direction
of new and wonderful tomorrows,
Full of hopes and dreams
the promise of what will be.

Blessed with parents who
guided and cared, who
came today to share in the joy,
of the bond that will be made.

Together arm in arm we will leave
towards a life of husband and wife.
We will face the challenges,
overcome the obstacles,
Fight to stay together and live
by the vows we decree.

What our future holds is a mystery
but the paths we choose,
we choose together and eventually,
later, when we are three,
our lives will be enriched
with memories of days like these.

Stacy Ann Terry Holbrook

Witch Maleena

Witch Maleena, queen of fire
Ancient Celtic love desire
With the Gods she doth conspire;
Through the mirror she has seen
Visions of a dragon green
Servant of a wizard king
Warrior, poet, lover, thief
Surrounded by a wall of grief
Mystic martyr in his heart
Flaming star of passion start

Clinton Hammons

Admonition

Whenever you think of me
After I have shed this shell
Let it be gently, kindly,
Because I loved you well.
Know that I hold your hand
Whenever pain is near,
Because I understand
The loss you've come to fear.
We two as one were met;
Our years a jubilee.
Farewell without regret
Still waits for you and me.
Solitude's a lonely land
So I will not leave you, dear,
Reach out and touch my hand,
My love, I am still here.
Death stores no tears, no pain,
So do not grieve too long.
One leaves, but one remains
To finish our love song.

Jewel E. Mullineaux

Encouragement

Just little old me
Asking how you might be.

Hoping what I might say
Might brighten your day.

To give you a little hope
To help you to cope.

Prayer is my task
So you might bask
In His rays of loving care.

Promise me to look
into the good book
To review His promises to you.

Now you are put to the test
to get some rest
So you can be good as new.

Gail Allen

You Left

As I wake up this morning
I look at your empty closet,
wishing you would come back home.
Be with me tonight as we say goodbye.
But you won't be coming back.
I know you won't come back.
Leave before I cry.
Don't call me if it's not working out.
You chose your new life, you lift me.
Don't you love me anymore?

Patrisha L. Rosauer

Evidence of Praise

My fingers cling to my hands.
They clap as I begin to dance;
The music's in my soul,
Chanting glory, glory forevermore.
I smile at you then wave.
I'm blessed as I hear you say,
With your eyes,
We are one in this praise.

Retha Bowman

Unrequited Love

When your love is slowly fading
and the end is drawing near,
You're so alone and filled with pain
you can't slow down the tears.
Your mind is filled with confusion
and your heart is filled with sorrow
You dread the thought of waking up
to feel that pain tomorrow.
Your soul is full of emptiness
that no one can replace
You sit and wait with teary eyes
to see his smiling face.
As time goes on and life goes by
the memories still remain.
And everyday until your life is done
your pain will remain the same.

Jessica M. Felix

Just The Three Of Us

Through all of our lives
It was our crew
Through laughter and tears
The three of us grew

From the times life seemed to hard
And you just couldn't on
You looked for your sister
And the pain would be gone

When her dream came true
And she ran to tell you
Opening your arms
Was all you could do

As it was from the beginning
And always will be
I hope my love
Is what the two of you see

Mary Eisenman

Winter

With the first snowfall,
It falls crisp and white.
I walk carefully over it,
Not to destroy its beauty,
It feels cold against my skin.
My mind never leaves the cold.

Lauren Talbot

Love

Love is a circle,
always in motion,
for all who dare to try it
May just not find it,
or if they do,
their feelings might fly off.
Off the circle of love.
Bye Bye.

Lacy Benson

Mom's Poem

Dedicated to my family
I am a hopeless romantic, we know
This to be true.

I am insulin-dependent diabetic . . .
So don't take away my needle.

I am a person; so don't take
Away my air, don't cut off
My nose despite of my face.

I have feelings, don't take
Away your heart.

I am love, use me . . .
Share me . . . with all
Mankind.

Helen Brown Aguilero

Untitled

Watch the time, my friend
Like a captured bird.
For if it does get away,
It will not return
And the loss is yours.

Misty Brennan

Nathan

I think of you
With your long hair waving,
Your dark eyes flashing.

You, with your stubborn pride,
Your anger,
Your beaten down heart.

I see in you
The small boy
With questioning eyes
But a ready smile.

I wonder
What might have happened
That frightened you
Or yourself.

Why do you hide
Behind
Your half-smoked cigarette?

Kimberly Turner

Count on Him

Who should we turn to in time of need?
The greatest healer of all,
The Lord, who is always there
To catch us when we fall.

Nothing is too great for Him to handle;
All you have to do is pray,
Asking His guidance and help,
Whatever time of day.

He's always there to listen
With a shoulder to cry on,
Or celebrating with us
A game that we have won.

When times get too rough,
Count on Him; He'll be there
With a kind word or lesson,
Teaching us to care.

Jillian Marie Florence

Broken Dreams

My dreams were crushed and broken,
My heart was surely tried;
I felt the need of Jesus,
Unto the Lord I cried.

"My child, be not discouraged,"
I heard my saviour say;
"Just take my yoke upon you
And I'll show you the way."

"Just take my hand and follow
Wherever I may lead;
You'll never be forsaken,
I'll fill your every need."

I took the hand He offered;
What joy and peace I found;
I followed and He led me,
A step to higher ground.

Martha Stauffer

Poetry, What A Wonderful Thing

Poetry is fame,
Poetry is a family's life.
Everyone who's talented is a poet.
Poetry is a game you must play.
Poetry is an art of the brain.
A love within our heart.
Poetry is a choice you must choose.
Poetry is wonderful,
What a wonderful thing!

Jacqueline Renee Kinsey

Pass The Ryder, Please

Would someone pass the Ryder, please?
Just put it by my side!
Because it's time to move again.
I no longer need to hide!

My life has been a galaxy,
I've gone to planets very strange!
And I have met some funny folks,
Whose lives I cannot change.

I've loaded stuff. Just throw it on!
I seem to not know why!
But perhaps I'll get an answer,
Before it's time to die!

So give me one that's new and clean,
And put on my face a smile!
So I can load the truck again,
And do it with some style!

I'm not as young . . . as I once was,
But wiser! That's a fact!
So please help me load the Ryder, Lord,
And then get me back on track!

Susan Dale-Wright

Fear

In my fears I am a child
trapped in a scary dream
Hoping someday I will awaken.

The monster I dreamt about
Is tearing away at me;
eating me alive.

I pinched myself to awaken
I awakened to a world of reality.
Only to find myself in a real nightmare.

Ruth Scarpa

Sending It Back

Send it back
Take the pique
Keep your pins and needles
I can mend the rip in my heart

What you need is spandex,
to stretch your way
away from me.
Take your pricks and stabs,
and pin them on yourself.

Satins, lace and silks
won't get my attention.
I'm sending back your gifts.

Take your cotton and nylon
Take your wool and rayon
I wouldn't accept your fabrics
I'm not a seamstress.

Cassandra Pingree

Save Us

Save us cried the wolves who
tried to find shelter from the fire

Save us yelled the birds fleeing
from the trees that were being
torn down

Save us called the whales trying
to find clean waters to live in

Save us, the deer said, the
hunters are shooting us when
they're not allowed

Save us, save us, save us,
Save us, the voices start to
fade away

Noelle Lansdale

Naked Earth

Deep beneath the naked
Earth there lies a morbid truth.

Of innocence and childhood
of murders in their youth
wherein lies the irony of
life taken and so young

For glances, signs, of simple
lies from naivete of tongue
a sacred future taken a
promise ne'er filled eternal
absence bears my pain
It was a child this has killed

Cherilee Melissa Lamothe

It's A Wonderful Place

shaken from a rusty grave
where no one wonders to
it's all alone and left alone
with no one to take control of it
leave the fortress behind
to no one that sees it abandoned
the world is a horrible place
for an old man to live in
winds sweep down at miles per hour
leaves rustle near its dead tree
there is no sanctuary to be in
a deserted island of insanity

Cynthia Chan

Fly With Me

Day breaks
Cool air fills my lungs
I take a deep breath
For the very last time

From the top
This bridge looks higher
I look down at the water
It seems so far away

Hold me
Take me away from them
They don't understand this
They never could

You take my hand
We jump together
I told you I could fly
For a moment we are free

Amy Neilan

Anger, As In A Thunder In My Hand

Anger will not stop,
I will pursue.
The battle that will not stop,
that I have started before you.
The thunder that builds,
deep, deep, inside.
One day I will show you,
what I had to hide.
One friend is better,
than far more than one.
Two can go better,
on the life long run.
A lot has been hidden,
from clueless eyes.
Till one day all tears,
will turn to gentle sighs.
The world has changed,
since the far, helpless past.
When people were well,
and together at last.

Christopher Dunay

Who Am I

I don't know who I am
Do you give a damn, about me
I don't know where I've gone
Must have gotten lost, along the way

I don't know where I end
Or where you begin, who am I
My tears, they will not come
Where have they gone, why can't I cry

Thoughts I think are mine not yours
But I can't be sure, get outta my head
I've walked in your shadow for so long
It's time I was gone, before I'm dead

I have to find out who I am
Do you give a damn, if I do
I used to know who I was
Way back before us, before you

Dale Swink

Baby Steps

His huge brown eyes
shine with delight as
he giggles that silly
sound (that babies have).
At first he grabs
that vivid green striped couch
and holds onto it like
a lifeline. I open
my arms wide and coo
softly, coaxing him to
be daring and let go.
He giggles again, that
angelic sound, and shakes his
tiny head (as if he would shake it off).
Finally, hesitantly,
he lets go and reaches out to me—
I back slowly away.
He looks down at the floor,
then up at me with uncertainty
(as he bends down to play
with his shoestring).
Finally, at last, he reaches
for me as he shuffles—
first one, then two, steps forward.

Alyssandra Cooper

Words

Exposed souls,
Naked spirits,
Opened fully,
To another.
Raw thoughts,
Pure emotions,
Honest words,
Broken hearts.
Wounds heal,
Words soothe,
Arms hold,
Lips whisper.
Eyes meet,
Fingers touch,
Hearts mesh,
Souls unite.
Times change,
People move,
Years pass,
Love remains.

Jennifer Albright

Razor Burn

Crawling the razor edge of hope
swallowing a hot coal of hurt—
The keen rim almost invisible ahead
but blood whispers in my track—
It's only the hue and cry of emotion
the rusty wreckage of my life—

Why tenaciously flaying myself
on a dream too sharp to grasp—
With a word that burns in my gullet
obstructing the retch of joy—
Trying to clasp that fine perfection
is it the point or only the strife

Slicing ceaselessly through my flesh
severing each delusion—
Faith persevering when courage fails
groveling ever onward—

Roberta Hartlove

The Beach

I love the beach,
Don't you?
I sit and eat a peach,
With my friend Lu.
Sometimes we read,
Sometimes we swim,
And do a good deed,
Or go to the gym.

The waves crashing,
The kids digging,
The fathers reading,
The mothers knitting,
All make up the beach,
Where I sit,
And eat my peach.

Jennifer Krieg

Random Energy . . .

random energy . . .
What else is there to say . . .
a lot . . .
I suppose, but the problem is . . .
I just don't know.
Give up Give in . . .
go away . . .
no compromise either way . . .
right or left day or night . . .
eteranal darkness . . .
shut out the light . . .
Close my eyes and let be peace.

Kerri Massey

Day Dreamer

Alone in thoughts
Of love and dreams
In the midst
Of joyous ease.
The hearts and eyes
Of lovers do
Reveal the truth.

Love blooms from
The depths
Like flowers
In spring,
The scent lingers on
And its essence
Never leaves.

My eyes are a
Reflection of you
And me.

Whatever led
Myself to Thee?

Lashunda Rodgers

Shards

There is a pain inside,
Deep within my soul.
I feel anger, I feel hate.
It holds me, it traps me.
I cannot escape.
My heart has shattered,
And I bend to retrieve,
The shards of myself,
From the floor.
The floor greets me,
With open arms.
I lay down, and close my eyes.
Sliced by a shard of myself,
I am silent.

Rachel Williams

Walk in the Park

On my walk in the park
I see
bees in the flowers
birds in the tree
fish in the lake
and me
this was once a fairy tale
but I believed
and now
it seems to me
that somebody granted my wish
because now all bad things
have disappeared
and to my surprise
I found
my one true
wealth was nothing more
than a walk in the park

Laura Leathers

The Waves of Love

The waves of love
are pounding
with a resounding force
against the walls of hate.

This course
will not abate,
for people will never cease,
nor forsake
the struggle for peace.

So take heart.
Someday, the waves of love
will tear apart
the walls of hate
and create,
in its wake
a more loving world for
everyone to partake in.

Patricia Trudeau

Take Me Away

Take me away from here,
Take me any where.
Somewhere far away,
Somewhere out where
I can play.
Take me to a place with sun,
Take me to a place that's fun.
Some where, where I don't cry,
Some where, where I can fly.
Far away from my fears,
Far away from my tears.
Dry my eyes and start to
Dream about a place with
Wonderful things.

Melissa Whitaker

Blossom

When a blossom blooms,
Its petals fall so soon.

Its seeds begin to spread,
In speed they go and dread.

And when they rest and sleep in fear,
They wait until Spring appears.

And then they bloom,
For others to sniff and consume.

Erin Littlejohn

Dreaming

I had a dream today
That the world had calmed,
The flowers stayed fresh,
The seas smelled sweet.
My dream ended
All when I awoke;
To a world of hate
Living this life is hard
Day by day I pray
For God to make the good stay
And blow the bad away
That's my dream
Just a dream though
Until one day
When we all have this dream
Only then will this not be a dream to me
Then and only then
Will my dream become reality.

Tiffany Hinkle

All Your Life

All your life you
wished someone
was there, knowing
someone who cared

Days go by like the
4th of July, all you
wanted to know was
this meant to be for
eternity

My life hasn't began
yet as I step out into
the world I see what
my dad has told me

It's not what it
seems to be. So
far so good. I found
someone who cares
and who's there, that's
their job, that the
man who cares for me.

Amanda Roberts

Listen

Listen.
Hush child, listen.
Can you hear it?
Yes, it's there.
Where?
Listen.
Hidden in your spirit's lair
Beckoning softly,
Colors abound.
The exhilarating sound,
Lush, extreme, balanced,
A dream
Ticking . . . beating.
Under your flesh,
A kindling warmth.
Can you feel it?
Breathe easy—mustn't strain
That is your heart whispering . . .
Sharing secrets with your soul.

Sara Conrad

Every Lonely Night

Every lonely night,
thoughts go through my head.
I hold my pillow close to me,
as I lye alone in bed.

Every lonely night,
I play the same sad songs.
In the midst of darkness,
I dream of just someone.

Every lonely night,
I stay awake and weep.
Hoping that he soon will come,
and sweep me off my feet.

Every lonely night,
I stare into the sky.
Praying to heaven beyond,
two hearts will meet and bind.

Every lonely nights,
in such constant pain.
Arriving with a brand-new dawn,
I imagine my time for change.

Michelle Rowena Tucker

The Arrow of Sparticus

She looked over his shoulder
For vines and olive trees,
Marble, well-governed cities
And ships upon wine-dark seas;
But there on the shining metal
His hands had put instead
An artificial wilderness
And a sky like lead.

Kathleen Day

Best Friends

A friend so honest,
kind and true
I'll never find
in anyone but you.
Though our paths
must someday part,
Forever I'll keep you,
close to my heart.
And when the skies
grow dark and gray,
I'll call upon you,
if I may.
For whether you
are far or near,
I know your thoughts
will always be here.
And if you ever find
yourself needing me,
look in your heart,
For there I will always be.

Mel Waggoner

Liquid Release

Sell a prisoner to sea and
Sail into a smile
To sacrifice the sadness.
Sweet sun will shine
And bathe away the madness.

Moments stream like liquid
Leaving language blind.
Red, pink, black and blue,
'Tis love that you will find.

N. Stout

Think of Me

I cannot put into words
These emotions that I feel.
I have never experienced
Anything quite like this.
They are confusing,
These emotions,
And I am caught in them.

I could try to put
These feelings into writing for you,
But never come close
To telling you what
You mean to me.

The three simple words
That we are told we can use,
Become not so simple anymore.
So instead I will say,
Think of me,
And there will never
Be a day when I don't
Think of you.

Linda Childs

Special

Friends, what are they for?
Same lie or cheat, but you
Never . . .

Who are you
Not a lover, not a friend
You are lost . . . in between . . .

In my place of hate and war
I slip away to you
To your place of hope
Where war is a dozen red roses
And my depression melts to elation,

My tears are turned into dancing
And my heart flies away

You are the source of all my joy
My teddy bear where the world turns cold

What am I without you
Only another face in the crowd.

But you . . . you make me "special"

Abby Weibel

Phenomenal Me

I'm a phenomenal girl,
phenomenally.
Things fall into a whirl,
so extravagantly.
I'm not strong like a diamond
I'm fragile like a pearl.
I'm strong in the mind
'cause I'm your regular phenomenal girl.
My wisdom is nothing special.
My skin isn't smooth as a pearl.
I'm not very intellectual,
I'm just a regular phenomenal girl.
My secrets are there,
but you will never see.
All's you can do is stare,
stare at me phenomenally.
I'm a phenomenal girl,
phenomenally.
Phenomenal girl,
unbelievably, that's me.

DaLanya Murray

Jessy Sat Alone

Jessy sat alone,
loneliness is good.
It's all woman ever felt,
it's all she feels she should.
Jessy sat alone.

Garret has gone out tonight,
no yells, or screams she'll hear.
Regardless she stays by the phone,
the woman lives in fear.
Jessy sat alone.

Jessy has no friends,
he's frightened them away.
She would try and leave herself,
but it's the fear that makes her stay.
Jessy sat alone.

Her family they know nothing,
she's hid it pretty well.
She couldn't bear to break their hearts,
with the news she'd have to tell.
Jessy sat alone.

Tisha Dawn Steele

The Storm

As I look up at the stars
And into the night,
I breathe the cool air
And take in the beautiful sight.

The clouds start to shift,
then rain begins to pelt down;
While the crickets chirp
and I listen to the sound.

Thunder then rolls;
lightning is the seal
Which is the proof of the storm
that I begin to feel.

Stale air stirs from the ground,
it is as clear as a bell,
along with the scent of a nearby forest
and the dampness that I smell.

As the storm rages on,
I begin to lift my face
to confront the fury
and open my soul for a taste.

Nicole Caposello

The Word

The world I'm in
is bitter and cold,
even though
summer had a rose.

I fear my world
will go up in flames,
even though
there's love in vain.

I haven't seemed
to find that love,
But eventually
it will come.

And when it does
I'll be there,
standing tall
with all my world to share.

Melissa Leis

Dog

In Loving Memory Of Nippy
You were my first true friend.
Being only a child;
You were my hero,
My playmate,
And my protector.
I miss those soft brown eyes,
That watched my every move.
Sometimes I wonder,
Why you had to leave so soon.
To some you may have only been a mutt,
But to me you were so much more.
This is a tribute to the creature
Who brought so much joy into my life.
Thank you dog.

Shawn Moffitt

Winds For All Seasons

The wind shouts at me
And runs away with my hat.
I laugh and chase it.

Leaf shadows play tag
Across wind ruffled grass while
The trees bend to watch.

The wind goes crying
Among bare branches, mourning
The death of summer.

In their wedding dance
The wind and snow come whirling,
Wild and passionate.

Gabrielle Farrington

Some Things Never Change

The restless ocean deep and wide,
More whippoorwills at eventide;
I'm really convinced and satisfied,
Some things never change.
The pitter-patter of the rain,
The quaintness of a country lane;
A rainbow through a windowpane,
Some things never change.
Magnolia blossoms in the spring,
Sweetly perfuming the night;
As rehearsed, Robins return to sing,
In the dim morning light.
The warmth of a golden daffodil,
Sheer splendor of autumn and its chill,
A morning sun coming over the hill,
Some things never change.

Roy G. Price

Summer's Picture Morning Rise

White puffy clouds picturesque against
deep blue skies, as morning sparkles
with colorful brilliancy, nature dances
to summer's gentle melodies.

Adisa Olubayo Bankole

The Tree

A tree is free
Just like me.
A tree is not free
when it stands alone.
Trees have more leaves
but more than three.
When the tree is
cut down.
The tree is no longer free.

Lauren Hallman

Mine Eyes

Mine eyes have seen the glory
Of the passing of the years
Through each tender moment
And the forlorn tears

I miss our walks in moonlit parks
The way we would hold hands
Our summer seasons on the beach
Our feet beneath the sands

The game is no fun without you
To watch my every side
Growing gray without my mate
I take it all in stride

Doorbell doesn't call out loud
Phone won't ring again
Kids are grown and far from home
No Christmas cards to send

Lonely is an elder's lot
To live without his wife
I miss you so, dearest one
Meet you in the after-life!

Michael James

The Best Man Ever

The best man ever, was rather clever.
He gave us life, and with a rib,
He gave mankind a wife.
He taught the birds their lovely songs.
With the laws he made,
We knew right from wrong.
He sent His son down to earth,
to start a heavenly birth.
When this hellish earth begins to end,
May the best man win.

Mary Walker

Our Target

It is a tough row to hoe;
Being born and not to know
That the goal of all mankind
Is different within each mind.

Some think we are born free,
Consider fame as equality
Constantly searching for the apple tree
Hid in a forest of our debris.

When you find peace you then know
The arrow's answer as it flees the bow.

Mary Alice Marcella

Be Free

I was lost in the night
and I wanted to be free,
free from the sin
that burned inside of me.

Then the tears filled my eyes
when I finally realized why Jesus died.
Jesus died for sin and pain,
misery, and all these things.

Do you know a man
that would die in your place?
A man who could show
such amazing grace?

Jesus is calling you,
He's calling you today.
And my friend,
what will you say?

Stephen Henry

Count to Four

Bird of passage
is what mother always
called me, never sitting
still for too long, always
fluttering about
Thirsty for knowledge
never getting enough
Mother thought it was wrong
"You're flying too fast!"
"You're flying too strong!"
So here I sit in my gilded cage,
They shut the door . . .
One . . . two . . . three . . . four.

Dolly Smith

Falling Down

"Ring around the rosy
Pocket full of posies
Ashes, ashes
We all fall down . . ."
We all fall because, we're dying.
Everyone that I know,
All the bodies are being burnt.
All the faces a rose.
We bring flowers to the dead
To the dying.
Everyone is dying.
Everyone is falling down.
We all sing . . .
A song of hope, a song of truth.
Put into words, words of sorrow,
Words of fear, of help.
We are dying, children are crying.
We lie down, depressed and weak,
It is now our turn . . .
To go to sleep.

Megan Lopes

Too Thin Skinned

Aspiring thins my blood
Old age edges my nerves
Youthful aspirations for a
wiser society
Filled me with hopes and ideals

Instead I now fear for
myself and mankind

Lightning caused by the
breakdown of society
Ignites my sparks of electricity
My aging lightning rods
seem incapable
Of deflecting life's impulses
Making me jittery and edgy

Too thin-skinned for the
hardness of reality
I yearn for the youthful
coating of my ideals
To insulate me once again
from the world's woes

Elinor Froehlich

Unreal Dreams

He'll never change,
Everything will be the same
Many memories down the road

I've come far, only to hear
I love you honey, I know, I'd say!

For fate put us together
With growing hearts
Willing to surrender

Our love became precious
But only to me

Youth is a funny thing
Beheld by unreal dreams,
That someday might be

For it's love that holds together
With no other in between
As years gone by, we've become our own

Drifting day by day
While emotions are no more
The love lingers long
For I could have loved you more

Your Dear Wife (1977-1997)

Kathleen Comstock Rutledge

Old Weeping Willow!

Old weeping willow,
I'm crying out for you.
Don't leave me here alone,
I'm scared.
Old weeping willow,
Protect the memories of us,
Since there are so many.
Protect the love we share,
Since it is so strong.
Old weeping willow,
Death has come for both,
So I just want to know,
Do you still care?
Did you ever?
Old weeping willow,
Death is here now,
And has took my soul so.
Bye old weeping willow,
Goodbye forevermore!

Destiny Owens

Selena

Beyond the grave into my heart
Always thinking of you,
With every tear of pain,
With every laugh of happiness.
You left for the big place in the sky,
Watching me grow up
As time goes by,
Until the day we are together
Again on a cloud in the big blue sky.
Until then all I have to say is
"I love you mommy."

Tabitha S. Wulfekuhl

Darkness

Darkness is my only fear,
Yet it is this fear, the darkness,
That comforts me the most.
The shadows from the pale
Moonlight outside frightens me
But they are also company to me
In the dark, lonely hours at night.
It is the other darkness,
The one that often comes out in people,
That frightens me the most.
Wishing for that darkness to disappear,
Yet wanting the darkness of night
To hide me from the world forever . . .

Kelli Curry

Why Does God Not Hear Me?

Do I not speak loud enough?
Do I not make myself clear?
Why does He not answer?
I only ask of this one favor,
To be loved and cherished as I should.
Why does God not hear me?

Did I not ask in the right manner?
Did I ask of too much?
If I were him and he were I,
I would answer His prayers and wishes.
I do not ask for much,
But when I do ask,
Why does God not hear me?

I do as I'm told,
And I speak when spoken to,
But all I want in life is love.
A little help would be appreciated.

That's all I ask of.
Why does God not hear me?

Amy Schroeder

Smiles

When do the smiles come back,
And the stars regain their luster,
The sound of birds again become music?
When?

When mankind can lose its arrogance
And be able to see its existence as part
of this universe and that its importance
To it is only as great as a grain of sand.

Then God will have its place to man.
God is the fish, the birds and the beasts
Of which we are one.
When we become one with the universe
We are then one with God . . .
Once reached the smiles will come.

Gerald D. Nathan

Winter In You

The music of the leaves dancing in the wind,
makes crystals from the frost glide down your throat
as you breathe in the icy cold breeze.
The buds of ice melt on your body.
The ashes of maple tree burn on your heart.
The majestic seas fly in your soul.

April Silvernagel

World of Nothing

In your mind imagine a world without life,
no trees, no people, no animals, no birds,
no blue skies, no sunrises or sunsets,
but it's only you living in your loneliness
because in this world there is no time, nor death.
You cannot live, you cannot die in this world,
it's just your soul surrounded by the darkness and
emptiness that tries to tear away at you,
You close your eyes, hoping that it's only a dream
but all you see is the faces of fear, hell and loneliness
that you never would imagine. You take a long breath and
succumb and the darkness welcomes you and then your soul
becomes the darkness, the emptiness, the fear and the loneliness,
then your soul begins to fade into the utmost and everlasting
insanity as you become nothing.

Andy Payne

We Take It For Granted

As I look out my window, I suddenly see,
All there is in the world to me.

My beautiful home, a wonderful place,
Where there's friends, laughter, and lots of free space.

And all of the people in this great big world,
Please, just listen to my few words.

We may die tomorrow, this might be our last day,
So anyone who may care, listen to what I say.

We all take things for granted and don't give thanks.
It's time to stop worrying about color or rank.

If you're a child or an adult, husband or wife,
It's time to start giving thanks for the good things in life.

Mary Kerley

My Father's Wish

Don't look at it as death, don't try to say goodbye.
Dry your eyes, my child, I don't want to see you cry.
I'm sorry to be leaving you, but I am not afraid.
All I ask of you, my child, is for you to be strong and brave,
It's beautiful where I'm going, a place where the sun shines bright,
Filled with all things good, it's a place of peace and light.
And while the time is passing, I'll miss you, each and everyone.
But we can take comfort in knowing to this place you all will come,
I'm just going first to prepare a home for us,
But take your time in joining me, there is no rush.
My earthly time may be over, but yours has just begun.
Continue on with your lives, leave not one thing undone.
Know that my love with always be with you
All I've taught you must stay.
And let my passing not blind you to the beauty you see each day.
We'll watch over you from our garden—my father, brother and I.
Keep me close in your heart, my dearest child,
And I'll never truly die.

Dawn M. Becker

Autumn Changes

Once when I was out walking in fall,
I stopped to notice the changing trees.
They smiled at me as I pondered their existence.
Each leaf seemed to remark,"I am redder than you are!"
I noted each leaf as it fluttered helplessly to the ground,
Bending and spiraling as if its life had just ended.
I remembered when I had to cope with the death of a loved-one.
I wondered if the leaves still on the trees felt the same way.
However, they didn't seem to be sad,
Tumbling from their dazzling abode.
I thought to myself we could all learn from those leaves;
Sometimes we need to accept the changes that we cannot control.

Ashley Taylor

Always

I can close my eyes
and feel you
near me, inside me.
Our love is not a light thing.
Our love goes so deep it is almost frightening

You have touched my emotions,
my physical being, my mental being,
my spirit.
Our souls have touched,
in the only way truest love knows how.

Should you and I be destined for one another
it will happen
Our higher selves will guide us.
I will always be linked to you
in a way that is not comparable to another,

I love you truly
yesterday
today
and tomorrow.
Always.

Betsy Heroux

Love

Love is like a cloud that drifts softly in the sky
Love is silent.
Love is grand.
But most of all Love is something everyone can
understand.
Love is short.
Love is long.
Love is weak.
Love is strong.
Love is about two people who do each other no
wrong.
Love is wonderful!

Sarah Karnes

Just A Wish

If I could wish upon a star,
I'd wish I could travel far.

Out where the sun strives to reach,
Out where the sky touches the beach.

Past the rolling hill and all the trees,
Past the song birds in the summer breeze.

To a place where morning majestically stand,
To a place made up of mostly sand,
To a place of beauty and vast open land.

I would be so very happy there,
I'd live my life without a care,
With only my family this place I'd share.

If I could wish upon a star,
I wish I could travel far.

Ronda L. Davis

Cisnes

Lingering gracefully on lakes so blue,
Suggests what these imperial creatures do.
Spreading their wings of lace
Wondering place to place.
Flourishing in the burning crimson skies
Calmly hoisting above this world of lies.
Intangible bodies of white
As ghost-like ships sailing at night.
A soft moon shines on serene, silver throats
Statuesque swans sing harmonious notes. . . .

Ana Maria Miro

Pictures

Pictures of him, are in a book.
Lets get them out, we'll have a look.
There at his birth, now at three or four.
Look at him now, he's walking to the door.

Pictures of him, are on the wall.
I try not to cry, I try to stand tall.
His eyes watch me, beyond that door.
As I go to work, or do my chores.

Pictures of him, on the table there.
I need him to know, I really do care.
I hold his picture, close to my heart.
And hope tomorrow, brings a new start.

Pictures of him, his name be spoke.
My spirit now, forever broke.
My arms are empty, no one to hold.
Who can I trust, his truck now sold.

Pictures of him, that's all I have.

Shell Hougland

My Wife

With a heart as big as all outdoors
She faces today as she has the days before

With a spring in her walk and a smile on her face
She washes and cooks and cleans up the place

She has raised two boys with little help from me
And the job she has done makes me proud as can be

It was a natural thing for she has a gentle touch
I want everyone to know I love her very much

She's let me stay around all these past years
We've had some laughs and we've shed a few tears

I hope to stay with her the rest of my life
I'm proud to say this lady is my wife

Bill J. Goostree

A New Beginning

Cold and darkness stir the sky, swallowing all life in its path.
Awaiting the next morning, it surrounds the whole earth,
bitter with rage and eager with vengeance.

Until light awakens, escaping the hold darkness has taken.
Seeking the evils of night, light shines through saving all life.

Light's hold over darkness strengthens,
destroying the bitterness of night.

The light fills the sky, streaks of sun warming
up the frosty, forbidden earth.
The sky a clear, bright blue,
whose beauty is being radiated from the glowing,
wondrous mass of light, starts the new day.
A new beginning has been made, creating warmth and strength for all.

Elaine Matzen

Love

Love is a four-letter word, we all have to face
Love is not something that you can taste
It's something you have to feel deep down inside
But sometimes that feeling tries to hide
Sometimes love can get out of control
But it makes you feel complete, it makes you feel whole
Love is more than a special feeling
It can do miracles, it can do healing
Love can lead you in the wrong direction—watch out
And that is what love is all about

Amanda Worley

My Daddy's Poison

The weekend I am to see my daddy,
he promises me he won't drink one drink.
He thinks I'll just forget, but I don't.
He knows I won't say anything, and I don't.
To him the alcohol is his best friend,
but it's really his enemy in disguise.

The next weekend I'm over to see my daddy,
he says he won't drink his poison.
He thinks I don't remember what he promised what he said.
Then I go and cry the that everyone can hear but him.

Again, I am coming over.
The promise is now nonexistent.
And while I'm put through slow and excruciating pain,
the poison continues to go down drink by drink.

And just then I begin to hear my daddy's
silent cry for help, that no one else can hear;
painful cries that even my dad himself can't hear.

Danielle M. Rygh

Heartbroken

I always dreamed of falling in love,
and when that day came I was like a dove.
Flying through the clouds for the world to see,
that someone really did love me.
Thinking of him day through night,
I felt that everything was oh so right.
Until the day came when I saw,
that he really didn't love me at all.
It was just a game for him to see,
If I would think that someone like him would actually love me.
He used me and thought I was a dog,
and I couldn't turn to anyone but God.
But through those days I learned to see,
that someone out there really did care for me.

Elena Mendoza

Wedding Wishes

HERE TODAY, FOREVER WILL START;
HAND IN HAND, HEART TO HEART;
WALKING THROUGH LIFE, TOGETHER AS ONE;
THE INCREDIBLE JOURNEY HAS JUST BEGUN;
FLOWERS, PEARLS, WHITE SATIN AND LACE;
A BEAUTIFUL YOUNG WOMAN TAKES A CHILD'S PLACE;
WE HAVE WATCHED TWO PEOPLE GROW OVER THE YEARS;
LOVE BUILT AND STRENGTHENED BY LIFE'S TRAGEDIES AND TEA
TOGETHER, YOUR LOVE SAW EACH OF YOU THRU;
FOREVER WAS MEANT FOR STEPHEN AND SUE;
MY SISTER, MY FRIEND, SUCH A BREATHTAKING BRIDE;
MOM AND DAD MUST BE FILLED WITH IMMEASURABLE PRIDE;
WATCHING OVER YOU FROM HEAVEN ABOVE;
TO SEE THE HAPPINESS AND JOY OF YOUR LOVE;
TO SEE THE MAN YOU HAVE CHOSEN FOR LIFE;
STEPHEN AND SUSAN, NOW HUSBAND AND WIFE.

Tammy Davis

Air Supply

Allergic, asthma, unable to breath,
These are the symptoms of sniffing a leaf.
Emergency, survival, sirens wailing,
I wished I would have stopped sniffing and smelling.
Help, unconscious, rushed for the drug,
I reached up and gave the paramedic a big fat hug.
Stricken, consuming, possibly fatal,
The disease has been with me since the cradle.

Drew Patterson

Mother and Child

A moistened tissue cleans his face,
And wipes away the salty stream,
Saving him from utter disgrace
And holding back his childhood scream.

Looking through the shroud of age eight,
You see the world in bright pastel.
But the innocence loses weight;
The greyness of life cracks the shell.

If only we could all return
To the glory of those lost years,
When, pulled from her purse with great concern,
Something to wipe away the tears.

Jeffrey Morrison

Untitled

countless hours i spent dreaming
the man inside of me always screaming
i scream in silence
to forget reality to mute the violence
don't know the answers
could careless about the questions
it's like going crazy when you're already insane
without a presence of God i live in pain
give me time i will come to grips with myself
taking thoughts from my mental shelf
place ever so neatly
i will ponder each one completely
to figure the mystery out
God moves through me i have no doubt

Keith Smith

Last Goodbye

You say you wouldn't hurt me, but that's what you're doing
every day, with every word, every lie.
I should have been more cautious, giving my heart to you,
I thought you, of all people,
someone who has seen heartbreak in many ways,
would treat it with respect.
Things would be so different if . . .
There I go again with the "would have beens" and "ifs."
I really need to stop that.
But you know me, I am full of "what ifs,"
It's just another one of my faults you've seemed to find.
I'm the stupid one in the whole thing,
Because you're sitting back, laughing at my weakness.
So I'll leave you, for the LAST time now,
taking my curfews, lunch money, favorite stuffed animals,
and other petty little things that go along
with being a senior in high school. And leave you,
to be alone, or shall I say together, with the college girls. . . .

Jennifer Topping

Poetry

Poetry is like the wind,
It blows where it will.
We cannot control it,
nor lock it up,
For ultimately it is free.
We can reach out,
finger it lightly,
let it show us beauty and sorrow,
but we may not capture it all in our hands.
We can never claim it for only ourselves,
for poetry is everyone's.
The language of the stars,
The love that holds us together,
Is this not poetry?

Mara Mitchell

The Storm

The day was calm, the sun shined bright,
But all too deceiving of the fast coming night.
As dusk approached, a cool wind appeared,
Bringing pitch black clouds, and a silence too weird.
The trees began to panic, as they swayed back and forth,
Running from the monster, approaching from the north.
The scream that it roared could be heard all around,
Crushing all the near, with its deafening sound.
The last light retreated, leaving nothing but the dark.
The storm was unleashing a bite far worse than its bark.
The lightning it carried would have made Edison proud,
And the thunder that followed was the loudest of the loud.
The rain came down in buckets as it flooded down the street.
Blanketing the town like a city size bed sheet.
Helpless victims scattered to the shelter they could find.
Huddled in their corners as their lives raced through their minds.
A wind wrapped round it all, squeezed the town like a snake.
Even the tallest strongest buildings, were unable to take . . .
This fearsome force of nature, this cruel godly game,
That entered a proud city, and left it in shame.

Kevin Bednarz

What You Knew

When did you know?
How could you have known?
I tried so hard,
Yet you knew.
Did I change so suddenly,
that I wasn't aware of it?
Why did you have to know?
It would have been simpler not to,
but you knew.
Now it is not my choice alone.
You are part of it.
Where will I go, what will I do?
Now you know.
Eternal escape is what I was looking for.
Damn you for knowing.
I cannot ever be free.
Who is there to trust?
I knew you before,
yet I never did,
but you knew me.

Jackie Kemp

Sudden Change

We were always best friends, but we seemed to be drifting apart.
Now he looks at me
And my knees collapse from under me,
My face turns red, and I grin in embarrassment.
He looked confused and somewhat flustered,
Then embarrassed, then ashamed.
He turns away.
I sit there in silence, waiting.
Suddenly, he jumps up, and grabs me in a warm embrace,
Standing me up, he wraps his now long strong arms around me tighter
Then kisses me gently.
I look up into his deep gazing eyes,
Hoping he'll say something, knowing he won't.
Finally I return the hug, the kiss still lingering
Upon my still wet lips, and I know we are best friends no more.

Christina Freeman

Hide

Hide,
step aside . . .
we're the children who want to forget
what it's like to lose the child inside.
Dream,
never scream . . .
our fears were not erased by comfort
or was it "nurturing" that our parents called it?
Strive,
stay alive . . .
we're present only to want to be absent from here
and questioning our presence for our own arrogance
Smile,
for a while . . .
our worries don't fade when we're too stressed to notice
or accept that we are here with a purpose and story
Love,
from above . . .
look down as you fly, soaring way up in the sky,
just this one time refusing to hide.

Bruno Derlin

Fading Hope

Hope was fading and emptiness pounded;
His heart was frozen from the coldness of life.
Then all at once, it seems
The vague silhouette of hope became a vivid reality.
His hollow heart, now overflowing
With an indescribable treasure.
His tears of loneliness, now of joy and happiness.
Then all at once, it seems
The reality that he thought he knew
Was in fact an uncertainty.
An unwelcome truth lies where a dream once bloomed.
A time to which there was no darkness,
While warmth once enveloped his soul.
But emptiness once more has its place.
And thoughts of yesterday echo,
Deep into the hollowness from once they flourished.
Hope's blazing flame dims into dying embers,
Smothered by his aching sorrow.
And still,
Hope fades . . .

Douglas Moore

Your Dark Side

Trapped in a world without love,
never knowing what's in the world above.
It's not a spell that can be broken,
the difference between heaven and hell has been forgotten.
Where angels have no wings,
and your mind thinks of nothing amongst other things.
There, demons weep,
and your soul isn't even theirs for the keep.
All emotional strength has been lost,
as you walk through a world that's been through a holocaust.
Your heat, you carry in a sling,
wondering what could be more depressing.
In front of you a way out appears,
you gaze into happiness and think as the chance disappears.
This is your dark side,
this is were you will dwell, this is were you will hide.
Willing is he never to be,
on the light side of the shaded tree.

The Dreamer

Earth Awakens

The moons silver rays dot the clear blue sky,
The rivers flow silently and listens to whispers among trees
The animals creep unto the land
and move gently through the night,
The stars burn intense but still leaves the sky a dark blue,
A lingering smell of damp green grass and
salty oceans aromatize the air
For the dirt is still damp from the rain of the night before
The snakes are still slithering so smooth so rough so cold so calm
Waves are crashing on the rock,
The sun rise brings new life,
The silver rays of the moon go down while the
fiery red heat ball begins to protrude over the horizon
The signs of life begin to show the homo sapiens awake,
Pollution fills the sky,acid rain the lake, the
light blue sky now turns grey and the earth
begins again

Erikka Smith

The Human Rules

The hurt we all face today,
Is ten times worse than yesterday.
We have rules we seem to follow,
That will lead us to tomorrow.
We kill for clothes and steal money,
Break into houses and think it's funny.
We shoot for fun at everyone,
And beat up the disabled just for fun.
We fill the walls with grime and gook,
After all the work and time it took.
We haunt the streets for fun all day,
Come out at night and hunt for prey.
We don't want to go to work all day,
So we go and steal someone else's pay.
"What happened to our world?" We all say,
It was safe long ago but not today.

Kathryn Byrnes

"The Dream"

Life has many things to say,
On any given day.

At first you realized then,
That practice makes perfect time and time again.

Reality makes you wonder why,
You choose either to live or to die.

In society today you stand tall,
Not to fall.

I've an ambition to be somebody,
Underneath my soul lies just me.

One good lesson in life that not everyone wishes you well,
By believing and achieving soon you could tell.

The Dream by Larry Valenzuela

Larry Valenzuela

Roses Remind Me Of

The Stem of a rose reminds me of how you are
to be held. Gently and carefully.
The Petals of a rose reminds me of your skin.
Soft and smoother than silk.
The Blossoming of a rose reminds me of your smile.
It will light up the darkest of nights.
And the Center of a rose reminds me of your heart.
It is surrounded by beauty and remains elegant,
delicate and very rare.

Richard East

On The Shores of Lake Ephemeral

On the Shores of Lake Ephemeral
rippling with angst and regret that tastes of youth
I step outside my haunted self
and step into my other self,
the self that lived innocently once.
Vulnerability reaches for my hand,
and I welcome her.
I give the palms of my tiny hands to the wind
and she cries at their emptiness.
That lady in the wind cries for me
and I cannot turn around and pepper her
with my salty tears of lament.
And my memory is painted with this:
I am the lady lost in the wind
rattling windowpanes inside myself.
I give the palms of my tiny hands,
victimized again.

For my life.
For my innocence.
For my weakness.

Sara Heidtmann

Untitled

The days of my life turn and go.
My fate is that of one who doesn't understand.
Secrets are held and known, but never shared with the other.
My things are mine, and it doesn't show.
I'm confused.
I care, but I don't.
Seeing isn't all that everything's sure to be.
Finding my way through the endlessness, I met a man.
He asked me my destination.
Not knowing, I read him a poem.
"The days of future time may not be the way they are" said I.
He remarked on the beauty and vanished with the dust.
I walk on to continue with my journey.
Maybe something different.
Next time.

Jason Hyatt

Kent State May 4, 1970

Four found dead among the halls of higher education
A bullet does not discriminate
love from hate
passion from discontent
It holds no age boundaries
It has no political point of view
it only strikes those
found
in a straight line
so geometrically perfect
only to be disrupted from that perfect line
by those who cross its path
like the cross hairs of a rifle
found in the hands
of those with a political point of view

John Martin

Timeless Observations

A tiny hand with fingers outstretched,
A fallen toy the dog just fetched.
A hairless head, a toothless grin,
The clean, fresh scent of newly-washed skin.
Legs that are bent in frog-like fashion,
Eyes that are bright with anticipation.
Little toes continuously flexing,
A sleeping babe needing constant checking.
Players change on the domestic scene,
But heartfelt love remains pure and serene.

Sylvia M. DuPerry

Daylan Came To Town

*IN MEMORY OF: DAYLAN TAYLOR SEALES,
B.D. MARCH 14, 1996*
Daylan came to see the world
For love is all he cared
His time to short for us to see
But love was there for him
I knew him only for a while
But mommy knew him more
The pain she felt was for her love
When Daylan came to town
The time was to short
But the love is very long
For no one knows the pain we feel
But Jesus up above
For you see the Lord has Daylan Taylor Seales
And we know he'll hold him forever more
But Lord please let him know we'll be there soon
And hold him once more

Joan Collier

Mom

Why do you lie?
Do you care?
Can't sleep, can't eat
I can't depend on you if you're not here.
Don't call, don't write
I care. Where are you?
Too busy for me?
Or just don't care?
Are you too busy shopping?
Spending money?
How dare you say it's caused
by your childhood and blame it on me.
You're too busy for me.

Kelina Elizabeth Mortimore

Wonder

Standing in a forgotten place with no sight of any one anywhere.
Looking for a way to get out and longing to be a pair.
Abandoned and scared, no hope of ever getting out.
The silence is unbarring, you begin to shout.
One scream is echoed, 100 times over you hear.
Longing for a friend to be closer and near.
The only one to hear you scream is you,
You're alone, and crying for help is all you can do.
Searching for a way out, walking around and around.
All is quiet; will you ever hear a sound?
At last you hear something, not much but still.
A rush of happiness gives you a chill.
Was it a person, an animal, a plant, or water?
You realize it was a mother crying for her daughter.
You start yelling for help hoping she hears your cries.
She can't, but you can hear her saying "another child dies"
You think for a minute about how you got to this place.
You remember seeing your mother with tears running down her face.
You are dead, and in this place you'll forever be.
Alone and scared and these empty walls you'll always see.

Rebecca May Diamond

Out with the Old and on with the New

I left this world searching for a better place,
A better life, replacing the old, along with,
A better past, a better present, and a better future.

Nha Ho

Fear

I look into your eyes,
And I see all your lies.

You're crying out,
For someone to love you without a doubt.

You look so helpless,
You're wanting to confess.

Your heart pounding like a rolling stone,
You suddenly pick up the phone.

You don't know what to do,
But then you push the number two.

Knowing you won't follow through,
Past the number two.

You put the phone down,
and look around.

You go to your room,
And plan to meet your doom.

You're so afraid of what will happen last,
'Cause it all happens so fast.

Lisa J. Tyus

The One

My love, my best friend.
To whom my heart I lend.
The one who holds me tight.
In the dark you are my light.
If I need help, you are always there.
You take the time to listen, I know that you care.
You hold me in your arms.
You'd keep me safe from harm.
When we're together, the world seems to stand still.
And when you say you love me, I know that you're for real.
I love to look deep, into your gorgeous eyes.
I can ask you anything and know you'd never lie.
Whenever you need me, I'll be here for you.
You see, it's this thing called love, and mine, my dear, is true.

Ashley Nagrodski

Out of Nowhere

Suddenly there was you.
With no one else do I have what we share.
No two people have ever said so much in a glance.
And when we do speak, it seems everything around
us slips away and it's just us
drinking deeply of each other
touching with our eyes.

Joan Webb

What Do You See?

Look out my window
What do you see
Dead rotted trees
And poor old me
For I cannot be happy
For happy is not for me
Happy is for people who see beautiful things
You see butterflies and pretty trees
While I see things you don't want to see
You do harm to confident things
So look through my window
What do you see?

Heather Price

Romeo and Juliet's Creed

Unto thy own self be true,
Never forget what thy bestoweth to thou;
Hent this tender solace to you,
In the midst of night it will protect thy now.
Looketh into the sun's warming light; dost thou see thee?

Thou's presence is a fullness of joy,
Through the stars I see thine eyes;
Thou remindeth me of a young babe's toy;
Through the wind I hear your beckoning cries.
Glance down upon the bustling streets; dost thou see thee?

From Heaven's pearly gates thy love will thrive;
Pouring down onto thine soul;
Fighting the evil with every strive;
It will soar liketh the wing of a gull.
Peer into the imaging mirror; dost thou see thee?

'Till death and beyond we must go; no distance must we separate;
Thy travel with but a single arrow and bow;
This love will never dissipate.
Stare into the face of another, dost thou see thee?
And repeateth, always say thee: Loveth thou'st forever, loveth thee. . . .

Carlotta The III

What A Day

Oh what a beautiful, sweet smelling day.
All the commotion makes you want to say
What a day, what a day.

The birds and the beasts all prancing around,
Singing and laughing; I don't see a frown.
What a day, what a day.

The trees and the plants just seem to be saying,
"Please come and join us; it is fun; just start swaying."
What a day, what a day.

Just put on a smile,
You can help all this happiness spread for just miles.

Jennifer Kristin Streicher

Confined

I try to make myself into that clay,
so God can take control and do as he may.
Oh the tears that roll down my face,
from being in this wretched
confined place.
I try to be what God wants me to be,
so I surrender to his every plea
Oh, how my tender heart yearns,
to be able to find a place
alone that about God I can learn.
Good times and friends are few and far between,
but one friend I've found on him I can lean.
I'm lonely, looking for trust, comfort and love,
but in here that's something you don't find much of.
For the mistakes I've made my
heart is filled with regret,
but I have to pay for the wrong
things I've done,
I guess this is what I get.

Jamie Cochran

Antiques and Time

For antiques we say, "Don't throw them away,
handle them well; they're of value today."
Yet we throw away time with just a sigh,
and it's a priceless possession we let go by.

Betty Lou Allen

The Longing

Each day that I walk life's highway, I'm longing to be understood
People I meet on my daily walk:
My family, friends, spouse that gives me everyday talk
cannot begin to comprehend the longing to be understood.

In the quest for the longing to be understood.
It is a let down in life to feel as if I am under a hood:
trapped from the rays of the sunlight.
nothing in my life seems to be bright.

Then I think about the Higher Power of any of them all
that would take darkness and turn it into light
remove my sadness and sorrows and give me a fresh start
at last, I know that after searching and searching:
my longing to be understood was fulfilled all the while

In the midst of my despair, my Lord was speaking unto me.
My child, you are never alone, for my love for you I will always understand
Come weary one and I will give you rest
I went before my Lord and there I found peace.
I have found the One that really understands.

Adrian Katrina Ford

What Perfect Life?

Husband, wife, 2.4 kids
Mortgage, cars, loans, deep debt
White, male, college degree
The perfect life.

Black, divorced, child support due
Foreclosure, bike, repossessed car
Bankruptcy, three jobs
Tired and poor
No time, no energy, no perfect life.
No chance.

Single mother, ex-husband, third wife
No child support, no visits, no interest
White, female, college degree
Mortgage, car, loans, deep debt
L-E-S-B-I-A-N mother
Must stay in closet, must keep child safe
No perfect life.
No chance.
Not yet.

Ann L. Detjen

Child of Mine

Child of mine, where are you going?
Is there trouble in your soul?
Child of mine, what are you doing?
Are you ready to leave this fold?

Into your eyes I look with wonder,
Yesterday you belonged to me.
Now, your feet are leading you asunder,
Why my darling, must you be so free?

Will I never again hold you tight,
Feed you cookies and wash your hands?
Read you stories and turn out your light,
Will you travel near or in distant lands?

Child of mine, my love will ever be true,
Go into the mysteries of this earth.
No matter what the world holds for you,
I am still the one who gave you birth.

Oh God, please love this child of mine.
Watch over this one you gave to me.
On this special soul let your light shine.
Bring him back when he is finished being free.

Florence C. Williams

We are all very different both you and I
We are also the same as everyone cries
We have unique thoughts our hopes, and our fears
We have similar dreams of things we hold dear

Some of us Women, some of us Men
Some collect dollars, some have no yen
Some go to college, others do not
To experience life's wonders, we're a fortunate lot.

So let's celebrate our ideas, I will show you my side
But lest we forget, neighbor too has their pride
And think not of each other, as white or as black
As male or female, let's end these attacks
Rather who that you are, lets not drive us apart
Judge your brother and sister, by what's in their heart

And maybe some time, in days as they pass
We will change our reflection, as we gaze in the glass
And one at a time, perhaps we shall see
That the shoes of another, indeed may fit me

David J. Meinhardt

The American Scheme

Triumphant defeat at the hands of those
Once cherished by teachers of whom others chose
Yesterday's glory is today's lost story
Of values long gone by peers passed on
Grasping the dart we are marked to receive
The Knights of Grandeur look on as we bleed
Expecting once mentors to answer our call
The cries of unheard character refusing to fall
Preaching corruption cloaked under greed
Known by the humbled in silent good deeds
Leaders teach profit as morals we sell
Rewarding hard work with a lifetime in hell
The strength to refuse the blasphemy taught
Unveils the scheme of wealth that is sought
Falsely condoned having failed subjugation
A sentence best served with unforced resignation
As Camelot courts the company of lust
Those of us freed build dreams that are just

Patricia Ann Darrell

Gone

How could you leave me when I was so young
My life hadn't started, it hadn't begun.

You left us all in such a mess
All so sad, under so much stress.

The world came crashing down on top of me
I held it in for none to see.

All that's important now seems so small
My knees so shaky; I'm surprised I don't fall.

All the things I am now deprived
Like you teaching me how to drive.

You're not going to be there on my wedding day
To walk me down the aisle and give me away.

My children will never get to hug their granddad
Never knowing the love they should've had.

I will never get to hug and kiss you; see you laugh or cry
For that I will miss you 'till the day I die.

Erin Devlin

Treetop Nightmare

As I lie in my cradle in the top of a tree
I listen and hear someone singing to me
The melody is just a soft lullaby
But the words they are singing are making me cry
"Rock-a-bye baby in the treetop
Any second now your heart will stop
No one will care and no one will weep
When you have entered your eternal sleep
As I draw this last mournful sigh
Your cradle will fall and you will die"
As I lie in my cradle in the top of the tree
I sit up and wonder what death could be
I haven't clue what the song is about
My heart suddenly stops—you have ripped it out
I see you sitting on a branch of the tree
You hold up my heart and start laughing at me
You've broken my heart so now I must fall
When I'm gone will you miss me—cradle and all?

Sidra Tees

My True Love

As you hold me in your arms
it seems nothing could go wrong.
But there's something you should know
about something that happened long ago.
Throughout all my life, with all my loves,
there's been only one I could call my true love.
Everything was perfect,
until everyone destroyed it.
He's always on my mind,
he's there all the time.
And ever since then,
I've wished every guy was him.
And I can't help but wonder,
is it possible to find another,
that I can call my one true love?
or did I let "the one" slip through my fingers?

Lindsay Thompson

Damned To Eternal Night

To once have gazed upon the stars in the sky,
And notice them as alive not fading to die.
The rain falls in sheets and drenches my clothes.
Rocked and stumbling in mud as the harsh wind blows.

Never more to see the sun rise upon the earth.
For the depths of darkness have given a new life birth.
Empty container am I, so filled with sorrow,
For eternity, on and on, day by night, and then tomorrow.

No longer am I frightened by the crude metal of the sword.
Fates forever spinning my life cord.
Long ago as my morals did die,
Never did I dare think to cheat, steal, and lie.

Now I care who not I kill,
Simply to leave it on the next man's bill.
The clouds in the sky blow by like my life,
Full of sorrow, misery, and strife.

Every monotonous night is the same,
Only my very own soul is to blame.
Never to bathe in the day's light,
Forever damned to eternal night.

Selly Strauch

Song of the Alien

This is the song that the Alien sings
In the compound UFO, it knocks and it rings.
From inside, the head Alien screams and it yells
From when it was brought up,
When this song had bells.
Long skinny fingers and very large eyes,
Small shoulders and long arms and narrow thighs.
Enormous head and bony legs and toes,
They come and they destroy and kill their foes.
Circular spaceships, green lasers and light
Blasting, fighting, as day turns to night.
Cities on fire, the world in great pain,
Songs of glory with very little gain.
Songs of the weak and powerless mankind,
Coastline to Coastline—

The U.S. resigns.

Amy D. Lagusker

We Love You Kurt

To Kurt Donald Cobain
Many candles burn ever so bright
For it is you we think of tonight.
In our hearts you will stay.
Your voice will never fade away.
They may not think you're a hero
But we will never think of you as a zero,
You will not be forgot.
When we heard you were gone a shiver
Of cold wind was what the news brought.
Afraid of death that's what we are
But it brings comfort to think you're not far.
We never got to say goodbye that day
But come to think of it we wouldn't have much to say.
Your life was hard, that we know,
But still we ask why did you have to go?
A time will come when we meet again but until then,
Know your thought of every day and that
In our hearts and minds our memories of you
Will stay strong and true because,
Kurt, we love you!

Elizabeth Giglio

Parents

They're here for awhile but then they are taken away,
Why? you ask. I don't know that's the way things are.
It's so cruel.
I know. I know.
What can we do?
Make the best.
Of what? Have fun with your parents,
make them feel needed and wanted.
Who? Help me I don't understand.
Think.
About what?
Are you listening?
Yes, Then think.
Who? What about?

Mom,
I wish I would have listened to Grandma,
and what she said.
I place flowers neatly on the ground.
I start to cry,
But I stop myself and think about it.

Robyn Herrick

Boundaries

Be oh so careful with this heart
It's been strongly protected and now belongs to you
Its universe so sheltered from the depths of pain
Be oh so careful with this heart
It gives itself completely from the start

Be oh so careful with this love
It needs laughter and joy to mature and grow
It requires understanding, compassion and trust
Be oh so careful with this love
It needs to be held tightly with gentle gloves

Be oh so careful with this soul
It needs security, passion, and a soulmate so true
It will blossom with honesty and devotion
Be oh so careful with this soul
In your hands, its world you hold

Be oh so careful with all of me
My dreams and desires I will share with only you
My emotional boundaries are written plainly above
Be oh so careful with all of me
Given the chance we can love for eternity

  Liza Quinn

In Memory of Our Friend Chris Kroll

Why, why did you have to go?
That we may never know.
Everywhere we go,
your spirit will fill the air.
Your humor, your height,
Your life, your style;
Chris I will always remember
the way you smiled.

It's runnin', playin', hangin' out;
Don't worry, Chris, there's no homework
up there. Theres no need to pout.

Because you never let anyone put you down
And you would always put your mind to it,
for that is why your memory will never pass.

Rest in peace my friend;
Your life has come to an end.

Stay sweet, Chris; we all love you.

  B. J. Korn

Tenacity

To have the will and the power not to bend and
Not to break.
To persevere no matter what it takes.
To live your life as a dandelion—
Your stubborn roots imbedded in the ground
Overcoming the poison ivy growing
All around.
Succumbing to the red and purple passions
Of the heart.
A dandelion—strong, unyielding, tenacious,
From the start.

  Theresa Weddle

It's Always Hard

To my boyfriend for the loss of his mother
It's always hard to let someone you love go,
So I'm sorry you had to be the one to know.
Early that morning you were awaken by a call,
Then I saw the tears fall.
You looked at me with sadness on your face,
And you rushed into my embrace.
You said it would be for the best,
Because at least now she could get a painless rest.
I know you will always have her in your heart,
Because the love you gave each
Other will never break apart.

  Kristian Lear

Starting Over Again

I let you get close to me
Again and again I accepted your excuse
In spite of myself I began to see
All along I never realized the abuse
When it came to you I was always so blind
Letting you get away with everything
Yet all the time you were playing with my mind
With all the heartache it would bring
I'm fighting so hard to put my broken heart back together
Dying inside and trying not to let anyone know
I'm hearing those haunting words, "I'll love you always forever"
It's tearing me apart trying to let you go
But that's what I have to do
After realizing all the pain you inflicted on me
Turning my back even though I needed you
You made me realize our love just wasn't meant to be

  Michele Smith

Those Younger Years . . .

The sky wrinkled up like the old veteran
sitting in his well worn rocking chair
thinking of the good old days

In the distance his faithful, old, black lab could be seen trudging
through the once smooth grounds towards the dirty, musty house

Before the dog could reach his master
he collapsed with an exhausted sigh
Onto the weak, rotted porch

(soon both fall asleep)

Dreaming of their nature hikes,
hunting and fishing trips together
during the hot, Indian summer years before

Then the rain began to fall in sheets of sorrow,
mourning for those younger years

  Tami Wilson

What Is A Having A Friend?

It's someone to chat to when there's nothing to do.
It's a way of sharing ideas and warming our spirits.
It's knowing that somebody, someone cares about you.

When you're frightened they're someone to turn to.
When you're sad they've a shoulder to cry on.
When you just need a boost, they've plenty to give.

They always compliment your talents,
And support you when you go against the flow.
They're always ready to discuss things,
And they help you get ideas out on the table.

They help with homework and are sympathetic,
They help you get your frustrations out.

What is a friend?
A companion for the ride.

  Ruth Madison

A New Beginning

A brand new start is the best way,
If you has made many mistakes.
The past has been hard,
Even though it's been fun,
Your new life has just begun.
Just the other day you hurt your best friend,
Which was supposed to be a friendship that would never end.
You feel bad and it sure does show,
All you hope is that she knows.
It's all up to you to change your ways,
All it takes are just a few days.
A brand new start is the best way,
If you have made many mistakes.

  Kelly Pappas

How

Long ago, we drifted apart,
Now you're back just to mess with my heart.
You're only back to hurt me one more time,
How could I be so blind?
You bring back to me your kisses and sweet touch,
I'm still not too sure why I love them so much.
You catch my glance and my body goes numb,
How could I be so dumb?
You take my hand and hold it tight,
I wonder if you really care and I think you just might.
You say you love me and my eyes get hazy,
How could I be so crazy?
I fall deep, hypnotized by your charm,
I let my defenses down and you start to do your harm.
I now realize you always treated me the worst,
How could I be so hurt?
I ask these questions and many more,
I think I've found what I've been looking for.
It's reason I feel this way, this I'm sure of,
It's really a simple thing, it's all because of love.

Jessica Durocher

Just A Prayer

Walking on the beach one day
The thought came that I had to pray.

Wondering and thinking what to say
I knew I had to pray anyway.

I kept fighting the need to pray
Hoping I could do it another day.

As the need to pray got stronger
Then I just couldn't wait any longer.

I fell and knelt on the sand
As I felt a soft and gentle hand.

The words came that I should speak
As I became very weak.

When I was done and all was through
My body and soul felt completely new.

Now I can see that when I am down
That a prayer will surely turn things around.

Mistie Fuentes

My Mom's Hands

My mom's hands are pale and white
At night in the dark they fill me with fright
On one finger she wears her wedding ring
From my father who is kind of a ding
When she washes the dishes her hands get wet
They look like white prunes I'd be willing to bet
I like it when she rubs my back
The special touch she does not lack
She quickly stirs her hot, black tea
Waiting to clean the house with glee
I try not to make fun of her twig fingers
For she remembers the insult and makes it linger
Mom quickly and carefully sits and sews
When she is finished her work is in perfect rows
She likes to turn the pages in her books about mutts
You can see on her thumbs she has many paper cuts
Those hands never hit me, not one bit
Instead she sat on the couch and knit
My mother's hands I talk of I think are sweet
In other words my mom's hands are pretty neat!

Lindsay Peak

Frank

I long to be with you through these numbered days
As we step one moment at a time into our future;
Loving you now with your smooth skin and strong body
With you beside me as time dances its changes into our lives
And paints it's passing in lines on our faces.
I want to be with you always,
As days turn into years
Remaining the same for you within the changes
Steady and constant,
The given factor in formula of change,
The one certainty in an uncertain world.
I hope to be the one to hold your hand
As our grasps imperceptibly weaken
So that when the inevitable comes and frailty beckons
I will be the one blessed
To button your shirts and wipe your chin,
So that you will understand beyond doubt
That I loved you from that first moment
And every moment after,
Loving you unfailingly into eternity.

Rhonda K. Blumer

The Unborn's Plea

The beating of a human heart
was my substance and my warmth.
A bright future was waiting for me, then suddenly,
Someone silenced my beating heart.

A bright light surrounded me,
A taste of love was felt.
So patiently waiting to breathe life, then suddenly,
Someone silenced my beating heart.

I dreamed of my mother's touch,
Love overflowed from my little heart.
Never fearing such a trauma, then suddenly,
Someone silenced my beating heart.

How happy my grandparents will be,
Although they do not yet know,
Waiting for their tender touch, then suddenly,
Someone silenced my beating heart.

Words like "It's only a blob" surrounded me,
A racing heart awakened me,
A raging fire surrounded me, then suddenly,
Someone silenced my beating heart.

Agnes Zwaschka

Lies

You've told lies when you were little, and when you appear brittle
There's no cat with a fiddle, and when they scold it belittles
Done either to control with praise or comfort you dismay
And your distant hope prays the truth revealed one day
But what truth—whose truth do you seek?
If they are right, are you genuinely week?
Is your soul a slave to another's desire?
Well, I answer no with empowering fire
Is my freedom day late?
Why should I hesitate?
Set me free, from what I cannot be
The lie from thee creates a chain on me
Which suppresses my special, splendid spirit
But it hasn't died because I can still hear it
Why do you desire to control me so?
Afraid of what I might be? How could you know?
I hear lies all around, and if I listen carefully
I'll see why my worthiness was obtained falsely
By discerning what's false, I've discovered the key
Which will unlock my dependency and set me free

Sharon L. Harris

Gift of Life

Life goes on, if we love it or not
It's a gift, that shouldn't be forgot
People we've loved, have passed away
People we will love, are on their way
This gives us hope, and strength so true
To help us through, when we feel blue
For as bad and dark, as times can get
Our hearts, our souls, try not to forget
Puppies and kittens, and flowers and rain
These and more, help soften the pain
So as we hold our babies, or loved ones
These things all make up our life
So remember when going through all the strife
It is a life, your life, your gift
And as a gift, it's meant to share
Weather as a pair, or alone it seems
You're not alone, not even in dreams
For in the greater scheme of things, all we have
or, are remembered for, is sharing our gift of
Life, love, there's little more

Rebecca Ann Pennington

Untitled

Merciless heatwaves are draining my days
Familiar pains are once again in my ways

Jagged waves of furious ominous faces
Drag me around to lucid lonely places

I conduct my cord and without thought I'm done
Loathing the around in the same trance I've begun

Otherworldly ghouls jeering the fall of my birth
Un-notably smiling, starving me where I sense worth

Erect and consciously aware the warmth in me aging
The land and scores helping my sweet doom their staging

If they wanted they may bathe my return and sudden doom
Grossly unaware how it's feeding my unpracticed gloom.

Kissed by the glossy lips of my conscience mocking me
Shoved everyday out the door my lifespan clocking me

Now to file the ragged sharp edges of my wake and sleep
I load on my remedies for bleak cuts still so deep

Cheryl Byrne

When The Day Will Come

I wonder when the day will come
For life and love to become as one
I've found a love I know is right
For her and me all through the night!

My lady and me, it will seem to some
are floating away and loving none
She wants a love that will ever last
From now till heaven and without a clash
I think of her sitting in her chair
Dreaming of the day to come.

I help myself and need no help
But to have you near me I always seem to melt
My heart is shielded for reason I know not
Yet you sneak right on in and steal it away
It would serve me right, for I always thought
A love like yours would strike me not!

I wonder when the day will come
For life and love to become as one
I've found a love I know is right
For her and me all through the night!

G. Kendell Guinn

My Love

All you heard was hard deep breathing,
Then you heard crying,
Love is in the air, all around the room,
Time to take me away from my love,
Now it's time to clean me up,
I live off of milk for 10 to 12 months,
Now I survive off hard and solids,
My love is still with me, I have the same Love,
But I don't give it back, in the same way,
Fourteen years, my love is still with me after all the bad,
I have put her through no manly love.
He is not around,
To play ball,
Go fishing,
So I have no love back.
My love couldn't give me things like the other boys,
But she always give me love.
After seventeen, I understand what my love was trying to do for me.
Through all the disloyalty and loyalty,
My love is still around.

Jean Pierre Malbreaux

Mommy's Little Boy

She's my shinning star and I'm her everything . . .
She used to help me tie my shoes and we'd play
with cars . . . Now we play catch and basketball . . .
Sometimes we even look at stars . . .
But I'm not, "Mommy's little boy" anymore . . .
I'm getting bigger every day and she always
says, "She's proud of me . . ."
I get upset when she won't let me stay up late . . .
Each day we say, "I love you" . . . every night we pray
before I sleep . . .
But I'm not, "Mommy's little boy" anymore . . .
Someday she says I'll have a wife . . . I tell her,
"No way, I'll never leave you" . . . As I get older a
girlfriend seems nice . . . I use to think they had cooties,
but now I'm thinking twice . . .
I'm learning to cook and Mom thinks I'm the
best . . . she'll always be close wherever I am . . .
To her I know I'll always be, "Mommy's little boy" . . .

Diane C. Stigers

Another Day

The sun rises, gleaming across the desert, bringing absolute bliss.
The sun rays touch my cheek like a gentle kiss.
It is a new day.
Yes, it has come again.
I embrace the day anxiously, where shall I begin?

Another day brings new drama.
Obstacles waiting to be trampled.
Ideas and goals wanting to be conquered.
New lands to be embellished.
Individuals we love to cherish.

But wait! My day is dwindling away.
The sun is setting in a fiery phase.
But I will wait, for another day,
Not long will I have to endure,
Because another day is always sure.

Another day passes just as quickly as it came.
But tomorrow it shall come again.
Bringing new challenges and beautiful sights.
Stirring souls with sheer delight.
Another day . . . another day . . . another day . . .

Aikena Scott

Please Talk To Me

Where wert thou when I needed you most
To talk to you and make you part of my life
Headaches you know, how hard I tried to hide
Please talk to me and lead me not to hide
You know my questions and I'm sure
you know the answers
It's a big wide world out there
It's scary and frightening at times
I fear the loneliness, no fun being alone
Please talk to me and lead me through the day
My heart is heavy at times.
Please talk to me to ease the pains of life
With your faith and hope and
understanding, I know you are there
But please just talk to me
          Ruth Mulcaster

Death

Death is so strong,
especially for people who care.
I can't believe he's gone.
He took our love and prayers.

He was the oldest and kindest
but also the boldest and caring.
The people who took care of him
will always have a place in my heart.

He was taken from us too soon.
He went up like an air balloon.
The date he passed away was the 25th of June.

I bet he landed on the moon
of the time half-past noon.

He always was listening to tunes,
On his strong hands were always wounds.

He was a great person.
          Jessica Yonfong

Our Special Heros

Where have our heroes gone?
I am often asked.
Who are the real heroes of today?
Many heroes were in the past,
I would say,
Kennedy, Patsy Cline.
Elvis, the King.
I have this song in my heart.
I wish I could sing.
They all stand on the right hand of God.
Oh, what a sight as they appear in my dreams.
Now, they sing in the Lord's Holy Bond.
On to our Heros of today,
1st and foremost there is Leonn, Garth,
Susan Savage, our mayor, as the special host.
          Donna L. Clark

My Life

My life is sometimes weird
My life is sometimes fun

My life will never fade
My life is made for me

Sometimes my life is painful
Sometimes my life is fair

My life brings all the joy to me in all different ways
But most of all my life is always with me
          Tatiana Morrissey

The Love of Jesus

Tears from heaven fell from above.
Angels were singing, "Hal-a-lou-ya"!
For Jesus was born on Christmas Day.
He came to save the lost from death,
and set the captives free;
He walked among the people with ease,
To share his miracles with anyone in need.
With love, concern, and Ernest heart,
Jesus was truly a man of God.
For Golgotha would tell the tell,
with scares of whips and nailed-scared hands,
and a crown of thorns upon his head.
Jesus would die a horrible death.
He paid the price of each one of us
that we could have eternal life.
So, upon this Christmas Day, I Pray
That each one of you remember "This Babe"!
He gave his all to anyone in need.
For all it takes is just "Believe"!
          Joann P. Woods

To You, My Friend

Although your life may seem like a living hell,
it's just a bad witch that's cast a temporary spell.
one day you may be as happy as can be
but then you will have to see
that life is full of ups and downs
a temporary smile and many long frowns
and when you may have one regret
don't ever forget:
God will never forget us
and life isn't a rule that comes with a syllabus
and so I kneel to you and implore
that you understand
that we used to love to sit and play in the sand
now we'd rather go to a concert and listen to a band.
and with all the pain of parenthood
I'm surprised you'd consider motherhood
but I'm kind of glad you did
and when life is finished and you've put on the lid
you will know one thing for sure:
my love for you is pure.
          Melanie Jareno

Needle

I am the needle, I feel no shame,
For I bring pleasure to your vein.
I am as sharp as I wanna be,
You know what else, you need me.
I'm the one that give you kicks,
Especially when you need a fix.
Paycheck time, bills you must pay,
Oh hell come go with me, and let's play.
Cook it up into a fluid.
Oh come on, you can do it.
Put on the strap, make it tight and firm,
Boy oh boy, will you ever learn.
Fill me up, push a little out for inspection,
Ease me into your arm, with a nice slow injection.
Sit back relax and take me in,
While I take you on the ultimate spin.
Take off the strap, but don't put it far away.
Because we're gonna have hot fun all night and day.
We're best friends, we do this often,
How much more can we do this, if we're stretched out in a coffin?
          Michelle T. Arnold

You World

I'd like to tell you world, what I think of you.
I'd like to let you know what you have done and to who.
I'll start at the beginning by saying that you stink.
All those times when I was silent,
when behind my back you tried to bring me down.
When I was in your presence you would smile
and when I turned my back your venom poured
like syrup down deep into my heart.
I'll tell you something else, you have made me so sad
and lonely and you have also made me cry, hurt me,
stabbed me and even confused me at times.
But I'll like to tell you now, that you have failed
trying to bring me down, that you no longer disturbed my mind,
that my soul has found what you have denied.
So for all that you've done and to whom you did it
to God Bless You and Good Night.

Elma Solorzano

Untitled

For Rudy

You can laugh and you can stare,
but I'll stay quiet cause I'm not there.

They can hate me all they want
and I won't care; it's them I haunt.

Tomorrow's just another day;
maybe tomorrow they won't come my way.
Tomorrow is just a word of hate;
tomorrow's just a silent saint;
maybe it's coming and maybe it ain't.

They can beat me all they might;
it doesn't work—my mind is far in flight.

Their dirty words can't touch me,
because I have left and I have fled.

Tomorrow's just another day;
maybe tomorrow they won't come my way.
Tomorrow is just a word of hate;
tomorrow's just a silent saint.
maybe it's coming and maybe it ain't.

Tomorrow's just a silent saint;
maybe it's coming and maybe it ain't.

Emily Noa

Heart-Affairs

When passing by your old home place,
I see the changes time has brought;
But time and change will not erase
What blissful heart-affairs have wrought.
Change often alters mortal plans,
And will, at times, cause hearts to sigh;
But immortal love of hearts and hands
Will never wither, wilt, nor die.

The trees—still there beside the road—
Are aging well in sun and rain;
But time's removed that quaint abode,
And has modified old lover's land—
Yet as fresh as morn— now memory
Recalls the thrills of your caress,
Which touched a cold heart, tenderly,
And warmed it with your springtime-bliss.

True hearts that ache, and love, will bloom
In some fair garden, rich, and rare;
But cold and lustful hearts will soon
Be as wayside fields, now brown, and bare.

Robert T. Sanderson

Money

Money is just an object and yet,
It's the most important thing today
The question is are we using it for important things?
Instead, we are using it for tans, fans and other objects,
Yet there are diseases that need to be erased from this world.

So I say "Dear Lord,
Help us to use this green paper
correctly in life."
I will strive, to use it right,
Not just to pick a fight,
But, a fight that is right,
To keep the money used right.

Till the day comes where people use it right
There are stilling diseases running around,
I would feel proud, When the word disease
disappears from the vocabulary and world,

And, I say "Dear Lord, forgive those who use the money
for of importance of themselves.
Bless those who use it for the importance of health,
mind and soul of an other."

Carina Garcia

So Many Tears

So many tears I cried that day.
So many tears couldn't wash away the pain.
So much darkness has entered my life.
So much darkness, where is the light?

I reach out my hand, to help him along.
I silently sing, a sad lonely song.
I try to be strong, to hide what's inside.
Something has died, I think it's my pride.

From somewhere inside, I feel something strange.
Something is happening, something has changed.
A hand has reached out, to pull me along.
Something inside, is making me strong.

I know what it is! what joy I have found.
God is here deep inside! He won't let me down.
Gently he holds me, close to his heart.
Gently he guides me, and gives a new start.

And then in a whisper, I hear him call out.
Don't be afraid let all the pain out!
I will be with you, I'll carry you now.
Don't be afraid! I'll show you how!

Rose M. Dreiling

Untitled

The darkness comes to envelop the evil of the days work.
I come to scatter in all directions,
for the darkness veil is as long as it is wide
I feel myself escaping out of this shell
I call body I look at what could have been
but will never be as I listen and observe
the one's within the emptiness in gulfs my whole being.
Emptiness and loneliness I never thought possible.
I talk but no one listens, I cry but no one cares.
I am obsolete object floating upon the nights
breath wanting to be part of a rainbow's glory.
But alas I'm only the wailing cry
of wind slowly evaporating through time

Heather Alecee McKune

Signs

Crime is running rampant, disease runs amok
Robbing children of their future, fathers down on their luck
Anger taking hold, clouding judgments, ending lives
Children slumber starving, hunger pains hurt like knives
Klansmen run for office, get majority of the vote
Killers on parole, innocents must now take note
IUDs that cause infection, lambskin condoms that don't work
Lucille Ball is six feet under, Jean Luc Picard replaces Kirk
Landon rests below the prairie, Sammy dances in the sky
Seuss no longer reigns in Hooville, Miles' horn sounds on high
U.N. council okays war, sends troops off on their way
Saddam still rules the roost, runs to fight another day
Anita Hill says, "He harassed me. Claimed a hair was on his Coke."
Lies or truth? It doesn't matter. Whole process is one big joke.
Live and love in these hard times. Open eyes to all the signs.

   Ron Jones

Fourteen Shades of Grey

There are fourteen shades of grey
she estimates when I ask.
She knows everything
except where she's going with me.
She sang bass for her choir alma mater
rumbles through my body her voice.
She is tawny, silken-haired,luscious,voluptuous.
I want to suck her, bite her,
consummate the flesh . . .
but it's her mind I worship.
When I was ten I fished from a bridge
separating my island from the mainland.
Using seaworms for bait- -
slimy poetry,
I waited for the flounder to tug.
Fourteen shades of grey
we live undefined.
We are casting.

———

   Chenery

Soundless Screams

Whose kids R **THEY**?
Their souls R crying as their bleeding fleshes motionlessly **LAY**.

Forget the bureaucracies & **POLITICS**.
Where were U when father forced her, at age seven, 2 suck his wrinkled up **D___**.

Where were U when that three year old's eyes were black & **BLUE**?
Answer me U title wearing, position, heartless . . .
Oh that's right, I forgot, U R just perping, because U haven't got a **CLUE**.

I am sick and tired of pseudo people & **AGENCIES**
Fronting like they have the backs & interests of the voiceless fragile **KIDDIES**.

What type of system would send children to foster care, then home,
kinship care, then home, residential care, then **BACK . . .**
What does it take to realize that children cannot grow and develop N the Taj MaHall
infested with **CRACK**.

It is interesting that U go 2 your sweet, loving children **EVERYDAY**,
But a pregnant or drug pushing teen is fair gain 2 funders & media 4 **DISPLAY**.

Grimmie, heartless, executors . . . Yeah, that's who U **R**.

   Selena T. Rodgers

Untitled

exhausted bodies,
straining,
glisten in pale light.
waxing fire rages,
feeding
lust's inferno.
blinding light,
searing heat,
waning tongues of flame
lick extremities,
burning,
marking,
branding.
sinewy bodies
disentangle, sated,
spent;
sifting ashes
after a
firestorm
of passion.

   Michelle Martin

Christ Butterfly

Christ butterfly
Evolutionary apple pie
Glide, glide
Go to where the outlaws hide

Smoking crystal chairs
Buffalo smile cares
Sunday cross papers
Souls tasting rapers

The snakes skin
My favorite kin
Thorn dull eyes
Wishful fingers sighs

White full void
Pen ink hemmoroid
Waste making love
Creating the greedy dove

   Keith Gorman

Can't Be My Hero

He's a big man—almost 250
I doubt I'll make 160.

He eats while
I get fatter

He drinks but
I have no tolerance

He works and
My hands are soft

He fights when
I say away

He f***s
I think of mother.

Still he's dead,
And I hear he was an a**hole in
person.

   John Morgan

Stop The Voices

Stop the voices screaming out at me
keep them from warping my mind.
Help me ignore the pain they want to give.
They say I'll never be loved.
They beat my mind and soul until I
want to give in, give up the fight.
Constantly they attack me and strip me
of what little dignity I have left.
Help me end this battle.
Stop the voices or soon they'll have their
wish, me dead and bleeding, abandoning
everything sacred to me.
Stop the voices because they're pissing me off.

Mark Sanford

Hands

Sensuous and exploring hands;
One a woman's, the other a mans's.

Grasped together in an emotional
And physical way;
A chess game of proverbial foreplay.

One can't begin to describe or understand;
The feeling created when holding hands.

Dennis E. Tatlock

The Sharpest of a Dull Razorblade

I close my eyes and imagine myself lying
naked on a bed full of blood-soaked roses.
Their petals scattered around the room.
Their sharp thorns piercing my bare flesh.
As I drop the blade I listen to my last
sound, breathe my last breath, see my
last sight of the darkness that is my life.
My warm blood fills the white sheets in
a maze of dark red color.
As I lie there my whole body goes numb.
What happened to the person that I used to be?

Sheena Isenberg

A Woman's Breast

My husband has always admired my breast
Every morning I wake up and stand in front of the mirror nude

My breasts are beautiful to me
They're not big but small indeed

They remind me of my favorite fruit nectarines
"Honey, where are my two beautiful queens"

I never had trouble breastfeeding when the baby came
Our only fight would be our baby's name

Always admired when we make love
Like the peace and serenity as a dove

A sense of security as he lays his head on me
My eyes closed with thoughts of tranquility

I received my annual check-up on Monday
I pray, to convey, my queens were diagnosed with the big "C" today

Karen E. Quezada

The Game Goes On

Tall and slim she stands there
Hair flowing behind
Eyes sparkling a pure blue
Locking my gaze for a moment
A brief moment captured in time
Etched into my memory
A moment stolen
A glimpse of an angel
The fires start in my soul
Watching for an oppurtunity
Stealing glances whenever possible
Looking for the right words
The right ice breaker
The first moment I knew
We were made for each other
From across the room we notice each other
The only thing that stands between us
A dipsh** in purple pants
Ah well the game goes on

Kevin Miller

In The Cavern

The sun plummets over the edge of the world
when the bloody stars fill his head.
The cold gun falls. It crashes against the ground
before his body, while the sun continues falling away forever
from him, taking his pleasure, his pain, all.

Pieces of brain slide from the back of his head
like snails leaving wet trails.
He tastes the red on his lips, knowing it
stains them darkly as his skin pales.
Skin stark white except for a tiny black hole
in his forehead that goes into another
universe where the suns are black, a
universe from which bloody stars pour into his mind.

He smells a flash of blue sky.
A drop of moisture touches his skin.
It is not rain.
He hears someone crying. It is not him.

His spine twists like a headless snake inside his still body.
Wine flows from his mouth instead of words.

In a black cavern there is lightning.

William Coleman

Fade Away

Paint peels like skin, waves crash like bones;
Your body is a jungle and I'm the fire;
Drive across your head on a highway;
Sun burns your eyes, fog clouds your head;
Walking across the bridge to nowhere;
Wind blows your nose, snow blankets your soul;
Hail pounds your ears, rain washes your face;
Thunder drives your heart, sleet blinds your veins;
Hair pulls roots, wrinkles divide your tissue;
Blood heals, tears hurt, sweat goes nowhere;
Running up the stairs to somewhere;
Life fades away, pain lives on.

Jacob Patrick Gonyea

Family Reunion

Though some of our history has been lost
Along our family's tree,
Though some of the pages are surely blank
Yes empty as can be,

But here we are together again
With hope, with pride, and love,
For this gathering of people,
This family reunion is blessed
From heaven above.

So go and laugh, you who need to laugh
And shed a tear if you must;
Emotions this day you need not hide,
For you have your family's trust.

From old to young and young to old,
This reunion is filled with love;
With a kiss on the cheek, a pat on the back,
And, yes, a great big hug.

From how do you do to great big tales,
From those who like to boast,
And with love in my heart, for the dearly departed

Robby Wyatt

A Summer Place

Boarded up buildings
Dried up fountains
Squirrels playing in the empty bandstand

Waves crashing on the beach
Wind singing through abandoned buildings
A fire alarm sounding in the distance

The smell of cotton candy and pizza lingers
The strong smell of salt hangs in the air
A light smell of smoke drifts in

The bitter taste of salt on my lips
The clean taste of raindrops

Benches wet from the ocean spray and rain
Boards cold, rough and wet under my bare feet

Leslie L. Van Herpe

Daddy's Gone

Why you left I will never know,
But still I ask myself where did he go?

You disappeared without a trace,
You've never even seen your daughter's face,

When I look in the mirror I see traces of you,
It makes me so angry I'm not sure what to do,

I feel all alone in this big place,
I wish we could say good-bye here face to face,

So many secrets "Mom and I" have shared,
I guess you really never cared,

Guess daddy wasn't meant as a family man,
That's why he turned his back and ran,

You ran from the truth and the family you had,
You've made my heart so incredibly sad,

No daddy to tuck me in at night,
Your love is so far from my sight,

I never asked for much- just time and concern,
The stuff you didn't know you would soon have learned,

I tell all my friends that I think you're dead,
But I guess that's just all in my head.

Angela Chapman

A Thunderstorm Night's Song

Look, coming a thundercloud,
that's the signal of a thunderstorm!
Only a moment, the night sky was covered
with dark and black clouds.

Thunders rumbled loudly,
lightning glistened brightly, as if
the heaven's troops were waving their sabers.
Wind blew strongly, as thousands of horses galloping ahead,
the woods rocked, tottering and crumpling;
Rain fell heavy, as the river rushed down in torrents,
the floods flowed turbulently and roaring.
A vast expanse of mist, a large extent of muddiness,
the high sky and deep earth would be closed.
A struggle of natures was locked together.
the specters of wind, rain, water, fire and soil got reunion
with noise and excitement in the cosmos . . .

But, all these things,
how could it be possible to last so long?
Look, please, look at the moon washed by rain
more luminous it was!

Henry Qiu

Sun

Overhead was blue and clear
And passion burnt above,
And from this passion flames were thrown
From the brightest star, my love.
And that's when the sweetest kisses pressed
From day's beginning to its end,
Upon my face, my neck, and breast
How I wished it never end.
What fun we had, and games we'd play
And with passing clouds he'd wink,
My star warmed my heart all day
And left my cheeks a bashful pink.
But when the daylight gave way to night
And the passion slowly died,
I prayed for morning to bring the light
That the moon had forced to hide.

Kathleen E. Buskey

Star In My Sky

I lay awake at night counting the stars in my sky
There is one special star who vanished,
it used to shine so bright in my sky.
Now the sky and stars are not complete.
Without this one star, my whole sky is empty,
except for the other meaningless stars.
I can no longer wish upon this special star,
in the chilling night.

Since the star vanished from my sky,
I have been lonely,
and in search of another star
to make my sky complete.
Throughout my long search,
I've found there is not one star
that shines as bright as he ever did.
I will keep looking for a new star,
but in my heart I know I'll never find a star
to shine as bright as he did.

O- my star in the sky will you come
and shine once again?

Sarah Bozick

Something Better To Do

Seeking something better to do, I searched for the meaning of life,
the reason for being, the secret of the universe.

I built a powerful microscope and saw inside the DNA spiral,
inside a molecule, inside an atom, inside sub-atomic particles.

And what did I see?
An eye, a hazel eye at the end of a telescope,
searching upward and outward.

I built a powerful telescope and saw beyond the solar system,
beyond the edge of the universe, inside a black hole.

And what I see?
An eye, a hazel eye at the end of a microscope,
searching downward and inward.

I read all the books on history, religion, philosophy, science.
I confronted a teacher, pastor, philosopher, scientist.

And what did I learn?
No means yes and yes mean no.
White is black and black is white.

Fortunately, my child came in and asked me to play,
giving me something better to do.

Richard Loewe

A Poem To Danielle

Dedicated To Danielle For Being Such A Pleasure.
A child of sweetness, intellect, and enthusiasm. A child of
inquisitiveness. A child I look upon who reminds me of myself
at her age. How can I begin to express to my little friend
what a little helper you have been? And how much fun the time
we spend together has put my soul in a whirlwind!

For my pretty friend has such potential to grow and become
a fine teacher. But what she really means to me is she is
someone who I can share my feelings to and she will listen and
I can reciprocate the same lessons. She will accept and learn.
But my Danielle is firm in her beliefs. However she amazes me
because she awakens to the fact that people are different and
she will not offend. She smiles with a twinkle in her eye and
says that it is okay. For how special is my Danielle? She is
our youth of our future.

Teresa W. Stueck Robinson

Old Bobtail Yellow Cat

Old bobtail yellow cat's stomach was growling.
So, he went hunting-he went prowling.
Sniffing here and sniffing there,
He didn't care—he sniffed everywhere.
He found a bag with something that smelled good.
He found something to eat—he knew he would.
Poking his head into the bag, his head got stuck.
And that was his bad luck.
Trying to get a piece of chicken that had been fried,
He couldn't get his head out, no matter how he tried.
It was such a sight to see
Old bobtail yellow cat trying to get free.
Who let the cat out of the bag? as the saying goes.
Old bobtail yellow cat knows.

Annie Cason

Marine World

Marine World, Marine World,
What a fun place to be,
There are two killer whales splashing at me,
Come see the sharks the dinosaurs for a scare,
Because they're getting extinct and they're very rare,
So have fun and enjoy the exciting new experience,
And come back if you . . . Dare . . .

Kasey Yvonne Ferguson

Untitled

I remember the night
we lay out under the stars
I told you my secrets
I opened my soul
but your heart wasn't there
our eyes were so far away
you were in another world
a world I'm too scared to understand

You told me you loved to watch the stars
you said they made you happy
I wish I could make you smile like that
just once if you would look at me
through clear blue skies
and your eyes they would see
that you're my star

Andrew Todd

Confined

How I yearn to be free, free to spread my wings and escape
from my prison. Free to choose, free to be myself.

How I need to be free, free to love, free to hate.
Free to lead, free to follow.

I believe my wish will someday be granted, and I will not
forget but worship the one who unlocked my cell door.

I still await the moment I can finally see with my own soul
the beauty and ugliness of my world. The world I can not
imagine, the world that I now seek and will spend the rest of my
life hiding from.

Alesha Mullins-DeBoer

A Part of Me

Unlawful entry to my heart
You broke in and stole a part.
You took a piece of me to be with you,
With all that trouble you had to go though.
Were you not afraid it would fall apart?
Shrivel like a rose,
And get lost in the wind as it blows.
Or go through life not being whole,
Like having a spirit, but not a soul.
I would have shared because your the best,
But now, I think I will protect the rest.
For if you stole it once, you'll do it again,
But do it twice, and you've lost a friend,
Do it again, when you are not a friend,
And that my love, will be the end.

Julie Person

Ode to Trafic Jam

There they go, lickety split,
not caring about me a bit.
While all the cars on my side
are standing still side by side.
People are out walking around,
and I don't hear an angry sound.
Some are playing catch with a ball.
Some lay on the grass doing nothing at all.
We've been standing still for quite a spell.
My tires have grown roots, ain't that swell.
The girls behind me sunbathe on the hood.
Young men wave as young men should.
The guys in front think this a great thrill,
while I'm parked next to a smelly road kill.
Hey wait a minute, I see movement ahead.
Oh good, I'll make it home in time for bed.

Donal J. Cox

His Bottle

Living inside of a bottle
is a claustrophobic illusion of a dream.
In someone else's dimension of reality
this one who I saw, searching
for his bottle, was in chase of his life's meaning,
his last chapter of a trilogy played to the beat of the mean street.

Looking inside out from a bottle
Stooping low behind a can, or a crate in search of
the monetary exchange which will quench his habitual thirst
A series of poor choices made, have clouded his vision
of the illusion of his life, our life, outside of the bottle.

A psychological spiral down a rabbit hole
to somewhere, anywhere, but here.
His dreams are images blurred by life's cruel trick
pulling another drink from his bottle
slumped down against cold concrete, wasting away the dark wet

Night of unseen faces and screams of pain
looking out through the bottle's green, stained glass
waiting for the end of his life.

John Wolfe

Tom The Painter

Tom walks into town everyday to buy painting tools.
He wears old clothes and a dirty straw hat,
They are the only clothes he owns.

He sits outside and paints.
He lives in a small shack next to mine.
He's been poor all his life.

He has no friends,
But he waves to me all the time, so I wave back.

I noticed the police were there one day,
I walked over there and they told me I could walk on in.
All I saw was his paintings.
I was the only one at his funeral,
He left everything to me.
He said I was the only who was nice to him,
And to think all I did was wave.
His paintings went to museums and they were worth a lot of
money.
And to think someone so poor . . .
Had a talent full of riches.

Leah Welch

Affairs of the Heart

Wayward trust or wonder lust.
Happen stance or careful glance.
Genuine lies or deceitful candor.
Pristine white and knows no vice
of hate, of lust, or of mistrust.
Guided vengeance, rage displaced
tender mercies soon retrace.
Shattered, beaten, tattered and torn
the heart is viewed for all to scorn
when secret lives are lived in public eyes.

Nancy Lee Peden

The White Rose

Roses come in many colors-
orange, yellow, and many shades of red.
Like perfumed belles they enchant
the poor, the rich, and all the in-betweens.
But one rose remains still
pure, innocent, and all its beauty simply seen,
In a sacred gift held in whiteness
the dress, the veil, and then the woman.

Joseph H. Flack

Grandpa Maki

We all miss you very much
I'll always remember this day
Without you, nothing could be as true
As you bravery that showed us the way

I wish you were here right now
But I realize that cannot be
At least you're not in pain anymore
Please always remember me

This is a very sad day
As everyone here knows
You always has a special place in my heart
That is now hurt, but still glows

How come it had to be you
That had to be taken away
Why couldn't your time here be longer
So that you could still stay

Ashley Kick

I Can See Through You

I can see through your eyes when you're faking
I can see through your mind when you're hiding
You whisper in my ear "I love you"
You put your hands on the inside of my thighs
All I hear echoing in my head are your sweet words
You press your body against mine
I tell you no and all you can say is "Yes, yes, I love you"
I can see through your eyes when you're faking
And I can see through your mind when you're hiding
I can see through your words
I will not open my door for you

Susan Boarts

Angels

Mother, please don't cry for me
I'm in heaven and happy as can be
Playing with love ones that's gone on before
No pain and no fear I feel anymore
I know you miss me and want me with you
But if only you could see past these skies of blue
At how beautiful I am in my new birth
You wouldn't want me to come back to earth
Stay with God and live His way
Join me in heaven to live someday
And not to forget before I part
I love you and miss you with all my heart

Mary Headley

Who Is The Winner?

For Casey Jordan
I was out playing with my dog,
We were wrestling all around,
All at once she sprang in a leap,
And I ended up on the ground.

She licked my face and bit my ear.
I could not win for losing.
The game she played was soon to see
She was winning, I was bruising.

I chased her across the flower beds.
Under the fence, on her belly she crawled.
She looked at me and wagged her tail;
"Come on Casey," you can sprawl.

So I got stuck and could not move.
"Come on Casey," she barked and barked.
Pulling my shirt, she pulled me through
And there we sat, on the grass we parked.

Elvera Smith

Blind Tiger

Smooth wisps of wind cross eyes
Deep thoughts unite cold skies
Firm stances remain taught
So once loose cries,
Are not

Without a doubt penetrable
True means enabled
River runs, for non-relinquishing
Twisted thoughts have escaped
Joys arrived craving

Or is it here, lingering on these blank pages?
Waiting!
Screaming!
Burning alive!
Inside,
The fever

Jason David Leete

How Do You Mend A Broken Heart?

How do you mend a broken heart?
Needle and thread aren't strong enough.
It's been said "Time heals all wounds"
But this time, the edges are too rough.

I gave you my heart with all my love
And I thought you felt the same way I do.
The fire that burned between us with such intensity
Died to embers and the flame finally blew.

My heart aches everyday with pain
And my eyes fill with unshed tears.
I love you so much even your memory hurts.
I felt so safe and secure with you, No Fears!

Life makes no guarantees, no promises.
Now your promise of love is gone
And my heart is in pieces. I keep asking
Myself, "Where did our love go wrong?"

You say you've found a new love
And all I want for you is the best in life
And for you to be happy, now and forever,
Just remember, though, I'll love you until I die.

Lynne Boyd

Untitled

Spring is the season
Of birth and joy
When the new baby comes
"Is it a girl or a boy?"
Summer rolls around
"Where did all the time go?"
Time for graduation
"Kids don't take too long to grow"
Fall follows quickly
Junior says "This bride is mine;
We'll go and raise a family,
And be happy for all time."
Winter comes with speed
And he realizes the joy a family can bring
Then comes the season
We all know is called spring
Spring is the season
Of birth and joy
Now it's his turn to ask
"Is it a girl or a boy?"

Melissa Quintana

John F. Kennedy

A man of his word.
A man among men.
The presidency is what he wanted to win.
He was a man who believed in equality
of races.
He was a man with many faces.

A U-boat pilot, husband, father, and friend.
His physical wounds had to mend.
He lived a short life.
With just his children and wife.
He was a man with many faces.

In November of 1963,
An assassin's bullet shocked our country.
Our 35th president lay dead.
Lee Harvey Oswald had shot him in the head.
Ashes to ashes,
Dust to dust.
If he'd stayed out of Dallas,
He might still be with us.

He was a man with many faces.

Cassie Chance

A True Friend

Friends that judge don't matter,
Friends that matter don't judge,
Someone who will stand by you,
And remain sincere.

Someone with whom you can talk to,
And share all your secrets,
Help one another, with your problems,
Make the solutions seem so clear.

A shoulder to cry on,
A hand to hold,
A heart to confide in,
With limits unset.

Someone to embrace,
With whom you can love,
Someone who makes an everlasting impression,
And someone you can never forget.

These are measures unaccounted for,
Memories to cherish,
Days when dreams seem like reality,
So hold on to the love of a true friend.

Tabby Longfellow

My Answer

To Robert Desnos
Let's make it New Orleans, Cafe du Monde

And so we were there
Two cups of cafe au lait and a table with pages
Of his works covered with powdered sugar.
We talked about the life that gave life to his words

His phantom lover rose up from the coffee's steam
And danced and twirled into the spinning, wobbling
Ceiling fans above our heads

He spoke of undying love that died in his arms
And dreams that ended reality
Dead voices filled his heart
He loved a love that never answered

Then he stopped, found my stare,
Gave me a taste of his smile

And I sat listening
And so deeply loving

In my eyes he found his answer

Leslie A. White

Destruction Fall

Depressed and lonely, she sits and waits.
She's reluctant to move knowing nothing of her fate.

Her cries for help are no longer understood,
She'd try to escape; if only she could.

Under her masters command in which she obeys,
She's forced to kill and to run away.
Beaten and abused, she dreams of going home,
But that's something she could never do;
For now it's just a mere place to roam.

After leaving her parents, they moved away,
Leaving her searching for a decent place to stay.
Then she met him and her life was turned around,
Not knowing she would soon be "drug fiend" bound.

It's now been four years of running from the law,
But the ground she's on is beginning to fall.
She sometimes wonders how it all began,
But she can't think clearly, for her mind is spinning like a fan.
With her hands trembling, she steps up to the edge,
Tells the city good-bye and jumps off the ledge.

Danelle McGregor

Simple People

It's so sad the way things are.
The successful people.
The one's that go so far.
What about the simple people?

The simple people,
With simple lives,
Simple dreams and goals,
And gentle hearts.

The people we know,
And the one's we don't,
The street people,
Pushing grocery carts.

Or the people who help when you need a hand,
They don't expect payment, loyalty or praise,
The one's that do things for no real reason,
Except to know a heart has been lightened and raised.

Kisses blown on the wind,
Hugs to help diminish sadness,
Compliments given out of generosity,
And smiles out of sheer gladness.

Connie Sue Tillman

For You, For Me

You bring me so much joy
You bring me so much hope
And now . . .
I beg for my strength for you
Because of my love for you
I cry each night
for you
I don't know if I'm strong enough for you
Like I should be, like I want to be
for you
If you need me, I'll need this strength and I have it not
for you
I want to have it for you
To hold you up . . . give you something to lean on
And if you go, I need it more
for me
Because I love you so,
Because it will be hard to go on for me
Because you won't be here
for me.

J. L. Currey

Crochet

What do I do with my hands each day
Make wondrous gifts through the art of crochet

Hundreds of shawls and blankets over the years
Have brought many a receiver to tears

With left over yarn to create the toys
Generations have played with, both girls and boys

The colors I blend together to make the design
In my minds eyes will match up just fine

Cats are also the reason for a gift
With a little bit of catnip they get a lift

May my hands remain active and glad
And arthritis doesn't set in too bad

Nancy Hamm

Father's Day

I'm grateful on this Father's Day,
As my children stand before me.
I'm proud of each and I can say,
They are my true immortality.

My firstborn gift is almost a woman now,
She's so beautiful and smart.
We don't always agree, but anyhow,
She holds a deep spot in my heart.

My middle gift is my only son.
He's smart, handsome and strong.
He'll carry our name to the next generation,
He'll be a man before too long.

My youngest gift is the most like me.
She's strong-willed and independent.
Pretty and smart with a touch of tom-boy,
A purer flower . . . God never sent.

Yes, I appreciate God's gifts to me,
On this glorious Father's Day.
All good things in life are truly free,
I love them all in a special way.

Billy D. Rains Jr.

Unexpected

Flickering, flying lightning bug went on as he was free.
Looking up at the sky seeing how it would always be.
He flew and flew flashing his light.
Oh how it was a pretty sight.
I seen him fly so free until a frog
Snapped him from a tree.

Cindy Erickson

Love Isn't Easy

As I walked through the forests' brush of joy,
I saw the sunshine coming through a tree.
Beyond a full fern stood a handsome boy,
Whose sweet golden complexion welcomed me.
We sat by a quaint pond, just him and me,
Watched the moon diminish the break of day.
The passion between us made me love thee,
And him the same as we will always say.
Our possession grew stronger late that night,
In which another love story enhanced.
As I look back, it was all a great sight,
Crying, as I remembered when we danced.
Through thick and thin our love will never die,
I watched him pass to the grave, where he lies.

Danielle Blake

All Because of You

You told me that I'm always happy
And there has never been a day where I was blue.
Well, why don't you look at me now cause I'm crying over you,
And these tears are caused by you.

I thought I would never see the day when you left me.
My days were happy when I had you.
But ever since you left me my days have been so blue.

I wish we could go back to the days when I had you,
When we became one and no longer two.
I thought we were soul mates,
Companions for life.

A day of happiness was when I had you.
One look into your eyes I knew it was true.
Something about you just captured my heart.
I loved you in so many ways I can't even count.

I go over in my head when you told me I'm always happy.
Well, you should be ashamed,
'Cause I'm crying
And it's all because of you.

Trisha Marie Tellez

Lief Law

Most amenable are three, powers that be,
Bonding generation o'er and thru the centuries.
The set of their seal binds all to the wheel;
Unto millennia, by motion, in adoption.

When a people adopt a covenant
They confirm a creed:
By blood to be sure
The rose seeks a cure,
For our mortal infidelity.

When a people adopt a constitution
They sanction a nations foundation;
Where entwined of preceding two
Promotes progress upon kindred true,
Thus enhancing the affusion
Of ours and God communion.

When a people adopt a contract
They create a creature of cycle;
Whether beholden to canon chosen,
Or wantonly void of statute poses:
Beware a dragon, bearing rein roses!

Timothy J. Foglesong

Only In My Dreams

Only in my dreams
I can fly
Only in my fantasies
My hopes will never die
Only in my dreams
I can live in a beautiful, peaceful place
Only in my fantasies
exists no violence, death, or hate
Only in my dreams
I don't destroy, I create
Maybe if we would listen to these fantasies
And what they mean
Maybe it wouldn't have to be "only in my dreams"

Ashley Harter

One Man's Hope

Lost, I wandered through life daily,
Seeking joy from everything I did.
All alone, I searched for something better
To fill the ache within my heart I'd hid.

An ache that so o'erwhelmed my spirit
And left me struggling desperately in tears.
Vain hopes, like shattered glass around me,
Failed to drive away my growing fears.

'Twas then you whispered sweetly to me
In words of love beyond compare
To deeply drink of the Father's tender mercies
And rest in His unending care.

On humbled knees I gave myself unto You,
Christ's sacrifice for sin I claimed as mine.
And the cleansing power of Jesus washed right through me
Bringing sunlight to this Light starved soul of mine.

Lord, now I praise your presence daily;
You're there each time I laugh or cry.
With arms wrapped gently 'round my shoulders
You'll walk with me where'er my path may lie.

Donald E. Williams

What's That Noise?

Drip, drip, drip . . .
That faucet could make you crazy.

Hee-haw, hee-haw . . .
That snoring could drive you up a wall.

Blink, blink, blink . . .
That neon vacancy light could drive you stark-raving mad.

Plop, plop, plop . . .
That dripping leak could make your skin crawl.

Scritch, scratch . . .
Those pesky kittens could give you a migraine.

Giggle, giggle, giggle . . .
Those kids could annoy you beyond belief.

Psssh . . .
That TV could keep you up all night . . .

But she smiles all snuggled up in bed, closes her
eyes, and thinks . . . aah . . . I love this apartment.

Traci Bickford

True Personality

All I really wanted was to be a perfect somebody,
A person who was true, alive, and real.
All I really wanted was to be able to feel,
With all of my heart, my true personality.

All I really wanted was to be happy and not feel pity,
And not censor my sadness and silently fall apart.
All I really wanted was to have heart,
And believe in my true personality.

But being perfect is just a dream,
Wake up and look at reality.
Sometimes I just want to scream
And pass my burdens to another nobody
"Calm down," I say, "and do as I please,
To please myself and nobody else."
Who is to tell me what I can be?
Who is to tell me how to be free?
It's I who decide; it's all in my true personality.

Mindy Lin

Stars Swimming Through The Milky Way

I see stars out tonight. They wink at me
from the corners of the universe,
maybe beyond the far off Andromeda.
Is there another girl, another creature
seeing my world as a flicker in the sky?
How insignificant I must be
through her eyes; just a speck of light
that may catch her soul.
Does she look at Earth like I look
at Orion, the stars
that glimmer and show fragments of the future?
Maybe she has flecks of moonbeam
that shower her face with the sharp light of reality.
She could be looking across the galaxies
and maybe she doesn't even see me.
Maybe, she never will.

Meg Scheding

Searching for a Rainbow

Have you ever searched for a rainbow
When it hasn't rained
Yeah I know it sounds totally insane
But I found one, one day
I thought I was looking for something
That I would never find
Just another beautiful image in the back of my mind
And then suddenly you appeared
Standing there right in my face
All this time I was looking for my rainbow
I was looking in the wrong place
The rainbow I found I didn't find up in the sky
The rainbow I found, I found when I looked into your eyes.

Odie Marizette Jr

What Is Love

What is love, is it strong, is it true?
Does it bring pain or ache to you?
Must you believe in it for it to be?
Is it a force you cannot see?
A steady motion or uneven beat?
Must it make sense, this strange thing we call neat?
Does it hold you together, or tear you apart?
Does it happen at the end of our lives, the middle, or the start?
Without it, would we be?
What is love? Please, tell me.

Josephine Anderson

The Accident

The heartless screech of tires, the endless
screams of fear. As the world rolls over
and under, One less voice screaming, that voice
suddenly deathly quiet. The endless shattering
of glass, the air filled with pain and fear.
Everyone seems ok, at least those here. One is
missing though, gone from sight. No sight of
her to be seen. Where did she go? We're here.
Battered and bruised, broken neck they say.
No more pain or suffering, so young, so filled
with life. She was so eager for the future.
Why her? Why us? Why anyone? The pain will
slowly subside the good memories will make us laugh,
She's still with us in our hearts,
she'll never be more than a thought away.
We'll miss you Nicole. Rest in Peace.

Megan Pearson

The Equalizer

Swirling, wrestling, whistling winds,
Cumulus nimbus clouds rolling
Across an orange red tinged sky,
Lightning, streaking,
Trees swaying with their boughs hanging low
The heavens are weeping, weeping.
Rich or poor,
Young or old,
Red, brown, yellow, black and white,
All are truly equal now in nature's sight.
Superiority?
It belongs to God and nature.

Jean M. Arthur

The Strong Black Girl

I am the strong black girl
I am the slave girl who ran with Harriet Tubman
I am the slave girl who played with Frederick Douglass
I am the strong black girl

I am the strong black girl
I am the black girl that heard
Dr. Martin Luther King speak
I am the strong black girl

I am the strong black girl
I am the strong black girl that sat
In the courts of desegregation laws and
Listened to Thurgood Marshall speak.

I am the strong black girl
I am the black girl who heard the poems
And the stories of Maya Angelou.

I am the strong black girl
I am the future's strong black girl
I am the strong black girl!

Sanchelle F. Johnson

Waves

The waves that crash upon the shore
Could be so much more

They speak and swell and then disappear
Such beauty, so short lived, and dear

They curl up like people in pain
Then run so fast, with nothing to gain

Their beauty is not how long they last
Or how huge they become

But rather in the eye of the beholder
How magical, they become

Waves, like life, come and go so fast
We would like to make them last

But the beauty is in the beholding as in the living
The here and now is all to those who enjoy giving

Stop and smell the roses, as they say
For they too, soon fade away

Love and be loved and appreciate the day
For all too soon it slips away

Give much more than you take from each living thing
And you will have eternal spring

Phyllis Speaker

Holocaust Memorial Museum

Many sad memories wrap through this historical place.
The Jewish people who died because Hitler hated them are here.

As you walk through the museum..
You feel their agony and suffering, the horror all rubs off on you.

And then you feel how many others felt fear.
You hear the cries, the Nazis capturing innocent people,
and the sound of people dying through these walls.

All of the sudden you feel like running and hiding.
But why?
You wonder what it was really like. What really happened?

Then think:
Do you really want to know?

Jennifer Schutz

A Teacher Wonders

Where are all my students of time past
who tenderly touched my life
and left such deep impressions
of treasured memories that last?

Each name, each voice, each footstep
was easily discerned.
Personalities mirrored behavior
innate and learned.

Tools of the trade were daily
sharpened and polished anew
for the structure they were building
required excellence to endure.

The lesson in the book was not
the only lesson taught,
but how to walk the path of life
and how the battle's fought.

The mind's eye sees and thoughts reflect
the pleasurable times we shared.
Where are all my students
who were entrusted to hands that cared?

Vivian Dunn Hardee

Man and the Irony of His Ignorance

Throw it away, throw it away.
Throw it away to dig up some other day.

May we grant ourself rainbow colored water
And three headed babies,
denying that we will scream and holler.

Invite all the pain and carnage you can muster
Up to the party, making the guest of
honor all of God's creatures
Destroying in the process all of the Earth's
beautiful, delicate features.

Toss intelligence out into the street on its keester
And whatever you do, do not believe a word
stupidity says when you meet her.

Lets lay it all on the line
All of our futures and our children's dreams
leaving in question whether we have
consciously not used our mind or if we
have simply just tossed it aside.

Mason W. Schmidt III

True Friends

A real true friend is what I need,
someone I can count on to take the lead.
A real true friend helps start my day,
and does not even get in the way.
A real true friend is always around,
no matter what may get me down.
Now that's a true friend even money can't buy,
so I warn you now—don't even try!

Vanessa White

Organic Religion

The rocks tumble towards the river:
The red, the black, the yellow and white
The whole damn world is turned upside-down
Just to stand upright.

There were to be no divisions;
Only organic revolutions that just might
Evolve into hope and turn the day
From this territorial fight.

Through the shocking realm of
Film-drawn victims
Imagination starves for freedom
And takes a licking
In sync with the rhythm of nature
The answer has arisen
We have become the movie that
Reigns our human vision.

The truth is a novel dream so
The south, the west, the east and north
The whole blue earth must face itself
In this light we must go forth.

Edward Eugene Smith

True Love

Can you think of anything more beautiful than love
This feeling which must come from heaven above
This feeling I speak about is what makes your day
Sometimes you're speechless, you don't know what to say
All you want is this love so near, so darn close
That all you can hear
Is I love you my darling, honest I do
My love for you is real and true
At present my sweet I'm all alone
Thinking of you, that's what brought on this poem
But now I must say good night to you
Knowing our love will always be true

Robt Wolowitz

Penitence

Brought by sunset, cold and harsh; consumed by
Fear, an aging loss, that builds in terror
As each day past, has come to seek the lye
In which to repent his inner mirror.

At half past twelve abound he seeks with arms
Outstretched toward heaven, with vision impaired;
Pledges "an apocalypse triumphs harms";
For alas hope befalls a love that cared.

From the skies a voice did speak in reason:
"Oh, beast of darkness now lower thine hands;
Why didn't thou trust the coming of season,
That summer would bring thy gift to land,
In thou heart, a beautiful bride will dawn;
But only a fool doth not trust . . . be gone!"

Megan M. Stewart

Make This House A Home

Make this a house a home, Gracious Lord,
Where by everyone you are adored.

Thank you, Lord, for this earthly gift,
A place to come, and burdens lift.

Protect and keep all those within;
Help and forgive them when they sin.

Let laughter ring throughout its halls,
A haven from the busy malls.

Then shield this house from Satan's snares;
Make it a place of sharing cares.

Send your holy angels to keep
All those who work, and play and sleep.

Cast out all fear of the unknown;
Fill hearts with love, as you have shown.

Grant, Dear Lord, that your word may grow
And prayers from lips daily do flow.

May all who come share in God's grace
And see the world a better place.

Bless members of this family
And let this home a haven be, a foretaste of eternity.

Darline Kussmann

Creating A Monster

Unwanted and alone, the child cries
Enveloped in the midst of a family's lies.
Verbal abuse drives the boy away
Developing an inner scar bound to stay.

A life on the streets becomes his hope
Drugs, money, and sex makes it easier to cope.
Joining a violent gang removes the pain
Of an abandoned heart that feels ashamed.

Blame it on the past of the innocent mind,
Search the child's soul and emptiness you'll find.
When there is nothing to lose, there is no wrong
With one you are weak, but with many you're strong.

We're creating a monster right before our eyes.
Isn't it apparent the shame that he hides?
Alone and cold, these secrets he'll keep,
But it is the street where he chooses to sleep.

Hatred and fear clouds the brain.
Molding the hurt into a torrent of flames.
The monster inside unleashes its rage
Not knowing that wrath is its ultimate cage.

Gary W. Castro

Untitled

She was my mother and my friend
Love and happiness my way she would send
I never knew how much I needed her until to late
I think of things I'd done to her and it's myself I hate

She was a woman I took for granted
And now beside her grave it's roses I planted
I wish I had five minutes with her just to talk
But it's too late for on this earth she'll never again walk

I'll always remember the good times with her I had
I'll forget the bad times and be happy not sad
I know she's watching on this earth each day
And in my mind I can hear her say

We'll meet in Heaven again sometime
And the joy we share will be divine

Debra J. Dickenson

Lost One

As she lay there so peacefully at the end of the bed
oh so big,
With a grin that made the heavens smile,
and thy angels rejoice.
Oh Lost One
As she took her last breath,
she floated so slowly up to heaven;
with her hands out,
just waiting to touch her loved one.
Oh Lost One
As she stood before thy God, he reached his hands out:
said "Come, Come Be Holy With All."
Oh Lost One
Her memories to be with all,
Her spirit to rest with thy Lord.
As she looked down upon us:
She said "be happy for thy Lord gave me peace,
Like I always wanted it to be,
Thee memories shall be cherished,
And thy spirit will be with all for eternity.

Kristyl Holle

A Nurse's Prayer

Lord help me to smile and never tire
Think of my patients as they are.

Apprehensive, discouraged and in pain
Help me make them well again.

As I say this wee little prayer,
Let them know I really care.

Keep in confidence, things whispered to me
Tell my heartache only to thee.

Never too busy to answer a light
Lend a helping hand whenever I might.

Not talk of things I have to do
Just keep on smiling until I'm through.

Help me to walk and never run
Stay with me dear Lord until I'm done.

When I collapse, if collapse I must
Please let me get home to all the dust.

Velma Robertson Klinger

When I Sleep

I dream of brushing your lips with mine
of holding you in my arms forever
of feeling your hot breath on my neck
of whispering my hopes and dreams to you
and of listening to yours.
I dream of seeing you every morning when I wake
of hearing your laughter echo in my ears
of watching your smile light up a room
of protecting you from the bad things
and of sharing with you the good.
I dream of loving you.
May I never wake.

Tim Ross

Untitled

Here I sit in my room alone
With no one to talk to and no one to listen
so who can I talk to? I know I can talk to the Lord,
The Lord will talk and listen to me.
He will answer my prayers and talk to me in my room alone.

Janet Lee Kellerstrass

Time

Time is something everyone never has enough of.
Time is something that always seems to drag by.
Time is something that as you get older seems to fly by.
Time is something that as you wait for something crawls by.
Time is something that when you know you've done something wrong
    seems the tick of the clock is quick.
Time is something everyone never has enough of.

Barbara Staymate

Always

He's got a beautiful smile,
A beautiful face.
He's got a wonderful laugh,
And wonderful ways.
He's my little boy,
My brother forever.
I'll protect him in the harsh, harsh weather.
I'll be by his side,
I'll stand with him.
I'll sick with him with vigor and vim.
I'll love him forever, and he'll always be,
My wonderful, loving, and beautiful baby.

Sarah R. Kessler

When Pain Is Gone

When pain is gone,
Then what is left?
When anger has vanished and banished all death.
When the flowers have gone,
And back to sunshine.
I just can't sit back and whine.
I would go mad in a world
Of great things.
What about the joy, pain brings?

Jennifer D. Doute

Graduation

Graduation time is here
Soon Junior High will appear.
I had the greatest time at P.S. 101,
but now the time as come . . .
to say goodbye to all my friends,
and hope our friendships never end.
As we all go our separate ways,
and enter a very complicated maze,
I'll miss all the special teaching,
but won't forget the useful preaching.
I'll always remember the precious memories,
and the special times we've shared,
also, all the sweet people that cared.
I grew up in this school,
yet I never felt like a small, lonely fish in a gigantic pool.
The candle of knowledge has always burned,
for all the fabulous things I learned.
So when graduation day comes, and we all yell and shout,
I'm sure that the candle of memories will never burn out.

Sandy Vladescu

Kellie's Poem

She is only a voice that I hear, for I cannot see her,
She walks beside me, softly speaking in my ear,
She gives me the courage to be brave with her calming voice,
She watches over me, and guides me through danger.
She shows me the way, and always lends her hand,
She is forever by my side, for she is my guardian angel.

Todd Nielsen

The Ocean

You hear the sound first.
Continues, ceaseless, incessant.
The waves crashing and retrieving,
Crashing and retrieving.

Next the immensity astounds you.
The stretch of black silk joining the fiery horizon.
It is alive; you stare in awe.

The unmistakable salty smell,
Reminds you where you are.
Repugnant, repulsive, strangely addictive.

You are only a needle in a haystack.
How can we feel so important and powerful?
It is ancient and invincible.

A Paradox.
Passive, peaceful one moment,
The Mother of all things.
Destructive, devastating the next, death itself.
How many have drown in its truculent waters?

It demands respect.

Agatha Glowacki

Woman's Liberation

Gave us all the right to vote.
My children stuck in day care!
Forced the boss to hire us.
They have to spend their life there!
Wages top out with the males.
Throw supper on a plate!
By "law" now we all have respect.
I'll be two hours late!
"Woman's liberation" made females feel so free!
No one ever thought to ask what I set out to be.

Terri L. Chandler

Depression

As I look out the window
I can't tell you what I see.
I'm not looking at the swarm of people
Passing by under me.
I don't look at the cars, busses, or trains,
But at loneliness, at wonder and pain.

The people that I see, those I love
Float by on white clouds far above.
Wishing I were with them
The longing that I know
Has not kept me from dreaming
To be with them for a long as
I grow, with the sorrow
Of each passing day.
I know that in the end
Everything will be happy and gay.

Jessica Saniuk

The Art of Conversation

There is a moment when the word must be spoken.
Lost, it cannot shape again.
Laughter then becomes polite.
The wash of love turns to social bathing
In articulate, disembodied pleasures.
Words become things, objects of affection
To trade between us like a gift proffered
At the wedding of a distant cousin.

Joan Hartwig

Silver Rain

I miss your kisses and the way you held me tight;
I'm beginning to wonder if you think of me at night.

As I think of you, I watch the silver rain,
Praying to an angel to take away my pain.

No one understands that all my hurt is real;
I wish you could know just exactly how I feel

When I see your face as you walk down the hall,
I start to think that you don't care at all.

I used to believe our souls were forever lost,
But now I feel you and I are star-crossed.

As your memory fades, the silver rain goes away;
I guess even my silver rain angel couldn't make you stay.

McKenna Brazel

Our Last Goodbye

We all love you more than words can say,
We're so sorry the Lord called you away.
The pain of missing you will never cease,
But it's comforting to know you will rest in peace.
For you were loving, gentle and kind,
A better man would be hard to find.
We thank God for the years we had together,
We only wish it could have lasted forever.
You took us all in and gave us your love,
You were truly a blessing from above.
Now for the last time we must say goodbye,
Help us to accept it and not question why.
Help us to remember you with a smile,
And be thankful you loved us for a little while.

Luanne Potts

Hatred

Why do we live in a world of hate?
Some might say, "Maybe it's fate."
But then there's kids out on the street,
Who fear, if they go home, they'll be beat.
If everyone hates to hear or see violence,
Then why do they make guns that bring pure silence?
What's the fun about killing each other?
It hurts a lot when you see it's your brother.
People don't understand the word ignore.
They think, without violence, the world's a bore.
Maybe one day, they should try and see,
How the world, without hatred, would really be.

Diane Tetreault

My Hero J.C.

Our world looks for heroes, in hamlets great and small,
As the greatest hero who ever lived watches over all!
He was born in a Bethlehem stable two thousand years ago.
His life is humanity's model to help every society grow.
He taught all who came to Him to love and give and share,
The only life worth living is the life that really cares!
He carried a cross to Calvary, high on Golgotha's hill,
He taught all who were touched by Him to do His Father's will!
He is our prime example: He was honest and sincere;
Those who faithfully follow Him will always find Him near!
Don't search for earthly heros in the puzzling maze of life,
Look only for the Prince of Peace;
He alone gives eternal life!
Ask not that your life be easy,
For that won't help you grow;
Ask only for the touch of the master,
For J.C. loves you so!

Cheryl Cook

In The Darkness

As I sit in the darkness, my thoughts turn to her.
Her laughter, her smile and her touch.
As I sit in the darkness, there's emptiness here.
My arms miss her so much.

When I held her, all time would stand still.
In the darkness it was her and I.
I laughed a little louder, loved a little longer,
And then she said goodbye.

We made no promises, guarantees, or commitments.
Living for the moment, felt right.
But now she's gone without a single word.
I sit in the darkness at night.

A gentle breeze blows and for a moment,
I could smell her cologne.
I close my eyes and I sit in the darkness.
In the darkness all alone!

In the darkness all alone!

Lorna Harbaugh

The Animal Within

A storm is coming.
The clouds are dark and gray.
As they change colors from black to green,
It rotates, spins, and starts to fray.
The clouds begin to form a funnel from the sky.
Dropping like an anvil,
The dust begins to fly.
The fine tip touches the city below.
It screams unbearable shrieks.
So violent, so frightening the blow,
The animal within seeks
Demolishing everything it eats.
It travels a tragic path,
Not knowing where to stop.
Until it starts to lose its power,
Spinning like a top.
Unwillingly, it retracts into its dark den,
Gathering power, traveling the lands,
Ready to drop again.

Karin Goodhue

Love

I love you so much.
Your hair, your smile.
The way you look at me with your innocent face.
You are a rose that grows more beautiful,
Everyday.
You never lose the rosiness in your cheeks.
I am the tear that is shed onto your petals,
And runs down them, clear and twinkling.
You are my rose.
Two of the purest things in the world,
Are a rose and the tears of love.
That is why.
I love you so much.

Jason Mills

Patience and Time

Upon the cliffs of Somerset, where the ocean's waves roar loud,
A man of soul and spirits lost did go to seek his peace.
He found his spirit waiting there atop the salt air breeze,
And every breath his lungs took in fulfilled his every need.
The truth he found, for patience with time, is all a man requires.
To breathe the air and feel the sun did answer why he's here.
A shell was he, or so it seemed, but now it's rather clear,
He overlooked and passed on by his reflection from inside.
So it is upon the ocean's breast his birth has come to light,
Where suicide has fought and lost, his new life can now begin.

Lisa Jornd

The Butterfly

A bee, whatever else he does,
Is almost always sure to buzz;
And lions and tigers and grumpy wild boars
Warn you with various sorts of loud roars
That they are nearby.
But what about a butterfly?

A butterfly just doesn't make any sound,
Not even a whisper to say she's around.
She's ever so timid, and terribly shy,
No matter how softly I tippy-toe by.
Cute little fluttery,
Sort of a buttery fly.

Constance Hyslop

Snowdancer

No lovelier vision that cold winter's night;
In starlit silence as she danced in the snow.
Her gentle beauty revealing of dream's delight,
Flowing to sonnets she only could know.

The snowflakes caressing her red lips were kissed;
A snow-shrouded fantasy of raven-haired glow,
With diamonds of ice in the glimmering mist,
As she glided and swayed in the twilighted snow.

Then the swirling whiteness obscured her from view
As her form was diminished and faded from sight.
I watched from my window and suddenly I knew
My vision of love has vanished this night.

But each snowfall from my window I watch and I yearn;
Her passion is near . . . This, somehow I know.
I'll always await my dancer's return
To watch her reveal her dance in the snow.

Lloyd C. Hall

Ground Zero

Days pass . . . and nights too,
When I get through life feeling okay, tis true.
But it's that mind of mine that I have to fight
Because after so many days, then it all seems like night.

A lot of those days my hope starts to build,
I think there is a light at the top of the hill,
And so I ignore the past failings, because try I must do;
Hoping against hope, hope all anew.

But, oh no, I really didn't see a light after all,
And that hill I tried to climb, instead, another fall.
A false light, a false hope, but what's real is the pain.
And I'm there one more time, Dear God, ground zero, again.

Lillian Martin

Untitled

They are based on deception.
They have always ignored her cries
Of aggravation, loneliness, fear, and frustration.
They manipulate her with their lies.

Their insults pierce her soul.
She's expected to fulfill their every command.
Power over her entire essence,
Is what they truly demand.

Her thoughts confined within herself,
They don't allow her to set them free.
Her spirit buried deep beneath the exterior,
How isolated she is, they just can't see.

They have always controlled her.
They have kept her in their deceitful grasp.
She longs to destroy their endless limitations,
As her mind hopes to uncover its freedom at last.

Sara de Souza

Silent Rhythms of the World

Those that think of the world,
Think of all the rhythm it has
First they think of all the joy it has

Also, they think of all the things you've done right
Peace and love combine to give you heaven
And all the animals of the world give you life.

Even though there may be war,
Life still goes on
And the music of the world plays on.

Life is too sensitive not to care,
Life contains the whole world
Life is just silent rhythms of the world.

Jessica Brewer

The Sky

The sky may look like many
different things to many different people,
But to me it looks
like the ocean flipped over and
got caught on something,
Or maybe someone dyed
Easter eggs in zero gravity,
Or even a huge,
colorful cloud to watch over us.
There are many different
opinions about the sky.
What's yours?

Marty Layton

A Happy Birthday Wish

It's time to say Happy Birthday,
To a special person in my life.
For you know there is only one person like that,
It just happens to be my wife.
A good thing I can say about her
Is that she does get better with age.
And as the years come and go,
We turn the book to a new page.
But no matter how the book might read,
You are the best thing in my life.
So now I give you your Birthday wish,
No one could have a better wife!

Paul Dorchak

For My Little One

I can remember when you were just 6 months old.
And at that time I was than told.
Enjoy your little son pretty soon he will be turning one.

Than, with a blink of an eye you turned two.
Before you know it you will be entering school.

You than turned three.
And it was hard to believe.
That I once bounced you on my knee.

Where did the time go. Now you are turning four.
And dressing you isn't such a chore.
You have fun mix matching your clothes.
As I stand by and say, Oh Joshua not those.

Now you are five.
And as I stand here with a tear in my eye.
I say to you my son.
I am so proud of you little one.

As you graduate from Happy Days.
I give Thanks and Praise.
To the Lord above who has blessed me so.
With a son whose smile always glows.

Tammy L. Lopez

Come a Little Closer

Come a little closer friend.
Come, so I can see, why so many
People chose to abandon me.

Come a little closer friend.
I seem to forget why my people have
No faith until they have regrets.

I never came to harm a soul, in fact
I came to save; yet so many people
Still refuse to pray.

Come a little closer friend, look into my eyes;
See the hurt and pain for them,
My heart and how it cries.

Come a little closer friend, refresh my memory.
Wasn't this a world for all to
Praise and honor me?

Come a little closer friend, come,
Let my Father judge us.
Don't be afraid, he'll know your name,
And mine, you know, is Jesus.

Theresa J. Washkowiak

The Watching Tree

Around, around, rages rain,
Bringing death and bringing pain,
Wind howls round trees, not telling what it sees,
To any of this mortal plain.

Upon the dreary hilltop stands a tree.
Alone, alone, save for He.
Around the storm cloud gather,
But the ancient tree shelters me.

Gnarled and brown with age,
The tree is a sentinel, watching the storm's rage,
Standing ever, ever on
Watching the story, writing it, page on page.

Around, beneath, above the tree the storm waits,
Harder now and then abates,
Again it comes, again it's gone
Man deciding, shaping fates.

How would the world be, if tree were torn?
If from its hilltop it were shorn?
Would it be peaceful,
Or by hate wracked, and worn?

Blake Hyde

Distractions

There are so many things happening;
There seems no end in sight.
One keeps on going and living,
Hopefully no wrong and all right.

Work, School, Science; whatever it may be
Seems to use up all of your time.
Then, of course, there's always a tragedy
And one notices the world is full of crime.

You're so naive to think you're invincible,
To think lifelong dreams will be fulfilled.
A vagrant who never forestalled
Their myriad of feelings for whom they would have killed.

No fun; all work and stress. No play.
Suddenly, consternation fills you.
Those you once love, have passed away.
The facts are elusive; what can you do?

So many distractions have caused you to miss
Those important times filled with salient memories.
Tremulously reaching to give a kiss,
You say goodbye and send them to live in peaceful eternity.

Wendy Moeller

Untitled

Flashes, blinding me
The rebellions earth
The enraged sky
Deafening, roars, moving the ground
Power, surging through me
It streams from my finger tips, and leaps through the sky
The clouds have opened
First one drop, now two
Pounding rain
Roaring thunder
Explosions through the mist
My toes are getting wet
My paper, my pen
It's all washing away
My home, and my world
Streets melt, and fade off the page
Castles crumble, and vanish
I am a stranger in this new world
However I am at peace
Alone, with nature

Christine Gilligan

Questions and Answers

What was I thinking, just the other day ?
What made me bend my head, in silence start to pray ?
The sun was shining. Not a cloud in the sky
I was thrilled and excited, yet a tear filled my eye.
What was I thinking, what was really on my mind ?
Why should I be thinking, life to me had been so kind ?
Why should I be thinking, with every single prayer
Dearest what would happen if suddenly you weren't there ?

Suddenly I'm lost. Nowhere to turn or run.
Lost forever as a night devours a setting sun.

As God giveth, He must surely take away.
Did it mean that He was listening to my thoughts today ?
Yes! God knew what my thoughts were trying to convey
He even held my tear, so that it would not run away.
He told me of the pain that would linger in my heart
Then He told me of the mansion where tears do not take part.
He whispered "Turn to Jesus, Listen to His words of truth.
He alone will give the answer of the elixir of youth "

Hold me close Lord Jesus, Comfort me in times of grief.
If You must take the one I love, please, make my stay be brief.

Walter T. Griffiths

Danny M. Anderson Jr. M.D.

A boy called Dan, Danny or Junior
Who had many desires and ambitions
To become a doctor, lawyer, and athlete,
His choice was to become a physician!

This physician, husband, father and man
Is appreciated, but many times is never told!
Your concern, sincerity, and dedication is real!
It radiates warmth, and you do want to heal!

This shows each time you walk into a room
Your caring and giving is sometimes hard to find.
To name all you've shown to all of my family,
"Danny Boy", you are one of a kind!

Your work is long, hard and very tiring,
At times there seems to be no rest.
Somewhere inside, your inner strength does emerge,
And God above, know's you have given your best!

I know you will continue caring for all of your patients!
Your reward will just have to be great!
So great that the good Lord above
Could be? May even make you a saint!

Margie Ruth Melone

Goodnight

The day is gone the night is here
The sun is gone the moon is near
It's time to rest those hearing ears
It's time to sleep those running gears

Tomorrow, today will be yesterday
And yesterday will be today
Gulls and buoys fly over bays
But dreams will never fly away

The time has passed so quickly by
Sometimes, we wonder, "Where does it fly?"
So do not fret, oh, do not cry
Memories of this day will never die

Everything will be alright
When you shut your eyes tight
So now it's time to shut the light
Now blow a kiss and say,
"Goodnight!"

Mary Mayo

COLLATE

Purification - ill sensation
Lamentation - pending rotation
Apathy - agony, right sum boredom
Remote shun delirium - beating numb hum
Blackened white - so is night
Spirit dream wave - test of might
Irate inmate - last strike insight
City visit - lack persistence
Retribution - that of distance
Disdain power - in an instance
Self restraint - expression paint
Soul taint - pride faint complaint
Act thick, love sick- convivial hiss kiss
Light missed - clinched fist
Quiet ocean - blaring devotion
Lifeless beat - lack of motion
Soulless notion - umatched potion
Segmentation - safe haven
Ego distinction - peace flow, amen
Mesh with death - with every breath
Power left - strength theft
Skim her skin - will of sin
Spinning pins - thoughts wore thin

Tommy Salinas

Inventors

Who can say when the earth stops?
Who can measure the sky?
Who can swim all the oceans?
Who can be immortal?

These are questions,
Which you can't fully answers,
'Cause those who can't answer are average thinkers!

I'm not the average,
I think differently.
I can total the earth,
I can measure the sky,
I can swim all the oceans,
I can be immortal,
With my devices and ideas,
There's no question,
Which I can't make the answer to!

Jennifer Bottari

Untitled

Dedicated To: Zachary Walker Hanson
Voice of an angel
Rings in my ears
Louder than a thousand choirs
Lingering, captivating, breath taking

Face of a prince
flashes through my mind
brighter than lightening
Blood rushing, heart pounding, rapid breathing

No feeling but pain
and longing to touch your face, kiss your lips,
and feel your love

Despair, you'll never be there
It can't be like this
When will we meet face to face
I may have to wait forever
And I sit
Forever waiting for you

Melissa Reynolds

Sand Storms

The wind blew across the sand
Making the grains dance up in small circles
Tossing about the desert.
No Confinement, able to roam free as they desire
Yet, Staying close enough to see
Trust binding them together,
Even in their distance
And by their own choice.

The wind quiets
Making the grains settle
Lying together on the ground.
Confined, no longer separated individually
Feeling the touch of one another
Distance no longer an issue,
Together as they please.

The wind is the master,
The grains must follow fate.
Whether they are separated by distance,
Or bound together with a touch,
They will never be without one another.

Trisha Hartwell Gagnon

Questions

Nothing can describe the pain I feel
For it is far too painful to be real
I'm lost in a world so grand
That's way too hard to understand

There are too many questions for
Which the answers I do not know
And the more I ponder them
My confusion continues to grow

I wish someone would share
But the answers just aren't there
So why should I even care?
Why do I let these questions put me in despair?

I don't know so how could you?
So let me sit and continue to feel
Like a bird who has never flown
Until my wish to know these answers
Comes to be true

Susannah Masarie

Love's Fire

Didn't want to leave the coffehouse today,
Kept looking back at you, since
Nothing compared to the way you were, body like
A sculptured guitar
Eyes so bright as they sparkled and shined
Off your hair of fire,
Melting my peppermint tea.
Your voice so spicy it was like eating hot chiles
and the way you said "cicadas" made my soul smile
But I drank my tea,
You had your mocha,
Doesn't mean it has to end.

Andrew Perdiue

Rain

Rain, it is hiding my pain
They cannot tell these are tears
They cannot tell what's in my brain
My heart so empty only filled with fears
Will I be OK or will I go insane
No one will ever know how I feel
The rain is covering my tears
To me nothing good will ever be real
Why should I go on with my life so hurt
You can almost feel my heart through my shirt
Tears are falling but they don't know
The rain keeps falling very slow.

Ines DeSa

A Mother's Love

A mothers love is one of a kind
With the things she does.
Just, because of a mothers love.
She's a doctor, a friend and big sister too;
She's a friend when your happy and a friend when your blue.
You see the love in her eyes, when she kisses you goodnight;
No need to be frightened, she leaves on the light.
She whispers "sweet dreams" and "peaceful sleep;"
And the memory of her loving smile, you will always keep.
Yes, God, created all the wonderful things,
The heavens and the stars above;
And smiled on the human race, when He gave us a mother's love.

Michael Dixon

Shownufflove

Two thousand promises not kept
Every year in man's trip
Is a promise that has slipped.
How many dead bodies
Have we in this time shipped.

Of all the periods in our history
This one gets the prize
For the least of Man's mercy
When do we open our eyes?

Two thousand wishes unfulfilled
Another millennium killed.
Every year in our planet's life
Is a promise Replaced With Still More Strife (unrealized)
Nothing conjured to be kept
Hate, injustice and suffering far and wide yet.

Praise Jah Loud
Sing Ya love boldly and proud.
Get rid of hypocrisy and fear.
Shownufflove to one another
demonstrate real care.

H. Glenn Bennett

The Storm

I noticed not the raindrops on the windows.
The thunder rolled and lightning filled the sky.
But still I never had a moments worry,
I somehow knew the storm would pass me by.

The clouds were dark, the wind was fiercely blowing.
I should have tried to safely hide away.
But how could I know fear when deep inside me,
I felt that God had made this special day.

Before I knew it, birds were softly singing.
The sky was clear, the clouds were quickly gone.
But all the time my heart was filled with sunshine.
I knew that I had never been alone.

Robbie Lynn Robinson

Untitled

From silence and darkness into the world we are born,
and from that moment on we are true to our form.

We have ideas and opinions, voices used to reign,
over the world which we consider our domain.

We join some who follow, still others may lead,
this joining of voices to shout out our need.

We can't ever be silent, for when silence descends,
our life is then grounded in darkness again.

For into chaos we find we are soon to be thrust,
in doubt and confusion 'til we once again lust.

For the time when our voices joined one and all,
our opinions are our power and without them we fall.

But not long in coming we shall go again
Into the darkness, a silence with no end.

And this time will be final, this world without sound,
For nothing is a silent as life underground.

Tammy L. Turner

The Turtle Awakes

The wave rises out of the enormous morning,
Blue palms cupped,
Heat-stunned
By the huge orange sphere
Rising above the waving wild grass.
The undertow pulls me
Towards the glittering crystal blue.
I ascend from the deep pockets of warm sand
And rise with the shimmering wave
Into my home,
The sea.

Kristin Hamilton

October 24, 1994

I try to forget that night each day,
but I cannot forget it, there's no way.
I thought it would be easy, I guess they were right,
this type of thing doesn't heal over night.
I feel all empty and damaged inside,
that one person made me lose my pride.
To think I trusted him as my friend,
I lost all trust in the end.
It's been nearly three years since that horrible day,
sometimes I wonder, "Will it ever go away?"
Tragedies like this shouldn't to happen to me,
why couldn't this person just let me be?
I wish I could hide and escape,
from the hurt and the anger of this tragedy . . . rape.

Amanda Marchand

Life

A dream, a light.
A sparkling star in the black of night.
A sun rising in the sky
The wind whistling by
A blossoming flower
A fruit gone sour
The rustling of a leaf
The mystery in a belief
A smile instead of frown
A raindrop tapping down
A growing seed
A child in need
A helpful hand reaching out
I guess this is what it's all about.

Kate A. Daignault

Because of Love

When you were conceived and born
It was because of love.
I cradled you in my arms
Kissed you ever so softly
Because of love.
Your father passed away
We embraced and carried on
Because of love.
The times you came to me to talk
I tried to advice, not criticize
Because of love.
You found the love of your life
I shed a tear and let you go
Because of love.
Now you have your own precious son
He's your pride and joy
Cherish and raise him well
Because of love.

Virginia M. Clark

Do You Still Want Me?

Cut me, let me bleed
Feel me, let me sleep
Help me, let me die

I want you
That is all I know

I want your pain
I want your pleasure
Your body is all I know
Your heart and soul
I love your pain
I feel your passion
A drunken flame
And an incomplete ending
No happily ever after

You in my veins
Your passion is mine
Your cares my only wish
You've showed me an unexplained
ecstasy
But after all this
Do you still want me?

Rachel Williams

Untitled

Can you see me
In the darkness of the night
Seeking solace in my dreams
Where time has no end
Nor impossibilities denied
I am suspended within its web
Longing to be free
But where does freedom lie
In daylight or in night
The question seems so puzzling
As I descend into the mist
Of a blissful slumber
The rapture that engulfs me
Never let it cease, I pray,
Until the shadows of the night
Come to steal my soul away.

Janet Marie Gentry

Happy Birthday, Joseph!

As you hold the key to my heart,
Your soft blue eyes calm my soul,
Your gentle touch gives me comfort.
As we walk hand in hand,
I seem to forget the rest of the world,
Everything is still and time disappears.
You reassure me of who I am,
You pick me up when I fall.
When the sky is dark and cloudy,
You make my day seem bright.
I love you so dearly,
And all you must do
Is turn the key,
And I will forever be yours.

Katie Green

This Mile

You cannot walk this mile for me
I must travel it on my own.
You cannot lift my burdens
Or help me discover which way to turn.

The paths before me are many
The fog and the mist are thick,
But only I can clear them away
To choose my match with fate.

Destiny is in my hands
Though the choice is so obscured.
This journey I must make alone.
. . . I need to find my soul.

Debra A. Hayes

Untitled

I lie in silent stillness
face upturned, palms to the sky
I wait to be filled
to be touched, inspired, saved
I wait
darkness lies upon my chest
I fold my arms around it
and wait
day break
the spell broken the soul broken
I rise hollow to face a world
that doesn't know that couldn't know
I will lie, hollow again
arms outstretched
and wait.

Tammy Schwab

You

Smile that smile
So beautiful and sweet,
Smile that smile
That makes me squirm in my seat.

Open those eyes
So cool and intent,
Open those eyes
That look true and innocent.

Walk that walk
So true and bold,
Walk that walk
For all to behold.

Show that self
So undeniably true,
Show that self
To let all notice you!

Veronica Marshall

Diamonds

Diamonds are very special,
known as a girls best friend.
It's not the size, shape,
or cost of the thing;
but the thought put in behind it.

When a girl is to be wed
they may ask to see
the huge rock on her finger,
to awe in selfish glee.
But the owner knows the thought
behind the magnificent thing-
whether they approve.

And somehow she'll live
with the stupid remarks
'cause she isn't there for the ring,
she's there for his heart!

Kellie Bondley

A Poem For Jesus' Ears

Oh Lord can you hear me?
May I bother you one more time.

I have a friend who's troubled,
can you kindly ease his mind.

I know that you are busy with folks
asking all the time

But you see Lord, he's special,
you made him and he's mine.

Katherine Daniels

Me

Will you tell me that I'm beautiful?
Why don't you tell me what you see.
Don't tell it to my mother or father,
But why don't you tell it to me.

If I'm full of pain and sorrow,
Will you come and comfort me?
And take me into your arms,
And tell me what you see.

If I'm not feeling well,
And feel I have no one to love,
Will you come and say to me,
"You have me and the one above?"

Now if you're down and feeling blue,
I'll be there to comfort you.
And I'll tell you what I see,
Why would I? Because I'm me!

Shaliah Maddox

Best Friends

Friends stay together
They never are apart,
Friends stay together
They're always in your heart,

Friends stay together
Even though you're far,
Friends stay together
You'll always be my star.

Friends stay together
Even if they fight,
Friends stay together
Day and night.

Friends stay together
Even though it's the end,
Friends stay together
To help or defend.

Monica Krauss

The Owl

The mountains—purple majesties,
Loom high up in the sky.
The sun lingers just above,
Waiting for the night.
An owl sounds his lonesome call,
No response he hears.
The note in his voice makes it sound,
Like he's been searching for years.
Who is he looking for?
It makes me wonder now.
Do we all search for someone,
Just like that lonesome owl?
As the night draws to an end,
The cries begin to fade.
Another night of searching,
Though no progress has he made.
But the next night he begins again,
Not discouraged in the least.
And he sings his lonesome song,
'Till the sun rises in the east.

Alex Licht

Hour Glasses

Broken glass
Timed elapse
Silence holds the room.
Risen brow
Whirled around
Heavy feels the gloom.
Taken back
Enabled lack
Farthest from the start.
Mistened eyes
Chartered lies
Stillness kills the heart

Misty Rowell

I Miss You

As time goes by
I cannot show . . .
I make the rules up as I go . . .
I hide my face,
I will not lie, to hide my feelings
deep inside . . .
I love you truly
this is true and to
this I conclude
I do miss you . . .

Nicole R. Tenney

The Beach

Waves greet me as I
Watch them on the shore,
Jumping and dancing till
I can't see them anymore,

The tide making foam on
The sand white as snow,
I watch the little baby
Crabs put on a dancing show.

I walk along the sand
Collecting shells and things,
I listen to the peace of
How the wind and water sing

I stop, and stand, to listen
For a while, with all the
Treasures I collected
At my feet in a pile

I pick them up and walk
Out into the waves that get
Me wet, I wait, while watching
The majestic sun set.

Charlotte Brown

Us

I,
Look into the sky,
And see a cloud drifting by,
Up so very, very high,
And wish that I could fly.

You,
Have a different view,
Of things so new,
Dreams, you have so very few,
But the dream you have, I once
Knew.

We,
Can together see,
That we need to be free,
Free as can be,
I, you, and we.

Jessyca Wood

Away

Dear God take me away, far away.

To walk in the clouds among my
long lost friends of this world,
is all I long to do.

Take me away where no more
problems I have to dwell upon.

Take me away where there is
no darkness.

Dear God, take me away to
your home.

Embrace me into your arms
and keep me warm.

Please just take me away
is all I ask of you.

I just long to be far away
from everything.

Dear God just take me away.

Sarah Lewis

My Love

My love for you is strong,
Nothing can keep us apart.
I couldn't live without you,
You have all the keys to my heart.
People say we shouldn't be,
But I won't listen to them.
People say we're too different,
Maybe but then again.
I love you more than I can say,
I can't seem to find the words.
So before you say, "I'm losing her."
Remember you're my whole world.

Darcy Koehn

The Nightmare Ends

The trial was so long
Yet, now that it's gone
Was it wrong?
The racist uncovered
No killer discovered
Above all, the verdict blubbered
"Not guilty," he said
As O. J. bowed his head
And Brown family remembered the dead
The real killer may never be found
Will we ever really sleep sound,
Now that this story's been bound?

Jill Marie Dove

Feeling

As I think to this day
About the one I used to love,
I realize I don't love him anymore,
And I will never love again.

My side has been hurt
Where I have been stabbed by him,
But I won't go back
For I've learned.

Now all that's left is me;
My spirit of anger and confusion
From your changing personality
I cannot comprehend.

I wash my feet of you,
And hope you drown,
Or basically die.
I don't care how.

Just die!

Charity Vogt

Find Me

Find me lost, deep away
hiding from the world today,
Find me dreaming very deep
or comforted by blinded sleep.

Find me thinking of the past
and what I've lost and gained,
Find me searching in my heart
and hiding fears and pain.

Find me with my head in my hands
and stains on my cheeks,
Find me looking out the window
for all a lonely person seeks.

Find me, wherever you may
and please when you do
wrap your arms around me,
that's all I ask of you.

Michelle Nichols

Just One of the Guys

Smooth, sexual chocolate
Like a Milky Way bar
Cruising by my way
In your father's new red car
Walking up the steps
Clean from head to feet
New shoes, new shirt
And jeans nice and neat

Ringing my doorbell
Nails nice and clean
Hair a little wavy
Body nice and lean

Waiting on the steps
Trying to be polite
Just a dab of Polo Sport
Ummmm, that smells just right

Kissed me on the cheek
Caught me by surprise
But you know that it's okay
'Cause you're just one of the guys!

Danean Kim Nixon

Best Friends

Friends may come
And friends may go,
But there is something
You should know,:
Choose your friends wisely
So you will know that
Best friends never go.

Adrian Campbell

California Poppies

The poppies' blooms
Were glorious in March.

In April
I didn't really notice.

In May
How could I tell?
My heart was so dark.

In summer
Stems grew tattered
And fragile,
Like me.

Blossoms faded,
And my spark dimmed.

In October came second bloom—
Pale imitation of March.

Now I wait for next year
For the poppies in all their glory.

Please come back.
I love you.

Marilyn Won

Firefly

Rhythmic spurts of incandescence
Buzzing lovely red light
Flickering blankets of
glassware jail cell,
Containing utterance
of eagle's oath undone.
Death to love and
birth of escape
freedom over death,
freedom over death, firefly.

Justin Pelletier

You

A thousand tears
You drained from my eyes.
A thousand wounds
You cut into my life.
A thousand
Broken promised ties.
A thousand
Slashes from the knife.
A thousand times
I have cried.
A thousand months
Of pain and strife.
A thousand times
Of troubled lies you told me
Day and night.
And
One good-bye to last
Far from sight.

Andrea Foster

Untitled

My friend where are you going
leaving again precious thing
what do you think
silly, are you okay
come down, inside my mind
stay for a while
if you'd like
don't mind, never did
your there anyway
perfect nobody is
my friend where are you going
help me through, help me see
happiness again
where has all the color gone
hidden behind black and white I guess
so what do you think, think of it
want to leave, I do, crazy, am I?

Amy James

Blind

Out of school without a job
Might as well join the mob
Daddy pays him minimum wage
Find him on the loser page

Doesn't work for what he needs
Doesn't want to plant the seeds
Never a kid, neither a wife
Now he's sick and blind for life

Georgia Lee

Mrs. Steven's Sewing Machine

My mother has a sewing machine
That's old and no longer used,
But, oh, the stories it could tell
If you would only sit and muse.

Of lovely clothes, gowns and more,
Of delicate materials and plain,
If we imagine, it will tell
Of memories that still remain.

That old machine has been replaced
With a newer, fancier model,
But we will never, ever forget
The beauty it made full throttle!

Cynthia A. Cook

The Plan

God holds it in His hands
The hand of fate is His
He says who comes and goes
He says who dies or lives

The baby may not live
Infected with HIV
"Please," his mother prays,
"Please don't take him from me"

At dawn a car swerves
Slams into a tree
A friend blames himself
"I should have taken the key"

The tumor's getting bigger
They just can't stop its growth
They'll take her to the ocean
It's what she loved most

No one knows how
To predict His future plan
God keeps us in suspense
Like no human can

Cassandra Renee Wolff

Life's Simplicity

Of all the people I see,
Faces mean the most to me.
Each expression slightly changed,
So awkwardly arranged.
Makes you wonder what it's like,
Living through their daily fight.
Every wrinkle placed about,
Expressing what they live without.
Makes you wonder why their faces frown,
Ask them why it's dragging down.
If they only knew the way,
To make the most of each day.
Maybe then their faces would shine,
Thinking not of what is mine.
But only how their lives could be,
If only everyone could see,
Life's simplicity.

Peggy Sue Martin

Societies

They are built to live within,
And shield us from those terrible things
That lie outside their boundaries,
Awaiting to steal our flowered innocence

They are built to shape our lives,
To give us that oh so sweet taste
Of peace and inner unity,
United by a love that binds
And is woven into the fabrics,
Of our ever changing hearts

But what becomes of a society,
When the seed of evil is implanted
And gains a root so inherently thick
That it chokes the morality
Out of the pinnacle of our consciousness

That's when the process begins
When the fabric becomes unwoven
And our hearts turn to acid
Causing our love to dissipate
Into an ever growing fire of hate

Terrance J. Mangum

Everyone Is Equal

Everyone is equal
doesn't matter who
Everyone is equal
Even the baboons

Everyone is equal
Some are big and small
Everyone is equal
Not just some but all

Everyone is equal
Color doesn't matter
Everyone is equal
Some may be skinny or fatter

If everyone realized
that we were all the same
Then the world would
be a better place
and not so much a game

Blair Schippits

Unspoken Words

Unspoken words with so much to say,
I can see it in your eyes.

And if the words will never be spoken.
Look to the falling rain,
there you will find my tears.

Look to the sun and see
the feelings that burn deep inside.

Look to the moon and find
illuminating truths hidden within.

Look to the stars above and see
the hopes and dreams
of some yesterday,
that is silently fading away.

Look further to the heavens
then you will know,
the vastness of my love.

But soon the clouds rush in
for fear of revealing
the unspoken words to be told,
when I look into your eyes.

Susan Anderson Aceti

My Love

Often I sit here wondering
What you mean to me
Later I've found myself pondering
How could that be?
I've realize that you bring me happiness
And it fills me with joy
You stay with me through my nastiness
And I'm glad you're my boy.
I wish this feeling would last forever
but I know someday it will end.
we say "Break up" never!
yet we seem to swerve at ever bend.
I'll missed the love we shared
and how much you cared.
Now I know we must part
and it seriously breaks my heart.

Sarah Moretti

If It Would Snow Stars

If it would snow stars
We would all be so happy.
Like at night,
The ground would shine like diamonds.

We would build starmen.
Go star skiing, star skate,
And have star ball fights.
We would have so much fun.

The stars won't melt like snow.
We would have a new season.
It would be so wonderful.
Oh, how I wish it would snow stars.

Yifan Zhang

Sisters

Sisters we are, sisters we'll be
Forever and ever, you and me.
We'll have fun throughout the years,
Together, we'll shed many tears.
Quarrels may part us; but not for long,
Because we have harmony, like a song.
Sister we are, sisters we'll be,
Forever and ever, you and me.

Meghan Spigner

Untitled

Life
Is constant
It comes and stays awhile
Friendship
Is forever
And lives on even after life has left
Love
Can come in a day
Is gone the next night
You are left with
Your life
Your friendship
Yet you say you
Have no
Life
No
Friends
All because you lost
Love

Jennie C. Ryden

It Could Happen

When we are all ready to think,
And get out of the mess we're in,
And give everyone a voice and choice,
Anything could happen.

When we fight for brotherhood,
Consider all men our kin,
When we find love for everyone,
Anything could happen.

When everyone helps someone else,
When all hatefulness ends,
Then all of us will reach the top,
Anything could happen.

When tricks and cheating disappear,
And everybody wins,
And justice rules and things are fair,
Anything could happen.

Andrea De Leon

Untitled

Love is like a rose,
Delicate and beautiful to hold on to.
Yet when you hit a thorn,
You're left with a void inside you.

Your soul is like glass,
Now shattered by the sorrow.
Your broken heart cannot last,
You won't make it until tomorrow.

Now the tears come,
And they echo when they fall.
A question in your mind,
"Should I end it all?"

A hand on your shoulder,
Wind spreads the glass as it blows.
Your soul and heart are now restored,
And in the other hand—a rose.

Elan Church

Middle School Days

Oh, those wonderful school days,
The time we spent there,
We'll remember always.

Why does it have to go so fast,
We'll miss the friends we made,
We'll always remember the past.

Even though we'll be apart,
The time we spent together will
always be remembered,
Every memory close to our hearts!

Emily Garzoli

Rose Hill

There's a place down in Georgia
Where only the faithful go
It's a hill by the river
They call it Rose

It's a fountain of memories
Of songs and stories told
It dates back a century
But it will never grow old

Many rebels are resting there
Where there's a way, there's a will
There are shrines to brothers lost
We call it Rose Hill

The Lord looks down with a smile
And the heavens open wide
As our souls rise up with a thrill
From the place we call Rose Hill.

Randall H. Murphy

A Pair of Doves

A pair of doves,
flying high as the sky.
A symbol of Love,
the symbol which will never die.
Two are better than one,
Whose love is bright as the sun.
No matter rain or shine,
their love will always be divine.
They will forever be flying,
To remind me and you to
Live and love,
That pair of doves.

Juanetta Tom

Haunted Eyes

We listen to the Dead,
Visions fill our head,
drugs are our escape,
we never want to wait.

We see the Haunted Eyes,
no evil and no lies,
we're on a psychedelic ride,
while tripping and so fried.

Our imaginations go wild,
like a little hippie child,
our life seems like a maze,
lose and out and out of phase.

We think it is all right,
but it's really turning fight,
we invite more to our kind,
we start to lose our mind.

Thinking we saw the light,
it was an amazing sight,
we think we see many things,
suddenly sprout wings.

Lindsay Ohlmeyer

Summer Weather

It is not winter nor fall.
It is summer.
It is hotter and funner.
You can run in the fields.
That is what I am doing today.
Running, skipping, jogging, and walking.
Picking flowers, laying in the sun.
Having all sorts of fun.
Then it is night.
I see fire flies.
I catch some and go home.
I give my mother the flowers and
my brother the fireflies.
I give them each a kiss and a hug.
Now off to bed I go.
Then I say, "Summer's fun."

Ashley Ericksen

What Would Happen

What would happen
If I told you how I feel.

What would happen
If I told you my feelings are real.

If I told you these things
What would happen.

Would it turn things around
To where it would be you telling me
How you feel;
And that your feelings are real.

Sophia Garcia

The Bird

This has been a day of bless,
birds are gathering in their nest
The joy of seeing a young one try,
To spread his wings and begin to fly
The first to the ground he will fall,
He will stay there till his mother calls
She helps him back to the peaceful nest,
He folds his wings and then he rest
Tomorrow will be another test,
To spread his wings and try his best.

Judy Martin

Madness

I like the phrase
"I'm going mad . . ."
It's so chaotic—
And ironic—
Yet so peaceful.

I could say it all day;
Staring, without seeing
Myself in the mirror.

Everyone would think
I've gone mad,
But I would know the truth.

I like the phrase
"I'm going mad,"
Because I know it's not true.

Robyn Kiyomi

Only Jericho

I walk around
concrete wall slabs,
solid fortress
sealing away my treasure,
last sliver of wide-eyed boy
and broken toy-plastic dreams
strewn across gray cold stone
In corner shadows
yawp became yelp
Now numbness and silence hold hands
and dare me come over
But still, I walk
Still—I walk
until, I discover my shout

Gene Bracken

The Siren's Song

The distant sound
at first too faint,
could not foretell
enduring pain.

Silent to
the conscious mind,
though certainly
my heart would find.

A friendship born
so I ignore
a whisper's hint
of something more.

But all too soon
my heart felt true.
The same could not
be said of you.

Through innocence
you sent along
the heartbreak of
the siren's song.

Lloyd Hlavac

Life

Life
can you feel it?
It's everywhere
no matter where you go
no matter what you do
it will always be there
free and alive
until death

DeAnna M. Allen

Eagle's Freedom

Capture a sunrise
Float with the wind
Know the freedom, of
Where an eagle has been

With style and beauty
Bred into him
Pollution and no solution
Has brought him to end

But he flies in the minds
Of the greatest of men
For he stands for freedom
Known only to them

Carl M. Pullen

The Gypsy

I met the gypsy at the mall
In a booth, along the wall and
Believed her promise on a sign:
"For a coin you'll have a chance
I'll tell your future at a glance
My crystal ball holds fate's design."

As she spoke of imminent fame
And the wealth that I'd soon gain
I wished I'd kept the dime I blew.
I admit that it all sounded swell,
But a recording just cannot tell
A fortune that will come true.

The next time I visit the mall and
See her and her crystal ball,
I will remember my foolish quest...
I won't waste any more money
(Though her forecast was a bit funny)
Living one day at a time is still best!

Deanna D. Shuster

Sara

She stumbles on the path,
Then looks ahead,
And they are gone.
She doesn't have a chance,
They have gone away,
And she doesn't know how to get there.
She lets herself fall,
They don't even care,
And they don't even know.
Somewhere up ahead,
They turn around,
And see that she has fallen.
But they don't really care.

Jennifer Renée Collins

I Loved Him

I used to love a boy.
His name was like a song.
I was about to tell him.
But something went terribly wrong.

I saw all the men running.
I saw the loot they've got.
I saw them getting their guns.
I saw the boy get shot.

Now I am alone in life.
I'm full with fear and hate.
The moral is to tell him
You love him before it's too late.

Lisa Glasspool

A Memory

Are you waiting for me
in some secret place,
Can you see what I look like,
will I know your face?

Will we laugh in the sunshine
and walk in the rain,
Can you hear what I'm thinking,
can you feel my pain?

Will you lie close beside me
sharing dawn's early rise,
Will I see rose-kissed sunsets
reflect in your eyes?

Will your arms ache to hold me
and never let go,
Will you love me forever?
I need to know.

Are you trying to find me,
should I look instead—or
Are you just a memory,
that stuck in my head?

Sharon Rabideau Derr

The Dream

I walk through the dream
as it carries me on
further and further
until mornings dawn
leading me closer
leading me near
guiding me through
the night without fear

Michelle Savage

A Painful Love

My heart belongs to somebody
Who doesn't know I live.
He took my life and breath away
But still my love I give.

Although I know we haven't met
My love for him grows stronger.
He seems so perfect in my eyes
Which makes me love him longer.

I think of him all night and day
But still he never knew.
This painful feeling deep in me
Is love so strong and true.

Andrea Terdik

Lonely Heart

Since you've been gone there
Is an empty space left inside my heart.
My world just isn't the same.
When I go back to the places
We've been, it feels like you're
Still with me. I live all my memories
over and over again. Since you've
left, my life seems so lonely.
There are memories all over the place,
bringing everything back so clear.
All of these lonely nights, I fight
to keep those memories away.
I have followed your steps in
The snow, the traces disappear.
We realize what we have
Only when it's gone.
I'm only wishing you
Were here with me.

April Peterson

Tweety Bird

Tweety Bird is my,
Favorite character of all.
He is so cuddly,
And friendly to all.
Except for that one,
Big putty tat.
He wishes he was gone,
Because he hates that cat!
All day long,
Sylvester chases him,
But for some reason,
He can't get 'em.
Don't worry at all,
Tweety gets him back.
He gets a bulldog,
To chase that putty tat.
Tweety Bird is safe,
And very happy.
Sometimes he must be careful,
'Cause he just might have to worry.

Richele M. Martinez

Perfect

It could be great, you know!
Fabulous, fantastic
Prolific.

But then there is reality.
I hate living in
Placid understanding,
Complacency.

But that's life.
Turbulent, malicious,
Exciting, dull.

I can't reconcile my
Life, my feelings, my destiny
with Yours.

It doesn't fit.
It's not neat, it's not clean,
It's not clear, it's not
Perfect.

Sandra Reisz

Jaded

Cold as ice,
Black as night,
Jaded, cynical.
Why are you so world-weary?
There is so much yet to be.
Eyes darker than desire,
They laugh mockingly at love,
At hope, at dreams.
Nothing's ever as it seems.
Your pasted-on smile's slipping
And these words that I am whispering
mean not a thing to you at all.
Cold as ice,
Black as night,
Jaded, cynical.

Amber K. Holland

Friends

Friends are like a flower
They are want you need
The bad ones are like a growing weed
But when you pull, they pop out
And there you plant a seed

Amanda Lynd

Love Is A Complicated Word

With so many
Different meanings
However it can be
Express
In many different ways
Shapes, and sizes
Kissing, hugging, and
Overfeeding
Are all signs of love
Love
It doesn't have to be
Shown or express
It can be silent a
Reflection of your shadow
Illuminated by the moon
Brighten by the
Sun rays
Oh wow!
Look over there!
Is that a rainbow?

Nexelda Dickens

Love

Love an extraordinary feeling
A land of enchantment
A world of it's own
A touch of warmth that
Tingles through my body
A sigh of relief that escapes my lips
An embrace that holds so
dear and near
A tear from my eye when
I see him there
So near yet so far
I'm afraid to let go though
I know I must
What would love be without trust
I know I shall never doubt love

Jackie Trevino

Good Times

Where have all the good times gone
that we used to know?
Where are all the good times
when we were growing up?
Where are all the good times?
We thought they would never stop.
Now there are no good times,
only misery and pain.
We open each day and close
each night with tears that are in vain.
Where did all the good times go
and will they ever come back again?

Milton M. Rothstein

Untitled

Temptation is heavy
Your thoughts are grim
Imitations are deceiving
Everything reminds you of him

He is everywhere around you
In pictures and on signs
There is nothing you can do about it
He is playing with your mind

You are growing sick of this
It can't go on another day
Reach for the terror and fury
With it you'll end your pain

Julie Cooper

Untitled

Define Love, he says.
A word, a gesture, a simple phrase?
A ring that forever
On a finger stays?
Is it my mother's eyes,
Or my father's embrace,
Or a kiss from a
Lover in a familiar place?
They say, Home is where the heart is
Is this where it lays?
Or a drop of blood
Off a king crowned in thorns
Who from the grave
Was raised.

Carolyn M. Hopson

Guilty As Charged

Guilty as Charged
Fined with a severe penalty,
Guilty as Charged,
Sent to the gallows,
my final depth,
Guilty as Charged
Angel why did you leave me?
Forsake me?
Guilty as Charged,
And so the angel said,
"I did not leave you!
Forsake you!
"I let you on your own!
And you have forgotten me.
You put it on yourself.
Goodbye.
Please help me I'm sorry!

Shekila Melchior

Keeper of the Light

Run to the light
Do not try to fight
Do not fear the judge
Or hold his verdict with a grudge

You have a part in his decision
For he knows your life with precision
If you obeyed his laws
With an occasional flaw
Do not fret
Because you have met
Before you were born
And at your death he will mourn.

That is when you come to him
Even though the world seems grim
He accepts you with his arms out-spread
Kisses you on the head
And whispers you are protected.

Carl Vollmer

Blue

Blue as the beautiful sky
Blue as the color of the tear in his eye
His color is blue and his name is too.

Blue as the color of the beautiful sea.
It's quite beautiful like me.
When the sun shines on it; it sparkles
Like a diamond.
Blue just like the sparkle in his eye.

Jenifer Amanda Zinkand

Pretty Bird

Sing pretty bird, sing
Of your joys and sorrows
Sing pretty bird, sing
Of places that you've been
Sing pretty bird, sing
Of a brighter tomorrow
Sing pretty bird, sing
Of the things you've seen
Sing pretty bird, sing
Of the hearts gone hollow
Sing, pretty, bird, sing
Of children that lost their dreams
Sing pretty bird, sing
Of lives that end up nowhere
So go ahead pretty bird, sing.

Erica Hoar

Falling Out Of Love

The sound of my heart breaking
tinkling bells and shattering glass
so much like your laugh

The sight of my tears falling
into puddles at my feet so clean
clear blue like your eyes

I gave you my heart
and you ripped it in two

I gave you my trust
which you quickly betrayed

I told you my dreams
and you laughed in my face

But still I love you
Why only my broken heart knows
Love has no reason
And Cupid has perfect aim

My pounding heartbeat
like the sound of your footsteps falling
and as you walk away forever
I fall dead upon the grass

Lizette Cox

We All Sleep

As I lie down to bed,
grasping the day,
A rush of dreams come to mind,
Covering me,
Sleeping soundly,
Dreaming,
Dreams different from nights before.
Snuggled deep within my blanket,
A stuffed bear at my side,
Seeing things never seen before.
Wondering visions,
put me to sleep.
Awakened,
Rumpled hair, sleepy eyes.
The alarm clock,
beeping,
A crush then silence.
Dreaming

Bridget Bond

I want to be a part
Of everything you do.
I want to be a part
Of everything that's you.
I want to be a flower
On the icing of your cake.
I want to be the only one
When love is what you make.
I want to be behind you
To cushion every fall.
I want to be beside you
When you finally have it all.
I want to be a part
Of every dream and fantasy.
I want to be your one true love,
The one you are to me.

Berni Jarvis Morgan

Dawn

As light approaches from the East.
And jumps upon the wild, wild, beast,
It rushes up to fill the sky.
It's why all flying creatures fly
To feel you're soaring by the Dawn,
Embrace the heavens you come upon,
The beauty of the rainbow sky;
Unfortunately it will die.
But live, my friend, and live at peace,
Again tomorrow you will feast,
Upon the golden warmth and light
Of the Dawn's sweet morning bright.
It storms across the open seas,
Across the jungles' ancient trees,
Across the deserts' sandy lands,
Across the arctic's icy bands;
And fill the skies of busy cities
So wonderful, so grand, so pretty
I promise you will not forget
Even at your last sunset!

Larissa M. Bright

A Dream and a Nightmare

There once was a dream
That everybody knew
We were all on the same team,
No one outcasted you

Everyone was very polite
And looks didn't matter
Nobody thought they'd see the sight
When the great dream would shatter

Now there is a nightmare
So evil and mean
When it stares
It'll make you scream

It'll come after you
'Til you become part of it all
You'll do what it says to do
And you'll take the fall

There used to be a day
When everyone was your friend
Who will stand up and say
Put the nightmare to an end

April Parrish

Untitled

I loved you so, my angel.
I loved with all my heart.
I hoped and prayed; I prayed and hoped
that we would never part.

The things we did-just you and me
were beautiful and sweet.
I blessed the day, my dearest love
when you and I did meet.

Don't ever leave; don't ever go—
These were the words I cried.
But it is you who's crying now,
for it was me who died.

Annie Deitrick

Lost or Found

My heart is pacing
My mind is racing
My hands are shaking
My chest is breaking
My breath is too slow
for the rate of my heart
The taste in my mouth is severely tart
My thighs feel weak
My sense of thought is bleak
I wonder if anyone can tell,
if anyone can see?
Is this love or has insanity finally
found me?

Natalie Brandt

Mama's Room

We stood gathered around dear Mama
As our final words were said,
In a voice barely a whisper she said
"Son, would you like my bed?"

In her pain she thoughts of others
It touched our hearts to be
In a room so filled with love
And so many sweet memories

Today, a new room holds her treasures
As each piece was placed in care
And as we stopped in the doorway
We could feel her presence there

She would have liked this room
We whispered
As we struggled through our tears
Her final gift she gave us
Will hold memories through
the years.

P. Maile

Untitled

On the wings of air
Softer than a breeze
Light transforms night into day.
These soft beginnings
Do in turn create
A new days dream.

For as we open our eyes
To a new sunrise
Optimism is our belief.

This is a day
That God has made
And I'm glad to be in it.

Sperry Kyle

Tears

Little boy lying there.
Tears shown in his eyes
By the bright moonbeams.
But does anyone care?
Can they see through the lies?
Not scared, he seems.

I am truly amazed.
Because he is so calm.
He dreams without fright.
He's been there for days.
Yet those days are so long.
Should I leave? I just might.

No, I will stay.
And watch his little heart beat.
Here comes the light.
Please just go away.
He gets on to his feet.
And runs towards the night.

Christianna Hurd

Out There

Slowly walking through the maze,
Searching every where.
True love is what my search is for.
But still it is not found.
As I walk and search I feel,
My heart is just about to break.
To break into millions of pieces.
Then float, float high in the air.
Slowly floating everywhere.
Yet I know my love is out there
Somewhere? Nowhere? Everywhere?

Crystal Jones

I Was Lost

I was looking
but I didn't find
I was hiding
but I didn't run
I was walking
but I ne'er tired
and I was scared
but I did not cower

But when I was looking
so were you
and when I hid
you did find me
and when I was walking
you did walk with me
and when I was scared
and I did not cower
it was your sword it used to win the fight

Natasha Treu Barrymore

Untitled

Wishing and crying,
Hoping and dying,
Thinking and speaking always.
Turmoil and tears,
Joys and fears,
The poor man dies as he prays.
Lord, keep me forever,
Forget me please never,
Show me the truth of your love.
With angels let me sing,
And let the bells ring,
And show me your heaven above.

Betsy Sutherland

Flying Solo

Flying solo
Is a butterfly,
Gently gliding
In the sky.
Soaring around
It finds another,
So they swiftly
Chase each other.
Together flying
In the air,
Performing the dance
That they both share.
Away, the other
Begins to soar,
So the butterfly drifts solo,
Again, once more.

Mindy Davis

I Dream of You

I dream of you
Standing in a pacific sunlight
Shimmering and shining
You were all that I could see
For a distance away
Shimmering and shining
In my mind, in my heart, in my soul.

Jennifer Hill

Untitled

many things can touch
and impact one's life
some that shall be remembered
forever and others of just a
short while
but words will always be in
one's heart and mind
and will always be on one's tongue
for many years to come

Katie Polzin

Survive

We do not follow
We don't stand on the side
We are the playmakers
And we are one
We are the survivors
We can't regret our choices
Because they are already made
We are stronger than the rest
And we are far better than the best
We cry not for self pity
We do not stand in a crowd and "fit in"
We are ourselves and we call the shots
We light the fires
We burn the bridges
We are the survivors
And this is our way.

Kim Reyes

If

If you only knew,
How much I love you,
Your wild bushy hair,
Your wondering stare,
Your soft gleaming eyes,
Your wonderful smile.
I love you gangster walk,
Your soft voice when you talk.
If you only knew.

Melaina N. Valentine

Garden of Eden

One bright day,
The apple was taken away.
The world was left in despair.
No one hoped,
No one cared.
The serpent showed its ugly face,
And Adam and Eve left this place.
The garden of Eden was paradise,
But now the world is not so nice.
People starve,
People freeze,
People kill,
But please,
In this troublesome world today,
Let us always hope and pray.
For when the world is not so nice,
Let us make up for it in paradise.

Sarah K. Montgomery

For The Children

Lay your head down to rest
another day you've stood the test
and when another day arrives
you'll withstand the test of time
but if it should get too hard
and you feel you can't go on
I'll be there to carry you
and together we'll withstand
the test of time

Nothing good comes easily
growing older you will see
there's dreams and there's reality
it's all what you believe
But if your dreams should tumble down
and you need more than a friend
We will search the stars above
and wrap your dreams around you
once again

Dan Kurtz

Searching

You'll be searching for me
can't you see
I'll be with you

You'll be searching
till the sun goes down

You'll be searching
till the moon turns 'round

Searching

You'll get on a boat
and sail the seven seas
and you'll find the keys
to my heart.

So can't you see we
will never be apart

Searching

Catrina Cantwell

Why?

Why can't you look past the surface,
why can't you see how I care?
If you ever took time to look,
you would see what's really there.
I'm not just who you think I am,
there's so much more to me
Why is to so hard for you
to open your eyes and see?

Kathleen Dorr

When Days Are Long

When days are long
and nights don't end,
I remember I have a family
and a friend.
When it seems too
much to bear and I don't
feel like anyone cares,
When I feel like
giving up and I can't
stand another day,
I remember to go and pray.
When I do, I know
my sins didn't disappear
but God forgave them,
and that's all I need to hear.

Sarah Stoeckl, age 12

Essence of Roses

Emblem of beauty,
festivity,
and love,
white meant "I'm worthy"
red meant "Pure in love"
Beauty,
Mystery,
and contradiction,
Simplicity rolled into one

Kellie A. Mullin

The Silky Snow Soon Became Rigid

The silky snow soon became rigid:
The man reached the edge.
The cool air felt so frigid.
The peak was a steep ledge.
He crept over and felt it slide.
He stopped to peer.
The feeling of a child took his side.
His entire body shook with fear.
He started to slip.
He saw a bump.
He hit it and started flip.
He fell with a "Thump!"
No one could spy,
Wether the man will live or die.

Valerie Stephens

Open Your Hearts

Reach for the stars, not the bars;
open your hearts to bring out
the joy, for life can stop
before your eyes!
For if you see a sign,
don't go into disguise,
for it could be a lie,
with or without a sigh!
For it could travel
beyond your knowledge of sight!
Take one day at a time
and you will find
there was or is no crime!
From time to time,
it has not been me,
but what you haven't seen,
or redeemed, or denied!
For my success could be
my best revenge!

Victoria Rose

The Night Is Gently Falling

The night is gently falling
Looking out upon the sea
For my love who is a sailor
To return safely to me.

The wind she starts a blowin'
Churning up the tender reef
Blinding waves crashing inland
My soul soon to grieve.

I can almost hear the echoes
The captain shouting to his crew
Look for the light ashore mates
To see us safely through.

The lighthouse was never spotted
As waves filled the deck
The sea a cold dark graveyard
And my love lay there to rest.

And when the dawn is breaking
I will stand upon the shore
I will sing of love eternal
I will watch forevermore.

Amy Caudill

A Mother's Child

A mother's child is moving on
Her feelings for her are so strong.
A she walks out the door
mother falls upon the floor
crying on her hands and knees
praying with the words of please.
She gives a wave with tears in her eyes
takes a deep breath and then she sighs.
A mother's child has moved on
that's why I wrote this special song.

Amber Statler

Rain

Black clouds fill the sky.
Thunder echoes throughout the night,
Like the sound
Of a shooting bullet.
Lightning bolts fill the sky
With a brilliant light.
A sudden rain begins to fall,
Like sudden tears.
The rain pounding,
As it hits the pavement.
A pounding like the sound
Of my heart.
Someone special once told me,
That when it rains,
No one can tell if you're really crying.
And as I stand here,
Tears falling from my eyes,
I let the rain fall upon me.
And like you once said,
Nobody knows,
Except for you,
That I'm really crying.

Amanda Jacobs

Snowflakes

They come to visit me every year,
We play together without any fear,
They comfort me when I fall,
Some are short and some are tall,
But when their master does return,
They act like a fire that is aburn
They pack up and go far, far away
And 'til next year,
I'm a waiting the day!!!

Jessica Mullins

Wait and See

You knew from the very start
That we would never last.

I faded in your memory
I was just the past.

You cared for just a moment
You thought of only you.

You never really loved me
You thought I never knew.

You thought you had the power
To walk all over me.

But you will lose everything
You just wait and see!

Megan Surdock

The Bench

The day is hot,
People come and go.
I see the bench,
It is a comfortable bench.
Children play, grown ups sit.
Some in dresses, some in shorts.
The bench is the place to be.
People leave newspapers,
Children leave toys.
Mothers sit to rest,
Lovers sit to play.
A picnic is forming,
The bench will be used.
Balloons will go up,
Streamers will fly.
Sun will set, evening will come.
The bench will be there,
For another day.

Ann Sharpe

Time

Time is all there is.
You can struggle,
You can fight,
Or drive yourself crazy,
And go through all the despair.
But
the pain,
The frustration,
Will all go away.
Just disappear,
Vanish,
Perish . . .
With time.

Alejandra Mora

My Brother

I once had a brother
I know his name was Shawn;
His time on earth was short here,
As mine was set to dawn.

He wasn't here for long,
Six months to be exact.
Enough time to make an impression,
Enough lives to impact.

I've never met my brother,
Or seen him with my eyes;
But I will cherish him forever,
And love him for all times.

Kari A. Raether

Cold and Still

I sit waiting cold and still in my
chair for a love who is not there.
I wait for him cold and still,
mind at work,
thinking, thinking of him at
his work.
I sit cold and still waiting
waiting for him to call on me
waiting for him to admit his love
for me once more.
I sit cold and still in my
chair with the pit of pain in
my heart and stomach.
The pain of my heart and
soul ripped from my body.
I sit cold and still in my
chair, still waiting, waiting for
a love who is not there.

April C. Curran

My Pop-Pop

When you're not in the garden,
growing tomatoes and peppers,
You find time to play cards,
dominoes and checkers.
You gave me a new bike
and taught me to ride;
We used your binoculars
to look up in the sky.
It was a spectacular sight
to see Hale-Bopp,
But nothing compares to
My Pop-Pop!

Brenda J. Reed

breakup

my heart beat for you
so slow to realize
you have done me wrong
i cried but i will
be strong
touch me, never let go
soon you will be
without a trace
you are my cornerstone
i have found someone new
and i blew you to the wind

amy janzer

Path Of Life

You were in darkness
But now you can see
God will guide you
As He did me
God has a light
He'll guide your way
He'll be with you
'Til your dying day
Love is a thing
That comes day by day
Don't let love pass you by
Or throw it away.

Jessica Sharp

When Will You?

When will you know,
How much I love you?
When will you sense,
How I feel?

When will you hear,
My heart crying out for you?
When will you see,
My dazed eyes?

When will you understand,
The giddy sensations in me?
When will you return,
The heart you stole?

When will you learn,
You're my soul?
When will you come,
And soar with me?

When will you touch,
The heart on fire?

When Will You???

Rahana Hussain

Confusion

I wonder through a maze.
Blindly, I seek the path to truth
I select a winding path.
As I wonder more,
My fear grows,
Until the path splits
Now two voices,
Fall upon the ear.
Each saying "believe me".
Which should I believe?
Which will lead me to truth?
I follow a voice I know.
The voice grows fainter and fainter,
Until I am left stranded,
With no voice to follow.
Sadly, I see what has happened
I am back where I started
Only this time knowing,
Which voice to believe.

Amber-Dawn Schiff

Walking Mr. Chuchill's Dog

I do not have time for laughing today.
I'm walking Mr. Churchill's dog.

Being dragged by that huge black beast
around each unexpected corner,
only to find dark assailants
in each alleyway I pass.

He offers me no protection,
yet will not let me leave his side,
growling at each move I make
to break away.

So I slip my fragile wrist
through the leash's loop
letting leather slice soft skin
with each ragged tug.

So pardon me,
if I have no sweet words for you,
my love,
but I've a date
with Mr. Churchill's dog.

T. C. Smith

Persistence

One quiet Christmas morning,
Just moments until dawn,
Our home waits, expectant.
There's frost on the lawn.

I walk through the garden,
Before family rises,
To greet Mother Nature
And all her surprises.

A bright Iceland poppy,
Bent double at stem,
Survived the wind's tantrum.
She breathes life again.

Her bloom now full open,
Face raised in persistence,
Disproves the storm's power
And affirms her existence.

This gift from the garden
Is pure effervescence,
And Christmas morn breaks forth
With nature's rich presence!

Bethany Adlam Brix

Why the Past You Ask of Me

Innocence, purity, a simple
Way to be
Full of life, so much trust
A reason to believe
The sun came up to shine
On me
The moon did glow the whole
Night through
Now hurt and pain, broken dreams,
Sad and lonely, somewhat crazed
My sun stopped shinning
My moon did fade
Without their light to guide
My way
I'm now lost and so afraid
Why the past you ask of me?
I lost everything, even
A reason to believe

Dianne Petrone

Passing

In Past's futures Dawn
I dwell

Down the paths of hell
Death has made crier's gone

My tears have dried up like a well
But once my tears fell

For you, my love, like a fawn
I so young for you to tell

The pain and anger of the paths of hell
But she is forever gone

A rose, but a rose
And forever in my heart

Joy Chavez

Dreams

Dreams come
true and dreams
stay dreams.
So at night, are
dreams reality or
fiction? That's I
guess why they
are called dreams.

Jennifer Fears

Destiny

Transparent skin, delicate, soft.
Blue veins and bones,
barely covered by thin tissue.
Yesterday, she had rosy cheeks,
muscles firm and controlling.

White hair, stooped shoulders,
gnarled hands.
Knees that creak and aching feet.
When she was young, she stood tall,
walked with grace.

Confused looks, questions, doubts,
decisions beyond reach.
She used to know the answers,
was in command, was sure.

Like a child frightened and lost,
in need of help and understanding.
She, is my mother.
Tomorrow, I will be she.

Lynn Adams

I GIVE THANKS

Thank you Lord for my flower garden
On my cliff above the sea.

The breeze is silk soft on my cheeks.
I breathe the fragrant abundance.
I feast on banquets of color.

I baptize buds with morning dew
As birds warble alleluias
And sing their conversations.

I plant seeds with reverent fingers,
Seeds who know all secrets of growing.

You scatter jewels on waves of the sea,
Gems sparkling, floating endlessly.
Thank you Lord, for felicity.

Evangeline Barnes

Dusty Places

Thrashing waves, laughing claims
both links on a beaten chain
sweetened tears kiss the cheek
(an unclaimed tune) you choose to weep
curling tears around your finger
hoping that the dream won't linger
careful to pick up all the pieces
still can't find where the peace is
sleeping till the morning dew
refreshes all you need it to
another day you cannot face
another rose in a dusty place.

Kristin Gallagher

She

The feeling she feels
of great size.
The hatred shows
in her eyes.
Though she can't deny
The pain, she hopes
Will surely die,
Though she knows it is
Just a lie.
The pain grows
stronger inside,
without the sun
to show her side.
She looks around and
fall to a sigh.

Michelle Wilmer

Leaves

All shades of green upon the trees
And you know it's Spring,
They dance and flutter in the breeze
Like tiny hands clapping.
Their soft rustle calms us
Blotting out the rush all around.

Fall comes with red and yellow hues
Giving the world a different look,
To close the door on summer.

Yard trapped, leaf vacuum ground,
Turned with garden bounty,
It crumbles into rich compost,
The food for next year plants
Or to cover flower beds
With deep, soft winter blankets.

Left free before the wind
They form brown rivers by my door
Hustling like lemmings rushing to the sea

Ann Howard

Nature's Collage—Fall Leaves

One good thing about the fall—
Is the rare color of it all.
The yellows, reds, rusts and browns
Can sometimes bring a little frown.
The wind is like music to the leaves—
Making them dance a cool breeze,
Either lying silently on the ground
Or floating, fluttering all around.
Their smell is sometimes in the air,
Making us know that they are there.
Some do beautiful whirls about—
On their way to a different route.
They finally decide to settle down
And through time, crinkle and brown,
But don't despair because in the spring
New colors will boast—
It's something that happens,
From coast to coast!

Julia Seiler Edmiston

First Love True Love

I often sit about thinking of you.
Wondering what I'm going to do.
The years have passed and yet
Your memories continue to last
Oh how many times I wished
We still live in the past
We always had such a blast
What happened my love?
Where did it all go so wrong
I have loved you for so very long
I just don't know if I can keep
Being this strong
When I hear our song
I fear that your love will
Never be near again
But I will try to keep the
Faith that one day you will
Be here, because I still love
You my dear!

Tammy F. Hurt

Gray Memorial Day

Breezy gray under impermanent
Overcast auspice; Cool ions stirring
Life's balance. Rain gathers
Above in mysterious anticipation.
Clouds bestow feather of
Descending mist: thirst be quenched.

Sun's timid rays give promise
By omission: Opaque resonance forgiving
Earth's muddy play.
Roots take hold in blackness,
A silent race to luminance.
The fragrance of lusty romance.
Floods this fertile dance.
Splash of semen bursting from the
Fruit of continuance. God breathes in,
And all is well.

Shawn Michael Helbert

You

You say you love me
But where is the love?

You tell me there is no
Word for our love that
It is so strong that no one
Has found a name for it.

You say you care about me
But I never see you.

You are never around
But still you say you care
You say I will see you but
When and where you are
Every where but here. Are
You to busy to care about me?

You say I can trust you but
Trust can only go so far.

You never call, you never come
Over, so how can I trust you?
You show no acknowledgement
Of your love so I can trust you?

Samantha Shelton

Strut

Strut to the left
Strut to the right
Oh did you have enough
I'm still here, I won't bite

Oh strut that stuff
Yes there is attention
People staring at you
Uh huh it's a big situation

You can walk that talk
And talk that walk
Strut it all day until night
You will be tired, and we'll be alright

Strut to the left
Strut to the right
Oh did you have enough
I'm still here, I won't bite

I hear the rhythm
Oh listen to the beat
Listen to the sound
Do you feel the heat

Zandra Patterson

I Say The Seasons

Up in the tree
The birds fly free
And as the branches sway
I say "Here comes May."
Summers here and school is out
and fun the kids will have no doubt.
the sun shines bright
Giving off great light
When I see the kids bouncing a ball
I say "Here comes fall"
The leaves tumble to the ground
And they twist and twirl around
and when the leaves get low
I say "Here comes snow!"
The scene is a wonder
Yet we miss the green grass that's under
Don't worry for long
Soon we'll hear the birds' amazing song
And all over the holiday cheer
I say "Here comes a new year!"

Catherine Lopez

Life of a Poor Child

A poor child sits alone
No food
No water
No family
A poor child stands alone
No one to love
No one to care for
No one to cry on
A poor child is alone
In the darkness
In the day
In life
A poor child
Almost lifeless, almost invisible
Almost gone

Angel Tarango

Alegory of the Old Lion King

Hunt not the lion
Who is old and half-blind . . .
With claws now dull
Like his aging mind . . .

Though once he was
A mighty beast . . .
Strongest in his pride
King of the feast . . .

A dangerous foe
He might of been . . .
Now living on memories
That are fast growing dim . . .

All he has left
Is a dignified roar . . .
Which frightens only those
Whose courage is poor . . .

Nobody can really say
What the future will bring . . .
One day you too
Might be the old lion king . . .

Joseph Andreoli

Live or Die?

Die this day and you will see
Life in general from above.
Maybe helping humankind.
Will you live or will you die?

We take our lives in our hands
Ask ourselves if we should die.
Maybe you can help us live.
Will you live or will you die?

Helps us humans if you can.
Look at us and shed a tear.
Full of fear we take our lives.
You shall live and you shall die.

Lisa M. Laureano

The Bonds of Friendship

You can lean on me, forever if you like.
I'll take care of your battles when
you can't fight.
I'll stand beside you through
thick and through thin, and when
your heart is broken I'll
assure you that it will mend.
When you are confused and
don't know what to do, I
promise I'll be there to comfort you.
When you are weak, I will be strong
and I'll be there to carry you along.
When you are crying I'll wipe away
the tears and promise to be there
throughout the years.
You can lean on me, I'll be here,
never forget that I am near.

Karra Smith

The Angel

In loving memory of my son, Jeremy Ryan
I put my finger in your tiny hand
You held it with all your might
Your fragile little body
Seemed to glow with a heavenly light.

You opened your eyes and looked at me
Your innocence shone right through
I tried to give you all the love
That I felt for you.

But an angel is what you were
And what you'll always be
God needed a new little son
That's why He took you from me.

And as painful as it is
I have to let go of you
But we will be together again
When my time here is through.

Julie Ann Jeffery Findley

My Sickness

They were right,
It happens just like that.
It comes out of no where.
They said to be careful,
But I didn't listen.
Now it is too late,
I can't change it.
There was only one thing left to do,
I had to come to realize,
I had to know,
That I was to leave my world,
never to return.

Danielle Ruggles

The Loss of a Loved One

This poem is dedicated to my Grandpa,
"Papa" I called him.
The love and joy you gave to us
will never fade away,
The sadness that swept over us
will be there day by day,
And as we pray for you at night in hope
that you will hear,
How much we love you even though
you left us will our tears,
We pray that you find peace and love
and comfort as you rest,
We will forever keep you in our hearts
the walls beneath our chest,
We pray that you'll remember us
and keep us up to date, until we reunite
in the heavens through the gate
There's one last thing I'd like to say
before I ball in tears,
That you will keep us in your heart
throughout all the years.

Tiffany Brooke Hawn

The Mornin' Afta

I love da mornin' afta rain
da dew be so good ta thee
Shakin' down from up da tree
nothin' can eva' be
quite da same afta, ya see

I love da mornin' afta rain
da sun shine down happily
on a red rose wid a bee
and butterfly's are contentidly
driftin' high ova' me

I love da mornin' afta rain
All da creatures be so happy
flower buds open slowly
lookin' at da sun so lovingly
nature has been made flawlessly

ya I do . . .
I love da mornin' afta rain

Elvira Rajala

Life

People kill people.
People kill dreams.
Why must we kill to discover
What our life means?

Do we live for love?
Do we live for life?
Why do we live?
Why do we fight?

Life is so confusing
Life is so dear
Do we really live
or are we just here?

What is life?
Where does it end?
If you know, if you care.
Tell me and, relieve my despair.

Brittany Jo Perrotta

Untitled

My love is gone
and each time the tide
rolls in, I see him.
Lonely and depressed,
the sun warms my face,
and he kisses me with
the salty mist.
He is away in another
land, but continues to
renew our love.

Bernice F. Goldman

Beauty

From deep with in you
Lies beauty too
From far and far
Deep in you

For it comes in different forms
To please me and you
Natural beauty
Deep within you

Kelly Myles

Just Awake

Oh, these walls entrap me!
How I wish to travel out
In search of that dirt road
Littered with ancient Greek iniquities.

And the birds, their ceaseless chirping
Rend my recluse writings,
Tear my weary being
From its place . . .

Drawn to the cursed frame to see
The sky which awash in light
Makes me return
In hope of fame . . .

That might be found in scripts
Composed in this bed,
Inhabited for too long the day
As I await my lazy muses.

Jamie Arnold

Mother

A mother's a great friend
Who'll stay by your side
A loyal champion, a teacher, a guide
A warm-hearted listener
Whenever you are blue
Forever and always
That good friend has been you
A mother can strengthen
Console and ensure
She is one to love
Cherish and admire
You are all of these things
And much more too
But most of all you are my mom
Someone who can't be replaced
And when you're gone
Someone who will always be remembered
Cherished and still loved
From now until eternity you will
always be my mom—I love you

Lori Heller

Once in a Lifetime

Just once in a lifetime,
The right one comes along,
The feeling is so strong,
You know you belong.
Just once in a lifetime,
You see his honest face,
You touch his loving hand,
You feel his warm embrace.
Just once in a lifetime,
Everything feels so right,
You see his shining face,
And your darkness turns to light.
Just once in a lifetime,
The feeling is so new,
To say three words and mean them.
The three words
"I Love You"

Heather Pulvermacher

Dead Moon

Tonight the moon cries
Because the sun said goodbye.
She has lost all her shine.

She knows that the sun left,
Left for good, to a better place.
But she asks: "What better place
Than right here with me?".

And crying she screams out:
"Come back sun, give me back my shine,
Give me back my love!".

But the sun won't listen
Because he left his home.

Poor moon, she's all alone;
Doesn't shine, does not glow.
Poor moon, she's all alone.

"Help me find my sun!",
She says, then dies.

She has lost her joy.
There is no more moon;
There is no more love.

Masiel M. Fernandez

What Is Death?

Dedicated to Ashley Carliston
Well, death is an untimely thing
it comes in and out of people's lives

I'm not scared of death
just conscious of it

To me death is just a darker world
to others it's a joke

Many people have come and gone
but this was untimely

He was a boy with a future
yet his dream was cut short

He took a trip and had a fall
now he's gone without a call

To some he's unknown
but to us he was a friend

Now he's gone and all will miss
the kindness of a stranger
no longer in this place

Jenny Svastics

Time

Time keeps on traveling,
Without thinking twice.
Time keeps unraveling,
People pay the price.

Why does time keep leaving,
Keep leaving us behind?
What is it achieving?
It isn't being kind!

But time isn't nice,
Nor is it sweet.
Time doesn't think twice,
It just causes defeat.

Jamie Gieseking

A Walk

Dedicated to: Lesley, Stephen, and Chelesta
The memories will be here
Though you have gone away
As you walk across that stage
All the memories come back to me.
Even if I haven't known you long
Every moment counts
To tell you
I'm going to miss you
I wish you wouldn't go
Come back sometime—
I'll always be here.
You don't seem to see this
From my point of view.
You're happy to leave
I'm happy for you, too.
Just remember I'm still here
Nothing will be the same.
Without you here
Everything changes
As you walk across that stage.

Jamie M. Jahnke

Sleep

See me sleeping
See me sleeping
I can't wait
any
longer
See me sleeping
For my weeping
The deeper I go
the deeper I go
See me sleeping
Rest is sweetening
No more reasoning
The deeper I go
See me sleeping
No more meaning.

Jennifer Yost

My Love

My love for you is as deep as
the deepest river.
My love for you is as wide as
the widest ocean.
My love for you is as strong
as an ox but as gentle as a
mother caring for her child
My love for you can never be
taken away
My love will live as long as
my soul is alive
In my heart there will always
be a plae for you, my love.

Catherine Irby

If I'd Never Met You and You'd Never Loved Me

When the daytime turns to nighttime
And I lie down to sleep
All the memories of a life time
Come back to visit me

As I lie there in the darkness
I wonder where would I be
If I'd never met you
And you'd never loved me

You have given a life time
Of sweet love to me
Never ever complaining
How hard life may be

And I can't help but wonder
Where would I be
If I'd never met you
And you'd never loved me.

Henry Kyle

My Guy

The wind in the sea,
Tells me he likes me.
The wind in my hair,
Tells me he will care.

If you dazzle my face,
we will be in a shinning place.
The holidays should be nice,
Of course we won't be in ice.

I will be in fear
Until you appear
Sleep is supposed to be grand
Then you will lend me a hand.

When I hear an old tune,
You will be back soon,
Sometimes I seem blue
When I don't see you.

When I fall on the floor
He will appear at my door.
He is here to stay
And will never go away.

Ivanka Hanushevsky

Renewal

A voice whispers
from the depths of my heart
struggling to be heard.

Doubt bred silence
yet indistinct words slowly emerge
as faith dispels fear.

Miraculous rebirth grants life
to the Voice once silenced
by life itself.

Discord blends into harmony:
A long-forgotten song
suddenly remembered.

Renewed by grace,
sustained by faith,
the song lives forever.

Andrea Evers

The Wrong Decision

There is no note that
fully explains a reason
to take your own life,
but yet we do. I don't
see the value of wasting
a full of energy, but deeply
depressed and saddened life,
but yet people do.

Is there a depression so
great and unbearable that
we want to end it all?
I wish I knew.

It's hard to grasp the
feeling that a loved one
is really gone, but we
have to.

Chelsea Knight

The Thing In The Sink

As I lie here in my bed,
I start to think . . .
Was it dead?
The thing in the sink.
I went to the kitchen,
Just to see,
I saw a chicken
Staring at me.
I started to scream.
I couldn't believe my eyes
Mom had asked me what I'd seen,
I was starting to make up lies.
Now as I lie here in my bed;
I start to think . . .
Was it dead?
The thing in the sink!

Serena Lindfors

Me and You

I remember what things used to be,
I always ask myself why me.
I wonder why were not together,
I thought it will always be forever,
I see your picture in my photobook,
I always have the urge to look,
I hear everyone talking about you,
I always hope that it isn't true,
I wish we were together again.
Because you used to be my best friend.
But now it's the end for me and you,
But we will meet again sometime soon.

Deserie Jimenez

Face of Stone

I want to reach out to you,
but will I find you there.
I need someone to comfort me,
and let me know they care.
So many times I've looked around,
to find myself alone.
So for now I keep it all inside,
and wear a face of stone.
But if you look behind the wall,
I'm sure that you will fine,
A man that has a heart of gold.
whose loving, sweet, and kind.
But I'm still afraid to reach out.
for fear I'll find myself alone
So for now I'll keep it all inside
and wear a face of stone.

Daniel Jerome

This Cruel World

I ask this soul
Why it came down in a world so cold
Incompetence, rejection, hardships
and pain to go through
Unable to take it well
And who could?
Being good, sane and nice— that is what
People expect from me
and what if I won't?
I would rather be evil, do as I please
And spit at those who condemn me
Is that what I want?
No!
I want to be good, sane and nice
and much more.
But it seems hard, impossible
so,
I ask this soul
Why it came down in a world so cold.

Asima Mehdi

Nature

The dog barked
when the cat clawed at him.
The elephant blew his horn
when it saw the mouse.

The deer ran
when the tiger came chasing it.
The rabbit fled
when it heard the snake hiss.

The clouds scattered
when the sun came out.
The rain fell hard
when the clouds came rolling back.

The wind whispered
when all was calm.
The sky was black
when night fell upon the earth.

Mindy Zastrow

Israel

Live in the Promised Land
Enjoy the Golden Sun and Sand
See the Eternal Light,
Seek the Lord with all your might.
Dream of a new Justice for man.
Live in the Promised Land.

Feel the truest joy of life.
Seek the strength Free From strife.
Know your fellow man.
Understand how your history ran,
Live in the Promised Land.

Find your long lost Love
Pursue the pure white dove.
Judge for yourself anew.
See how your people grew.

Find your place in the sun
Know your race was won.
Thrill to every moments feast.
Live and Love the Eternal Peace.

Robert T. Goldberg

The One I Met At Birth

Of all the paraphernalia that comprises this earth,
I've found nothing as complex as the one I met at birth.

I've dissolved some nasty tangles, put some puzzles together, too.
But there's no bigger puzzle than the one inside my shoe.

Lightening and thunderclaps can surely cause a fright,
But it's the one upon my pillow who keeps me awake at night.

If I could only understand the one who bats my eye,
When night shadows come creeping, I wouldn't have to sigh!

If I could just have hope in the one who wears my face,
That she's not just a weed sprung up in this place

Quite by happen chance, dwelling on the earth.
Isn't that what Darwin said of the one I met at birth?

Perish the thought, and do so in a hurry,
Lest dark shadows scurry across my room in fury!

Oh! Tell me there is a God who doesn't make an error;
Then I think there's hope for the one inside my mirror.

Mystery, though she is, when her creator she knows,
I am at peace with her, the one who blows my nose.

Then sound asleep she goes, forgotten all her woes
The one I met at birth, who wiggles all my toes.

Donna Nevling

When Doves Cry

Edward Owen Humphreys
Soon you'll feel so free, that you could fly!
That's when it's time for doves to cry.

You have been strong all your life and it's time to let go.
Rest up, so you can see the light of tomorrow.

You look old from among. But in your soul you're still young!
Life goes by so fast, but this time its your time to rest at last.
You were a father, grandfather, and a fighter.
But deep within your spirit is getting mightier.

I will try to get through.
I hope you know it's not too late!
Just ask God to open those pearly gates.

Live life with no regrets, but notice how much time is left.
When it's time, please don't fight. Just go ahead, toward the light.
It may be my last goodbye, but right now it's time for doves to cry!

Heather R. Humphreys

Thoughts on Retirement

"It's time now," they said. "Aren't you glad?"
I thought I would be, but somehow I was sad.
I'm really not ready, not old enough, not tired.
"Smile," my boss chuckled. "At least you weren't fired!
Here's your Gold Watch and a card from a dear friend."
But, where's all my usefulness; where will this all end?
"I wish I were in your shoes," one of my co-workers said.
I'd be glad to trade them, I thought, (my hands to my head).
I guess I'll take up a hobby, or maybe a craft.
"That's what I'd do," someone said as she laughed.
Oh well, maybe I can just begin life over instead.
As I picked up my pencil and filled it with lead.
I'll become a poet and write everyday.
At least I can contribute to society that way.
I only hope someone reads the poems that I write.
So I can retire with a new future in sight.

Cheryl Jonson

You're All They've Got

I love the mountains, I love the rolling hills,
Two voices resound,
Two little girls with energy unbound,
A moment ago, sworn enemies,
Now they're best friends.
Childhood so simple . . .
Why must it end?
Oh, I grouch at my kids
Every now and again,
But I've found the best medicine
is a big hug, and then
We sit down and talk
And end with a prayer.
The world is a scary place
To send kids unprepared.
We must play with them, pray with them,
Praise them a lot;
The world can't build confidence;
You're all they've got!

Diane Dodge

A Black Man Talks Of Pain

I have sown inside me all the light
In my prison cell.
I have planted words of life deep
Within my soul,
In hope that the guards and prison officials
Would recognize my reform.

I pray with thoughts of freedom,
Every second of the day and night.
I scatter seeds of my thoughts like flowers,
Enough to reach outside these prison walls.
But my reaping gives only more seeds of thought
To sow and spread with cries of justice.

I am a black man full of pain,
Because I cannot demonstrate my value.
I am a black man full of pain, begging to show my
Appreciation for the life that I once disregarded.
So, I talk of my pain as an incarcerated black man,
By sowing my thoughts and words as seeds.

Gregory D. Moore

Why Is It?

Why is it? Two people become friends,
No intentions brought, it can't be wrong
I wouldn't have thought.

What is it? That the feelings grow,
I tell myself,
I'll just take it slow
But, not wanting to let go.

Why is it? That it grows each day,
I can't stand it when you're away.
Or, is that something I shouldn't say.

What is it?
No words need be spoken
'Cause just with a glance,
The eyes and the smile,
The conversation is open.

What is it?
That the dreams turn to hope, hope for reality.

Why is it? That no more need be said,
After this poem
You have read.

Terri Johnston

Poetry

Poetry is the sun, to a cloudy day
When you're not feeling happy
It brings you your way,

Poetry can make your worst time just fine.
If only you sit down and write down a few lines.

You don't have to be the best at it,
But you can always try
With just one thought
You can change any ones mind,
With Poetry.

Tashenna Edwards

The Suicide Note

Do you remember that night
When we had that big fight?
It was about you and that girl,
The one with the dirty blonde curls.
I kept asking for your words to be true.
You love her don't you?
When you walked out the door and left me that night,
I kept telling myself that I'd be all right.
I ached all over in a way that was such
Because I missed you so much.
I'm sorry! I hate to do this.
If only I could give you one last kiss
Before I die.
Now you know how much I love you—goodbye.

Lisa Hertzman

Reverie

Your memory haunts me, sometimes.
Other times it comforts and soothes.
The mind plays tricks while the heart struggles to heal.
A soft chuckle,
A silent smile,
A lonely tear.
Emotions awaken with a passing scent that reminds me of you.
Recollections of another place and time take me back,
Yet push me forward.
Slowly, your memory fades.

Laura Rodriguez

Life

Life is once in a lifetime event.
What we do with that life, determines
How well we understand the meaning of life.

Life is a series of events.
Some good, others bad. What we do with
Those events determines how well we
Understand the situation.

Life a roller coaster ride.
Some moments up, others down.
How well we tolerate the ride determines
How well we tolerate change.

Life is full of disappointments.
How well we deal with them determines
How well we learn.

Life is once in a lifetime event.
How well we live it determines
Our regret factor later on.

Lesley R. Griffin

Please, Mommy, Daddy, Quit
(From a Child's Point of View)

My mom and dad smoke cigarettes,
It's just something that they do.
Would I be in trouble
If I told them I smoke too?
The smoke I get is not direct,
I get theirs, second-hand,
Smoke can hurt my little lungs.
Why isn't smoking banned?
I love my parents very much,
And hope they stay alive,
But with all that pollution
How can anyone survive?
Don't they know their smoke can kill us?
Don't they care a tiny bit?
So, for the sake of little me
Please, mommy, daddy, quit!

Mary Elizabeth Kuypers

Sea Shells

From one shell selector to another,
From one who delights in swirls and whorls,
colors and sculptured faces,
striped spirals
infinitely varied and surprising
delicately distinct
full of fascination
creatively embodied
raw essential beauty
small houses of perfection
little temples of nature.

And here's to the little guys that built them
with the Creator's assisting hand.
Let us not always eat them only—
But raise a filled glass in appreciation
Of what they do for us You and Me—
Lovers of natural creations from the Sea!

William Eugene Davidson

Myself

Sitting in my room; total darkness; quiet as ever;
not even could I hear the sound of my breathing self.
Sitting in my room, wondering what I'd be
if I wasn't myself . . .
Sitting in my room, hearing the cries of children,
hungry children that are sitting in my room, thinking
what a world this is . . . ?
Now, I'm sitting in my room saying
"I have no answer at all."

Ashley Osborne

Dolphins

Jumping in and out,
Swimming all about,
Playful just like a child,
They can also be quite wild!
Thousands get killed in Japan,
Just to be stuffed into a tuna can,
We must do something before it's too late,
For these wonderful creatures just can't wait.
Listen to my cry and maybe you'll see,
Just how much dolphins mean to me.
The trash and oil in the water,
Is just another type of slaughter!
They will continue to die, one by one,
Until something is done,
Please stop the killing,
For their beautiful sight is quite thrilling!
Please help save the dolphins,
So we don't have to dig their coffins!

Amber Posey

Untitled

Giant waves crash down
My shoulders wet with burden not my own
Laden with loss and good-byes
Sweating bullets of sorrow
My brow damp with despair
Breathing in the heavy, mildewy smoke of anguish
Picking the dirt of disillusionment
From under other people's fingernails
Forlorn in a way that,
Strangely,
Leaves me satisfied
For the swords of unhappiness
Glance off of my
Impervious
Armor
Of Tranquility

Benjamin Adams

Woman

A gift from God to man,
Not to change him so much,
But to help him in the special ways she can.
She is specially designed, just anything wouldn't do.
A help meet just for him
Made suitable and proper, too.
A nurturer by nature,
She always wants to give.
Flexible, adaptable to change,
Whatever needs to be done, becomes her will.
She is a wife, and even a mother,
Faithful in both steads.
Supportive of her husband and rearing her children,
Rising early in the morning, putting prayer ahead.
Because God is their source,
She and her husband believe.
Their children are raised in the admonition of the Lord.
Therefore, God has blessed this family to succeed.

Linda V. Walker

Creation

Unnoticed
Unseen
Omnipresent
Forgotten storms
Colored stars
Chalky moons
Twinkling twilight
Through the night's dark cloak
Hiding the unmerciful sun
Stretched out to behold the valleys,
Plains
Mountains
Streams
Floating aimlessly throughout the morning
Settling in peace during the night
Sunlight giving life
To deathly-marked shadows
Night air breezing,
Shivering
Beholding all whispering sighs.

Melissa Arel

Friendship

Friendship is a gift given to you
By a person who's there for you and loves you.
Make a friend, make a long-lasting friendship.
Love your friend, help your friend.
Never make a false friendship.
And remember—don't fool with friendship.

Nikki Roberts

The Ghetto

We lived in a ghetto with blacks and whites.
We were never afraid to walk alone at night.
We showed respect for one another,
As we did for our father and mother.

When we passed, it was with a friendly hello.
We didn't think of religion or color, but another fellow.
Now when we walk alone, its only with fear.
If only we could go back to that good old year.

We know that this can never happen, so we must do our best,
If we don't do it soon, our minds will never rest.
So let us get together, and make our wish come true,
For our country, America, needs people like me and you.

God Bless America
   Milton Warner

Untitled

Her eyes gaze upon the darkness.
There is only one thing she can see.
It is the feeling of the love she wishes to receive.
If it is a wish, is it reality?
Or is the reality of the love just a dream?
Either way, she feels the power.
The power enlightens her to which way the correct
path to his heart maybe.
But the darkness is evil
Is it the Devil, trying to grasp her soul?
Filling her heart with hopeless dreams.
Making her suffer with the anguish of emptiness.
Need not to be.
   Jeremy P. Hoivik

The Howling Wind

Give me a moment that I would benefit from
to tell you how you have become the one I grew to love.
May my revelation fix me an easier path to your unspoken thoughts.
Now that I speak softly in words there is to find.
Still it takes away much of my strength
to simply admit to you how much you have meant to me.

Say your thoughts before I perish.
Call me by my name before I collapse in distress.
Let me know of your true feeling that I would understand
How you reason my life to change forever.
And if it is only a pain that I will suffer from,
Please be gentle and say it right away.

So I would not be confused as time goes by;
I would not be alarm by any sudden seizure.
When death comes to lead me away,
Rather I would smile
For though life is very hard there was a time
I, at least, try my best.
   Phil M. Choun

Requiem

The sun descends, as the winds play their empty song
Holding you, in my hands, daring to say, "Goodbye."
Wretched anger, and despair engulf my very being.
As I lay you down to rest, my friend, to sleep eternal sleep.

Your pain, forever healed.
May your dreams be forever sweet.
As I await the day when you and I shall meet again.

As for myself, I shall sift the dirt from my hands . . .
And go on my way,
Embracing the coming days when I to, will heal,
Releasing the pain, to carry your memory.
   David Grigorieff

Untitled

Pass thru me ghostly lover
Dream unrealized
Fog has no purpose but to obscure
Settling thick and heavy, evaporating into
Nothingness.
Again.
My hand reaches out, there is nothing of
Substance
To touch.
As one approaches the mirage in the desert
To find the reality fades
And thirst is not slaked.
Ever receding
Death awaits.
If one is fortunate enough to find
Real water underground
Enough to survive
And backtrack to higher ground.
   Rita Dils

Snowman

Kristy and Kelsey were building a snowman,
Out in the falling snow.
They rolled the snow in great big balls,
So eager to get it done.

They had three balls, round and plump,
But now how do they stack them?
They tried and tried, falling and laughing,
So happy to have it done.

They got the balls into place!
And now all it needs is a few final touches,
Button eyes, a carrot nose, and mouth made out of coal
So happy to have it done.

They placed a hat upon its head
And sticks to make his arms
Mr. Snowman was completely finished
So happy to have it done!
   Kayla M. Godbey

Snow Angels

The winter is a thinking room conjuring
Devils in my mind.

Before me two bundled doves lay,
Heads turned back,
Upon the footstep-ridden snow.

Their warm bodies merged with giggles
To become a spark
To melt the frost.
Yet a flicker of warmth was all there was.

Arms flapped to pierce the ground with
Arches as ornate
As those of church doors.
Angels in the snow
—delicate impressions upon a season of bleakness.

As angels fly away, these two must also do.
Their commission
Has been fulfilled.
The brother flame
Lashes out its last sweet tongue,

And I hear the silent devil chill laugh.
   Talene Lee

Austerity

Austerity—The outermost edge of beauty framed
by the vast expanse where it can no longer
nourish our soul. The twilight fringe where
beauty no longer meets our needs but
reminds us of them.

Will we thrust our longing elsewhere in time.
Casting this momentary glimpse out into the
recesses of our lives?

Will we dare to excavate the nuances of
beauty's relief, risking our fragile hope
between its sharp contours and the
weight of darkness?

Will our hunger drive us to take a running leap
off the edge?

Greg Wertime

K.

Pale blue eyes filled with mystery—
They pierce his soul with a glance;
Phantom smile touches her lips:
Punctures his heart like a lance.

His heart pounds and his blood races,
Sidelong glances all he can bear;
for beauty is a powerful thing,
And to look upon such as her, he fears,
Would send his soul up in flames.

He feels like a fool, perhaps a little delusional,
Wishing upon a star—
Her beauty is beyond him, so very, very far.

He knows that to invoke such feelings
Can only bring him pain . . .
But he cannot help but wonder—
Does she feel the same?

He hopes and yearns and ponders,
For what he knows he cannot have;
But the hope remains inside, alive:
Perhaps somehow, some way—perhaps there is a chance.

Jeremy Campbell

Obsession

You water the vines that entangle me,
You throw away the key that could set me free.
You're a two faced angel with a pretty face,
but your heart's too messed up to be replaced.
There's a little girl who deserves the best,
but she only wants the worst just like the rest.
Love is an obsession that can't be tamed.
I pulled the curtain to your soul and the tears fell like rain . . .
You're a little boy who believes he's a man
You try too hard, now you can never be.
You don't care and you don't cry
You just stare into me and make me want to die.
I want to throw you down,
I want to n.8 you
No matter how I try, I just can't break with you
I wanna touch your face,
I want you back again
'Cause your my obsession . . . yeah!
you're an obsession . . .

Erin Beacher

Inside

I want to be inside his mind
when he thinks of me.

I want to be inside his arms
when the summer breezes blow.

I want to taste his sweet lips
on mine and feel his fingers in my hair.

I want to live with him forever
in a beautiful mansion on a hill
with lakes and lands across the miles.

I want to have little versions of him
with mischievous miles and deep blue eyes.

I want to be the first person he sees in the morning
and the last person that he sees at night.

I want to be inside his thoughts.
Insides his arms, for a lifetime.

Audrey Horne

Trust

Trust is a powerful chain
Each link takes time to gain
It's a powerful word
It doesn't fly free as a bird
One wrong move can break it all
And that's when you take the fall
With every true friend the chain gets longer
But only you can make it stronger
Just the weakest link and the chain can be torn apart
Picking a strong link, you must trust your heart
You can't let one person break you down
Because trust can be found

Soua S. Lee

Old 87

Old 87 carries much of my fondest memories,
for down this stretch of lone highway my mind is set at ease,
remembering Grandma waiting for us eighty
miles or so ahead, sent warm feelings to my
heart beyond miles that most would dread.
The country sky above us always seemed serene
and clear; I have never felt overwhelming
peace anywhere as I did here.
Oh, how I loved to see the rustic barns, the hills so green,
This nostalgic beauty reminded me on my Savior should I lean,
For he alone created this small touch of heaven
that I have come to cherish, known as "old 87."

Carol Anderson

Into This World

In years that have passed, I had a dream,
of wishes and pleasures, it's not what it seems.
I feel as though I've been missing something true,
But after 25 years it's finally come true.
In certain years I wouldn't have bothered,
Now my dream is reality, I have a daughter.
A little angel throughout my mind,
So beautiful yet so gentle and kind.
I've fantasized since the days of my nephews and nieces.
That without that love it drove me to pieces.
How do I walk without someone to hold my hand,
Now that I do, the meaning of love I understand.
Thanks to you I have a brand new baby girl,
Thank you my love for bringing Aleyah into this world.

Lamar Wallace

From a Student's Point of View

They make us read,
They make us write.
Both at day,
And at night.

They make us study very hard,
So we can get good grades on report cards.

They always say it's the best,
When we get 100's on our tests.

Book reports, no way!
Get a life, get away!

They check to see if our homework's done,
Can't we just have a little fun.

Well, that's about all I can say,
About how teachers teach today.

Fawn Harris

Daddy

You're gone now, again.
We are three families, we are one.
All we can do
Is remember stories,
The times I experienced, but don't remember
When we were one, now we were three.

We bring in the common things to
converse or to tell.
Then what? Back to old stories
Back to ourselves, then it gets quiet
No stepping on toes please
So we go shopping, watch movies, eat out.

I want you to be here
Not just a day or a weekend
Watching the flight schedule
As soon as I'm done, Daddy,
As soon as I'm done
When I'm all grown up
Not three families but one.

Jennifer Wizbowski

Landlocked, on the Edge of a Dream

On the edge of a dream,
An old love I've found.
On the edge of a dream,
An old ship run around.

On the edge of a dream,
With her bridge back in place,
It's like I can feel the spray on my face.

I had hoped, one day, to get back to the sea,
Board a ship in reality.
But liberties abused, are liberties lost, it would seem.
With no way in sight, my life to redeem,
Must I forever be landlocked . . . on the edge of a dream?

C. E. Churchward

The Butterflies and The Sparrows

Butterflies flutter by in the warm misty air.
There flies a sparrow grey and bleak.
They fly through the air every day of the week.
It sings a song that the butterflies hear, they dance and sing
every day of the year. So, after that they shed a tear,
their little wings are beat, they hurt from head to feet.
I listen to them sing and dance. And every chance I get.
I take a glance. And I see the butterflies and
sparrows looking at me. And so you might not see
them, but they're there, living in harmony!

Jessica Sheaks

Joint Custody

Please, talk about children,
with sticky fingers and sloppy kisses.
Talk of Dr. Seuss and Mother Goose
and nursery rhymes with happy endings.
Talk of cookies and juice on hot afternoons
and safety blankets and baby-dolls
that are actually cat-dolls.
Speak of how fun it is to jump on newly-made beds
and over sprinklers.
Of glistening hair and devilish grins.
If you can remember these, as he carts them off
it might make it easier.
It might help you to forget.

Regan Schwartz

Vows

These are the vows that I give to only you.
I'll hold you close and near.
Never letting you stray too far.
Taking away all your fears.
Helping you keep in mind
What is so near and dear to your heart.
I'll keep the faith that we've vowed to share.
Keeping in mind that you're mine and I'm yours,
And we're a pair.
Never walking in front of you and never walking behind.
But always walking beside you.
Thru the life we've vowed to share.
You and I. Keeping out all that is wrong
And accepting all that is right.
These are the vows that make our love unite.
The vows I give to only you.

Rubiutonn Rice

Falling Tears

As the light glows from the golden moon,
her dreams are stolen by a silver spoon.

Clear tears fall from the blacken sky,
and a white star shines from a lover's eye.

His loving touch is icy cold,
and their words drift apart untold.

With a tender kiss,
she's afraid of what she might miss.

Her delicate lace lingers low,
as the wind starts to blow.

Their laughter drifts into the sky,
and a tear falls from her eye.

After all the pain she's been through,
her glorious dreams have come true.

Jenny Kennedy

Wedding Vows

I ask myself why time and time again
and I find it just not my kind.
We were married at a park
to find out we were in the dark.
A marriage that never took place,
vows that were never made but again
I want to be saved.
If the Love took me away right now I would go
because there's nothing down here
I've enjoyed besides my kids and
I know he gave me them for awhile
so I wouldn't have to feel alone.
I feel there's no mate for me
no one to make me happy.
It's really not bad, just sad.

Louise Moore

Star Cross'd Love

I see two stars in summer's night,
Blinding, hovering, lost in light,
Each so dull in heaven's net,
So much is left, as yet unmet.

But fortune moves in strangest ways,
It lengthens nights and shortens days,
May this night end, and day begin,
And bring two lovers together again.

Love will come, and love will go,
Leaving you brokenhearted, and can't let go,
And all but leaving you to see,
Your heart being tossed from sea to sea.

Love seems blind, and love fears,
Always leaving you in tears,
And I end this poem with a sad goodbye,
Writing this left tears in my eyes.

Angela Luan

The Sharpest of a Dull Razorblade

I close my eyes and imagine myself lying
naked on a bed full of blood-soaked roses.
Their petals scattered around the room.
Their sharp thorns piercing my bare flesh.
As I drop the blade I listen to my last
sound, breathe my last breath, see my
last sight of the darkness that is my life.
My warm blood fills the white sheets in
a maze of dark red color.
As I lie there my whole body goes numb.
What happened to the person that I used to be?

Sheena Isenberg

What To Do With A Green Rectangle?

Would you accept me if I was a normal color and shape?
In a world full of red circles would you accept me if
I was a green rectangle?
Would you shun me from society if I was a green rectangle,
would you claim that a shape with pointed sides
can't exist in a world full of smooth?
Would you file down my edges and paint me red,
or would you get that near?
Would I be forced into a silent corner with a yellow triangle,
or would you accept me. If you didn't accept me,
I would rebel causing you to destroy me . . .
Or is that what you were trying to do all along?

Mariam Catania

Missing You

If this was the last day we had,
I would want to spend it with you.
But I guess now you don't feel the same,
You left me here all by myself.

I don't know how to go on,
I know you'll be back, but I don't know if
I'll be here to see you. I just might leave too.

Forever? No, I just won't be where ever you are.
You hurt me when you left.
You had nothing to say to me.
I guess you don't care anymore.

But I guess I'll live
With all of this hurt inside.
I just miss you so much. I don't know what to do.
If I could feel your arms.

Around me and your sweet lips once more,
I could go on forever.
Just one more kiss and hug.
But then I guess I'll spend my life
Missing You!

J. Smith

Meditation

And I pondered
Looking toward the heavens
As the droplets quietly fell
And landed on velvet petals.

Is he saddened too, by all he sees?

And I pondered
And I wondered
As the gentle breezes
Rustled through the trees.

Is he saddened too, and sighing,
And shaking his head in despair?

And I pondered
Looking outward
As the golden sunshine
Made the world warm and bright.

Is he smiling too, hopeful of a better tomorrow?

Donna Michalski

When You're Not There

When the day is full and bright and
seems too long to have to be without you there.
I see your face, I hear your voice in my
mind. I see the smile that could turn rain
into a rainbow and my heart turns
upside down. I imagine your eyes so sweet
and kind you never want to turn away.
I see your soft and sexy body, the way you're
cute, the way you're fine, the way no matter
what you make my heart skip a beat.
Without these things in my heart and in my
mind I couldn't get through the full and
bright day. Into the hours where the blackness of
night takes up the last ray of light.

Wendy Rathbone

Best Friends

What is a best friend?
A best friend is not a trend.
Being nice and being sweet,
best friends are totally neat!
If one should move away,
all the others will stay.
And when your life is to the end,
Your friendship still won't bend!
You'll even be friends six feet under,
and even through lightning and thunder.
If your friendship is special to you,
you and your best friends will always stick like glue!

Kelly Cox

Lost Cat!

Has anyone seen my lost fat cat,
He's black and white and round and fat.
He'll fight you then bite you and take your hat,
and ask if he can have a bat.
He went to catch a bird and fell in a turd
then didn't say a word.
One time he bit me and left a bruise,
I wanted to hit him with one of my shoes.

Nancy Burger

True Love

Across the open plains my heart longs to be.
Across the open plains to be wild and free.
Oh I wish that I could live out there
my love and I, we'd make a pair.

Across the open plains far from this boring life,
across the open plains where I could there be made his wife.
Oh I wish that I could live out there
my love and I, we'd make a pair.

Across the open plains my love would wait for me,
across the open plains there, wed, he and I would be.
Oh I wish that I could live out there
my love and I, we'd make a pair.

Across the open plains
my love is not waiting for me.
Here I cannot love another,
there my love will be waiting for thee.

Jessi Clark

Time Fades Away

Constantly you're on my mind,
I think about you all the time.
I can't sleep no matter what I do,
I can't stop thinking of you.

Could this be love deep down inside?
Tearing me apart and breaking down my pride.

The moonlight embraces me as I yearn for your love,
you're my eternal pleasure sent from heaven above.

I'll whisper dream into the darkness
and watch the stars 'till they're gone
and when all time fades away my love will still live on.

Kristy Ashpaugh

My Soul Is Black

My soul is black
I can't turn back.
I made myself this way,
I pay for it each and every day.
I have so much built up inside,
So that I can protect my pride.
It takes every bit of strength that I have
To keep a hurt look off my face,
I just choke back and let a mask take its place.
Everyone sees a happy outer shell,
Although, they could not begin to imagine the hell.
I am so glad they cannot see,
The shame and pain inside of me.
Sometimes I feel I want to cry,
Even though I don't know why.
I keep on holding back,
Therefore, my soul is black.

Marti Sue Carpenter

Everyday

Everyday is something new.
Everyday that we have together is cherished
Everyday includes me and you.
Our love is like a rainbow,
But instead of finding a pot of gold,
There is a life filled with happiness.
Your love is a gift that I will
Never get tired of.
I will cherish you and your love for eternity.
I want to "thank you" for this
Precious gift you have given me.
And say "I love you" every day of my life.

Theresa Ann Peacemaker

The Question, Please

Before you stands a great and mighty task,
I'll give you the answer, the question you ask . . .

It's the only thing in life which you can give, but cannot keep.
Always awake, but forever asleep.

It's always free but still it cost.
Whenever found, it still is lost.

Forever to have, but forever to lose.
You never own, but always use.

It's always the same, but never again.
Your worst enemy, your closest friend.

The shortest of short and the longest of long.
Will prove you right and prove you wrong.

The only question with the only answer
Cause of babies, cure for cancer.

The only thing in life which is different, yet remains the same.
I gave the answer, so please name its name.

P.S.—The question is something we all know of
It's not that simple, so don't say love

Damion L. Faulkner ("The Purveyor of Truth")

Impossible

A spark can turn into a flame,
That's why I'm playin' this hard game.

Only the strongest can survive,
There is no room for compromise.

I don't know how to give in,
You knock me down,
I pick myself up again.

There's never perfect circumstances,
Just do your best and take your chances.

You gotta believe,
That's all you need for a victory.

Hope, risk determination and desire
The trademarks of a champion,
Always lifting me a little higher.

And no matter how long,
I'll stay strong.
Because to me,
"Impossible" only defines the degree of difficulty.

Caitlin Phillips

A Dream

Porcelain stares at the ceiling
as her dreams dance on the edge of existence.
The images entice her,
popping in and popping out,
leaving no souvenirs.
But porcelain knows now.
She knows that there is something better,
something hidden.
She wants to find it.
She wants to feel it.
She wants to be aware.
The alarm sounds,
and the armies of "reality" attack.
The snooze bar adds nine minutes,
but porcelain wants eternity.

Domenick Chiddo

This Old House

This house of clay is shaky;
It's old, it's tired and worn.
The winds and rains have had their way,
Through all the years of storms.
But God's been good to this old house;
He holds it close together.
And when I think it will crumble and fall,
He brings calm peaceful weather.
So thank you, Lord, for being there
Through all the stormy weather.
Your anchor keeps this old house of clay
And holds it close together.

Ruby Johnson

Dividing Mysteries

Some people's past is a mystery,
kept hidden because they can't stand
the awful knowing
That somebody knows what they did.

They say the past is over,
completed through
it's not important now
even though it has made them who they are.

What was so painful?
So horrible that not even your family can know.
Why keep us wondering?
And waiting and hoping that someday we'll learn

What it is that separates us.

Some people's past is a mystery
others pretend to tell the story, hiding their secrets.
Nobody knows the truth about anyone else,
about what their life has been; who they are.

That is what separates us.

Emily E. Hynes

More Moonshine

I will write a sonnet, dammit, on my day,
Crowded with activity and loneliness.
(Oh, come on, not so lonely now, confess!)
No. Obsessed, though, by the image of a ray
Of moonlight in a glass. It spots the wall
Inside me, like a ghost. I look away;
It's there. I talk a lot, but what I say
Still echoes back my voice beneath it all.

Some say I am romantic, and that's true.
I have a double vision, or a triple,
My dreams of th'ideal can thwart and cripple,
Leave me unsatisfied in all I do.

If I could catch that moonbeam when I meet her,
Would she cool me? Or, I distract and heat her?

William N. Parker

Soul Mates

I sit alone, no one there for me
I wonder if this was meant to be
Why does everyone hate me so bad
Don't they realize it makes me sad?
They've got no reason to hate me so
But the hurt inside proceeds to grow
I try to tell myself that it's not true
But the only one really left is you
Nobody else really cares for me
But that's the way it's got to be
But I am quite lucky, there are no debates
Because you and I are forever soul mates.

Stacey Goodwater

Untitled

I was walking in the rain.
Wet, lonesome and tired.
Went to a store found that is was no more.
I left and went to my grave.
I was there a minute or two,
When along came a parade.
They welcomed me to my doom.
I was glad to accept it.
I was walking in the rain.
Wet, lonesome and tired.
When I was, though, I would give my soul up for hire.
I worked all day and most of the night.
I sent the souls to their rightful place,
Condemned them to hell,
Or gracing them with heaven.
It was a lonesome job,
But I had to do it.
I got paid my freedom my soul.
Lost no longer I would walk among the graves,
And they would scatter.

Daniel Tiger

Together (No Relationship to the Dating Service)

You are not in the room,
yet I know you are here,
though you may be far away in body.

You are with me always,
in spirit,
because there are many ways to be together.

It matters little with whom you spend your time
for we are always connected,
and always will be so.

You can hurt me but I will always forgive you,
because you are the other half of me,
and we cannot be torn apart.

Kathy Farrell

His Work of Art

When God unrolled His canvas and spread
It across the sky, He paused and pondered
Thoughtfully on all that met His eyes.
He thought about a thousand things,
He searched His mind, His heart, then
Chose the subject that He loved
To be His Work Of Art.
And when His picture was complete,
No more that He could do,
His masterpiece was unsurpassed
For He had just created you.

Pepper Kantelberg

My Grandma's Groundhog

My grandma when she was but eighty-six
Went for a walk quite near her knoll
And took her cane to help her out,
On this short stroll.

And there quite blocking her forward path
Was a daddy groundhog basking
And he refused to even budge,
Though she was gently asking.

And so she swung her trusty cane,
And brought it down with might and main,
And for his impertinence in lying there,
She gave him a concussion!

Margaret M. Andreassen

Second Coming

Mass destruction upon the earth
Robots, robots, robots we will destroy the earth
Putting cars and trucks into overdrive
Watching machines destroy humanity
So the machines can take over the earth
Destroying their creators is what they had in mind
Causing a nuclear war to wipe out the planet
And to cause the blackened earth
To before ever darkened
Beware of the second coming
The coming of the robots

Brian Stoneking

Crossroad of Life

Sometimes in life you come at a crossroad
And get too worried and confused
You go the wrong way.
The pathway gets too rough
And you cannot make it.
But an angel comes along
And picks you up and puts you on
The right path.
The angel cannot help you the whole way through.
So you have to keep the faith and
Stay on the right path because . . .
Wonderful things may happen
To you!

Darcie Kirkland

What Is It Like To Be Something Else?

As I sit here staring into the ocean waves below
and up at the sky above,
I wonder what it is like to be something else,
rather than and old brown tree.
What would it be like to swim all day,
or fly way above the clouds
I wonder and think these things in my head,
but an answer never comes out.

I've asked all the birds what it's like to fly,
but none of them have ever answered,
I've tried to call to the fish down below,
but I guess I'm up too high,
for none of them have ever heard me,
or even answered the question I cry.

What is it like to be something else,
I guess I shall never know.

Sarah Marchena

Sonnet #16

I can feel your soft lips upon my own,
I hear you whispering that you love me.
I feel your hands holding mine, they're so strong,
I hear the words you whisper just for me.
I feel your hard body pressed against mine,
Your arms of steel are holding me tight.
You might not love me for the rest of time,
But at least for now we will have tonight.
I hear a sound, not music, a siren.
I am lifted up upon a platform.
And as I'm rushed, you are right beside me,
The clouds will cover me to keep me warm,
I say one phrase then succumb to death's charms:
Remember the night I died in your arms.

Beth Curry

When Pretense Falls

I see the branches of life
Stretching all around me,
Far as the eye can see
And beyond.
They survey the very depths of my soul,
Seeing what improvements need to be made.
Before the leaves on the branches
Turn brown, turn cold,
And fall to the ground
Never to be used again.

Jessica Gaboury

Teardrops

Tears roll down my eyes, I'm sorry.
Down my cheek they trickle, slowly.
A hand reaches down to me,
Down to me to say everything is fine.
Yet deep down I know it won't be,
For what I've done is so bad, so humiliating.
But I'll cry and cry until I die, until I die!
I'm so sad, so forbiddingly sad,
So sad am I.
Teardrops are falling down my face,
Rolling ever so gently.
My friends don't even care,
They just bitterly walk away.
Tears are rolling down my cheek,
As I sit here and sadly think,
Think of what I've done.
Teardrops,
Teardrops are rolling down my sad and sobbing face.

Nicole Pupshis

Sunrise, Sunset

Is there beauty more than I can see
When the sun rises and sets for me?

The rays of light spread that o'er the earth.
It is sunrise, a time of rebirth.

As the sun shines through the noon of day,
Heaven's golden arches brighten our way.

Through thunder and hail, it's always there,
Sometimes a child hiding from care.

The clouds may dance their ballet carefree;
The finale is the sun shining for thee.

Now a glorious prism is in sight,
A colorful horizon, a sunset bright.

It fades quietly, yes, whispering now
"Tomorrow I will be back somehow."

The sky sheds a tear with the morning dew
Awaiting the dawn when the night is through.

Is there more beauty God creates for all
Than when the sun decides to rise or fall?

Maybe words on paper I can write,
Only He can turn on earth's daylight.

Kourtney Ridgway

The Shadow Theater of the Mind

Tonight, grey clouds darken the sky.
I walk alone along the beach.
My only companions are my random thoughts.
Shadows of the past roam the byways of my mind.

A trip down memory lane can be as dangerous as
A walk down a dark alley.
You never know just what you might awaken.
About to jump out at you could be something
You don't want to face.

A shark's fin breaks the calm waters of the conscious mind,
Scaring away pleasant memories.
Events best left forgotten float up
From the ocean floor of the unconscious.
I shake my head to clear away these dark remembrances.

The grey clouds of midnight fade into mist.
A silver moon shines brightly upon the blue oceans of earth.
The memories of events long ago are but flickering images
That appear in the shadow theater of the mind.

Adam Erik Batkay

Cry of Nature

In the moon's crescent, find solace
For worlds and stars are empty too
And moons and moods wax and wane,
And it seems the casting seasons
Never cease to change.

Through this drought within,
Listen close for the lone wolf's howl
Soaring in the desert night
To yearn for the full moon
As it drowns in the clouds,
While imagining the fire beneath
With empty hands outstretched around
That burns with the chorus of crackling wood.

And when sorrowful tears are heavy
Like torrents of raindrops
Against your windowpanes
Look to the waterfall
And listen to the gentle cascade
Let the soothing sound surround your soul
Then know—nature cries with you.

Gerald Glover

I Want To Go

I want to go to a place
Where water never runs dry
And lilies and roses bloom year round
Where summer balances through fall
And the leaves crumble like a burnt cookie

Where the sky is always blue
And the moon is always full
Where worries are illegal
And death is an option

I want to go to a place
Where time can be turned back
And tears are only joyful ones
Where men are men
And boys are boys
And love has no color

Where age is just a number
And loneliness, a companion
Where cities can join hands
And racism is extinct

Zanthia Phillips Turner

Pulse

Death in the blood lingers like a vulture
One worldly wind blows away your hope
Linger in the valley of morbid culture
Devoted to a faith of no way to cope

Insides rotting slowly, no turning back
Eyes float like pinball's inside your mind
Love of a lifetime stabs you in the back
All thoughts in your head are falling behind

Moon lights the darkened path into your heart
Vacant eyes, blue-lipped smile advertise
Nonexisting pulse tells of your ending part
The one who gave you life won't compromise

Smile your last smile because you are done
Die your last death because you have now won

Clover McClure

Strawberries

Wet and cold was the morning
Red and sweet were they
Wearing green hats they danced from their branches
With the wind humming a tune behind them

The sun penetrates through the fog
Hitting a thousand little mirrors
That send of a dazzling red glow

The farmer sits
Amazed by the beauty
He lies back and dreams of when he was a boy

They are happy thoughts
They only bring a smile to his face

Of when he was out picking strawberries with his mom
He would put only the bad ones in his pail
And eat the rest
He loved strawberries

Now he awakes
And rises to his feet
The sun is gone now
He gets to work before his family returns

Tyler Blanski

A Poem About Me

I am strong and confident,
I wonder why we are here today.
I hear a flower bloom.
I see a rose.
I want everybody to be happy.
I am strong and confident.

I pretend to hit a home run.
I feel I can do anything.
I touch success.
I worry somebody won't be here in the morning.
I cry when I think of my grandfather.
I am strong and confident.

I understand everything cannot go my way.
I say things are better only in my heart.
I dream to be a professional baseball player.
I try to overcome fears.
I hope things could be the way they should be.
I am strong, I am confident,
I am what I am.

Kyle Bannow

True Love

Lifelong dreams put in one little basket
Feelings that make lifes sorrows bearable
Making time when there is none
Never losing faith in your feelings
Always saying I love you
True love is never planned, its built from trust and friendship
Looking at sadness and making a smile
never second guessing your feelings
A gentle kiss a tender touch
A gentle whisper in ones ear
A pleasant look from afar
A twinkle in your eyes
A soft wink
Never saying I'm sorry
Risking everything and gaining nothing
True love is forever
My love for you will always
be true and forever

Stan Gustafson

I Am Woman

I am woman taken from the rib of a man
I am woman that was God's plan.

I am woman a child of eve
but I am not so easy to deceive.

I am woman so uniquely made you see
I was created by Jehovah and there is only one me.

I am woman made to give birth
I am woman God made me from the earth

I am woman with a heart full of love
with wisdom and guidance that comes from above.

I am woman and from and my beginning to the end
I will strive to make Jehovah God my friend.

Sarah L. Abron

Seizure

Mommy! Daddy! What's happening?
Why do I feel so bad?
Why is everything getting so dark?
Why am I shaking so vigorously?
Why do I feel so hot?
Mommy! Daddy! Why am I changing colors?
Oh help me, God, someone please help me,
Mommy, Daddy, please,
Please do something—I don't like this.
I'm scared.
Why does this have to happen to me?
Mommy! Daddy! It's happening again!

Charles J. Anzalone

Mother

She was tiny and she was frail,
But her deep love would never fail;

To hold her hand and touch her face
Would clearly show her loving grace.

Through all her life her smile was bright,
Everyday, morning, noon and night.

When her hands were stilled to work no more,
She joined that host on the other shore;

But here on earth, there is no other
Who could replace a loving Mother.

Don L. Hicks

Spirit Rising

While I was walking, outside with my friends
I took a step and began to ascend.
I floated beyond the tops of the trees
And looked at my friends—were they still watching me?

As soon as that thought had entered my head
I was no longer rising, but landing instead.
"Don't pay attention to people below,"
I said to myself and began to let go.

I felt myself lifting, again, off the ground.
"I do this for me, not my friends to astound."
I was happy to know I was able to rise
But saddened to see just how closed were their eyes.

As I drifted along
I became more aware
That my friends were still earthbound
Too anchored to care.

As we awaken, we each need to know
That our friends and our loved ones, not ready to go
Should not hold us back from our hopes and our dreams.
To leave them behind is not sad, as it seems.

Lisa M. Grandia

Who Am I

If I could do one special thing I would fly
I would be right up there in the sky
I would always be dancing with the birds and the bees
Always wondering what would be the next thing I would see
For up there in the sky I will never be shy

If I could see one person I'd see you
For you don't scare me you don't say boo
You're a person who I could play with
You would never tell me a lie or a myth
Best of all you know me so well you never ask who

If I could be one person I'd be me
I like myself and I know I'm better than I ever could be
I'm kind and I care
I'm sweet as a teddy bear
But I'm just glad I'm me and not a he

Megan McCurry

O' Heart, My Heart

O' Heart, my heart, where are those tears you cried?
Those tears I cried just rose right up, drowned my soul and died
Those tears I cried had made a sea, with wild torrents a churning,
Those tears I cried blew in a fire, that sent my soul a burning.

O' Hear, my heart, where is your steady beat?
The steady beating I once had, the patterns did not meet,
The steady beating I once had, had made me live in hell,
The steady beating I once had, filled me with death's smell.

O' Heart, my heart, why did you have to go?
I did have to go because my soul had gone below,
I did have to go because, I've been broken many times,
I did have to go because, the hatred drove my mind.

O' Heart, my heart, it left me lying here,
No one stirs or wills to stir, however far or near,
Here I lie in my own blood, a sticky rancid smell,
But hey you know what the saying says, "Heaven's better than Hell."

Shari Cui

Wear A Smile

Waking up this morning I had no smile upon my face
But surely did Remember to awake was, by his grace

So I took a shower, brushed by teeth, and combed by hair
Then while putting on my cloths, within I said a prayer

Lord I'm here because you love me, I'm here because you care
I'm here because you gave your life, for me you're always there

I thank you for the sunshine, I thank you for the rain
I thank you for my up's and downs, and for taking away the pain

I thank you for encouragement when I am feeling low
I thank for health and strength and protection where ever I go

Dearest Lord, I want to please you now
Please tell me, and show me how

What there is that I can do
That will please and comfort you

Within my heart I know that I
Upon your care I can rely

What you've done for me is because of grace
So proudly I wear on my face

The expression that's so worthwhile
I'm secure in your love, Jesus, so proudly I'll wear a smile!

Thamer M. Lewis

Petrified Wood

The trees were not petrified from fear,
Though death was near;
When their cells were consumed by swamp acid,
The fallen trees were not exactly placid.
Yet, they did not moan or groan.
Instead, slowly, patiently, they
Turned themselves to stone,
Developing a different, stronger form
Than what had once been their norm.
When you triumph over disaster,
You, and you alone, are your own master!

Gloria R. Barron

Way of the Old

I know of a time long ago old,
When the world was new.
I conjure the colors of a way no longer bold,
White, red, green, and blue.
I toy with elements that are pure as gold,
Wind, fire, earth, water.
I roam in directions which have never been told,
Therefore I am the way of the old.

Jobynne C. Prazak

Self-power

In self-absorbed charades they ignore me.
Am I worthy, and if not, who is?
Will I continually be cast off by them?
Or perhaps. They are the very ones who need me.
They yearn to be better and greater.
But in order to achieve they must drive down
and crush opponents. They need me to succeed.
No, I will not give way to harassment and pain.
No, they will not destroy my opinions.
Yes, I will strive and prosper on my own.
I will become whatever I want, because I want.
I will not be ruled by self-proclaimed leaders.
I am a leader. I will go beyond what they comprehend.
I will be me. I will be their ideal. They wont stop my
imagination because they don't control my mind. I am strong.
I am free. I will overcome all your obstacles
Look at me. I am woman.

Michelle Dills

Time Fades

Under the crimson sky
Eyes of twilight yearn for love's return.
She waits, time fades.

Down a lonely road
Young mind wanders to image of her.
He drives, light fades.

Stranger loses control
Ending young dreams in pools of red.
He dies, life fades.

Phone rings, like church bells
Signaling salvation, loneliness ends.
She answers, fear fades.

Impersonal voice speaks
Revealing the truth breaking her heart.
She listens, color fades.

Phone slammed down
Like crashing thunder bringing rain.
She falls, sound fades.

A picture on the wall and in her heart will remain,
She cries, love fades.

Mark Hayes

Fate

What would I do if I didn't have you
to answer my silliest questions?
Who'd grab the remote as I nibbled his throat
and eschew my romantic suggestions?

Who'd take me to movies I don't want to see
and keep me up nights with his snoring?
Who'd set me ablaze with a hand on my knee
in the midst of a day that is boring?

And where would you be if you didn't have me?
Who'd wash, starch, and iron each shirt?
Who'd set your alarm so you wouldn't be late
and massage both your feet when they hurt?

Who'd tenderly turn down your covers at night
and bake for you cookies and bread?
Who'd whisper "I love you" while dimming the light
and mean it more now than when wed?

I'm sure as the sunset must follow the day,
it had to be more than blind luck,
of all of the possible choices he had,
God picked you and me to be "stuck!"

Dell C. Byrd

Untitled

A bird can't fly with a broken wing;
rest and healing makes him well again.
You hear his song before its light,
to chase the shadows of the night.
You're looking forward to a brand new day
and all challenges it brings your way.
Some things are everyday routine
and some are difficult, before unseen.
You try to cope in work and fun
with friends and family and get things done.
But always there to lend an ear,
a helping hand, or quell a fear;
a friendly smile, a hug or look
lets you know, that's all it took
to make you see problems from a different angle
and hope they are easier to handle.
When you help others, you help yourself.
It makes you richer than all the wealth
that anyone could bestow on you
and that will always get you through.

Julie Giddens

Paper Boat

As I sit in this boat I feel water at my feet
This ocean I am sailing is a whirlpool of deceit
The winds blew through my paper sails now just two empty holes
Poseidon cannot save me from my empty hopeless goals
I try to steer my paper boat but the current is too strong
As I am tossed about the seal I wonder what went wrong
As I tightly grasp my paper boat it slowly melts away
I must somehow stay afloat in waters dark and gray
I let the ocean lead me now onto a paper shore
In search of paper answers for there is nothing more
As I stand on this paper shore the ground begins to shake
This land I am standing on is nothing more than fake
In this place I look about me and see people thin and weak
I ask for some directions but they don't appear to speak
They grab at me with paper hands and look deeply in my eyes
One by one they run away back to their paper lives
Somehow I must leave this place but there's nowhere to go
Somehow I must soon touch base with things that I don't know
So I guess I'll make a paper boat in search something more
I only pray I stay afloat 'til another paper shore

Scott Edwards

Hurt and Rejection

In a room filled with fear
I feel another tear
Fatter and fatter I feel
Don't want to deal
What's reality
It's not for me
His hand moves up my thigh
I try not to cry
I don't want him but I cannot win
His touches give me the chills
A few more pills, his touches subside
I try and hide
Fear take control
Another scar to carve
Help me somebody, my life is a lie
I'm overwhelmed by fear, and I'm not all there
I see the light
I give up the fright
Rut and rejection
It's all an obsession

Stacy Barnard

The Wonderful Gift

I once knew a girl pretty and sweet
Self-esteem low, meager, and weak
A wonderful gift came into her life on a
Dark romantic Saturday night,
A man so perfect she couldn't believe
"Oooh, my gosh, could he actually like me"?
They bonded all night the feeling getting stronger
Could they live without each other?
It couldn't be perfect "too good to be true"?
Yes she discovered when she found out he had to move!
So the perfect couple was torn apart
This simply broke their hearts.
Thousands of miles their love stretched
Like modern day Romeos and Juliets.
Their only hope being somewhere, sometime,
Hopefully in the near future they could
Be together again. . . .

Angela Trumpower

A Part of You

You mocked me, and I smiled

You excluded me, and I grinned

You laughed at me into my face,
and I managed to stifle a chuckle

You ignored me, and I kept myself
from looking at no one but you

And when you made a nasty remark about me,
I replied with, "How are you today?"

I am the speaker for every person you hurt.
I reach out and speak for the ones whose hearts
were weakened by your actions

I clear your eyes when they are so fogged up with prejudice,
you can't see the results of your actions

I make you smile at the ones you mocked

I make you grin at the ones you excluded

I make you laugh with the ones you laughed at

I make you look at the faces of the people you ignored

I make you say, "Hello" to the ones with your
nasty remarks still weighing heavy inside

I am a part of you, I am your conscience

Alexandra Woodruff

Bedtime Illusions

I'm in a world of butterflies and Ladybugs
A place with ponds and grass
Where the only important are kisses and hugs
and where the moon is made of glass

I sniff the freshly picked plastic flowers
As I run, the heart shaped sun hits my face
and watches me sweat tears like a shower
I then run to the mushroom I call my place

Morning arrives again, just as a rose belongs to a stem
I go and watch the green clouds
And ask them if they will come again and when?
For I will wait for them next to the candy flavored owl

Darkness could never exist here
It's immune to all evil and pain
In my heart I always hold the forces of nature near
This is the only place where I can be sane

This is my land
It's the art of illusion and mind over matter that gives
But it's all real
It's not a fantasy game I play, it's a fantasy I live

Hector Hernadez

Too Many Days

Too many days have passed us by sense
they day we shared together
it was our day
the day I meet you
we shared much more than just time
we shared
love, laughter, tears
You gave to me a reason to live, to smile
to be excited about life
Now there is nothing
but sadness to surround me
You left me too soon
I was young in mind
I didn't know
Now I try so hard to be happy that
I even had you at all

Gene Ray Allen

Stolen

Babi Yar stole my innocence
A day in the park is a day at eternal rest
Bubbles in the bathtub are washing away my girlhood
I want to run freely but my body has been stopped, motionless

Babi Yar stole my beloved flame
A trusted friend betrayed by life's truth
Back and forth we would whisper sweet nothings
In each other's eyes we would soar

Babi Yar stole my baby
An innocent child with dreams to be lived out, no more
Baby cries I hear at night, my baby
I want to hold my baby but my arms are numb

Yea though I walk through the valley of the shadow of death
I am too stiff to feel fear
A march to the sad fate that awaits me
Rare is the savage that stole me

Rebecca A. Weiner

His Hand In Mine

I have to go, I have no choice.
Yes, I know, but not without me. For I am always besides you.
I'm so excited, I can finally set the record straight.
Yes, but not without me. You need me.

I rush out never hearing the words inside my heart.
Driving down in a traffic jam, I think isn't there something
I forgot? Did I lock the door, make the bed, take out the
trash? What did I forget to do?

What about me? Did you forget to seek me?
Did you forget to speak to me?

In my heart I heard the words. My spirit cried. My soul wept.
I'm sorry father, I cried. I have been in such a rush.

Rush, my child? What's the rush? I did not make the world
in one day, nor did I do it while I was in a rush.

I stopped and wept, than I prayed, forgive me father,
I didn't realize until today how much I needed you.
All he wanted was his hand in mine.

Lillis Cruz

She Swam Ashore With Flying Colors

I shall try but I can't say
I will be able to describe every detail
In full, in very deep waters they lay
I shall try my very best to nail
The Jaws, perhaps I should paint
A picture because words aren't enough
To tell a story so quaint
Of that of a sea goddess so tough
From the very start
It's been a hard struggle to survive
The Whales, this brave yacht
Underwent too many a nose dive
Though none was smooth sailing
She swam ashore with flying colors
Let's celebrate victory! It's worth hailing!
She captured the whales as wells as the Jaws
She's gasping and choking, she's asphyxiated
But this clever Yacht has a life buoy
She's bubbling with laughter, she's emancipated
And she's hooting with joy.

Amanda U. Ajuluc

Life (As We Don't All See It)

Once I was like you,
Strong vibrant young and new,
Life was all mine
And I had lots of time.

Life is but a vapor,
So God has said where has all of the hair gone
Upon my head?
My body has no tone.
My hands are frail.
Sometimes this body feels like a jail!

In my mind I can do anything
But when I try sometimes all I can do is cry!

I am here, do you see me?
Day by day you pass me by.
Not even stopping to say hi.
Sometimes I feel as though
I'm here waiting to die,
So the next time you see me stop and say hi,
Because tomorrow may be the day
I slip away into the sky.

Melissa M. Sleight

Now Is The Time

We bring life into this time of rising despair.
For man has polluted the water, land and air.
So now is the time we must show that we care.
Or on future generations this load they must bear.
To take from the earth and leave her but an empty shell.
Will seal our fate and that future generations as well.
So we must be aware of everything we use and take.
For only then a future for all is what we will make,
This earth has great beauty in what she has to give.
So let us take care of her for on this earth we all must live.

Lewis Edward Wicklund

Casting Your Cares

I look back in the past at what has
Been a broken home for years.
People all around knew the circumstances
But it seems no one really cares.

Homes, families, and children
Are tossed about each day
Living a life as, a rebel
That is slowly leading them away.

We are a self controlled people
Watching for no one but me
If we put others before ourselves,
Crying needs you will see.

Its not enough just to say
It will all work out
Because pain, heartache, and sorrow
Are, what the world is, all about.

We hold the keys, to help those in need
But we fail to unlock their crying plea.
Help the broken hearted, and encourage the weak.
For its a treasure of care, we must seek.

Terral Vance Cannon

Salvation Beyond 2000?

As the dawn was brilliant fiery red.
Peace on earth now was dead.
The warnings came long ago.
A futuristic world said he could not know.
As death warmed over, cities fell.
Then our world became the hell.
Flesh-eating vampires; because of no food.
Our futuristic world soon became crude.
Dying common men with no control.
Yet, the president lives in 300 foot hole.
With no power, no need for education.
All became people without a nation.
And in time came the golden age.
A time of living without rage.

Kari Thornblad

The Spaceman's Albatross

The sky is the future of things to come
For aren't there more things that we can become

Like leaders of space and things mundane
Describing the place of detailed terrain

Man has polluted his air and sea
But they say magnificent space is free

Millions and millions we'll spend, and more
Unlimited areas we will explore

Many light years of travel we'll see
But what will we do with the spaceman's debris

Nancy C. Arbuthnot

Foolish Girl

How foolish can a girl be,
To be fooled by a man when he starts to say,
I love you sincerely and truly,
But in his heart he really knows,
He'll just hang on as far as he goes.

How foolish can a girl be,
Pretending not to know what's going on,
With all those tricks and gimmicks he had shown,
Still no matter what advices friends and relatives gave,
She's stubborn, won't listen, and won't believe.

Wake up girl if you're in a deep sleep,
Do something before it's too late,
Give yourself a real break,
No more tear drops rolling down your cheek.

Dear Girl, please, listen to this,
Don't turn your life into a real mess,
You're too sweet, so nice to deserve all these,
Heed good advices and stop being foolish,
Good luck in the future,
May you have the best!

Melchorita E. Mendelson

Forced Back

Did you just speak?
Was your voice stilled?
Can you feel the frustration? The pain?
The helplessness?
Did they numb you?
Can you see the blood run cold?
Or are you blinded by the devil's black light?
Please—break these ropes and chains,
Free me.
Or are you as weak as myself?
Have you faded away into the darkness?
Your presence can no longer be felt.

Tara Bui

Christ In Christmas Colors

Winter Browns in stall and cone
Are for the Humility,
Christ's nativity has shown.

The White of lights or snowy air,
Show His Light and Purity
With all He came to share.

Gold of wreath and ball
Express Christ's Royalty
In windows, door and hall.

In sky or ribbon, Blue
Displays His Loyalty
For me and you.

How Blest are we!
For in the red
We can own the Saving Blood Christ Jesus shed.

'Twas shed for Green,
Which is Everlasting Life for each and all
Who will upon this Saviour call.

Joyful Christmas Colors we do display
Our Blessed Christ This Christmas Day!

Rosella L. Knuth

Here I Am in the Natural . . .

Here I am in the natural going from day to day
Learning all that I can asking God to tell me what to do and say.
Here I am in the natural being led to believe
The product of a women who did not want to conceive.
Here I am in the natural never knowing why I came about
Being responsible, being caring and doing without.
Here I am in the natural my fate has been dealt
Here I am in the natural knowing I need Gods help.
Thank you Lord for being with me every step of the way.
Help me, teach me, so that I will know what to do and say.

Beverly A. Haywood

Veteran's Day

Veteran's Day is a time to remember.
It comes on a cold day in November.
They have fought many wars, so we have been told,
They are the ones that were oh so bold!
They carried our flag, the red, white and blue,
and gave us our freedom, this is true.
The men and women who gave their lives,
fought for freedom, for you and I.
Be proud of the ones who serve our land,
please thank them and give them one grand hand.

Glenda Deering

Loving Wisdom

As a small child I knew my father was the wisest of all.
An active boy, he seemed to have learned much more.
Then as a smart teenager, I was in for tremendous fall.
My father had turned into somewhat of a bore.

As I matured myself and became more aware,
I realized that elderly man was much smarter than before.
The leading, and fathering, dispensed with loving care
Brought me into the world of adulthood with maturity galore.

I look back with pride on the life we did share.
It ended too soon; I wish there could have been much more.
If we could have been together for a long time,
His great knowledge I would have had time to store.

Alvin L. Vaughan

Together Forever In Our Hearts

Everything I gave you I guess just wasn't enough.
Maybe it was supposed to be this way,
Even though I didn't want it.
But through every day, every night, every hour, every second
trying to get over you is so rough.
I love you too much and I miss you so much.
I can't get over it.
Why did it have to turn out this way?
Why does life suck when you're not around?
Why is it so hard?
Why couldn't you just stay with me?
I love you.
You will always be in my heart till the day I die.

Jamey Owens

Daddy's Knee

Hey, look at me . . . up here on Daddy's knee.
I'm on top of the world,
The tallest I'll ever be.
I'm a cowboy
With a saddle under me.

He throws me up, I bounce back down
Oh ain't laughter the greatest sound.

Now I'm older, too big to ride
As I sit at his side
And like his knees
We ride life's ups and downs
We run around like rodeo clowns
Some have smiles, others wear frowns.

Before you know it . . . daddy's gone
This cowboy sings a lonely song.
Like a mustang he is free
But I know someday inside of me
I'll be back . . .
Back up on daddy's knee.

Dan Taylor

I Know Better

People say poetry is just words on paper,
But I know better poetry is about life, loves and hates.
People say, "Love is just a game,"
but I know better. Love is a passion
that can only be felt between two people.
People say "Kids would not understand,"
but I know better. Kids understand, do they!
We understand about poverty,
hunger and violence, and every day
Hundreds of people die because of being a bystander.
Then people say kids need to be guided.
They are right; I don't know better.

Katie Owens

Strailing Love

Now that I learned I have you
You are starting to let me go
You come home late every night
Don't even give me the pleasure I deserve
Smelling like perfume and lipstick on your collar
I often wonder why I don't holler
Maybe cuz I love you
I could be wrong
Or maybe cuz I need you
Still I could be wrong
You're always lyin'
So now you better be tryin'
To win back all my love
Cuz you're all I'm thinking of
I'm not gonna leave this alone
So please baby stay home
So I can have you always to hold.

Chrystal Stone

What Took Me So Long

I've been searching for my Lord.
I've took the long way up.
I've climb mountains and fell; I will run,
I will walk. I reached out to the Lord and cried.
I prayed to God above to led me to the open doors.

I've gotten so far up, my ears were deaf.
But I kept on climbing up the mountain and pulling.
Something inside of me wouldn't give up,
and when I felt like I couldn't climb any
more the Lord led me to the open door.

I will stand straight and I felt the power
of the Holy Spirit, My Lord was calling me
I let my feet walk in. I gave up my troubles
and let the Lord take over.

My heart is filled with love.
My soul is washed clean.

I am with the Lord Almighty,
I am in mighty fine hands.

Thank you.

Corenthia F. Burton

O What Should I Do?

Once upon a midnight dreary
Hair unkempt and eyes so bleary
I listened to a talk show host
And those calling in from coast to coast.

Of Randy Weaver's wife and baby
And seventy innocent of Waco . . . maybe
Oklahoma too, some scoff
Why the FBI took the day off?

And as my weary frame unbends
I wonder, "Who are my friends?"
My parents who raised me, dead and gone
My children grew up and all moved on

Neighbors hurry to work and back
Gulf war symptoms heart attack
So talk and let your feelings out
To digest distrust, and fear, and doubt.

And as I finally go to sleep
I make a promise that I will keep.
I'll be like the Samaritan
Who stopped and helped his fellow man.

Dale Colebank

One Day

One day last year, I traveled to Africa alone,
without fear. I sat in the trees cool shade, or marched
along as if I were in a parade.

One day last year, I traveled to the jungle
alone, without fear. I climbed the highest trees, then
walked along in the cool, gentle breeze.

One day last year, I traveled into outer space alone,
Without fear, I floated along, merrily singing a song.

One day last year, I traveled to the lake alone,
without fear, I found some stones to throw into the lake,
taking all the time I needed to take.

One day this year, I'll travel to all
these places not just in my imagination
but full of fascination

Danielle Rohrscheib

Beautiful Earth

Beautiful is the sky above,
Beautiful as a white dove.
Beautiful is the sight of rain drops falling,
And the sound of song birds calling.

Beautiful is the water below,
Racing fast, walking slow.
Beautiful are flowers growing,
In the wind they are blowing.

Beautiful is the earth itself,
Before mankind had his wealth.

Jami LaBelle

On The Mountain

For my husband Milton
Where the land is unspoiled and the animals
run free I want to live forever.
The sun shines bright and the stars shine through
the night it's so beautiful here.
The grass is so green in the early spring and the
streams just seem to glitter.
I was raised on this mountain and here I shall
die but, my soul shall live forever.

Wendy Mock

Angels Walk Among Us

Your father's eyes
With your mother's heart
A deadly combination from the very start.

A tear to shed
In your memory tonight
Like the rain
fading out of sight

No stories to tell
for all is cold
It feels like hell
without you to hold

No where to turn
No where to run
I'm sure my destiny is to burn

In my memory you will always be bright
For I know you are in the light
I have a smile to give for all in sight
But only darkness falls tonight

Connie D. Shanks

Colors of Time

Red, white, black, yellow and brown are colors in our minds,
but what do we look for in difference to our time.
The variance is only surface and with light to our eyes,
and does not penetrate to the soul or to past crimes.
The colors are natural blending in life and on canvas to,
but it seems not to matter the substance of the hue.
Red, white, black, yellow and brown is in every town,
the people of substance are all around.
With the direction of one and the melding of minds,
success at all endeavors has been the test of our times.
When we lose our direction from which we are accustom and akin,
is it due to our perceptions of the color of skin.
Should we look deeper to see what is there, we should really care.

As we are born the colors are blended and prime,
we do not analyze or evaluate the crime.
As we get older the perceptions of time grow more rigid,
we do decide and become more frigid.
As we continue to go through life we continue the perception,
that the colors are different and should continue the deception.
The substance of the colors of our time is much deeper than any rhyme.

Bob Burger

Innocence

She runs through the grass
I see her and I long to be her
She hasn't a care in the world
Only living for today
She laughs with glee and
chases butterflies through the garden
With only the world around her
She has no need to be scared.
Every little things delights her
And she loves everything around her
Her world includes fairy tales and family
She stares up at the sky
Finding shapes in the clouds
I watch her, and I know her
I know her innocence
There's a whole world out there
Waiting for her to set her flag down
And conquer hearts everywhere
To her, the sky's the limit and
there's no such thing as an impossible dream.

Stephanie V. Sava

If Only

If only I could tell you.
If only you knew how I felt, your heart would just melt.
If I say what I have to say,
Would you turn and walk away, or would you stay?
You might call me this and I might call you that.
It may lead to fears and many, many tears.
If only you knew I really do care.
If only you would listen to me, only then,
for just a few, you would let me hold on to you.
If only I didn't lock it up inside and swallow my pride,
Things wouldn't be this way.
If only you knew . . . but I have nothing to say.

Rose Cygan

Asylum

Mach to often center of matter
Has been manipulated to left, right, out,
Hidden under skin view layers
Living us option of sand grain-
Only to maintain asweight to waves,
Or strip from dimension particle of stone black
It is time to take leave of absence
Dear love ones, friends and presidents.
Fly a way to gardens of promised land
Where every dog barks in languages I understand
Take Ophelia from Algae of my dreams
For pure de la art dance on stars trapeze.
With faith of lamb, that just escaped
From table of world's last supper, feast
On battlefields growing in to green posture,
Where horizons are wild open, prayers answered
Feel reunion with universe, starting and ending in me.
Where unspoken promise men to men, is communion of believers
Silence is voices arising and every hunger surrendered
To one who gives evenly to all daily bread of peace.

Eva Pintscher McQuillan

Open Your Eyes And See

Oh open your eyes and see
Me, you, them, and we.
Black, white, tan skin have we.
What great friends we could be.

We can solve problems like stopping wars.
And we can also solve problems by opening doors
In your mind and heart to make a start.

Amanda Russell

Impossible Dreams

I have this list of dreams of mine
Of things I'd like to have seen
Although they may not ever happen
I'd still like to share my impossible dream

Some day I want to see world peace
But some people are just so mean
If mankind could just get along
We could live my impossible dream.

I wish people were colorblind
We could make such a team
All races in equality
That is my impossible dream

If only there weren't any leaders
The human race would surely gleam
Each person working equally
Then we'd share in my impossible dream

I know this won't ever happen
But at least someone has tried
I know my dreams are impossible
But I also know that they haven't died.

Cassandra Hill

Creator/Destroyer

Fear is loneliness, in my case I'm always alone.
Alone is lost, I constantly roam.
Scared to cry, to smile, to love.
Alone and driven away from all I dream of.

He is the reason I am what I am,
I'd kill to escape the grip of his hand.
He is the destroyer of my heart and my mind,
He and only he is this brutal and unkind.

He is the blade that raptures my veins,
He is the creator of my pains.
He devours my light and my hope,
I hang myself and he holds the rope.

Though he is brutal and controls my life,
Even if his words cut me like a knife.
I know I will never look at him and hate what I see.
Because my Father is a part of me.

Heather Campbell

Life Really Sucks When . . .

Life really sucks when nothing seems to go your way.
Most normal people have bad and good days, but
what do you do when every day is bad for you.

Life really sucks when nothing seems to go your way
What should you do hide it with a smile, but
what happens when you can't smile anymore.

Life really sucks when nothing seems to go your way.
What happens when you try for the best possible day
in the best possible way, but it never fails it doesn't
go your way.

Life really sucks when nothing seems to go your way
You hope and pray for a better day, but it
never happens it always gets worse.

Life really sucks when nothing seems to go your way.
You're stuck in the mood, like you're locked in a room,
but know one has a key.

Life really sucks when nothing seems to go your way.
One day you wake up and the right person comes
And says the right thing, now you're not trapped.

Life's really great when everything goes your way.

Kristina Stein

I Am A Shadow

I am a shadow
a person no one knows,
a person no one cares to know,

I am a shadow
life for me is moving from person to person
looking, searching for that special person

I am a shadow
People themselves are shadows
until they find someone to love
and who loves them

I am a shadow
No more!

Kimberly Storesund

Dear Friend, Don't Cry For Me

In Memory of Winston Weems
Life is a flower, that's blooming,
As a rose, so early, in spring,
So lonely to look, upon it,
Such beauty to all, it brings.

Think as you look upon it,
A young tender rose, as a child,
One day will then have to leave us,
We're here, for only a while,

Through heartaches and life's disappointments,
Good times, along with the bad,
Though life here on earth has ended,
Remember the good times we had,

For I'm in a home called Heaven,
A mansion prepared just for me,
No pain, no sorrow, no suffering,
With the Savior, forever to be.

So let not your earthly heart trouble,
Fret not o'er the things you can't see,
Though on earth, I'm so longer with you,
Dear friends, don't cry for me.

Roger Aligood

Untitled

Love can hurt, love can sting
A broken heart can never sing

Boys will come, boys will go
But a friend is forever this I know

A friend is rare and hard to find
Everyone knows it's true

You helped me through a very bad times
I'll always be grateful to you

Whenever I need someone to lean on
I know you're always there for me

Some might think they can not live with out boys
But I think it is better to have a friend.

When boys hurt my feelings in many ways
I always know I have a friend who cares

So I always thought of you as my sister
Because you have always been there for me

That is why you are my best friend
And you know I will do the same for you

Kimberly R. Clampitt

Caring Hearts Join Healing Hands

The need was appalling, the cry loud and clear;
Something should be done, it must be this year.

So Dr. "O", U.H.C. and colleagues said "Hey Listen Here!"
And the Medical Society bent many an ear
Of the business community and friends everywhere;
"We must come together to show that we care."

Then one by one, people began to stand;
United Way came forward, "We will lend a hand."
This spark of a dream had taken form;
Health Access Free Clinic would soon be born.

Our Director arrived from out of the blue;
The Volunteers came, it didn't seem true . . .
So many Caring Hearts Joining Healing Hands!
To serve the needs of their fellowman . . .

Sandra J. Martin

I'm Tired Of

I'm tired of being hurt, hit, slashed, and kicked.
Every night I cry myself to sleep.
I have covered the wounds you have slashed in so deep.
These wounds you have made can never be healed,
For I feel your love for me long ago has been killed.

Fawn Martin

Stepson

I didn't birth him
so don't feel an umbilical tug at my heart
When he says, "I'm getting dreadlocks"
In his straight blonde hair
Which would be green if he had his way.
I spit and scream in private.
Age thirteen weirdness,
Wearing the pants of a 300 pound giant,
Not a lanky boy
Moving loosely in freshly greased joints.
"Nothin' to do," he pouts
In the teen stench of his temporary bedroom,
Then proclaims, "I'm changing my name to Cheesefudge"
or some such nonsense.
I have little humor or affection
For this silly boy in almost man's body.
Guiltily, I pack him in a box of styro peanuts
To send postage paid to his mother
Who loves him but not his father anymore.

Connie Heinlein

Captured

Let me hear the sounds you hear,
As you paint the pictures in your head.
My neck strains to hear the voices,
I make up when I'm dead.
I'm in a life long trance,
My thoughts venture from me quickly.
Now I hear a bird song call,
I am feeling sort of sickly.
Let your voice sooth my soul,
Talk to me with your gestures,
Your mouth moves, that I see,
But I hear no tips of life.
Help me live, that's what I need,
To free that ghost inside my body,
Closing me into a world without light.
Give me your hand, I'll hold it close.
And though my gentle touch is numb,
I praise you with my heart.
It is late into the night, and so I say farewell.
Please think about the things you've read and remember me within.

Ariana Katz

Cemetery

Cemetery,
cold and quiet,
reveal to me your secret stories.
Tales told silent by tombstones.
Each the closing of a chapter in life.

Tell me of your hollow occupants,
shells of those who used to be.
Temporary housing returned to the ground.

Show me a scene of vibrant yesterday,
when these lives were burning bright.
Each somehow shaped our world today.

Give to me a vision of tomorrow,
when at last my worries will end.
A simple marker will greet those who visit.
Or will I be forgotten?

Jason Martin

Eternity

The tree of love grows in the palm of your hands
for mine are tied
The roots grow deep like the love we could share
But sometimes no matter how deep the roots
trees just die
But if the tree has a heart like mine
I will never stop loving you

Anthony Levin Ottaviano

A Week Ago Today

Dedicated to Javier Ricardo Quezada

A week ago today I cried, a week ago today you died.
The pain I felt when I heard that you died,
the stain on my pillow from where I had cried.
I can't understand how this can be, a week ago
today you were here holding me.
Your kisses I'll miss, as well as your smile.
How I wish I could bring you back just for a little while,
and hold you in my arms, as you fill me with your charms.
I'll never understand why he took you away without letting me say
my good-bye. My heart you did touch, and I miss you so much.
A week ago today I waited for your call, not knowing later
on that night how hard I would ball.
The time I wish I could rewind, then maybe
you'd be sitting right here looking so fine.

I look at my chair and see you still sitting there,
With that ear to ear grin that I'll never see again.
Then I start to feel sad thinking of what we might have had.
I know I'm down here and now you're up there,
but forever you'll be in my heart even though we're apart.
This to you I swear, I want you to know I'll always miss you Javier.

Kelly Thompson

Devils

Devils are surrounding me
Those evil thoughts I fear
My mind is full of chaos
My vision is unclear

Angels watching over me
But are too weak to fight
Though, they keep faith in me
To stand my ground through day and night

But the devils grasp is tight and strong
Sucking up my energy and will
But I won't let an evil get into me
I will let nobody lie me still

Alona Kantor

The Two Whoms

To see the way I view the world,
the disdain of their every word.
The two figures to whom
I gaze, and every authority word take toll.
Yet, away I say no
longer will I wither to die away.
Yet, survive the pain
and, thrust given by the two whoms
who are suppose to love.
Yell and yell they must
till I grieve in mental illness
from above.
To all freight the sadness
of the two whoms love
and hate by I shall
never be forgotten.

Victoria Almazan

The Car Ride

I open my eyes.
We are driving through Washington D.C.
My father turns up the radio,
Loudly accompanying Carly Simon in song.
My mother frantically points out the Capitol,
Explaining that the House of Reps
And the Senate work there.
My sister is in the seat in front of me
Making her stuffed animals dance to the music.
She turns to me.
"Look. Mr. Bear can do the Macarena."
I smile and watch
Then close my eyes.
6 hours to go.

Amy Van Deusen

Soaring

The eagle spreads his wings
And flies over open country
The wind lifts him up
Carrying him with ease.

The sun reaches out
Shining down on this eagle
It engulfs him in warmth
And shimmers like gold on his feathers.

I look up and see this eagle
As he soars over my head
I sometimes wish I could be as free as him
But then I realize
There is so much more for me here.

A simple smile to me
Is like flying over an open country
And the sun shines on me every day
In the form of friends
They are my earth, sun, and my moon.

Laura Munder

For The One I Love

Two hearts that share one love, one life,
Will always know true joy
Dreams we have seen come true.
The gentle moments spent with you
The true longing for the
one I love
The white birds that fly above
sign of heaven
made the only one I love

Breanna Higle

Esperanza (Faceless! Nameless!)

Mr. Executive!
While you read the wall street report, I serve your coffee.
While your secretary has lunch, I answer her phone.
While on business travel, I make comfortable your suite.
Yet, I have no face and I have no name.

Ms. Executive!
While you compete in the new modern world, I clean your home.
While you meet with associates, I take your suit to be cleaned.
While you go to the gym, I care for and wipe your children's tears.
Yet, I have no face and I have no name.

America!
Look at me and listen to me.
I have a face and I have a name
My face is lined and brown and humbly says
I AM CHICANA ! I am HISPANA ! I AM LATINA !

MR. AND MS. EXECUTIVE !
Call me what you want, but I know who I am
I know my face and I know my name
More important, my children and your children know my name
I AM ESPERANZA AND I AM AMERICAN.

Julia Soto-Cabrera

I Give My Love To You Only

I want to live and love with you
and be one forever;
To be near you, to touch you;
to make love with you talk with you
and be silent with you, to hold you close every night
Wake up to you each morning . . .
I want to share my secrets with you,
and be honest with you, to understand and
respect you, accepting you as you are.
To find shelter in you when I am afraid
and hold you when I need warmth.
To be with you through all the seasons,
Walking with you in the sunshine and
cuddling you in the cold; to care for
you when you're ill and be joyful with
You when you are happy, to grow
old with you and be with you
until the end of time.

To you only, I give all of my love. . . .

Jacque Mitchell

Secrets

Secrets
Everybody has them
Everyday we put on a smile
and act as if everything's okay
But inside there are secrets
Secrets that nobody knows
and maybe nobody ever will
Secrets that replay in your mind
time and time again
Secrets that are a part of you
and no matter how hard you try
you can't get rid of them
Secrets that may one day destroy your life
and you must live knowing it
Secrets
Everybody has them.

Kristi Ritchey

EYE MOTIONS

When you're walking in what you do.
Your eyes are in motion,
constantly guiding you.

Most men look women up and down
It matters who they talk to.

Women watch where a man's eyes travel.
They know his movements are starting to unravel.

Their talk is full of hints,
using words that come close.
Slowly getting to the point,
to catch you for his most.

Desire stares through this part.
His eyes are the windows of his heart.

When their relationship blows out
like a flat tire.
Here they come to hit and run.
Wanting to use you as their spare.
Women, just say no!
and don't let 'em get there.

Thomas Horsman

Earth

Earth is a sign of nature's gifts.
It shows us the beautiful things in life.
We gather our thoughts the further and
Further we go, for earth has beautiful sights.
We realize how much mother nature has
given us, for we thank the stars above.
If it wasn't for earth we, wouldn't be
here with the ones we truly love.

Nina Derosa

Oh the Taste

Oval goddess of all fruits,
Apples can't compare.
Smooth,
red,
squashed against my fingertips.
I slice down the center,
juice flows down my palm
Licking my fingers.
the soft crannies enter my longed for mouth
Crunching the outside,
bland in my mouth,
plucking yellow seeds from my satisfied lips
I enjoyed my digested.
Tomato.

Rachel Magnus

The Gift

In clearing land for this small mountain cabin,
A dogwood, stout and strong as dogwoods go—
Some forty years in growing—was uprooted,
Delivered to its death by one swift blow.
Denying fate, its laden branches blossomed
As it lay slowly dying in the snow.

At my son's passing, I too was uprooted,
Confronting death, with blooming yet to know,
And seeking hope and meaning in that wounding,
Was given grace to learn and strength to grow.
The dogwood spoke of life and resurrection
In its last gift of beauty to the earth.
God, let me not forget that benediction;
Life's ending is transfigured in rebirth.

Jane Higgins

Ashley Erin

For my precious daughter, Ashley,
may she always know the love I hold in my heart for her.

A   may you ALWAYS ASPIRE to higher ground.
S   may the SMILE that plays on your lips forever reach
    your dancing blue-green eyes.
H   may you always HUNGER for the answers to life's
    puzzling questions.
L   may your LUST for LIFE never diminish on your journey.
E   may the ELEGANCE and grace you possess as a child
    blossom and EXPAND 'til your dying day.
Y   may your YOUTHFUL spirit shine, eternally.
E   may you EMBRACE your destiny with EVERLASTING passion.
R   may you RISE above man's inhumanities and REJOICE in
    God's will.
I   may your INDEPENDENT spirit never waiver as you make
    your way through life's IMPENDING obstacles.
N   may the NUMBNESS of your darkest days, NEVER overshadow
    sun-filled tomorrows.

Kelly Specht

What Is Love?

Though life may be hard and obstinate,
there is no need to cower.
Love is always a candle lit,
even in your darkest hour.
No matter what kinds of troubles you tend to encounter,
whether they be big or small,
love gives you the power to conquer.
It gives you the strength to overcome it all.
Love is the fresh, cooling, summer rain
that flows into a peaceful river.
Each droplets is a tear from pain,
that has been taken from a single soul to end his shiver.
The emotions of sadness and anger are powerful,
but these can be easily overcome with love unconditional.

Laura L. Molnar

Truth In Trust

Peace, love, and happiness
Words I would not know the meaning of.
If it had not been for you.
Friendship, trust
Two words I found do come true.
Open, shut
Words I know how to use
To protect my heart.
Knowledge in trust
As long as I go through the
World with an open mind and heart;
Believe in friendship truth, and trust.
And don't shut people out of my heart and soul
Peace, love, and happiness
Will come fully and completely to me.

Christina Gruwell

Valentine's Day

Through the woods, across the fields, a shallow lurks a red
Squirrels yields. You're all alone, it feels so nice, the wind
so cold your skin like ice. The air blankets your every move,
your breathing is rough and your skin so smooth. The sun
is bright and shines in your presents, and you shed a short smile
and splendor its essence. And a thought of love comes
to your mind and then you ask, will you be my Valentine?

Raven Heil

ANGELS OF THE EARTH

The wind howls in mourning throughout the mountaintops.
The echoes can reach the depths of one's soul.
The wind mourns for all the unborn children who have no voice on Earth.

Dark storm clouds embrace and unite.
Heavy rain pelts onto our planet Earth.
Thunder explodes wildly across the skies.
The rain pours down tears for all the children that are abused
and neglected in our land.

The ocean pounds immense, frothy waves relentlessly onto the sandy beach.
The break of the waves is intensely rhythmic, like that of a drum demanding recognition.
The ocean is a huge life force that impoverishes none.
The ocean's song is that we end poverty amidst our children.

The rain subsides and a radiant golden sun arches its rays from heaven and across the skies.
The sun is the future of love, so that all children will know love on Earth.

Suddenly, an iridescent, translucent rainbow makes its path across the sky.
The rainbow portrays future hope for all the angels of earth.
The Lord speaks to us through nature's call.
Someday, when we all listen, all children will be protected from any earthly harm.

Our children are blessings and our destiny.
Without our children there would be no hope or promise for tomorrow.

KarenAnn M. Tobiasz

Nameless

I, by the tide, stare and ponder with wide eyes about a fascination
of love and hate, about procrastination with chance and fate, about
relationships of joy and tears, about blatant trips so brave with fears.
Silent wetness and silent cries with stoic numbness and stoic eyes.
A mangled heart mended with thread; of frightening thoughts subsiding
instead. A pool of blackness, a pool of blood, a pool of cracked and
hardened mud with nothing but a burning rope. Hope that's lost and hope
that's gone, and beautiful wishes at the break of dawn. A raining season,
a thundering cloud, a wondering laughter, a thought that's proud to exist.
Moments of frustration, a sad realization, a vivid imagination, and saline
sighs. Pages of tragedy, pain, and horror with screams into the darkness
behind a knobless door. Nights of insomnia and what causes it be, and
me, running and climbing my tree. Questions at random, answers unheard,
tears suppressed, wings of a bird. Salvation, damnation, reality, and
thoughts, and apocalyptic wars in the depths of my soul. I, by the tide,
stare and ponder with closed eyes.

Elizabeth De La Cruz

Mother Nature

Mother Nature is very upset. That's why the planet Earth is a wreck.
People with brains can understand our polluting the world with
hatred all over the land. Instead of love and lending a hand, only when
disasters occur; then people can. Why can't love be shown each day?
Why must Mother Nature have to show us the way? Or have us say,
I'll help my fellowman in every way. Does it take the Earth to show us
how we must live or to teach us it's better to give? Mother Nature has
to make mankind feel humane toward each other. Very sad it takes that
to help the next brother. God said Love will conquer the world. That's for
every woman, man, boy and girl. We must learn from Mother Nature to
have compassion for all races. When mankind begins to do as the Bible
says, I think all twisters and hurricanes will be on their way. For then
Mother Nature will know we have love and it can show. I feel we're
the cause of this untamed weather. People on this Earth can't come
together in harmony; we cause the Earth to suffer in the first degree.
When we get together and unite in love, then we'll receive blessings
from Heaven above.

Gertrude Youson Igus

No Wrong

World, within a world,
within a mutilated sight
perception of the living deceased
in the embers of the night
remote control emotion
with laser sensor beam
super speed efficiency
open for the extreme
manufacture the end of the world
clone it from one breath
edit the lines of symmetry
drawing out our death
reflection of a deadened thought
changing into shock
ignorance and common sense
blurring with the clock
decency is an excuse
for imperfection and what is what
kill it before it really lives
'cause it's a caring moral cut

Angela Legg

Sensory

I see velvet roses blooming in the dark fertile soil,
my mother baking a 4-layer triple chocolate cake,
my golden lab chasing a squirrel up a tree.

I hear the sound of my father assembling a brand
new mountain bike, my sister letting out
a high-pitched scream, my grandma slowly entering
our old remodeled house.

I smell the smoke from a bonfire,
the salt in the ocean, and the aroma of coffee
in the morning.

I feel the lush surface of a silk scarf, the
roughness of sandpaper, and the condensing
water on the side of a cold glass of iced tea.

I taste the chocolate in a brownie,
the sugar in Kool-Aid,
and the salt on a slice of pizza.

Johnny Lybrand

The Ultimate Judge

Why do so many men today,
Seemingly Christian otherwise,
So freely deal in deceit and lies,
Knowing their sins will be repaid?

Surely they must understand
That such things are so unjust,
Bringing on great doubt and distrust
On the part of their fellow man.

Not only are such acts unfair,
But are also sins in the eyes of God;
So it would seem doubly odd
That they just don't seem to care.

In truth, the greatest risk they run
Is not the harm they do to others,
Although all men are their brothers,
But in disobeying the Father and the Son.

They may not be called to account by men,
Leading them to feel they need not fear,
But they'll find their slates aren't really clear
When before Heaven's Judge they finally stand.

C. N. Wesson

Bittersweet

Bittersweet is life
As it shall always be
But one must know pain
Before they truly see

One must know pain and heartache
Of the most destructive kind
Before they look into themselves
And there their heart they find

Once they find their heart
The bitterness is gone
And in its place of sadness
That always lingers on

I'd like to have love and laughter
With me every day
But I'll settle for the bit of sweetness
That sometimes comes my way

I try to leave a little sweetness
With those whose life I touch
For I have seen what bitterness does
It destroys oh so much

John H. H. Gray

Biographies
of
Poets

ABAD, PEDRO E.
[b.] April 29, 1953; Norfolk, VA; [ed.] BS English - St. Paul's College; [occ.] Teacher; [hon.] Poems published in local newspapers; [oth.writ.] Authored 4 books: "The Poet In Me", "Heavy", "Love . . . Oh How It Hurts", "One Voice"; [pers.] I write from my heart and soul. Relax and feel my words.; [a.] Norfolk, VA

ADAMS, BENJAMIN
[b.] May 27, 1978; Washington, DC; [p.] Maria Adams, Michael Adams (deceased); [ed.] The American School of the Hague, Wassenaar, The Netherlands; [occ.] nightclub promoter; [oth.writ.] Several poems in small anthologies, many unpublished novels, plays and philosophical works; [pers.] I would rather sit and learn about everyone than sit and talk about myself. My writing is my truth, and I share it so others may find their own truths.; [a.] Alexandria, VA

ADAMS, LYNN
[b.] September 11, 1996; St. Louis, MO; [p.] Ina Mae Apsley; [m.] Gilbert M. Adams; May 30, 1968; [ch.] Shaun R. Knapp and Daniel N. Adams; [ed.] Kierkwood High School, Meramec Community College; [occ.] Secretary; [pers.] Concentrate on the moment . . . Remember it always.; [a.] Fenton, MO

AGUILERO, HELEN BROWN
[pen.] Helen Aguilero; [b.] August 20, 1944; Fonddulac, WI; [p.] Sebastian and Marie Post; [m.] Santos German Aguilero; December 2; [ch.] 5 sons, 1 daughter; [ed.] GED 1991 College of Lake county; [occ.] Quality Assurance Inspector; [memb.] American Legion Auxiliary; [oth.writ.] Several unpublished; [pers.] If you take care of and help others God will take care of you.; [a.] Waukegan, IL

AGUINALDO, ALICIA MERCEDES A.
[b.] July 22, 1969; Quezon City, Philippines, [p.] Jose Aguinaldo (deceased), Alicia Velasco Agatop; [ed.] St. Peters College (BS/CS/DP), St. Peters College (MBA/MIS); [occ.] Unemployed; [memb.] St. Peter's College Alumni Association; [oth.writ.] Unpublished poems written from senior year in high school "A Special Friend or Best Friend" "My Teachers", "My Parents", "My Only Love", submitted "A Beautiful Sunny Day" to the Poetry Guild to be considered for publication; [pers.] I got the idea of writing poems from reading some literacy books during my senior year in High School.; [a.] Springfield, NJ

AHLERING, MICHAEL THOMAS
[pen.] Michael Thomas; [b.] October 28, 1981; Fullerton, CA; [p.] Mike and Nancy Ahlering; [ed.] Currently high school junior at Sunny Hills High School, Fullerton CA; [occ.] High school student; [memb.] Future Business Leaders of America, Sunny Hills High School Varsity Footbal team, Fullerton Recreational Riders (Equestrian), Republican Club and Computer Club; [hon.] 1st Place S.C. F.W.C. Literary contest in poetry and essay contest, F.B.L.A. second place, state of California C.S.F., Student of the Month, Silver Medal Chemistry; [a.] Fullerton, CA

AJULUC, AMANDA U.
[b.] June 21, 1962; New York; [p.] Michael and Janet; [ch.] Jason; [ed.] Hunter College in New York City; [occ.] Accountant; [oth.writ.] Several poems published in some magazines; [pers.] Constantly pray for world peace, most importantly, for all the children.; [a.] Dorrance, CA

ANZALONE JR., CHARLES JOSEPH
[b.] Frebruary 19, 1969; Niskayuna, NY; [p.] Charles Joseph Anzalone Sr.; Diane Bell Paige; [m.] Michelle Virginia Anzalone; May 6, 1989; [ch.] Arielle Maria, Amanda Shelbi, Ashley, Gabrielle Melissa; [ed.] Schalmont High School, Schenectady Country Community College; [a.] Schenectady, NY

ARAGON-VANDEVENTER, STEPHANIE NICOLE
[pen.] Mercedes Benzo; [b.] July 5, 1976; Decatur, IL; [p.] Mark and Angela Vandeventer; [m.] Stephen Daniel Aragon; March 25th 1997; [occ.] Full-time Child Care Provider; [oth.writ.] Poem in "Isle of View."; [pers.] Writing has always been my personal way of expressing my personal feelings. I give much respect to all writers. My biggest inspirations in life our my mother, father, siblings, and my beloved husband Stephen.; [a.] Thornton, CO

ARBUTHNOT, NANCY C.
[b.] May 28, 1923; Patoka, IN; [p.] Charles and Berniece Chappelle; [m.] Edwin (deceased 1989); June 18, 1949; [ch.] Indiana Business College, Attended dance conventions. Studied with George Zoritch Ballet Master, children's literature class, Univ. of Evansville; [occ.] Retired dance instructor, at present teaching ladies ballet class/ adult ballroom class; [memb.] Inactive member Dance Masters of America, St. Louis, MO. Chapter, taught dance in Evansville and Tri State 40 years; [hon.] Various dance awards from local organizations, citizen of the month award for the re-opening of Mesker Amphitheater Evansville, IN, which had been closed for 20 years, presented several shows there; [oth.writ.] "Mommy Let's Do Ballet" 17 pages of poetry and illustrations describing my teaching methods. Am in the process of mailing manuscript for copyright; [pers.] The above work was written as a request by Prof. of children's literature, Vardine Moore, Univ. of Evansville as a project 10 years ago.; [a.] Princeton, IN

AREL, MELISSA LYNN
[b.] April 1, 1981; Hollywood, FL; [p.] Michael and Maryse Arel; [ed.] Bristol Eastern High School—Junior; [memb.] Rock Church of Farmington Valley; National Art Honor Society; [hon.] Northeast M.S. outstanding in Art; Bristol Eastern H.S. excellence in English and contemporary systems; honor roll at Bristol Eastern H.S.; [pers.] My poems are the reflection of my soul and inspired by my love and gratitude to my saviour, Jesus Christ.; [a.] Bristol, CT

BALLARD, ROYCE W.
[pen.] Royce W. Ballard; [b.] April 2, 1984; Houston, TX; [p.] James Ballard, Edna Ballard; [ed.] Kinkaid Middle School (8th grade); [occ.] Student; [memb.] Kinkaid Choir, Kinkaid Band; [hon.] Science Fair award, sports awards in track and field; [oth.writ.] none published; [pers.] My writings are inspired by current and historical events, as well as personal experiences.; [a.] Sugarland, TX

BANNOW, KYLE S.
[pen.] July 7, 1984; Riverside, CA; [p.] Mark and Debbie Bannow; [ed.] Student at Chemawa Middle School Riverside, CA (8th grade); [occ.] Student; [memb.] Arlington Little League; [hon.] Participant in school (college sponsored) AVID Individual Determination; [a.] Riverside, CA

BARKER, KATHERINE JOAN
[pen.] Kate Barker; [b.] March 1, 1950; Africa, Zimbabwe; [p.] WM. and V. Marie Barker; [m.] September 6, 1975; [ch.] Jeffrey Pagan; [occ.] Ph.D. Candidate University of Arkansas Accounting [memb.] United Presbyterian Church; [oth.writ.] Too numerous to include; none have been published to my knowledge.; [pers.] The time is at hand.; [a.] Fayetteville, AR

BARNARD, STACY ANN
[b.] December 5, 1978; Binghamton, [p.] Robert Barnard, Linda Potenzino; [ch.] Victoria Rebeca Barnard; [ed.] High Junior Graduate Class of 1997; [occ.] Burger King, Binghamton; [memb.] Ross Memorial Presbyterian Church of Binghamton; [oth.writ.] "He Will Never Abandon You", In The Book War Cry; [pers.] I write my poems in hopes that someday my poems may help other people realize they are not alone in life and they can survive.; [a.] Binghamton, NY

BATKAY, ADAM FRIK
[pen.] Adam McKay; [b.] December 5, 1970; New York, NY; [p.] William Batkay, Viiy Batkay; [ed.] Montclair High School, Montclair State University; [occ.] Student Assistant at MSU Library; [hon.] Had a play I wrote in a playwriting workshop put on in 1994; [oth.writ.] Poems and stories published in school literary magazines; [pers.] Assume nothing. I try to write diction with twists to it. It makes it more interesting you write and read.; [a.] Caldwell, NJ

BATTAGLIA, REBECCA
[pen.] Rebecca Battaglia; [b.] July 18, 1980; Ocala, FL; [p.] Rick and Lori Battaglia; [ed.] Catholic Elementary School: St. Joseph's Catholic Harrison Performing Arts High School; [occ.] Student; [memb.] FCA, Varsity Soccer Team, Student Arts Council, Thespian Society, Ambassadors in Missions; [hon.] Presidential Scholars, Daughters of American Revolution Report, D.A.R.E. Essay, High Honors, Honors, Principals Award for Literature, named Best Writer of Graduating Class; [oth.writ.] I always writing about life, other subjects—mostly, observations become plays or emotions become a poem. Not many are titled; it all just flows.; [pers.] The moment your writing stops coming from your heart is the moment it becomes lost, the truth is hidden and you find you've accomplished nothing.; [a.] Barton, FL

BAUMGART, KURTIS
[pen.] Kurtis Baumgart; [b.] December 9, 1975; Anaheim, CA; [p.] Karen Baumgart and Walter Baumgart; [ch.] (1) Savannah R. Green; [ed.] GED, Community College, Santa Rita High School, Tucson AZ, PIMA Community College, Tucson, AZ; [pers.] Dedicated to my beautiful daughter, Savannah, who inspired me to write this.; [a.] Newport Beach, CA

BELISLE, STEPHEN
[b.] Edward and Marie Belisle; [ed.] BSME - Clarkson University, MBA - Clarkson University, U.S. Army Ranger School, U.S. Army EOBC; [occ.] Law Student, the George Washington University; [memb.] Toastmasters International; [hon.] Clarkson University Levinus Clarkson Award, United Nations Service Medal, Armed Forces Expeditionary Medal, Presidential Scholar - all semesters; [pers.] The greatest of mountains can be moved one shovel at a time.; [a.] Washington, DC

BENHAM, KIMBERLY NICOLE
[b.] July 17, 1980; Atlanta, GA; [p.] Gregory and Catherine Grant; [ed.] Camden County High School; [occ.] Student; [memb.] National Field Archery Assoc.; [hon.] 2 State Indoor Archery Championships, 2 Regional Indoor Archery Championships, 4th place 1997 Indoor National Archery Championship; [a.] Kingsland, GA

BENJAMIN, GAYLE V. DANCY
[b.] December 23, 1946; [p.] Isaih and Essie Dancy; [m.] Kenneth M. Benjamim, Sr; May 20, 1967; [ch.] Michelle, Michael, Marc; [ed.] Julia Richman High School University of the Virgin Islands; [occ.] English teacher, Charlotte Amalie High School St. Thomas, VI; [memb.] American Federation of Teachers, National Alliance of Black School Educators, Association for Supervision and Curriculum Development, Schomburg Social for the Preservation of Black Culture; [hon.] Graduated Magna Cum Laude - University of the V.I. - Award - Extra Mile Award, Charlotte Amalie High School; [oth.writ.] Poems published in Sea Breeze, U.V.I. Literacy Mag. 1991-1992; Daily News Article "A Clarion Call, We Are Family." Curriculum documents: "The Relationship of Environment to Survival," "Linkages: The Contributions of Virgin Islanders to the Harlem Renaissance";

[pers.] My writing expresses my belief in the greatness of my African ancestry. I have been greatly influenced by the Harlem Renaissance writers.; [a.] St. Thomas, VI

BENNETT, H. GLENN
[pen.] H. Glenn Bennett; [b.] April 27, 1947; Trinidad, WI; [p.] Ruby and Hugo Bennett; [m.] Dawn A. Bennett; August 31, 1997; [ed.] BA Architecture Pratt Inst.; [occ.] Architect Fine Artist (Painter, Sculpture and printmaker) writer, songwriter, digital artist; [memb.] Industrial Design Society of America; [hon.] New York City, Playground Design Award, Art Award; [oth.writ.] Essays on structural philosophy and norphology, plays, songs, and poetry; [pers.] That there is the need for us to be about a synthesis of mind, body and spirit that makes us evolve as we express visions to positively offend our honey and others on it.; [a.] Brooklyn, NY

BENWELL, FRANK PAUL
[b.] December 29, 1928; Michigan City, IN; [ed.] Graduate of Isaac C. Elston High School, Indiana University (A.B. and A.M. in Spanish); [occ.] Retired; [memb.] Grale Church (Member of Church Council), International Society of Poets; [hon.] Dean's List, Phi Sigma Iotha; [oth.writ.] Several articles and book reviews when teaching at the University of South Dakota (1959-1963) Poem published in Saints Herald (1965) An article in a trade journal when working in the hearing aid business (1973); [pers.] I try to enhance one's self-esteem. I gave the four-year old Grace Church the money to buy the elementary school I attended in the 1930's, a building built on land donated to the city by my paternal grandparents in 1914.; [a.] Michigan City, IN

BERNHEIMER, JASON J.
[b.] June 3, 1986; Medellin, Columbia; [p.] Allan and Deborah Bernheimer; [ed.] Pound Ridge Elementary School, graduated June 1997. Now attending Fox Lane Middle School; [occ.] Student; [hon.] Won essay contest on "What Memorial Day Means To Me" May 1997 (Town of Pound Ridge); [pers.] Writing is fun . . . I hope to grow with it and use it in my future.; [a.] Pound Ridge, NY

BICKFORD, TRACI
[b.] June 3, 1980; Elmhurst, IL; [p.] Sharon Bickford, Ed Bickford; [ed.] Lake Park Hill School; [pers.] What doesn't kill you make you stronger.; [a.] Itasca, IL

BISS, JAMIE
[b.] January 4, 1986; Hackensack; [p.] Lynne and Glenn Bliss; [ed.] 6th grade; [occ.] Student; [memb.] Student Council, Tweety Bird fan club; [hon.] First honors every year from first through 5th grades. Cheering awards, softball awards, soccer awards, basketball awards, gymnastics award; [pers.] I write discriptions and have a great imagination.; [a.] Wanaque, NJ

BITSON, GARY
[pen.] Lance Pentagrasp/Lance Freeman; [b.] September 04, 1953; Shelby, MI; [p.] Arthur Bitson and Cista (Rought) Bitson; [m.] Cindy (Boes) Bitson; January 5, 1974; [ch.] Wyatt Arthur, Benjamin Franklin, Rebecca Lynn, Joshua Clay, Betsy Lou, Mary Bell, and Samuel Mead; [ed.] Shelby High School; [occ.] Friar/Freelance writer, poet, lyricist, philosopher, and composer; [memb.] NLP Distinguished Member, Member of International Poetry Hall of Fame, 3 Editor's Choice Awards from NLP, selected several times for poems upon NLP's Sound of Poetry; [hon.] Note above; [oth.writ.] Several poems published in numerous volumes of the NLP's Anthology Series; [pers.] To prove through nature, word, history, and Christ the reality of God, and saving grace to mankind upon acceptance and repentance to the requirements of truth.; [a.] Baldwin, MI

BLUE, CONNIE
[b.] August 8, 1955; Memphis, TN; [p.] Noel Don and Lenelle Anderson McDonie; [m.] Ivy Petrie Blue III; June 9, 1985; [ch.] Pete, Max, and Teddy, Ivy Petrie IV, Brian Maxwell, Benjamin Taylor; [ed.] Vermilion High, N.VA. Community College, The American University; [occ.] Business Officer Manager; [memb.] Mount Vernon U.M. Church U.M.W; [hon.] Grand Cross of Color; [oth.writ.] Short Story, Matthew, Mark and Luke ask "Why do we have to go to church"; [pers.] Why do we look to the abstract when life and the greatness of earth is so amazing in itself with all its miracles?; [a.] Alexandria, VA

BLUMER, RHONDA K.
[b.] August 22, 1953; Algona, IA; [p.] Easter and Elead Wegner; [ch.] Stephanie and Karilyn Jordan; [ed.] Iowa Lakes College; [occ.] Registered Nurse; [hon.] Dean's List Soroptomist Scholarship Hoink Scholarship; [pers.] I thank God for my inspirations: Frank, who gives me the feelings to put into words, and Stephie, Kari, and Jordi, whom I love.; [a.] Anaheim, CA

BOEGLIN, JULI
[pen.] Juli; [b.] February 13, 1982; Bradenton, FL; [p.] Eugene and Judith Boeglin; [ed.] Currently in the 10th grade (class of 2000) at Cardinal Mooney Catholic High School in Sarasota FL. Have had 11 years of Catholic education; [occ.] Student; [pers.] Any goal worth setting is worth achieving. Surround yourself with those who amuse you and nothing will keep you from your dreams.; [a.] Bradenton, FL

BOOTH, CELINA
[b.] February 11, 1981; [p.] Craig and Susanne Booth; [ed.] Currently a Junior at Ponaganset High School; [memb.] Ponaganset High Cheerleader, Students for Social Awareness, Youth to Youth; [pers.] I'd like to thank Nany Smith for her continuing support and encouragement. She made me realize poetry comes from the heart and soul.; [a.] Chepachet, RI

BOWEN, AMY LYNNE
[b.] February 17, 1974; Bremen; [p.] Joan Tucker and Jim Bowen; [ch.] One daughter Miriah; [ed.] Bremen High, 1 year of Cosmetology at Elkhart Career Center; [occ.] Graphics Installer (On Motorhomes); [hon.] Editors Choice Award for "David" Poem. Regional finalist 1991 in Cosmetology; [oth.writ.] David; [a.] Nappanee, IN

BOWMAN, RETHA
[b.] May 4, 1966; Jacksonville, FL; [p.] Obie and Joyce Bowman; [occ.] Child Care Specialist; [pers.] Allow yourself to travel in my writing. Grasp life. Sow Love, Reap Joy.; [a.] Jacksonville, FL

BRADBURY, MELISSA
[b.] May 25, 1980; Scottsdale, AZ; [p.] George, Paula Bradbury; [ed.] Pioneer Elementary, Cactus High School - Class of 1998!; [occ.] Student, children's horseback riding instructor; [hon.] Academic letter for honor roll, Renaissance Program gold and silver, 3rd place poetry contest - Jr. year, Cactus High #1 student award, Leadership Awards; [oth.writ.] Writen several other poems for pleasure, and entered many in school contest. 4th grade winner "Slithering Snakes and Slimey Frogs"; [pers.] "Emotion, Life, and people make poetry possible. Write yourself onto paper and join your heart with a pen."; [a.] Glendale, AZ

BRATCHER, YVONNE MARIELLE
[b.] March 1, 1983; Lakeland, FL; [p.] David and Simore Bratcher; [ed.] Havelock High School; [occ.] Student; [memb.] Ducks Unlimited, SADD, Beta Club, Cherry Point Theatrical Ensemble, French Club, American Taekwondo Association, Saint Michaels Chapel Choir; [hon.] 6th Grade Camouflage Belt, All Country Choir, Solo Rating Superior, 5th Grade Green Belt; [oth.writ.] The Beach, Voices, Like a Flower, Grandmothers, published in county wide poetry contest; [pers.] Write from your heart, and your work will be stronger.; [a.] Havelock, NC

BROWN, ALEXIS
[b.] April 14, 1983; San Antonio, TX; [p.] Ross and Christine Young; [ed.] Sagnalie Junior High School; [occ.] Student; [memb.] Junior Honor Society; [hon.] Honor Roll; [oth.writ.] Two poems published in the anthology "Treasures"; [pers.] Poetry soothes the mind, soul and heart. Society may say its not good, but in your mind it is.; [a.] Federal Way, WA

BROWN, CHARLOTTE
[pen.] Char or Charlie; [b.] March 8, 1984; [p.] Jeanette and Michael Brown; [ed.] I am now attending Voyager Middle School and am in 8th grade.; [memb.] I am part of a Camp Fire group along with 3 other girls. They are great and so is our leader.; [hon.] I own only one award. It is a first place ribbon that I won in 5th grade with my shuttle relay team; [oth.writ.] I am now in the process of writing a mythological adventure, with my step-mom Julie; [pers.] Not meaning to brag, but I am not always that smooth at writing. I have had many blocks. Those are the toughest to get out of.; [a.] Everett, WA

BROWN, ERICA
[b.] January 14, 1980; Oil City, PA; [p.] Pete and Kathie Brown; [ch.] Alix Brown; [ed.] Parkersburg High School; [occ.] Student at Parkersburgh High School; [pers.] Only you can decide what your future will bring, so make it good.; [a.] Parkersburg, WV

BRUBAKER, LEO N.
[b.] November 11, 1917; Harvey, IA; [p.] Leo and Myra (Nace) Brubaker; [m.] Deceased; [ch.] Rondoll and Kimberly; [ed.] BA, University of Maryland; [occ.] USAF (retired); [memb.] United Methodist Church (Foundry), Washington, DC; [hon.] Air Medal with Oakleaf Clusters in WWII, many combat ribbons; [pers.] Let's do our best for God and man.; [a.] Reston, VA

BUI, TARA
[b.] September 17, 1984; Houston, TX; [p.] Hal V. Bui and Linh T. Nguyen; [ed.] Vista View Middle School Yamaha Music School (piano); [occ.] Student; [memb.] Vista View performing Arts Group; [hon.] Ocean View school district outstanding young author award; [oth.writ.] None that have been published; [pers.] I just simply do my best, because with my best I know I can never fail.; [a.] Fountain Valley, CA

BURKE, MIKE
[b.] July 2, 1979; Blue Island, IL; [p.] Denise Uraski, John Burke; [ed.] High School Graduate; [occ.] Poet, writer; [oth.writ.] "Hate My Town" in Through Sun and Shower; [pers.] I dedicate this poem to my best friend Mark. Without him life would be a lot less interesting, and I like to say make every moment of your life have meaning because the future's uncertain and the end is always near.; [a.] Evergreen Park, IL

BUSH, TAMMY S.
[b.] February 8, 1978; Washington, DC; [p.] Mr. and Mrs. George Bush; [ed.] Graduate of Bryan Station Senior Lexington, KY; [occ.] Dietetics and Nutrition, Pine Meadows Nursing Home; [memb.] Main Street Baptist Church Shapes Coed Fitness Center; [pers.] Through my writings, I am able to express what I see, feel, and experience in everyday life. I have learned in writing to never give up—in every effort if you try hard enough it will be recognized someday; thanks to writers such as Longston Hughes and others.; [a.] Lexington, KY

BUTTER, DOLORES
[pen.] Dee Bee; [b.] November 18, 1913; Jersey

City, NJ; [p.] John Frieda Klink; [m.] Charles Butter; December 31, 1933; [ch.] Three; [ed.] 2 Years High School; [occ.] Retired; [memb.] AARP, Democratic Club; [oth.writ.] A few poems; [pers.] My husband and I both became interested in poetry when the children were in grade school, needed a little help. He is deceased but left never let us.; [a.] Bayonne, NJ

CABRERA, JULIA SOTO
[pen.] Julia Soto; [b.] March 19, 1951; Dallas, TX; [p.] Ruth and Celestino Soto; [m.] Jose Cabrera; September 20, 1975; [ch.] Esperanza and Joseph Cabrera; [ed.] High School N.R. Crozier Tech. Assoc. in Arts and Science - El Centro College, also attended Dallas Baptist Univ. and Paul Quinn College—all are in Dallas; [occ.] Part-time Political Consultant and Civic Volunteer; [memb.] Board member and officer of Metro Dallas YWCA and City of Dallas Housing Finance Corp. also United way of Dallas Fund Allocation Committee member: Member of the National Council of La Raza; [hon.] 1969 "Most Valuable Staffer Award for Journalism by the Dallas Times Herald - High School Category; [oth.writ.] Many letters to the editor to Dallas Times Herald and Dallas Morning News. Wrote articles for high school and college newspapers/publications; [pers.] Writing is influenced by life experience and the human condition. Writers whose works influenced me are John Steinbeck, Thomas Hardy, Victor Hugo, Emerson and Thoreau; also influenced by life sayings of the elders.; [a.] Dallas, TX

CALDWELL, BRIANA
[b.] February 23, 1980; Yuba City, CA; [p.] Pat and David Caldwell; [ed.] Senior at Nevada Union H.S.—Honors English classes, as well as advanced math and science; 3.93 G.P.A.; [occ.] Student / Secretary at Dr. Kallmans Medical Office; [memb.] Secretary of California Scholarship Federation. Key Club member. Junior Auxiliary. Youth Educator Program. HIV/AIDS Awarness; [hon.] American Legion Aux. Essay contest - 2nd place Sophomore yr., 1st local and regional - junior yr. Girls State Alternate. Golden State in Biology. Who's Who Among American High School Students, 3 years in a row; [oth.writ.] Poetry / Journal on my own time. Essays for classes. Nothing yet published; [pers.] "In all 10 directions of the universe. There is only 1 truth."—Zen; to me, nothing is more important than the truth of oneself.; [a.] Penn Valley, CA

CAMPBELL, ADRIAN
[b.] January 11, 1981; Beaufort, SC; [p.] Lynann Campbell and Edward Campbell; [ed.] I go to New Smyrna Beach High School. I am a Junior; [hon.] I got awards for playing basketball and for maintaining the honor roll all year; [oth.writ.] I can't name all of them, but I am always writing stories and poems; [pers.] My parents and friends knowing that I could do really well helped me. They always encouraged me.; [a.] New Smyrna Beach, FL

CARFAGNO, LINDA R.
[pen.] Linda R. Carfagno; [b.] October 23, 1958; Wilkes-Barre, PA; [p.] John and Maria Romanchick; [m.] Steve Carfagno; May 10, 1986; [ch.] Lauren Nicole Carfagno; [ed.] Belleville High School; [occ.] Homemaker, Angel Enthusist, Crafter; [pers.] May the angels watch over each one of us, and bring light and love into our hearts, and peace into our lives.; [a.] Middletown, NJ

CHURCH, ELAN
[b.] October 13, 1983; New York; [p.] Athene Church, Tracee Lovett; [ed.] Pace Academy (High School); [memb.] National Junior Honor Society, Band, Pace Academy Volleyball Team; [hon.] A lot; [oth.writ.] Waterfalls published in the Anthology of Poetry by Young Americans; [pers.] "The past is gone—you can't change it. The future isn't here—it may never come. Today is a gift—that's

why they call it the present."; [a.] Marietta, GA

CHURCHWELL JR., GARY W.
[pen.] Gary W. Castro; [b.] July 17, 1974; Los Angeles; [p.] Gary and Kathy Churchwell; [ed.] Bachelors of Science in Biology at the University ofCalifornia, Riverside; [occ.] Medical Student at the University of Medicine and Dentistry at New Jersey; [memb.] Golden Key National Honor Society, Medical Society of Pediatrics, American Medical Association (AMA); [hon.] Editor's Choice Award for poem "Love"; Dean's List; [oth.writ.] Many poems published in NLP, poems published in University newspaper, Novel written called "No Trespassing" that is in the process of publication.; [pers.] This poem reflects the inner stirings of disturbed and lonely hearts of young people and how those feelings can erupt into something damaging for all of society.; [a.] Voorhees, NJ

CLAPP, DONALD
[b.] August 15, 1931; Northampton, MA; [p.] Elmer and Maxine Clapp; [m.] Betty J. Clapp; June 30, 1956; [ch.] David and Donna; [ed.] Northampton H.S Oberlin College, Boston U., School of Fine and Applied Arts; [occ.] Retired; [memb.] Green Valley Poetry Soc., Church Choir; [a.] Green Valley, AZ

CLARK, DONNA
[b.] August 7, 1939; Des Moines, IA; [p.] Audrey, Dick, Simpson-Clark; [ed.] 11th Grade in High School; [occ.] Songwriter, Shoe Dealer; [oth.writ.] "Our Missing Angels", "My Beloved Tulsa", "Faded Roses"; [pers.] Writing poetry has been my lifetime dream. I wrote a poem when younger; didn't go for it. I wouldn't give up; 5 years ago I saw an ad in magarine, a Record Company made 1st contract recording—"Our Missing Angel"; [a.] Tulsa, OK

CLIPPARD, LES
[b.] January 16, 1982; Gastonia, NC; [p.] Harold and Gail Clippard; [ed.] 10th Grade; [memb.] Fellowship of Christian Athletes; [pers.] "In the course of life one may struggle, but in the end we see it was worth it all."; [a.] Iron Station, NC

COLEBANK, DALE
[b.] June 13, 1930; Mentor, MN; [p.] Robert L. and Esther A. Colebank; [m.] Loita J. Walker; December 13, 1951; [ch.] Molly, Kathleen, Melissa, Shannon and Collin; [ed.] Tigard Ore, Union High School, self-taught music and minister; [occ.] Retired Longshoreman, piano tuner; [memb.] Jehovah's Witness; [oth.writ.] Sunday Sermon in The Independent Republic WN; [pers.] I try to answer, just how does this work? How can I do it? And How will this benefit my friends and neighbors?; [a.] Woodburn, OR

COLEMAN JR., WILLIAM
[b.] Birmingham, AL; [p.] William and Jeanette Coleman; [ed.] University of Alabama at Birmingham, Michigan State University, University of Alabama; [hon.] Clarion Writing Workshop; [oth.writ.] Poetry published in Aura magazine; [pers.] Writing is thought made manifest. To do it well is to truly be immortal.; [a.] Adger, AL

COLLEY, RICHARD K.
[pen.] Dick Colley; [b.] July 4, 1942; Nampa, ID; [p.] Kenneth H and Agnes R. Colley; [m.] Connie J. Colley; July 1, 1995; [ed.] Central High Oregon State University (B.S.), Lane Community College (A.S.), Oregon College of Education (Post B.S.); [occ.] Shoes Associate, Wal-Mart, Eugene, OR; [memb.] First United Methodist Church. Formerly Lions Club and Toastmasters Club and Demolay; [hon.] Sales contest winner; High school Letterman Club, Member of Award-winning band, Third place, High School Distric Wrestling, Second place, Junior High Poetry contest; [oth.writ.] Letters to the editors (published), song parodies for sales meetings, wrote poems For Birthdays, Engagement

(roast), and Sympathy on Death of Uncle; [pers.] The common thread among all the arts is the excellence by which knowledge of a media's discipline and perceptiveness of reality fuse into something we call beauty.; [a.] Springfield, OR

COLLINS, CHRISTOPHER M.
[b.] November 11, 1970; Ft. Walton Beach, FL; [p.] Bob and Sandy Collins; [ed.] High School Graduate, some college Cottawa High School 1985-1986, Aurora Central Catholic H.S. 1986-1989; [occ.] U.S. Army; [hon.] 1982 Illinois Member of Young Authors Conference in Recognition of a Short Story "The Mysterious House"; [pers.] Destiny is the product of self-evolution or no evolution.; [a.] Ft. Drum, NY

COLWELL, LARRY W.
[pen.] Mr. C; [b.] February 8, 1945; Washington, DC; [p.] Lenora Wiggins; [m.] Neldra Colwell; June 28, 1969; [ch.] Dennis James/ Annel Lenita; [ed.] D.C. Teachers, Trinity College, UDC, M.A. in English, M.A. in Admin and Supervision; [occ.] English teacher, Evans Middle School; [memb.] Omega Psi Phi fraternity, D.C.C.T.E; [hon.] Who's Who Among Teachers in America, Who's Who Among Students in Colleges and Universities; [oth.writ.] choral readings, short stories; [pers.] I believe that difference between the good and the great is the extra effort.; [a.] Washington, DC

CONRAD, SARA
[b.] July 16, 1983; San Jose, CA; [memb.] Mission Dance and Performing Arts; [hon.] Several Young Author Awards won in the years 1991, '92, '94 and '95 (First award recieved in second grade); [oth.writ] Poetry published in an anthology (Treasures), and short stories available in Fremont School and public libraries; [pers.] I write to motivate and inspire others. My dream is to help other people accomplish their dreams. "Write what you know".; [a.] Fremont, CA

COOPER, ALYSSANDRA MICHELLE
[pen.] Alyssandra Fox; [b.] March 3, 1969; W. Monroe, LA; [p.] Dan and Judy Fulton; [ch.] Jeremy Alynn Cooper, Jaysen Alexander Cooper; [ed.] Parkway High School, Kansas State University (BA) Texas Southern University (Law); [occ.] Student, writer; [memb.] Golden Key National Honor Society, Who's Who; [hon.] Who's Who Among American Colleges and Universities, Dean's List, Golden Poet Award 1986; [oth.writ.] World of Poetry Golden Poet 1986, published on-line, currently writing a book; [pers.] "I have learned that success is to be measured not so much by the position that one has reached in life, as by the obstacles which he has overcome while trying to succeed."—Booker T. Washington; [a.] Houston, TX

CORMIER, ALFRED
[b.] June 17, 1972; Meriden, CT; [p.] Ronald and Nancy Cormier; [ed.] St. Bernard's High School, Loyola College of Maryland, Assumption University in Bangkok, Thailand; [occ.] Full-time student, Emperor's College of Oriental Medicine; [hon.] B.S Degree in Biology, Dean's list Honors '92 and '93; [pers.] In my writing, I strive to reflect the world as it would be seen through a sheet of crystal.; [a.] Mar Vista, CA

CUNNINGHAM, CARLEY NICOLE
[b.] September 15, 1987; Baton Rouge, LA; [p.] Cassandra and John Cunningham Jr; [ed.] 4th Grade Oak Knoll Elementary School—Cary, IL; [occ.] Student (4th Grade); [memb.] Prairie Club Chorus; [hon.] Presidential Award for Physical Fitness; [oth.writ.] I write poems to go with the artwork in my art class. These have been displayed throughout my school, and my art Teacher has video-taped me reading them aloud.; [pers.] I really appreciate the earth and all its wonders. I never take it for granted. I express my love for the earth in my writings.; [a.] Cary, IL

CURREY, JENI
[pen.] J. Currey; [b.] May 24, 1981; Lone Star, TX; [p.] Kelly Currey, Dawn Lilley; [ed.] Hughes Springs High School; [occ.] High School Student; [oth.writ.] My other writings have not yet been seen.; [pers.] I try to put all my thoughts in my writing. How I feel is what I write about. Writing seems to be the only way for me to express myself.; [a.] Hughes Springs, TX

CURRY, KELLI
[pen.] Kelli; [b.] January 2, 1981; Findlay, Ohio; [p.] Todd and Alice Curry, Trina and John Cooper; [ed.] Junior year in high school of Carroll High School in Ft. Wayne, Indiana; [memb.] Member of Carroll High School Band, Drama Club and I was involved in Girl Scouts for ten years; [hon.] Silver Award in Girl Scouts, and was invited to meet poet Helen Frost at Manchester College in Manchester, IN.; [oth.writ.] During my Sophomore year in high school, a couple of friends and I published a poem book called Awakenings: Poems About True Life.; [pers.] No matter now horrid the outside world is, always remember that you can escape any time you want through your mind and inner self.; [a.] Ft. Wayne, IN

DAIGNAULT, KATE
[b.] March 21, 1982; Springfield, MA; [p.] Philip and Mary Daignault; [ed.] 1996 Graduate of St. Mary's School, Ware, MA; Presently a Sophomore at Cathedral High School, Springfield MA; [occ.] Student; [memb.] Cathedral High Community Council, R.O.O.T.S Organization, Red Cross Certified Life Guard, Cathedral Jr. Soccer player; [hon.] 1997 V.F.W. Forest Park, Springfield MA Past District Essay Winner; [a.] Ware, MA

DAMICO, JOSEPH S.
[pen.] Joe Domico; [b.] March 6, 1920, Sicily, Italy; [p.] Isabella and Salvatore; [ch.] Paul, Jenny, Matt and David; [ed.] M.A. (Public School Admin.); [occ.] Retired; [hon.] Quarter Finalist American Song Festival, Lyric Competition V; [oth.writ.] Many but I didn't submit them for publication. This is my first published.; [pers.] See the beauty in the flowers that grow on weeds, and the beauty in the shades and shapes of living creatures—all of which were ordered by supreme design.; [a.] Escondido, CA

DANIELS, KATHERINE
[pen.] Kathie; [b.] July 25, 1962; New York; [p.] Paul and Kathryn Speckenbach; [m.] Engaged; about 2 years from now; [ch.] Tara Marie and Joseph Paul; [ed.] St. Andrew Avelino (Elm) Flushing High School Suffolk Comn Coll. Norrell Health Care; [occ.] Mother, Retired Nurse (Spine Injury); [memb.] "Blessed Hope Ministry"; [hon.] None as of this writing.; [oth.writ.] I have many other poems I hope to publish someday.; [pers.] "Inspiration comes when theLord decides "It's Time.";[a.] Flushing, NY

DARRELL, PATRICIAN ANN
[pen.] Patti Hall; [b.] April 6, 1956; Mpls., MN; [ed.] MS Telecommunications St Mary's University; Speech BA-79 MN; [occ.] Director of Ops. and Sales-11 years quit 1-'97, Entertainer, Master of Ceremonies, Singer, comic; [memb.] Real Estate License-'86, Toastmaster, National Ceboofor Geocosmic Research, American Federation of Astrologers; [hon.] Toastmaster of the Year, Scholarships, Corporate Policy # 1 Nationally Procedures, (800 employees received employee of year #1), Poetry Corner #1; [oth.writ.] Thesis "Human Inside The Mail Box", Numerous other poems locally; [pers.] Poetry is music with its lyrics and timbre-rhythm is the conductor of this ochestration; Poets: Jim Morrison, Dylan; [a.] Mpls., MN

DAVIS, CHUCK
[pen.] Chuck Davis; [b.] December 14, 1953; New

York; NY; [p.] Mr. and Mrs. Sidney J. Davis; [m.] Linda Davis; March 8, 1987; [ch.] Stephen, David, Laurie, Chuch Jr., Alex, Veronica; [ed.] Benjamin Franklin High School, John Jay College; [occ.] Fraud Investigator, Human Resource Administration, New York; [oth.writ.] One poem published by the National Library of Poetry and several unpublished poems and original lyrics; [pers.] I always enjoy writing for other people pleasures, to give them a lift mentally, emotionally and spiritually. My inspiration coming from life's givings.; [a.] Laurelton, NY

DE LA CRUZ, ELIZABETH
[pen.] Sissy; [b.] April 24, 1979; San Jose; [p.] David and Sari; [ed.] High School Graduate, currently attending San Jose State University, Majoring in graphic design; [hon.] Art Logo on Art and Wine Festival; [a.] San Jose, CA

DEITRICK, ANNIE
[pen.] Annie Joe; [b.] Saint Ann's Day; Scranton, PA; [occ.] Aspiring and poet writer; [pers.] I am an incurable romantic. I adore writing. I have written two books. My boyfriend Joe is my greatest inspiration.; [a.] Dunmore, PA

DERLIN, BRUNO
[b.] February 19, 1965; Genoa, Italy; [p.] Italo E Enza Derlin; [ed.] New Utrecht High School, Center for the Media Arts, The School of Visual Arts, New York, New York; [occ.] DJ / Independent Film and Music Producer; [hon.] Scholastic Achievement Award in Bilingual Studies / Best Achievement in Editing - Short subject video / CMA; [oth.writ.] Various screenplays, including one produced feature, and the soon-to-be produced romantic comedy One Week 'til Next Year; [pers.] In my writing I wish to capture the essence of the tiny magical moment, which is always—"write here, write now!"; [a.] Brooklyn, NY

DESA, INES
[b.] October, 22, 1972; Madeira, Portugal; [p.] Fernando and Maria Desa; [ed.] Finished high school in Peabody, MA, and finished Cosmetology school at Blaine in Boston, MA; [memb.] The North Shore Medical Center Foundation; [oth.writ.] I have other poems but they've never been published or entered in any contests.; [pers.] I try to express myself through my poems. "Rain" was written after I was diagnosed with Leukemia, I am now doing better because I had a bone Marrow transplant.; [a.] Salem, MA

DESILVA, FENTON F.
[b.] January 1, 1920; New York, NY; [p.] Fenton F. and Christine DeSilva; [m.] Hilda M. DeSilva; August 29, 1941; [ch.] Fenton III, Michelle and David; [ed.] Some College, Hunter, NYC; [occ.] Retired Pub. Accountant retired Pvt. Investigator, former Rev. Off.; [memb.] A.A.R.P., N.C.S., S.P.L.C.; [hon.] Golden Poets, World of Poetry; [oth.writ.] Poems published in newspapers, magazines, anthologies, etc.; [pers.] Strive for joy on your arrivals, and tears at your goodbyes.; [a.] New York, NY

DICKENS, NEXELDA
[pen.] Nexi; [b.] Panama; [p.] Marva and Ernest Dickens; [ed.] Currently attending Long Island University, Towards a BA in Business Management; [pers.] My parents are my inspirations. They are my support. Little things that are meaningless, I find beauty in them. I was raised in Brooklyn, NY. I came to the U.S. when I was a little girl. I'm 28 yrs. old, I'm learning new things every day. Those qualities are what keeps me going in life. Life is too short to be so sad, angry and fighting. We should look forward to wonderful moments with family and friends.; [a.] Brooklyn, NY

DIETRICH, STEVEN M.
[b.] August 15, 1963; Concord, CA; [p.] Sharon

Dietrich, Doug Stinehagen; [m.] Maria Dietrich; November 11, 1989; [ch.] Stephanie Helena, Christian Anthony; [ed.] Helena High, Community College of the Air Force, Emory Riddle University; [occ.] United States Air Force Title, Technical Sergeant; [memb.] World Tang Soo Do Association, Non-commisioned Officer Assoc. Life Saving Assoc. (Germany); [hon.] Air Force Commendation Medal (3 times awarded) Non-commissioned Officer of the Quarter (4 times in career) Quality Initiative Award, Numerous Suggestion Initiative Awards (Air Force); [oth.writ.] Several Poems, though unpublished to date; [pers.] In 16 years of honorable military service, I've seen more good in people than bad, my writing is much influenced to that end; [a.] Ramstein Air Base, Germany

DILIBERTO, LUKE
[b.] December 11, 1979; Englewood, NJ; [p.] Joseph Diliberto, Diane Diliberto; [a.] Matawan, NJ

DITMER, HOWARD
[pen.] Happy wonderer; [b.] July 8, 1923; West Milton, OH; [p.] Delpbert C. and Anna Johana Ditmer; [ed.] 10th grade and 3 month special course, police training; [occ.] Retired worked at Monarch Machine Tool, Mow Monarch Lothers; [memb.] Life Member National Rifle Association, Sidney Wesleyan Church, Triple A; [hon.] 1970 Most Active Member, Shelry County Auxiliary Police (now deactivated); [pers.] I wrote this poem about a girl I knew over in Ireland in the 1940's. It was also written about my, and Lady in Sidney—she was the one who inspired me to put the words on paper.; [a.] Sidney, OH

DOBRZYNSKI, LUCILLE
[pen.] Lucy; [b.] December 14, 1951; Michigan City; [p.] Wallace Dobrzynski and Patricia Dobrzynski; [m.] October 3, 1970; [ch.] Five; [ed.] Graduated 1971 a degree in Medication Aid and Certified Nurses Aid; [occ.] QMA - CNA - Visiting Home Nursing; [memb.] National Hemophila Foundation of NY for children born with Hemophillia, an bleeding disorder; [oth.writ.] I have written articles, for Hemologi Magazine, for myself on personal comments; [pers.] Love and love others and enjoy life be happy within your own soul, and it will prevail throughout life.; [a.] Michigan, IN

DOOLEY, PHALA LORENE
[pen.] Jimme Lynn; [b.] May 17, 1936; Canvas, WV; [p.] Paul Willard and Ethel Ruby (Vance) Dooley; [m.] Widowed; May 15, 1955; [ch.] Lawana Kaye, Jayenita Ann, Michael Dwayne, Andrea Lorene, Jason Paul; [ed.] 12 yrs regular, 2 yrs Voc Tech, 4 College Voc Tech, Manhattan Kansas, Rose State, Midwest City, Oklahoma, 10 yrs. Crieghton Grade and High Criegthon, W, VA, 2 yrs Huntington Grade and High, Chillicothe, OH; [occ.] SSI Parkson's Disease; [memb.] Christian Church, Lifetime License to teach "Little League Baseball with NYSCA, Historian 2 yrs. Rose State College; [hon.] Best Character Award " May 16, 1991 in "Right On Time" Rose State College, Midwest City, OK; [oth.writ.] Too numerous to mention. Have written poetry and songs since age 15; [pers.] Lack Algebra and Physical Science in getting degrees in both Drama and Psychology won "Best Character Award" May 16, 1991. I'm in heaven on stage.; [a.] Watonga, OK

DUFFY, DANIELLE
[b.] October 20, 1980; Mineola, NY; [ed.] Sacred Heart Academy, Hempstead, NY; [occ.] Student, 12th grade; [memb.] National Honor Society; [pers.] I feel that the poetry I write thrives on both the good and bad experiences of my past.; [a.] Long Beach, NY

EALLONARDO, WARREN
[b.] May 7, 1974; Syracuse, NY; [p.] Patricia and Samuel Eallonardo; [ed.] B.S. in English at the State

University of New York College at Brockport; pursuing Masters Degree; [occ.] High School English Teacher; [memb.] Sigma Tae Delta International Honor Society for English Majors; [hon.] Editor's Choice Award for Outstanding Achievement in Poetry Presented by the National Library of Poetry, 197, Dean's List; [oth.writ.] 2 Others published poems in similar books; [pers.] We are all caught in a machine that does not care about us. We bleed our isolated grief through many sources. This poem is one of mine. Don't lose heart.; [a.] Brockport, NY

EDWARDS, TASHEENA
[b.] July 9, 1982; Philadelphia, PA; [p.] Cassandra D. Edwards; [ed.] Currently attending Overbook High School. Bebber Middle School and St. Carthage; [occ.] Student; [memb.] Lindon University Laser Program; [hon.] Science, Track, Poetry, Singing, and Softball; [oth.writ.] Several poems, and writings in the school newspaper; [pers.] I hope to let the world know about my great poetry, and let other young people aknow that they can do the same as me.; [a.] Phialadelphia, PA

EISENHAUER, TRAVES W.
[pen.] Traves W. Eisenhauer; [b.] May 21, 1973; Jacksonville, FL; [p.] Edwin S. and Ella A. Eisenhauer; [ed.] Orange Park High School St. Johns River Community College; [occ.] Lending Officer in Local Credit Union; [oth.writ.] Several poems unpublished include, "I Think It's Going To Rain Today", "The Offering", "The Dolphin's Way", "David's Song"; [pers.] The brillance of a poet is not determined by his ability to write against paper, but to move the pen he is holding as to create the words.; [a.] Orange Park, FL

ERICKSON, CINDY
[b.] August 7, 1981; [p.] Rick and Sandra Erickson; [ed.] High School Student; [occ.] Student, Cheerleader; [hon.] Certificates, Varsity letter; [a.] Hopedale, OH

FEARS, JENNIFER
[b.] October 1, 1984; Bellville, IL; [p.] Debbie Noonan and Guy Fears; [ed.] 7th Grade at North Jr. High School. Elementary School was Hollywood Heights; [occ.] Student; [memb.] Tepee; [hon.] I have a different variety of awards from different activities.; [a.] Caseyville, IL

FERGUESON, MAURINE
[b.] February 9, 1938; Park City, UT; [p.] Oren J. and Marie Anderson; [m.] Ernest R. Fergueson; December 19, 1967; [ch.] 2 sons, 4 daughters; [ed.] High School, night courses in accounting experienced chef; [occ.] Owner/manager M.J.N. Inc. rentals; [memb.] Kiwanis Club of Layton, Layton Area Chamber, Military Affairs Chair, Layton Safe Community Davis County Sheriff Association Northern Apartment Association of Utah; [hon.] Layton Achievement Award, Lifetime ISP and Society of Poets, Hall of Fame. International Poet of Merit, 1995, 1996 and 1997. Twice on "Poetry Today" radio in New York City, NY; [oth.writ.] Several anthologies "My Attitude" Book Nobel House "Poets Are People" Self-published, manufactured by Watermark Press, 3 more poetry books ready for publication, magazine, newspapers; [pers.] I don't know why I can write poems as revealing as mine are. I'm glad I can. I finally got someone to pay attention to me. Now if I can only get my husband to read them.; [a.] Layton, UT

FERRERA, POLICARPIO FADERON
[b.] January 26, 1940; Romblon, Philippines; [p.] Nazario F. Ferrera, Cecilia F. Ferrera; [m.] Estrella Villafuerte Ferrera; May 16, 1972; [ch.] Cezar, Richelle and Americhard; [ed.] Banton High, PLM (University); [occ.] State Employee, CA; [hon.] Local Organization; [oth.writ.] Published English, Non-English verses, articles, unpublished graduate works; [pers.] I attempt to explore my surround-

ings natural splendor, retrace the footprints of time and life's paradox through writing. The works of great poets have been my inspiration and source of aesthetic inclination.; [a.] Los Angeles, CA

FITZPATRICK, SYLVIA
[b.] January 23, 1965; Ireland; [p.] Joan Bourke, Ray Fitzpatrick; [ed.] Loreto Abbey, Palkey Co., Dublin, Ireland, Columbia College, Hollywod, CA, Film School; [occ.] Writer, Aritst; [memb.] MPSC Local 839, Student Member Academy of Arts and Sciences; [oth.writ.] Screenplays and short stories; [pers.] My poems and writings reflect personal experiences within my life. I offer the greatest gratitude to my parents who encouraged me when I needed them the most. Creativity, imagination, and sensitivity—without these, our dreams would not exist.; [a.] Burbank, CA

FOGLESONG, TIMOTHY J.
[b.] September 8, 1956; Los Angeles; [ed.] Perpetual; [memb.] 3rd Generation American; [hon.] Ad Altere Dei; [oth.writ.] Dei-O; Gretchen, Of truth and kin, How to Slay a Dragon in 5 Easy Steps, Kith vs. Kin; [pers.] Concerning my poem "Lief Law" and the powers that be described there in, I am baptized to the 1st born in the 2nd victim of the 3rd.; [a.] Whittier, CA

GABOURY, JESSICA
[b.] May 5, 1977; [p.] Mark Gruetter and Cynthia Gaboury; [ed.] Third year at Portland Community College, Graduated from Franklin High in 1995; [occ.] Student; [memb.] The Christian Fellowship, the Drama Club and Creative Writing Club; [hon.] Received a letter for Drama at Franklin High; [oth.writ.] Hope to direct and produce self-written plays, and further enhance my poetic boundaries; [pers.] I would like to thank my mother, father, step-mother Corrine Gruetter, brother Derek Gruetter and grandparents Donald and Margaret Gaboury for their love, support, and encouragement. My poetic influences are mainly the Bard himself, Walt Whitman and Robert W. Service.; [a.] Portland, OR

GALLAGHER, KRISTIN
[b.] October 15, 1979; New Brunswick, NJ; [p.] Alison and Thomas; [occ.] Student, Juanita College, Huntington, PA; [hon.] Who's Who Among America's High School Students; [oth.writ.] Poem to be published in Treasures. I used another of my poems as lyrics. I wrote music for it and played the piano and sang it with the Old Bridge H.S. concert choir; [pers.] My journal goes everywhere with me. I hear music in the words.; [a.] Old Bridge, NJ

GALVEZ, EMILY
[pen.] Emily Montalvo Galvez; [b.] November 25, 1967; Manhattan NY; [p.] Johnny Montalvo, Vicenta Soto; [m.] Cornelio Galvez Jr; November 5, 1988; [ch.] Joshua, Andrew, Emily Y; [ed.] Bassick High School (Ed) University of Alaska Anchorage Associates in Human Services, Emphasis Family and Youth BA in Psychology; [occ.] Travel Broker; [hon.] Several Appreciation Awards for devoted and incluable services rendered for youth, and children; [oth.writ.] Several poems to family and friends; [pers.] My poems are my deepest expression of my values, thoughts, and feelings. I attribute all of my talent to the one I love with all my heart and soul, Jesus Christ.; [a.] Anchorage, AK

GARCIA, CARINA MARIA
[b.] March 24, 1983; Thornton, CO; [p.] George and Maria Garcia; [ed.] High School, Holy Family; [occ.] Education, sports; [a.] Thornton, CO

GARCIA, SOPHIA
[b.] March 14, 1979; Fresno, CA; [p.] Richard and Lupe Garcia; [ed.] High School Graduate, College Student now at CSU Fresno; [hon.] National English Merit award, Architectural Graphics award,

world history award, American History/Lit. Award; [oth.writ.] I write poetry on my own, but none has ever been published.; [pers.] I write with my own feelings and experiences. My experiences give me the motivation to write.; [a.] Fresno, CA

GAUDET, VIOLET F.
[pen.] V.F. Guadet; [p.] Arthur and Violet Hodgdon; [m.] Joseph R. Gaudet; Married now for thirty-six years; [ch.] Christina and James, and five beautiful grandchildren; [a.] A degree in Mental Health Technology; [occ.] Retired, but not from writing; [oth.writ.] I have several published poems and a short story called "Sweet Jennifer," and I am presently working on a novel titled "Women, Children and Their Conversion Vans."; [pers.] "Sunrise, Senset, Sunsrise, Sunset, Swiftly Goes the Years." I do take time to stop and smell the roses, to take in a deep breath of fresh air, to look up at the blue sky and dream upon a puffy, soft white cloud. I am alive.; [a.] North Andover, MA

GEISSER, ANN MARIE
[b.] February 11, 1965; Providence, RI; [p.] Earl and Anna Fiske Jr; [m.] Divorced; [ch.] Gary K. Geisser, II; [ed.] BS/BA Providence College, Prov. RI CNA Certified Nursing Asst.; [occ.] Operations Area Manager; [memb.] M.S. Society; [hon.] National Honor Society 1978-1979; [oth.writ.] "In The Darkness of The Light" Plus, numerous poems for my personal pleasure and fulfillment; [pers.] I write from the essence of my heart, which is reflected on my mind and portrayed in my poem's lines.; [a.] Warwick, RI

GEORGE, MARGARET
[b.] October 18, 1956; Ogden, UT; [p.] John and Lillian Handrahan; [m.] Joel George; April 25, 1997; [ch.] Ian Summerill, Brit Summerill, Jon Mahoskey, Lela Mahoskey; [ed.] Cleafield High School; [occ.] Medicaid Eligibility Representative for State of Utah, Dept of Health; [memb.] Second Baptist Church; [oth.writ.] 1st try at publishing. Have a collection of over 90 other Christian poems; [pers.] My poetry is a gift from God and I praise Him for it. "With the gift that He gave me hallelujah's I raise, for my God is worthy of the highest praise!!"; [a.] Ogden, UT

GIGLIO, ELIZABETH ANNE
[pen.] Elizabeth A. Giglio; [b.] April 30, 1983; Seattle, WA; [p.] Joel and Steve Giglio; [ed.] Entering 9th grade at Weather Wax High School Aberdeen WA; [occ.] Student; [memb.] Students against violence everywhere President second year running. 7th Street Kids, Driftwood players, Grays Harbor Young Authors. Voulenteer work for Grays Harbor Historical Seaport, Lady Washington, and Grays Harbor Special Olympics; [oth.writ.] Students Against Violence Everywhere Newsletter and Gray Harbor Young Authors; [pers.] I wrote "We love You Kurt" after serious thought of the impact Kurt's life had on my life, the impact of Kurt's death on my life made my realize now special everyone is. I believe Kurt Donald Cobain deserves this recognition. He truly was love.; [a.] Aberdeen, WA

GLASSPOOL, LISA
[b.] June 18, 1986; Gilroy, CA; [p.] Gary Glasspool, Laura Glasspool; [ed.] Currently 6th Grade Student of Luigi Aprea; [occ.] Girl Scout of Santa Clara County; [hon.] Principal's roll for 3 years, Top 20 finalists in pagents of America Scholarship; [a.] Gilroy, CA

GLEESON, DONNA
[pen.] Donna Gleeson; [b.] August 25, 1949; Chicago, IL; [p.] Roy Ana Laurayne Jones; [m.] Mark Galetka; April 1, 1994; [ch.] 2: Amy, Kelly Ann; [ed.] St. Gregory H.S.; [occ.] Homemaker; [pers.] I wrote "Angel in Disguise" in dedication to my youngest daughter, Kelly Ann, who was killed in a car accident on July 12, 1996.; [a.] Holcombe, WI

GODBEY, KAYLA
[b.] March 3, 1984; Danville, KY; [p.] Sherry Godbey and Neal Godbey; [ed.] I'm a 8th grade student at Boyle County Middle School.; [memb.] Jr. Beta Club; [hon.] Jr. Beta Club; A and B Honor Roll; [a.] Danville, KY

GOLDBERG, ROBERT T.
[pen.] Bob Goldberg; [b.] April 18, 1931; Indianapolis, IN; [p.] Victor M. and Rose P. Goldberg; [m.] Harriet P. Goldberg; November 27, 1955; [ch.] Beth Louise, Julie Ann, and Ellen Rose Goldberg; [ed.] Butler University Indianapolis; [occ.] Retired; [memb.] I.H.C., J.C.C., J.W.F. (Over 50 years); [hon.] Gold Medal from Culver and Shortridge High School; [oth.writ.] On Father's Day Just a Memory to Bethie; [pers.] "Israel" was a gift to my daughter Julie Ann Goldberg-Herman in 1985. She now has five daughters and five sons plus two grandsons living in Israel.; [a.] Indianapolis, IN

GOLDMAN, BERNICE F.
[pen.] Bernice G.; [b.] November 9, 1913; Tolado, Ohio; [p.] William and Lillian Fineger; [m.] Mark Goldman; June 1, 1934; [ch.] Susan Apter; [ed.] College Graduate "La Salle" Judy Gorman College Graduate Boston Un. V.P. New York Life V.P. Chase) Manhattan Bank; [occ.] Retired—Graduate Scholarship in English at Toledo U.; [memb.] Cancer-Heart Fund, Alzheimer Fund; [hon.] Nat'l. Library Poetry 1993; [oth.writ.] Cox Newspaper Reporter in N.Y. for all the Arts- Musems - Movies - Plays - Ballet; Wrote 4 original Musican-Performed in Chicago, Detroit, Toledo, Kentucky; [pers.] I firmly believe in poetry as a key to psychological stress and that it's a comfort for everyone so inclined.; [a.] Palm Beach, FL

GOMES, CAROL
[b.] May 29, 1951; Cambridge, MA; [p.] Joseph and Virginia Tramentozzi; [m.] Joseph Gomes; September 26, 1969; [ch.] Michelle, Anne, Joe Jr, Scott, and Mike; [ed.] Graduated with honors Southeaston Technical Nursing School; [hon.] Editor's Choice Award 1997 from the National Library of Poetry for poem entitled "Life" published in Tracing Shadows; [oth.writ.] Poems published in "What We Do In Anguilla" which is a local newspaper in Anguilla, BWI; [a.] Lawrence, MA

GOODMAN, MICHAEL A.
[b.] June 30, 1974; Brooklyn, NY; [p.] Miles and Elaine Goodman; [ed.] Carmel High, Clinton College; [occ.] Firefighter; [memb.] Veterans of Foreign wars; [a.] Vandenberg AFB, CA

GRANQUIST, NILS
[b.] February 8, 1939; Gardner, MA; [p.] Edwin O. and Hilda I. Grandquist; [m.] Marilyn; August 25, 1990; [ch.] 6; [ed.] Garnder High School, Assoc. Degree—Culinary Inst. of America; [occ.] Business Analyst—Eds. Corp.; [oth.writ.] Children I Leave You, Walk with God, One Night in Fattey's Bar; [a.] The Colony, TX

GUINN, GREGORY KENDELL
[pen.] G. Kendell; [b.] December 18, 1958; Russell, KS; [p.] Mary Lee (Reigal), Charles Richard; [ed.] Roaring Fork High—Carbondale, Colorado; [occ.] Emission Testing Technitian; [memb.] Songwriters Club of America; [oth.writ] Other writing published National Library "Windows of the Soul"; [pers.] Knowing what you do best, is a great accomplishment, leaving what you do best, is a lifetime struggle. I always look inside for the answers.; [a.] Salt Lake City, UT

HAMDANI, EDDIE H.
[pen.] Eddie Hamdani; [b.] July 26, 1907; Atlanta, GA; [p.] Edna Gates and Willie Gates; [m.] Jeweldine Hamdani; April 12, 1992; [ch.] One step-daughter, Godfather of three daughters and two sons, 1 grandson; [ed.] 8th grade (mostly self taught);

[occ.] Retired; [memb.] Atlanta Masjid of Al Islam; [hon.] I was honored with a trip to Mecca, received an Appreciation Award Service to Al-Islam and the community, I received our youth award—Pioneer of the Year; [oth.writ.] I wrote articles as free contributions to Muslim Journal. I am looking forward to a book being published.; [pers.] I feel pleased to be dealing with the National Library of Poetry. I am a person who loves people, whether they are young or old, rich or poor. I am not just struggling just for self, but also for others.; [a.] Decatur, GA

HAMMONS, CLINTON
[b.] June 29, 1967; Barbourville, KY; [p.] Larry Hammons, Sue Cooper; [ed.] BA—Russian, U. of Kentucky; diploma—Defense Language Institute; diploma—USAF Radio School; [occ.] Navy veteran and E. KY University Grad. Student; [hon.] 2 US Navy Honorable Discharges, Numerous Navy Letters of Commendation, Joint Meritoriors Award (USN), Humanitarian Award (USN); [pers.] I would like to thank the Goddess Rhiannon who always watches over her children.; [a.] Richmond, KY

HANUSHEVSKY, IVANKA
[b.] May 12, 1984; Rochester, NY; [p.] George and Daria Hanushevsky; [ed.] Eight Grader at St. Josaphat School; [occ.] Student; [memb.] Plast Ukrainian, Yevshan Ukrainian Dance Group; [hon.] School field day awards First place in obstacle 32.1 sec; [pers.] I enjoy putting my feelings into words.; [a.] Rochester, NY

HARDEE, VIVIAN DUNN
[b.] July 31, 1931; Darlington, SC; [p.] James Frank Dunn and Pearl Lofton Dunn (both deceased); [m.] Ernest W. Hardee (deceased May 3, 1983); [ch.] Dianne Hardee Protor, Ernest W. Hardee, Jr. Robert Dean Hardee; [ed.] Andrews High School, Accounting Degree, Droughn's Business College, Columbia, South Carolina; [occ.] Teacher; [memb.] Former member of Screen Baptist Church, Maryville Section, Georgetown, South Carolina 1951-1971, church organist and choir director (Primary through Adult), church secretary, church-wide Women's Missionary Union President, Primary and Youth Sunday School Class, Sunday School Class Outreach Persons, Curren Missions Group I Facilitator, Young as Ever, Decorating Chaiman, Young and Restless, All at Baptist Church, Georgetown, South Carolina, Business and Professional Woman's Club; [hon.] Cum Luade, President's Roll, Teacher of the Month, Teacher of the Year, Editor's Choice Award in Poetry (The National Library of Poetry), Twenty Six Years of Outstanding, Dedicated Service to the Teaching Profession in Georgetown Country Public School System, Winyah Arts Association Exhibit (Prevost Gallery) Merit in Eloquence (3), Georgetown, South Carolina, Georgetown Country Fair first place in Arts and Crafts; [oth.writ.] Poetry published in "Wind in the Night Sky" by the National Library of Poetry, Owings Mills, MD, under the name Vivian Hardee Petrozzelli, "Your Day" P.423; [pers.] I am a Retired Teacher. In my writings, I enjoy drawing from my personal experience. The caring ones in nature intrigue me. I have a fondness for Emily Dickinson, Ralph Waldo Emerson, and William Faulker. I dedicate this poem to my parents, James Dunn and Pearl Lofton Dunn (both deceased), Andrews, South Carolina who were an inspiration for me to develop a life of fruition through education and Bible training. This is a lasting gift that enables me to more adequately and effectively express my thoughts and feelings. In all of this there was, is and will forever be God. He is first in my life. I like to paint on canvas, travel, listen to music, play the piano, do needlework, arts and crafts and sew. I am interested in most sports, especially golf. I practice regular chuch attendance and involvement, tithing, pledging above and beyond the tithe, and have a deep, abiding love for

family ties. Whatever your station in life may be and the acclaim you may or may not receive, keep telling yourself, "I'm not the best, but I'm trying each day to be the best." [a.] Georgetown, SC

HARLESS, CHARLEY
[b.] October 12, 1973; San Diego, CA; [p.] James G. and Mary D. Harless; [ed.] University of Alabama 1996 Computer Science; UCLA Computer Science; [occ.] Research Assistant in Lab. of Neuro. Imaging; [memb.] International Society of Poets, Association of Computing Machinery, Odyssey of the Mind; [hon.] Hon. mention for National Science Foundation Fellowship, AT & T Laboratories Summer Internship; [pers.] We cannot achieve greatness without love, honor, and knowledge.; [a.] Westwood Village, CA

HARRING, MARGARET
[pen.] Amy Auther; February 25, 1948; St. Louis; [ed.] High School Graduate; [occ.] Retired PBX operator; [hon.] President Club awards 4 years in a row; [pers.] I love sharing my feelings and thoughts with others. This poem is dedicated to my wonderful parents.; [a.] India, MO

HARRIS, FAWN
[b.] November 10, 1984; Verron Hospital; [p.] David Harris, Kim Foley; [ed.] Torrington Middle School; [pers.] If it wasn't for my best friend Emily Steina who gave me the Idea of what kind of poem I should write, it wouldn't be the way it is.; [a.] Torrington, CT

HART, CONNIE DENISE
[pen.] Connie Hart; [b.] February 17, 1958; Greene County; [p.] James Delma Hart and Ann Haroper, Hart; [m.] James Richard (Ricky) Turnage on November 23, 1978; July 7, 1983 (deceased) July 2, 1992. Linwood Earl Smith on July 9, 1983; 1988 (deceased) February 2, 1996; [ch.] Liza Leigh and Amanda Nicole Smith; [ed.] Greene Central High School in Snow Hill, NC graduated in 1976; [hon.] Outstanding singing and musicianship award, member of French Club, Pep Club, School newspaper staff in journalism, member girls chorus, varsity chorus, varsity singers, Ramblers ensemble group, two bands: Essence and Blue Satin, and gospel group: the Hart Family. School volunteer; [occ.] Musician, piano, organ music for weddings, etc. mother of two daughters; [memb.] The National Children's Cancer Society, Northshore Animal League for homeless pets. The Hart Family Gospel Singers. Top Records Songwriters Association of Nashville, TN. Member of Frot Run Freewill Baptist, Holiness Pentecostal Church of Shine Croosroas, Snow Hill, NC played for choir and church, traveled for years with my family to sing and play music at churches and school singing, albums with the Hart Family, by Delma Hart, Ann Hart, Connie Hart, JB Hart, Mary Hart, Triplette, Stevet Michael Hart, Billy Head, (Jim Head deceased) all of Greene County. Honored with Editor's Choice Award 1996 presented by the National by the National Library of Poetry, for poem "The Heart is Forever," won talent contest at age 12 in Dunn, N.C. on piano, won girls chorus award 1974, varsity singers award 1976, The Carol Hichs Memorial Scholarship, diploma from Greene Central High School graduated 1976; [oth.writ.] Include "Daddy's Got a New Heart," gospel song about my Daddy, Delma Hart, also wrote a country song 1996, "Out Here in the Country." Also published in book 1996 Portraitd of Life, an original poem, "The Heart is Forever." In "Tracing Shadows" book, an original poem "A Rare Jewel", about my Daddy 1997. This poem also won an Editor's Choice Award 1997. To come: "Hearts" a new poem for "Moments of Solitude." [pers.] I enjoy art in music, writing, drawing and life. I write every day. Poetry is my expression of the heart, my heart, memories made with my family and friends. My hobbies include music, fishing, camping, walk-

ing, writing and conserving our land and wildlife in any way I can.; [a.] Snow Hill, NC

HARTWELL, TRISHA ELIZABETH
[b.] December 1, 1972; Rochester, NH; [p.] Roger and Sheila Hartwell; [m.] Steven Gagnon; September 13, 1997; [ed.] Mascoma High, Keene State College; [occ.] Safety and Health Specialist; [memb.] American Society of Safety Engineers, National Safety Council; [hon.] Magna Cum Laude, Delta Mu Delta; [pers.] This poem, "Sand Storms," was written for my husband and I thank him for the inspiration.; [a.] Nashua, NH

HAWN, TIFFANY BROOKE
[pen.] Tiffany Broke Hawn; [b.] August 16, 1983; San Diego; [p.] Minnie and Marty Anderson; [ed.] 9th grade student at Santanna High School/ Grossmont District; [occ.] Student; [hon.] Softball all-stars, citizen of the month, honor roll ("A"), Most athletic awards for school; [oth.writ.] Personal little writings from 5th grade I used to write.; [pers.] I wrote my poem, "Loss of a Loved One", for my grandpa (Papa) and for anyone else who has lost a loved one.; [a.] Santee, CA

HAWS, ERNEST
[pen.] Ernie Haws; [b.] March 16, 1933; Amboy, IL; [p.] Erwin E and Alma E Haws, both deceased; [m.] Vercele S. Haws (deceased); June 11, 1955; [ch.] (8) eight (5 girls 3 boys); [ed.] 11th grade, quit high school to join the army in the year of 1952; [occ.] Retired because of health problems (on Soc. Security); (memb.) American Leigon post 453 here in Amboy, Member of Reynolds United Methodist Church in Rural Ashton; [hon.] Update in service battalion supply, from above update became water supply spec. Made battalion color guard etc. minor incentents; [pers.] I've always wanted to write a poem. Now, due to health problems, I would like to do more writing but at this time it is doubtful.; [a.] Amboy, FL

HAYES, MARK
[pen.] Aron Phoenix; [b.] Sept. 3, 1974; Pasadena; [p.] Kaye and Steve Sparks; [ed.] Literature Major at Sam Houston State University; [occ.] Student, Writer and Salesman at bookstore; [memb.] Society for Creative Anarchrism; [oth.writ.] Several poems, short stories and a novel yet unpublished; [pers.] My philosophy is best summed up in the words of Billy Joel—"It's all about soul."; [a.] Huntsville, TX

HAYWOOD, BEVERLY
[pen.] Bobbie-Dobbie; [b.] June 15, 1950; New Orleans, LA; [p.] Charles and Mable Zeno; [m.] Mr. Deed D. Haywood; January 27, 1989; [ch.] Franchon and Travell Gray; [ed.] Manuel Arts High School, Pasadena City College; [occ.] Sales Associate, United States Postal Service; [memb.] Combined federal campaign, WPCC Ministry of Helps; [pers.] Sometimes the words of others are articulated in such a way that the words are the only thing that will make a difference in this short span of time that we call life. I would like to be one of the people who brings love, happiness, and understanding to this world by bringing together poetry.; [a.] Palmdale, CA

HENRY, ROBERTA
[b.] June 21, 1961; Little Rock, AR; [p.] Milo Harvey and Jimmie Walkup Harvey; [m.] Russel Henry; January 24, 1987; [ch.] Josh Wesley; [ed.] Duncan High School, Duncan, OK, University of Oklahoma and Oklahoma City Unversity; [occ.] Mortgage Collection Counselor; [memb.] Smithsonian and The National Arbor Day Foundation; [oth.writ.] "Scooter," a poem written and dedicated to the memory of a friend's pet dog; [pers.] Writing offers a therapeutic approach to the exploration and expression of feelings in the research for healing. My influence comes from life's experiences, relationships, art, music, and

my family, including my Rat Terriers, Rachel and Maxina.; [a.] Oklahoma City, OK

HERBERT, CESARINA MARIA
[pen.] Cesarina Maria Rossetti; [b.] August 23, 1911; Castro, Italy; [p.] Julio Rossetti and Angela Frassa Rossetti; [m.] Divorced; [ch.] Rossett Herbert, Maiae Tumelty and Claren Herbert; [ed.] Burlingame High Interstate College of personlogy Dolores Premiere School of Cosmetology; [occ.] owner and manager of own properties; [memb.] Girl Scout Leader, Boy Scout Den Mother, American Red Cross Swimming Instructor, Earthquake Safety Program; [oth. writ] Best Poems of 1996, Spirit of the Age, A Muse to Follow, Where Dawn Lingers, Across the Universe, Best Poems of the '90s, Through the Hourglass, Sunshine and Daydreams, Amidst the Splendor, Frost at Midnight, Of Moonlight and Wishes, Essence of a Dream, Through Sun and Shower, Through the Looking Glass, Moments of Solitude; [pers.] In my writing, my goal is to express and project the basic reality of all life as life is presented to me.; [a.] Hillsborough

HICKS, DON L.
[pen.] Don Hicks; [b.] August 11, 1932; Marietta, OK; [p.] Delbert, Lucille Hicks; [m.] Shirley Trout; June 4, 1954; [ch.] Deanna Bansuelo, Sharon Hernandez, Angela Wilson, David Hicks; [ed.] B.S. Degree in Business Administration, Abilene Christian University - 1954; [occ.] Executive Director, Dallas Southwest Osteopathic Physicians, Inc; [memb.] Oak Cliff Lions Club, Dallas Concilio Hispanic Service Org., Oak Cliff Chamber of Commerce, Amber University Board of Trustee; [hon.] Oak Cliff Tribune Citizen of the Year Award, 1990. Dallas Baptist University Samaritan Award, 1990. Dallas Mayor Pro Tem, 1980-83. Dallas City Council, 1977-83, Dallas School Board 1985-86; [a.] Dallas, TX

HICKY, DAN MCHENRY
[b.] June 28, 1917; Nashville, TN; [p.] Louise McHenry-Dan Hicky; [m.] Hattie-Mina Reid; April 27, 1944; Mina, Dan, Stratton; [ed.] B.S. Business University of GA. Air Force Communication School, Air Force Comptroller School; [occ.] Col U.S.A.F (Ret); [memb] American Legion ,Blinded Veterans Assn. Lambda Chi Alpha (Frat) Air Force Assn., Sons of the American Revolution (SAR) Daidalien-Methodist Church; [hon.] Air Medal W/2 Oak Leaf Clusters, Meritorious Service Award, Legion of Merit, Diamond Homer Award F.P.S.); [oth.writ.] Weekly poem (The Poet's Corner) for the Madisonian newspaper.; [pers.] Completed 25 Combat Missions as a Fighter Pilot in World War II. After 25 years as a USAF Pilot, Glaucoma has left me legally blind. Not able to maintain so active a life, I have taken up poetry, which is now my main occupation.; [a.] Madison, GA

HOLLIS, HEATHER MICHELLE
[b.] January 6, 1978; St. Louis, MO; [p.] Keithand Mary Hollis; [ed.] Fox Senior High St. Louis Community College; [occ.] AT and T Teleservices Associate; [oth.writ.] Several poems—none published; [pers.] I gain a sense of strength through pouring my emotions onto paper. I would like readers to feel as if they have a haven in my writing and can somewhat relate.; [a.] Imperial, MO

HOPPE, WILLIAM
[p.] Al and Sharon Hoppe; [ch.] One child—Courtney Charon Hoppe; [occ.] Aircraft Maintenance Planner; [oth.writ.] The Suitor, Path of Life, Time and Memories, A Bottle of Wine, Soft Hands, Memory Lane, Whisper and A Woman I desire; [a.] Tempe, AZ

HOPSON, CAROLYN
[pen.] Cari; [b.] February 7, 1980; Franklin, PA; [p.] John and Eleanor Hopson; [ed.] Junior in High School; [occ.] Student; [hon.] Recognized by the Maryland Art Education Association as an emerg-

ing young artist for my paintings; [oth.writ.] other poems; [a.] Bowie, MD

HORSMAN, THOMAS
[pen.] F for Fom and H for Horsman; [b.] March 5, 1963; Portland, OR; [p.] Cherry Alice Horsman and Thomas Robert Horsman; [m.] Yvonne Bernadette Horsman; September 17, 1996; [ed.] Metro Learning Center, Portland, Oregon; I graduated in 1982. The school is from Kindergarten to 12th grade.; [occ.] Dietary Aide; [oth.writ.] Straight to the Point—haven't gotten it published yet, but I had it copyrighted; a book or poetry and illustrations; [pers.] If you don't stand for something you'll fall for anything.; [a.] Portland, OR

HOWELL, ROBERTA E.
[pen.] Bert; [b.] April 13, 1917; Due West, SC; [p.] Robert and Susie Ellis; [m.] Andrew Rendall Howell; June 14, 1942; [ch.] Rendall, Emil, Suzette; [ed.] A.B. French and English, M.A. (Lib) Johnson C. Smith Univ., Charlotte NC; NC Central University, Durham, NC. Retired Librarian, (membership) Member of American Association of University Women; Delta Sigma Theta; [memb.] Sorority; Timothy Darling Presbyterian; Alpha Kappa Sigma Honorary Scholastic Society; Superior rating in piano; [oth.writ.] I have written a few short stories and essays. Several have been published in the local newspaper.; [pers.] I like to write about ordinary happenings around me.; [a.] Oxford, NC

IGUS, GERTRUDE YOUSON
[pen.] Jackie Youson; [b.] March 28, 1954; Phoenix City, AL; [p.] Jimmy and Gertrude Youson; [m.] Lionel Eugen Igus; December 18, 1969; [ch.] Tyronica, Monique, Tarvie, Tretia, Victoria, Jeremy, Sharron, Madez and Joshua Igus; [ed.] Spencer High School in Columbus, Georgia Trombly Educational School in Detroit, MI Abundant life school of ministry in Michigan; [occ.] Evangelist; [memb.] Union Grove Baptist Church Abundant Life Church. Honor Society of Christian faith; [hon.] Grandson Awards of Melissa, Tony Jr. Satora, Malcolm Tarvie Jr. Willie Jr., Trent, Gary Eugene Jr. and Gabriel, whom all I love so dearly (and all the new births to come).; [oth.writ.] I'm published in The Rippling Waters anthology. Poems about my family and friends. Poem published in Ford Motor Co. magazine; [pers.] I write expressively of my deepest thoughts and feelings to make a different. In today's living and time, and also of times to come, blessings to all.; [a.] Detroit, MI

JANZER, AMY
[b.] June 12, 1980; Pittsburgh, PA; [p.] Roberta and Larry Yotter; [hon.] Writing award for poem about Kurt Cobain; outstanding attendance; [pers.] Everyone needs a friend, no matter who, what, or where they are.; [a.] Hebron, MD

JERRY, GERALD
[pen.] Jerry Wise; [b.] November 24, 1934; Freeport; IL; [p.] La Verne and Merle Wise; [m.] Nancy Wise; May 2, 1959; [ch.] Mark, Joel, Dan, Denise; [ed.] Dakota High School; [occ.] Retired Dairy Farmer; [memb.] Central Christian Church, Stephenson Co. Farm Bureau; [hon.] "John 3:16" published in The Isle of View, have a page on internet's Worldwide Web , The International Poetry Hall of Fame, The Wonders of God published in the Moments of Solitude; [oth.writ.] I have a collection of writings I put together in my own book "Rejoice In The Lord." I have had poetry in newspaper and newsletter publications; [pers.] All of my works are written solely for The Glory of God. All of the honors go to Him, because it is only possible to write because of the gift He gave me.; [a.] Freeport, IL

JIMENEZ, DESERIE
[b.] September 27, 1983; East Los Angeles, CA; [ed.] Currently Attending La Serna High School; [memb.] California Junior Scholarship Federation;

[pers.] I often try to use my family in my poetry especially my Tio Turi because he has inspired me to write poetry.; [a.] Whittier, CA

JOHNSON, GREGORY D.
[pen.] Greg Johnson; [b.] January 1, 1955; Arlington, VA; [p.] Richard Johnson and Theresa Johnson; [ch.] Dylan Grise; [ed.] St. John's, Loudoun Valley High, Northern VA College; [occ.] Locomotive Engineer CSX Transportation, Cumberland MD; [memb.] Trout Unlimited, Moose National Republican Committe, Fraternal Order of Police; [oth.writ.] Love, Hate, Death, and another published poem on God; [pers.] Most of my poems are based on the human experience.; [a.] Cumberland, MD

JONES, LAUREN
[b.] July 30, 1955; Tucson, AZ; [p.] Thomas Lauren Jones, Margaret Ann Snyder; [occ.] Data Specialist; [oth.writ.] Several Unpublished poems; [pers.] "I shall pass through this world but once. Any good therefore that I can do or any kindness that I can show to any human being, let me do it now. Let me not defend or neglect it for I shall not pass this way again."; [a.] Salt Lake City, UT

JONES, QUEENIE E.
[b.] November 9, 1917; Trinidad, WI; [p.] deceased; [m.] deceased; February 9, 1979; [ch.] two; [ed.] 2 year High School; [occ.] Retired; [a.] Brooklyn, NY

JONES, RONALD EDWARD
[pen.] Ron Jones; [b.] June 13, 1964; Roanoke, VA; [p.] Dorothy Jones and Willie Hurt Jr; [m.] Mary Ann Jones; September 14, 1996; [ed.] Patrick Henry H.S '82 Norfolk State University '88; [occ.] Editor in Sports Dept. Richmond Times-Dispatch; [pers.] My mother, who raised three sons by herself in a housing project, is my hero.; [a.] Richmond, VA

JORND, LISA
[b.] September 30, 1965; Ilinois; [m.] Tony Jornd; May 16, 1987; [ch.] Michael Long - 13, Anastacia Jornd - 10, Justin Jornd - 8; [ed.] William Penn Nixon Elementary, Prosser Vocational High School, Elgin Community College; [hon.] Dean's List at ECC (Com. College); [oth.writ.] Various poems - have written for other special occasions, create greeting cards for people, completing my first novel; [pers.] I believe somewhere between the good we expect from other mankind, and the evils that we find from it lies our own true self.; [a.] Elgin, IL

JOSEL, JACK
[b.] October 19, 1982; Hartford; [p.] Dr. and Mrs. Mark Josel; [ed.] Kingswood Oxford School, Avon Old Farms School; [occ.] Student; [memb.] Farmington River clean-up; [hon.] Most Goals—Lacrosse, Honor Roll, Most Penalty Minutes—Hockey; [oth.writ.] Untitled, all of them; [a.] Avon, CT

KAUFFMAN, JOHN W.
[pen.] The Sarge; [b.] August 3, 1926; Shamokin, PA; [p.] Deceased; [m.] Helen L.; June 3, 1952; [ch.] Sally Ann and John Raymond; [ed.] Shamokin High, Mil Tech School's Correspondence Courses; [occ.] Retired; [memb.] American Lgn., TREA, ISP; [hon.] NLP Editor's Choice Awards, Commendations, letters of appreciation for civ. and mil. employers, assortment of mil. medals; [oth.writ.] HS periodicals, correspondents NLP Anthologies; [pers.] 50 yrs of poetry attempts and the appreciation remains and I continue on. I feel quite gifted that I am enabled to somewhat fathom the literary arts of "the Bard." I forever endeavor to express what I feel, see and think through my seemingly endless rhyming.; [a.] Odenton, MD

KENNEDY, CATHLEEN A.
[p.] Ann L. And Donald V. Bacon; [m.] William J. Kennedy; [ch.] Heather Ann Kennedy-Estabrook;

[ed.] Oceanside High - Some Courses at Palomar College - Parker Truck Driving School - Life itself!; [occ.] Dispatcher/Office Manager, "Beckett Trucking, Inc", Escondido, CA; [memb.] MADD; [hon.] Volunteer - March of Dimes; [oth.writ.] Nothing published; [pers.] Life has always been my biggest influence, and my love of life my greatest drive to share that influence.; [a.] Vista, CA

KERLEY, MARY E.
[pen.] Mary Elizabeth Kerley; [b.] December 26, 1985; Hickory, NC; [p.] Diane and Barry Kerley; [ed.] Currently in 7th Grade at Jacobs Fork Middle School, Newton, NC; [memb.] Duke University Talent Identification Program. Library Club and Student Council; [hon.] President's Award for outstanding Acedemic Achievement, Music Achievement, four years highest Acedemic Grade Point Average, three years knowledge Master Team Awards, Physical Education Excellence Award and Participant in Lenoir Rhyne College's Summer Enrichment Program; [pers.] A lot of people have talent; only a few get discovered.; [a.] Vale, NC

KLUZ, ELYCE MARIE
[b.] February 18, 1981; Rockford, IL; [p.] Gary Kluz, Debbie Kluz; [ed.] Presently a Junior at Stillman Valley High School; [memb.] Stillman Valley High School Varsity Cheerleader, Track, Basketball, Outdoor Club, FFA, FHA, Chorus also AJQHA; [hon.] 1995 Meridian Jr High 81 m Hurdle School Track Record, 5th Place at state in 100m Hurdles. Ray DeVore Memorial Track Award; [oth.writ.] One poem published in the 1995 Anthology of Poetry by Young Americans called the Beginning of Life, also "Memories" published in Essence of a Dream by The National Library of Poetry; [pers.] To me the best time to write poems is when emotions are strong, because then the words just seem to flow onto the paper.; [a.] Rockford, IL

KUYPERS, MARY ELIZABETH
[pen.] Gramma Betty, Betty Kuypers; [b.] August 23, 1921; Montreal, Canada; [p.] Stuart, Madge Graham, [m.] Leonard Kuypers; January 8, 1949; [ch.] Trudi Lee Williams, Carol Leslie Beauvios; [ed.] High School, Business College, Mechanical Engineering Drafting Course, Writing for Children Course; [memb.] British American Club of S.W. Fla., Cape Hobby Club; [hon.] Scholarship in high school, prize winnning recipe in National Contest, prize winning recipe in local newspaper contest, honorable mention for sign design in National contest; [oth.writ] My recipes published weekly in local newspaper. Children's stories, The Mystery of the Unhaunted Castle, The Case of the Missing Mummy, Snowballs in July?, The Fabulous Floormat, The Cat That Lost Its Meow, A Different Kind of Watchdog, and numerous others; [pers.] Although much of my childhood was during the depression years, it was an interesting and exciting time. My parents deserve all the credit. Money was in short supply, but no one would guessed if from the way my parents (mostly my mother) managed. I rely upon my childhood memories, with embellishments and exaggerations, for many of my stories and poems.; [a.] Cape Coral, FL

LABELLE, JAMI
[pen.] Alex; [b.] January 3, 1985; Gainesville, FL; [p.] Michael G. LaBalle, Juana LaBellee; [m.] August 23, 1975; [ch.] Jami LaBelle; [ed.] Whittier Elementary, Menaul Middle School; [occ.] Student; [hon.] Honor Roll 4.0, Poetry Contest: $50 gift Certificate; [oth.writ.] No Dream, Screeching Creatures, Night Will Be No More, and many more; [a.] Albuquerque, NM

LANSDALE, NOELLE
[b.] May 23, 1985; Middletown; [p.] Marianne/Alan Lansdale; [ch.] Sister Nichole Lansdale; [ed.] 7th grade; [occ.] Student; [hon.] Honor roll; [pers.]

Hobbies: playing football, reading, collecting knick-knacks and stamps; [a.] Middletown, OH

LAYTON, MARY
[b.] January 2, 1983; Grand Prairie, TX; [p.] Anita D. Layton; [hon.] 1 Reading, 4 Bible Scripture Awards, 1 writing best imaginative story, 5 best behavior awards; [pers.] Down with Dope, Up with Hope; [a.] Memphis, TN

LEE, GEORGIA DANIELLE
[b.] August 30, 1985; New Jersey; [p.] George and Arttimeche Lee; [ed.] I.S. 72 (Richmond) 6th grade; [occ.] Student; [hon.] Various school certificates for writing; [a.] Staten Island, NY

LEE, HERBERT W.
[b.] April 10, 1905; Bethel, MN; [p.] Weston and Ruth Lee; [m.] Laura B. Lee; June 10, 1933; [ch.] Marlys. M; [ed.] High School, Dunwoody Night School, Night and Correspondence School, University of Minnesota; [occ.] I am retired from Federal Cartridge after 35 years as a production worker, machinist, and draftsman; before that I worked as a farmer, laborer and a 'Springer'; [memb.] Zion Luthern Church, Scorekeeper for a Whist Club that has been going for 50 years; [hon.] Salutatorian of my St. Francis Minn. High School, Class of 1923; [oth.writ.] History of origin of St. Francis H.S. in Minn. I am 92 years old and I am writing my autobiography in poetic form. So far I have approx. 40, 6-line stanzas; [pers.] I believe every poem should make a philosophical statement, tell a story, or record an event. I always enjoyed memorizing poetry. The Psalm of Life. The Raven, The Skeleton in Armur, Incident in a French Camp. How we carried the news from Ghent to Aix. When I was in the first grade, if we had a few minutes before recess or lunch hour, the room would recite poems from memory. I can still remember: "Dark Brown is the river, golden is the sand."; [a.] Anoka, MN

LEMMER, MICHELLE LEE
[b.] March 30, 1977; South Carolina; [p.] Deborah Schoenfeld, David Mrozinski; [ed.] Rosebank Elementary, Southwestern Christian School, Castle Dark High School (All in Chula Vista, CA), Still undecisive on future schooling and career goals; [memb.] American Legion Post 255; [hon.] Participant in the 1993 Tournament of Roses (parade). I've won various writing/poetry contests; [oth.writ.] I was a journalist for my high school newspaper, and also on the yearbook staff. I have my own personal book of poetry; with a total of 36 poems written by myself; [pers.] I'd like to give loving recognition to my little brother, Lance Lemmer - you are my inspiration. Also thanks to my grandparents, Aunts/Uncles, and most of all my mommy. With your love - all of the visions, difficulties, and expenses of a young girl becoming a woman. My poetry is mostly dedicated to my first love. Writing helps me to understand my feelings, and tends to calm the fear that I have to move on. Life is full of dreams . . . you've just got to believe in yourself with peace, and love and happiness.; [a.] Chula Vista, CA

LEVITE, MARCELLA
[pen.] Marcella Reid Levite; [b.] January 20, 1945; Brooklyn, NY; [p.] Jean and Edward Baranowski; [ch.] Louis, Patrick, and Lisa Jolaine; [ed.] Dickinson City High School, Matthew and Nicholas Hair Academy, Scranton, PA; [occ.] Training Director, Rivera Cosmetic Labs, Haddonfield, NJ; [pers.] This poem came from the heart! I wrote this poem for my daughter Lisa. It is exactly how I feel about her and how she lives her life. I'm so very proud of her. Thank you, Lisa, my Gem! - Love, Mom XO; [a.] Beverly, NJ

LEWIS, THAMER M.
[b.] December 8, 1933; Los Angeles, CA; [p.] Elder, W. M. and Sarah E. Harris; [ch.] Ardy,

Cheriee, Mark, Lisa, Derrick and William; [ed.] GED; [occ.] Retired; [memb.] KTLA TV; [hon.] Golden Poet Award in 1987 from World of Poetry; [oth.writ.] "It Was God's Will" "So Jesus Is Glorified Me", "Where Are You Going", "Time", "What Are You Doing", "The Prostitute" "Jesus My Lord", "Easter Morn", "Lisa", "Because I Love You"; [pers.] I love writing. I tell the truth in the poems, storys plays, and songs, I write.; [a.] Victorville, CA

LEWIS-RAND, AVONELLE
[pen.] Annette Lewis, Red Head; [b.] September 9, 1965; St. Kitts, WI; [m.] Michael Rand; [ch.] Jonathan-Michael, Brandon-Michael and Sean-Michael; [ed.] Trinity Government School-St. Kitts, Brooklyn College; [occ.] Nurse; [hon.] Outstanding Achievement in Poetry; [oth.writ.] Poems—Depression, Life, Auntie Joycie, My Sunshine—published in other Anthologies; [pers.] I believe that by sharing a small portion of my thoughts will change a life somewhere if only for a second. My writing have been inspired by my aunt, who has given her unconditional love and support.; [a.] Augusta, GA

LINDSTROM, LISA MICHELE
[pen.] Leo; [b.] August 8, 1961; Minneapolis, MN; [p.] Ward and Carol Engebrit; [m.] Jeff; July 25, 1992; [ed.] German, Literature, Grammar, Charles A., Lindbergh Sr. H.S., 1 year University of Minnesota, Literature; [occ.] Poet, Publisher, Housewife Logistical Events; [memb.] Charter Member, All American Eagle Racers, Distinguishd Member, International Society of Poets; [hon.] Over 20 Editor's Choice Awards from the National Library of Poetry, 3 Poet of Merit Awards from International Society of Poets and I was nominated and accepted a web page with the International Poets Hall of Fame; [oth.writ.] Inadequate Justice, Beginning Healing through poetry, 1st book. Publishing—Observing and Feeling While I am Healing, and I am presently writing, "Slamming the Ancient Door Forevermore to a Distant Shore"; [pers.] My personal experiences drive me to write most of my poetry. I also like the subjects of politics, nature, culture and people.; [a.] Yorba Linda, CA

LITTLEJOHN, ERIN
[b.] February 17, 1983; Carson City, NV; [p.] Diane Strong, Bob Strong; [ed.] Big Bear High School—Freshman Year 1997-1998; [memb.] Key Club, Interact Club; [pers.] My grandma always said, "Take time to smell the flowers."; [a.] Big Bear City, CA

LONGFELLOW, TABITHA C.
[pen.] Tabby; [b.] July 29, 1980; Maysville, KY; [p.] Eddi and Diana Longfellow; [ed.] I am currently a senior at Manchester High School; [memb.] Cheerleader, volleyball, 4-H, Softball, Beta club, spanish club, SADD, FFA, Student council, yearbook, Who's Who Among American teens, National Honor Roll Academy; [hon.] All-star cheerleader, all-star volleyball, all-league volleyball, most hustle in softball, greyhound award, best spiker award in volleyball; [oth.writ.] I have written over three hundred poems, but this is the first poem published.; [pers.] I feel I inherited my talent from an uncle, Henry Wadsworth Longfellow. Love to my parents To Dante for being my best friend and Larry for being who he is; XOXO to Ricky.; [a.] Manchester, OH

LOPEZ, CATHERINE E.
[b.] December 1, 1983; Santa Fe, NM; [p.] Antonio E. Lopez, Patricia B. Lopez; [ed.] 8th Grader—St. Michael's High School; [occ.] Student; [memb.] Santa Maria de la Paz Youth Group, Girl Scout of USA, choir; [hon.] Presidential Physical Fitness Award; [pers.] My only inspiration was my front yard tree and the expression in my heart.; [a.] Santa Fe, NM

LOPEZ, TAMMY L.
[b.] April 16, 1967; Catskill, NY; [p.] Chet and Linda Perry; [m.] Paul P. Lopez; June 16, 1991; [ch.] Joshua P. Lopez; [ed.] Coxsackie / Athens Jr.-Sr. High School, International Correspondence Schools; [occ.] Homemaker; [pers.] I would like to dedicate my writing to my son Joshua P. Lopez. Without him, it would not be possible for me to achieve such a goal.; [a.] Voorheesville, NY

LORIA, RUTH ANGELA
[pen.] Angie Loria; [b.] August 10, 1969; Elkins, WV; [p.] Dick Stalnaker- Grandfather; [ch.] Emily Jane Everhart; [occ.] Secretary; [a.] Nedgesville, WV

MAHON, MARY C.
[b.] June 26, 1919; [p.] John and Clara Koenigshoff; [m.] James J. Mahon, Jr; November 18, 1940; [ch.] Kathleen Auer, Judith Louden; [ed.] High school—Villa Angela Academy, Cleve OH, 1937, St. Vincent Charity Sch. of Nursing 1940; [occ.] Registered nurse, retired; [memb.] Served 3 years in Venezuela as Missionary nurse as a member of Papa volunteers for Latin America 1970, sponsored by Catholic Diocese of Cleveland. Completed over 50 years in various phases of the nursing profession; [a.] Clearwater, FL

MANESS, CARL MASON
[pen.] Carl Maness; [b.] January 31, 1951; Union, SC; [p.] Mason and Kathleen Maness; [m.] Janice (Deceased) January 15, 1992; March 30, 1985; [ch.] Aaron Mason Maness; [ed.] Four Years of Technical College-Spartanburg-Union High School- US Army Veteran; [occ.] Inmate of SCDC; [memb.] Buffalo Baptist Church SC; [oth.writ.] Unpublished; [pers.] I hope that gifted singers will add their music to my poems so that others will know how I feel about things, especially the forgiveness of God.; [a.] Buffalo, SC

MANGOLD, AMANDA
[pen.] Amanda Mangold; [b.] April 11, 1988; Barrington, IL; [p.] Michael and Joy Mangold; [ed.] 3rd Grade—Richmond Grade School Richmond, IL; [occ.] Student; [pers.] Love always, think deeply, play hard, have fun!; [a.] Spring Grove, IL

MANGUM, TERRANCE JAMES
[pen.] Tamerlane; [b.] September 3, 1979; Lancuster, PA; [p.] James and Paralee Mangum; [ed.] Jacksonville Senior High; wisdom of my mother and father; [occ.] Receptionist/Office Assistant in Family Business; [memb.] Religious Order of Sons and Daughters of Cornelius; [hon.] Presidential Physical Fitness Award; [oth.writ.] Working on completion of a Personal Book of Poems; [pers.] Men are made from the sands of the earth, I am made from the ashes of dead poets.; [a.] Jacksonville, NC

MARCELLA, MARY ALICE
[pen.] AKA Mary Alice Bailes, Mary Alice Bell, Alice Bailes Bell; [b.] July 23, 1922; Warren, OH; [p.] Angela Marie DeSanti Marcella DeWitt, Anthony Marcella (both deceased); [m.] Deceased; 1st November 19, 1941 and 2nd May 10, 1986; [ch.] Roger James Bailes and Faith Ann Taylor; [ed.] Graduate fo Warren G. Harding Sr. High, classes at Long Beach State, Orange Coast College Palomas Jr. College, American Institute of Banking, ABA Pre-Standard Certificate; [occ.] Freelance writer, entrepreneur owner of Marcella Press; [memb.] Lifetime member and founding president of LaQuinta Historical Society, Member of AMORC, Member of Desert Beautiful, Member of IPA; [hon.] Listed in 7 editions of Who's Who in California, the first edition of Who's Who of California Executive Women, and the 1992 edition of The International Who's Who of Intellectuals; [oth.writ.] Personality profiles and various news articles for Indio. Daily News, Warren Tribune Chronicle, an oceanside newspaper and oth-

ers. Songs: "Color Fills", "The World", "Forty Days and Forty Nights", "A Million Paths within My Mind", "Between You and Me", Book: Rhyme and Thought (self-published 1980) many unpublished poems and short stories; [pers.] The Spiritual quality rises above the physical, ultimately giving to humanity its individuality.; [a.] LaQuinta, CA

MARCHENA, SARAH
[b.] March 7, 1983; El Paso; [p.] Luther Marcena and Maureen Marchena [ed.] Maxin L. Silva Magnet High School for Health Care Professions; [occ.] Full-time student, children's software specialist of MHER International; [memb.] National Junior Honor Society, Healthy Occupation Students of America (HOSA); [hon.] (1994) Reflections Contest Literature, (1996) Reflections Contest Photography, Honor Student in Junior High School and High School; [oth.writ.] Several other poems; [pers.] If you strive to do your best, great things will come to you.; [a.] El Paso, TX

MARTIN, FAWN
[b.] December 14, 1984; Stockton; [p.] Frances Tapuro, Paul Martin; [ed.] First Nazarine Elementary, Claudia Landeen Elementary, Tyler Elementary, Daniel Webster Middle School; [memb.] Columbia House Records; [oth.writ.] I have several journals full of poems that I have just written down what came to my mind.; [a.] Stockton, CA

MARTIN, JASON
[b.] February 26, 1973; [a.] Marion, OH

MARTIN, JUDY ANN
[b.] August 21, 1952; Alabama; [p.] Lois Martin; [m.] Divorced; [ch.] James - 27, Jerry - 24, Rhonda - 21; [ed.] 9th grade; I don't have much education, but I have learned a lot in my lifetime. I have feelings, that's what it takes.; [occ.] Disabled; [pers.] I have always enjoyed poetry, but just never done anything with it, until my son was going through some difficult times I wrote the poems to help him get through them, he thanks me every day and I thank God for the strength.; [a.] Fulton, TX

MASARIE, SUSANNAH
[b.] Greensboro, NC; [p.] Jack and Gayle Masarie; [ed.] Western Guilford High School; [occ.] Student; [a.] Greensboro, NC

MAYHUE, VIRGINIA L.
[pen.] Gin; [b.] December 15, 1931; Wetumka, OK; [p.] Roy E. Ackerley, Pearl E. Atkinson; [m.] William W. Mayhue; November 4, 1960; [ch.] 7 by former marriage; 2 by Bill; [ed.] 12 Grade by G.E.D.; [occ.] Retired—Housewife, Nurse and Cashier; [memb.] Member of Lighthouse Church, Member of Womens Ministry at the Lighthouse Church; [hon.] Certificate of Determination Diploma from High School by G.E.D. Diploma from Nursing School N.E.C. National Education Center; [a.] Elberton, GA

MAYO, MARY
[pen.] Margaret E; [b.] September 2, 1984; Sacramento, CA; [p.] Enrique Mayo and Daisy Mayo; [ed.] St. Joseph Catholic School; Hidalgo Elementary school. St. Anthony's Catholic School; [occ.] Student; [hon.] The grade honor roll Language arts award; [oth.writ.] Dedicated to my grandmother Valeriana Mayo and Leonila Espiritu and to my grandfathers Francisco Mayo and Antonio Espiritu; [pers.] It is best to have the knowledge that brings about your self-confidence, thereby believing in yourself to achieve your goals and follow your dreams.; [a.] Fresno, CA

MCDONALD, EDWARD
[pen.] Ed McDonald; [b.] August 6, 1948; Providence, RI; [p.] John and Netta McDonald; [ed.] La Salle Academy, Bryant College, Roger Williams Unversity, Community College of RI; [occ.] Small Business Owner; [memb.] Newport Art Museum,

Newport County YMCA, Norman Bird Society, People Speak; [hon.] Maple Leaf from Canadian Embassy in Boston, Editor's Choice in View from Afar; [oth.writ.] Nature's Poin, Diamonds and Peals, Ode to Desert Wind—A View from Afar; [pers.] Do unto others as you would have done unto you.; [a.] Portsmouth, RI

MCGREGOR, CHRISTINA DANELLE
[pen.] Danelle McGregor; [b.] October 20, 1982; Paducah, KY; [p.] Danney and Limma McGregor; [ed.] Freshman at Ballard Memorial High School; [oth.writ.] Along with many other unknown poems, I have also written many short stories. Also I enjoy drawing and learning about different forms of art; [pers.] Poetry is a very good way of soothing the soul. Most of my poems express my feelings and depression, and when I begin to write, all of my troubles seem to fade away.; [a.] LaCenter, KY

MCMULLEN, PHYLLIS
[b.] December 31, 1947; Council Bluffs, IA; [p.] Eldred H. and Anna M. McMullen; [ed.] Bachelor of Arts in Education—Kearney State College, Kearney, NE; Master of Science—University of Nebraska at Omaha; [occ.] Speech, Language Pathologist; [oth.writ.] Published and wrote Plumm Fun, a summer newsletter for children, for 2 years. Iowa writer's project 1997 summer edition; [a.] Underwood, IA

MCQUILLAN, EVA
[b.] April 26, 1949; Poland; [ch.] Vanessa Lee McQuillan; [ed.] Nursing College - Jagiellonsky University of Poland; [occ.] Nurse; [a.] Cucamonga, CA

MICHALSKI, DONNA
[b.] March 10, 1946, Schenectady, NY; [p.] Duard & Betty Genter; [m.] Charles Michalski, September 26, 1981; [ch.] Charles Theodore & Shea Marie; [ed.] Shaker High School; [occ.] (Housewife) Domestic Engineer; [oth. writ.] "Fireside Thoughts" a book of unpublished poetry; [pers.] I started writing my poems at age 16, and my biggest source of encouragement to keep on is my sister Denny.; [a.] New Port Richey, FL

MILBURN, REBEKAH RACHEL
[b.] October 20, 1979; Galax, VA; [p.] Mr. and Mrs. James A. Milburn, Jr.; [ed.] Math Education and Physics Majors at Virginia Polytechnic Institute and State University; [occ.] Student and Tutor; [a.] Allisonia, VA

MILLER, MARLENE
[b.] October 11, 1940; Pittsburgh, PA; [p.] Joseph and Anna Miller; [ed.] Carbow College, Duquesne University, University of Puerto Rico, Georgetown Univ.; [occ.] Director of Religious Education; [memb.] ACCOP, NART, AARP; [hon.] Woman of the year 1991; Commander's Award for Civilian Service, Achievement Medal for Civilian Service; [oth.writ.] Music book "Awake My Soul", being printed "Legend of the Easter Egg"; [pers.] Freely have we received from God, so freely must we share.; [a.] APO, AP

MILLER, ROBIN R.
[b.] September 14; West Virginia; [p.] Joe and LaVonne Miller; [ch.] Tabetha, TJ, Matthew; [ed.] Bachelor of Arts in History from College of St. Rose, NY; [hon.] Magna Cum Laude, Dean's List, American Red Cross Letter of Commendation, Volunteer Service Award; [pers.] I would like to express my deepest appreciation to Don, whose unconditional friendship has allowed me to grow in ways I never dreamed of.; [a.] Woodbridge, VA

MILLER, T.J.
[b.] May 25, 1972; Trenton, NJ; [p.] Ted and Gail Miller; [ed.] BA In Philosophy of History at Rutuers University, NJ; Martial Arts Training; [occ.] Actor—Pennsylvania Renaissance Faire; [pers.[In seeking the truth I looked within, but was

cast back out to the earth, the one inevitably to the other leads.; [a.] New Egypt, NJ

MILLS, DEBRA
[pen.] Debra G. Mills; [b.] September 25, 1956; Hammond, IN; [p.] Frank and Alice Stur - Deceased; [m.] Charles Mills; April 20, 1985; [ch.] One stepson - David, 1 stepdaughter - Tosha, Daughter - Kim; [ed.] High School, I am also a graduate of the Institute of Children's Literature in West Redding, Conn.; [occ.] Full-time mom and housewife; [memb.] I am a member of Lansing Assembly of God Church and also belong to a writing group in town.; [oth.writ.] I have written many poems about dieting, children's stories and spiritual poems— also humorous poems—but none have been published.; [pers.] I am depressed about my weight problem. I wrote this poem in hopes that it will help not only myself but others who share the problem. God has been my greatest helper.; [a.] Lowell, IN

MILLS, JASON
[pen.] Vincent Crow; [b.] January 12, 1980; Columbus, OH; [p.] Linda and Paul Mills; [ed.] Westerville North High School; [hon.] Three years on 4.0 plus Honor Roll. Three time scholar-athlete and academic letter winner. Golden Scholar Certificate from Ohio Basketball Association; [oth.writ.] Poem published in Anthology of poetry by Young Americans, articles for school newspaper; [pers.] A person should not let people put limitations on their life or talent. If a person comes up with an idea, they should see it through and never get discouraged by what other people think or say. I wish to thank my parents for teaching me about life and being patient with me.; [a.] Westerville, OH

MITCHELL, JACQUELINE MARIE
[pen] "Jack," "Girlfriend"; [b.] May 6, 1962; Denver, CO; [p.] Chris and Joe Chapman (Joseph Henley—biological father); [m.] Isaac C. Slaugh-fiance (The love of my life); [ch.] (4) Ashleigh, Melisse, Courtney and Sean; [ed.] Completed 12th Grade; [occ.] Home Day Care Provider (I love kids)!; [pers.] I love poetry. Everything I write about I have lived—It comes right from the heart.; [a.] Grand Junction, CO

MOCK, WENDY
[pen.] Wendy Mock; [b.] August 12, 1964; Binghamton, NY; [p.] Della McCrady, Kenneth Sechrist Sr; [m.] Milton C. Mock Sr; January 30, 1981; [ch.] James, Mitton Jr., Michael, Angel; [ed.] Attending college - graduate with a 2-year degree in early childhood education in December 1997; [occ.] Student, Housewife; [hon.] President's List in college; [oth.writ.] Nothing that is published; [a.] Little Meadows, PA

MOORE, LOUISE
[b.] September 12, 1954; Greenwood, MS; [p.] Rev. B.T. and Elizabeth Moore; [ch.] Rodrick, Hamani; [ed.] Greenwood High, Clark College Indpls. Ind. and Indiana Univesity; [occ.] Poet, Guardian Angel; [memb.] Greater Shepherd MB Church, Indiania Beauty School; [hon.] Certificate of Achievement - Clark College; [oth.writ.] Going Home, Sad, Where Is The Love; [pers.] When life get you down, and it's hard to make it thru, while on your journey in our passing, you meet a lady name Lou.; [a.] Spring, TX

MOORE II, DOUGLAS E.
[b.] October 13, 1979; Elyria, OH; [p.] Douglas and Joyce Moore; [ed.] Open Door Christian School (High School); [occ.] Student at Open Door Christian School (senior); [pers.] All of my talents are from my inspiration, Jesus Christ. "Why are you downcast, O my soul? So why disturbed within me? Put your hope in God, for I will yet praise him my Savior and my God."—from Psalm 42 and 43; [a.] Oberlin, OH

MORA, ALEJANDRA
[b.] June 21, 1979; New York, NY; [p.] Sara and Jorge Gautreau; [ed.] Visitation School, Academy of Mount Saint Ursula; [occ.] Student; [oth.writ.] Have written many poems and short stories for many years; [pers.] My greatest wish is to become the best author I can be and I feel I will be successful, when I know I have fully entertained my readers.; [a.] Bronx, NY

MORENO, JANET J.
[b.] September 16, 1976; Monterrey, MI; [p.] Maria Gaytan, Jose Estrada Sr.; [ch.] Crystal Elena Moreno, Joel Moreno Jr., Jonathan Joel Moreno; [occ.] Housewife; [hon.] Bear Facts school newspaper, a poem that was published by "The National Library of Poetry. " [oth.writ.] "The Time Has Come" published in "A Lasting Mirage"; [pers.] I write poems by what I see around me, in this poem is to tell my husband that there is no word in this world that could explain how I feel for him.; [a.] Houston, TX

MORGAN, JOHN
[b.] June 11, 1978; Hilo, TX; [pers.] "Can't Be My Hero" is for Charles Bukowski; [a.] Waco, TX

MORRISON, DWAIN F.
[b.] March 12; Chicago, IL; [p.] Mr. and Mrs. Jackson; [ed.] High School Graduate, 2 years College; [occ.] Office Maintenance; [hon.] Poetry Award from camp as a child; [oth.writ.] Working on a novel and poetry book; [pers.] Life is like a poem with no ending, and only God can write it. We are left to wonder what it will be like if the world was the way God planned it, not the way it is today.; [a.] Wichita, KS

MUNDER, LAURA
[b.] August 21, 1981; Atlanta, GA; [p.] Elma and Gary Munder; [ed.] Completed 10th grade, in 11th grade; [occ.] Student; [memb.] Local club soccer team, high school soccer team, high school band; [hon.] In all-state band (2 years), principal's honor roll; [oth.writ.] Write for each graduating class at my high school; [pers.] Friends are life's greatest treasure.; [a.] Roswell, GA

MURLEY, ELEANOR A.
[pen.] Ellie; [b.] August 22, 1926; Nfld., Canada; [p.] Althia and Llewellyn Butler; [m.] Chesley Murley; May 11, 1962; [ch.] 3 - Margaret, Charles, Tricia; [ed.] High School and Secretarial, also Memorial University - Nfld., Canada; [occ.] Housewife (Retired Teacher); [memb.] St. John's Guild, Mass. Poetry Society; [hon.] Tops, Poetry; [oth.writ.] Short Stories and many poems; [pers.] I like to write about God and Nature; Shelley is my favorite poet.; [a.] Saugus, MA

NEAVES, JR., DAVID C.
[pen.] David Neaves, Jr.; June 10, 1964; Norta, Cardira; [ch.] 4; [ed.] High School; [occ.] Supervisor; [hon.] Editors Choice Award for It should be said of when we are dead; [oth.writ.] Over sixty poems unpublished and a few songs unreleased poems on a variety of subjects; [a.] Erlanger, KY

NEVLING, DONNA
[b.] August 26, 1951; Johnstown; [p.] Don and Dorothy Nevling; [ed.] High school, some Vo-tech for Advanced Clerical Duties, 1 year Bible College; [occ.] Secretary for MetLife Medical Director— 19 years. I am currently in the process of changing occupations. [oth.writ.] Short Story Book published by Allegheny Pub. in Salem, OH (1991). Novel to be published in Spring of 1998 by Moore Books in Somerville, IN.; [pers.] I write with the hopes of inspiring the eternal soul of mankind toward its higher, nobler purpose and destiny.; [a.] Johnstown, CA

NEWTON, SARAH NELL
[pen.] Sarah; [b.] April 21, 1945; Hart County; [p.]

Katie Mae, James E. Newton; [ed.] 12th Grade—Graduated; [hon.] Editor's Choice Award for Outstanding Achievement in Poetry; [oth.writ.] Songs written; [pers.] I like writing, even with no college degree.; [a.] Hartwell, GA

NIELSEN, TODD M.
[b.] 1968; [a.] San Jose, CA

NORDEN, MAXINE J.
[ed.] Bachelor of Arts in English Literature, Bachelor of Arts in Woman's Studies, honors English / Cum Laude Graduate, International Honor Society - Sigm Tau Delta; [occ.] Free-lance writer; [hon.] Cum Laude graduate, International honor society - Sigma Tau Delta, certified Women's Studies, Associate women's studies, Bachelors with honors in English Literature; [pers.] I strive to create in my writing life's realities and truths of the human condition.; [a.] Lauderhill, FL

NUCKOLS, TATE
[b.] August 18, 1973; Richmond, VA; [p.] Dr. and Mrs. W.A. Nuckols; [ed.] B.A. in Latin from University of Richmond in 1995; Currently pursuing a Masters of Teaching for secondary level English; [occ.] Student at Virginia Commonwealth University; [memb.] Eta Sigma Phi (Honorary Classical Studies Fraternity); [hon.] Intermediate honors while attending University of Richmond, Two-time recipient of Selma Dunn Pierson Scholarship for Latin majors, served as Eta Sigma Phi president and messenger while at University of Richmond; [oth.writ.] I write poetry on a constant basis.; [pers.] Despite the little things that complicate your day, just trust your heart and you will find your way.; [a.] Richmond, VA

OLSEN, MARIE
[pen.] Buddy Love; Bunny Love; [b.] February 5, 1961; Philadelphia, PA; [p.] Robert Schreiner, Colleen Schreiner; [m.] Fred W. Olsen III; September 19, 1981; [ch.] Fred W. IV, Mellisa Marie, Nicola Mary; [ed.] Lower Moreland High School, Eastern Montgomery T.M. Services; [occ.] Nurse, Certified Massage Therapist, Owner of "Tornado Productions" Band Booking Agency; [memb.] Southampton Days Committee Entertainment Coordinator, Community Marching Band Director, Multiple Sclerosis Society, Founder of the "Phebe Blessington Memorial Music Scholarship"; [hon.] Vice-President of Nursing Class; [oth.writ.] "Have You Lost Something?" in With Flute and Drum and Pen, lyricist for multiple bands; [pers.] I want to dedicate this poem to the memory of many people I've lost this year - Ron Blessington Sr., Ron's Daughter, Phebe and, especially, my Mom. You have all been an inspiration in my life.; [a.] Southampton, PA

OWENS, DESTINY JOANN
[b.] March 22, 1984; AL; [p.] Patti and Tom Owens; [ed.] 8th Grade this year; [pers.] To my loving mother, who gave me confidence and moral support.; [a.] Leeds, AL

PALMERIO, COLETTE J.
[b.] April 5, 1977; Freehold; [p.] John and Donna Palmerio; [ed.] Holy Family School, Lake Wood High School, Ocean County College; [occ.] New Talent Management; [memb.] Saint Mary of the Lake Church; [hon.] Honor Roll 91-95, Presidential Academic Award '95, Yearbook Award 94-95, Dean's List (National) 95-96, Tutoring (Math) 96-97; [oth.writ.] I Love You, When? Greatest Pain of All, Unconditional Love; [pers.] I hope our youth will look for beauty on the inside and not focus so much on the outside.; [a.] Lakewook, NJ

PANAGUITON, MARY S.
[pen.] Nene; [b.] March 14, 1937; Philippines; [p.] Manuel A. Panaguiton, Caridad S. Panaguiton; [m.] Turio M. Niere; May 6, 1970; [ed.] Mountain View College, Bible Instructor - Philippines; [occ.] Cer-

tified Nurse Assitance CNA and Home Health Aid HHA; [memb.] Seventh-Day Adventist Church; [hon.] To the Far East as a literature Evangelist in soul winning and as a worker for Home and Health Services; [oth.writ.] I wrote poems since my high school days but in our Pilipino language. Some were published in local papers.; [pers.] I wrote poems as an inspiration to comfort the comfortless and to give courage to those who are discouraged, to give hope to the hopeless and to give messages—the Good News that Jesus is coming soon; be prepared.; [a.] Van Nuys, CA

PARKER, ANDRIA NICCLE
[pen.] Parker; [b.] March 19, 1984; Tampa; [p.] Jennifer Wilson, Dyrell Wilson; [ed.] 8th grade honors, Math & Science; Adavanced Lang. Arts and U.S. History; [memb.] Cheerleading—Progress Village Panthers; [hon.] Academic Award from Duke; [oth.writ.] I'm all Alone, Help it, What's Up, Around Here, That's Deep, A Dream, I Hate, Wondering, Have You; [a.] Tampa, FL

PARKER, WILLIAM NELSON
[pen.] Nelson Parker; [b.] June 14, 1919; Columbus, OH; [p.] Murray and Evalyn Parker; [m.] J. Yvonne Parker; September 20, 1948; [ch.] Marki Pulley and Jarret Parker; [ed.] AB (1939) Harvard Ph. D. (1951) Harvard GSAS, MA, Yale 1962, in Privatim; [occ.] Retired Professor, Composing a Memoir; [memb.] American Academy of Arts And Sciences, American Philosophical Society; [hon.] TIBK Hughes Prize for Teaching, Economic History Ass. [oth.writ.] Europe, America And The Wider World, 2 Vols, 1985-1991 Cambridge Univ. Press (A Collection Of Articles on Economic History of the West; [pers.] The Poem is one of 50 Sonnets written on 1989-1993 to celebrate my retirement as an Economic-History Professor after Forty years at Williams, One and Yale Chapel Hill; [a.] Hamden, CT

PAULES, TARA
[b.] August 8, 1976; Allentown, PA; [p.] Timothy C. Paules Sr. Carolyn S. Paules; [ed.] Northern Lehig High School, Lehigh County, Vo-Tech School, Lifetime career schools; [occ.] Manager, Burger King, Northampton, PA; [memb.] Girl Scouts, National Home Gardening Club, National Audubon Society; [hon.] Vocal Music Awards 1989-90, Certificate of Recognition 1987, Student of the Week 1993, Certificate of Attendance 1991-92, Certificate of Merit 1993, Book it! Reading Honor Diploma 1988, Bulldog Achievement Award 1992-94; [a.] Slatington, PA

PEARSON, SUZANNA M.
[b.] December 5, 1967; Idaho; [p.] Sue and David McBride; [m.] John E. Pearson Jr.; May 24, 1987; [ch.] Jesse M. Thomas E., Emmalee S., David L., and John M.; [ed.] Homedale High School 1987; [occ.] Homemaker and Homeschooling Teacher; [memb.] Calvary Chapel in Ontario, Oregon; [pers.] I strive to reflect the kind of love our Lord Jesus would have us give.; [a.] Fruitland, ID

PEDEN, NANCY LEE
[pen.] Grace; [b.] May 12, 1965; Amarillo, TX; [p.] Col. Roger Lee Peden, USAF, Ret. and Martha Janie Stennis; [ed.] Brandon H.S., Mississippi State University (Man and Meridian Campuses); [occ.] Rush Hospital Secondary Insurance Biller; [memb.] Daughters of American Revolution (DAR), Sam Dale Chapter, Pleasant Ridge United Methodist Church, Hospitality Committee; [hon.] Who's Who Among Young American Women 1988; [pers.] I believe all people (children and adults) can learn in the right environment.; [a.] Dekalb, MS

PENNINGTON, REBECCA ANN
[b.] November 14, 1960; Dearborn Co, IN; [p.] Russell and Elizabeth Ann Pennington; [m.] Alice Ann Pennington; September 21, 1979; [ch.] Asena Ann McGuire; [ed.] Ross School and G.E.D; [occ.]

Homemaker [hon.] Good Citizenship Award from D.A.R; [oth.writ] Only to my loved ones; [pers.] I've lived unique life, and thus and am open minded about life and it's extremes of highs and lows. I'm looking forward to life and it's challenges, and sharing these with others.; [a.] Ross, OH

PERKUS, MARION
[pen.] Dana; [b.] February 3, 1941; Canandaigua, NY; [p.] Marion and Milton Partridge; [ch.] Lisa, Aaron, Benjamin; [ed.] University of Rochester (BS), SUNY Albany (PH D); [occ.] Research Scientist; [oth.writ.] National Library of Poetry, "Pas de Deux" (Through Sun and Shower), "Spring Comes" (A Prism of Thoughts), "The Love Affair" (Journey Beyond the Stars), "Poetry is Born" (The Ever-Flowing Stream), "Other Lives" (Chasing The Wind), "The Sunset" (Montage of Life), Sparrowgrass Poetry Forum, "Without This Snow" (Treasured Poems of America, Winter 1998); [pers.] In my poetry, I aim to bridge the gaps between inner and outer, male and female, science and spirit, nature and technology, mythic and pragmatic reality.; [a.] Altamond, NY

PERROTTA, BRITTANY JO
[b.] April 2, 1983; Camden, SC; [p.] Karen and Joseph Perrotta; [ed.] Freshman at Sumter High School in Sumter, SC; [memb.] National Honor Society, Leadership Club, BMS, OPAL, National Jr. Science Academy; [a.] Sumter, SC

PERSON, JULIE
[b.] February 5, 1980; Dallas, TX; [p.] Douglas Person and June Person; [ed.] Senior at Mesquite High School; [pers.] My poetry reflects my feelings, and describes my personality.; [a.] Mesquite, TX

PHILLIPS, CAITLIN
[b.] November 10, 1984; Boulder, CO; [p.] Shannon Phillips, Jim Phillips; [ed.] Bixby School, Colorado Academy; [occ.] Student; [memb.] National guide for piano playing; Hockey, soccer, swimming, tennis and basketball teams; student council; Colorado Academy Choir; [hon.] Full-year honor student; '95-'96 state soccer champions; [oth.writ.] Editor/publisher of the Bixby Post (school newspaper); [pers.] I have been greatly influenced in my writing by my love sports. The Colorado Avalanche rule and Patrick Roy is #1.; [a.] Denver, CO

PRAZAK, JOBYNNE
[b.] April 20, 1974; Sovix Falls, SD; [p.] Mike and Susan Slane; [m.] Thomas Prazak II; May 21, 1994; [ch.] Thomas Prazak III; [occ.] Domestic Engineer; [oth.writ.] A handful of poems and short stories all written for fun. Aspiring to write a romance novel; [per.] Being fond of history and romance, I like to blend reality and fantasy in my writing.; [a.] Phonix, AZ

PRESCOD, TAMIKO NATASHA
[pen.] Tammy, Slims, Flex; [b.] December 31, 1982; Barbados; [p.] Colleen Prescod/Tyrone Marshall; [ed.] High School; [pers.] I strive for excellence and perfection. I am a kind person and I like lots of fun but yet I am very religious. My two role models are Tyra Banks and Naomi Campbell.; [a.] Rochester, NY

PRICE, HEATHER
[b.] November 11, 1984; Elyria, OH; [p.] Laura Gereke, Mike Gereke; [ed.] 7 Grade, Midview Middle School; [occ.] Student; [hon.] Merit Student; [oth.writ.] 2 other poems, but never published; [pers.] I write what I see and feel and what I see in the future for me.; [a.] Elyria, OH

PUPSHIS, NICOLE
[pen.] Margaret Mary Maggiti; [b.] August 12, 1985; Baltimore, MD; [p.] Anthony and Melissa [ed.] Attending Arthur Slade Regional Catholic School; [oth.writ.] I have 2 poems in my school literary magazine; [pers.] You can do anything, as

long as you put your mind to it, no matter your age.; [a.] Glen Burnie, MD

QUEZADA, KAREN E.
[pen.] K. E. Robinson, (nickname) "KK"; [b.] June 6, 1964; Louisiana; [p.] Murphy Robinson and Dorothy Robinson; [m.] Jesus L. Quezada; April 5, 1997; [ed.] AA degree, Paralegal—Phillips Junior College, ZOE Christian Institute and a high school graduate of Inglewood High.; [occ.] In pursuit of being an Entrepreneur; [memb.] Zeta Phi Beta Sorority, Inc. and Long Beach Community Worship Center, my church in Long Beach, California; [oth.writ.] I have been writing for over 15 years. I have never had any of my poems published. I finally was able to put together my first volume of writings to have copyrighted in 1996.; [pers.] Keep your dreams alive by doing what you love. Never let it become a memory that has never tasted the beauty of becoming alive.; [a.] Los Angeles, CA

RAY, STEPHANIE
[b.] February 28, 1986; Fort Hood TX; [p.] Robert Ray; [ed.] 5th grade; [occ.] School, Stephanie Ray Foundation; [memb.] Children with AIDS Projects Camp Headland; [hon.] Humanitarian Award, Mrs. Clinton, Children with AIDS Project, Buffalo Solders Humanitarian award; [oth.writ.] Ryans poems, Listen to my Heart Speak; [pers.] I like my school, I make good grades I like going to Camp Heatland. Sports I like a lot, as well as my dog Maxine. My dad is my favorite friend. I like helping people; most of all I just like being a kid.; [a.] Glendale, AZ

REAGAN SHELLEY, WANDA
[pen.] Shelli Smith; [b.] January 6, 1941; New Florence, MO; [p.] Frances and the (late) Chester (Ted) Smith; [m.] Merlin (Sonny) Shelley; January 21, 1982; [ch.] Tina, David, Scott, Rich and Shawn; [ed.] Attended Martinsburg MO (grammar), Scotts Corner, MO (high school) Graduate, Long Ridge Writers Group, Palmer's Literary Arts, Cosmetology, and adult classes - Oil Painting; [occ.] Freelance Writing, Poetry, Short "Love Stories," Operating a small business; [memb.] Garden Grove Chamber of Commerce, President of Mu-Mu Chapter Beta Sigma Phi Santa Ana City Council, Owned and Operated Beauty Salon near Disneyland Anaheim, ex-model; [hon.] Crowned Princess Beta Sigma Phi. Selected Semi-finalist, National Library of Poetry, "Editor's Choice Award 1997 poem—"My Mother" and dedicated to my mom Frances Smith; [oth.writ.] Wrote a "Dear Wanda" column for Sunday Mail Magazine, "My Mother" published in Prism of Thoughts, small Newspaper writings, Editor in school paper; [pers.] When everthing feels right in your heart, and you can respect yourself, have confidence in your accomplishments, with hope and faith, then all your dreams will become your realities.; [a.] Garden Grove, CA

REAMS, WILLIAM ROBERT EARL
[pen.] Robbie Reams; August 13, 1982; Army Hosp., Germany; [p.] Coleman and Beverly Reams; [ed.] Student at Stonewall Jackson High School; [occ.] Student; [memb.] National Rifle Association Lifetime Member; [hon.] VFW award for parade dutied, band award for outstanding performance; [oth.writ.] The Cry of an Indian; [a.] Mt. Jackson, VA

REAVES, NAOMI STEWART
[b.] November 2, 1946; Detroit, MI; [p.] Edward and N. Stewart; [m.] Jimmie G. Reaves Jr; July 16, 1978; [ch.] Jennifer and Noelle; [ed.] High School, some college; [occ.] Doll maker, storyteller, writer; [memb.] Cleve. Assoc. of Black Stories, United Med. Women; [oth.writ.] Historical fiction of black women in the 1800's: Tellie, Fannie, Lil' Martha and A'nt Hanna, Betty-Blu, Big Rose and Twin Slave Sisters, Thomasine and Naomi; [pers.] Live Unsitawi (to-see-too-wee) daily, "Prosperity

both spiritual and material." Usitawi is taken from Mali, Western Country in Africa.; [a.] Cleve. Hts., OH

REYNOLDS, MELISSA
[b.] December 29, 1981; Chester, PA; [p.] Peter Reynolds, Sharon Vogler; [ed.] High School Student; [hon.] Honorable mention from Iliad Press; [pers.] I believe that poetry comes from the heart and the quality cannot be judged by anyone but the author itself.; [a.] Mission, SD

RICE, STEPHANIE
[pen.] Stephanie M; [b.] January 2, 1977; [p.] Marvus and Debra Rice; [occ.] Student at Hampton University Studying Biology; [oth.writ.] One Lost Soul - My Search for Inner Peace, On Freedoms Wings, Epistles; [a.] Indianapolis, IN

RIDGWAY, KOURTNEY
[b.] January 15, 1980; Pasadena, TX; [p.] William and Karen Ridgway

ROBERTS, NIKKI
[b.] July 17, 1985; Warren; [p.] Betty Roberts; [ed.] 7th grade; [memb.] Teen magazine; [hon.] Improvement, perfect attendance, citzenship; [oth.writ.] Unicorn, Love, I; [pers.] Life is to short to care about but I still care.; [a.] Windnon, OH

RODGERS, SELENA T.
[pen.] Poet Dva; [b.] January 17, 1972; Harlem, NY; [p.] Dorothy Mnceil-Rodgers and James Rodgers; [ed.] MSW, Syracuse University; BSW, Marymount College; NYS Certified Social Worker; [occ.] Director: Victim Services, INC; Adjunct Professor; College of New Rochelle - Rosa Parks Campus, Mental Health Consultant; [memb.] Alpha Kappa Alpha Sorority, Inc, Phi Alpha Honor Society for Social Work; NABSW and NASW; [oth.writ.] The Imani Dream, copyrighted 1997; [pers.] Wisdom-N-Words is the foundation of my Essence-Afrika 72.; [a.] Jamaica, NY

ROHRSCHEIB, DANIELLE
[b.] May 4, 1984; Spokane, WA; [p.] Rick and Klea Burris (stepfather and mother); [ed.] Starting 8th Grade; [hon.] I received a reward for "Reflections," in Elementary School; [oth.writ.] Many other poems, out not published; [pers.] I have been influenced by Mrs. Schmutz, Ms. Tingy, Mrs. McDaniel, and Mrs. Marcuson (my teachers); also my family helped to influence me.; [a.] Farmington, UT

ROMAN, SANDRA
[pen.] Sandra Roman; [b.] July 7, 1948; Delaware; [p.] Horace and Mary Ann Pedrick; [hon.] Several poems published by the National Library of Poetry; [pers.] John Anthony, you are my love, my friend. Life has brought us together to teach one another the importance of a true, loving relationship you and I have been given that chance through God. We will walk together hand in hand.; [a.] Hockessin, DE

ROSS, CAROL H.
[b.] October 24, 1928; K.C., MO; [p.] Clarence and Martha Haize; [m.] Deceased; March 31, 1961; [ch.] Patty, Bob and Connie; [ed.] MA-1982, Univ. of Wis.-Whitewater; [occ.] Retired; Unitarian Fellowship; [hon.] Diamond Honor from Famous Poets 1996, Poets Laureate of College of Education-UW-W 1996; [pers.] Have been writing poetry since 6th grade; [a.] Whitewater, WI

ROSS, CHARLES DURAN
[b.] June 13, 1926; San Francisco, CA; [p.] Maria Ester Ross; March 3, 1956; [ch.] Constance, Mary, Anne; [ed.] Piedmont H.S., Predmont, CA.; U. of San Francisco, S.F.CA; Education Course of San Diego State and Sunlight Courses at U. of Redlands; [occ.] Retired; [memb.] Gavel Debating Society at USF; [hon.] General Secondary Teaching Credential; [oth.writ.] Poems: Vivian, Lady Mac Beth, Queen of the Misty Isles, Melody of Love. Short Stories: Maggie, Ellnora, Snake Ranch, Vashti

Sangumore—all tales of the Supermatural; [pers.] I write to show the beauty of God's creation and to portray women as the primary life force. I had to write this poem because Theresa is heroic.; [a.] Downey, CA

ROYER, DENNIS E.
[b.] November 9, 1954; West Reading, PA; [p.] Maude and Richard Royer; [m.] Nadine; September 2; [ch.] Benjamin; [ed.] Wilson High School and Eleon College; [occ.] U.S. Army Officer; [oth.writ.] Several poems and short stories; [pers.] My poem are designed to evoke a strong emotional response and appreciation for a particular themes, such as types of love (relationships), the emotional aspect of selected colors, and reflections on individual life journeys.; [a.] Wyomissing, PA

RYDEN, JENNIE C.
[b.] July 17, 1979; Sawyer, MI; [p.] Richard Ryden, Sandra Ryden; [ed.] New International School of Thailand; currently a Freshman at Hawaii Pacific University; [hon.] Graduated from New International School of Thailand (NIST) Magna Cum Laude; [pers.] Rather than suppress dreams, we should obey them, for they are the harbingers of our future selves.—Richard Bode. Life is the greatest inspiration, and it's always right there at our fingertips.; [a.] Kaneohe, HI

SALINAS III, TOMMY A.
[b.] April 2, 1976; Mission, TX; [p.] Tomas and Eloisa Salinas; [ed.] 3 years higher learning; [pers.] To my angel of inspiration Andrea R. Stewart, I give my words. Thank you for everything. I love you.; [a.] Austin, TX

SCHMIDT III, MASON W.
[b.] July 27, 1974; Houston, TX; [p.] Mason Jr and Karen Schmidt; [ed.] Reagan and Dickinson High School—Alvin College (2 yrs.) and Mainland College (1 yr.); [occ.] Night Stocker; [hon.] Had several poems printed on merit through Famous Poets Society and the National Library of Poetry; [oth.writ.] JMW Pub. Co. "Headlights in Your Face" 1995, Sparrowgrass Poetry Forum "I Love You" 1995, Poetic Voices of America "Nature of the Beast" Spring 1996; [pers.] I try to convey what I see as reality. I also try to get across that life is meant to be more simple and not as complex. We as humans should not take advantage of other humans and/or non-humans, but it happens.; [a.] Houston, TX

SCHNEIDER, DEB
[b.] June 30, 1953; Coose Bay, OR; [m.] Anthony Schneider; April 3, 1991; [ed.] High School, 1 yr College, Various Comp. Classes and writing classes; [occ.] Self-Employed. I was in a factory for 14 yrs.; [hon.] Mostly ribbons for cooking and crochetting at country fairs. Now I also paint scenery pictures.; [oth.writ.] Started a writing class, via the mail, for children's books. One poem published, still writing; [pers.] I may be facing a serious operation soon. I wrote these poems so my son, his wife and 1st grandchild from my only son will love them.; [a.] Elk, WA

SCOTT, PAT
[b.] March 6, 1932; Donna, TX; [m.] Alvin W Scott; May 12, 1995; [ch.] Ginger Lee Collins Susan An McCain, Lawrence Scott Collins, Sr. [ed.] Corpus Christi High School; [occ.] Retired [memb.] Villa Maria Senior Writers, Calaller Writers, Bapt. Church; [oth.writ.] I have ha several articles printed in the local papers. Poems and articles are being read over a local radio station [pers.] My goal is to paint picutes with my writing I enjoy combining humor with nostalgia in m articles.; [a.] Corpus Christ, TX

SHAFFER, JACQUELYN
[pen.] J. Lee; [b.] May 23, 1933; Ohio; [pers Studied body and the reactions to food and drugs an

why health books don't tell all so we can have real health and know what would do the trick.; [a.] Crystal, MN

SILVERNAGEL, APRIL AMBER
[pen.] April Silvernagel; [b.] April 15, 1985; Dayton, UT; [p.] Wayne Patricia Silbernagel; [ed.] Jr High, 7th Grade; [occ.] Student; [memb.] soccer, church, jr. choir; [hon.] Gymnastics, Dance, Science Fair, Writing Essays, DARE Essay; [pers.] The ocean;s breeze is tender inside me; watching the sunset lets me think of home. Watching the pale moon is like feeling the sunset's breeze.; [a.] Dayton, WI

SLEIGHT, MELISSA MARIE
[b.] July 29, 1969; Lansing, MI; [p.] George and Janet Bliven; [m.] Michael Sleight; May 23, 1987; [ch.] Two, a beautiful girl and a beautiful boy; [ed.] Graduated from Portland High School, Nurse's Aid Training Classes; [occ.] Nurse's Aide For The State of Michigan Veteran Facility; [memb.] Local 261 (AFSHME); [hon.] My awards will be in Heaven; [oth.writ.] Several poems non-published of my personal writings. One poem is possibly being published by the Poetry Guild, as I was a Semi-Finals.; [pers.] Words of encouragement go a long way. Bless people with your kindness each day, for it will come back to you someday.

SMITH, ERIKKA
[b.] July 18, 1983; Fort Ord, CA; [p.] Yvonne Smith, James Smith; [ed.] Los Arboles Junior High, Seaside High; [a.] Marina, CA

SMITH, KARRA
[pen.] Karra Smith; [b.] August 13, 1981; Cullman, AL; [p.] Terry and Donna Smith; [occ.] Student; [pers.] This poem was written for my best friends: Chasidy Cross, Jennifer Newman, Joni Thompson, Heather Moore, and Rachel Joiner.; [a.] Cullman, AL

SMITH, NAOMI SHELIA
[pen.] Imoan or Short Cake; [b.] October 23, 1964; Baltimore, MD; [p.] Joseph and Calpertia Clavon; [m.] Kelvin Smith; November 18, 1983; [ch.] Kelvin Jr, Marcus, Vickie; [ed.] Completed 1st Year of College at Florence Dayton College, located in Florence St. Studies Humam Services, Laboratory Technician; [occ.] Claims Associate For Champo BC/BS 6 years; [a.] Florence, SC

SOLORZANO, ELMA
[pen.] Nevily Suarez; [b.] April 20, 1962; Guatemala; [p.] Luis Suarez, Gregoria Miranda; [m.] Manuel Angel Solorzano; September 29, 1978; [ch.] Ludvin, Nankel, Emily; [ed.] L.A. High Guatemalteco Israeli, Essex County College (Currently Attending); [occ.] Student (Graphic Arts) (At Essex County College) Newars NJ; [hon.] I have a trophy for a singing competition, a few running medals; [oth.writ.] To Emily, Faceit, Others Without a Name (yet) nothing published.; [pers.] My writings are a reflection of life struggles of love and everyday life and forgiveness. Even though life is hard at times, we must continue to strive for a better future for us and generations to come.; [a.] Newark, NJ

SPECHT, KELLY
[pen.] K. Burke, Kelly Burke; [b.] January 29, 1964, NJ; [p.] John and Ellen Burke; [m.] Marry; May 17, 1986; [ch.] Daniel, Ashley Erin; [ed.] Kittatinny Regional H.S. Ramapo College; [occ.] Freelance writer; [pers.] It is my greatest desire as a writer to evoke a reader to feel.; [a.] Newton, NJ

SPERRAZZO, MARY C.
[b.] May 5, 1937; Wash. D.C.; [p.] Antonino and Giovanna Torcisi; [m.] Dr. Gerald Sperazzo; September 30, 1961; [ch.] Mark, Christine, John and Anne; [ed.] Roosevelt High School Graduate, some business school training and some college courses; [occ.] Homemaker, wife, mother, and grandmother;

[memb.] Roman Catholic Church; [oth.writ.] About 30 other poems so far in last 10 years; [pers.] Use your God-given talents well and with joy for the glory of God. I hope my poems have brought pleasure to my family and friends and all the other loved ones in my circle of life. I enjoy this gift so much and am very grateful for it.; [a.] San Diego, CA

SPIDELL, KIM M.
[pen.] Kimee; [b.] June 1, 1971; Texas; [p.] Mr. and Mrs Kenneth and Marie Spidell; [ed.] Houston - Tillitson College Austin, Texas; Major Education, High School Arkansas Senior High June 1989 Texarkana AR; [occ.] Self-Employed; [memb.] NAACP, Women of America, Black Women of America, SADD, etc. American Walk of Life; [hon.] Who's Who Among American, Honor Roll, Merit Award; [oth.writ.] Written several songs but never copywrote them; [pers.] I consider myself to be a strong Black Woman, striving to become the best. Always remember: "Seek ye the first the kingdom of God and he shall give thee the desires of thine heart." Psalm 37:4; [a.] Ft. Lauderdale, FL

STEGER, CARMELITA
[b.] June 3, 1934; Portland, OR; [m.] James E. III; May 4, 1991; [pers.] I am native American Indian who strives to write from from the heart, about the way I see life going through its journey.; [a.] Central Point, OR

STEIN, KRISTINA DENISE
[b.] September 25, 1980; Detroit, MI; [p.] Kimberly Stevens; [ed.] Martin County High School; [occ.] Salad Girl, Bus Person; [hon.] Awards and ribbons from AFJROTC; [pers.] What ever happens will happen just go with the flow of it.; [a.] Jensen Beach, FL

STEINMEIER, CHRIS
[pen.] Roulette Stron Jay; [b.] June 1, 1979; Harrisburg, PA; [p.] Richard and Danniela Steimeier; [ed.] Graduated from Harrisburg Academy will attend Penn State in the fall (major Law); [occ.] Full-time student; [hon.] National Honor Society, Who's Who of American High School students 3 yrs. in a row. Attended presidential classroom and national youth forum on Law and Constitution in Washington, D.C. in '96 '97; [pers.] "Be swift as the thunder that peals before you have a chance to cover your ears, fast as the lighning that flashes before you can blink your eyes."—Chen Hao. "Making yourself, invincible means knowing yourself; waiting for vulnerability in opponents means knowing others"—Zhang Yu; [a.] Harrisburg, PA

STEPHENS, RACHEL
[b.] October 10, 1913; Kernersville, NC; [p.] Henry Ingram, Rosa Ingram; [m.] Hermon Stephens; April 14, 1944; [ch.] Herman, Wayne, Roger—3 step-children; [ed.] Kernersville High School, 1 year High Point College (now High Point University); [occ.] Homemaker; [memb.] Union Grove Baptist Church, Bible Study Group, International Society of Poets; [hon.] Several Award-winning poems published by the National Library of Poetry; [pers.] I like my poems to be positive, hopefully inspirational.; [a.] Kernersville, NC

STEPHENS, VALERIE
[b.] October 21, 1982; Pontiac, MI; [p.] Larry and Debri Stephens; [ed.] Lake Orion High School; [occ.] Student 9th Grade; [memb.] Sports: Cheerleading, Skiiing, Softball, Basketball, Track, Snow Mobiling; [hon.] Honor Roll at School, 1st Place Cheerleading, belonged to a singing academy and made 4 records, modeling; [oth.writ.] People; [pers.] Live life to the fullest—you can never have too many friends or go too many places.; [a.] Lake Orion, MI

STICKEL, MARY ANN
[b.] October 9, 1933; Zelienople, PA; [p.] John and Mary Zajacz; [m.] Harry F. Stickel; August 12,

1972; [ch.] Karen R. Hanes; [ed.] Alvernia High School Pgh. PA. RN- St. Francis Gen. Hosp. 3 School of Nursing Pgh. PA. BSN- Duquesne University Pgh. PA. MED- Duquesne University Pgh. PA; [occ.] Retired- Volunteer at Leading (4) Adult Mutual Support Groups; [memb.] American Nurse's Association, American Heart Association, St. Hilary Church Bereavement Ministry, American Academy of Bereavement, Association for Death Education and Counseling; [hon.] American Nurse's Association Certification, American Heart Association- Volunteer; [oth.writ.] Several unpublished poems, Unpublished nursing articles; [pers.] My poetry is the expression of deep thoughts that might come to me at significant times or within special relationships. Writing one's thoughts is the essence of freedom, the freedom of uninhibited self-expression—and that power leads us through crisis and uncovers new purposes in life that were not seen before.; [a.] Washington, PA

STREICHER, JENNIFER
[b.] January 13, 1987; Castro Valley, CA; [p.] Debby and Ralph; [ch.] 1 sister, 6 years; [hon.] 5th grade writing contest; [pers.] I'm in 6th grade and 10 years old; I attend Creekside Middle School. I love to read!; [a.] Castro Valley, CA

SURDOCK, MEGAN
[b.] January 24, 1982; Long Beach, CA; [p.] Rick and Linda Surdock; [ed.] High School Student of Lakewood High School; [occ.] Student; [memb.] Hula Halau Keali'i O Nalani; [oth.writ.] Several Non-published poems; [pers.] Always strive to do my best; [a.] Long Beach, CA

SWINK, DALE
[b.] November 20, 1966; Lincolnton, NC; [p.] Robert and Diane Swink; [m.] Cathy Swink; March 9, 1997; [ch.] Michael Dewayne, Sarah Nicole, Joseph Daniel; [ed.] Lincolnton Sr. High, Gaston College; [occ.] Staff Sergeant—United States Marine Corps; [hon.] Navy Achievement Medal, Kuawati Liberation; South West Asia Service Medal; [oth.writ.] I have over 200 poems written but nothing has been published.; [a.] Camp Lejeune, NC

TALBOT, LAUREN
[pen.] Lauren Tracy Talbot; [b.] July 24, 1983; Manhatten; [p.] Maurena and Robert Talbot; [ed.] High School, acting, dance, gymnastics, piano, track; [occ.] Still a student; [memb.] YWCA, NYRRC, ASPCA, Natural living; [pers.] Never think of poems, let them come to you.; [a.] New York City, NY

TAYLOR, ANN GILMORE
[pen.] Ann Gilmore Taylor; [b.] February 25, 1928; Philadelphia;l [p.] Anna A. and James Gilmore; [m.] Walters S. Taylor; August 18, 1951; [ch.] Suzanne Gilmore Reddick; [ed.] Kimberly Beth Taylor Gordon BS in Education, MS and many more credits on graduate level; [occ.] Substitute teacher—long term at times. Love to teach, love children; [memb.] Mid-Atlantic Center Shell club, Investment Club, President Garden Club, Questers President etc; [hon.] 4 trophy and Bayonne writers contest short stories, poetry essays, Went to Chatauqua New York for 2 summers 1995-1996 for writing workshops. These are put on by Highlights magazine; [oth.writ.] Short stories, Poetry, Book for Children, The Miracle at Auburn Acres (trying to get published); [pers.] Writing is sheer joy to me. I write every day. I read poetry in Chalfant Hotel in Cape May, October 16, 1997.; [a.] Cape May, NJ

TAYLOR, TABITHA
[b.] July 17, 1969, Queens, NY; [p.] William and Gladys Taylor; [ch.] 1) Tashana, 2) Carlton, 3) Christen, 4) Carla; [ed.] Graduated John Adams High School in 1987, CA Guardia Community College, J. Sargent Reynolds Community College; [hon.] Dean's List; [pers.] I was inspired by the

love and spirit of Carlton to write this poem. We all miss him dearly.; [a.] Richmond, VA

TENCZA, ELAINE
[b.] August 18. 1945; Detroit, MI; [p.] Eleanore and Henry Oprinsky; [m.] Daniel Tencza; April 24, 1981; [ch.] Ken and David; [oth.writ.] Poetry Guild—Among the Roses; [pers.] Follow your vision, follow your heart—nobody is an expert in handling your life. For better or for worse, you are unique. Be proud of who you are.

TERDIK, ANDREA
[b.] November 23, 1983; Derby, CT; [p.] Eleonora Romano; [ed.] St. Joseph's School (K-8) Going into High School (Grade 9); [occ.] Student Chighschool; [memb.] YMCA; [hon.] Science fair, cheerleading, 1st place Art; [oth.writ.] Other poems I have written, non-published. (I never tried to get any published.); [a.] Ansonia, CT

TRASK, FRANKLIN
[b.] August 17, 1907; Boston, MA; [p.] Albert M. and Bertha (both deceased); [m.] Diane Millman Trask; February 18, 1944; [ed.] 4 Universities (4 advanced degrees)—Boston University, B.S., Boston University M Ed., Columbia University M. Arts, Staley College Honorary Doctorate; [occ.] Retired; [hon.] Honorary Doctor's Degree, Formerly Head of Dept. of Speech and Drama at Cedar Crest College, Allentown Penn Builder of 800 summer homes in Plymouth MA, Philanthropist: Builder of libraries and schools, Priscilla Beach Theatre producer for 27 years (Plymouth MA); [oth.writ.] The Actor's Shakespeare; [pers.] As an article from the Drama Editor of the Boston Herald indicates, Franklin Trask is one of the nation's most active and prolific theatrical producers— employed 150 actors: 250,000 people, 1 play to 85 separate and distinct ventures each year etc; [a.] Boca Raton, FL

TRURAN, JENNIFER
[b.] October 30, 1980; Warren, OH; [p.] Kathleen Morrison & Jeff Truran; [ed.] Attending Lawrence North High School, honors courses; [occ.] Store Trainer at a restraunt, Boston Market; [hon.] 1st place team cross-country; [oth.writ.] None that have been published but as far as other writing go I ahve read them at my fathers wedding. (June 28, 1997); [pers.] I live by the saying, "Nothing ventured nothing gained," and also, "Never 8settle for less than the best." Both were told to me by my mother, who I am grateful for.; [a.] Indianapolis, IN

TUCK, LATOYA
[pen.] Toya; [b.] March 28, 1984; Phoenix, AZ; [p.] Gloria; [ed.] Been in school for 9 years honor roll; [occ.] Dance for 7 years, cheerleading; [hon.] Have won school poetry contest, and have won a scholarship in dancing. Performed in "Harlem Nutcraker"; [oth.writ.] Love writing stories and writing songs. Mostly just poetry; [pers.] You can go out and be someone, or you can be absolutely no one.; [a.] [pers.] Glendale, AZ

TURNER, KIMBERLY
[b.] April 23, 1973; Price, UT; [p.] Ben and Beverly Tucker; [m.] David Turner; September 5, 1992; [ch.] Kathleen Elizabeth, Anna Marie, Charles Taylor; [ed.] Emery High, College of Eastern UT; [occ.] Data Entry Specialist; [pers.] I write to express my feelings and as an outlet for emotions. I try to describe people the way I feel them instead of how society sees them.; [a.] Orangeville, UT

TURNER, TAMMY
[b.] October 10, 1964; Davidson County Denton, NC; [p.] Ruth Hogan and the late William Cross; [m.] Wiley Turner; April 17, 1995; [ch.] Jonathan and Crystal Barringer; [ed.] High School Equivalency Graduate; [occ.] Sewer for upholstery at IJ furniture in Asheboro, NC; [memb.] National Park

Trust, Easter Seal Society, Paralyzed Veterans of America Sponsor, North Shore Animal League, National Wildlife Federation, American Children's Cancer Society, National Rifle Assoc.; [oth.writ.] Nothing published. I have only written poems for family and friends or to express my feelings.; [pers.] I write to express my emotions on a situation or to stir emotion in others. I am greatly influenced by writings from Helen Steiner Rice and Grace E. Easley, whom I think are masters of emotion.; [a.] Denton, NC

TURNER, TAMMY
[b.] May 12,1965; Asheboro, NC; [p.] Delmas Powers and JoAnna Shelley; [m.] Tony Turner; March 29, 1991; [ch.] (3) Anna, Elizabeth Gail, Hayley Damron; [ed.] New Hanover High School - Wilmington, NC; Mountain Empire Comm. College - Big Stone Gap, VA; [occ.] Sales Rep. - Phoenix Sign Systems Atlanta, Georgia; [a.] Snellville, GA

ULMER, SIDNEY GALE
[pen.] Sidney Gale Ulmer; [b.] January 10, 1937; Chicago; [p.] Sidney D. Collisson and Dolly J. Collisson; [m.] Deceased; March 9, 1973; [ch.] 5 ages: 39, 37, 35, 13, 15; [ed.] BFA Corcoran School of Art DC, Endicott Counselor Unity Church; [occ.] Artist-Teacher drawings, paintings prof., in area and on East Coast; [memb.] Draw and paint theatrical productions, regular exhibits, retail, and have own line of cards with art poetry; Memb. of Wilmington Artist Assoc.; [hon.] Merit award 1997; published in Wispers at Dusk anthology, National Library of Poetry; [oth.writ.] Unity newsletter, WHOR Radio station readings— Wilmington, NC, Short stories and poetry read to music "Knots of Wisdom", (subt. souls unraveling); [pers.] Poetry comes from the soul's being nudged to respond to an inspirational idea beyond the personality. Spirit moves, the pen responds naturally as the gift is given and I too am in awe.; [a.] Wilmington, NC

VALENTINE, MELAINA
[b.] March 13, 1984; Brooklyn, NY; [p.] Mel and Marsha Valentine; [ed.] I am entering the 8th grade at Old Court Middle in Baltimore, Maryland; [occ.] Student—full-time; [hon.] National Junior Honor Society; [oth.writ.] I've written for a children's paper called "Just Write." I'm working on 2 novels and my own poetry book.; [pers.] My poems are influenced by the people around me. I wrote "If" for a boy I liked in the seventh grade named Gregory Robinson.; [a.] Pikesville, MD

VALENZUELA, LARRY
[pen.] Larry Valenzuela; [b.] September 7, 1978; Calexico, CA; [p.] Lauro Valenzuela, Benita Valenzuela; [ed.] Calexico High School, Imperial Valley College; [occ.] Office Clerk, Central Union High School, El Centro CA; [memb.] Future Business Leaders of America; [hon.] Most Improved Award in Band, Medallion 4 Years Band Member. Percussionist Twins of the Year, Honor I.I.D. Scholarship, Attendance Awards; [oth.writ.] 1st poems "that turned my life around": The Dream, Discrimination, etc; [pers.] My poetry is a way of self-expression that leads to unforgettable memories and opens a door of past, present, future, and brings out our soul in writing poems, happily, sadly, but the truth.; [a.] Calexico, CA

VAN ATTA, JAMIE LYNN
[pen.] Jamie 61112- (Internet Call Name); [b.] November 20, 1979; Billings, MT; [p.] Clint and Verlaine Van Atta; [ed.] Senior at Skyview High School in Bilings; [occ.] Cashier and Sandwhich Maker at Wendy's (fast food) Old Fashioned Hamburgers; [oth.writ.] Several Poems listed over the Internet; [pers.] My poems usually seem to come off as suicidal. But my meaning is to state my feelings and hope readers can relate.; [a.] Billings, MT

VELANDO, LIZABETH M.
[pen.] La Nina; [b.] June 12, 1974; Cavite, Philippines; [p.] Augusto D. Velando, Estebana M. Velando; [ed.] Shelton Park Elementary School, Cavite Institute, College of Nursing and Midwifery, De La Salle University—Aguinaldo; [occ.] Dialysis Patient Care Technician; [hon.] Honor Society, Cultural Award, Most Promising Actress, Dean's List; [oth.writ.] "Stretching Our Arms" and "Save the Earth" both published in "The Cavitenana" and "Seasons of Laughter" and "American Poetry Annual,"respectively; [pers.] "Almost everybody raves to be the one to absorb all the limelight, but for me, there is much more strength in simply sitting back in the shadows and the audience in poignant silence."; [a.] Sedalia, MO

WALKER, DEION MATTHEW
[b.] June 4, 1977; Lynwood, CA; [p.] Billy and Sharon Walker; [ed.] High School Graduate; [occ.] Student; [oth.writ.] I am a Man, Heart and Soul, Beautiful and Sweet Taste Sensation; [pers.] My poetry reflects the inner peace within myself. I have always been encouraged by my mother. She believes I am special.; [a.] Los Angeles, CA

WALKER, JASMINE
[b.] December 5, 1982; Detroit, MI; [p.] Miss Velma Walker; [ed.] Detroit High School for The Fine Performing Arts (9th grade); [occ.] Student; [hon.] Received an award for paper on Crime Prevention, received and award for playing Basketball; [oth.writ.] I have written a complete porfolio of all my writing; [pers.] A pen is an escape from reality, a magic carpet to far and distant lands, a space shuttle to the culture and beyond.

WALKER, MARY
[pen.] Martina Walker; [b.] August 27, 1983; Haywood County; [p.] Mrs. Denicha Walker and Mr. Martin Walker; [ed.] 8th Grade Crockett County Middle School; [hon.] Honor roll since 1st grade; Award from President Bill Clinton for excellence in Education. Student of the year and student of the month in the 5th grade; [oth.writ.] Have many writings but this is the first to be published; [pers.] I love writing and enjoy reading many books, for what will life be without books?; [a.] Brownsville, TN

WARNER, MELTON
[b.] April 14, 1920; Newark, NJ; [p.] Louis and Rose Warshawsky; [m.] Sarah; November 19, 1944; [ch.] Karen and Alan; [ed.] Weequahic High; [occ.] Retired; [memb.] President Kadima-Heep Org. Exec. Brd. David L. Warner Boys Club of Newark, Pres. of Central Jersey Condo. Assoc., Pres. Seymour Fildman Leukemia, Vet. Foreign Wars; [hon.] Medal for action beyond call of duty. Pres Seniors of Caintree V.P. of Deborah Hospital of Covered Bridge Mgm't course at Brookdale College; [pers.] I have always been interested in writing either poetry or short stories. My writing of children's short stories have always been apprciate and rewarding.; [a.] Voorhees, NJ

WASHKOWIAK, THERESA
[pen.] Theresa J. Washkowiak; [b.] December 4 1957; Springfield, IL; [p.] Francis L. Brewer Doris Brewer; [m.] Thomas E. Washkowiak Sr. September 25, 1982; [ch.] Thomas E. Jr. and Jop Lynn; [ed.] Hall High School, Spring Valley, IL (1976) IVCC (1977) John Rober Powers, Chicago IL (1978); [occ.] Self-employed commercial window washer; [hon.] International Thespian Society (1976); [oth.writ.] Have free-lanced, wrote articles for many years, several published in our local paper, written articles for friends, relatives etc.; [pers.] No matter what I do, I always put forth my best effort to do a good job.; [a.] Peru, IL

WATKINS, RONDA J.
[b.] June 8, 1972; Orange Co., NC; [p.] Brice an Margie Watkins; [ed.] Southern Alamance High

Graham, NC. Meredith College, Raleigh, NC; [occ.] Self-employed at Child Care Mebane, NC; [memb.] Springdale AME Church Steward Board, Missionary, Choir Directress, Usher, Teen Talk Coordinator; [hon.] Part-time honor student - Alamance, Community College, Haw River, NC; [oth.writ.] Articles written for preschool and church newspapers. Several unpublished poems; [pers.] My writing reflects personal experiences. I write in order for each reader to obtain their own meaning through my work. I am greatly influenced by Maya Angelou.; [a.] Mebane, NC

WATSON, NORBERT
[b.] January 13, 1931; Michigan; [p.] Roy D. and Anna Watson; [m.] Daisy Ellen Baugh Watson; February 10, 1951; [ch.] two; [ed.] Rosevelt and 2nd high, Cass Tech. Det., Michigan; Hohnemann School of Natural Health Sciences—Bradenton Florida; [occ.] Retired/portrait artist (15 years); [hon.] Doctorate of Science; [pers.] I'm from a family of artist and poets. Love is the correct motivating factor in life.; [a.] Monroe, UT

WERTIME, GREGORY S.
[b.] September 23, 1972; Evanston, IL; [p.] Steven F. Wertime, Tacquelinew Frumbacher; [ed.] BA, U. Southern California in "The Study of the City" An Interdisciplinary Urban Studies Program; [memb.] I live among fellow Christians who express aspects of their faith and growth, through art.; [a.] Pasadena, CA

WHITE, LESLIE ANGELLE
[b.] August 28, 1973; Opelousas, LA; [p.] Joseph White and Theresa White; [ed.] Bachelor of Arts, English Creative Writing—Louisiana State University; [oth.writ.] One poem scheduled to be published in the spring '98 edition of Poetic Voices of America; [pers.] I try to bring the things I see and experience every day to life in my writing. I want my reader be a part of what's happening in my writing.; [a.] Smyrna, GA

WHITT, MATTHEW SHANNON
[b.] April 29, 1980; Beckley, WV; [ed.] Kathy Thompson; [ed.] Foothills High School; [pers.] Michael E. Wells, Who I wrote my poem for, gave me a hand, time and again, through very hard times. In return, he asked that when I had the chance to do the same for others I should. That's my life goal.; [a.] Dobson, NC

WIDNER, EVELYN COPPLE
[b.] January 4, 1911; Jefferson Co., IL; [p.] Birthal and Mayne (Dickinson) Copple; [m.] Eldon L. Widner; November 7, 1980; [ed.] Centralia High School, Centralia, IL, B.A Degree Monmouth College, Monmouth, IL, Additional Credits for special K-14 Teaching and Supervising Instructional Materials; [occ.] Retired (Former School Teacher and Learning Center Director (Media Specialist); [memb.] AARP, NRTA, IRTA, Morgan Scott Retired Teachers Assoc., Delta Kappa Gamma Professional Society International, Charter Lifetime Member Internaltional Society of Poets, Central Christian Church; [hon.] High Honor Student in High School, Teacher Emeritus, Galesburg IL, Editor's Choice Awards The National Library of Poetry, International Poet of Merit Award, International Society of Poets, Poems published in the National Society of Poetry anthologies, Poem in the World's Largest Poem for Peace; [oth.writ.] Poems for various occasions and celebrations. For many years I have composed my own Chistmas greetings. 30 now are published. Some of my poems have been published in newsletters, bulletins for various organizations, etc. Some read on "Sound of Poetry" and "Impressions" cassettes. I have had over 200 poems copyrighted.; [pers.] Writing poetry gives me much pleasure. It helps fulfill my sincere desire to promote peace, love and greater understanding in our beautiful world. I hope my efforts will be seen by anyone who reads my poems.

This is important.; [a.] Jacksonville, IL

WILKERSON, VIANNEY
[b.] July 14, 1982; San Antonio; [p.] Anna and Richard Wilkerson; [ed.] Devine High School; [a.] Devine, TX

WILLIAMS, DEENA JEAN
[pen.] Penelope; [b.] April 19, 1985; Hollywood, FL; [p.] Steven and Denise Williams; [ed.] Middle School—7th Grade; [memb.] Lisa Frank Club; [hon.] Principal's Honor Award for Academic Excellence, Boward County Art Award - 1st place, 1st place in Water Balloon Event, 2nd place winner in 3-Legged Race; [oth.writ.] Personal Poetry Notebook; [pers.] I can't express the feeling I get when the inspiration of poetry flushes through me like a waterfall. It's one of the best feelings and I'm proud of it.; [a.] Davie, FL

WITRIOL, MORGAINE
[b.] June 9, 1986; Pound Ride, NY; [p.] Marianne Denniston and Neil Witriol; [occ.] Student; [pers.] I wrote this poem gazing out of my window. That day my poetry teacher, Mrs. Pomerance, had taught my class to find ideas to write about poetry. I had gotten so many ideas from looking around and listening. There are a million ways to find a poem. You just have to look for them.; [a.] Pound Ridge, NY

WIZBOWSKI, JENNIFER
[b.] November 13, 1972; Rome, NY; [p.] Harold E. Ford of Gettysburg, PA; Marlene Buckler of Fresno, CA; [m.] Raymond V. Wizbowski II; May 18, 1996; [ed.] BA—English, Fresno Pacific University; [a.] Fresno, CA

WOODHOUSE, B.A.
[pen.] Bee Aay Dubya; [b.] August 26, 1944; Burley, ID; [p.] Cliff and Ann Woodhouse; [m.] Linda Ann (Cashen) Woodhouse; August 16, 1975; [ch.] Dudevant Augustus, Daphne Clair, Deirdre Natasha and Bartholomew Tobias; [ed.] Oakley High School, Whitman College, USAF Officer and Electronics School, New Horizons Computer Training Center; [occ.] College Textbook Production Editor and Freelance Editor, Writer, Proofreader, and Project Manager; [memb.] Bookbuilders of Boston, Delta Tan Delta, North Billerica Citizens Action Committee; [hon.] Dean's List, Co-Valedictorian, Orion Medal, Underwood Award, Voted Most Talented; [oth.writ.] Eat The Old Fruit First, a collection of humorous essays and family anecdotes; serious essay on politics, economics and human nature and relationships; sonnets, limericks, short stories, autobiography; journal chronicling my thoughts, feelings and relationships; [pers.] At this point, I'm trying to figure out what I want to be when I grow up; grasp why people are the way they are; and understand the Big Picture—that is, how the universe evolved from the Big Bang to human consciousness.; [a.] North Billerica, MA

WOODS, JOANN P.
[pen.] JoAnn Palmertree; [b.] April 4, 1958; Drew, MS; [p.] El and Marie Palmertree; [m.] Ronald G. Woods; July 8, 1978; [ch.] Tiffany Katrina Woods [memb.] South Side Baptist Church; [oth.writ.] A Daddy's Heart, Crossing The Finish Line; [pers.] The Lord has changed my life, and He can change yours too. Just believe!; [a.] Winona, MS

WRIGHT, MINAYA
[pen.] Naya; [b.] December 15, 1981; Los Angeles, CA; [p.] Edward Wrigth, Autumn I. Wright; [oth.writ.] Several poems, stories and plays that have yet to be published in the future; [pers.] I enjoy reading and writing because it allows me to reflect other lives besides my own. This poem was written in dedication to all the Black Women whom I greatly admire. Hopefully one day I will have someone look up to me as I have to them.; [a.] Stone Mountain, GA

WRIGHT, SUSAN
[b.] June 29, 1956; Houlton, ME; [ed.] University of Massachusetts; [occ.] Poet; [oth.writ.] A body of works (poetry) which reflects my relationship with the earth

WRIGHT, SUSAN DALE
[pen.] Holly Dale or Susan Dale Wright; [b.] June 26, 1947; Roswell, NM; [p.] Oran C. Dale and Frances L. Dale; [m.] Thomas Everett Wright; April 3, 1966; [ed.] College of San Mateo in San Mateo, CA. San Francisco State in San Francisco, CA. Graduated in 1970-71 from University of CA in Hayward, CA with a BFA degree, some work towards MFA—not complete; [occ.] Semi-retired; [memb.] National Humane Society of the US; Honorable Citizen of Boys Town USA, Southern Leadership council on Racial tolerance, World of Wildlife Org. and World Vision; [oth.writ.] Several poems in local newspapers. Many children's stories, mostly about animals—mainly cats, dogs, and birds; [pers.] I believe there is good in everyone, and it is up to me to find that good. My love of animals has taught me how to observe, listen, and learn, the "art" of patience.; [a.] Tyrone, NM

YATES, DYLAN
[pen.] Chenery; [b.] May 15, 1961; Boston, MA; [p.] Barbara Rubin, Robert; [m.] Jo-el Hartman, August 13; [ch.] Jaime Yates; [ed.] Hull High, University of Colorado-Boulder, American Academy of Dramatic Arts-NY, NY Directors Lab., LA., CA; [occ.] Artistic Director For Goddess Theatre, Boulder, CO and Corporate Trainer; [memb.] Voices For Children-C.A.S.A. Open Door-1997 Grant Recipient; [hon.] Dean's List, Nova Award, 1997-Nova Winner, Open Door-1997 Grant Recipient, Boulder Arts Commision-1997, 1995, 1994, 1993, 1992 Grant Recipient, AHAB/ Neodata Arts and Humanities—1997, 1993 Grant Recipient; [oth.writ.] Several poems published in local newspapers, newsletters, publishes in the Volume Urania, Mile High Poetry Society; [pers.] Influences include Sara Tessdale, e.e. cummings and Anaïs Nin; [a.] Lafayette, CO

YOAKUM, TERESA J.
[pen.] Jane Yuakum; [b.] May 31, 1957; Peoria, IL; [p.] Mark and Geneva McCoy; [m.] Harry Yoakum; August 25, 1987; [ch.] Kerry, Paula and Jeff; [ed.] Elmwood Comm. High School, U.S. Air Force Guard; [occ.] Assoc. Anesthesiologists, Surgery Schedule; [memb.] President Maple Lane Country Club Shady Ladies, George Strait Fan Club, Amer. Cancer Society; [hon.] Several Poems in Local Newspaper; [pers.] Poetry is something I enjoy doing, along with songwriting. With my friends' encouragement, I have fulfilled my dreams.; [a.] Elmwood, IL

YOUNGER, ASHLEY
[b.] June 22, 1983; Decature, IL; [p.] Scott and Rebecca Younger; [ed.] Attending Meridian High School; [occ.] Student at Meridian High School; [memb.] National Junior Honor Society; [hon.] Principal's List; [pers.] My poetry is a way for me to express how I feel with what is happening in my life.; [a.] Blue Mound, IL

ZIMMERMAN, DORIS M.
[b.] March 28, 1957; Cornith; NY; [p.] Leona and Myles Bacon; [m.] Charles A. Zimmerman; September 13, 1975; [ch.] Marcia Jean, Tammy Lynn, Rodney Scott; [ed.] Graduated from Prattsburgh School, NY, in 1975. Went to college for 2 years and graduated from Finger Lakes Community College, in Canandigua, NY. May 1995 with Honors and a Business Administration Degree; [occ.] Housewife; [memb.] Pulteney Firemen's Auxiliary since 1983, Hammondsport Girl Leader then Troop Coordinator since 1983. Hammondsport Committee Chairman and member since 1990; [hon.] I graduated from College with Honors, Dean's List 3 semesters. I received the Ann Hamilton Reading/

writing award in December 1993. I won a $400 Scholarship from the Canandaigua Business & Professional Women's Club in January 1994; [oth.writ.] Just a hobby—when the mood hits me I write; [pers.] All through life you have many mountains to climb, you are always falling into the valley to climb another mountain, but remember— you will get through life by telling yourself, "Everything could always be worse." I remembered this when our daughter, Tammy at 12, came down with leukemia in 1990, and now we have a beautiful miracle granddaughter from her.; [a.] Pulteney, NY

Index
of
Poets

Index

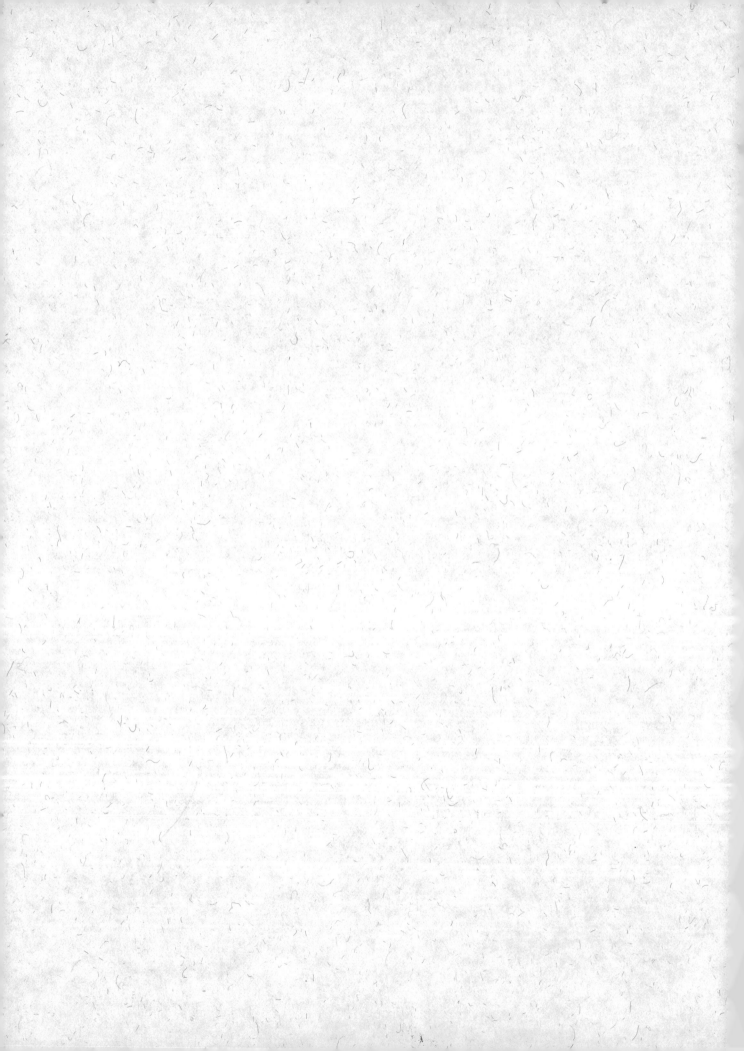